Financial Derivatives

Markets and Applications

5th Edition

Financial Derivatives

Markets and Applications

5th Edition

Obiyathulla Ismath Bacha
INCEIF University, Malaysia

Contributions by
Pattarake Sarajoti
SASIN School of Management, Chulalongkorn University, Thailand

NEW JERSEY • LONDON • SINGAPORE • BEIJING • SHANGHAI • HONG KONG • TAIPEI • CHENNAI • TOKYO

Published by

World Scientific Publishing Co. Pte. Ltd.

5 Toh Tuck Link, Singapore 596224

USA office: 27 Warren Street, Suite 401-402, Hackensack, NJ 07601

UK office: 57 Shelton Street, Covent Garden, London WC2H 9HE

Library of Congress Cataloging-in-Publication Data
Names: Ismath Bacha, Obiyathulla, author.
Title: Financial derivatives : markets and applications / Obiyathulla Ismath Bacha,
    INCEIF University, Malaysia ; contributions by Pattarake Sarajoti,
    SASIN School of Management, Chulalongkorn University, Thailand.
Description: 5th edition. | New Jersey : World Scientific, [2023] |
    Includes bibliographical references and index.
Identifiers: LCCN 2022022527 | ISBN 9789811261473 (hardcover) | ISBN 9789811262166 (paperback) |
    ISBN 9789811261480 (ebook) | ISBN 9789811261497 (ebook other)
Subjects: LCSH: Derivative securities--Asia.
Classification: LCC HG6024.A45 I75 2023 | DDC 332.63/2095--dc23/eng/20220914
LC record available at https://lccn.loc.gov/2022022527

British Library Cataloguing-in-Publication Data
A catalogue record for this book is available from the British Library.

Copyright © 2023 by World Scientific Publishing Co. Pte. Ltd.

All rights reserved. This book, or parts thereof, may not be reproduced in any form or by any means, electronic or mechanical, including photocopying, recording or any information storage and retrieval system now known or to be invented, without written permission from the publisher.

For photocopying of material in this volume, please pay a copying fee through the Copyright Clearance Center, Inc., 222 Rosewood Drive, Danvers, MA 01923, USA. In this case permission to photocopy is not required from the publisher.

For any available supplementary material, please visit
https://www.worldscientific.com/worldscibooks/10.1142/12999#t=suppl

Desk Editor: Lai Ann

Typeset by Stallion Press
Email: enquiries@stallionpress.com

Printed in Singapore by Mainland Press Pte Ltd.

Preface

This book is the result of my many years of teaching the Derivatives course, first at the International Islamic University Malaysia and then at INCEIF University. As any teacher of the subject would attest, it is an inherently difficult subject, made all the more so by the discussion in current texts of largely American instruments/contracts. Though the mechanics may be the same, the settlement procedures, trading methods, and the contracts themselves are vastly different. This often makes it difficult for Asian students to visualize and connect the pieces in order to have a holistic understanding. My main objective in writing this book is to provide an Asian perspective without compromising on the academic rigor of typical American textbooks on derivatives. While the first four editions of this book were Malaysian in orientation, this fifth edition has been designed to be more comprehensive with an Asian perspective by including contracts and derivative markets in Singapore, Hong Kong, and Thailand. The key strength of the book, its emphasis on application, has been maintained. Rather than the use equations to prove a theoretical argument, I have made extensive use of illustrations and write-ups to provide an understanding of the underlying logic and intuition. This is further augmented by way of illustrative boxes in each chapter.

This book is designed and developed explicitly for a foundation course in derivatives. It can be used at the undergraduate level or at the MBA level (with supplementary material). While it assumes no previous knowledge or familiarity with derivatives, readers should have had at least one basic course in finance. Several chapters in this book have appendices of additional materials for flexibility in customizing the course content to suit students' need. The materials in the appendices should be covered when the book is used for the MBA/Masters level course. To suit student abilities, certain sections of chapters may be ignored without losing the overall flow. The chapters are arranged to build from the simple to the more complex. Chapters 1, 2, and 3, for example, provide the basis for the in-depth examination of stock index futures contracts, and the interest rate futures contracts covered in Chapters 4 and 5. Similarly, Chapters 6 and 7 provide the foundation for the later chapters on options.

The book covers key financial derivative contracts traded in Malaysia, Singapore, Hong Kong, and Thailand. While minimizing duplication in each case, the book illustrates the three common applications for these contracts: hedging, arbitrage, and speculation. In the earlier chapters, to make it easy for students to understand the mechanics of derivatives trading, I deliberately use the example of physically-settled commodity contracts. The use of commodity futures as example makes it easier for a student to visualize the flow and understand what happens at contract initiation, the margining process, and final settlement.

A derivatives textbook can be extremely dry. To avoid this and to show how to use the concepts/tools in real life, I have used a variety of detailed worked-out, real-life examples. Each chapter also has a series of boxes highlighting key concepts/relationships. All chapters end with a chapter summary which provides a synopsis of the chapter. A section titled Key Terms lists the important terms used within the chapter. The End-of-Chapter Questions provide students with the opportunity to practice and improve comprehension. Most of the questions are designed to test the student's analytical ability. Solutions to a selected number of questions from each chapter are provided at the end of the book.

About the Book

This book is designed for beginners who possess no previous knowledge or familiarity with derivatives. Written in an easy-to-read style, it guides readers through the challenging and complex world of forwards, futures, options, and swaps. The emphasis on Asian markets and contracts enables easier understanding. Financial derivative contracts from Malaysia and select contracts from Thailand, Singapore, and Hong Kong derivative markets are covered. For each derivative contract, their three common applications hedging, arbitrage, and speculating are shown with fully worked out examples. Extensive use of illustrations, graphics, and vignettes provide for easy comprehension of the underlying logic of derivatives.

New to This Edition

This fifth edition is the result of substantial revision to the previous edition. In addition to updating the trading information/data, this edition includes many new materials. Much of these changes and inclusions were based on feedback from instructors using the book as text for their Derivatives courses. The main change from the previous edition is the expansion of the book's scope to include the other key Southeast Asian markets: Thailand, Singapore, and Hong Kong. In addition to Malaysia's Bursa Malaysia Derivatives Berhad, Thailand's TFX, Singapore's Singapore Exchange (SGX), and Hong Kong's Stock Exchange (HKEX) are covered. Among the new material in this edition are:

— The SET 50 Index futures contracts
— Single stock futures contracts traded on TFX
— Currency forward and futures contracts
— Currency option contracts — the US$/CNH contracts
— The pricing of currency forwards, futures
— Valuation of currency options using the Garman–Kohlhagen model
— Stock index option contracts — the SET 50 Index option contracts
— The SGX Nikkei 225 Stock Index option contracts
— The pricing of stock index option contracts
— The 3-month Bangkok Interbank Offered Rate (BIBOR) futures contracts traded on TFX
— Japanese Government Bond (JGB) interest rates futures contracts traded on SGX
— Non-deliverable forward contracts (NDFs)
— Islamic structured products
— *Sukuk* with embedded options

I have kept what works well but added depth where necessary. Given the expanded scope of the book, most chapters have undergone extensive new additions and sections. There is an increased number of illustrative boxes. All chapters have these boxes to both provide better understanding and show the connection with the real world. This is done in two ways, either by describing a real-world event related to the topic and/or reporting evidence from empirical studies that have used actual market data. These boxes bring reality and relevance to material covered in the respective chapters. The inclusion of new material includes additional end-of-chapter problems/questions. In summary, this fifth edition has undergone substantial change from the previous four editions.

About the Author

Obiyathulla Ismath Bacha hails from the southern state of Malacca. He is currently Professor of Finance at INCEIF University in Kuala Lumpur, Malaysia. He was the President of the Malaysian Finance Association (MFA) for the 5-year period 2012–2017. He received his primary and secondary education at the Banda Hilir English School and SMJK St. Francis, Malacca. He graduated with a Bachelor's Degree in Social Science, majoring in Management from the Science University of Malaysia in 1984. His graduate studies were at Boston University, USA where he received the Masters of Arts in Economics, Masters of Business Administration with High Honours in Finance, and Doctorate in Business Administration, specializing in Finance. His doctoral thesis was an empirical study of the multi-market trading of the Nikkei Stock Index Futures Contracts. His paper on the Nikkei Stock Index Futures, Regulation & Volatility won the Chicago Mercantile Exchange Competitive Research Award. He has authored and published numerous research papers in the area of derivatives, international finance and Islamic finance. Prior to his current position, he was a Professor of Finance at the International Islamic University Malaysia and an Assistant Professor of Finance at Boston University, USA.

Acknowledgments

Numerous individuals had helped in one way or other to make this book possible. I would like to thank everyone who had contributed towards the success of this book. I am thankful to my many students and the instructors at various universities who had provided feedback and comments on earlier editions over the years. These feedback had helped improve subsequent editions. I am also grateful to my research assistants, Ikhlas Amatullah, Muhammad Mahmudul Karim, and especially Nurlina Shaharuddin, who had painstakingly gone through the manuscript and updated the statistics, graphs, and charts. Professor Pattarake Sarajoti, the contributing author, was instrumental in accessing the Thailand Futures Exchange (TFX) and contributed the material on the TFX and Singapore Exchange derivatives. I am also indebted to Lai Ann of World Scientific Publishing, Singapore, for undertaking the numerous tasks involved with getting this edition published. Last but not least, special thanks to my wife and children, Hafiz Raziq and Hafeeza Alysha, for all their support and understanding.

Professor Dr. Obiyathulla Ismath Bacha
Department of Graduate Studies
INCEIF University
Kuala Lumpur, Malaysia
June 2022
obiyathulla@yahoo.com; obiyathulla@gmail.com

This book is dedicated
to the memory of my
late parents

Contents

Preface — v
About the Book — vii
New to This Edition — ix
About the Author — xi
Acknowledgments — xiii

Chapter 1 Derivatives: Introduction and Overview — 1
   Introduction — 1
   1.1 What are Derivative Instruments? — 2
   1.2 Common Derivative Instruments — 3
   1.3 Evolution of Derivative Instruments — 3
   1.4 OTC versus Exchange-Traded Derivatives — 7
   1.5 The Main Players in Derivative Markets — 8
   1.6 Commodity versus Financial Derivatives — 10
   1.7 Types of Risks — 11
   1.8 Overview of Global Trading in Derivatives — 15
   Summary — 17

Chapter 2 Derivative Markets and Trading — 19
   Introduction — 19
   2.1 Trading Methods — 19
   2.2 The Role of a Derivatives Clearinghouse — 23
   2.3 Derivatives Trading in Malaysia — 24
   2.4 Hong Kong Exchanges and Clearing — 29
   2.5 Derivatives in Singapore — 33
   2.6 Derivatives in Thailand — 35
   2.7 Relative Trading Performance of the Four Derivatives Exchanges — 39
   Summary — 41

Chapter 3 Forward and Futures Markets: Pricing and Analysis — 43
   Introduction — 43
   3.1 Forward Contracts — 44
   3.2 Futures Contracts — 46

	3.3	Mechanics of Futures Trading	49
	3.4	Margining and Marking-to-Market	50
	3.5	Forwards, Futures: Zero-Sum Game	53
	3.6	Futures Markets — The Main Players	54
	3.7	Determination of Futures Prices	58
	3.8	Issues in Futures Trading	59
	3.9	Types of Orders	66
		Summary	70
		Appendix	74

Chapter 4 Stock Index Futures Contracts: Analysis and Applications — 81

		Introduction	81
	4.1	Why Use SIF Contracts?	84
	4.2	Index Construction and Types of Indexes	86
	4.3	FBM KLCI Futures, Contract Specifications	88
	4.4	SIF Trading — The Main Players	91
	4.5	The Pricing of SIF Contracts	91
	4.6	Applications of SIF Contracts	94
	4.7	SIF in Thailand	105
	4.8	SIF Contracts and Portfolio Management	114
	4.9	Issues in SIF Pricing	117
	4.10	Issues in SIF Trading	119
	4.11	Growth and Trading Performance of the FBM KLCI and the SET 50 Index Futures Contracts	121
	4.12	Single Stock Futures	123
		Summary	132

Chapter 5 Interest Rate Futures Contracts and Currency Futures Contracts — 139

		Introduction	139
	5.1	Interest Rate Futures Contracts	139
	5.2	What Is Interest Rate Risk?	140
	5.3	Bond Pricing, Yields, and Interest Rate Risk	141
	5.4	The 3-Month KLIBOR Futures Contract	145
	5.5	Contract Specifications — 3-Month KLIBOR and 3-Month BIBOR Futures	146

5.6	Determining the Equilibrium Price: The Implied Forward Rate	149
5.7	3-Month IRF: Applications	151
5.8	Singapore Exchange's IRF Contract: The 10-Year Mini Japanese Government Bond Futures Contract	159
5.9	Determinants of IRF Prices	165
5.10	Contract Performance	168
5.11	Currency Forward and Futures Contracts	171
5.12	The HKEX's US$/CNH Currency Futures Contract	174
	Summary	186
	Appendix	192

Chapter 6 Introduction to Options — 201

What Are Options? — 201

6.1	Calls and Puts	201
6.2	Payoffs to Investing in Stocks versus Options	203
6.3	Expectations and Option Positions	213
6.4	Options: Uses and Applications	214
6.5	Option Moneyness	218
	Summary	227

Chapter 7 Equity, Equity Index, and Currency Options — 231

Introduction — 231

7.1	Trading Option Contracts	232
7.2	Option Premiums and Underlying Asset Price	234
7.3	American-Style Options and Early Exercise	236
7.4	Intermediation and Margining	237
7.5	Option Classes and Series	239
7.6	Malaysia's FBM KLCI Options: Contract Specifications	240
7.7	Stock Options Traded on Hong Kong's HKEX	243
7.8	Stock Index Options in Thailand — The SET 50 Index Options	246
7.9	Currency Options	257
	Summary	264
	Appendix	268

Chapter 8 Option Strategies and Payoffs — 279

Introduction — 279

8.1	Uncovered/Naked Positions	280

8.2	Hedge Strategies	280
8.3	Spread Strategies	288
8.4	Combination Strategies	295
8.5	Covered Call Strategy	303
8.6	Butterfly, Condor, Ratio, and Box Spreads	308
8.7	Summary of Strategies by Market Outlook	314
	Summary	316

Chapter 9 Option Pricing   323

	Introduction	323
9.1	Asset Valuation in Finance	324
9.2	The Binomial Option Pricing Model	325
9.3	The Black–Scholes Option Pricing Model	334
9.4	Determinants of Option Prices	341
9.5	Illustration of Price Dynamics — Changing Call and Put Values	345
9.6	Issues in Option Pricing	346
9.7	Implied Volatility	350
9.8	Valuing Equity Index Options	353
9.9	Valuing Currency Options	357
	Summary	361
	Appendix 1	366
	Appendix II	376

Chapter 10 Replication, Synthetics, and Arbitrage   381

	Introduction	381
10.1	Replication and Synthetics	382
10.2	Put–Call Parity and Arbitrage	388
10.3	Put–Call Parity, Conversion and Delta Neutral Trading	396
10.4	Put–Call Parity — Empirical Evidence	398
	Summary	399

Chapter 11 Options in Corporate Finance and Real Options   405

	Introduction	405
11.1	Levered Equity: An Options Approach	405
11.2	A Rights Issue	411
11.3	The Value of Underwriting a Securities Issue	411

	11.4 Securities with Option-Like Features	412
	11.5 Real Options and Capital Budgeting	415
	11.6 Exotic Options	420
	Summary	423
	Appendix	427

Chapter 12 Interest Rate Swaps, Credit, and Other Derivatives — 433

	Introduction	433
12.1	Interest Rate Swaps	433
12.2	IRS — Applications	436
12.3	Pricing IRS	442
12.4	Currency Swaps	444
12.5	Nondeliverable Forward Contracts	448
12.6	Forward Rate Agreement	451
12.7	Credit Derivatives	453
12.8	Credit Swaps	455
12.9	Credit Options	459
12.10	Credit-Linked Notes	460
12.11	Contract for Difference	461
	Summary	466

Chapter 13 Derivative Instruments and Islamic Finance — 471

	Introduction	471
13.1	Necessary Features for Islamic Financial Instruments	472
13.2	Islamic Finance Instruments with Features of Derivative Instruments	473
13.3	The *Ba'i -Al-Urbun*	477
13.4	The *Bai bil-Wafa* and *Bai bil-Istighlal* Contracts	478
13.5	The Islamic Profit Rate Swap	479
13.6	Islamic Structured Products	481
13.7	*Sukuk* with Embedded Options	487
13.8	*Shariah* Views on the Trading of Currency and *Shariah*-Compliant Tools for Managing Currency Risk	489
13.9	Islamic View of Current-Day Derivative Instruments	492
13.10	The Need for Harmonization	497
	Summary	499

Answers to Select End-of-Chapter Questions	503
References and Further Reading	521
Formulas	523
Index	529

CHAPTER · 1

Derivatives: Introduction and Overview

> ## Objectives
>
> This chapter is intended to provide an introduction to derivative instruments and its trading. On completing this chapter, you should have a good overview of derivative instruments and their markets.

Introduction

Derivative instruments, in their current form, are relatively new instruments. Compared to financial assets such as stocks and bonds which have been exchange-traded for more than a century, derivative instruments, especially **financial derivatives**, are very new instruments. For example, even the world's oldest exchange-traded financial derivatives, interest rate **futures**, is hardly 40 years old. Most of the more exotic forms of **derivatives** are instruments that did not even exist a decade ago.

Despite their newness, derivative instruments have turned out to be very popular. Trading volume in derivatives has shown impressive growth in recent years. Interestingly, the volume of trading in several derivative contracts has outpaced the trading volume of the **underlying assets** on which they are based. Despite their obvious popularity, derivative instruments have been blamed for having precipitated several financial scandals that resulted in spectacular losses. Examples of these are Barings PLC, Sumitomo Corporation's losses ($2.6 billion) on Copper derivatives, Metallgesellschaft AG's (DM 1.8 billion) losses on oil futures, and Orange County California's losses on interest rate derivatives. The most recent derivatives-induced loss occurred in 2008 when the French bank Societe Generale announced futures-related losses exceeding 4 billion euros, the largest derivatives loss in the history. Until then, the largest derivative-related loss (approximately $4 billion) occurred when Long-Term Capital Management (LTCM), the United States (US)-based hedge fund, blew up in late 1998.

All of these abovementioned losses have been widely reported. Given the size of the losses, they had attracted much attention. Since each of these scandals involved derivative instruments, a widespread misconception appears to have occurred with regard to derivative instruments in general. The misconception is that there is something inherently risky about derivatives and that prudence would require one to avoid these instruments. As the reader works his way through this book, it would be clear that the common perception of derivatives is untrue. Derivatives are "powerful" financial instruments, which if improperly used can cause serious problems. If used intelligently, derivatives can reduce the risks and allow for flexibility. Indeed if one examines each of the abovementioned scandals in detail, it will be evident that in every case, the problem was not the use but the *misuse* of derivatives that caused the problem. In each case, the players involved had used derivatives to take huge speculative positions, almost all of which were irrational and greed driven.

1.1 What are Derivative Instruments?

Derivative instruments are essentially financial instruments that **derive** their value from the value of an underlying asset. As such, a derivative instrument has little value in and of itself. Its value is entirely dependent on the value of its underlying asset. For example, suppose I buy and hold a Crude Palm Oil (CPO) futures contract. The value of this contract will rise and fall as the value or price of spot CPO rises or falls. Should the underlying asset, CPO in this case, rise in value, then the value of the CPO futures contract that I am holding will also increase in value. Alternatively, should the spot price of CPO fall, then the value of my CPO futures contract will also fall. This happens because a derivative is in essence a "claim" on the underlying asset at a predetermined price and at predetermined futures period(s).

Note
A derivative instrument is a financial asset that derives its value from the value of its underlying asset.

So, unlike spot market transactions, where assets are bought/sold for cash at prevailing spot prices for immediate delivery, derivative market transactions allow for future transactions at prices determined today. The term "derivative" denotes the fact that these instruments **derive** their value from elsewhere (the word "derive" being the root word for derivative).

Though the analysis and pricing of derivative instruments can be complicated and highly quantitative, the basic principles and logic of derivatives are relatively straight forward.

Today, there is a broad spectrum of derivative instruments, many with very exotic names and highly specialized purposes. This chapter (and book) focuses on three main derivative instruments: **forwards**, **futures**, and **options**. In fact, forwards, given their fairly simple structure, are discussed only as a precursor to futures contracts.

Thus the main focus of this book will be on the more popular derivative instruments: futures and options.

1.2 Common Derivative Instruments

As mentioned earlier, forwards, futures, and options are probably the three most common derivative instruments. A fourth and an increasingly popular derivative is the swap contract. As derivative instruments, forwards, futures, options, and swaps derive their value from their underlying assets. However, key differences in some of their features lead to substantially different payoffs and, therefore, purpose of use. We examine below the basic definition of each of these four derivatives.

A Forward Contract: A forward contract can be defined as a contract between two parties agreeing to carry out a transaction at a future date but at a price determined today.

A Futures Contract: A futures contract can be simply defined as a standardized and exchange-traded form of forward contract. As in a forward contract, a futures contract represents a formal agreement between two parties to carry out a transaction at a future date (contract maturity date) but at a price determined at contract initiation. Thus, from an operational viewpoint, forwards and futures are essentially the same, the difference being that futures are standardized and exchange-traded.

An Option Contract: An option contract provides the holder the right but not the obligation to buy or sell the underlying asset at a predetermined price. While a call option provides the right to buy, a put option would provide the right to sell.

A Swap Contract: A swap can be defined as a transaction in which two parties simultaneously exchange cash flows based on a notional amount of the underlying asset. The rate at which the amounts are exchanged is predetermined based on either a fixed amount or an amount to be based on a reference measure. (The reference measure could be an interest rate like 3-month KLIBOR.)

1.3 Evolution of Derivative Instruments

As in the case of any other product, derivative instruments evolved as a result of product innovation, which was in response to increasingly complex needs. As business environments became increasingly sophisticated, new and better financial products were needed to manage changed needs. The requirement that every newly evolved product must provide increased benefits or "value added" over existing products in order to survive applies equally to derivatives. We examine the evolution of financial derivatives and how each step down the evolutionary chain lead to value-added products. We restrict our discussion here to the three main instruments, namely forwards, futures, and options.

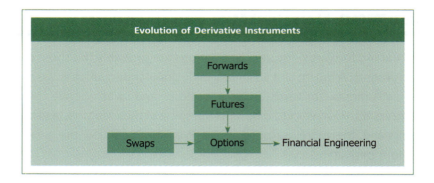

1.3.1 Forward Contracts

Chronologically, the first derivative instrument was probably the forward contract. Not surprisingly, forwards were also the simplest type of derivatives. In a forward contract, two parties undertake to complete a transaction at a future date but at a price determined today. The two parties could be a producer who promises to supply the product (underlying asset) and a consumer who needs the product at a future date. Clearly, both parties here are faced with risk, essentially price risk. While the producer would be fearful of a fall in the spot price between now and 6 months from now, the consumer would be susceptible to an increase in the spot price. Since they both face risk but in the opposite direction, it would be logical for both parties to meet, negotiate, and agree on a price at which the transaction can be carried out at the future date. Once the terms are formalized and documented, we have a forward contract. The benefit of such a forward contract is that the parties have *eliminated* price risk. Both parties have "locked-in" their price/cost.

Note
Forwards are customized contracts between two parties to carry out a transaction at a future date but at a price determined today.

1.3.2 The Need for Futures Contracts

The next step in the evolution from forwards was futures contracts. Futures contracts were innovated to essentially manage risk. One would be tempted to ask why futures were needed if forwards were sufficient for risk management purposes. As pointed out earlier, a newly innovated product will not survive unless it has some value added over existing products. The fact that futures contracts have become increasingly popular and have huge trading volume is testimony to its benefits over forward contracts. The need for futures contracts came about given the problems associated with forwards.

The forward contract has a number of problems. We will examine the three main problems here. The first problem may be classified as that of *multiple coincidence*. Here, the party to a forward contract would have to find a counterparty who not only has the opposite needs with respect to the underlying asset but also with regard to timing and quantity. The counterparty must need the product in the right quantity at the right time. Thus, a number of factors will have to coincide before a forward contract can be drawn up. A second problem with the forward contract often lies in the way the forward price is arrived at. Typically, the ***forward price*** is arrived at through negotiation. Depending on the bargaining position, however, it may be possible that a forward price is forced upon the other party. This may either be due to urgency on the part of one party (e.g., perishable goods) or more commonly due to informational asymmetry. A third and probably most important problem with forward contracts is ***counterparty risk***. Counterparty risk refers to the default risk of the counterparty in the contract. Though a forward is a legally binding arrangement, legal recourse is slow, time consuming, and costly. Default risk in forward contracts arises not so much from "dishonest" counterparties but from increased incentive to default as a result of subsequent price movement. When spot prices rise substantially above the forward price, the seller has the incentive to default.

The buyer would have the incentive to default if the opposite happens, i.e., spot price decreases.

As these shortcomings of the forward contract became apparent over time, a new instrument was needed that would provide the risk management benefit of forwards while simultaneously overcoming its problems. The resulting innovation was the futures contract. A futures contract is essentially a standardized forward contract, standardized with respect to contract size, maturity, product quality, place of delivery, etc. With standardization, it was possible to trade them on an exchange — which in turn increases liquidity and therefore reduces transaction costs. In addition, since all buyers and sellers transact through the exchange, the problem of multiple coincidence of wants is easily overcome. One would transact in the futures contract maturity closest to needed maturity and in as many contracts as needed to fit the underlying asset size.

With exchange trading, the second problem with forward contracts — that of being possibly locked into an ***unfair price*** — would not exist. This is because each party is a price taker with the futures price being that which prevails in the market at the time of contract initiation. As exchange-quoted prices are market clearing prices arrived at by the interaction of many buyers and sellers, they would by definition be "fair" prices.

The problem of counterparty risk is overcome in futures contracts by means of the ***novation principle***. The exchange being the intermediary "guarantees" each trade by being the buyer to each seller and seller to each buyer. What this means is that each party transfers the counterparty risk of forwards onto the exchange in the case of futures contracts. This transfer of risk to the

Note
Futures are a standardized and exchange-traded version of forward contracts.

exchange by parties to the futures contract has to be managed by the exchange, which now bears the risk. The exchange minimizes the potential default risk by means of the **margining process** and by **daily marking-to-market**. The basic idea behind the margining and marking-to-market process is to reduce the incentive to default by requiring initial deposits (initial margins) and recognizing losses as they occur and requiring the party whose position is losing to pay up as the loses accrue (margin calls).

These margining and marking-to-market process has been refined and fine-tuned over the years by futures exchanges to such an extent that incidences of market cornering and systemic defaults have been reduced to negligible rates.

1.3.3 The Need for Options

Though futures contracts have been able to overcome the problems associated with forwards, they were still inadequate in some respects to later-day business needs. In particular, there were two inadequacies that stimulated the search for further product innovation. The first is the fact that while futures enabled easy hedging by locking-in the price at which one could buy or sell; being locked-in also means that one could not benefit from subsequent favorable price movements. Wouldn't it be wonderful to have an instrument that protects you from unfavorable price movements while at the same time enables you to take the advantage of favorable price movements? This is precisely what options do.

In essence, options have at least three important advantages over forwards and futures. First, options provide the best of both worlds: downside protection and upside potential. Second, options are extremely flexible and can be combined in various ways to achieve different objectives/cash flows. Finally, as we will see later, there may be complicated business risk situations that cannot be handled with forwards/futures but can be easily handled with options.

> **Note**
> Options provide their holders the right but not the obligation to buy/sell the underlying asset at a predetermined price.

Following the advent of options, a whole new area of finance known as **financial engineering** came about. Financial engineering revolves around the designing of risk management solutions to complex risks. Since derivatives, particularly options, are extremely flexible instruments, they form the building blocks of financial engineering.

1.3.4 The Advent of Swaps

Swaps are a fast-growing category of derivatives. They are customized bilateral transactions in which the parties agree to exchange cash flows at fixed periodic intervals. The cash flows to be exchanged are based on an underlying asset. One could think of a swap contract as a series of forward contracts. Being customized, swaps are **over-the-counter** or OTC instruments. Depending on the kind of underlying asset, there are different kinds of swaps.

A currency swap, e.g., is one where parties exchange one currency for another; a **commodity** swap is one where parties exchange cash flows based on either a commodities index or the total return of a commodity in exchange for a return based on a market yield. Equity swaps constitute an exchange of cash flows based on different equity indices. An interest rate swap (IRS), on the other hand, is a transaction in which the parties exchange cash flows based on two different interest rates. Since its introduction in 1981, IRS has become extremely popular. Transacted volume, measured by total notional amount, exceeds US$ 50 trillion according to the International Swaps and Derivatives Association (ISDA); the IRS has become so popular in developed markets despite being an OTC instrument has to do with the initiatives of ISDA. ISDA had streamlined and standardized much of the paperwork for IRS, making the process much more simplified and thereby incurring lower costs. As an IRS is a highly effective instrument with which banks can manage their interest rate risk, an Islamic variant, known as the Islamic Profit Rate Swap, has been innovated for Islamic banks to manage their profit rate risk. We examine swaps in detail in Chapter 12 and Islamic profit rate swaps in Chapter 13.

1.4 OTC versus Exchange-Traded Derivatives

Derivatives may be categorized according to where they are available. There are two broad categories: *exchange-traded* derivatives and *OTC* derivatives. An **exchange-traded derivative** is one that is listed and traded on an official exchange. These exchange-traded derivatives tend to be of standard contract size, maturity, delivery process, and, in the case of commodity derivatives, also of standard quality. Every exchange-traded derivative would have a *contract specification* that specifies these features in detail. So, when one trades an exchange listed contract, one is transacting in standardized contracts. Furthermore, with exchange trading, the exchange becomes the intermediary between the buyer and the seller. In doing so, the exchange guarantees the contract. This effectively transfers *counterparty risk* or the risk that the counterparty to the transaction will default onto the exchange. As we will see in Chapter 3, the standardization and risk transfer element of exchange trading brings many advantages. In addition to increased trading volume and liquidity, which reduces liquidity risk and transaction costs, exchange trading helps in the key function of price discovery.

OTC trading, on the other hand, refers to customized transactions between parties in a bilateral arrangement. The two parties to the transaction agree on all the terms. Thus, all elements of the transaction are negotiable, including pricing. In the case of derivatives, OTC transactions typically take place between a corporate client and a financial institution like an investment bank. For example, a corporation which is an exporter may be receiving foreign currency payments in the future. Fearing a potential depreciation of the currency, the company may want to hedge its position by using currency derivatives like perhaps forwards or swaps or in some cases, even customized currency options. As a bilateral

Table 1.1 OTC versus Exchange-Traded Derivatives

OTC		Exchange-Traded	
Advantages	**Disadvantages**	**Advantages**	**Disadvantages**
• Customization possible	• More costly	• Lower transaction cost	• Customization not possible
• Can fully hedge a position	• Not liquid	• Very liquid; can be easily reversed	• Some basic risk arising from mismatch in asset, quality, maturity, and size is possible
• Can be tailored for specific needs	• Cannot be reversed/offset	• Market clearing prices (transparent)	
	• Potential for "unfair" price	• No counterparty risk	
	• Little transparency in pricing		
	• Counterparty risk		

transaction, counterparty or default risk by either party is possible. As such, a financial institution would not want to go into an OTC transaction with any entity, only those which it deems to be credit worthy. Counterparty risk is always present in the case of OTC transactions. Table 1.1 shows the advantages and disadvantages of both transaction types.

Though each type of transaction has its strengths and weaknesses, the key decision criteria would typically be the need for customization. If the need for customization is important, a customer may opt for an OTC contract even though an exchange-traded contract may be cheaper. Of the four types of derivatives discussed earlier, forwards and swaps are OTC instruments, whereas futures and options are exchange-traded. However, in the case of options, customized ones may also be available in OTC markets. In many countries where exchange-traded derivatives are not available, there is usually an active OTC variant.

1.5 The Main Players in Derivative Markets

As is the case with other financial markets, there are thousands of institutions and traders involved in derivative markets. However, they could all be classified into three broad categories, namely (i) **hedgers**, (ii) **arbitrageurs**, and (iii) **speculators**. If hedging is the *raison d'être* for derivative markets, then obviously hedgers would be major players.

Note
Hedgers are players whose objective is risk reduction.

Hedgers use derivative markets to manage or reduce risk. They are typically businesses that use derivatives to offset exposures resulting from their business activities.

The second category of players — arbitrageurs — use derivatives to engage in arbitrage. Arbitrage is the process of trying to take advantage of price differentials between markets. Arbitrageurs closely follow quoted prices of the same asset/instruments in different markets looking for price divergences. Should the divergence in prices be enough to make profits, they would buy in the market with the lower price and sell in the market where the quoted price is higher. Since most financial markets are integrated by computer networks, arbitrage activity boils down to hitting the right keystrokes. As arbitrage opportunities can quickly disappear, quick action is needed. Thus, institutions (commercial banks, investment banks, currency dealers, etc.) that engage in arbitrage activity invest huge amounts of money in global computer networks and telecommunications equipment.

In addition to merely watching the prices of the same asset in different markets, arbitrageurs can also arbitrage between different product markets, for example between the spot and futures markets, between the futures and option markets, or even between all three markets. It is in this type of arbitrage that sophisticated financial engineering techniques come into play.

> **Note**
> Speculators are players who establish positions based on their expectations of future price movements.

The final category of players is the speculators. Speculators as the name suggests merely speculate. They take positions in assets or markets **without** taking off setting positions. For example, if they expect a certain asset to fall in value, they would short (sell) the asset. Should their expectation come true, they would make profits from having shorted the asset. On the other hand, should the price increase instead, they would make losses on their short position. Speculators therefore expose themselves to risk and hope to profit from taking on the risk.

Having described the activities of the three major categories of players, it would be pertinent to ask whether these activities are useful from a societal viewpoint. Hedging is undoubtedly useful. Aside from enabling businesses to plan better, the reduction in fluctuation of their product prices can help reduce costs and thereby provide a tangible benefit to society. Consumers would benefit since producers, being able to hedge, would need to charge lower risk premiums. Societal benefits from arbitrage activity is much less direct. The benefits accrue from the proper realignment of prices. Arbitrageurs, by means of their activities, ensure that prices in the different markets (spot, futures, and options) do not diverge from each other. Because product prices are perhaps the most important signal in market economies, proper price discovery has serious implications on resource allocation. Arbitrage activity enhances the price discovery process. For example, arbitrage between markets in different countries "internationalizes" product prices. This forces less efficient producers to enhance productivity in order to remain in business. Arbitrage also helps reduce the distortionary effects of government regulation/intervention.

Speculative activity tends to hurt more than help. The evils of speculative activity are well documented. Although speculative activity is harmful, there are some benefits. First, speculative trading increases trading volume. This in turn provides two benefits: (i) increased trading volume reduces transaction costs, thereby making it cheaper for genuine hedgers to hedge and (ii) it increases liquidity. As a result, markets become deeper and broader, thereby reducing execution risk. Finally, the fact that speculators are willing to take risks means that hedgers have someone to pass on their risks. Despite these, it will be difficult to make a case in favor of speculation. Speculative activity can be disruptive. Yet, regulators have often been unable to keep such activity under control. This has largely to do with the fact that it is a very fine line that separates hedging and arbitrage from speculation.

1.6 Commodity versus Financial Derivatives

Today, derivative contracts are available on several types of underlying assets. In developed markets such as the United States (US), futures and options are available on several categories of assets. Among the underlying assets are agricultural commodities, metals, energy, currencies, and stock indexes. Table 1.2 shows examples of some of the underlying assets within each category.

Broadly speaking, these underlying assets can be divided into two categories, namely **physicals** and **financials**. All commodity derivatives, such as those from agricultural commodities, metals, energy, etc., which have a physical underlying asset, have what is known as actual or **physical settlement**. This means that on maturity of the derivative, there is actual physical delivery of the underlying asset.

Table 1.2   Underlying Assets, Categories, and Types

Category	Asset Type
Physicals	
• Agricultural commodities	— Wheat, soybean, crude palm oil, citrus, coffee beans
• Metals and energy	— Gasoline, gas oil, propane, etc. — Gold, silver, copper
Financials	
• Foreign currencies	— US$, ¥en, DM, Can$, SFr, Eurodollar, Euro
• Equity and bond futures	— T-bills, T-bonds — Kuala Lumpur Interbank Offered Rate (KLIBOR) futures, t-bill futures, etc. — Various stock indexes

Unlike the commodity derivatives which call for physical delivery at maturity, financial derivatives such as foreign currencies, stock indexes, and interest rate derivatives have what is termed **cash settlement**. Cash settlement means that the buyer does not receive the actual underlying asset but the monetary equivalent of the asset. Cash settlement happens either because the underlying asset does not exist in a tangible form (interest rate derivatives) or because physical settlement could be very cumbersome; e.g., in the case of stock index futures. So, in the case of cash-settled contracts, the parties simply "take-out" the money left in their margin accounts with profits and losses having been adjusted to these accounts.

> **Note**
> Commodity derivatives have tangible underlying assets and physical settlement at maturity.

> **Note**
> Financial derivatives have financial assets as underlying and are cash-settled at maturity.

1.7 Types of Risks

As mentioned earlier, the key function of derivatives is in risk management. In this section, we will do a quick overview of the different types of risks commonly found in today's markets. Risk in finance refers to the uncertainties associated with returns from an investment. Fluctuations in prices would mean volatility of returns. Thus, the common measure for risk is **standard deviation**. Any asset that does not come with "guaranteed" fixed returns has some amount of uncertainty. In fact, even a "guaranteed" instrument has risks if the issuer's credibility is questionable.

(a) Market/Price Risk

Price risk refers to changes in an asset's price due to changes in market conditions, either demand/supply conditions or sentiments. Any number of factors can cause changes in demand/supply and market sentiments. Thus, price risk is quite encompassing. All market-traded asset instruments have exposure to this risk.

(b) Inflation Risk

Inflation risk refers to the loss of purchasing power resulting from inflationary conditions. In highly inflationary environments, future investment returns would be worth much less, given the loss in purchasing power. Long-dated investments and assets with income generated mostly in the distant future would suffer relatively more from such distant cash flows.

(c) Interest Rate Risk

Interest rate risk refers to the changes in asset values because of changes in nominal interest rates. This is a particularly important source of risk for fixed income securities as it is the result of discounting to find prices. In the case of fixed income securities, the numerator (coupon or interest) is unchanged, whereas the denominator increases with an increase in nominal interest rates. Interest rate risk can also be in the form of funding or financing risk. Here the risk is that a change in interest rates can change the cost of funds or financing.

(d) Default/Credit Risk

This risk, which is also sometimes known as counterparty risk, refers to the changes in financial integrity of the counterparty or the issuer of the asset. When an issuer of financial instruments, e.g., bonds/stocks, gets closer to bankruptcy, there is increased default risk. On the other hand, if the issuer's financial position improves, there would be a resultant decrease in default risk. Though investors can lose their entire investment when an issuer goes bankrupt, it is often the case that there would be huge *anticipatory losses* even before bankruptcy actually happens. As such, although outright bankruptcies are a rare occurrence, default risk is relevant because of the possible anticipatory losses. As a result, a financial instrument could go down very substantially in price (close to worthless) even though the issuer has not technically declared bankruptcy.

(e) Liquidity Risk

Liquidity risk refers to risk that arises from thin or illiquid trading. When an asset is thinly traded, two possible sources of liquidity risk could arise. First, there is empirical evidence that thinly traded instruments have higher price volatility, i.e., price changes tend to be larger between trades as opposed to those of highly liquid, continuously-traded assets. Second, in thin, illiquid markets. One cannot dispose off an asset quickly. The only way to quickly sell the asset would be by taking a big discount on the price.

(f) Currency/Exchange Rate Risk

Currency or exchange rate risk refers to changes in investment income as a result of changes in exchange rates. Such a risk arises every time someone engages in a foreign currency-denominated transaction or invests in a foreign currency denominated asset. Even if the income is unchanged in foreign currency terms, the amount could vary in domestic currency terms if exchange rates have changed.

(g) Political Risk

This refers to risks faced by international investors. Most political risk is of a regulatory nature. It refers to risks such as expropriation/nationalization, imposition of exchange controls that disallow foreigners to withdraw their funds, the imposition of unfavorable tax or ownership requirements, etc. Political risk therefore refers to the diminution in the value of a foreign-held asset as a result of unfavorable regulatory change overseas.

As we will see later, different derivative instruments are intended for managing different types of risk. **Risk management** refers to the process/techniques of reducing the risks faced in an investment. What makes risk management challenging is the fact that risks and returns are generally positively correlated, hence the **risk-return trade off**. The challenge of risk management is to protect the expected returns while simultaneously reducing or laying-off the risks.

Risk management generally involves three broad steps: (i) identifying the source and type of risk, (ii) measuring the extent of the risk, and (iii) determining the appropriate response/methods. Traditional risk management methods were largely **on-balance sheet** techniques. On-balance sheet methods of risk management essentially involve the adoption of techniques that often change the way we do business in order to reduce risk. For example, in managing equity risk, an on-balance sheet method would be to diversify the investment and/or use asset allocation strategies. Similarly, in managing currency risk, an on-balance sheet technique would be to quote only in Ringgit, even for foreign customers. There are two problems with on-balance sheet techniques. First, there are limitations. For example, there is a limit to how much equity risk can be reduced with diversification (systematic risk remains even with full diversification). Asset-allocation strategies can be touch-and-go, its efficacy being dependent on the fund manager's ability to time the market. The second and perhaps the bigger problem with on-balance sheet techniques is that adopting the techniques may require us to change the nature or the way a company has been doing business. For example, a fund manager with a sectoral view cannot be sector-specific if he is also needed to diversify. Nor can a company engage with foreign customers or remain competitive if it is required to quote only in Ringgit.

It is in overcoming such limitations that **off-balance sheet** techniques come handy. All risk management techniques involving derivatives are off-balance sheet. What this means is that the hedging mechanism/method is "detached" from the underlying transaction. The advantage is that there is no need to change the way one does business. There is neither loss of competitiveness nor customer inconvenience. Thus, the fund manager can take as large a sectoral exposure as he wants and still manage the risk using stock options. He could also choose the extent and duration of equity exposure by using equity derivatives. For example, he can fully hedge his position for a duration of his choosing by means of stock index futures. In the case of currency exposure, the company is free to quote in any desired foreign currency that would win it the business and then hedge the exposure using currency derivatives. Being off-balance sheet, hedge positions involving derivatives do not show up in the balance sheet. Though not a disadvantage, this has been a key source of apprehension for regulators.

Box 1.1
The Virus Fires Up the Derivative Markets

Derivative markets across the world appear to have had a stellar year in 2020 despite the pandemic. This is according to the World Federation of Exchanges (WFE) Annual Survey 2020. The survey covered a total of 49 derivative exchanges across the world. Overall, there was a 40.4% increase in aggregate traded volume across all derivative categories. This was the highest growth rate in traded volume in 15 years. It was also more than a threefold increase from 2019, when volume growth was 11.4%. The heightened uncertainties arising from the COVID-19 pandemic appears to have been the driver for the increased use of derivatives. It is obvious that hedging needs to be increased when the environment is uncertain. The lockdowns and disruptions in economic activities across the globe obviously increased systemic risks. Being systemic, it affected all players in the value chain: producers, manufacturers, wholesalers, retailers, traders, etc. The most logical and efficient way to manage these risks was through the use of derivatives, thus the huge increase in total traded volume. In terms of breakdown by category, options appear to have grown faster at 44% while futures grew 37.5%. They had grown at 15% and 12%, respectively, in the prior year, 2019.

In terms of product categories, exchange-traded fund (ETF) derivatives, which have a listed ETF as underlying asset, have had the highest growth of 65% in 2020. This was followed closely by equity derivatives that grew 56.5%. Within equity derivatives, index futures grew 60%, whereas index options approximately 43%. Single stock options had 56% growth, whereas single stock futures grew nearly 100%. This should not be a surprise as equity markets had demonstrated spectacular performance in 2020. The ultra-loose monetary policies adopted by central banks in response to the pandemic and the historically low interest rates fueled the equity markets across much of the world. Ironically, though real sector growth suffered across the world, equity markets boomed. Elsewhere, the traded volume of commodity derivatives rose 34%, whereas currency derivatives grew about 31%. The only dark spot appears to have been in interest rate derivatives, which declined 12% in volume terms. This negative growth in volume of interest rate derivatives follows years of tepid growth. The obvious explanation is the very low interest rate regime that has prevailed over the last many years. When interest rates are near zero or negative in the developed world, managing interest rate volatility becomes much less important from a risk management viewpoint, and so the need for interest rate derivatives.

1.8 Overview of Global Trading in Derivatives

Much of today's derivatives had their beginnings in the exchanges of Chicago. Located in the Midwestern grain belt of the US, Chicago is the birthplace of three of the world's most renowned derivative exchanges: (i) the Chicago Mercantile Exchange (CME), (ii) the Chicago Board of Trade (CBOT), and (iii) the Chicago Board Options Exchange (CBOE). Though these exchanges trade a wide variety of derivatives with a range of underlying assets, their origins lie in agricultural commodities. The first exchange in Chicago was the Chicago Onions and Potatoes Exchange, which evolved into the CME. Being at the agricultural heartland of the US, it is no surprise that these exchanges began by offering instruments to hedge agriculture-related risks. Today, much of the action is in financial derivatives rather than commodity contracts. Accordingly, the Chicago exchanges, though still prominent, have lost their monopoly as the world's top exchanges. As will be evident in Chapter 2, a number of other exchanges have grown to challenge the dominance of the Chicago exchanges.

Figure 1.1 shows the trading performance of the two main categories of exchange-traded derivatives: futures and options. It is obvious that both categories of derivatives have had very impressive growth over the 19-year period from 2002 until 2020. Over the 19 years, traded volume for both categories had increased more than sevenfold. Beginning with a total traded volume of about 6.2 billion contracts in 2002, total volume has increased quite steadily to reach 46.7 billion contracts in 2020. As is evident from Figure 1.1, both futures and option contracts have grown steadily in volume over the period. Futures contracts, however, continue to dominate options in volume terms.

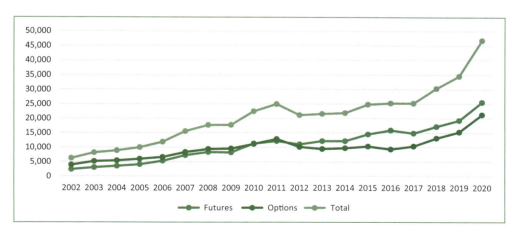

Figure 1.1 Global Traded Volume of Futures and Options (Contracts in Millions)
Source: Futures Industry Association www.futuresindustry.org.

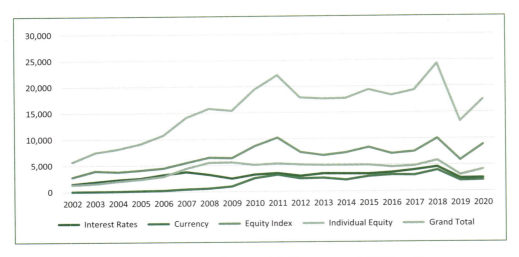

Figure 1.2   Total Traded Volume of Financials (Contracts in Millions)

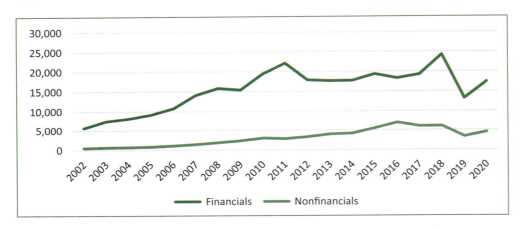

Figure 1.3   Traded Volume Financial versus Nonfinancial Derivatives (Contracts in Millions)
Source: Future Industry Association, www.futuresindustry.org.

Figure 1.2 shows the performance of financial derivative contracts over the 19 years from 2002 to 2020. The main categories within financials are equity index futures and options; single stock futures and options, which are often classified as individual equity products; currency; and interest rate derivatives. As the total line shows, financial derivatives experienced a sharp fall in volume in 2019 with the onset of the COVID-19 pandemic. The decline, however, appears to have turned around in 2020.

Figure 1.3 shows the relative performance of trading activity between financial and nonfinancial derivatives. Nonfinancials constitute derivatives based on agricultural commodities, metals, energy, and other commodities. Though financials were introduced much later than nonfinancials, they clearly dominate trading. The total traded volume of financial derivatives is easily three to four times higher than that of nonfinancial commodity-based derivatives. As mentioned earlier, while financial derivatives are cash settled, commodity based derivatives are physically settled.

SUMMARY

This chapter provided a basic introduction and an overview of derivative instruments. We examined the evolution of derivative instruments from forwards to options and financial engineering. This chapter provided the rationale for the evolution and how the latter instruments were an improvement on existing ones. The key players in derivatives markets were also discussed. Hedgers use derivatives for risk management. Speculators use derivatives to bet on price movements of the underlying asset. Arbitrageurs use derivatives to take advantage of price differentials.

The difference between commodity and financial derivatives was also examined. Although commodity derivatives have tangible underlying assets and have physical settlement, financial derivatives have financial assets as underlying and are cash settled at maturity. The different types of risks common in today's investment world were described. Different derivative instruments are intended to manage the different risks. For example, while stock index futures and options would be used to manage market/equity price risk, interest rate futures/options can be used for managing interest rate risk. Credit derivatives would be used for managing credit risk, whereas currency derivatives for exchange rate risks.

KEY TERMS

- Derivatives
- Underlying asset
- Commodity
- Forwards
- Hedgers
- Financial derivatives
- Arbitrageurs
- Financial engineering
- Physical settlement
- Options
- Speculators
- Cash settlement
- Standard deviation
- Risk management
- Off-balance sheet techniques
- Exchange-traded derivatives
- OTC derivatives

End-of-Chapter Questions

1. What is a derivative instrument? How is it different from stocks and bonds?
2. State four common categories of derivative instruments.
3. The evolution of derivative instruments means that each new derivative is an improvement on its predecessor. State the operational advantage(s) of (i) futures over forwards, and (ii) options over futures/forwards.

4. What is meant by financial engineering? What is the role of derivative instruments in financial engineering?
5. Who are the key categories of players in derivative markets? Briefly describe the objective of each category of players.
6. What benefit(s) do arbitrageurs bring to derivative markets?
7. How might the absence of speculators/speculation hurt hedgers?
8. What benefit(s) do speculators bring to derivative markets? In what way might some of their activity hurt markets?
9. Differentiate between commodity and financial derivatives.
10. State an advantage of cash settlement over physical settlement. Does the absence of physical delivery make financial derivatives any less suited for hedging, arbitrage, or speculation?
11. Outline some of the key types of risks and identify the appropriate derivative instrument to manage the risk.
12. Differentiate between on-balance sheet and off-balance sheet hedging methods. Where do derivatives fit in?
13. Compare OTC with exchange-traded derivatives. What are some of the advantages/disadvantages of each?
14. Why have interest rate derivatives become less popular in recent years? What does this imply about the main use of derivatives?
15. If the world moved to a fixed exchange rate regime where all currencies are "fixed" against each other, what would it imply about the need for currency derivatives?

CHAPTER · 2

Derivative Markets and Trading

Objectives

This chapter discusses the trading of derivatives in Malaysia, Hong Kong, Singapore, and Thailand. It provides an overview of the derivatives exchanges in each territory and the products traded and examines their trading methods/mechanisms. On completing this chapter, you should have a good understanding of exchange structures, their functions, trading methods, and regulatory systems.

Introduction

Although most modern-day derivatives are exchange-traded, many are not. Exchange-traded means that the instrument is designed by, listed, and traded on a formal centralized exchange. Though most exchanges have a centralized physical structure, exchanges are increasingly becoming more electronic and virtual with minimal physical size. Thus, derivative instruments may be either exchange-traded or traded over-the-counter (OTC).

As we saw in Chapter 1, futures and options are mostly exchange-traded, whereas forwards and swaps are largely OTC-traded. Unlike exchange trading where the contracts are standardized and governed by formal rules/trading procedures, **OTC markets** are informal markets that have negotiable arrangements and customized contracts. Both systems, as seen in Chapter 1, have their own advantages and disadvantages. Exchange trading through standardized contracts has several big advantages like efficient price discovery, increased liquidity, reduced transaction costs, and easy price dissemination. However, not all exchanges have the same trading system. There are alternative methods. We will now discuss the two common trading methods used in exchange trading of derivatives.

> **Note**
> OTC markets are informal markets that have negotiable arrangements and customized contracts.

2.1 Trading Methods

Trading methods on derivative exchanges can be divided into two broad categories: (i) the **open-outcry** or auction method and (ii) the **computerized** or screen-based method. Though the open-outcry method of trading has historically been the mainstay of exchanges, computerized electronic trading is now the norm. While the older exchanges, like the Chicago and London exchanges, which have always had open-outcry systems, have been forced to also introduce electronic screen-based systems, the newer exchanges are entirely screen-based. We examine below the features of each of these trading methods.

2.1.1 Open-Outcry or Auction Methods

Until quite recently, the open-outcry or auction method has been the mainstay of derivative exchanges. Today most of the world's exchanges are computerized screen-based systems. Despite the excitement and color of manual trading, the system is now being viewed as outmoded. Open-outcry, as the name suggests, is the manual trading of financial instruments by shouting out buy or sell orders and prices. In essence, it is competitive bidding based on prices as in an auction. Exchanges with open-outcry trading methods typically have huge **trading floors** within which all trading takes place. The large trading floor is subdivided into smaller areas known as pits or trading pits. Each trading pit is designated to trade one derivative contract. Some contracts that are very popular may have more than one pit assigned to its trading. In such a case, different pits may trade the same contract but of different maturities.

Trading is done by means of shouting out orders and use of hand signals. A standard set of hand signals using the palm and fingers are used. A trader wanting to sell would signal his intention by facing his palm outward and the number of extended fingers signaling numerical prices. Numbers 1 through 5 are represented by vertically extended fingers, whereas the numbers 6 to 9 with the fingers of the same hand extended horizontally. For example, the number 2 is represented by two vertically extended fingers, whereas two parallel (horizontally) pointed fingers would denote the number 7. Both the numbers 10 and 0 are quoted by a closed fist. Finally, a buy signal would be indicated by the palm faced backward. The numerals for the number of contracts and prices are indicated by extended fingers.

> **Note**
> In an open-outcry system, trading is done in a trading hall by means of shouting out orders and by the use of hand signals.

2.1.2 Order Routing/Trade Execution

In a manual system such as an open-outcry, order routing goes through several steps. A client who wants to trade derivatives would first call his futures broker (usually a company), and the brokers representative who takes the call processes the order and time stamps the order form before passing on the information to the trading floor. On arrival at the company's booth near the trading floor, the order form is again time stamped before being delivered to the respective trading pits by runners. The forms are delivered to the company's floor traders or **locals** for execution of the trade. It is these locals who actually carry out the trade. Once a floor trader receives the customer order, he signals the customer's buy or sell request and the prices. Should he find a match, the trade is executed, a trade form is filled out and sent out for clearing, and the customer is informed.

Depending on the structure and trading method used, an exchange would have several categories of intermediaries for the execution of trade, for instance broker members, clearing-members, non-broker members, locals, and trade affiliates. Each category of membership enables certain specific activities while disallowing other tasks.

2.1.3 Computerized/Screen-Based Trading

The alternative and increasingly popular trading method is the computerized or screen-based method. Under this method, there are no trading floors nor floor traders. The system works by means of a distributed computer network. Instead of being routed to a trading floor, customer buy or sell orders are keyed in directly into dedicated terminals in futures broker's offices. These terminals are connected to a mainframe central processing unit (CPU) which acts as a matchmaker. The terminals display the few best bid (buy) and offer (sell) prices. For example, the current five highest bid prices and the five lowest offer prices may be displayed at any one time. Once a bid price is equal or higher than the lowest offer price, a transaction goes through.

Note
In a computerized/screen-based system, trading is done by means of a distributed computer system. Buy and sell orders are entered directly into the system with the computer playing matchmaker.

The derivative exchanges in all the four territories covered in this chapter/book operate on fully automated electronic trading systems. As such, "trading" can take place at any futures broker's office anywhere in the territory. Since execution takes place almost instantaneously once a match is found, there is little time lag between when a customer order is placed and execution begins. Still, as in the case of an open-outcry system, customer orders are time stamped. The need for time stamping in both trading methods arises from the need to avoid "front-loading," that is, brokers taking advantage of customer orders to trade for their own account. For example, suppose a broker receives a big buy order from a customer. The broker knows that in carrying out this large buy order, prices are likely to be pushed upward. The broker stands to gain if he front loads, i.e., enters his own buy position before executing the customer's order. The impact that the arrival of big orders has on market prices is known as ***market impact costs***.

2.1.4 Open-Outcry versus Computerized Systems

Both trading methods have their advantages and disadvantages. Still, the fact that electronic screen-based systems have become increasingly popular, forcing some exchanges that have for decades used open-outcry systems to switch, implies superiority of screen-based systems. The open-outcry system does indeed have some shortcomings relative to computerized systems, the most severe being that it is much more error prone. Errors in documentation and communicating have remained a problem. On the other hand, open-outcry systems have the advantage that they are less prone to trading halts caused by order imbalances. Although open-outcry systems may be more adaptable at absorbing price jumps, computerized systems appear to be less so and subject to trading halts. Table 2.1 outlines some of the advantages/disadvantages of each system relative to the other.

Table 2.1 Comparison of Trading Methods

Open-Outcry System	
Advantage	**Disadvantage**
• Can handle order imbalances — smoother trading	• More prone to errors
• More transparent since less anonymity of traders	• More costly
• Traders can sense immediacy/urgency of other traders/markets	• Longer time lag — execution risk
	• Easier for orchestrated trading/ramping by syndicates
Computerized System	
Advantage	**Disadvantage**
• Less error prone	• More prone to trading halts
• Lower transaction costs	• Anonymity of traders/investors
• Faster execution — less execution risk	• Traders cannot tell urgency/immediacy

Box 2.1
Europe's Largest Open-Outcry Pit at London Metal Exchange, Reopens Following Pandemic Closure

The London Metal Exchange (LME), which despite changes in trading technology and trends continues to hold on to its pit trading, announced the reopening of its trading pit following a near 18-month closure due to the COVID-19 pandemic. The LME's pit trading tradition goes back more than 140 years from 1877. During the pandemic, while pit trading was closed, trading on its electronic platform continued. Though the exchange had proposed to permanently close the trading pit, its trading members were strongly against the move. The economics of costs and trading efficiency would not justify the continued the use of open-outcry trading pits, however, so the LME had to compromise with its long-standing trading members. The prices resulting from pit trading have traditionally been used as reference prices for transactions in the underlying commodities in other markets, including overseas. The LME's daily closing prices, which are used by banks and other market players for their daily marking-to-market valuation, are generated from the electronic trading platform. Despite all the nostalgia, the long-term viability of open-outcry pit trading remains questionable.

2.2 The Role of a Derivatives Clearinghouse

The **clearinghouse** is a key component of any well-functioning derivatives market. As the name suggests, a clearinghouse has the main objective of **clearing** trades. Simply put, clearing trades means identifying who has bought, who has sold, what amount, who needs to pay, who needs to deliver, to whom should delivery be to, etc. Though mundane, these are highly essential functions. Problems with any of these basic functions could seriously affect the integrity and credibility of the system and potentially lead to systemic risk.

A clearinghouse's functions can be broadly categorized into two basic areas: (i) **record keeping** and (ii) **risk management**. In its first function as a record keeper, the clearinghouse registers all trades that take place on the exchange. When a customer does trade, his broker has to clear the trade with the clearinghouse. The broker does it directly if the broker is a clearing member. Otherwise, the broker clears through another broker who must be a clearing member. Thus, every transaction that takes place on an exchange ultimately gets channeled for registration with the clearinghouse. Aside from being able to record the positions taken by customers/traders, this activity forms the basis by which the clearinghouse is able to carry out its second function, risk management. There are two levels of risk that the clearinghouse has to manage. The first is the risk faced by clients/traders. Notice that when a customer takes a long or short position, he or she is faced with counterparty risk, that is, the risk that the other party to the transaction might default. By means of the **novation principle**, the clearinghouse imposes itself as the intermediary in every transaction done through the exchange and sent to it for registration. In essence, the clearinghouse substitutes itself as the buyer to seller and the seller to every buyer. This substitution by the clearinghouse is a key facility in enhancing liquidity since it enables buyers and sellers to enter and exit markets easily. Since the clearinghouse, upon registration of the trade, guarantees the transaction, customers eliminate their counterparty risk.

Now that the clearinghouse has guaranteed every transaction, it has to make sure that neither of the two parties to any derivatives transaction will default. This it does by means of the *margining* and *marking-to-market process*. We examine the margining process in detail in the next chapter. Both the novation and margining processes are intended to ensure the integrity of transactions. The clearinghouse, however, has to further ensure the financial integrity of the intermediaries, i.e., the brokers through whom customers trade. The clearinghouse does this by requiring and monitoring performance bonds from its clearing members. The clearing members would require such bonds from the nonclearing brokers who clear trades through them.

It should be obvious that given the heavy transaction processing, clearinghouses would have high overheads. As such, unless there is sufficient trading volume, it would not make sense to have more than one clearinghouse. Thus, in all four territories, Malaysia, Hong Kong, Singapore, and Thailand, all clearing functions are consolidated within a single centralized clearinghouse.

2.3 Derivatives Trading in Malaysia

Malaysia currently has a single derivative exchange offering several derivative contracts. The single exchange is named *Bursa Malaysia Derivatives Berhad* (BMDB). Prior to the demutualization of Bursa Malaysia, BMDB used to be known as the Malaysian Derivatives Exchange (MDEX). As the country's sole derivatives exchange, BMDB trades both commodity and financial derivatives. Box 2.2 provides a brief overview of the historical evolution leading to the establishment of BMDB.

Box 2.2
Malaysia's Derivative Exchanges and Products — A Brief History

Currently, Malaysia has a single derivatives exchange known as Bursa Malaysia Derivatives Berhad or BMDB. Prior to the demutualization of Bursa Malaysia, BMDB used to be known as Malaysia Derivatives Exchange (MDEX). MDEX, which began on June 11, 2001, was the result of a merger by Malaysia's two previous derivatives exchanges, Commodity and Monetary Exchange of Malaysia (COMMEX) and the Kuala Lumpur Options and Financial Futures Exchange (KLOFFE). Though COMMEX was the older of the two, KLOFFE was the exchange that introduced Malaysia's first financial derivative. For the sake of historical perspective, the following is a quick overview of BMDB's predecessors, COMMEX and KLOFFE.

Commodity and Monetary Exchange of Malaysia

COMMEX, which was the result of a 1998 merger of two exchanges, had its beginnings in the Kuala Lumpur Commodity Exchange (KLCE). The KLCE, which was Malaysia's first derivative exchange, was established in 1980. As the name suggests, the KLCE was established to introduce and trade commodity derivatives. The first derivative contract introduced by the exchange was the Crude Palm Oil (CPO) futures contract in 1980. Subsequent to the successful launch of CPO futures, the KLCE introduced several other commodity futures contracts. These were:

- 1983: Rubber futures contract (RSS1, rubber futures)
- 1986: Rubber futures contract (SMR 20, rubber futures)
- 1987: Tin futures contract
- 1988: Cocoa futures contract
- 1990: Palm Olein futures
- 1992: Crude Palm Kernel futures

The CPO contract is the most actively traded contract and has been the key to the exchange's survival. This may in large part be due to the fact that unlike cocoa, tin, and rubber futures that are also traded in foreign exchanges in London, Tokyo, etc., CPO

Box 2.2
(*Continued*)

futures are only traded in Malaysia. As such, the CPO futures settlement prices in Malaysia are often used as reference prices in third-party trades elsewhere.

Just prior to the establishment of the KLCE, the Malaysian parliament had enacted the Commodity Trading Act, 1980. Following a market-cornering attempt in 1984, a new statute was introduced in 1985. Known as the Commodity Trading Act, 1985, this new act tightened the regulation and established a new regulatory authority known as the Commodities Trading Commission (CTC). The CTC was under the auspices of the Ministry of Primary Industries.

The year 1996 saw a major development at the KLCE with the establishment of a wholly owned subsidiary known as the Malaysian Monetary Exchange (MME). The MME was tasked with the objective of introducing and trading financial futures contracts. The need to establish a subsidiary to trade financial derivatives arises from the fact that several aspects, in particular the settlement procedures, are quite different for financial as opposed to commodity futures. MME initiated its first contract, an interest rate futures contract known as the 3-month Kuala Lumpur Interbank Offered Rate (KLIBOR) futures contract.

MME could not continue on its own with the single contract it had. In early 1998, at the urging of the Ministry of Finance, the two exchanges worked on a "merger." This resulted in the KLCE absorbing MME in December 1998. The new entity came to be known as COMMEX.

The Kuala Lumpur Options and Financial Futures Exchange

KLOFFE, Malaysia's first financial derivatives exchange, was established in July 1993 by a consortium of private companies. This first product was a stock index futures contract based on a revamped Kuala Lumpur Composite Index (KLCI). With the introduction of this index futures contract, KLOFFE became the second derivative exchange in Asia, after Hong Kong, to trade its own equity derivative. Exactly 5 years later, on December 1, 2000, KLOFFE introduced its second product, index options. The KLCI options, as they are known, have call and put options of varying strike prices available for investors.

Despite an independent beginning, KLOFFE's owners sold the exchange to Bursa Malaysia's predecessor, the Kuala Lumpur Stock Exchange (KLSE) in early 1999. For a time, KLOFFE was a wholly owned subsidiary of the KLSE. In December 2000, KLOFFE was merged with COMMEX to form MDEX. With the merger, all derivatives trading in Malaysia was consolidated under a single exchange, MDEX. MDEX itself was a wholly owned subsidiary of KLSE; KLSE become Malaysia's single exchange, trading stocks and both commodity and financial derivatives. With the demutualization of the KLSE and its renaming as Bursa Malaysia Berhad, MDEX was renamed Bursa Malaysia Derivatives.

2.3.1 Bursa Malaysia Derivatives

Until September 2009, when the Chicago Mercantile Exchange (CME) went into a strategic partnership with Bursa Malaysia and took a 25% equity stake, BMDB used to be a wholly owned subsidiary of Bursa Malaysia. The entry of CME as an equity holder of BMDB represents a major milestone both for the exchange and the country's derivatives market. Following this investment by the CME, BMDB's derivative products are now available for trading on CME's global electronic trading platform known as GLOBEX.

As for the products on offer, BMD currently trades a total of 12 derivative contracts. Of these 12, six are financial derivatives consisting of equity and interest rate derivatives, whereas the remainder six are commodity contracts.

These contracts are the following:

Equity Derivatives
 (i) Financial Times Stock Exchange (FTSE) Bursa Malaysia KLCI Futures (FKLI)
 (ii) SE Bursa Malaysia KLCI Options (OKLI)
 (iii) Single Stock Futures (SSFs)
 (iv) Mini FTSE Bursa Malaysia Mid 70 Index Futures (FM 70)

Interest Rate Derivatives
 (v) 3-month KLIBOR futures (FKB3)
 (vi) 3-year MGS futures (FMG3)
 (vii) 5-year MGS futures (FMG5)
 (viii) 10-year MGS futures (FMGA)

Commodity Derivatives
 (i) Crude Palm Oil futures (FCPO)
 (ii) USD Crude Palm Oil futures (FUPO)
 (iii) Crude Palm Kernel Oil futures (FPKO)
 (iv) USD, RBD Palm Oil futures (FPOL)
 (v) East Malaysia Crude Palm Oil futures
 (vi) Options on Crude Palm Oil futures (OCPO)
 (vii) Gold futures (FGLD)
 (viii) USD Tin futures

While the first four contracts are equity derivatives, the latter are interest rate derivatives. The 3-month KLIBOR futures contract, which enables one to borrow or lend RM 1 million for 3 months at the futures yield rate, can be used to hedge short-term interest rate risk. The MGS futures contracts, which have Malaysian government securities (or Malaysian government bonds) as their underlying, can be used to manage interest rate risk of medium and longer term. In the case of equity derivatives, aside from an index futures contract, index options are also available. In both cases, the underlying index is the FTSE Bursa Malaysia KLCI (FBM KLCI). SSF are futures contracts on a select group of individual stocks. We examine

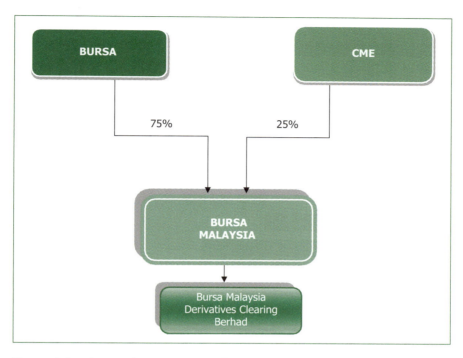

Figure 2.1   Ownership Structure of BMDB

all these financial derivative contracts in detail in later chapters. The CPO futures contract, which is by far the most actively traded derivative contract in Malaysia, is examined in the Appendix of Chapter 3.

Figure 2.1 shows the ownership structure of BMDB.

2.3.2 The Regulation of Derivatives in Malaysia

The objective of regulation is always to ensure fair and transparent markets by enforcing ethical behavior on the part of all players. In May 2007, the Malaysian Parliament consolidated three existing acts, the Securities Industry Act, 1983; the Futures Industry Act, 1993 (FIA); and part of the Securities Commission Act, 1993, into a single new act known as the **Capital Market and Services Act**, 2007 (CMSA). The regulation of derivatives now come under this new act, the CMSA, 2007.

Continuing from the FIA 1993, under this regulatory structure, an exchange is deemed a *self-regulatory organization* (SRO). This means that the exchanges are responsible for their operational compliance with the CMSA. Aside from ensuring self-compliance, an exchange

Note
A clearinghouse plays two key roles: record keeping and risk management.

Note
The regulatory framework for the financial derivatives market in Malaysia is embodied in the *Capital Markets and Services Act*, 2007.

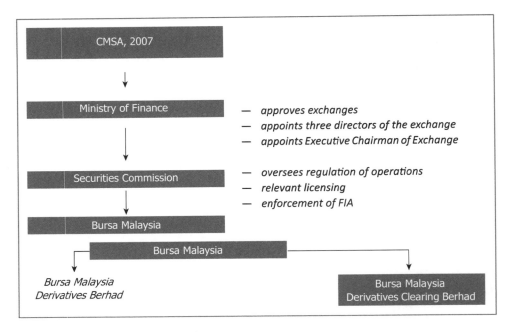

Figure 2.2   Derivatives: Regulatory Structure

is also responsible as a SRO for the compliance of their members with the act. The exchange does this by means of the various internal committees.

Figure 2.2 summarizes the current layout of the regulatory structure.

Note
The "novation principle" refers to the fact that as intermediary, the exchange becomes the buyer to every seller and seller to every buyer.

2.3.3 Trading Performance of Derivatives in Malaysia

Figure 2.3 plots the total annual traded volume for all derivative contracts available on BMDB. Looking at the trend, it is obvious that overall growth in volume has been impressive. Over the 13 years, total volume has gone from 6 million contracts to 18 million contracts, an increase of about threefold or an average annual growth rate of about 20%.

When we examine the decomposition of traded volume, the predominance of the CPO-based derivatives becomes clear. Averaging across the years, some 60%–80% of trading volume in each year was for CPO derivatives. Equity derivatives, the equity index futures, were a distant second. Thus, the growth rate in trading activity is heavily concentrated on a single product, CPO futures. Over the long run, BMDB should look into broadening the growth base.

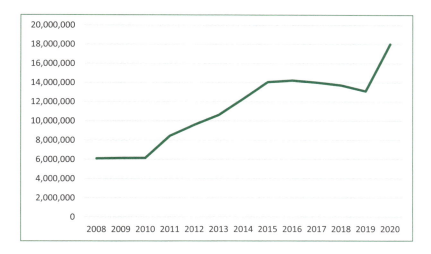

Figure 2.3   Malaysia — Total Annual Volume (All Derivative Products-Contracts)

2.4 Hong Kong Exchanges and Clearing

Hong Kong is undoubtedly one of Asia's key financial centers. Until Asia's largest territories like China, India, Vietnam, and such began to liberalize and open up their economies, Hong Kong, which was rooted in laissez-faire trade and capitalism, was a major player in Asia's financial space. Over the 1980s and much of the 1990s, Hong Kong had the third largest equity market in Asia after Japan and Australia. Leveraging on its huge hinterland, China, which was closed for much of the last century, Hong Kong built its markets as the gateway to China. Hong Kong, which has always been highly accessible to international investors, has now met its match and may soon be overtaken by China's own financial markets centered in Shanghai and Dalian.

Hong Kong established its first derivative exchange in 1976. This was the Hong Kong Commodity Exchange. The main products traded were futures contracts on agricultural commodities such as sugar, cotton, and soybean. A gold futures contracts was the only metal product traded. With a view to expand into financial derivatives, the Hong Kong Commodity Exchange was renamed the Hong Kong Futures Exchange (HKFE) in 1985. The following year, 1986, saw the introduction of the first financial derivative, a stock index futures (SIF) contract, named Hang Seng Index (HSI) futures. The underlying HSI has 50 constituent stocks accounting for about 58% of total market capitalization. The HSI is Hong Kong's most popular and most referenced stock index. This was Hong Kong's only financial derivative until the introduction of an interest rate futures contract in 1990, Hong Kong Interbank Offered Rate (HIBOR) futures, the underlying being the 3-month HIBOR.

2.4.1 Market Crash and Reform

The global stock market crash of 1987, which originated in the United States as the Black Monday crash, had a huge impact on Hong Kong. It laid bare the weaknesses of gung-ho capitalism. Hong Kong's stock exchange and the HKFE were shut down for 4 days supposedly to avert an even larger crash. For the futures exchange, HKFE, the closure, however, brought its own problems. Margins were triggered and difficulties with executing and administering the margining process nearly caused the HKFE to collapse. To avert such disaster, the Hong Kong government initiated a "lifeboat fund" with HK$ 2 billion injected to keep the exchange afloat. In addition, the government undertook major regulatory reforms to strengthen the HKFE. The main regulatory reform was the establishment of the Securities and Futures Commission (SFC). The SFC was made the direct watchdog of the HKFE. This was followed by major changes to the structure and organization of the HKFE, putting it on a template similar to the most advanced futures exchanges of the world. Further, in 1989, an independent clearinghouse known as the HKFE Clearing Corporation (HKCC) was established to undertake the clearing, record keeping, and guarantee functions for futures contracts. A similar clearinghouse for options was established as the Stock Exchange of Hong Kong Options Clearing House (SEOCH). Finally, since 2014, the clearing for all OTC contracts was centralized within a single entity, the OTC Clearing House.

2.4.2 The Regulatory Framework for Derivatives

All regulatory matters, execution, and oversight are vested with a single centralized entity, the SFC. The SFC, which was established as an independent statutory body in 1989, regulates the stock and derivatives exchanges and the OTC market. Being independent of the government, the SFC is funded by licensing fees and transaction levies. The SFC sets licensing standards, evaluates and approves new licensees, monitors the compliance and financial soundness of licensees, and undertakes investigation of misconduct. Though banks come under the purview of Hong Kong's Central Bank, the Hong Kong Monetary Authority (HKMA), banks that undertake securities and derivatives businesses are also required to be registered with the SFC.

If the events of 1987 led to the establishment of a centralized SFC that streamlined regulation, the Hong Kong government's subsequent initiatives led to the streamlining of the trading and organizational structure. In March 2000, three exchanges, the Stock Exchange of Hong Kong Limited (SEHK), the HKFE, and the Hong Kong Securities Clearing Company Limited (HKSCC) were demutualized and merged into a single entity known as the Hong Kong Exchanges and Clearing (HKEX). The three exchanges were merged through a share swap with HKEX listing itself on the stock exchange as a public listed company. HKEX was one of the world's first exchanges to be listed. Figure 2.4 shows the overall regulatory framework for derivatives in Hong Kong. HKEX, the holding entity, has three subsidiary exchanges: the SEHK, the Hong Kong Futures, and the London Metals Exchange (LME), which it acquired in 2012. The mutual market access that HKEX worked out with Shanghai in 2014 substantially added to the vibrancy

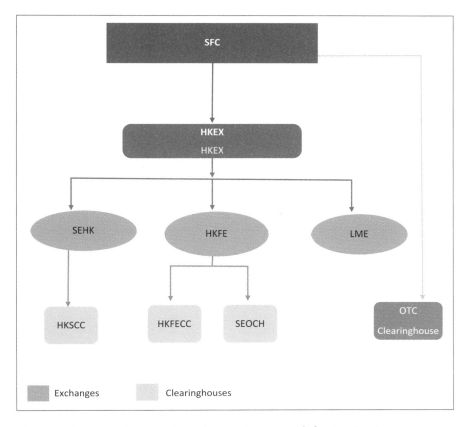

Figure 2.4   Hong Kong — Regulatory Framework for Derivatives

of Hong Kong. Known as the Shanghai–Hong Kong Stock Connect, it enabled traders to trade listed products seamlessly between exchanges in Hong Kong and Shanghai.

Where derivatives are concerned, HKEX currently offers listed futures and options in equity index, single stock, foreign exchange, interest rates, and commodities. As for OTC derivatives, Interest swaps, cross currency swaps, and nondeliverable forwards are offered.

2.4.3 Trading Performance of Hong Kong Derivatives

2.4.3.1 *HKEX Futures Contracts*

Figure 2.5 shows the traded volume performance of all futures contracts traded on HKEX over the 35 years from 1986 to 2020. Recall that the first financial derivative, the SIF contract based on the Hang Seng Index, was launched in 1986. As is evident from the graph, the overall performance of traded volume is nothing but impressive. Following what appears to be a difficult few years in the beginning, growth in traded volume has been strong. Annual traded volume, which in 1986 was 791,305 contracts, increased more than fourfold (450%) to 3,611,329 contracts the very next year. However, given the stock market crash and the events of 1987 as described earlier, total annual volume fell to a mere 140,155 contracts in 1988, which was less

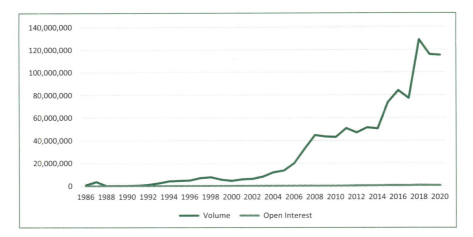

Figure 2.5 Hong Kong — Total Annual Traded Volume of Futures Contracts
Source: Based on data from https://www.hkex.com.hk/Market-Data/Statistics/Derivatives-Market/Yearly-Statistics?sc_lang=en#select1=0.

than 20% of volume in 1986. Traded volume remained low for the following 5 years and only started picking up from 1993 onward. It was from 2004 onwards that traded volume took off exponentially. The peak volume in 2018 of about 128.8 million contracts was approximately 160 times larger than 1986 volume. Over the 35-year period, the compound annual growth rate (CAGR) has averaged 15.3%. This is indeed impressive growth by any measure.

Within financial futures, the HKEX offers five main products. (i) HSI futures based on the HSI. (ii) The Mini-HSI futures which is aimed at retail investors with a contract multiplier of HK$ 10, which one-fifth that of HSI futures. (iii) HSCEI futures which is based on the Hang Seng China Enterprises Index (HSCEI). The HSCEI is an index developed by the Hang Seng group constituting listed companies from mainland China. The HSCEI futures were introduced in 2003. (iv) The Mini-HSCEI futures which is again aimed at retail investors and has a smaller contract multiplier. (v) SSF. In terms of popularity, going by 2020 numbers, the HSI futures accounted for about 36% of total futures volume, the HSCEI futures had about 31% of the volume, while the Mini-HSI futures accounted for some 24%. The Mini-HSCEI and SSF contracts accounted for a mere 4% and 1%, respectively, of total futures volume in 2020.

2.4.3.2 *HKEX Option Contracts*

Figure 2.6 shows the annual traded volume growth for HKEX option contracts. Though introduced in 1993, it was not until a dozen years later in 2005 that options became active and traded volume took off. Relative to futures contracts, volume growth of options has been even more impressive. From a total annual volume of 295,215 contracts in 1993, annual volume had grown to exceed 167 million contracts in 2020. The CAGR averages 25.4% for the 28-year period. Again, very impressive performance for a listed derivative product. In terms of products, several types of options are listed. By far the most active in terms of

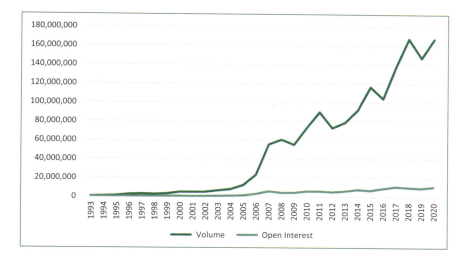

Figure 2.6 Annual Volume and Open Interest Growth 1993–2020
Source: Based on data from https://www.hkex.com.hk/Market-Data/Statistics/Derivatives-Market/Yearly-Statistics?sc_lang=en#select1=0.

volume is the single stock options. Based on 2020 volumes, options on single stocks account for about 78% of total HKEX option volume. This is followed by options on the HSCEI at 12% a d HSI options at a mere 6%. Several other options are offered, including Mini-HSI options and weekly HSI and HSCEI. These options have minimal volume. The weekly options expire on the last trading day of each week. They are designed for investors wanting to manage short-term risks or traders wanting short-term exposure to the underlying index.

There is no doubt that HKEX has been a success. According to the World Federation of Exchanges' 2020 Survey, HKEX offers 10 derivative product lines, and is among the world's top 10 exchanges for single stock options, stock index options, SIF contracts, and short-term interest rate derivatives.

2.5 Derivatives in Singapore

The derivatives market in Singapore can be dated back to the early 1980s. In 1984, Singapore International Monetary Exchange (SIMEX) was founded as the first financial futures exchange in Asia. In the same year, SIMEX launched the Eurodollar futures contract, the first futures contract in Singapore. SIMEX collaborated with the CME and pioneered the first international linkage known, which enabled the world's first mutual offset system (MOS). The system enables players on one market to offset their transaction on another market after hours. The MOS was used for the Eurodollar futures contract. This linkage with CME gave SIMEX the much-needed boost in its early years. In 1986, SIMEX launched the Nikkei 225 futures contract, the first Japanese stock market futures contract in the world. In its subsequent years, SIMEX introduced several derivative products including futures and/or options in equity, currency, energy, metal, and interest rates. In 1999, SIMEX, CME, and Paris Bourse together offered their derivative products on a single electronic trading platform, which is known as GLOBEX. In December 1999, three separate entities, the Stock Exchange of Singapore (SES), SIMEX, and the Securities Clearing and Computer Services (SCCS) were merged into single entity known as the Singapore Exchange (SGX). SGX is regulated by the Monetary Authority of Singapore (MAS), which regulates all securities and derivatives trading in the island nation.

2.5.1 SGX — Trading Performance

Toady, SGX offers access to a wide range of derivative products including equities, equity index, foreign exchange, dividend index, interest rate, iron ore and steel, freight, rubber, coal, oil, petrochemicals, and electricity. Currently, SGX's equity index derivatives are said to offer exposure to more than 80% of Asia's economies.

Figure 2.7 shows the annual turnover and open interest of all futures contracts traded on the SGX from 1993 to 2020. Today, there are more than 180 different futures contracts available on SGX. As is evident from the graph, the overall performance of traded volume has been impressive. Total annual turnover, which in 1993 was 14,768,322 contracts, increased more than 15 times (1,500%) over the 28-year period to more than 230,000,000 contracts traded in 2020. That is a CAGR of 10.4%.

At the end of 2020, SGX offered 20 option contracts on a variety of underlying assets. Options are available on shipping charter/freight rates, on currencies, equities, stock indexes, and commodities such as iron ore, coal, rubber, and precious metals. Figure 2.8 shows the traded

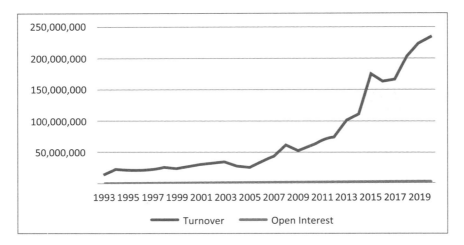

Figure 2.7   SGX — Volume Growth of Futures Contracts
Source: Based on data from https://eservices.mas.gov.sg/statistics/msb-xml/Report.aspx?tableSetID=III&tableID=III.8.

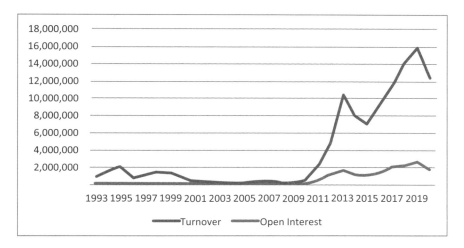

Figure 2.8   SGX — Volume Growth of Option Contracts
Source: Based on data from https://eservices.mas.gov.sg/statistics/msb-xml/Report.aspx?tableSetID=III&tableID=III.8.

volume performance of all option contracts traded on SGX over the 28-year period from 1993 to 2020. There were less than one million option contracts traded in 1993. The traded volume remained relatively low until it reached more than 4.7 million contracts in 2012. At the end of 2020, the total traded volume for options was 12,480,306 contracts, with the CAGR of 9.6% over the 28-year period.

SGX is undoubtedly one of Asia's premier derivatives exchange, according to the Futures Industry Association (FIA), a global industry association. SGX is ranked 20th globally among all derivatives exchanges based on traded volume and clearing activity for 2020. SGX has a total offering of nine derivative product lines. According to the World Federation of Exchanges (WFE) Derivatives Report 2020, SGX is placed in the fifth position globally for traded volume of SIF contracts. Although the SGX offers several SIF contracts, its most active SIF is the FTSE China A50 index futures contract. SGX is also placed in fifth globally for volume traded on nonprecious metals and ninth for currency options and currency futures contracts. For the trading of long-term interest rate options and futures, SGX was in 10th place globally. SGX has obviously been instrumental in placing Singapore as a premier financial center in Asia together with Hong Kong and Tokyo.

2.6 Derivatives in Thailand

The securities market in Thailand began in 1962 with the establishment of the Bangkok Stock Exchange. For several years of the early period, trading activities were not very active. In 1971, the trading volume only approximated $900,000 (30 Baht per US$ 1). To further develop and promote the capital market in Thailand, the Stock Exchange of Thailand (SET) was established in 1974 with the support of the Thai government. The SET is regulated and overseen by the Securities and Exchange Commission (SEC) of Thailand.

Following the boom in economic growth in Southeast Asia over the 1980s, the Thai equity market boomed with participation from domestic and foreign investors. Total market capitalization, which was estimated at US$ 1.9 billion in 1985, grew to US$ 24 billion in 1990, a massive 1,200% increase in market capitalization over 5 years. The privatization efforts of the Thai government, coupled with market liberalization, helped in a big way.

The SET's main index is the SET composite index that measures overall market movements. It constitutes all listed stocks on the SET and is calculated as a capitalization weighted index. The SET Index, which was launched in 1975 with an initial value of 100, was at 1616 on September 29, 2021. Thus, the SET index has had an average annualized return of 6.24% for the past 46 years.[1] The stock exchange also calculates the SET 50 Index. The SET 50 launched in 1995 is an index of 50 top SET-listed stocks.

Agriculture is one of the main sectors of the Thai economy. In order to support the growth and stability of this sector, the Agricultural Futures Exchange of Thailand (AFET) was established as the exclusive agricultural futures exchange in Thailand in 2001. AFET, which was Thailand's first derivative exchange, offered commodity derivative contracts on rubber, rice, and tapioca. Two years later in 2003, in order to support the growth of Thailand's capital market, the country's first financial derivatives exchange, the Thailand Futures Exchange (TFEX), was established. TFEX allows market participants to have access to a wide range of derivative products, both futures and options. In 2006, it introduced its first equity derivative product, an SIF contract based on the SET 50 Index. The SET 50 Index options were subsequently introduced in 2007. In 2016, TFEX merged with the AFET. Today, TFEX covers derivative products in several segments, including agricultural, currency, equity, interest rate, and metal.

2.6.1 Financial Crisis and Derivative Markets

The Asian financial crisis of 1997, also known in Thailand as the Tom Yum Kung crisis, started in Thailand and rapidly spread across Asia. Prior to the 1997 financial crisis, the Thai economy was booming because of huge capital inflows from abroad. The economic growth which was the result of liberalized economic policies led to appreciations in both real and financial asset values. Prior to the crisis, Thailand operated under a fixed exchange rate policy. Faced with speculative attacks, Thailand used its foreign reserves to support and stabilize its currency.

---

[1] The stock exchange also calculates the SET Total Return Index (SET TRI) to measure overall market performance in terms of both capital gains and cash distributions. The SET TRI started in 2002 with the base value of 1,000. As of September 29, the SET TRI was at 11,068. Thus, over the 19-year period, the SET TRI has an average annualized return of 13.5%.

These support measures resulted in a significant erosion of foreign exchange reserves.[2] In July 1997, Thailand was forced to abandon its fixed exchange rate policy and switched to a managed float. The result was an immediate depreciation of the Baht by 20%. The Tom Yum Kung crisis led Thailand to initiate several amendments of its laws and regulations on banking, finance, and securities business,[3] including new laws such as the Agricultural Futures Trading Act B.E. 2542 (1999) and the Derivatives Act B.E. 2546 (2003), by which the AFET and the TFEX were brought under these provisions.

2.6.2 Trading Performance of Thailand Derivatives

2.6.2.1 *TFEX Futures Contracts*

Figure 2.9 shows the traded volume performance of all futures contracts traded on TFEX over the 15 years from 2006–2020. The first equity derivative contract traded on TFEX was the SET 50 Index futures. In its first year, 2006, the total traded volume of merely 198,737 contracts. Traded volume, however, increased more than sixfold (610%) to 1,228,238 contracts in the following year. Interestingly, the traded volume was not affected much by the 2008 financial crisis. The traded volume was between 2,099,098 and 2,522,465 contracts between 2008 and 2010. As is evident from Figure 2.9, the growth rate in traded volume was slow in the first few years, but increased significantly in subsequent years. Even with the COVID-19 pandemic in 2020, the total traded volume reached 118 million contracts, the highest total traded volume since the contract was launched in 2006. Over

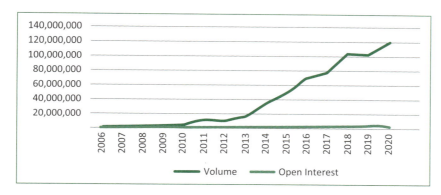

Figure 2.9   TFEX Futures — Total Annual Traded Volume and Open Interest

Source: Based on data from https://marketdata.set.or.th/tfx/tfexyearlymarketsummary.do?locale=en_US.

---

[2] Report of the Bank of Thailand's financial position in 1997, No. 16/1998.

[3] Apisith John Sutham, The Asian Financial Crisis and the Deregulation and Liberalization of Thailand's Financial Services Sector: Barbarians at the Gate, *Fordham International Law Journal*, Vol. 21, no. 5 (1997), pp. 1890–1940.

the 15-year period, of all futures contracted traded on TFEX, the CAGR has averaged 53%, a very impressive growth rate.

Currently, TFEX offers several futures products within equity futures. There are three main products: (i) the SET 50 Index futures which is based on the SET 50 Index, (ii) sector index futures which has a sector index as an underlying, and (iii) SSF contracts. Based on volume numbers for 2020, the SET 50 Index futures was the most active contract, accounting for 48.5% of the exchange's total traded volume. The SSF contracts were the second most popular futures product with about 40% of the traded volume.

2.6.2.2 TFEX Option Contracts

Figure 2.10 shows the annual traded volume of TFEX option contracts. Launched in 2007, the SET 50 Index option was not as active as the SET 50 futures in its early years. Index option volume, which peaked in 2020 at 1,698,625 contracts traded that year, is small compared to the more than 57 million SET 50 Index futures contracts traded during the same year. However, the growth rate of the traded volume of options has been impressive. In 2007, when the contract was launched, it had total traded volume of only 8,467 contracts. With traded volume 1,698,625 contracts in 2020, the CAGR averages an impressive 93% for the 8-year period.

In terms of its relative position worldwide, the FIA places the TFEX in 25th position for total volume of derivatives traded in 2020. Going by the WFE Derivatives Report 2020, TFEX offers five derivative product lines and is placed fifth globally for volume traded of precious metal contracts. TFEX is also ranked in seventh place for the number of SSF contracts traded.

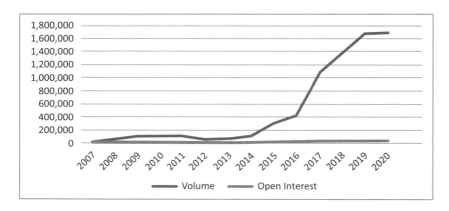

Figure 2.10   TFEX Options — Total Annual Traded Volume and Open Interest
Source: Based on data from https://marketdata.set.or.th/tfx/tfexyearlymarket summary.do?locale=en_US.

2.7 Relative Trading Performance of the Four Derivatives Exchanges

Table 2.2 shows a sample list of the world's derivatives exchanges ranked by traded and/or cleared volume as at the end of 2020. The four exchanges covered in this book are highlighted. Of the four exchanges, despite its relatively early start with financial derivatives, Bursa Malaysia is ranked the lowest at 33rd position. At the time of its introduction in 1995, the KLCI SIF contract was the first in an emerging Asian market. Only Hong Kong and Japan had SIF contracts traded based on their domestic stock indexes. Singapore's then SIMEX traded Japan's Nikkei 225 SIF as an offshore contract. Thailand's first financial futures exchange was only established some 8 years after Bursa Malaysia in 2003. Yet, as Table 2.2 shows, Thailand's future exchange has overtaken Malaysia's and ranks in 25th place. Hong Kong's HKEC is by far the most active of the four exchanges. It ranks 17th, ahead of Singapore's 20th position. While both these exchanges have tried to leverage on their ties with China by offering various China linked products, Hong Kong has been better able to capitalize on its proximity and its "Stock Connect" platform which links Hong Kong's stock exchange directly with exchanges on the Chinese mainland.

Table 2.2 Sample of Derivatives Exchanges Ranked by Traded and/or Cleared Volume

Rank	Exchange	Jan–Dec 2020 Vol
1	National Stock Exchange of India	8,850,473,823
2	B3	6,307,562,139
3	CME Group	4,820,589,858
4	Intercontinental Exchange	2,788,944,012
5	Nasdaq	2,660,595,514
6	CBOE Holdings	2,614,108,017
7	Dalian Commodity Exchange	2,207,327,866
8	Korea Exchange	2,184,930,969
9	Shanghai Futures Exchange	2,128,613,700
10	Moscow Exchange	2,119,939,033
11	Eurex	1,861,416,584
12	Zhengzhou Commodity Exchange	1,701,847,321
13	Borsa Istanbul	1,517,476,458
14	BSE	924,427,025
15	Miami International Holdings	827,454,642
16	Japan Exchange Group	454,261,835
17	**Hong Kong Exchanges and Clearing**	**437,073,315**

(Continued)

Table 2.2 (*Continued*)

Rank	Exchange	Jan–Dec 2020 Vol
18	Taiwan Futures Exchange	341,393,346
19	TMX Group	318,018,983
20	**Singapore Exchange**	**247,149,451**
21	ASX Australia	224,853,882
22	Multi Commodity Exchange of India	221,016,837
23	Euronext	175,583,217
24	JSE Securities Exchange	169,728,724
25	**Thailand Futures Exchange**	**120,193,573**
26	MATba ROFEX	117,485,220
27	China Financial Futures Exchange	115,281,396
28	Tokyo Financial Exchange	49,688,268
29	Tel-Aviv Stock Exchange	42,406,411
30	MEFF	40,476,929
31	London Stock Exchange Group	28,911,476
32	Indian Commodity Exchange	25,504,933
33	**Malaysia Derivatives Exchange**	**18,233,788**
34	Dubai Gold and Commodities Exchange	12,732,560
35	North American Derivative Exchange	11,737,457
36	Warsaw Stock Exchange	11,489,849
37	Metropolitan Stock Exchange of India	10,268,717
38	National Commodity and Derivatives Exchange	10,247,119
39	Athens Derivatives Exchange	9,975,260
40	Asia Pacific Exchange	8,823,345
41	BMV Group	6,847,410
42	Budapest Stock Exchange	6,378,441
43	LedgerX	3,537,129
44	Pakistan Mercantile Exchange	3,230,197
45	OneChicago	3,186,854
46	Minneapolis Grain Exchange	2,766,442
47	Dubai Mercantile Exchange	1,176,519
48	Bolsa de Valores de Colombia	697,016
49	Osaka Dojima Commodity Exchange	461,209
50	Indonesia Commodity & Derivatives Exchange	403,865

Source: www.futuresindustry.com.

Derivative Markets and Trading

SUMMARY

This chapter examined the operational and structural features of derivative markets. The differences between OTC markets and exchange trading were discussed. While OTC markets are informal markets that have negotiable arrangements and customized contracts, exchanges are formal, trade-standardized derivative contracts. The two types of trading methods for exchange-traded contracts were also discussed. The open-outcry or auction method involves competitive bidding by traders on a designated trading floor. Trading is carried out by the use of hand signals and shouting out orders. A screen-based system on the other hand works by means of a distributed computer system. Bids and offers are keyed directly into terminals. The computer plays matchmaker to the buy and sell orders. The advantages and disadvantages of each system were outlined. With the exception of a few hold-outs, most of the world's exchanges have moved to computerized screen-based electronic trading systems.

The chapter also examined the derivatives exchanges in Malaysia, Hong Kong, Singapore, and Thailand. Hong Kong's HKEX is the highest ranked of the four exchanges in terms of trading activity. Singapore's SGX has the second highest trading. Both HKEX and SGX offer a wide range of futures and option contracts. With Hong Kong and Singapore being international financial centers, both HKEX and SGX offer contracts on currencies, stock indices, and commodities from several countries, not just domestic ones. HKEX has benefited tremendously from mainland China-listed stocks/derivative products and as the investment gateway to China. Thailand's TFEX is the youngest of the four exchanges, having being established in 2006. Despite its newness, TFEX has had impressive growth in traded volume. TFEX currently offers SIF, stock index options, SSF, and agricultural commodity futures. TFEX is placed fifth globally by volume for trading in precious metal futures contracts. BMDB, despite its early start with financial derivatives, has the lowest total traded volume among the four exchanges. Though volume growth has been rising over the years, it has fallen behind the other three exchanges in relative terms. Today, its CPO futures contract, a commodity contract, is its main traded contract. This is unlike the other three exchanges where financial derivatives dominate.

KEY TERMS

- OTC markets
- Open-outcry
- Screen-based trading
- Market impact costs
- Trading floor
- Clearinghouse
- Novation principle
- Risk management
- Capital Markets and Services Act
- Locals

End-of-Chapter Questions

1. Differentiate between exchange-traded and OTC instruments. Under what circumstance might one prefer an OTC instrument to an exchange-traded one?
2. From a transaction cost viewpoint, how would OTC instruments compare with exchange-traded ones?
3. Derivative exchanges have traditionally had open-outcry systems, yet the trend now is towards computerized screen-based trading. Outline some of the causes for this trend.
4. Briefly explain the order routing process in an open-outcry system.
5. Compare and contrast the open-outcry and the screen-based system. Why has there been resistance from brokers to move from an open-outcry to a computerized screen-based system?
6. Derivatives exchanges in Malaysia, Hong Kong, Singapore, and Thailand have undergone several mergers. What were the key reasons for these mergers?
7. Describe the regulatory framework for derivatives in Hong Kong, Singapore, Thailand, and Malaysia.
8. Look up the websites of the derivative exchanges in Hong Kong, Singapore, Thailand, and Malaysia. State the main financial contracts currently traded. Which contract has the largest trading volume? Which has the lowest?
9. As a self-regulatory organization, how do derivatives exchanges ensure compliance?
10. Which are Asia's top derivative exchanges currently? Use the Internet to determine what their top derivative contracts are.
11. Despite being one of the earliest exchanges in Asia to have introduced derivatives, Malaysia has lost its relative position in terms of traded volume and activity measures. Briefly explain why this has been the case.
12. Among the three categories of derivatives available on HKEX, SGX, BMDB, and TFEX, commodity, equity, and financial derivatives, which is the most popular by traded volume? Why is this so?
13. What explains the rising popularity of financial derivatives even though they came about much later than commodity derivatives?

CHAPTER · 3

Forward and Futures Markets: Pricing and Analysis

Objectives

This chapter is designed to provide an in-depth understanding of forward and futures contracts. The mechanics of trading these contracts, their pricing, and related issues are analyzed. The evolution from forwards to futures, the exchange trading of futures contracts, and the exchange's risk management process through margins are examined. This chapter lays the foundation for the more complex contracts in the forthcoming chapters.

Introduction

Forward and futures contracts are two very common and highly popular derivative instruments. Recall from our definition in Chapter 1 that a derivative instrument is essentially a financial asset that derives its value from the value of its underlying asset. Thus, the value of both forward and futures contracts depends on the value of their underlying asset. One may be tempted to ask why such derivative instruments are necessary if the underlying assets themselves are being traded. Is this not an unnecessary duplication? The answer is no. Recall that derivative instruments were innovated in response to the needs of traders/investors. Thus, unless the newly innovated products have distinct value-added over existing products, they would be a mere duplication and will not survive over the long term. The fact that derivatives have been around for a while and have become increasingly popular globally implies that investors must derive utility from them.

The key utility that users can derive from derivative instruments is help with managing their risks. Risk management is the *raison-d'être* for the existence of derivatives. The original justification for derivatives was risk management. It is true, however, that given the features of these instruments, they could just as easily be used for speculative and arbitrage purposes.

If the need to manage risks was the original need for derivatives, the need to manage increasingly sophisticated risks led to the evolution of these instruments. As we saw in Chapter 1, there were two driving forces behind the evolution: first was the shortcomings associated with certain derivatives instruments themselves, and second, the evolving nature of risks. The evolution process, however, did not result in the substitution of the existing instrument by the new; rather the evolution has been complementary. That is, both the old and new instruments have coexisted.

This chapter begins with an examination of the most basic derivative instrument, the forward contract. We then examine in depth the futures contract, the mechanics of using these contracts, and their pricing and related issues.

3.1 Forward Contracts

Chronologically, the first derivative instrument was probably the forward contract. It was also the simplest type of derivative instrument. It is believed that variants of present-day forward contracts were in use in Japan, among rice farmers and dealers, as early as the 17th century. Even elsewhere, in Europe and in the United States (US), forward contracts appear to have had their beginnings in agribusiness, i.e., agriculture-related businesses/commodities. It is easy to see why this has been the case. Agriculture has several random elements beyond the control of man: the weather, insects, diseases, etc. These factors directly affect the supply conditions and therefore prices. Both products (farmers) and their customers — food processors, millers, etc. — were subject to these price fluctuations. Managing the price risk became critical not only for protecting their incomes but also for purpose of business planning. Life can be miserable if your income is entirely dependent on the vagaries of fluctuating marketing prices. Thus was born the need for forward contracts.

We now examine the mechanics of a forward contract. We do so by working through an easy example of a farmer and a confectioner. We then use this same example to examine the mechanics of a futures contract. In order to make it easy for a beginner to understand these contracts, we use the example of a commodity contract, i.e., a cocoa contract. We use a commodity contract as illustration here, simply because it is much easier for a beginner to understand given the physical flow of product (underlying asset).

Forward Contract: An Illustration

Assume there are two parties: a cocoa farmer who has planted cocoa on his farm and is expecting to harvest the cocoa in 6 months and a confectioner who produces chocolate using cocoa powder. Assume further that the confectioner has in his inventory sufficient cocoa to last him for the next 6 months, but would have to replenish his stock at the end of the 6th month. Clearly, both parties here are exposed to risk, in this case *price risk*. The cocoa farmer faces the risk that the spot price of cocoa could fall between now and 6 months from now when he completes his harvest. Such a fall will obviously reduce his revenue and profits. In fact, if the fall in spot price is sharp enough, he could even face outright losses. The confectioner faces a similar risk but in the opposite direction. The spot price of cocoa could increase between now and 6 months from now when he needs to replenish his inventory. Any increase in price will increase his costs and reduce his profits.

Since both parties face price risk and neither party can tell which way prices would go, it would be in their interest to go into an arrangement that could protect them from this price risk. Such an arrangement would be the forward contract. Under the forward contract, the farmer would agree to deliver and the confectioner to take delivery of cocoa of an agreed quantity on a mutually agreeable date and at a price determined now, i.e., at the time of initiation of contract. Notice that all items — quantity, maturity, and price — are negotiated. By means of such a forward contract, both parties eliminate price risk, in that they know exactly the price at which the transaction would be carried out at the future date. Aside from eliminating the uncertainty or price risk, such certainty would also help both parties with business planning. A forward contract, being a customized and documented agreement, is therefore an obligatory (legally binding) contract between two parties.

> **Note**
> A forward contract is a customized arrangement between two parties to carry out a transaction at a future date but at a price determined today.

The seller in the forward contract, the cocoa farmer, is said to be in the **short position**, whereas the buyer (confectioner) is said to be in the **long position**. Essentially, the short position is the party that promises to make delivery, whereas the long position is the one that promises to take delivery. Notice that at this point, nothing changes hands; what takes place at the time of contract initiation is merely negotiation and an agreement to carry out the transaction on the maturity date. So a forward contract can be thought of as involving two steps. A first step of negotiation and agreement at the time the contract is initiated and a second step on the maturity date when the contract is consummated. It is on the maturity date that the transaction takes place. On this day, the farmer will deliver the cocoa of the agreed quantity and quality while the confectioner will pay the agreed amount. This forward contract is summarized as follows:

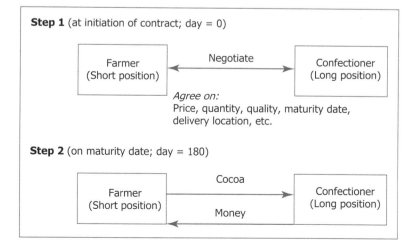

Figure 3.1   A Forward Contract

The forward contract, which is a relatively simple form of derivative instrument, was the only derivative available until the advent of futures contracts. As is evident, in a forward contract, both parties eliminate price risk by "**locking-in**" the price at which they would carry out the transaction at the future date. Once the forward contract is mutually agreed upon, neither party has to worry about subsequent price changes. It is by means of this price "lock-in" that both the farmer and confectioner hedge their price risk.

> **Note**
> The long position agrees to take delivery (buy) of the underlying asset, whereas the short position agrees to make delivery (sell).

3.2 Futures Contracts

Though the forward contract is simple in design and easy to execute, there are a number of problems with forward contracts. It is the existence of such problems that made it necessary to have futures contracts. Futures contracts can be simply defined as **standardized and exchange-traded forward contracts**. To reiterate from Chapter 1, forwards had three problems: (i) **multiple coincidence of needs**, (ii) **potential for price squeeze**, and (iii) **counterparty/default risk**.

> **Note**
> A futures contract is essentially a standardized and exchange-traded forward contract.

3.2.1 Multiple Coincidence of Needs

The first problem refers to the fact that at least three things must match before the two parties in a forward contract can even begin to negotiate prices. There must be (i) **asset match**, i.e., both the long and short positions want the same underlying asset; (ii) **maturity match**, where both parties find the maturity suitable to their needs; and (iii) **quantity match**, where both parties find the transaction quantity appropriate to their needs. In addition to at least these three matches, there could be others such as delivery location. As is obvious, such needs do not always fall neatly in place for two given parties. The result is that there could be substantial "search costs" involved. One party will have to search out the other thereby incurring costs in terms of time, advertisement, etc.

3.2.2 Potential for Price Squeeze/Unfair Price

The second problem with forward contracts has to do with price. Recall that in a forward contract, the forward price is arrived at through negotiation. The problem with negotiation is that bargaining position matters. If one party is in a weak bargaining position, he could be squeezed by the other. Typically, the "fair" forward price should equal the current spot price plus the cost of carrying the underlying asset to maturity. However, if there is only one confectioner (potential buyer of cocoa) in the district but several cocoa farmers, the long position has the bargaining power and could dictate on price. In such a situation, even if the cocoa farmer feels the price offered may not be fair, he may have little choice but to accept the price. This would be particularly so if the product is perishable and could spoil shortly after harvest. The short position does not have much of an option to wait and see whether he could fetch a better price post-harvest. An implied gain of RM 30 per ton since he gets to sell for RM 100 something that is now worth only RM 70. So, when the spot price subsequently falls, the long position stands to lose while the short position gains. On the other hand, at a price of RM 120 per ton, the farmer faces an implied loss of RM 20 per ton since he could now have sold the cocoa at RM 120 per ton instead of the forward price of RM 100 per ton. The confectioner on the other hand stands to gain RM 20 per ton.

3.2.3 Counterparty/Default Risk

Counterparty risk or default risk refers to the possibility that one of the parties to the transaction could default. Such default could happen not so much because the party is "dishonest" but rather due to the incentive to default given changes in the spot price. Recall from the earlier discussion that the forward price is usually arrived at by adding the carrying cost to the prevailing spot price at the time of negotiation. This then becomes the agreed price at which both parties lock themselves into. However, if spot prices subsequently begin to fall, the long position (confectioner) begins to hurt since he has agreed to a forward price based on the higher previous spot price. The opposite is true if spot prices begin to rise after the forward contract is negotiated. Now, the short position, the farmer, begins to hurt since he would feel that his cocoa could now be sold at higher prices. He would regret having locked himself into the "low" forward price. Table 3.1 shows the effect on each party if spot prices change subsequently. We assume that the two parties had agreed on a forward price of RM 100 per ton. We examine what will happen if say the spot price on maturity day is at RM 70 per ton or RM 120 per ton.

At a price of RM 70 per ton at maturity, the long position makes an implied loss of RM 30 per ton. This is because, had the confectioner not entered the forward contract, he could have bought the cocoa at the lower spot price of RM 70 per ton instead of RM 100 per ton. The farmer on the other hand makes an implied gain of RM 30 per ton since he gets to sell for RM 100 something that is now worth only RM 70. So, when the spot price subsequently falls, the long position stands to lose while the short position gains. On the other hand, at a price of RM 120 per ton, the farmer faces an implied loss of RM 20 per ton since he could now have sold the cocoa at RM 120 per ton instead of the forward price of RM 100 per ton. The confectioner on the other hand stands to gain RM 20 per ton.

Table 3.1 Payoff to Long and Short Positions

Spot Price at Maturity	Forward Price	Implied Profit/Loss	
		Farmer (Short)	Confectioner (Long)
RM 70 per ton	RM 100	+RM 30	−RM 30
RM 120 per ton	RM 100	−RM 20	+RM 20

To summarize from Table 3.1, the relationship between spot price movements and position is as follows:

- *Falling spot prices* are favorable to short position but unfavorable to long position.
- *Rising spot prices* are favorable to long position but unfavorable to short position.

And herein lies the issue of incentive to default. When spot price falls, the long position has incentive to default; on the other hand, when the spot price has risen, the short position has the incentive to want to default. The larger such price movements have been, the greater the incentive. Though the forward contract is legally binding, defaults can and do happen.

It is the need to overcome these three problems of forward contracts ((i) multiple coincidence of needs, (ii) unfair forward price, and (iii) counterparty risk) that futures become necessary. As mentioned earlier, futures can be thought of simply as standardized and exchange-traded forward contracts. As we will see later, such standardization enables exchange trading and together, these features enable futures contracts to overcome the problems of forwards. Table 3.2 outlines the key features of forward versus futures contracts.

Note
The long position gains when spot prices rise, while the short position gains when prices fall.

In order to enable exchange trading, the key features of a contract have to be standardized. Features such as maturity, quantity, quality, and place of delivery are determined by the futures exchange that offers the contract for trading. Each and every futures contract has its own "contract specifications," which lays out these standardized features. In deciding on these standard specifications, the exchange relies on judgment and on the existing business practices of players who would potentially use the contract.

Table 3.2 Forwards versus Futures

Forwards	Futures
• Over-the-counter (OTC) contract	• Exchange-traded, market prices
• Customized to needs of parties	• Standardized as per specifications of the exchange
• Parties deal directly with each other	• Clearinghouse is intermediary
• No margin payments	• Margins and marking-to-market processes
• Illiquid/untradeable	• Highly liquid/easily tradable
• Prices are negotiated	

3.3 Mechanics of Futures Trading

In discussing the mechanics of futures trading, we use the same example of the cocoa farmer and the confectioner. We do, however, need to add a little more details. Assume that the farmer is expecting to produce 120 tons of cocoa in 6 months and wishes to eliminate or hedge his price risk. Suppose further that cocoa futures are available in 3-month cycles (maturing in 3, 6, 9, and 12 months from now) and have a standard size of 10 tons per contract. The current quoted price for 6-month cocoa is say RM 100 per ton or RM 1,000 per contract. For simplicity, assume that the confectioner also requires 120 tons in 6 months.

Each party can do their hedging through the futures market as follows: The farmer would call his futures broker and short (sell) 12 cocoa futures for 6-month delivery while the confectioner would instruct his broker to long 12 such contracts. At this point, both parties would be fully hedged since in 6 months the confectioner knows he will have to pay exactly (RM 1,000 × 12) = RM 12,000 for the 120 tons of cocoa he needs, whereas the farmer is assured of RM 12,000 as payment for his cocoa. Notice that neither party needs to know who the counterparty is. Yet, each party is assured of delivery/payment because the exchange (through its clearinghouse) becomes the counterparty to both the farmer and confectioner. On registration of the trade, the clearinghouse guarantees the transaction. Assuming both parties hold their position to maturity, the cocoa futures contract will be settled on its maturity day (day 180) as follows:

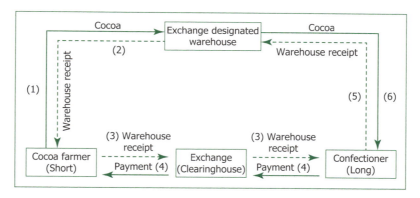

Figure 3.2   Settlement of a Futures Contract
Note: Numbers within brackets show the sequence of events.

Though the settlement (completion) of a futures contract appears much more complicated relative to a forward contract, as we will see, such a process enables futures contracts to overcome the problems a sociated with forwa ds.

The first problem of multiple coincidence of needs in forward contracts is overcome, since futures are exchange-traded. Since the exchange is the central point through which all trading is done, it becomes the focal point for **all** buyers and sellers. As such, finding a counterparty becomes much easier. Furthermore, since futures contracts are of standard sizes, ***divisibility*** is possible. That is, a seller does not necessarily have to find a counterparty who needs exactly the same quantity that he has available for sale. The seller's counterparty in futures could be several buyers, each taking his or her needed number of contracts. This ability to divide the sale to several buyers leads to a substantial increase in liquidity of trading.

The second problem of forwards, the potential for unfair price, is also overcome with futures. Recall that the forward price is a negotiated price that can lead to an unfair price to one party if the other has substantial bargaining power. Since futures prices are arrived at through the interaction of hundreds of buyers and sellers, such prices are by definition "market-clearing" prices. These prices would reflect currently available information and demand–supply conditions.

The third problem of forward contracts, that of counterparty risk, is also overcome with futures. Recall that the futures exchange, through its clearinghouse, becomes the intermediary in each trade. Once the trades are registered with the clearinghouse, the clearinghouse **guarantees** the trade. In doing so, the clearinghouse stands ready to complete the trade, even if one of the parties default. As such, buyers and sellers of exchange-traded futures contracts eliminate counterparty risk. In fact, traders of futures contracts would have no idea who their counterparties are and would have no interest in knowing so.

Our discussion thus far of the mechanics of futures trading has shown how futures had overcome the problems associated with forwards. Still, the careful reader would have noticed that while the three problems were indeed overcome, a new "problem" now exists. That is, all default risk has now been transferred onto the clearinghouse. It is obvious that with centralization of risk, the clearinghouse will have to carefully manage this risk in order to prevent systemic problems. The clearinghouse does this by protecting itself by means of **margining** and **marking-to-market processes**. We now turn to an examination of this critical risk management process of the clearinghouse.

3.4 Margining and Marking-to-Market

The transferring of risk onto the clearinghouse is not something unique to futures trading. In fact, most financial intermediaries such as insurance companies, finance companies, and banks take on risk transferred to them and manage these risks. Insurance companies may examine the safety and impose conditions on insurance that they underwrite. Banks manage their risks by undertaking credit analysis, requiring mortgage, a certain payment schedule, etc. Clearinghouses, on the other hand, manage their risk by means of margins and marking-to-market.

There are two types of margins in derivative markets: an ***initial margin***, which has to be deposited on the day the futures contract is entered into, and *variation or **maintenance margin***, which is essentially additional margin payments that would have to be paid if the initial margin falls below a certain level. The marking-to-market process can be thought of as the process by which the clearinghouse recognizes gains/losses incurred by the long and short positions and adjusts their margin accounts accordingly.

We now examine how this process works by using our example of the cocoa farmer and the confectioner. At the time of initiation of contract, both parties would be required to post margins. This margin is the ***initial margin***. The reason both parties are required to post margin is because both the long and short positions could potentially lose depending on which way prices move. The initial margin is typically a percentage of the total value of transaction, usually 10%–20% (depending on whether it is individuals or institutions and the perceived credit risk by brokers). The maintenance margin is usually a percent of the initial margin, e.g., 70% of initial margin. For simplicity, let us say the initial margin is 10% and maintenance margin is 70% of initial margin. Thus, both the farmer (short) and confectioner (long) would have to place an initial margin of RM 1,200 (10% of RM 12,000) with the clearinghouse (through their broker). Subsequent to this, each party's margin position will be adjusted as prices change.

Note
The clearinghouse protects itself from the default risk of participants by means of margins and marking-to-market.

Let us now examine the type of adjustment that will take place for a given range of futures prices. In essence, the marking-to-market process, which is done on a daily basis, recognizes the gains and losses of each party as futures prices change subsequent to their having entered the contract. This recognition is done by crediting or debiting each party's account at the end of each trading day. Losses result in debits (minus) or reduction in margin balance, whereas gains are recorded as credits or additions to existing margin. Table 3.3 outlines the process for a small range of futures prices.

Table 3.3 illustrates the margining and marking-to-market process for the first 5-day period using hypothetical futures settlement prices. On day 0, which is the day both parties enter

Table 3.3 Margins and the Marking-to-Market Process

(1) Day	(2) Cocoa Futures Sett. Price (RM per ton)	(3) Margin Account Farmer (Short Position) (RM)	Balance (RM)	(4) Margin Account Confectioner (Long Position) (RM)	Balance (RM)
0	100	1,200	1,200	1,200	1,200
1	98	+240	1,440	−240	960
2	97	+120	1,560	−120	840
3	98	−120	1,440	+120	960
4	96	+240	1,680	−240	720*
5	95	+120	1,800	+480*	1,200
				−120	1,080

*Margin Call is triggered as balance is below Maintenance Margin.

into the contract, the settlement price happens to be the same as the price they went into. On day 0, columns (3) and (4) show a margin balance of RM 1,200. This is the initial margin (10% of **contract value**) which has been arrived as follows:

Initial margin (I.M.) = 0.10 × Contract value
I.M. = 0.10 [(RM 100 per ton × 10 tons) × 12 contracts]
I.M. = RM 1,200

The assumed maintenance margin is 70% of initial margin. Thus, the Ringgit amount of the maintenance margin would be:

Maintenance margin (M.M.) = 0.70 × I.M.
= 0.70 × RM 1,200
= RM 840

This means that if either party's margin balance falls below RM 840, he would receive a margin call from his broker. A margin call is simply a requirement that the eroded margin account be brought back to its **initial margin level** by paying an additional margin.

On day 1, the futures price falls to RM 98 per ton. As we saw earlier, a fall in price would profit the short position but work against the long position. As such, we note that the clearinghouse adjusts for the price fall by debiting the confectioner's account and crediting the farmer's account. Essentially, this represents a movement of funds out of the "losing" account and into the "gaining" account. Since day 1 price fell RM 2 per ton (RM 100 − RM 98), the adjustment amount would be:

RM 2 × (10 tons per contract × 12 contracts)
= RM 2 × (120 tons)
= RM 240

On day 2, the price falls another Ringgit to RM 97, thus another RM 120 is deducted from the long position and the same amount added to the short position. Notice that after the deduction on day 2, the long position's margin balance is RM 840, which is the maintenance margin level. Since maintenance margin level is not breached, he does not receive a margin call yet. On day 3, the price goes higher to RM 98. This is favorable to the long position and so his account receives a credit of RM 120, bringing his balance to RM 960. The short position's account meanwhile is

Note
The initial margin is the margin required at the time the contract is entered into. The maintenance margin is the minimum amount to which a margin account can fall.

debited the RM 120 amount. On day 4, however, the futures price falls to RM 96. At this point, after day 4 marking-to-market, the long position's margin balance falls to RM 720. As this is below the maintenance margin level of RM 840, the long position will receive a margin call from his broker, requiring him to pay an additional RM 480 (RM 1,200 − RM 720) of margin. This amount has to be paid within a stipulated time the next day. Failing which, the long position would be deemed to have defaulted, his position closed out, the remaining margin forfeited, and he would be blacklisted from future trading. The RM 480 additional margin payment is shown in Table 3.3 with an asterisk.

The basic idea behind this marking-to-market is to make the players pay up the losses as the losses are incurred. In doing so, the clearinghouse protects itself. With such a process, players will have no incentive to default at maturity since they would have already paid for losses caused by unfavorable price movements along the way. For example, let us say that on day 180, i.e., 6 months later at maturity, the futures settlement (and spot) price is RM 80 per ton. If there were no margins nor marking-to-market, the confectioner will have a huge incentive to default on the futures contract since he can get the same cocoa at the prevailing spot price of RM 80 per ton (or RM 80 × 120 tons = RM 9,600 in total), a price much lower than the RM 100 price for the futures. However, by means of the margining and marking-to-market process, he will have no incentive whatsoever to default. This is because the system would have required him to pay additional margins as the price kept falling to RM 80 from RM 100. The amount of total margins that he would have paid would equal RM 20 per ton (RM 100 − RM 80) or RM 2,400 in total. That amount would have been moved to the farmer's account. Thus, the remainder amount that the confectioner will have to pay in order to take delivery will be RM 80 per ton, which is the RM 100 per ton original futures price, less margins already paid of RM 2,400, which is equivalent to RM 20 per ton. There will be no incentive for the confectioner to default since he would either pay the remainder RM 9,600 (RM 80 × 10 tons × 12 contracts) on the futures or default on the futures and still pay RM 9,600 for spot purchase of the cocoa (RM 80 per ton × 120 tons). The margining and marking-to-market process is therefore a very clever way by which the clearinghouse prevents defaults and protects itself.

3.5 Forwards, Futures: Zero-Sum Game

Notice that like a forward contract, futures enable the hedger to "lock in" the price he would pay or receive. In locking-in the futures price, the hedger eliminates price volatility, which is after all the objective of hedging. Still, the hedger who uses a forward or futures contract, while eliminating unfavorable price movements, will not be able to take advantage of favorable price movements. Thus, in our example, the cocoa farmer cannot benefit from subsequent higher spot prices once he has entered the futures contract. If spot cocoa prices are indeed higher than his RM 100 per ton (futures price) at maturity, he makes an "implied loss" of the difference. Similarly, the confectioner makes an "implied gain" of the same amount since he pays only the RM 100 (futures price) even though the spot price then is higher. This is evident from Table 3.3 earlier. Summing across columns 3 and 4, notice that the gain to the farmer equals the loss to the confectioner and vice versa. This is what in economics is known as a **zero-sum game**. In a world of limited/finite resources, most financial transactions, including all derivatives transactions, are zero-sum games, i.e., one party's gain is at another party's expense.

Also as with forwards, the long position in futures gains when prices rise, whereas the short position gains when prices fall. These implied gains can be summarized as follows:

If spot prices rise:
Profit to long = spot price at maturity − original futures price
(The short position's implied loss equals this amount)

If spot prices fall:
Profit to short = original futures price − spot price at maturity
(The long position's implied loss equals this amount)

3.6 Futures Markets — The Main Players

As is the case with other financial markets, there are hundreds of institutions and traders involved in futures markets. Categorizing them by their objective, we generally have three broad categories. There are (i) hedgers, (i) arbitrageurs, and (iii) speculators. We now examine how each of these categories of players would use futures contracts.

3.6.1 Hedgers

Hedgers use futures contracts to manage their price risk. While potential purchasers of the underlying asset would use futures contracts to lock in their price, producers would use futures to lock in their proceeds/revenue. Hedgers in futures markets are typically businesses that use derivatives to offset exposures resulting from their business activities. As in the case of the cocoa farmer and confectioner, when their underlying business activity creates the exposure, they use futures contracts to offset the exposure. For

Note
The basic idea in hedging is to establish a position in derivative instruments that would provide a pay-off opposite to that of the underlying asset.

example, once the farmer has planted the cocoa on his farm, he can be said to be "long" cocoa since he is committed to harvesting the cocoa pods in 6 months. To offset this underlying "long" position in cocoa, he takes the short position in cocoa futures. In doing so, he hedges his price risk. Should the spot price of cocoa fall, the loss will be offset by the gain on the futures contract. The basic idea in hedging is to establish an opposite position in derivatives such that the gain/loss from the derivatives position cancels out the loss/gain from the underlying transaction.

Price Movement	Impact on *Long* Underlying Position	Impact on *Short* Futures Position	Impact on Hedged Position
Increase	+	−	0
Decrease	−	+	0

From the viewpoint of the confectioner who **needs** cocoa in 6 months and is therefore in the "short" position, the profit or loss will be as follows:

Price Movement	Impact on *Short* Underlying Position	Impact on *Long* Futures Position	Impact on Hedged Position
Increase	−	+	0
Decrease	+	−	0

We have seen how a hedged position offsets gains/losses in order to provide a locked-in value. But how do we determine what is the correct hedging strategy? That is, when should we long a futures contract and when should we short? There are two equivalent ways to determine the appropriate hedge position. The first is to view the hedge from the underlying asset position. That is, if you are long the underlying asset, then the position in a futures contract of the same underlying asset should be short and vice versa. The second way to determine the appropriate hedge strategy would be to view from the point of price risk. To protect yourself from rising prices of the underlying asset, long the futures contract. To protect against falling prices, short the futures contract.

One should realize the congruence of both viewpoints. Someone who is currently long underlying would be afraid of falling prices and so, viewed from either of abovementioned viewpoints, should short futures contracts to eliminate the price risk. The relationship between underlying position, price risk, and hedge position can be summarized as follows:

Position in Underlying	Potential Price Risk	Appropriate Futures Hedge Position
Long	Falling prices	Short
Short	Rising prices	Long

An Anticipatory Hedge

Often, producers may not have an immediate position in an underlying asset but a potential position. That is, they anticipate having a position in the underlying asset at a future point. Notice that the cocoa farmer in our example did not have an immediate exposure. He is expecting to harvest cocoa in 6 months. Yet, he hedges the position today. This is what is known as **anticipatory hedge**.

3.6.2 Arbitrageurs

The second category of players, arbitrageurs, use derivatives to engage in arbitrage. Arbitrage is the process of trying to take advantage of price differentials across different markets. For example, many commodities and currencies are traded in several markets. Arbitrageurs closely follow quoted prices of the same assets/instruments in different markets looking for price divergences. Should the divergence in prices be enough to make profits, they would buy on the market with the lower price and sell on the market where the quoted price is higher. Since most financial markets are integrated by computer networks, arbitrage activity boils down to hitting the right keystrokes. As arbitrage opportunities can quickly disappear, quick action is needed. Thus, institutions (commercial banks, investment banks, currency dealers, etc.) that engage in arbitrage activity invest huge amounts of money in global computer networks and telecommunications equipment. These computers are programmed to track in real-time prices in different markets, identify arbitrage opportunities, and use the right arbitrage strategy. This process, which is known as **program trading**, has been an important contributor to trading profits of large investment houses. Since the underlying asset is the same, a given pricing relationship should hold between the spot and futures. (We will examine this pricing relationship in the next section.) Once this pricing relationship is violated, riskless arbitrage is possible. Table 3.4 shows the arbitrage strategy if the futures were *mispriced* relative to spot.

Table 3.4 Mispricing and Arbitrage Strategy

Nature of Mispricing	Arbitrage Strategy
Futures overpriced relative to spot	Short futures and long spot
Futures underpriced relative to spot	Long futures a d short spot

3.6.3 Speculators

Speculators are players who use futures contract to profit by taking speculative positions. In essence, speculators take long or short positions in futures contracts based on their expectation of the underlying assets price movement. For example, if they expect the underlying asset's price to rise over the immediate future, they would long futures contracts on that asset. On the other hand, if they expect the asset's price to fall, then they would short the futures contract. Notice that unlike hedgers and arbitrageurs who always have two net positions, speculators typically have a single position. For example, the speculator who expects rising prices would long the futures contract without any offsetting position in the spot market. As such, if the expectation comes true, the speculator makes a profit, otherwise he makes losses. So unlike hedgers who are risk reducers, speculators are risk-takers who often have uncovered positions.

Overall, speculators can be classified into three categories: (i) *day traders*, (ii) *scalpers*, and (iii) *position traders*. The day trader does mostly intra-day trading and on relatively small volumes. The typical day trader would take long or short positions of a few contracts and reverse out the positions later in the day when prices would have moved. The scalper is essentially the same except that the scalper takes big positions (large volumes) and goes for small price fluctuations. That is, a scalper would, for example, take a long position on a large number of contracts and then get out of the position once prices have moved up a little. He aims to make small profits on large volume. The third category, the position trader, is a relatively longer-term player. He often takes and hold positions for several weeks/months before getting out.

Box 3.1
Spot, Futures, and Competitive Strategy

A recent Bloomberg report argues that the Organization of the Petroleum Exporting Countries' (OPEC) attempt to curtail US shale drillers by increasing output and thereby causing spot prices to fall has had no impact whatsoever on shale oil production. The reason being that US shale oil producers had locked in their revenues by hedging with oil futures for the rest of the decade. The shale oil producers had undertaken anticipatory hedges by shorting oil futures contracts equivalent to their expected output levels. As such, OPEC's actions, which had caused spot prices to fall 14%, would have had no effect because the fall in spot prices would have been exactly offset by the gains in their short futures position. It appears that shale oil producers had learned their lessons from the oil price rout of 2014–2016 to better manage their price risks. The real loser in this episode would be the OPEC members, whose attempt to use pricing to curtail the competition had failed. The price cut would have reduced their contribution margin and revenue but not their market share.

The entire episode points to a key fact about the use of derivative instruments such as forwards, futures, options, and swaps. Aside from hedging, these instruments can be a strategic competitive tool. For example, an importer who had taken a long (buy) call option position would have a huge competitive advantage against competitors if the currency in which the imported product is denominated appreciates against home currency. The option position enables him to undercut prices and gain market share against unhedged competitors. Similarly, an exporter who has shorted currency futures or bought currency puts would be able to gain market share at the expense of unhedged competitors by keeping foreign currency price the same even as the foreign depreciates. The gains from the derivative position offset the losses from the depreciating foreign currency. In the earlier episode, OPEC could not kill off a marginal competitor because that competitor had protected their revenue from falling spot prices. Revenue had been detached from spot prices through hedging. By way of such hedging, the US shale oil industry has changed the industry's dynamics. Though small, they need not live at the mercy of OPEC. That derivatives can do all these is not obvious to many.

Source: Adapted from the author's op-ed piece, May 2017.

3.7 Determination of Futures Prices

Having discussed the mechanics of futures trading and its key players, we now turn to an examination of futures pricing. How are futures contracts priced? To answer this, recall from our earlier discussion the following two factors: (i) futures are like forwards except for standardization and exchange trading and (ii) futures like forwards are derivative instruments. First, since a derivative derives its value from its underlying asset, the starting point in futures pricing is the spot price of the underlying asset. Next, as in the case of forwards, the price has to be determined by adjusting the spot price of the underlying asset by the carrying cost. Carrying cost refers to any additional costs that would be incurred in the case of forwards/futures. Since a futures contract calls for delivery at a future date, the short position (seller) will have to incur additional costs like storage and handling costs, etc. Furthermore, as the payment for the futures will be received only at maturity and not immediately as in the case of a spot transaction, the short position incurs the **opportunity cost** of later payment.

Given the stated logic, it should be clear that to arrive at a futures price, we would first need to start with the current spot price of the underlying asset and then adjust for additional costs. Notice that there are two additional costs: (i) cost of storage which includes the costs of handling, spoilage, shrinkage, etc., and (ii) the opportunity cost of having to receive payment only at maturity of the futures contract. Obviously, both these costs should be **added** to the current spot price. Finally, there is one other adjustment that may be necessary. This refers to something commonly known as **convenience yield**. Convenience yield refers to any benefits that could accrue to the short position (seller) from holding on to the spot asset until maturity. In the case of most underlying assets, there is little or no benefit that arises from holding the asset, as such in most cases no adjustment is necessary for convenience yield. However, in the case where a benefit does exist, an adjustment is necessary. Since this benefit accrues to the seller, the convenience yield should be **deducted.**

To summarize our discussion thus far, a futures contract should be priced by first determining the current spot price of the underlying asset and then **adding** both the cost of storage and the opportunity cost. The sum of both these costs is known as carrying cost. Finally, any convenience yield should be deducted. Deducting the carrying cost by the convenience yield gives the net carrying cost or simply net carry. Mathematically, the futures price can therefore be written as:

$$F_{t,T} = S_o(1 + rf + c - y)^{t,T} \qquad (1)$$

where

$F_{t,T}$ = futures price for a contract with maturity from t to T (t = today, T = maturity)
S_o = current spot price of the underlying asset
rf = annualized risk-free interest rate (being the proxy for the opportunity cost of later payment)

c = annualized storage cost in percent (inclusive of shipping and handling, shrinkage, spoilage, etc.)

y = convenience yield (annualized percentage)

Equation (1) is commonly known as the **cost-of-carry model** (COC). Since the equation also tells us what the equilibrium futures price should be given the spot price, it is also known as the **spot-futures parity** equation.

> **Note**
> The logic of the COC model is that the futures price should equal the spot price adjusted for net-carry.

Using the COC Model: An Example

Using our example of the cocoa farmer and confectioner, let us determine what the correct price of a 6-month cocoa futures should be given the following information.

- Spot price of cocoa = RM 98.00 per ton
- Risk-free interest rate (*rf*) = 6% annualized
- Storage cost = RM 5 per ton/year
- Convenience yield to farmer = Nil

$$F_{t,T} = S_o(1 + rf + c - y)^{t,T}$$

$$\begin{aligned}
F_{180} &= \text{RM } 98(1 + 0.06 + 0.051 - 0)^{0.5} \\
&= \text{RM } 98(1.111)^{0.5} \\
&= \text{RM } 98(1.054040) \\
&= \text{RM } 103.30
\end{aligned}$$

The correct price of a 180-day (6-month) futures contract according to the *COC model* is RM 103.30. Notice that the **storage cost** of RM 5 per ton per year is entered as a percentage in the equation. The conversion from Ringgit amount to percent is done as follows:

$$\frac{(\text{RM amount of storage cost})}{(\text{Spot price})} \times 100$$

Also notice that the equation is raised to the power of 0.5. This is to denote the 6-month or half-year period. For a 90-day or 3-month contract, the exponential would be 0.25.

3.8 Issues in Futures Trading

In this section, we examine a number of key issues relevant to futures pricing and trading.

3.8.1 The Convergence Property

The **convergence property** is a key principle in futures pricing and price dynamics. Just as a bond's price at maturity must equal its face value, the convergence property states that the price of a futures contract on the day of its maturity must equal the spot price of the underlying asset on that day. The logic for this is that, on its maturity day, a futures contract is essentially a spot asset. A spot price is a price for immediate delivery. A futures contract on its maturity day is also for immediate delivery. Thus, since the underlying asset for the spot and futures is the same and there is no time difference between the two, it follows that the prices should be equal. In fact, the prices must be equal otherwise there would be a riskless arbitrage opportunity. One could even argue that the existence of such arbitrage opportunity would **ensure** convergence.

Notice that according to this property, convergence should occur only at maturity. Prior to maturity, the spot and futures prices would not be equal. There is a logical reason for why their prices would not be equal. Even though the underlying asset is the same, the spot and futures prices should not be the same since there is clearly a time difference between the two. The spot contract calls for immediate delivery, whereas the futures, delivery at a future date. This time difference brings into play the earlier mentioned opportunity costs, storage costs, etc. The net carrying cost therefore drives a wedge between the spot and futures prices.

However, as time passes by and the futures approaches its maturity, these net carrying costs would obviously reduce, thereby reducing the difference in prices. At maturity, the net carrying costs for the futures will be essentially zero. Thus going by Equation (1), the futures price will equal its spot price. Figure 3.3 shows this price dynamics.

Note
By the convergence principle, the price of a futures contract on its maturity day should equal the spot price of the underlying asset on that day.

Notice from Figure 3.3 that futures prices move in tandem with spot prices. This should not be surprising given that futures, being a derivative, derives its value from the

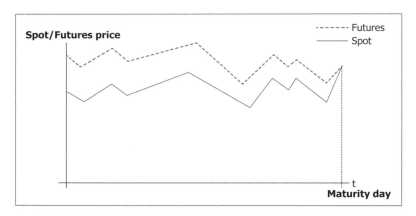

Figure 3.3   Spot–Futures Convergence at Maturity

underlying spot price. Also, notice that the difference between the two prices narrows as maturity is reached. At maturity, the two prices converge.

3.8.2 Basis and Basis Risk

The difference or spread between the futures and spot prices is often known as the **basis**. Going by Equation (1), the basis should equal the net carrying cost. As Figure 3.3 showed, the basis narrows over time to reach zero at maturity. Given convergence at maturity, basis must be zero. Prior to maturity, however, the basis would be positive or occasionally negative.

$$\text{Basis} = F_{t,T} - S_o$$

Basis risk can be thought of as tracking error. Such a tracking error happens when there are mismatches. For example, suppose the underlying asset of the futures contract and spot is different; then obviously there would not be convergence at maturity nor close comovement/correlation in the two price movements. This is basis risk. Basis risk would be present whenever there is any of these three mismatches: (i) asset mismatch, (ii) maturity mismatch, and (iii) quantity (or contract size) mismatch. A maturity mismatch happens when the hedging horizon does not match contract maturity. For example, you might need to hedge for 45 days but the **nearby contract** may have 30 days left for maturity while the later or **deferred contract** 60 days to maturity. In such a case, the hedge will have to be lifted/reversed before maturity, thereby incurring basis risk. A quantity mismatch might mean that either you overhedge or underhedge. For example, suppose you need to hedge 45 tons and contract size is 10 tons; you would either have long 4 contracts and leave the remaining 5 tons exposed or long 5 contracts and be overhedged. By definition, the existence of any one of these mismatches would mean that a hedge strategy would not be perfect — and so subject to basis risk.

3.8.3 Cross-Hedging

Cross-hedging refers to the use of a futures contract with an underlying asset different from that of the asset to be hedged. In essence, cross-hedging implies an asset mismatch. This happens because often there is no futures contract on the asset to be hedged. Cross-hedging is used extensively in currency futures. Often a currency to which a company is exposed may not have futures contracts; rather than leave the position unhedged, the company might use the futures contracts of other currencies that might have a high correlation with the currency to be hedged.

Since almost no two asset returns can be perfectly correlated, cross-hedging will always be exposed to some degree of basis risk.

3.8.4 Leverage and Transaction Costs

Among the many reasons for the huge popularity of futures contracts and derivatives in general are transaction costs and leverage. The much lower transaction costs of futures contracts relative to spot markets is a big attraction. Taking the case of the Malaysian stock market and index futures, the transaction cost of using futures is substantially lower. Often, transaction costs in index futures are a tenth of stock market transaction costs based on Ringgit value. Even among derivative instruments, the transaction cost for futures contracts is typically cheaper than those of forwards, which in turn are much cheaper than options. The reality of lower transaction costs makes futures contracts attractive, particularly to institutional investors. Since they buy and sell in large volumes, the savings on transaction costs could be substantial.

The other major attraction of futures (and derivatives) is the inbuilt **leverage**. Leverage refers to the use of other people's money in the financing of an asset. To use debt financing is to use leverage. As we know from finance theory, leverage magnifies returns. It is this magnification of returns that is attractive to traders, especially speculators.

Futures contracts have inbuilt leverage since one needs to only pay the initial margin and not the full amount. For example, if one were to buy the asset in the spot market, full payment would be due immediately. However, in the case of futures, one has to only pay the initial margin and not the full amount. Recall that the full amount is only due at maturity. Thus, if the initial margin is say 10% of contract value, then the trader who goes long is effectively leveraging the remainder 90% of contract value. It is the need to pay only the initial margin that provides the automatic inbuilt leverage in futures.

3.8.5 Margins and Leverage Factor

The initial margin and the extent of leverage are obviously related. The **higher** the initial margin, the **lower** is the leverage factor or leverage multiple. That is, if the initial margin is 10%, the leverage factor will be 10 times. This is because a trader pays only the 10% margin, or 10 sen per RM 1 of exposure. On the other hand, if the initial margin was raised to 20%, then the leverage factor would be 5 times. The leverage factor can be determined as the reciprocal of the initial margin.

A trader in futures could therefore control 10 times the value of the underlying asset if the initial margin is 10%. This means that his percentage returns would be 10 times more than that in the spot market. As such, a 10% fall in asset prices can wipe out all margins placed in futures, effectively a negative 100% return!

As should be evident, an exchange can control speculative activity by increasing the initial margins. In fact, exchanges often use what is known as **risk-based margining** for exactly this purpose. Where a futures contract is designated to have risk-based margining, the exchange is allowed to increase margin at times of abnormal volatility in underlying asset markets.

However, there is a tradeoff involved. While raising margins would indeed dampen speculative activity by increasing the amounts speculators have to place as initial margin, it would at the same time also hurt hedgers, since increased margins would mean more of their funds being tied up. This effectively increases the cost of hedging.

3.8.6 Contango and Normal Backwardation

Contango and backwardation refer to the pattern of prices between the spot and futures contracts. When the futures price is higher than the spot price and the distant futures contracts have higher prices than nearby contracts, the prices are said to be in **contango** formation. (*Note: Though the COC model would dictate such a price formation, contango really refers to the situation where the more distant futures are priced higher than the COC model would dictate.*)

$$F_6 > F_3 > F_1 > S_0$$

Backwardation is the opposite situation. Backwardation occurs when the futures price is lower than the spot price and the distant futures are priced *lower* than the nearby futures.

$$S_0 > F_1 > F_3 > F_6$$

The reason for such price formations has to do with "expectations." For example, when the market expects increased supply of a commodity in the future or decreased demand, one would see backwardation. If a supply shortage or increased demand is expected in the future, then a contango formation is likely. It should be noted that these price patterns are more likely to occur in the case of commodity futures rather than financial ones since it is in commodities, especially agricultural commodities, that supply shocks and the like can happen.

3.8.7 Open Interest and Trading Volume

Both **open interest** and **trading volume** are indicators of how active trading in a futures contract is. While the daily trading volume is simply the aggregate of total trade that took place in a particular contract for the day, open interest may be a more meaningful item where derivatives are concerned. Open interest is the total number of outstanding contracts for a particular contract month, for example the June cocoa contract or the March cocoa contract and so on. An outstanding contract is a contract that has not yet been offset. Since for every buyer there must be a seller, open interest is measured from either the buy or the sell side. So, a reported open interest number might be based on all long positions in the contract that have not been offset. Obviously, the total of the short positions must equal this number too.

Note
Open interest refers to the total number of outstanding long or short contracts for a given contract month.

Box 3.2
Schools of Thought on Asset Price Behavior

Forecasting the future price movement of an asset has preoccupied investors for a long time. As the ability to predict an asset's future price is a guarantee for profits, investors have always looked for ways and means to predict and explain these price movements. Over time, several schools of thought have evolved to explain the behavior of asset prices. Though these schools were mostly focused on predicting stock prices, their logic has been extended to other market-traded assets, both commodity and financial assets. Since a derivative contract derives its value from its underlying asset, the logic has also been extended to traded derivatives. Among the various schools, the two most commonly used for derivative instruments are Fundamental Analysis (FA) and Technical Analysis. We now briefly discuss each of these schools.

Fundamental Analysis
According to FA, an asset's price behavior is rooted in its fundamentals. In the case of stocks, it would be fundamentals of the underlying firm's performance. Thus, the fundamentalists, as the adherents of this school of thought are known, would examine the issuing firm's growth in revenue, profitability, market share, and factors like quality of management in trying to predict future performance of the stock. For a commodity derivative like the Crude Palm Oil (CPO) futures contract, fundamental analysts would examine factors like current yields, changes in hectarage, current inventory, expected output and weather patterns that could affect CPO output. In addition, they would also examine the output and prices of substitutes like soy bean oil and other edible oils. All of these factors go into deriving the expected future price of CPO and thereby of CPO futures. As any of these input factors change, so would their forecast price. Fundamentalists can therefore be thought of as Rationalists, in that, they attribute asset price changes to changes in the asset's underlying fundamentals. Much of what is taught in Finance courses in universities really belong to FA.

Technical Analysis (Chartism)
Technical Analysis or Chartism as it is often known is based on the philosophy that history repeats itself. Technical Analysts or Chartist as its practitioners are known, attempt to predict an asset's future price movements by analyzing its prior price pattern. The idea is to look for buy and sell signals from graphical analysis of price plots, and thus the name Chartism. Chartists depend on price/volume patterns, charts, and numerous graphical indicators to look for identifiable signals. For example, a head and shoulders pattern would signal the end of a bull market and the beginning of a bear market (down market) for the asset. Alternatively, the formation of a "W" (double bottom) pattern or

(*Continued*)

> ## Box 3.2
> (*Continued*)
>
> a "reverse head and shoulders" would signal the end of a bear market and the beginning of a bullish trend. This would arguably be a very strong buy signal. Technical analysis has literally tens of such patterns and indicators. Some technical analysts appear to prefer certain patterns/buy–sell signals over others. Although it is hard to rationalize the use of these graphical analyses, the underlying logic is that investor's psychology rather than fundamentals is what drives stock/asset prices. And since humans are creatures of habit, they behave in certain predictable ways. Thus, to tell whether investors will chase up or pull down an asset's price, look at the underlying psychology as portrayed in its current price.

To illustrate the difference between trading volume and open interest, we examine the following: suppose Trader A and Trader B who had no position enter a futures contract. Trader A longs the contract while Trader B goes short. The result of this transaction between Trader A and Trader B will mean that the trading volume rises by 2 since there are two transactions. However, the open interest only increases by 1. This is because, measured from either the total of long positions or total of short positions, open interest only increases by one, as a result of the trade between Trader A and Trader B. Suppose a week later, Trader A offsets his long position in the contract by going short (selling) to Trader C, who takes over the long position from Trader A. Trader A is now out of the picture. It is now Trader C who is long against Trader B who is short. On the day of the transaction between Trader A and Trader C, trading volume rises by 2, whereas open interest would be **unchanged**. Open interest is unchanged since neither the **total** of long nor short positions have changed. If a few days later, Trader B now reverses his original short position by going long against Trader D, a new entrant, once again, trading volume on that day will increase by two since Trader B is buying and Trader D is selling but open interest will be unchanged.

It should be evident by now that open interest should vary over time for a given contract. When an exchange first lists a contract for trading, open interest will begin at zero and must end at zero on its maturity day. Typically, one would see open interest increasing shortly after its listing and peaking close to its maturity. It should be noted that unlike forwards that are mostly held to maturity and result in delivery, futures contracts are mostly reversed out before maturity. In fact, empirical studies show that close to 95% of all futures trades are reversed out before maturity.

3.9 Types of Orders

There are several types of orders that one could place with brokers when transacting in futures markets. Though there are several types, they can be categorized into three major categories according to whether they are:

(a) Price-related orders
(b) Execution-related orders
(c) Time-related orders

In making a price-related order, a trader specifies or "qualifies" the prices at which the transaction should be done.

3.9.1 Price-Related Orders

(1) The Market Order
It is simply an order by an investor, requiring the broker to buy or sell at prevailing market price. The broker will execute the order *immediately* upon receipt at the best possible price. For example, suppose a trader wants to buy and so places a market order with his broker. Upon receipt of the order, the broker will try to execute the order at the last done price, if he cannot execute at that price, he will have to keep bidding higher until the transaction is done. As such, market orders are relatively safe in high volume, highly liquid markets. However, in thinly traded markets that have high volatility, placing such an order could mean execution at a price quite different from the intended price.

(2) The Limit Order or Price Order
In placing a limit order, a trader specifies the price at which he wants the transaction to be executed. The broker will then wait to complete the transaction if and when that price is reached.

(3) A Stop Order
A *stop order* may be either a *buy-stop* order or a *sell-stop* order. Essentially, it is very much like a *stop-loss* order which is intended to cut losses.

A *buy-stop* order is an order instructing a broker to buy at a specified price *above* the market price. For example, if you feel that CPO, which has been trading in the RM 950 – RM 980 range, could really gain in price if it breaks out of the RM 980 resistance level, then you might place a buy-stop order at say RM 985. The broker will execute the buy order when the market hits that price. The intention of the trader in placing a buy-stop order is to catch an upside rally at an early stage.

A *sell-stop* order is the opposite. Here, a trader instructs the broker to sell at a price *lower* than the current market price. The broker will execute when the market hits that price level (not immediately). Going back to the earlier example, suppose a trader feels that if CPO falls below the downside support level of RM 950, then it is likely to fall substantially in price, he might want to take advantage of the falling prices by initiating a *short* position early in the price slide. As such, the trader might place a sell-stop order on CPO at RM 945. If the specified price is not reached, the order is never executed.

3.9.2 Execution-Related Orders

(1) Market if Touched Order

A Market if Touched (MIT) order is a specific order to a broker to buy or sell if and only if the market price hits a certain price. The broker will begin to fill the order only after the market has hit the price. For example, suppose I place an MIT order to buy June CPO at RM 980; the broker will do nothing until the market price of June CPO futures hits RM 980. At that point, he will seek to fill my order. He may not be able to buy at RM 980, since the market has already hit RM 980. He might end up buying at say RM 985.

(2) Market on Open and Market on Close Orders

A *Market on Open (MOO) Order* is simply an instruction to a broker to either buy or sell at the market opening price.

A *Market on Close (MOC) Order* is an instruction to transact at the last minute, such that the transaction price will be the closing price.

Depending on demand and supply conditions, the MOC or MOO order may or may not be filled. Sometimes, it may be filled several ticks away from the closing price.

3.9.3 Time-Related Orders

(1) A Fill or Kill Order

A *fill* or *kill (FOK)* order is an instruction to a broker to either buy or sell *immediately or cancel* the order. If the broker is unable to execute immediately, he cancels the order. An FOK order is usually used for quick entry or exit.

(2) A Good till Canceled Order

Also known as an open order, a *Good till Canceled (GOC)* remains active either until it is filled by the broker or is canceled by the trader. A GOC order could therefore be on the broker's books for several days.

(3) A One-Cancels-the-Other Order

A *One-Cancels-the-Other (OCO)* order is used when a trader wants to catch a price breakout on *either* side. An OCO is essentially two orders placed simultaneously but with the stipulation that if one order is filled the other must be automatically canceled. For example, suppose you now have a long position in June CPO futures. It is currently trading at RM 930. You do not want to keep the position much longer. You want to take profit if the prices goes up or stop loss and get out if the price falls. In such a case, an OCO that constitutes the following two orders would be useful.

(i) Buy June CPO at RM 940
(ii) Sell June CPO at RM 920

As one order is executed, the other is automatically canceled. You achieve your objective of getting out of the market at either a slightly higher or lower level than the current price.

(4) A Day Order
It is essentially an instruction to a broker to transact at a specified price **within the day**. Thus, if the market does not reach the price level to enable the broker to transact by the end of that day, the order is canceled.

Box 3.3
Yet More Competing Schools of Thought on Asset Price Behavior; Efficient Market Hypothesis and Behavioral Finance

In addition to FA and Chartism that we discussed in Box 3.1, there are other schools of thought of asset price and market behavior. These are the Efficient Market Hypothesis (EMH) and the more recent Behavioral Finance School. EMH argues that market participants being rational would have priced in all publicly available information into an asset's current price. As such, prices will only change with the arrival of new information. Since the arrival of new information itself is random, prices move randomly. An efficient market is one in which information is available cheaply, publicly, and in a timely fashion.

Fama refined the argument and showed that different markets may have different levels of efficiency. He put forth three versions or levels of market efficiency, these being the weak-form EMH, semi-strong-form EMH and strong-form EMH. Weak-form EMH argues that future stock price movements are independent of past price changes. This effectively precludes the use of Technical Analysis or Chartism. Semi-strong-form EMH postulates that all available public information is reflected in a stock's price. Since a stock's current price already reflects all known information, researching a stock's fundamentals or analyzing its past price behavior is irrelevant and will not yield excess returns, effectively

(*Continued*)

Box 3.3
(Continued)

implying that in a semi-strong-form efficient market, both fundamental and technical analyses are useless. Strong-form EMH argues that a stock's price reflects not only all public but also private information about the stock. Thus, in a market that is strong-form efficient, even insider information will not lead to excess returns. Though there has been much empirical support for weak and semi-strong-form efficiency, strong-form EMH appears to be a difficult proposition to accept. There has also been consistent evidence of systematic patterns in stock returns. The presence of systematic patterns obviously flies in the face of EMH since a systematic pattern is by definition non-random. Systematic patterns in stock returns have been documented in several areas, notably day-of-week returns, a January effect, a small-firm effect, and the consistent outperformance of value versus growth firms. The presence of these inconsistencies has given rise to a new school of thought, the Behavioral Finance School.

Behavioral finance uses psychology-based arguments to explain investor behavior. Since other theories in finance assume rational investors, they are unable to explain the many market anomalies. Behavioral Finance makes no such assumption but accepts the reality of human emotion and psychology in decision making. Irrational financial decision-making that leads to market bubbles and panics are explained using cognitive theories from psychology in combination with conventional finance theories. Behavioral finance has its origins in the work of Daniel Kahneman and Amos Tversky, two cognitive psychologists who began examining the role of rationality in economics. It was Richard Thaler, an economist, who saw the value in Kahneman and Tversky's work to explain the many phenomena that conventional finance and economic theories could not explain. Together they laid the foundations of behavioral finance, though still new, behavioral finance has made much headway in recent times. In explaining "irrational" markets, behavioral theorists often point to investors making decisions based on "heuristics" or approximate rules of thumb and not necessary logic. In addition, different investors react differently based on their "mental emotional filters" or "framing."

SUMMARY

The chapter examined in depth the operation of forward and futures contracts. Futures, which are a standardized and exchange-traded version of the forward contract, were needed to overcome the problems associated with forwards. With futures trading, counterparty risk is transferred onto the clearinghouse. The clearinghouse manages this risk by means of the margining and marking-to-market process. Margining and daily marking-to-market reduce the incentive of both the long and short positions to default by forcing payment for losses as the losses accrue.

Futures prices are determined by adjusting the spot price of the underlying asset with the relevant carrying costs. The COC model shows the equilibrium between spot and futures prices. The chapter also examined related issues such as the convergence principle, basis risk, cross-hedging, price patterns/formation, and open interest.

Despite all the advantages of futures over forwards, futures contracts did not really replace forwards but are complementary. Forwards are still useful where customization is important. Thus, both instruments have coexisted in several asset markets. In the case of some assets where the forward market is highly active and deep, futures have failed to make inroads. In Malaysia, e.g., the existence of an efficient forward market in currencies has meant that exchanges have had no incentive to offer currency futures contracts.

Though in terms of transaction costs, futures are usually cheaper than forwards, one should note that forwards do not have margins. Thus, no funds are tied up for margins. Since default risk is a serious consideration in forwards, forward players like banks may not want to enter into contracts unless they *trust* the counterparty. Occasionally, a counterparty may require a margin even in a forward contract in order to protect itself.

KEY TERMS

- Price risk
- Short position
- Long position
- Multiple coincidence of needs
- Counterparty risk
- Divisibility
- Initial margin
- Maintenance margin
- Contract value
- Zero-sum game
- Locking-in
- Anticipatory hedge
- Mispricing
- Cost-of-carry model
- Spot-futures parity
- Convergence property
- Convenience yield
- Storage cost
- Opportunity cost
- Basis/basis risk
- Cross-hedging
- Leverage
- Contango, backwardation
- Open interest

End-of-Chapter Questions

1. Define what is meant by basis? State three situations that could result in nonzero basis at maturity.

2. You have gone long 4 September CPO futures contracts. The futures price is now RM 1,800 per ton. Assuming a counterparty has the same total value, determine the daily marking-to-market adjustment to both accounts and the balance on the 5th day.

   Contract size = 25 tons
   Initial margin = 10% of total value
   Maintenance margin = 70% of initial margin

Day	Price				
0	RM 1,800	___	___	___	___
1	RM 1,820	___	___	___	___
2	RM 1,790	___	___	___	___
3	RM 1,770	___	___	___	___
4	RM 1,800	___	___	___	___
5	RM 1,810	___	___	___	___

3. If the main difference between a forward and futures contract is that futures are standardized and market traded, how are futures contracts superior to forwards?

4. If the inherent leverage of derivatives is what causes increased volatility, why is it that derivative exchanges do not choose the easy route of increasing margins to reduce volatility?

5. Evaluate the following statement: Since the trading in derivatives is a zero-sum game, society has no benefits from such trading.

6. Define basis risk. State three instances in hedging where basis risk would be present.

7. a. You have gone long 10 June copper futures contracts. The futures price is RM 2,000 per ton. Given the following information, determine the daily marking-to-market adjustment to both your and the counterparty's account. (Assuming same total value.)

   Contract size : 10 tons per contract
   Initial margin : 10% of total value
   Maintenance margin: 70% of initial margin

Day	Futures sett. price
0	RM 2,000
1	RM 2,010
2	RM 1,980
3	RM 1,970
4	RM 2,000
5	RM 2,020

   b. If futures contracts are really market-traded forwards, what was the need for such an evolution?

8. What is the convergence property? Why is it that convergence must occur at maturity?

9. Suppose it is June 2016; you expect the price of rice to increase over the next 3 months. (Assume rice futures are traded on Bursa Malaysia Derivatives Berhad (BMDB) on the typical 3-month cycles.)

   Initial margin = 10%
   Contract size = 5,000
   Current spot = RM 3 per kg
   Transaction cost = RM 40 per contract (per round trip)

   a. Given the following information, what can you do to take advantage of your expectation? You have RM 10,000 to invest.
   b. Suppose rice goes to RM 3.50 per kg over the next 3 months. What is your net return in RM and % given your position in (a)?
   c. What would your net return in RM and % be if rice is at RM 2.25 in 3 months?
   d. Explain why the results in (b) and (c) are so different.

10. A farmer shorts cocoa futures contracts for 500 tons at RM 6,000 per ton. The exchange requires him to post RM 300,000 as initial margin. If the maintenance margin is RM 250,000, what price change (per ton) would lead to a margin call? What price change could lead to RM 30,000 being credited to his margin account?

11. Suppose that on September 15, 2016, you sell €100,000 forward for delivery on January 15, 2017. On September 15, 2016, the spot price of a € is $0.95 (i.e., the exchange rate is $0.95/€), and the forward price for delivery 4 months later is $0.92/€. Then, on January 15, 2017, the spot price of a € is $0.93, and the forward price for delivery 4 months later (i.e., for delivery on May 15, 2001) is $0.94/€. Determine your profit or loss on the transaction.

12. Suppose you bought one gold futures contract for August delivery at its April 2 settlement price of $279/oz. Assume that both the last trading date and the delivery date are August 27. Assume that your borrowing and lending rates are 8% per year, and that you borrow to meet any mark-to-market cash outflows and lend any mark-to-market losses.

    a. If the gold futures price remains unchanged until August 26, then falls to $250/oz. on August 27, what is your profit or loss per ounce?
    b. If, instead, the gold futures price falls to $250/oz. on April 3 and stays there until the delivery date, what is your profit or loss?
    c. If, instead, the gold futures price rises to $420/oz. on April 3 stays there, and then falls to $250/oz. on August 27, then what is your profit or loss?
    d. Given that money has time value, which of the foregoing price scenarios is most attractive: a, b, or c? Briefly explain why.

13. A corporate treasurer who was long 3-month futures contracts on British pound sterling for 400,000 pounds subsequently goes short 3-month pound forward contracts for 400,000 pounds. Assume the exchange rate in both cases is equal. What is his net position in British pounds?

Use the following information for Questions 14 and 15.

The spot price of tin is now RM 14,000 per ton. The annualized 3-month Kuala Lumpur Interbank Offered Rate (KLIBOR) rate is 8%. While there is no yield from holding tin, there is a storage cost. Currently, the storage cost is about RM 420 per ton per year. Futures contracts on tin are quoted as follows:

3-month futures = RM 14,171.80 (90 days)
6-month futures = RM 14,395.73 (180 days)

14. Assuming the contract size of the futures contract is 10 tons per contact,
    a. Prove that there is mispricing
    b. Outline the arbitrage strategy and show the profit if you took a position equivalent to 10 contracts. Assume the spot price of tin on day 90 is RM 14,300 and on day 180, it is RM 14,700.

15. You work at Datuk Keramat Smelting, Malaysia's largest tin smelter. Your company will have a large output of 120 tons available for sale in 4 months. Your boss wants you to design a 4-month forward hedge.
    a. Outline your hedge strategy using forwards (show the diagram).
    b. Given the background information above (before Question 14), what Ringgit amount can you lock-in with your forward hedge strategy?
    c. If your company's cost of funds is 12% annualized and the brokerage/transaction costs are similar between forwards and futures, which would you choose, a forward or futures contract? Explain your choice.

16. You want to hedge a large exposure in Renminbi (RMB). Suppose both currency forwards and futures are available for RMB.
    a. State the circumstances under which you may want to use forwards instead of futures.
    b. What key advantages do futures have over forward contracts?

17. An importer with €25 million payable in 90 days wants to hedge his exposure. He has the following information:
    - RM/€ spot rate = RM 3.95/€
    - RM/€ 60-day forward rate = RM 3.89/€
    - RM/€ 90-day forward rate = RM 3.80/€
    a. Based on the earlier quotes, what is the market's expectation about the € relative to the Malaysian Ringgit?
    b. State the hedge strategy using forwards with which the exporter can protect himself.
    c. If the importer were to ask your opinion on appropriate strategy, what would you advise him?

Appendix

The Crude Palm Oil Futures Contract

The Crude Palm Oil (CPO) futures contracts is a commodity futures contract and therefore beyond the scope of this book of financial derivatives. The underlying asset is crude palm oil. Even so, we take a quick look at the CPO futures contract as palm oil is one of the world's main edible oils and a key export of the southeast Asian region. The CPO futures contracts are currently Bursa Malaysia Derivatives Berhad's (BMDB) top futures contract by trading volume and open interest. It is also Malaysia's oldest derivative contract. CPO futures began trading on the BMDB's predecessor, the Kuala Lumpur Commodities Exchange, KLCE, in 1980. The CPO futures contract's popularity lies in the fact that Malaysia is the only country that has CPO-based derivatives. Indonesia, which currently is the world's top producer of CPO, does not have CPO derivatives, and thus, third country trades in CPO often use BMDB's prices for invoicing/settlement. BMDB has introduced a number of related contracts like futures on Palm Kernel oil and futures on refined, bleached, and deodorized (RBD) Palm Olein which is traded in US dollars. In addition, an options contract on CPO futures and a US dollar-based CPO futures contract have also been launched over the years. Despite the variety, the basic CPO futures contract denoted (FCPO) is the most active by traded volume. Figure 3.4 shows the trading performance of the contract.

Unlike financial futures (stock index and interest rate futures) which are cash settled, CPO futures call for physical settlement. Thus, unless a long position is reversed out, the long position will take delivery of the physical quantity. The short position that is kept open until maturity must deliver the underlying quantity. The form of delivery, quality of delivered product, place of delivery, etc., are prespecified and standardized. The CPO futures contracts have a contract size of 25 tons and matures every month for the immediate 6 months and every alternate month up to 24 months ahead. Thus, CPO futures could be used for

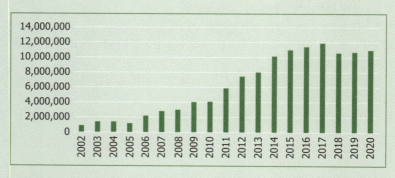

Figure 3.4   Total Annual Traded Volume of CPO Futures Contract (FCPO)

transactions up to 24 months ahead at any one time. As the only exchange-traded CPO futures contract in the world, the futures prices are used as reference price for palm oil trade elsewhere. Thus, third country trade in CPO is often based on BMDB settlement prices as reference price. Since September 2009, the CPO futures contracts are available for trading on GLOBEX, a global electronic platform hosted by the Chicago Mercantile Exchange (CME). The existence of physical settlement does not in any way impede the trading activity. That is, hedging, arbitraging, and speculation are not impeded. With physical delivery, however, arbitrageurs would have to offset their positions just before maturity. Hedgers may or may not close out their position before maturity. For example, a refiner who had short hedged his inventory of CPO would close out his position, but a manufacturer who had long hedged and needs the product might keep his position open in order to take delivery. Since long positions still open at maturity will result in delivery, a trader who does not want to take delivery of CPO must close out his position just before maturity.

Pricing CPO Futures Contracts

The same spot-features parity or cost-of-carry model can be used in pricing CPO futures contracts. However, since there is no yield on the underlying commodity, the term "y" is dropped from the earlier model.

$$F_{t,T} = S_o[(1 + rf + C)^{t,T}]$$

where

S_o = current spot price of CPO
rf = risk-free interest rate
C = annual storage cost as percent

CPO Pricing: An illustration

Suppose the spot price of CPO is quoted at RM 1,100 per ton. The annualized rf rate = 6% and annual storage cost per ton = RM 44 per ton. What is the fair price of a CPO futures contract maturing in 3 months (90 days)?

$F_{t,T}$
$\quad = 1,100 (1 + 0.06 + 0.04)^{.25}$
$\quad = 1,100 (1.10)^{.25}$
$\quad = 1,126.53$ per ton
Price per contract = RM $1,126.53 \times 25$ tons
$\quad = $ RM 28,163.25

Unlike financial futures that have virtually zero storage cost and no "spoilage" due to limited shelf life, CPO does have storage cost and a limited shelf life.

As such, the futures-spot parity condition may be somewhat *loose*. This is partly due to the fact that storage cost which includes spoilage could vary from time to time. As a result of seasonal production patterns, etc., commodity futures contract have a better chance of being in *normal backwardation*. Normal backwardation refers to the situation where futures prices are at a discount or lower than current spot prices. Usually, this happens when the market expects either the demand to be less or the supply to be higher in the future. Additionally, in the case of commodity futures, one has to be wary of several external factors that might influence current futures prices. The demand and supply of substitutes, weather patterns elsewhere where the substitutes are produced, possible production or transportation bottlenecks, etc., could all affect current futures prices. Although external factors are relevant to financial futures too, these have a more direct effect in the case of commodities.

Contract Specification: FCPO	
Underlying Instrument	Crude Palm Oil
Contract Size	25 metric tons
Minimum Price Fluctuation	RM 1 per metric ton
Daily Price Limits	Varies by time to maturity. See BMDB website for details
Contract Months	Spot month and the next 5 succeeding months, and thereafter, alternate months up to 24 months ahead
Trading Hours	First trading session: Malaysian 10:30 a.m. to 12:30 p.m. Second trading session: Malaysian 3:00 p.m. to 6:00 p.m.
Contract Specification: FCPO	
Speculative Position Limits	The maximum number of net long or net short positions which a client or a participant may hold or control is: • 800 contracts for the spot month • 10,000 contracts for any one contract month except for spot month • 15,000 contracts for all months combined The above position limit will be a combined limit for FCPO Contracts and Options on FCPO. (Please note that spot month futures limit will not be applicable to the options.)
Final Trading Day and Maturity Date	Contract expires at noon on the 15th day of the delivery month, or if the 15th is a non-market day, the preceding Business Day.
Tender Period	First Calendar Day to the 20th Calendar Day of the spot month, or if the 20th is a nonmarket day, the preceding Business Day.
Contract Grade and Delivery Points	CPO of good merchantable quality, in bulk, unbleached, in Port Tank Installations approved by the Exchange located at the option of the seller at Port Kelang, Penang/Butterworth and Pasir Gudang (Johor). Free fatty acids (FFA) of palm oil delivered into Port Tank Installations shall not exceed 4% and from Port Tank Installations shall not exceed 5%. Moisture and impurities shall not exceed 0.25%. Deterioration of Bleachability Index (DOBI) value of palm oil delivered into Port Tank Installations shall be at a minimum of 2.5 and of palm oil delivered from Port Tank Installations shall be at a minimum of 2.31.

(Continued)

Contract Specification: FCPO	
Deliverable Unit	25 metric tons, plus or minus not more than 2%. Settlement of weight differences shall be based on the simple average of the daily Settlement Prices of the delivery month from: (a) The first Business Day of the delivery month to the day of tender, if the tender is made before the last trading day of the delivery month (b) The first Business Day of the delivery month to the last day of trading, if the tender is made on the last trading day or thereafter

Source: Bursa Malaysia website.

Notice that the contract specifications clearly outline the several features of the contract. Minimum price fluctuation and daily price limits are intended to check excessive price volatility. Specifying the grade of product to be delivered and point of delivery avoids problems with delivery. Note that items such as moisture content and impurities that could affect quality are also clearly laid down. This is intended to prevent the delivery of poor quality material and to ensure fair play. Finally, reportable positions, speculative position limit and transaction limits are put in place to curb excessive speculative activity.

CPO Futures Contracts: Applications

This subsection discusses the applications for CPO futures contracts. Recall that there are generally three broad application for derivatives: hedging, arbitraging, and speculating. (Note: These applications are dealt with in greater depth in Chapters 4 and 5.)

(I) Hedging with CPO Futures

A refiner has 250 tons of CPO in inventory. He will be holding this over the next 3 months. He intends to protect himself from a fall in the price of CPO which could cause him losses since his output price is tied to CPO prices. He has the following information.

Current inventory	= 250 tons
Spot price	= RM 1,100 per ton
rf rate	= 6% per year
Annual storage cost	= RM 44 per ton (4% per annum)
3-month CPO futures	= RM 1,126.53 per ton

How can the refiner use the CPO futures contract to protect himself from falling CPO prices?

Answer: Short 10 three-month CPO futures contracts

To prove that the hedge strategy will "lock-in" the value of his inventory, we examine two possible price scenarios for the CPO in 90 days.

Scenario 1: Suppose CPO Price Falls 20% (to RM 880 per ton)

Action	Position Today	Position at Maturity	Profit/Loss
Long inventory position	RM 275,000	RM 220,000	(RM 55,000)
Short 10 CPO futures	RM 281,632.50	(RM 220,000)	RM 61,632.50
Less storage cost	–	(RM 2,750)	(RM 2,750)
			Net gain = RM 3,882.50

(Storage cost = RM 44 per ton/4 = RM 11 per ton for 3 months. RM 11 × 250 tons = RM 2,750)

Scenario 2: Suppose CPO Price Rises 20% (to RM 1,320 per ton)

Action	Position Today	Position at Maturity	Profit/Loss
Long inventory position	RM 275,000	RM 330,000	RM 55,000
Short 10 CPO futures	RM 281,632.50	(RM 330,000)	(RM 48,367.50)
Less storage cost	–	(RM 2,750)	(RM 2,750)
			Net gain = RM 3,882.50

Analysis of Hedged Position

Scenario 1: CPO Price ↓ 20%

Initial value of position	= RM 275,000
• Unhedged value at maturity	= RM 220,000
• Profit from short CPO futures	= RM 61,632.50
• Less storage cost	= (RM 2,750)
Value of hedged position	= RM 278,882.50

Scenario 2: CPO Price ↑ 20%

Initial value of position	= RM 275,000
• Unhedged value at maturity	= RM 330,000
• Loss from short CPO futures	= (RM 48,367.50)
• Less storage cost	= (RM 2,750)
Value of hedged position	= RM 278,882.50

Notice that regardless of whichever way CPO prices go, the value of the hedged position is the same. This is precisely the objective of hedging — to "lock-in" a value. You would also notice that under both scenarios, the value of the hedged position is higher than the initial value by RM 3,882.50. This gain, which was shown in the tables, represents the return to the hedged position. In percentage terms, the RM 3,882.50 would approximate the risk-free rate. Since a fully hedged position is riskless, one earns a return approximating the risk-free rate of return.

(II) Arbitraging with CPO Futures

Suppose on a certain day, you notice the following quotes.

CPO spot price = RM 980 per ton
rf rate = 6% per year
Annual storage cost = 4% per year (RM 39.20 per ton)
3-month CPO futures = RM 1,013.63 (90 days to maturity)

Is arbitrage possible? If so, how would you arbitrage?

Step 1: Determine correct price of futures and compare with futures price quoted.
$$F = 980(1 + 0.06 + 0.04)^{0.25}$$
$$= RM\ 1,003.63$$
Thus, the 3-month futures contract is overpriced by RM 10 per ton.

Step 2: Given the mispricing, determine arbitrage strategy.
Arbitrage strategy: Long Spot, Short Futures (Cash and Carry Strategy)
Suppose the price at maturity is RM 1,015, what would your profit be if you are willing to invest in 50 tons?

Action	Position Today	Position at Maturity	Profit/Loss
Long 50 ton spot	(49,000)	50,750	1,750
Short 2 futures contracts [(1,013.63 × 25) × 2]	50,681.50	(50,750)	(68.50)
Carrying cost $[(1.10)^{0.25} \times 49,000] - 49,000$	–	–	(1,181.57)
			Net gain = 499.93

This net gain of RM 499.93 is really the mispricing of the futures contract (RM 10 per ton × 50 tons = RM 500). Note that this amount is pure arbitrage profit. It is riskless profit since your exposure was covered by the offsetting position.

(III) Speculating with CPO Futures

Suppose a trader with no current position in CPO is bullish about CPO spot and futures prices over the next 3 months. He believes CPO prices are headed higher and wishes to profit from his expectation. He observes that the 3-month CPO futures with 90-day maturity is quoted at RM 980 per ton.

What is the appropriate speculative strategy? Since he is bullish and expects prices to go up, the appropriate strategy would be to long CPO futures contracts. Suppose the speculator goes long on 3-month CPO futures contracts.

Scenario 1
Suppose CPO price in 90 days (at futures maturity) is 20% higher at RM 1,176.
Profit on futures = (Exit Price − Entry Price) × 25 tons
Profit on futures = (RM 1,176 − RM 980) × 25 tons
             = RM 4,900

Scenario 2
Suppose CPO price in 90 days is 20% lower at RM 784.
Profit on futures = (RM 784 − RM 980) × 25 tons
             = (RM 4,900)

In Scenario 1, when CPO prices go up as per his expectation, the speculator makes a profit of RM 4,900. However, when the price goes down by an equal quantum, he losses RM 4,900. This is precisely the danger with speculative positions. One makes money if prices go as per expectation, otherwise losses are incurred.

Unlike the hedge and arbitrage positions that involved simultaneous positions in both the spot and futures contracts, speculative positions typically only involve a position in either. For example, in the earlier example, the speculator uses only the futures contract. Though most speculative trades are as such, one variant of the speculative strategy, the spread position, involves the use of both. This strategy is examined in Chapter 4.

CHAPTER · 4

Stock Index Futures Contracts: Analysis and Applications

Objectives

This chapter examines equity futures contracts like stock index futures (SIF) and single stock futures (SSF) contracts. In-depth analysis is undertaken for two SIF contracts, the FTSE Bursa Malaysia Kuala Lumpur Composite Index (FBM KLCI) futures (FKLI) traded on Bursa Malaysia Derivatives Berhad (BMDB) and the SET 50 Index futures contract traded on the Thailand Futures Exchange (TFEX). The chapter describes how these contracts can be used for hedging, arbitrage, and speculative purposes. SSF contracts available on both BMDB and TFEX are also examined. On completing this chapter, you should have a good understanding of SIF and SSF contracts and their applications.

Introduction

Exchange-traded equity futures contracts are generally of two kinds, stock index futures contracts (SIF) and single stock futures (SSF). An SIF contract is an exchange-traded futures contract that has, as its underlying asset, a basket of common stocks. The basket of common stocks would together make up an index. An index is simply a composite of several stocks traded in an exchange. For example, the Dow Jones is an index made up of 30 stocks traded on the New York Stock Exchange (NYSE). The FTSE Bursa Malaysia Kuala Lumpur Composite Index (FBM KLCI) is an index of 30 stocks traded on Bursa Malaysia, while the SET 50 is an index of the top 50 stocks listed on the Thai stock exchange. The purchase of an SIF contract entitles one to "take delivery" of the group of stocks that make up the index at a prespecified price and at a predetermined future date. As the underlying asset is an equity index, SIF contracts are equity derivatives.

Note
An SIF contract is an exchange-traded equity derivative. Its underlying asset is the basket of common stocks that make up the index.

Since all SIF contracts are ***cash-settled***, the long position receives a cash settlement equivalent to the value of the underlying stocks, instead of the underlying group of stocks. The long position would have made a profit if the cash received on settlement is higher than what was paid in margins. This would be the case, if the index closes at maturity at a higher point, then when entered into. The need for cash settlement arises from the fact that physical delivery of the group of stocks that make up an index would be very cumbersome and costly. If the contract is physically-settled, the short position (seller) would have to buy each stock in the correct proportion according to its weight in the index in order to deliver. Aside from the unnecessary transaction costs that would be incurred in purchasing each of the component stocks, there could also be problems with odd lots, stock registration, etc., for the long position who receives the stocks. With cash settlement, all of these problems are overcome.

> **Note**
> SIF contracts are cash-settled. With cash settlement, the problems associated with physical delivery of the stocks that make up the index are overcome.

The Financial Times Stock Exchange (FTSE) Bursa Malaysia Kuala Lumpur Composite Index Futures Contract, which is an SIF contract, began trading on December, 15, 1995. Designated as FKLI, the contract was designed and introduced by the Kuala Lumpur Option and Financial Futures Exchange (KLOFFE), the predecessor to Bursa Malaysia Derivatives Berhad (BMDB). This SIF contract was Malaysia's first financial derivative and in 1995 Asia's only emerging market SIF contract. Now designated as the FBM KLCI Index futures contract, it experienced impressive growth in trading volume and open interest in its initial 2 years. The contract was popular with foreign fund managers who had exposure to the Malaysian stock market; however, with the imposition of capital controls in September 1998, trading volume saw a substantial decline. Still, relative to other financial derivatives in Malaysia, the index futures contract is by far more popular. It is currently the second most active derivative contract in Malaysia after Crude Palm Oil (CPO) futures.

Today, SIF contracts are very actively traded on several exchanges in various countries. The world's first SIF contract was introduced in 1982 (Kansas City Board of Trade on the Value Line Index). Today, trading in SIF contracts has increased tremendously. In Asia, SIF contracts traded in Thailand, China, India, Singapore, and Korea have been very successful. Table 4.1 lists the Global Ranking of SIF Contracts by traded volume in 2020.

Going by Table 4.1, the popularity of SIF contracts appears well spread out. Even though the Chicago Mercantile Exchange (CME) accounts for three of the top 10 contracts of the world, exchanges in Latin America, Asia, and Europe are also well represented. Thus, SIF's popularity appears to be truly global and not restricted to some parts of the world. Of the four derivatives exchanges covered in this book, Singapore Exchange's (SGX) FTSE China A50 SIF contract is in 12th place, whereas TFX's SET 50 SIF is in 13th place. Hong Kong Exchanges and Clearing's (HKEX) Hang Seng index-based SIF is in 27th, whereas its China H-Shares-based SIF is ranked 31st. Despite its early start, BMDB's FBM KLCI (FKLI) SIF is ranked 77th. Interestingly the trading volume (by value) of some SIF contracts has overtaken the trading volume in the underlying stock market. For a new financial instrument to succeed, there must be some advantages to using them. Without a net benefit, trading in the new instrument is unlikely to take off.

Table 4.1 Global Ranking of Stock Index Futures Contracts by Traded Volume

Rank	Exchange Name	SIF Contract Name	2020 YTD
1	B3	Bovespa Mini Index	2,888,021,160
2	Chicago Mercantile Exchange	E-mini S&P 500	502,227,405
3	Eurex	Euro Stoxx 50 Index	352,195,151
4	Chicago Mercantile Exchange	Micro E-mini S&P 500 Index	226,808,530
5	Chicago Mercantile Exchange	Micro E-mini Nasdaq 100 Index	178,531,164
6	Osaka Exchange	Nikkei 225 Mini	321,718,519
7	Moscow Exchange	RTS Index	156,014,870
8	Chicago Mercantile Exchange	E-mini Nasdaq 100	146,717,097
9	Eurex	Euro Stoxx Banks	92,545,411
10	Korea Exchange	Kospi 200	90,553,417
11	Borsa Istanbul	BIST 30 Index	98,651,034
12	**Singapore Exchange**	FTSE China A50 Index	96,578,641
13	**Thailand Futures Exchange**	SET 50	57,465,829
14	ICE Futures U.S.	Mini MSCI Emerging Markets	46,022,840
15	Taiwan Futures Exchange	Mini Taiex Futures (MTX)	60,051,670
16	National Stock Exchange of India	Bank Nifty Index	76,245,807
17	Chicago Mercantile Exchange	E-mini Russell 2000 Index	51,918,970
18	Korea Exchange	Mini Kospi 200 Futures	39,357,509
19	ICE Futures Europe	FTSE 100 Index	37,140,466
20	Taiwan Futures Exchange	Taiex (TX)	46,324,077
21	Chicago Board of Trade	E-mini $5 DJIA	59,371,718
22	National Stock Exchange of India	CNX Nifty Index	54,753,338
23	Osaka Exchange	Topix	27,702,276
24	B3	Bovespa Stock Index	41,414,065
25	CBOE Futures Exchange	CBOE Volatility Index (VX)	48,574,180
26	Chicago Board of Trade	E-micro $5 DJIA	32,643,055
27	**Hong Kong Exchanges and Clearing**	Hang Seng Index	41,635,063
28	China Financial Futures Exchange	CSI 300 Index	29,998,722
29	China Financial Futures Exchange	CSI 500 Index	32,755,439
30	Nasdaq Exchanges Nordic Markets	OMX (Index)	43,195,648
31	**Hong Kong Exchanges and Clearing**	H-Shares Index	36,256,445
77	**Malaysia Derivatives Exchange**	KLSE Composite Index (FKLI)	3,497,416

Source: FIA Futures Industry Association.
Note: Volume is reported as round-trip.

4.1 Why Use SIF Contracts?

The popularity of SIF usage arises from the many advantages of SIF contracts. We examine below five of the key benefits of SIF contracts.

4.1.1 Diversification Benefits

Diversification benefits refer to reduction in risk as one diversifies across assets. Investment in a SIF contract as opposed to direct investment in stocks provides **instant diversification**. This diversification benefit arises from the fact that an SIF contract has as its underlying, an index that constitutes several stocks. Thus, purchasing an SIF contract is akin to **buying each of the component stocks in the index**. The benefit of diversification lies in risk reduction. Recall, that according to Portfolio theory, investment in a broad range of stocks reduces **unsystematic risk**. Thus, investment in a broad based SIF contract like the FBM KLCI, S&P 500, or Nikkei 225 would mean that one is exposed only to **systematic risk**. This inbuilt diversification is a key advantage of SIF contracts over stock market positions.

Note
SIF contracts provide automatic diversification. They are therefore exposed to only systematic risk.

4.1.2 Lower Transaction Cost

A second major benefit of SIF over stock market transactions is **lower cost**. There are several reasons why transaction costs are lower in SIF than in stocks. First, brokerage costs like commissions are lower on a percentage of face value basis. Second, the margins that need to be posted for SIF contracts are also much lower relative to full payment on stock purchase. As such one need not tie up too much money in margins. A saving that results from this is that it reduces the cost of funds. (Since posting margin means losing the opportunity of alternative investment.) Finally, if one thinks of the transaction cost that will have to be incurred if one were to buy each of the index stocks, it is obvious that transactions in SIF are a lot more cheaper and hassle free.

4.1.3 Provides Leverage

The fact that margins in SIF transactions would mean investment outlays that are much lower than transactions in the stock market, it implies that there would be **automatic leverage** with SIF contracts. This benefit, however, is true of most derivative transactions and is not unique to SIF. As we saw in Chapter 3, leverage is attractive, in particular to speculators since it implies a higher return for a given investment.

4.1.4 Market Exposure and Stock Selection

Since an index is representative of the underlying market, a position in SIF contracts allows for exposure to the entire market, that is exposure to broad based market movements. Such a benefit is especially useful in international portfolio management. For example, suppose an American mutual fund manager is bullish about the Malaysian economy and wants exposure to Malaysian stocks. He gets instant exposure to the overall market by going long an FBM KLCI futures contract. In the absence of SIF contracts, the foreign fund manager would have to engage in individual stock selection to assemble a portfolio of Malaysian stocks. Such a process can be time consuming, costly to conduct and hazardous (since he might not have a good understanding of local conditions).

Exposure to the overall market through SIFs can also be useful to a *local* **investor** who adopts a passive investment strategy. Numerous empirical studies have shown that achieving consistently superior returns through a stock selection and/or timing strategy is not sustainable over a long term. Thus, a passive investment strategy can be an intelligent one. Since a long position in an SIF contract is essentially like taking a long position in each of the constituent stocks that make up the index, it would be ideal as part of a passive investment strategy.

> **Note**
> SIF contracts offer broad market exposure, and are suitable for passive investment strategies.

4.1.5 Hedging, Portfolio Insurance, and Risk Management

Perhaps one of the most useful aspects of SIF contracts is their use in hedging. There are two ways in which SIF contracts are particularly suited for hedging purposes:

(i) For managing systematic risk
(ii) Hedging overall portfolio value

(i) Managing Systematic Risk

Recall that **systematic risk** is the risk that remains even after one has put together a broad portfolio of assets. This is why it is also known as undiversifiable risk. Thus, a mutual fund manager would have eliminated all unsystematic risk through diversification but would still be faced with systematic risk. SIF contracts can be used in managing this systematic risk. As a simple example, suppose a fund manager has a fully diversified portfolio of RM 10 million of stocks. How can he use SIF contracts to reduce the systematic risk?

Answer: By taking a short position in SIF contracts.

Suppose he wants to reduce the systematic risk by half, he should then short approximately RM 5 million worth of SIF contracts. This of course implies two things: first that there is minimal basis risk between his portfolio and the index on which the SIF contract is based (beta is equal) and second, the reduction in systematic risk holds only until the maturity of the futures contract.

> **Note**
> Systematic risk can be managed by the use of SIF contracts.

(ii) Hedging the Overall Value of a Portfolio

As with other futures contracts, SIF contracts are used extensively in managing risk. In the context of equity investment, SIF contracts provide a very effective, easy, and low-cost method by which equity exposure could be hedged. Later in this chapter, we use numerical examples to examine how SIF contracts can be used for hedging equity price risk.

4.2 Index Construction and Types of Indexes

A stock index is essentially a barometer of stock market performance. As mentioned earlier, an index is made up of a basket of stocks. This basket of stocks that make up the index is usually carefully chosen to be representative of the market it is measuring. Indexes are essentially statistical sampling. There are essentially three types of stock indexes:

(i) An equally weighted (price weighted) index
(ii) A value weighted (capitalization weighted) index
(iii) A geometrically weighted index

Though the objective of measurement is the same, each of the above type of index varies in the way it is computed. Such a difference in computation can lead to small differences in market performance. Each method of computation has its own advantages and disadvantages. We discuss briefly the three types of indices and their computation.

4.2.1 An Equally Weighted Index

Examples: Dow Jones Industrial Average (DJIA), Major Market Index (MMI), and Nikkei 225

An **equally weighted** or **price weighted index** is computed by adding the closing prices of the component stocks and dividing by a **divisor**. Mathematically this is done as:

$$Index = \frac{\sum_{i=1}^{n} P_i}{Divisor}$$

where

P_i = closing price of each component stock
Divisor = statistical adjustment factor for capitalization changes; stock splits, bonus issues, rights, and stock substitution

In a price weighted index, every stock has equal weight. Although it is simple in computation, the fact that every constituent stock has equal weight can cause problems. Since every stock has equal weight, it has "equal influence" on the index's closing value. Because an index should be representative, small companies are often also included. As such, a small company with only a couple million shares

Note
In an equally weighted index, all component stocks have equal weight. The size of the firm is not adjusted for.

outstanding would have the same influence as a large conglomerate would. This often leads to increased volatility of the index even though most component stocks may be very stable. The Nikkei 225 Index is plagued by such problems.

4.2.2 Capitalization Weighted Index
Examples: S&P 500, TOPIX, FBM KLCI

Unlike an equally weighted index, which has equal weights for each constituent stock, in a *capitalization weighted index*, each component stock has a different weight in the calculation. The weight of each stock will depend on its market value proportionate to the market value of the total index. Market value or market capitalization refers to the price per share multiplied by the number of shares outstanding. Thus, the capitalization weighted index gives a larger weight to big firms, which have a large number of shares outstanding. For a given firm, its capitalization can also increase if its share price rises faster relative to other shares. A value weighted index is therefore computed as:

$$Index = \frac{\sum_{i=1}^{n} N_{i,t} \cdot P_{i,t}}{O \cdot V} \times M$$

where

$N_{i,t}$ = number of stocks outstanding for firm i on day t
$P_{i,t}$ = price per share of firm i on day t
$O \cdot V$ = original value, that is the index value on the day the index computation was begun
M = an arbitrarily set multiplier usually 100

Computation Example
Suppose there are three stocks in the index and computation begins on day $t = 1$.

Stock	Number of Stocks Outstanding	Close Price on Day, $t = 1$	Close Price on Day, $t = 2$
A	5,000	5.00	5.40
B	10,000	7.00	6.80
C	6,000	6.00	6.50

$$Index_{t=1} = \frac{5,000(5.00)+10,000(7.00)+6,000(6.00)}{5,000(5.00)+10,000(7.00)+6,000(6.00)} \times 100$$
$$= 100 \text{ points}$$

$$Index_{t=2} = \frac{5,000(5.40)+10,000(6.80)+6,000(6.50)}{5,000(5.00)+10,000(7.00)+6,000(6.00)} \times 100$$
$$= \frac{134,000}{131,000} \times 100$$
$$= 102.29 \text{ points}$$

On day $t = 2$, the index would be reported to have gone up 2.29 points (or 2.29% in this case since base is 100). In a capitalization weighted index, larger capitalized firms would have more influence. As such, in the case of the FBM KLCI, the three top capitalized stocks, Telekom, Maybank, and Tenaga have the most influence. As such, increases in the price of these three stocks would be enough to move the index even if the other stocks were largely unchanged.

> **Note**
> A capitalization weighted index accounts for differences in firm size by weighting for relative market capitalization of component stocks.

4.2.3 Geometrically Weighted Index

The third method of index computation is the **geometrically weighted index**. This method of index computation is neither a common method nor very popular. This is due to the fact that it is very difficult to replicate such an index. The valueline index uses this method of computation. It is computed as:

$$\text{Index} = \sqrt[n]{[(P_{it} \mid P_{it-1}) \ldots (P_{nt} \mid P_{nt-1})]}$$

where

P_{it} = price per share of firm i on day t
P_{it-1} = price on day $t - 1$

4.3 FBM KLCI Futures, Contract Specifications

Contract specifications are basically the ground rules by which a derivative contract's trading is dictated. Every exchange traded derivative contract has its own contract specification. The objective of a contract specification is to lay out in clear and uncertain terms the features and trading rules of the contract. This ensures fairness to all parties involved and a clear and transparent process in settlement, margining, etc. Table 4.2 shows the contract specifications for the FBM KLCI futures contract extracted from Bursa Malaysia's website.

A number of items from the abovementioned contract specifications will now be briefly examined. First, note that the contract size is the FBM KLCI multiplied by RM 50. This RM 50 is known as the **Index Multiplier**. The size of this multiplier is determined by the exchange when designing the contract. The index multiplier used to be RM 100, but was changed to RM 50, in order to reduce contract size and thereby increase liquidity. Different exchanges may use different size multipliers. For example, the Nikkei Index Futures contracts traded on the Osaka Securities Exchange have a multiplier of ¥en 10,000 (Nikkei spot index × ¥en 10,000), whereas the

> **Note**
> Contract specifications lay out in clear and uncertain terms the features and trading rules of a contract.

Table 4.2 Contract Specifications: FBM KLCI Futures

Contract	FKLI
Underlying Instrument	FBM KLCI
Contract Size	FBM KLCI multiplied by RM 50
Minimum Price Fluctuation	0.5 index point valued at RM 25
Daily Price Limits	20% per trading session for the respective contract months except the spot month contract. There shall be no price limits for the spot month contract. There will be no price limit for the second month contract for the final 5 business days before expiration.
Contract Months	Spot month, the next month, and the next 2 calendar quarterly months. The calendar quarterly months are March, June, September, and December.
Trading Hours	First trading session: Malaysian 08:45 hours to 12:45 hours. Second trading session: 14:30 hours to 17:15 hours.
Final Trading Day	The last business day of the contract month.
Final Settlement	Cash settlement based on the final settlement value.
Final Settlement Value	The final settlement value shall be the average value, rounded to the nearest 0.5 of an index point taken at every 15 seconds or at such intervals as may be determined by the exchange from time to time from 3.45:30 p.m. to 4.45:15 p.m. plus one value after 5.00 p.m. of the index on the final trading day excepting the three highest and three lowest values.
Speculative Position Limit	10,000 contracts, for all months combined

Source: Bursa Malaysia website.

same futures contract traded in Singapore International Monetary Exchange (SIMEX) has a multiplier of ¥en 5,000. The idea behind a multiplier is to make the size of a contract appropriate for potential players, i.e., fund managers, etc. A small multiplier would mean small contract size, thus requiring fund managers to transact in numerous contracts to suit their needs. On the other hand, if the multiplier was too large, contract size would be huge, potentially reducing liquidity.

The **Minimum Price Fluctuation** is also known as tick size. A tick size of RM 25 means that a buyer willing to offer a higher price than currently prevailing, must bid at least RM 25 higher. He cannot, for example, offer to buy at say RM 2 above current price. Similarly, a seller willing to sell at a lower price must offer a price at least RM 25 lower than current price.

Daily Price Limits determine the extent to which prices can fluctuate in any given trading session. Note that there are two trading sessions per day. A 20% price limit means that prices can go up or down a maximum 20% over the previous close price. Technically, if prices go out of the 20% range, trading is halted until bid and offer prices come back within the 20% range. Sometimes known as "***circuit-breakers***," the idea behind such price limits is to check excessive price volatility which may be due to speculative play. Exchanges also have what are known as **Position Limits** and **Reportable Positions** to limit excessive speculative activity.

Contract Months tells us the fixed maturity periods of the contracts. Recall, that a contract is identified by its contract month. As per the contract specification, four FBM KLCI futures contracts would be available for trading any one time. The closest or nearby contract at any one time would be the spot month contract, whereas the furthest deferred contract 6 months away (nearest second quarter).

Trading Hours of the futures contract shows something interesting. Notice that trading begins 15 minutes **before** the stock market (Bursa Malaysia) opens and ends 15 minutes **after** the Bursa closes in each session. This delayed close of the futures market is not unique to Bursa Malaysia but quite common to derivative exchanges worldwide. The 15 extra minutes after the stock market closes is to enable fund managers and other institutions to hedge out whatever net positions that may have resulted from the day's trading and which the fund manger may not wish to carry overnight. The 15-minute earlier open is to enable futures market participants who may wish to take preemptive positions before the stock market opens. As we will see later in this chapter, the first and final 15 minutes typically account for most of a day's trading volume in derivative markets.

Final Settlement Value of the contract at maturity is determined by averaging the value of the index for the 30-minute period, 3.45 p.m. to 4.15 p.m., plus one observation at 5.00 p.m. on the maturity day. The index value is taken at 15-second intervals over the 30 minutes of trading. The three highest and lowest of the price observations are dropped. The average of the remaining price observations is used as the final settlement value. The need to use such an averaging process is to eliminate the possibility of last-minute market manipulation influencing final settlement values. For example, in other countries, it used to be that the final settlement value of the futures contract was simply the close price of the stock index on maturity day. Experience has showed that such a settlement value determination is subject to easy manipulation. For example, speculators with long positions in futures need merely place last minute buy orders in the underlying index (stock market) in order to push up the settlement value of their futures contracts. In fact, such manipulation is easier if the underlying index is an equally weighted index.

Transaction Costs would typically be around RM 60 per contract per transaction.[1] A round trip (long and short or vice versa) would cost RM 120. It was mentioned earlier that low transaction costs are a major attraction of futures relative to underlying market transaction. To see how the transaction costs compare, we offer the following simple example.

Assume the FBM KLCI is now at 1,000 points. (Ignore margins or more specifically, the opportunity costs of funds paid as margins for the futures.)

---

[1] Transaction cost of RM 60 per contract used to be stated on the contract specification. Currently, since commissions, especially for large trades are negotiable, costs are more flexible.

The value of each futures contract is: 1,000 points × RM 50 = RM 50,000
Cost per long position = RM 30
Transaction cost as % of value: (RM 30/RM 50,000) × 100 = 0.06%

A RM 50,000 position established in the futures market has a transaction cost of RM 30 or 0.06%.

How does this compare with stock market transactions? Broker's commissions excluding stamp duty, clearing fee, etc. is currently around 1% of contract value for smaller trades. Taking only the 1% broker's commission, costs for a RM 50,000 transaction in the stock market would be RM 50,000 × 0.01 = RM 500.

Thus in percentage terms, index futures transactions are approximately 16 times cheaper (RM 500 versus RM 30) than stock market transactions. This multiple would of course depend on the level of index.

4.4 SIF Trading — The Main Players

The main players in SIF markets are institutional investors. This is largely due to the fact that the money amounts involved in SIF trading is large. Since the SIF has a multiplier, in the case of FBM KLCI futures contracts, the multiplier is RM 50. This means that a single contract would be worth in excess of RM 50,000 if the FBM KLCI is above 1,000 points. As the exposures are huge, there would be very few retail or individual players. SIF contracts are really intended for the big players. The main players would therefore be institutions like pension funds, insurance companies, fund management operations of merchant banks, asset management companies, mutual funds, etc. Aside from wanting exposure to stock investment through SIF contracts, these institutions may also be involved as hedgers, arbitrageurs, or speculators.

4.5 The Pricing of SIF Contracts

Recall from our earlier discussion in Chapter 3 of the Spot-Futures parity condition that the cost of a futures contract should be:

$$F_{t,T} = S_o (1 + rf + c - y)^{t,T}$$

where

rf = risk-free interest rate
$F_{t,T}$ = future prices of maturity t to T
S_o = spot price of the underlying asset
Y = yield if any from holding the underlying asset
c = storage and handling costs

The underlying principle of SIF pricing is the same. Thus, the spot-futures or cost of carry model can be used in pricing SIF. Adjustments, however, will have to be made given the fact that the underlying is a financial asset and not a commodity. There are really two needed adjustments to the aforementioned model.

(a) The storage/handling cost of financial futures contracts like SIF is practically zero. Thus, the variable c drops off from the equation.
(b) Since holding a portfolio of stocks would enable one to receive any dividends declared, the variable y can be replaced with d, to denote the **dividend yield**. However, since holding an SIF contract as opposed to the actual stocks would mean that we do not get the dividends when they are declared, d is deducted.

Thus, the spot–futures parity or cost of carry model for SIF contracts is:

$$F_{t,T} = S_o(1 + rf - d)^{t,T}$$

where

$F_{t,T}$ = the correct price of a SIF contract with maturity t to T
S_o = current value of the underlying index
rf = risk-free interest rate
d = the dividend yield of the underlying index

4.5.1 Using the Cost of Carry Model: An Example

Assume the following: (i) The spot index, the FBM KLCI is now 960 points; (ii) the average annual dividend yield of the FBM KLCI is 2%; (iii) the risk-free interest rate is 6% annualized; and (iv) index multiplier is RM 50. What would be the correct price of a SIF contract if it matures in (i) 3 months, (ii) 6 months, and (iii) 1 year?

3-Month Maturity

$$\begin{aligned} F_3 &= S_o(1 + rf - d)^{0.25} \\ &= 960(1 + 0.06 - 0.02)^{0.25} \\ &= 960(1.04)^{0.25} \\ &= 960(1.01) \\ &= 969.46 \text{ points} \end{aligned}$$

The correct price/fair value in points of a 3-month FBM KLCI futures contract is 969.46 points. Since the index multiplier is RM 50; thus, 969.46 points × RM 50 Ringgit value per contract = RM 48,473

6-Month Maturity

$$\begin{aligned} F_6 &= 960(1 + 0.06 - 0.02)^{0.5} \\ &= 960(1.04)^{0.5} \\ &= 979.01 \end{aligned}$$

The equilibrium price of a 6-month FBM KLCI futures contract is 979.01 points.
Ringgit value = 979.01 points × RM 50
= RM 48,950.50

1-Year Maturity

$F_{1yr} = 960(1 + 0.06 - 0.02)^1$
$= 960(1.04)^1$
$= 998.40$

The fair value of a 1-year FBM KLCI futures contract is 998.40 points.
Ringgit value = 998.40 × RM 50
= RM 49,920

4.5.2 Dividend Yields and Dividend Payment Patterns

Notice from the earlier computations that the futures price increases as the futures maturity gets longer. The reason for this is that the net carrying cost ($rf - d$) gets compounded for a longer period as the maturity increases. For the 6-month futures, the net carrying cost is approximately 2%, whereas for the full year maturity it is 4%. Thus, it is logical that the net carrying cost would get smaller with shorter maturity or as one approaches maturity. At maturity, the net carrying cost (which accounts for the basis, $F-S$) will be zero.

Does this mean that the futures price will always be greater than the spot price before maturity? Or that the distant futures contracts would always be higher than nearby contracts? Not necessarily. The futures price will always be higher than spot when the net carrying cost ($rf - d$) is positive. However, if the net carrying cost is negative, then the futures price would be less than the spot price. Can the net carrying cost be negative? Yes. This is largely due to the fact that dividend payments tend to be "*lumpy*." The dividend yield of 2% that is imputed in the earlier equation is the ***average annual dividend***. The way it appears in the equation implies that dividends are paid in equal amounts across the year. In reality, this is not the case. Though companies pay dividend on different dates, most dividend payments tend to spike around

Note
Dividend patterns that tend to be clustered can result in negative net carrying and SIF prices being lower than spot value.

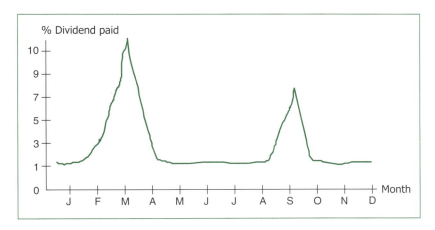

Figure 4.1   Typical Dividend Pattern by Month

two periods, March and September. This clustering has to do with the fact that most companies pay dividends twice a year, an interim dividend and a final dividend. As most companies have end December as their fiscal year end, the declared final dividend gets paid typically in March. An interim dividend which is announced in the middle of the fiscal year, June, usually gets paid in September. As such, some contract months for example, the March Contract could see futures prices **lower** than spot prices on several trading days. Figure 4.1 illustrates the typical pattern of dividend payments.

4.6 Applications of SIF Contracts

In this section, we examine the application of SIF in investment management. Specifically, we look at how SIF contracts can be used in hedging, arbitrage, and in speculation. We work through numerical examples of each of these three applications.

4.6.1 Index Arbitrage

Arbitrage, as we have defined earlier, refers to the process of taking advantage of the existence of mispricing. Thus, the first step in arbitrage is always to check for mispricing. Index arbitrage is the term used to describe the process of arbitraging between SIF and the spot market. Technically, arbitrage is possible whenever the Futures-Spot parity is violated. For example,

If $f_t > S_o(1 + rf - d)_t$, then the futures is overpriced relative to spot or equivalently, the quoted futures price is higher than what it should be.

To take advantage of this "mispricing," an arbitrageur would:

Short the futures contract, and long the spot market.

This goes back to the basic arbitrage rule; buy low, sell high or, buy/long the asset that is underpriced and sell/short the one that is overpriced in relative terms.

If $f_t < S_o(1 + rf - d)_t$, then the futures is underpriced relative to spot or the quoted futures price is lower than what it should be. Here an arbitrageur would:

Long the futures contract, and short the spot market.

There are two things to note here. First, the arbitrage here is riskless since there is no net exposure; further the arbitrage should require no net cash outflows. That is, the arbitrage strategy should self-finance such that the arbitrageur has no out-of-pocket outlays. Thus, it is essentially a risk-free strategy. The second point to note is that, the size of the arbitrage profit will depend entirely on the extent of mispricing. Underlying market movements will have no bearing on the profit.

Note
Index arbitrage is the process of arbitraging mispricing that may exist between the SIF and the stock market.

To prove the aforementioned points and to see how SIF arbitrage would work, we work through the following example.

Suppose you observe the following quotations today:

3-month SIF price = 1,210
Index value = 1,200 points
rf rate = 4%
Dividend yield = 2%
Time to maturity of SIF = 90 days

To see whether arbitrage is possible, we first check for mispricing. The correct value of the 3-month SIF should be:

$F_t = 1,200(1 + 0.04 - 0.02)^{0.25}$
$= 1,200(1.02)^{0.25}$
$= 1,205.96$ points

Given the earlier information, the futures is clearly overpriced relative to spot. The futures price should be 1,205.96 points, yet it is quoted at 1,210 points and is overpriced by approximately 4 points.

Since there is mispricing, arbitrage is possible. By using the following arbitrage strategy, a riskless profit can be made. *(Note: No cash outlay is needed today.)* To see how much profit would be made and to prove that the profit will be *independent* of stock market performance, we will look at two market scenarios. *(Note: Current stock index value is 1,200 points.)*

(i) Index rises to 1,225 at maturity.
(ii) Index falls to 1,175 at maturity.

Scenario 1: Index Rises to 1,225

Action		Position Today	Position at Maturity	Profit/ Loss
(a)	Short 1 SIF contract	60,500	(61,250)	(750)
(b)	Long spot	(60,000)	61,250	1,250
(c)	Borrow RM 60,000 @ 4% for 90 days	60,000	(60,591.20)	(591.20)
(d)	Receive dividends and invest it @ 4% for 90 days	0	303	303
			Net =	211.80

(Assumption: Dividends are received immediately and reinvested the same day) (Dividend amount = 60,000 × 0.02 = 1,200/4 = RM 300)
(Reinvested dividend amount = RM 300[1 + (0.04)/4] = RM 303)

Scenario 2: Index Falls to 1,175

Cash and Carry Arbitrage

Action		Position Today	Position at Maturity	Profit/Loss
(a)	Short 1 SIF contract	60,500	(58,750)	1,750
(b)	Long spot	(60,000)	58,750	(1,250)
(c)	Borrow RM 60,000 @ 4% for 90 days	60,000	(60,591.20)	(591.20)
(d)	Receive dividends and invest it @ 4% for 90 days	0	303	303
				Net = 211.80

Notice that regardless of whether the index went up or down, you still make the same RM 211.80 of profit. This proves the point that the arbitrage profit is independent of market performance. The arbitrage profit which is 0.35% (RM 211.80/RM 60,000) approximates the percentage deviation in the actual futures price from theoretical price, [(1210 − 1205.96) × 50]/60,000 = 0.34%. Thus, the size of the arbitrage profit is determined by extent of the mispricing. As with all other arbitrage activity, the arbitrage will continue until the equilibrium is reached. As more and more arbitrageurs long the spot market and short the SIF, spot prices will rise and SIF prices fall until equilibrium is restored.

Reverse Cash and Carry Arbitrage

Suppose in the earlier example, the futures price today is quoted as 3-month SIF price = 1,201. Now, the SIF is *underpriced* relative to spot. In order to arbitrage, we need to do the reverse of the earlier strategy. The following ***reverse cash and carry arbitrage*** would be appropriate here.

Index Rises to 1,225

Action		Position Today	Position at Maturity	Profit/Loss
(a)	Long 1 SIF contract	60,050	61,250	1,200
(b)	Short spot	60,000	(61,250)	(1,250)
(c)	Lend RM 60,000 @ 4% for 90 days	(60,000)	60,591.20	591.20
(d)	Borrow RM 300 @ 4% for 90 days to replace dividends on borrowed shares (shorted)	0	(303)	(303)
				Net = 238.20

Index Falls to 1,175

Action		Position Today	Position at Maturity	Profit/Loss
(a)	Long 1 SIF contract	60,050	58,750	(1,300)
(b)	Short spot	60,000	(58,750)	1,250
(c)	Lend RM 60,000 @ 4% for 90 days	(60,000)	60,591.20	591.20
(d)	Borrow RM 300 @ 4% for 90 days to replace dividends on borrowed shares (shorted)	0	(303)	(303)
			Net =	238.20

Notice that once again, the profit amount is the same regardless of index movement. The percentage profit will approximate the percentage mispricing or deviation of the actual from the theoretical futures price. As in the earlier case, there is no net exposure; thus it is riskless arbitrage and the profit is pure arbitrage profit.

In index arbitrage, we take positions in both the SIF and the spot index. For example, in a **cash and carry arbitrage**, we long the spot index and short the SIF contract. Going long the spot index does not mean that one has to buy each and every one of the component stocks of the index. It may be possible to design a customized index of far fewer stocks that has a high correlation with the market index. For example, the FBM KLCI may be "replicated" by a portfolio of perhaps 30 stocks of different weighting that has a very close correlation with the FBM KLCI. Thus, one needs to only long these select 30 stocks and not the entire index in order to arbitrage. Alternatively, a fund manager who already owns a diversified portfolio of stocks could do the cash and carry arbitrage by shorting the SIF contract alone. He does not have to long the spot index since he already owns a portfolio of stocks that is correlated to the spot index. This kind of arbitrage is often known as *quasi arbitrage or quasi-index arbitrage*.

4.6.2 Hedging

The second application we examine is hedging equity risk with SIF contracts. Suppose you are a foreign fund manager with exposure to Malaysian stocks. You intend to keep your position in the stocks since you think the underlying fundamentals are good. However, you are worried about volatility that could erode the current value of your portfolio. Is there any way by which you could use SIF contracts to protect your portfolio's value? Answer: Yes, you can do a **short hedge**.

Example
The following information is available to you today.

Current value of portfolio = RM 1,200,000
rf rate = 6% per year

Dividend yield on portfolio = 2% annualized
Spot index value = 1,200 points
3-month SIF futures contract = 1,211.82 points
(Assume the futures will expire in exactly 90 days.)

Since you now have a long position in stocks, hedging would require that you establish an offsetting short position in SIF contracts. But how many SIF contracts should you short? The answer depends on how closely your portfolio is correlated to the market index. If your portfolio exactly tracks the FBM KLCI, then you do a **base hedge**.

$$\text{Base hedge} = \frac{\text{Current Ringgit value of portfolio}}{\text{Current Ringgit value of index}}$$

$$= \frac{\text{RM } 1,200,000}{1,200 \text{ points} \times \text{RM } 50}$$

$$= 20 \text{ contracts}$$

Thus, going by the base hedge computation, you should **short 20 SIF contracts**. This, however, assumes that your portfolio is **exactly** like the portfolio of stocks that make up the index. In such a case, the correlation between your portfolio and the index would be **perfectly positive** (correlation = +1.0); there would be no tracking error whatsoever. In reality, your portfolio may not be exactly like the index. (Why spend effort/time assembling a portfolio that resembles the index when the index itself is traded with the advent of SIFs?) When your portfolio is not exactly like the index, an adjustment has to be made in base hedge calculation. This is really an adjustment to the difference in the relative betas of your portfolio and the index. Suppose the beta of your portfolio is 1.20 (weighted average of individual stock betas in your portfolio). Since, by definition, the beta of the index = 1.0, the number of SIF contracts needed can be determined by either of the following two ways.

(a) Base hedge × Beta of portfolio
    20 × 1.2 = 24 contracts
(b) Or by the following equation:

$$\text{Number of contracts} = \frac{\text{Ringgit value of portfolio} \times \text{Beta of portfolio}}{\text{Ringgit value of index}}$$

$$= \frac{\text{RM } 1,200,000 \times 1.2}{1,200 \times \text{RM } 50}$$

$$= \frac{\text{RM } 1,440,000}{\text{RM } 60,000}$$

$$= 24 \text{ contracts}$$

Note
In determining the number of SIF contracts to hedge with, the base hedge is applicable only if the portfolio beta equals market beta.

Having determined that you need 24 SIF contracts, you establish the **short hedge** by going short 24 SIF contracts while holding onto your current portfolio. To see how your portfolio value would be protected by the hedge, let us examine two possible market scenarios over the next 90 days. If the hedge strategy is appropriate, you should be able to lock in the same value regardless of market performance.

Scenario 1: The Stock Market Falls 20%

Action		Position Today	Position at Maturity	Profit/Loss
(a)	Portfolio value	1,200,000	912,000	(288,000)
(b)	Short 24 SIF contracts	1,454,184	1,152,000	302,184
(c)	Dividends received till maturity	–	–	6,000
				Net = 20,184

Note: (1) Since beta of portfolio is 1.2; portfolio value falls 24% when market falls 20%.
(2) At maturity, index value is 1,200 pts × 0.80 = 960 pts. SIF value at maturity = [960 pts × 24] × RM 50.
(3) Dividends received over the 90-day period until maturity equals portfolio value multiplied by the annual dividend yield and divided by 4 to adjust for the 90-day period which is one calendar quarter. [RM1,200,000 × 0.02] ÷ 4.

Scenario 2: The Stock Market Rises 20%

Action		Position Today	Position at Maturity	Profit/Loss
(a)	Portfolio value	1,200,000	1,488,000	288,000
(b)	Short 24 SIF contracts	1,454,184	(1,728,000)	(273,816)
(c)	Dividends received till maturity	–	–	6,000
				Net = 20,184

Note: (1) Portfolio value rises by 24% since beta is 1.2.
(2) At maturity, index value is 1,200 × 1.20 = 1,440 pts. SIF value at maturity = [1,440 pts × 24] × RM 50.

Analysis of Hedged Position

Under Scenario 1
Initial value of portfolio = RM 1,200,000
Unhedged portfolio value = RM 912,000
Profit/Loss from SIF contracts = RM 302,184
Dividends received = RM 6,000

Value of portfolio with hedge = RM 1,220,184

Notice that with hedging, your portfolio has grown by RM 20,184 over the 90-day period even though the market fell 20%.

Under Scenario 2

Initial value of portfolio	= RM 1,200,000
Unhedged portfolio value	= RM 1,488,000
Profit/Loss from SIF contracts	= (RM 273,816)
Dividends received	= RM 6,000

Value of portfolio with hedge = RM 1,220,184

With hedging, your portfolio has grown by RM 20,184 over the 90-day period, even though the market went up by 20%.

There are two essential points to note about the earlier hedging:

(a) Regardless of market movement, your portfolio value is the same. This is precisely the point about hedging, i.e., preservation of value.

(b) Under either scenario your portfolio grows by RM 20,184. Why this amount? When annualized and adjusted for transaction costs, this amount will approximate the risk-free return. The logic is straightforward. Since your portfolio was fully hedged, the return you can expect should approximate the risk-free rate of return. A fully hedged portfolio is essentially a riskless asset; the return from a riskless asset equals the risk-free rate of return. In the example here, the approximate transaction cost of the SIF contracts would be [RM 60 per contract × 24 contracts] RM 1,440. Thus, the fully hedged annualized return in percentage is:

> **Note**
> Since a fully hedged portfolio is riskless, it provides a return that approximates the risk-free return.

$$\frac{RM\ 20{,}184 - RM\ 1{,}440}{RM\ 1{,}200{,}000} \times 4 = 0.062 \text{ or } 6.2\%$$

(Note that we have ignored the opportunity cost of margins posted on the SIF position; taking this into consideration will make the returns closer to the risk-free return.)

Notice that the annualized return closely resembles the risk-free return in the example of 6%. In addition to proving that the return from a fully hedged position approximates the risk-free return, there is an important implication. We now examine this implication.

4.6.3 Creating Synthetic Position (Replication)

Suppose in the earlier example, you had liquidated the portfolio of RM 1,200,000 and invested the cash in a risk-free asset; you would have earned an annualized return equal to 6%. Since you also earned approximately the risk-free return with the hedged portfolio, you have essentially created a **synthetic cash position (or synthetic T-bill position)**. To understand synthesizing or **replication**, note the following:

(a) Long futures ⇒ we pay premium of 4%; (0.06 − 0.02) ($rf - d$)
    Short futures ⇒ we receive premium of + 4% (0.06 − 0.02) ($rf - d$)

(b) Long stock portfolio ⇒ we receive the dividend yield; +0.02 or 2%
Short stock portfolio ⇒ we pay the dividend yield; 0.02 or 2%

Recall that the hedge abovementioned involved the following: short futures and long (hold) stock portfolio.

$$\text{Short futures} + \text{Long stock port} = \text{Risk-free rate } (rf)$$
$$\Downarrow \qquad\qquad \Downarrow \qquad\qquad \Downarrow$$
$$4\% \text{ received} + 2\% \text{ received} = 6\% \text{ received}$$

When shorting futures, you received the 4% premium; then in holding the stock portfolio, you received the 2% dividend yield. Together it adds up to the 6% risk-free rate.

Alternatively

$$\text{Long futures} + \text{Long } rf \text{ asset} = \text{Long spot return}$$
$$\Downarrow \qquad\qquad \Downarrow$$
$$4\% \text{ pay} + 6\% \text{ received} = 2\% \text{ received}$$

What this says is that by going long futures and T-bills, we could get a return that would be earned by owning a portfolio of stocks. In other words, we can replicate a long stock position by going long SIF and long treasury bills.

To summarize, the following replication strategies hold:

> ***Synthetic T-bill Position = Short Futures + Long Stocks***
> ***Synthetic Stock Position = Long Futures + Long T-bills***
> ***Synthetic Futures Position = Long T-bills + Short Stock***

4.6.4 Speculating with SIF Contracts

The third application of SIF contract that we examine is speculation. As mentioned earlier, SIF contracts can also be used for speculative purposes. A speculative position is simply establishing a position in the SIF market without any offsetting position in the underlying stocks/index. The established position in SIF could be long or short according to whether the speculator is bullish or bearish about market performance.

Bullish Expectation: Illustration

Suppose a speculator believes that the remaining four trading days of the week is likely to see an increase in the stock market index and SIF contract value. Recall from Chapter 3 that a long position gains from rising prices, whereas the short position gains from falling prices. Since the speculator is bullish, the appropriate speculative strategy would be to long the SIF contract. We examine below the pay-off to a speculator who goes long one SIF contract for an assumed market movement over the next few days.

Strategy: Long One SIF Contract

Day	Index Close	Amount (RM)	Profit/Loss	Accumulated P/L
0	1,200	60,000	0	0
1	1,212	60,600	600	600
2	1,208	60,400	(200)	400
3	1,205	60,250	(150)	250
4	1,214	60,700	450	700

The speculator had been correct in his expectation. Since the index was up 14 points from initial value, he gets an accumulated profit of RM 700 (14 points × RM 50). The profit could also have been determined as: (Exit Value − Entry Value) × Multiplier = (1,214 − 1,200) × RM 50 = RM 700. Since the speculative position has no offsetting position, someone who had been bearish and gone short on day 0 would have lost RM 700.

Bearish Expectation: Illustration

Suppose a speculator expects stock and SIF prices to decline over the next several days. In order to take advantage of falling values, the right speculative strategy would be to short the SIF contract.

Strategy: Short One SIF Contract

Day	Index Close	Amount (RM)	Profit/Loss	Accumulated P/L
0	1,200	60,000	0	0
1	1,188	59,400	600	600
2	1,182	59,100	300	900
3	1,187	59,350	(250)	650
4	1,183	59,150	200	850

Since the index had fallen 17 points (1,200 − 1,183), the investor had been correct in his expectation. His speculative position would earn him a total RM 850. (Entry Value − Exit Value) × Multiplier = (1,200 − 1,183) × RM 50 = RM 850.

A speculator who had been bullish and had gone long an SIF contract on day 0 would have lost RM 850 by day 4.

4.6.5 Spread Trading

Notice from the discussion that the typical speculative strategy involves taking a single position, either long or short according to the speculator's expectation. The speculator goes long if he is bullish and short if bearish. As there is no offsetting position in typical speculation, the speculator is basically placing a bet based on his expectation. This is of course a high-risk strategy. A speculator would either make huge profits or huge losses.

> **Note**
> Spread trading is essentially a speculative strategy but one that has a safety net.

Spread trading is essentially a speculative strategy but one that has a safety net. Unlike an outright speculative position, which is a single long or short position, spread trading involves taking *simultaneous* long and short positions in the derivative asset. The basic idea here is to take a speculative position but cut losses if the market moves in an unexpected way. There are several kinds of spreads. A ***time*** or ***calendar spread*** involves going long and short in two futures contracts of different maturities. An ***intermarket spread*** involves going long in one market and going short the same asset in another market. For example, long Nikkei Futures on SIMEX and short Nikkei futures on Osaka Securities Exchange (OSE). One might also do an inter-asset spread across two markets. For example, long CPO futures on Bursa Malaysia and short Soybean futures on the Chicago Merchantile Exchange (CME). The basic idea in all spread trading is to speculate and to have a safety net, or cut losses if prices move opposite to expectations. We examine below a common type of spread trading, a time spread. A ***bull time spread*** is established if the trader/speculator is bullish while a ***bear time spread*** if he is bearish.

Bull Time Spread: Illustration

Suppose an investor believes stock prices are likely to increase over the future. To profit from this expectation, the investor could establish a bull time spread in SIF contracts. This could be done by purchasing a longer maturity contract and selling the shorter maturity or nearby contract. That is, long the distant or deferred contract and short the nearby contract. The logic behind such trading is that, longer term contracts are generally more sensitive and would move more than the shorter term contracts. Though both contracts will rise as stock prices rise, the distant month contract would rise more. As such the *basis spread* between the two contracts would *widen*. Time spread trading seeks to take advantage of this change in spreads.

Example: Today's date : Jan 15
Prices quoted
March SIF contract = 1,100 points
June SIF contract = 1,104 points

Strategy: Short 1 March contract
Long 1 June contract

	(Today) January 15	(2 Weeks later) January 30	Gain/Loss
Mar SIF	1,100	1,108	(8 points)
June SIF	1,104	1,118	+ 14 points
Spread	4.00	10.0	6 points

Suppose the SIF price on January 30 was as above, the spread trade would have profited RM 300, derived as follows:

$$\text{Loss on March contract} = 8 \text{ points} \times \text{RM } 50 = (\text{RM } 400)$$
$$\text{Gain on June contract} = 14 \text{ points} \times \text{RM } 50 = (\text{RM } 700)$$
$$\text{Net gain} = \underline{\text{RM } 300}$$

The gain of RM 300 came from the *increase* in the spread from 4 points on January 15 to 10 points on January 30.

Box 4.1
Does the Introduction of SIF Increase Underlying Market Volatility?

The question of whether the introduction of SIF contracts or more generally, derivatives, induces additional volatility in the underlying spot market is a common one. As usual there are two sides to the argument. Critics of derivatives argue that the introduction of derivatives ought to have a destabilizing effect, implying increased volatility in the underlying cash market. They attribute this to the presence of speculators attracted by the inbuilt leverage and the ease with which derivatives could be used for speculation. This line of thinking received support from the Brady Commission's report of the October 1987, Black Monday stock market crash in the US. The blame for the crash was placed on 'program trading' by the fund managers using portfolio insurance strategies. It was argued that program trading led to heavy selling of futures as underlying markets fell. Falling futures prices caused spot values to be overvalued inducing their further sell down. This resulted in a virtuous circle and a downward spiral in prices. This argument overlooks the fact that arbitrage between the derivative and spot markets would prevent price movements that are out of line. For example, as the spot markets goes overvalued relative to futures, short selling of the spot must be accompanied by long positions in the futures. The long futures position will act to limit further falls in the spot. So, movements in one market counterbalance the other.

(*Continued*)

> # Box 4.1
> (*Continued*)
>
> The other side of the argument is that the presence of derivatives should act to minimize price fluctuations or volatility in markets. The reasoning here is as follows: first, the presence of derivatives allows risk managers to hedge their positions without having to sell off their underlying holding. In the absence of derivatives, fund managers seeking shelter from temporary market turbulence, e.g., impending elections, would have no choice but sell their holdings in order to protect themselves, post elections, they would have to move back in by buying back the stocks they sold. The aggregate impact of fund managers first selling and then coming back in is likely to be volatility inducing. With derivatives, there is no need to liquidate. Thus, markets ought to become more stable. A second line of reasoning here is that, with derivatives, syndicated ramping up or artificially pushing down stock prices becomes less feasible. Speculators who try to artificially push down the price of an asset will be themselves being taken advantage of by arbitrageurs who can take advantage of the artificial mispricing by way of arbitraging with derivatives. So, in many ways, the presence of derivatives helps to check market manipulation.
>
> Several studies have examined the above arguments. While a few studies have shown that markets have become more volatile post introduction of derivatives, the majority of the studies, across different countries, appear to find either no increase in volatility or an actual reduction, post derivative introduction.

Bear Time Spread: Illustration

A bear time spread is the opposite of the abovementioned. When prices are expected to fall, the distant contract would typically fall more than the nearby contract, once again causing a widening of the spread. The spread trader, establishes the bear time spread as follows:

> **Strategy:** Long the near by month contract.
> Short the distant month contract.

4.7 SIF in Thailand

The SET 50 Index futures contract, began trading on April 28, 2006. The contract was designed and introduced by the TFEX, a subsidiary of the Stock Exchange of Thailand (SET). This SIF contract was Thailand's first financial derivative. Since its launch, the SET 50 Index futures contract has experienced impressive growth in trading volume and open interest. Compared to other financial derivatives, the index futures contract is currently the most popular financial derivative in Thailand. The SET 50 Index futures contract is an exchange-traded futures contract which has the SET 50 Index, a basket of the top 50 stocks listed on SET, as its underlying asset. Like other SIF contracts, the SET 50 Index futures contract entitles the buyer to "take delivery" of the group of stocks that make up the index at the prespecified price and at a predetermined future date. The SET 50 futures contract is cash-settled; the long position receives a cash equivalent instead of a group of the 50 stocks. Table 4.3 shows the contract specifications for the SET 50 Index futures contract extracted from the TFEX's website.

Selected terms from the above contract specifications will be briefly discussed. First, the contract size is the SET 50 Index multiplied by THB 200, i.e., the **index multiplier** which is determined by the exchange when designing the contract.

The **Minimum Price Fluctuation** or tick size of the SET 50 Index futures contract is THB 20, meaning that a buyer willing to offer a higher price than currently prevailing, must bid at least THB 20 higher. He cannot, for example, offer to buy at THB 10 above the current price. Vice versa, a seller willing to sell at a lower price must offer a price at least THB 20 lower than the current price.

Daily Price Limits determine the extent to which prices can fluctuate in any given trading session. The SET 50 Index futures contract has a 30% price limit meaning that prices can go up or down a maximum 30% over the previous settlement price. Should, prices go above or below the 30% range, during a session, trading is temporarily halted under "**circuit-breaker**" rules.

Table 4.3   Contract Specifications: SET 50 Index Futures

Contract	SET 50
Underlying Asset	SET 50 Index which is calculated from the prices of 50 selected SET stocks
Contract Size	SET 50 multiplied by THB 200
Minimum Price Fluctuation	0.1 index point at THB 20
Daily Price Limits	30% of the latest settlement price
Contract Months	3 nearest consecutive months plus the next 3 quarterly months
Trading Hours	Morning pre-open: 09:15–09:45 hours. Morning session: 09:45–12:30 hours. Afternoon pre-open: 13:45–14.15 hours. Afternoon session: 14:15–16:55 hours.
Final Trading Day	The business day immediately preceding the last business day of the contract month.
Final Settlement	Cash settlement based on the final settlement price.
Final Settlement Price	The final settlement price shall be the numerical value of the SET 50 Index, rounded to the nearest two decimal points as determined by the exchange, and shall be the average value of the SET 50 Index taken during last 15 minutes and the closing index value, after deleting the three highest and three lowest values.

Source: TFEX website.

Contract Months of the SET 50 Index futures are the 3 nearest consecutive months plus the next 3 quarterly months. This means that a total of six SET 50 futures contracts would be available for trading on any given trading day. For example, if today is November 15, 2021, the 3 nearest consecutive months would be November, December, and January 2021, and the next 3 quarterly months would be March, June, and September 2022. **Trading hours** of TFEX equity futures contracts begin 15 minutes before the stock market (SET) opens and ends 15 minutes after the SET closes in each session. Similar to other exchanges, the extra 15 minutes before and after the stock market opens and closes allow investors such as fund managers to initiate and/or hedge their positions, especially, if they do not wish to carry their position overnight.

Final Settlement Price of the contract at maturity is determined by averaging the value of the index during the last 15 minutes and the closing index value. After removing the three highest and lowest values during that 15-minute period, the average of the remaining observations are rounded to the nearest two decimal points.

Transaction Costs would typically be around THB 78 per contract per transaction.[2] To see how these transaction costs compare with that of the underlying stock market, we work through the following simple example.

Suppose the SET 50 Index now at 1,000 points, the value of each futures contract is:
$$1,000 \text{ points} \times \text{THB } 200 = \text{THB } 200,000$$
$$\text{Cost per long position} = \text{THB } 78$$
$$\text{Transaction cost as \% of value} = (\text{THB } 78/\text{THB } 200,000) \times 100$$
$$= 0.039\%$$

A THB 200,000 position established in the futures market has a transaction cost of THB 78 or 0.039%.

By comparison, for stock market transactions in Thailand, the Internet brokerage commissions excluding stamp duty, etc, is currently around 0.207% of transaction value.[3] Thus, the transaction cost for a THB 200,000 transaction in the Thai stock market would be THB 200,000 × 0.00207 = THB 414. Thus in percentage terms, index futures transactions in Thailand are approximately five times cheaper (THB 414 vs THB 78) than stock market transactions. This cost advantage would obviously depend on the level of index and the number of contracts traded.

As discussed earlier, SIF contracts like all other derivative instruments can be used for hedging, arbitrage, and speculation. The principles and underlying strategies for all three applications are the same as that of the KLCI SIF contract seen earlier. We examine below the application of the SET 50 Index futures contract for arbitrage, hedging, and speculative trading.

---

[2] Internet transactions.

[3] Cash account. Internet transactions.

4.7.1 Index Arbitrage with SET 50 Index Futures Contracts

Suppose you observe the following quotations today for the SET 50 Index and SIF contract:

3-month SIF price = 1,012
Index value = 1,000 points
rf rate = 6%
Dividend yield = 3%
Time to maturity of SIF = 90 days

To see whether arbitrage is possible, we first check for mispricing. The correct value of the 3-month SIF should be:

$$F_t = 1,000(1 + 0.06 - 0.03)^{0.25}$$
$$= 1,000(1.03)^{0.25}$$
$$= 1,007.5 \text{ points}$$

Given the earlier information, the futures contract is clearly overpriced relative to spot. The futures price should be 1,007.5 points, yet it is quoted at 1,012 points and is overpriced by approximately 4.5 points.

4.7.1.1 Cash and Carry Arbitrage

Since there is mispricing, arbitrage is possible. As the SIF is overpriced, the appropriate arbitrage strategy would be the cash and carry arbitrage. By using the following arbitrage strategy, a riskless profit can be made. *(Note: No cash outlay is needed today.)* To see how much profit would be made and to prove that the profit will be *independent* of stock market performance, we will look at two market scenarios. *(Note: Current stock index value is 1,012 points.)*

(i) Index rises to 1,025 at maturity.
(ii) Index falls to 975 at maturity.

Scenario 1: Index Rises to 1,025

	Cash and Carry Arbitrage			
	Action	Position Today	Position at Maturity	Profit/Loss
(a)	Short 1 SIF contract	202,400	(205,000)	(2,600)
(b)	Long spot	(200,000)	205,000	5,000
(c)	Borrow THB 200,000 @ 6% for 90 days	200,000	(203,000)	(3,000)
(d)	Receive dividends and invest it @ 6% for 90 days	0	1522.5	1,522.5
			Net =	922.50

(Assumption: Dividends are received immediately and reinvested the same day) (Dividend amount = 200,000 × 0.03 = 6,000/4 = THB 1,500)
(Reinvested dividend amount = THB 1,500[1 + (0.06)/4] = THB 1,522.50)

Scenario 2: Index Falls to 975

	Cash & Carry Arbitrage			
Action		Position Today	Position at Maturity	Profit/ Loss
(a)	Short 1 SIF contract	202,400	(195,000)	7,400
(b)	Long spot	(200,000)	195,000	(5,000)
(c)	Borrow THB 200,000 @ 6% for 90 days	200,000	(203,000)	(3,000)
(d)	Receive dividends and invest it @ 6% for 90 days	0	1522.5	1522.5
				Net = 922.5

Notice that regardless of whether the index went up or down, you still make the same THB 922.50 of profit. This proves the point that the arbitrage profit is independent of market performance. The arbitrage profit, exclusive of transaction costs, which is 0.46% (THB 922.50/THB 200,000), approximates the percentage deviation in the actual futures price from theoretical price, $[(1012 - 1007.5)/1007.5] \times 100 = 0.44\%$. Thus, the size of the arbitrage profit is determined by extent of the mispricing. As with all other arbitrage activity, the arbitrage will continue until the equilibrium is reached. As more and more arbitrageurs long the spot market and short the SIF, spot prices will rise and SIF prices fall until equilibrium is restored.

4.7.1.2 Reverse Cash and Carry Arbitrage

Suppose in the earlier example, the futures price today is quoted as 3-month SIF price = 1,002.

Now, the SIF is *underpriced* relative to spot. In order to arbitrage, we need to do the reverse of the earlier strategy. The following **reverse cash and carry arbitrage** would be appropriate here.

Scenario 1: Index Rises to 1,025

Action		Position Today	Position at Maturity	Profit/ Loss
(a)	Long 1 SIF contract	(200,400)	205,000	4,600
(b)	Short spot	200,000	(205,000)	(5,000)
(c)	Lend THB 200,000 @ 6% for 90 days	(200,000)	203,000	3,000
(d)	Borrow THB 1,500 @ 6% for 90 days to replace dividends on borrowed shares (shorted)	0	(1,522.50)	(1,522.50)
				Net = 1,077.5

Scenario 2:   Index Falls to 975

Action		Position Today	Position at Maturity	Profit/Loss
(a)	Long 1 SIF contract	(200,400)	195,000	(5,400)
(b)	Short spot	200,000	195,000	5,000
(c)	Lend THB 200,000 @ 6% for 90 days	(200,000)	203,000	3,000
(d)	Borrow THB 1,500 @ 6% for 90 days to replace dividends on borrowed shares (shorted)	0	(1,522.50)	(1,522.50)
			Net =	1,077.5

Notice that once again, the profit amount is the same regardless of index movement. The percentage profit approximates the percentage mispricing or deviation of the actual from the theoretical futures price. The percentage mispricing of the SIF contract is $[(1{,}002 - 1{,}007.5)/1{,}007.5] \times 100 = 0.54\%$. The percentage arbitrage profit is [THB 1,077.5/ THB 200,000] × 100 = 0.53%. As in the earlier case, there is no net exposure; thus it is riskless arbitrage and the profit is pure arbitrage profit.

In index arbitrage, we take positions in both the SIF and the spot index. For example, in a **cash and carry arbitrage**, we long the spot index and short the SIF contract. Going long the spot index does not mean that one has to buy each and every one of the component stocks of the index. It may be possible to design a customized index of far fewer stocks that has a high correlation with the market index. For example, the SET 50 Index may be "replicated" by a portfolio of perhaps 30 stocks of different weighting that has a very close correlation with the SET 50. Thus, one needs to only long these select 30 stocks and not the entire index in order to arbitrage. Alternatively, a fund manager who already owns a diversified portfolio of stocks could do the cash and carry arbitrage by shorting the SIF contract alone. He does not have to long the spot index since he already owns a portfolio of stocks that is correlated to the spot index. This kind of arbitrage is often known as *quasi-arbitrage or quasi-index arbitrage*.

4.7.2 Hedging with SET 50 Index Futures Contract

Hedging is one of the applications of SIF contracts. The SET 50 Index futures allow investors to hedge their positions against volatility in the underlying stock market. Suppose you are a fund manager with exposure to the Thai stocks. You have concerns about near term volatility but would like to hold your position in the stocks. To hedge, you initiate a short position in the SET 50 Index futures to protect your portfolio's value.

Example

The following information is available to you today:

Current value of portfolio = THB 1,000,000
rf rate = 6% per year
Dividend yield on portfolio = 3% annualized
Spot SET 50 Index value = 1,000 points
3-month SET 50 index futures contract = 1,004.96 points

Because you have a long position in stocks, the hedge should be an offsetting short position in the SET 50 Index futures contracts. To determine how many SET 50 Index futures contracts you should short, you need to adjust for the correlation between your portfolio and the SET 50 Index. If your portfolio exactly tracks the SET 50 Index futures, then you do a base hedge.

$$\text{Base Hedge} = \frac{\text{Current Baht value of portfolio}}{\text{Current Baht value of index}}$$

$$= \frac{\text{THB } 1{,}000{,}000}{1{,}000 \text{ points} \times \text{THB } 200}$$

$$= 5 \text{ contracts}$$

Thus, from the base hedge computation, you should short *5 SET 50 Index futures contracts*. This assumes, however, that your portfolio is *exactly* like the portfolio of stocks that make up the SET 50 Index, and that the correlation between your portfolio and the SET 50 Index would be *perfectly positive* (correlation = +1.0), with no tracking error. In reality, when your portfolio is not exactly like the index, an adjustment has to be made in the calculation to reflect the difference in the relative betas of your portfolio and the index. Let's assume that the beta of your portfolio is 1.40 (i.e., weighted average of individual stock betas in your portfolio). The number of the SET 50 Index futures contracts needed to fully hedge, can be determined by either of the following two ways:

a) Base hedge × Beta of portfolio = 5 × 1.4
   = 7 contracts
b) Or by the following equation:

$$\text{Number of contracts} = \frac{\text{Baht value of portfolio} \times \text{Beta of portfolio}}{\text{Baht value of index}}$$

$$= \frac{\text{THB } 1{,}000{,}000 \times 1.4}{1{,}000 \times \text{THB } 200}$$

$$= 7 \text{ contracts}$$

Based on the above computation, to fully hedge your current portfolio, you need to short 7 SET 50 Index futures contracts. The following two possible scenarios over the next 90 days illustrate how the portfolio value would be protected by this hedging strategy.

Scenario 1: The Stock Market Falls 20%

Action		Position Today	Position at Maturity	Profit/Loss
(1)	Portfolio value	1,000,000	720,000	(280,000)
(2)	Short 7 SET 50 Index futures contracts	1,406,948	(1,120,000)	286,948
(3)	Dividends received till maturity			7,500
				Net = 14,448

Note: (1) Since beta of portfolio is 1.4; portfolio value falls 28% when market falls 20%.
(2) At maturity, index value is 1,000 pts × 0.80 = 800 pts. SET 50 Index futures value at maturity = [800 pts × 7] × THB 200.
(3) Dividends received over the 90-day period until maturity equals portfolio value multiplied by the annual dividend yield and divided by 4 to adjust for the 90-day period which is one calendar quarter [THB 1,000,000 × 0.03 ÷ 4].

Scenario 2: The Stock Market Rises 20%

Action		Position Today	Position at Maturity	Profit/Loss
(a)	Portfolio value	1,000,000	1,280,000	280,000
(b)	Short 7 SET 50 index futures contracts	1,406,948	(1,680,000)	(273,052)
(c)	Dividends received till maturity			7,500
				Net = 14,448

Note: (1) Portfolio value rises 28% since beta is 1.4.
(2) At maturity, index value is 1,000 pts × 1.20 = 1,200 pts. SET 50 Index futures value at maturity = [1,200 pts × 7] × THB 200.

Analysis of Hedged Position

Under Scenario 1

Initial value of portfolio	= THB 1,000,000
Unhedged portfolio value	= THB 720,000
Profit/Loss from SET 50 Index futures	= THB 286,948
Dividends received	= THB 7,500
Value of portfolio with hedge	= THB 1,014,448

Note that with hedging, your portfolio has grown by THB 14,448 over the 90-day period even though the market fell 20%.

Under Scenario 2

Initial value of portfolio	= THB 1,000,000
Unhedged portfolio value	= THB 1,280,000
Profit/Loss from SET 50 Index futures	= (THB 273,052)
Dividends received	= THB 7,500
Value of portfolio with hedge	= THB 1,014,448

With hedging, your portfolio has grown by THB 14,448 over the 90-day period, even though the market went up by 20%.

Two interesting points about the earlier hedging:

(a) Regardless of the market movement, your portfolio value remains the same. This is exactly the point about hedging, i.e., preservation of value.
(b) Under both scenarios your portfolio grows by THB 14,448. The reason for this is that since your portfolio is fully hedged, it is essentially a riskless asset. Thus, the return to your portfolio should be approximately the same as the risk-free rate. When annualized and adjusted for the round-trip transaction costs that we have excluded, the amount should approximate the 6% risk-free return.

4.7.3 Speculating with SET 50 Index Futures Contracts

Another application of the SET 50 Index future that we examine is speculation. A speculative trade is essentially a position in the SIF market without an offsetting position in the spot market. The speculative position with the SET 50 Index futures could be either long or short depending on the speculator's view on the market.

4.7.3.1 Speculative Position: Bullish Expectation

Suppose speculator believes that the market is like to rise in the next 4 trading days. As such, the appropriate speculative strategy would like to long SET 50 Index futures contracts. The following table shows the pay-off to a speculative position of going long one SET 50 Index futures contract.

Assuming the underlying index has the following price movement over the next 4 trading days:

Strategy: Long 1 SET 50 Index Futures Contract

Day	Index Close	Amount (THB)	Profit/Loss	Accumulated P/L
0	1,000	200,000	0	0
1	1,012	202,400	2,400	2,400
2	1,010	202,000	(400)	2,000
3	1,007	201,400	(600)	1,400
4	1,015	203,000	1,600	3,000

Since the speculator's expectation was correct and the index rose by 15 points from his initial entry value, the accumulated profit is THB 3,000 (15 points × THB 200), which could have also been determined as: (Exit Value − Entry Value) × Multiplier = (1,015 − 1,000) × THB 200 = THB 3,000. On the other hand, suppose another speculator, with a bearish outlook, had established a short position on day 0, he would have lost THB 3,000. The danger with naked short positions is that the outcomes are binary, you make profits if your expectation turns out correct and losses otherwise.

4.7.3.2 Speculative Position: Bearish Expectation

Assume a speculator expects the market and the SET 50 Index futures prices to decline over the next few days. To take advantage of the price decline, the appropriate speculative strategy would be to short the SET 50 Index futures contracts.

Strategy: Short 1 SET 50 Index Futures Contract

Day	Index Close	Amount (THB)	Profit/Loss	Accumulated P/L
0	1,000	200,000	0	0
1	993	198,600	1,400	1,400
2	996	199,200	(600)	800
3	989	197,800	1,400	2,200
4	987	197,400	400	2,600

Since the SET 50 Index had fallen by 13 points (1,000 − 987), the speculator had been right with this expectation. His speculative position would provide him a total profit of THB 2,600. Computed as (Entry Value − Exit Value) × Multiplier = (1,000 − 987) × THB 200 = THB 2,600. By contrast, a speculator who had been bullish and had established a long position by holding one contract of the SET 50 Index futures on day 0, would have lost THB 2,600 by day 4.

4.7.4 The Congruence in Strategies Amongst Contracts

Having examined in-depth two SIF contracts, the FBM KLCI of Malaysia's BMDB and the SET 50 of Thailand's TFEX, it should be obvious that the underlying logic of the strategies used in the three applications, hedging, arbitrage, and speculation are exactly alike. This should not be surprising. The strategy to arbitrage a mispriced contract would be the same regardless of which SIF contract is to be arbitraged. In other words, the underlying logic of the strategies are universal. Thus, the hedging strategies would be the same no matter the SIF contract. The only needed adjustments in the applications would be for market microstructure differences like, exchange rules, size of index multipliers, position limits, contract sizes, and such. The currency denomination of the contract should also be adjusted for where needed.

4.8 SIF Contracts and Portfolio Management

In addition to the earlier three applications, hedging, arbitrage and speculation, SIF contracts are also used for other portfolio management purposes. We examine two other common uses of SIF contracts by portfolio managers as follows. These two other applications are (i) **Adjusting Portfolio Betas**, and (ii) **Asset Allocation**.

4.8.1 Adjusting Portfolio Betas with SIF Contracts

Portfolio managers would often want to adjust the beta of their stock portfolio. Beta, as we know, is the measure of a stock's systematic risk. Portfolio managers who typically hold a diverse range of stocks would largely be focused on managing the systematic rather than total risk. Total risk, which is made up of both systematic and unsystematic risk, is not the object of focus since unsystematic risk would have been diversified away when putting together a portfolio of stocks. Thus, it is the systematic risk or beta of the portfolio that a manager would want to manage. Going by modern portfolio theory, the beta of a portfolio is the weighted average of the betas of the stocks that make up the portfolio.

$$B_{port} = W_1 \times B_1 + W_2 \times B_2 \ldots W_n \times B_n$$

As is evident from the earlier equation, changing the beta of a portfolio is no easy task. In order to achieve a desired portfolio beta, much portfolio rebalancing may be needed. Such rebalancing would requireweight re-adjustment which in turn means selling different proportions of various stocks and adding (buying) different proportions of yet other stocks. Portfolio beta adjustment is a tedious, time-consuming, costly, and iterative affair. Yet, portfolio managers would necessarily have to undertake such a task if they wish to improve their returns performance. Fund managers often try to adjust their portfolio beta according to their expectation of stock market performance. For example, if a manager expects a bull run in the near future, he would want to increase the overall beta of his portfolio. The opposite would be true if he is bearish.

We have seen earlier that systematic risk can be easily handled with SIF contracts. Since betas are the measure of systematic risk, the same logic applies. A manager could easily reduce the beta of his portfolio by going short SIF contracts equivalent to a proportion of his portfolio value, in essence hedging a portion of his portfolio. As to what proportion of the portfolio should be hedged would depend on how low he wants the beta to be. The portfolio beta could be reduced to zero by going short SIF contracts with a total value equivalent to the value of the portfolio. Since a fully hedged portfolio with zero beta would only provide returns equivalent to the risk-free return, portfolio managers would often want to do a partial rather than full hedge. We examine below how SIF contracts could be used to adjust portfolio beta.

Adjusting Portfolio Beta: Illustration

You currently hold a portfolio that has a beta of 1.5. You are worried about impending volatility in the stock market over the immediate future. With a beta of 1.5, your portfolio would be 50% more volatile than the stock market's volatility. As such, you want to reduce your portfolio beta to a more acceptable 1.0 beta. How can you use SIF contracts to do this?

Information
Current portfolio value = RM 6,000,000
Portfolio beta = 1.50
Index level = 1,000 points
Intended portfolio beta = 1.00

Since this is a partial hedge, what proportion of your portfolio should you hedge?

Answer:

$$\text{Amount of portfolio to hedge} = \text{Portfolio value} \times \left[1 - \left(\frac{\text{Intended beta}}{\text{Actual beta}}\right)\right]$$

$$= \text{RM } 6{,}000{,}000 \times \left[1 - \left(\frac{1.00}{1.50}\right)\right]$$

$$= \text{RM } 2{,}000{,}000$$

So, RM 2 million worth of your portfolio should be hedged.

$$\text{Number of SIF contracts} = \frac{\text{RM } 2{,}000{,}000}{1{,}000 \times \text{RM } 50}$$

$$= 40 \text{ contracts}$$

$$\text{New portfolio beta} = \frac{\text{RM } 4{,}000{,}000}{\text{RM } 6{,}000{,}000}(1.50) + \frac{\text{RM } 2{,}000{,}000}{\text{RM } 6{,}000{,}000}(0)$$

$$= 0.67(1.50)$$

$$= 1.00 \text{ beta}$$

4.8.2 Adjusting Asset Allocation

SIF contracts can also help portfolio managers with implementing dynamic asset allocation strategies. Asset allocation involves the allocation of funds among several asset categories, e.g., among stocks, bonds, and T-bills. T-bills are a key element in asset allocation. When markets are deemed bearish, portfolio managers would increase the weighting in T-bills (cash) and reduce the weighting in stocks. The opposite occurs when markets are expected to be bullish. Adjusting asset allocation would therefore require buying/selling shares and T-bills as the case may be. This is an expensive proposition when viewed from a transaction cost perspective.

Asset allocation becomes a much cheaper strategy with SIF contracts. As we saw earlier, SIF contracts can be used to synthesize or "create" T-bill positions with stocks. A fund manager could easily mimic the desired T-bill position by simply combining the right proportion of SIF contracts to his current stock position. To increase the T-bill position, he would short more SIF contracts and do the opposite if he wants to reduce the T-bill position. Recall that a long stock position when combined with a short SIF position results in a synthetic T-bill position. Thus, the desired proportion in T-bills can be created by shorting an appropriate amount of SIF contracts. The portfolio manager has no need to buy/sell stocks or T-bills in order to adjust his asset allocation. Transaction in SIF contracts alone is sufficient to achieve the desired allocation.

4.9 Issues in SIF Pricing

Violations to Spot–Futures Parity

Theoretically, sustained deviations from spot-futures parity is not possible since it would be arbitraged away. However, the reality is that deviations do happen and quite often too. Some of the reasons for this violation are given below:

(a) *Transaction Costs and the No-Arbitrage Bounds*

Arbitrage as we know, takes advantage of mispricing or price deviations from parity. However, while arbitrage is always possible whenever there are price deviations, it may not be profitable when the mispricing is small. Recall that when the SIF is overpriced relative to stocks, the appropriate arbitrage strategy would be a cash and carry strategy, i.e., long stocks, short futures. When the SIF is underpriced, the appropriate arbitrage strategy would be the reverse cash and carry. Here, we would long the SIF and short the stocks.

Each strategy, whether cash and carry or reverse cash and carry, has its transaction costs. For example, in cash and carry transaction, costs will be incurred in going long stocks and shorting the SIF contracts. Generally, the cost of the reverse cash and carry is slightly higher since one does not get the full proceeds from shorting the stock. The existence of these transaction costs creates an upper and lower bound around the fair value (correct value) of the futures price. This area around the fair value or theoretical value of the futures contract is known as the **no-arbitrage bound**. Mispricing that falls within this bound is not arbitrageable. Mathematically, the no-arbitrage bound is given as follows:

$$F_t^+ = S_t(1+C^+)(1+r-d)^{t,T}$$
$$F_t^- = S_t(1+C^-)(1+r-d)^{t,T}$$

where

F_t^+ = theoretical futures price adjusted for the transaction cost of the cash and carry strategy
F_t^- = theoretical futures price adjusted for the transaction cost of the reverse cash and carry
C^+ = transaction cost of cash and carry
C^- = transaction cost of reverse cash and carry

Figure 4.2 shows the no-arbitrage bound, given movements in the fair/theoretical value.

As the transaction costs form a bound around the fair/theoretical value, **mispricing that falls within the bound is not arbitrageable**. This is because, mispricing that falls within the bounds is too small to cover the transaction costs of the arbitrage. Only mispricing that falls outside the bounds are arbitrageable.

Note
The no-arbitrage bound is the band created around the theoretical price by transaction costs. Mispricing that falls within this bound is not arbitrageable.

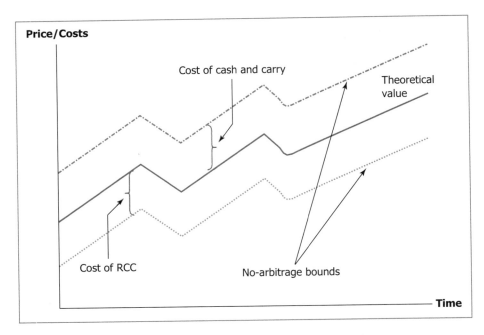

Figure 4.2   Theoretical SIF Value and No-Arbitrage Bounds

There is an implication of this from a market development/efficiency viewpoint. Well-developed and highly efficient markets have low transaction costs and therefore **narrow no-arbitrage bounds**. On the other hand, less efficient markets that have higher transaction costs would have **wide** no-arbitrage bounds.

(b) **Inefficiencies**

In markets where information flow is not efficient, a number of reasons could lead to violations in the parity. First, quoted prices may be **stale**. Because the reported prices may not be current prices, "implied" deviations may really be nonexistent.

Second, in such markets there could also be more **execution risk**. That is, an attempt to arbitrage may not work because the prices at which transactions are executed may not be at the prices quoted. This often has to do with the lag between when the order is placed and when it is executed. In inefficient markets, this lag can be long enough to prevent sufficient arbitrage.

(c) **Order Imbalances**

Occasionally, deviations from parity may be due to order imbalances in the futures and/or spot markets. For example, if there are much more sell orders than buy orders in futures, the futures price is likely to fall below parity without being arbitraged immediately.

(d) **Regulation and Other Hindrances**

These may also cause violations from parity. For example, government restrictions on short selling, exchange requirements on margins, tick-rules, etc. are often the main reasons for deviations from parity. This is because such hindrances may prevent or at least reduce arbitrage activity. Furthermore, the existence of regulation often *increases* the transaction costs and therefore restricts convergence to parity. Some exchanges have thrived on helping investors overcome such hurdles by listing foreign indices. A classic example would be the Singapore's SGX has grown successfully to become one of Asia's largest derivative exchange by allowing the listing and trading of other foreign indexes but without the regulation. This lack of regulation is a "value" created by exchanges like SGX and has attracted investors who would otherwise not use the indexes. The very successful listing and trading of the Japanese Nikkei SIF contract is a good example.

4.10 Issues in SIF Trading

Since the advent of SIF contracts and given their huge popularity, SIF trading has been subject to much academic research. Much of the empirical work has revolved around several issues related to SIF trading. We examine some of these issues here.

4.10.1 Volatility of Underlying Stock Market

The advent of SIF contracts has often been blamed for having increased the volatility of the underlying stock market. Critics have blamed **index arbitrage** activity, especially program trading for causing increased volatility. Program trading is simply large-scale computer-triggered index arbitrage. It was blamed for the 1987 stock market crash on the NYSE. Critics argued that index arbitrage activity between the futures market in Chicago where the S&P 500 Index futures contracts are traded (on the CME) and the NYSE in New York accentuated the crash. This led to several studies on whether SIF trading does indeed cause increased volatility of the underlying market. The results however appear mixed. Though some of the earlier United States (US)-based studies did find evidence of some increase in volatility, the later US studies based on larger data sets did not. Empirical work in other markets too found no evidence of an increase in underlying stock market volatility. In fact, several later studies had found quite the opposite, i.e., underlying stock market volatility had reduced. It is a logical outcome given the fact that with derivatives, the big players in stock markets, the portfolio managers, asset management institutions, etc. Have no need to enter and exit markets according to their expectations. For example, if a portfolio manager is worried about short-term volatility, he need not sell off his holdings, as he would have to do in the absence of derivatives. With SIF contracts, the portfolio manager can easily hedge his position without selling out. It is when the big players exit and reenter the markets that they cause slumps and run ups in the stock market — thereby increasing market volatility.

Subsequent research on underlying market volatility has also focused on expiration day volatility, i.e., to examine stock market volatility on the days when the SIF contracts expire (maturity day). In the US, underlying markets were indeed found to have higher than average volatility on "*triple-witching days*." These were the days when the three equity derivative instruments, the S&P 500 Index futures, index options, and stock options expired, all on the same day. Such early experience of increased volatility on expiration days has led exchanges to stagger expirations. Thus, the impact is now reduced. Several studies of non-US markets have found no significantly higher volatility even on expiration days.

4.10.2 Volume Migration from Spot to SIF

Several studies have also shown that with the introduction of SIF trading, there is often a migration in trading volume from the stock market to the SIF market. This has been most evident in the Nikkei SIF markets; by about 3 years after the introduction of Nikkei SIF contracts in Osaka, volume as measured by ¥en value had already matched trading value in the underlying stock market, the Tokyo Stock Exchange. By the fifth year, trading value of SIF had overtaken that of the underlying stocks. This had largely been because volume had migrated. Stock market volume had shown a steady decline, whereas Nikkei SIF contract volume, a steady increase. Part of the reason for this migration is the lower transaction costs of SIF compared with similar size transactions in the underlying spot/stock market. We have discussed these lower costs earlier in the chapter. In addition to costs, the derivative markets given their microstructure and lighter regulatory framework offer players much more flexibility.

4.10.3 Lead–Lag Relationships in Returns and Volatility

Several previous studies, particularly of US markets, have documented evidence of a **lead–lag relationship** between the index futures and stock markets. It appears that the SIF market is usually the first to react to news, whereas the stock market follows. Several reasons have been put forth to explain this relationship. Among these are: (i) infrequent trading of stocks comprising the index; therefore, the index reflects "stale" prices and so lags futures; (ii) differences in liquidity between the stock and futures markets; (iii) informed traders may have a preference to trade in one market and not the other depending on whether the information is firm-specific or systematic; and (iv) due to market frictions such as transactions costs, capital requirements, and short-selling restrictions that may make it more optimal to trade in the futures markets.

4.10.4 Patterns in Intraday Trading and Volatility

Analysis of timed interval intraday transactions data of stocks have shown systematic patterns in returns, trading volume, and volatility. Typically, intraday volume and volatility have portrayed U-shaped patterns. A number of researchers has presented evidence that these same patterns exist in futures markets too. Most of the recent studies had used intraday data of 15-minute intervals. The results show that both return volatility and trading volume show a prominent U-shaped pattern. It appears that most of a trading day's volume and price action are clustered around the immediate period of the morning open and last half hour of the trading day.

4.10.5 Intermarket Spread Trading

With the launch of SIF contracts in various exchanges across the world, there has been a boom in **intermarket spread** trading. Spread trading between different SIF contracts, e.g., between the S&P 500 Index futures and the Nikkei Index futures has also been popular. With increased globalization and cointegration of markets, such intercontact spread trading is likely to gain popularity. The most interesting form of intermarket spread trading has however been in cases where the same or similar index futures contracts are listed on more than one exchange. The best example being the Nikkei SIF contracts which are traded in Singapore (SGX), Osaka (OSE), and in Chicago (CME). With multimarket trading such as this, it becomes possible not only to engage in spot-futures arbitrage but also in futures — futures arbitrage across markets. Indeed, this kind of spread trading between SGX and OSE had been very popular in the initial years of the Nikkei SIF's introduction. This huge popularity stemmed from the fact that Japanese regulatory intervention gave rise to easy arbitrage opportunity between the OSE and SGX. Essentially, Japanese government intervention in the form of margin rules, uptick rules, and other restrictive requirements had led to the Nikkei futures on the OSE to being overpriced relative to the same contracts traded on SGX. Since both OSE and SGX were trading contemporaneously, it was easy to make arbitrage profits by shorting the contracts on the OSE and going long the same contracts on SGX. Regulatory intervention gave rise to these arbitrage opportunity and the opportunity remained for quite a while until Japanese regulation was changed. The infamous Barings PLC scandal was in some ways related to this situation. It appears that Barings PLC got into this intermarket Nikkei arbitrage at the tail end. The Singapore branch of Barings PLC had made good arbitrage profits initially, but as Japanese regulation changed, the arbitrage opportunity disappeared. It was at this point it appears that their trader Nick Leeson began to take speculative positions in order to keep making the same level of profits.

4.11 Growth and Trading Performance of the FBM KLCI and the SET 50 Index Futures Contracts

Figures 4.3(a) and (b) show the growth in annual traded volume of the two SIF contracts discussed in the chapter. Though the FBM KLCI was introduced a good 10 years earlier, in 1996,

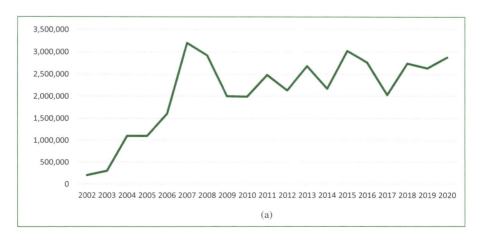

Figure 4.3(a)   FBM KLCI Index Futures Contracts-Growth of Annual Traded Volume (2002–2020)

its trading performance pales in comparison to Thailand's SET 50 Index futures. The most active year for FBM KLCI index futures was 2007 when volume reached 3.2 million contracts. Since then, volume appears to be fluctuating between 2.5 million and 3 million contracts per year. In 2020, total traded volume for the contract was approximately 3 million contracts. Relative to the SET 50, trading activity for the FBM KLCI was about 20 times lower in 2020. Not surprisingly, in terms of global ranking of traded volume, the FBM KLCI Index futures are ranked at the 77th position. Even the introduction of another SIF based on mid-cap stocks, the **Mini FTSE Bursa Malaysia Mid 70 Index Futures (FM70)** seems to have done little improve overall interest in Malaysian SIF contracts. The FM70 has a smaller contract multiplier of RM 4 and so has smaller contract value. Exchanges introduce such "mini" contracts to attract smaller players and hope for higher activity/liquidity. That, however, does not seem to have been the case. This despite the fact that like other derivatives offered by Bursa Malaysia, both the SIF contracts are available for trading electronically on CME Globex.

Figure 4.3(b) shows the trading performance of Thailand's SET 50 Index futures contracts. The SET 50 Index futures was first equity derivative contract traded on the TFEX. In its first year, 2006, the total traded volume of merely 198,737 contracts. Traded volume, however, increased more than six-fold to 1,228,238 contracts in the following year. Interestingly, the traded volume was not affected much by the 2008 financial crisis. The traded volume was between 2,099,098 and 2,522,465 contracts between 2008 and 2010. As is the case with most newly introduced derivatives, the growth rate in traded volume was slow in the first few years, but increased significantly in subsequent years. The takeoff point seems to be 2013 when 5.7 million contracts were traded. Growth has been exponential since then. The following year, 2014, total volume was close to 14.5 million. Based on volume numbers for 2020 of 57.5 million contracts, the SET 50 Index futures is TFEX's most active contract, accounting for 48.5% of the exchange's total traded volume. In global ranking of the most active SIF contracts as seen in Table 4.1, the SET 50 index futures contract occupies a highly respectable 13th placing. For a contract that is just about 15 years old, this is quite an achievement.

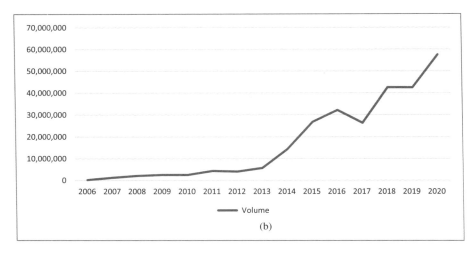

Figure 4.3(b)   SET 50 Index Futures Growth of Annual Traded Volume (2006–2020)

4.12 Single Stock Futures

SSF are a fairly new equity derivative product. All the four exchanges covered in this book, BMDB, TFEX, SGX, and HKEX, have introduced SSF contracts. In this section, we will examine SSFs traded on BMDB and TFEX. SSF is a futures contract on an individual listed stock. Since the underlying asset is an equity instrument (individual stock), SSFs are equity derivatives. SSFs are a new derivative instrument, having been introduced in the US less than 15 years ago. Currently, SSFs are listed and traded on exchanges in several countries.

Note
A SSF is an equity futures contract which has a single stock as its underlying asset.

Being an equity futures contract, SSFs share many common features with SIF contracts. We have seen the many advantages of SIF contracts. SSFs also share many of the same benefits. Like any other derivative, SSFs can be used for the three key applications: hedging, arbitrage, and speculation. In addition, being based on an individual stock, SSFs offer several stock specific advantages. We will examine some the uses of SSFs below.

4.12.1 SSFs in Malaysia

Since the launch in April 2006, Bursa Malaysia (BMDB) has offered SSF contracts on 10 underlying stocks. Some 15 years, though some of the underlying stocks have changed, it is still 10 stocks that are being offered now as SSF contracts. These are the following:

- CIMB Group Holding
- DRB Hicom
- Gamuda
- Genting Bhd
- Top Glove
- Hartalega Holding
- Inari Amerthon
- My EG Service
- Telekom Malaysia
- Genting Malaysia Bhd

All 10 stocks are main board listed have fairly large market capitalization and have good liquidity and depth. Tables 4.4(a) and (b) show the contract specification for SSFs listed on Malaysia's BMD and Thailand's TFEX.

Table 4.4(a) Contract Specification for Single Stock Futures — BMDB

Contract Code	SSF
Contract Size	1,000 shares
Contract Months	Spot month, the next month and the next 2 calendar quarterly months. The calendar quarterly months are March, June, September and December.
Trading Hours	First trading session: Malaysian Time 8:45 a.m. to 12:45 p.m. Second trading session: Malaysian Time 2:30 p.m. to 5:15 p.m.

Table 4.4(a)   (*Continued*)

Contract Code	SSF
Minimum Price Fluctuation	0.02 point valued at RM 20
Daily Price Limit	None
Speculative Position Limit	Maximum number of net long or net short positions to be held: 1,350 contracts, or 2,300 contracts (if the Average Daily Trading Volume [ADTV] of the underlying stock is more than 20 million for the most recent 6-month period).
Final Trading Day	The last Business Day of the contract month.
Delivery	Cash settlement based on the Final Settlement Value. The Final Settlement Value shall be the Weighted Average Price, rounded to 2 decimal points, or in the event the final settlement value is equidistant between 2 minimum price fluctuations, the value shall be rounded to the higher minimum price fluctuation of the underlying share prices traded for the morning and afternoon trading session on Bursa Malaysia on the Final Trading Day.

Source: Bursa Malaysia website.

Notice that the contract months, trading hours, final trading day, etc., are the same as that of SIF contracts. In the case of SSF, the contract size is 1,000 underlying shares. Thus, a long position in one SSF contract would allow the trader to *buy* 1,000 of the underlying stock on maturity at the predetermined futures price. Similarly, a short position in SSF would allow the trader to *sell* 1,000 underlying stocks at the predetermined futures price. Though one is entitled to buy or sell the underlying stock, note that as a financial derivative, SSFs are cash-settled. As such, no delivery of the underlying stock takes place. Instead, the contract is cash-settled. As shown in the earlier contract specification, the final settlement value is the weighted average price of the underlying stock on the final trading day.

Note
Like other financial derivatives, SSF contracts are cash-settled at maturity.

4.12.2 SSF in Thailand

In addition to SIF, TFEX also offers SSF. Launched on November 24, 2008, SSFs offer investors an alternative instrument to investing in the underlying stock directly. Since 2008, TFEX has registered seven batches of SSFs and in total there are 128 SSFs registered on TFEX as of December 2021. Table 4.4(b) shows the contract specifications for SSF contracts on TFEX.

Table 4.4(b) Contract Specifications: SSF in Thailand

Underlying Asset	128 Listed Stocks in Stock Exchange of Thailand (SET)
Contract size	1,000 shares
Minimum Price Fluctuation	THB 0.01 (or THB 10 per contract)
Daily Price Limits	30% of the latest settlement price
Contract Months	March, June, September, December, up to four nearest quarters
Trading Hours	Morning preopen: 09:15–09:45 hours. Morning session: 09:45–12:30 hours. Afternoon preopen: 13:45–14.15 hours. Afternoon session: 14:15–16:55 hours.
Final Trading Day	The business day immediately preceding the last business day of the contract month.
Final Settlement	Cash settlement
Final Settlement Price	The volume weighted average value of the underlying share trading transaction during last 15 minutes and at the closing on the last trading day, rounded to the nearest two decimal points.

Source: TFEX website.

TFEX's SSF contracts were the second most popular futures product with about 40% of the traded volume.

4.12.3 SSF — Trading Mechanics

Operationally, trading SSF contracts is very similar to that of SIF contracts. In both bases, at maturity, one closes out one's position by taking out the profits in the margin account if a profit has been made or closing the position, having already paid the margins if a loss has been made. No physical delivery takes place in both cases.

Trading SSF Contracts — An Illustration

Mr. Tan is bullish about demand for medical gloves and intends to participate in a potential rally. He thinks Top Glove Bhd. would be a big beneficiary of rising health and sanitary awareness following the pandemic. It is now June 2021; he therefore goes long 1 September 2021 SSF contract on Top Glove Bhd. at RM 15. What this means is that he gets to "buy" 1,000 Top Glove Bhd. stocks on the maturity day of the SSF contract at RM 15 each or RM 15,000 for the 1,000 stocks. On the day he initiates the contract, Mr. Tan will have to place an initial margin. Depending on his futures broker, this can vary between 10% and 25%. Variation margins also apply. Depending on which way the underlying stock performs, Mr. Tan may receive margin calls if the stock's price declines subsequently. On the other hand, his margin account will increase if Top Glove Bhd.'s stock rises.

Suppose on September 29, the final trading day, Top Glove Bhd.'s stock settles at RM 15.80, Mr. Tan would make a profit of RM 800 as follows:

(Buy) Entry Price ⇒ RM 15.00 × 1,000 = RM 15,000
(Sell) Exit Price ⇒ RM 15.80 × 1,000 = RM 15,800
Profit to long position = RM 800

Being a cash-settled contract, this RM 800 would have been added to his margin account. Mr. Tan therefore, simply closes his margin account to realize the RM 800 profit.

A seller, or short position in a SSF contract would benefit if prices fall. A short position in a SSF contract entitles one to sell the underlying stock at the predetermined exercise price. As we saw in Chapter 3, the profit to the short position would be:

> Profit to Short = Original Futures Price − Settlement Price

The lower the settlement price at maturity, the higher the profit to the short position.

4.12.4 Why Use SSF Contracts?

It should be evident from our discussion thus far that SSF contracts are operationally similar to SIF contracts. As such, it should not be surprising that SSFs provide many of the advantages that SIF contracts offer. Being a derivative instrument requiring only initial margins, SSFs provide automotive leverage. They have lower transaction costs, can be used to lower risk (hedging), to short a stock, and like SIFs, they can be used to alter the beta of a portfolio. We will discuss some of these applications later.

Note
SSF contracts can be used for hedging, arbitrage, and speculation, in addition to other stock specific use.

4.12.5 Pricing a SSF Contract

Pricing a SSF contract is based on the same logic of SIF contracts. An SSF contract is priced based on the cost of carry model.

$$SSF_{t,T} = S_o(1 + rf - d)^{t,T}$$

where

S_o = current price of underlying stock
rf = risk-free interest rate
d = expected dividend yield in %
t,T = time to maturity

Notice that the earlier equation is identical to the model used in pricing an SIF contract. Indeed it is a cost of carry model, based on an individual stock and the expected dividend yield of that stock.

SSF Pricing — Illustration

A stock is currently selling at RM 12. The stock is expected to pay a dividend of 30 sen over the next 90 days. If the risk-free interest rate is 6%, what should the correct price be for a 90-day SSF contract on the stock?

$$SSF_{t,T} = S_o(1 + rf - d)^{t,T}$$

Since a 30-sen dividend per stock is due, the dividend yield on the stock is:

$$\left[\frac{RM\ 0.30}{RM\ 12.00}\right] \times 100 = 2.5\%$$

$SSF_{t,T}$ = RM 12(1 + 0.06 − 0.025)$^{0.25}$
 = RM 12(1.035)$^{0.25}$
 = RM 12(1.008637)
 = RM 12.10

The 90-day SSF would therefore sell at a 10-sen premium over the spot price. In most cases, since the dividend yield would be smaller than the risk-free rate, there would be positive carry. A positive net carrying cost would imply that SSF prices would usually be higher than the stock's price. As in the case of SIF contracts, a large dividend payment could cause the net carrying cost to be negative; in which case, the SSF contract would be at a discount to spot. Given the cost of carry model, the following relationships hold between the SSF value and its determinants.

For an Increase In	Value of SSF
Stock price (S_o)	Increases
Interest rate (rf)	Increases
Dividend yield (d)	Decreases
Time to maturity (t, T)	Increases

4.12.6 SSF — Applications

SSF contracts, as mentioned earlier, can be used for several purposes in addition to hedging, arbitrage, and speculation. In this section, we examine these applications.

Note
SSF contracts are priced using the cost of carry model. The underlying stock's price, its dividends, and the risk-free rate are the key determinants.

(1) Hedging with SSF Contracts

Since an SSF contract has as its underlying asset a single stock, it can be used to hedge exposure arising from that stock. Given the lower transaction cost and the automatic leverage, SSF contracts would be a cheap and sensible instrument to hedge with. The hedging principle is the same. One should take a position in derivatives that would exactly offset movements in the underlying.

Illustration: Hedging a Long Stock Position
A fund manager had been accumulating a large position in the banking stock, CIMB Group Holdings. He had been proven right thus far. However, with the recent resignation of key personnel and the surrounding uncertainty, he is worried about the stock. The stock price had not reacted to the resignation but the fund manager feels subsequent events might cause a negative reaction. He intends to lock in his gains on the stock thus far and remain hedged for at least the next 10–12 weeks, after which he believes things should settle down. How can he hedge his position?

Answer: Since he is long the underlying stock and would fear a fall in the stock's price, he should short, 3-month CIMB Group Holding SSF contracts. The number of contracts to short would depend on the size of his holding and the extent of hedging cover he wants.

For example, if he is long 50,000 stocks and wishes to be fully hedged, then he should **short 50 three-month CIMB Group Holding SSF contracts**.

Hedging a Short Stock Position
An investor had shorted Genting Berhad stocks on hearing that the company had failed in its bid to secure Singapore's new casino project.

He had shorted a total 6,000 stocks. He thinks Genting Berhad stock is likely to continue falling for a while. Yet, he is uneasy about rumors that Singapore might be considering another casino. Although he does not think this rumor has much credence, he would nevertheless like to cover his exposure. How can the investor protect himself?

Answer: Since he fears a rise in the price of the underlying stock, he should **long 6 three-month Genting Berhad SSF contracts**.

To recapitulate our discussion on hedging with SSF contracts:
To hedge: Long underlying position, short SSF contracts.
To hedge: Short underlying position, long SSF contracts.

(2) Arbitraging with SSF Contracts
Recall that arbitrage is essentially the process by which one tries to profit from mispricing. The general rule being, to long (buy) the underpriced asset and short (sell) the overpriced one. The same applies in this case. We compare the quoted SSF price with its theoretical fair value.

If $SSF > S_o(1 + rf - d)^t$: SSF is overpriced relative to its underlying stock.

Arbitrage strategy: Short SSF, long underlying (**and borrow to finance the purchase of stock by borrowing at rf rate**)

If $SSF < S_o(1 + rf - d)^t$: SSF is underpriced relative to its underlying stock.

Arbitrage strategy: Long SSF, short underlying (*and lend the proceeds from short sale of stock at rf rate*)

Illustration: Arbitraging with SSF Contracts

You work at the arbitrage desk of a large mutual fund. You observe the following quotes on your Reuters screen.

Top Glove Bhd. stock = RM 15.00
Top Glove Bhd. 3-month SSF = RM 15.48
Risk-free rate: (3-month KLIBOR) = 6% (annualized)

You know that Top Glove Bhd. stock just went ex-dividend and so no dividend is expected over the next 3 months. Given the above prices and dividend information, you are wondering whether arbitrage is possible.

Answer: To check for potential arbitrage opportunity, we calculate the theoretical price of the SSF and compare it with the quoted price. The theoretical price should be:

$$SSF_{3\,mth} = S_o(1 + rf - d)^t$$
$$SSF_{3\,mth} = RM\ 15.00(1 + 0.06 - 0)^{0.25}$$
$$= RM\ 15.00(1.06)^{0.25}$$
$$= RM\ 15.00(1.014674)$$
$$= RM\ 15.22$$

Since the fair value is RM 15.22 whereas the SSF is being quoted RM 15.48, the futures is overvalued. The arbitrage strategy would be to short the SSF, long the underlying stock and finance the purchase of stock by borrowing at the *rf* rate. Notice that this is essentially the cash and carry arbitrage we saw in the earlier section on SIF contracts. To work through the example here, suppose you can invest around RM 150,000 for the arbitrage and Top Glove stock is at RM 16.20 in 90 days. Your profits would be:

Cash and Carry Arbitrage with SSF

Action		Position Today	Position at Maturity	Profit/ Loss
(i)	Short 10 SSF contract	RM 154,800	(RM 162,000)	(RM 7,200)
(ii)	Long stocks (10,000)	(RM 150,000)	RM 162,000	RM 12,000
(iii)	Borrow RM 150,000 at 6% for 3 months	RM 150,000	(RM 152,201)	(RM 2,201)
			Net =	RM 2,599

This arbitrage profit of RM 2,599 comes from mispricing and is independent of movements of the underlying stock price. Recall that we saw in the case of SIF contracts, that arbitrage profit remained the same regardless of whether the index rose or fell. It will be the same here. You can try the earlier exercise for any value of Top Glove Bhd. stock price in 90 days, the arbitrage profit should be the same.[4]

(3) Speculating with SSF Contracts

To profit from expected fall in stock price: Mr. Tan is convinced that the recent rise in oil prices is likely to have a negative impact on the airline industry. He has been looking to short the two airline stocks in the country, Malaysia Airlines (MAS) and AirAsia. However, regulation against short-selling prevents him from doing so. How can Mr. Tan profit from his expectation? Answer: If SSF contracts are available on AirAsia stocks, he can profit from his expectation by going short on AirAsia SSF contracts. The size of his profit would obviously depend on how much AirAsia stock falls and the number of SSF contracts he shorted. Should Mr. Tan's expectation not come through and AirAsia stock rise instead, he would make losses on his SSF position.

> **Note**
> Using SSF contracts in hedging, arbitrage and speculation is operationally identical to that of SIF contracts.

To profit from expected increase in stock price: Mr. Ali has just finished reading the latest report on Global Infrastructure needs. The report shows a huge increase in demand for new infrastructure. The report also points to the launch of a World Bank infrastructure fund. Mr. Ali thinks all of these bodes well for infrastructure firms. He has been looking at infra stocks listed on Bursa Malaysia, in particular Gamuda Bhd. He thinks that given lower transaction costs and inbuilt leverage, the SSF contracts may be a more sensible instrument to use. What should Mr. Ali do to profit from his expectation? To profit from the expected increase in underlying stock price, a long position in the stock's SSF contract would be appropriate. Thus, Mr. Ali should ***long SSF contracts*** on Gamuda Bhd.

To recapitulate our discussion of appropriate strategy for speculating with SSF contracts:

To benefit from:
falling stock price, short SSF contracts.
rising stock price, long SSF contracts.

---

[4] The percentage mispricing of SSF was approximately 1.71%. The profit of RM 2,599 on an investment of RM 150,000 approximates the percentage mispricing.

Other Applications for SSF Contracts

In addition to the earlier three common applications, hedging, arbitrage, and speculation, SSF contracts, given their specificity have other uses:

(i) One obvious use of SSF contracts would be to hedge or take advantage of firm-specific events. For example, if you think a particular firm is likely to benefit as a result of an event, like new regulation, SSF contracts if available on the stock would enable you to gain quick easy exposure to the stock. Similarly, if a firm is likely to suffer a temporary setback due to a firm-specific event, SSF contract on the stock would allow us to hedge the **specific corporate event**.

(ii) SSF contracts are often used by fund managers to lock-in a **target sell price** on a stock.[5] By shorting an SSF contract on a stock already owned, we will ensure that we sell the stock at the futures price on maturity of the SSF contract.

(iii) SSF contracts are also popularly used by fund managers to temporarily alter the beta of a portfolio. With SSF contracts, a fund manager alters the overall portfolio beta by adjusting the **beta of a single stock** within the portfolio. Suppose a fund manager has a narrow portfolio of say 10 stocks. He obviously cannot use an SIF contract to alter his portfolio beta. The more logical step would be to use SSF contracts. If some of the stocks within his narrow portfolio have SSF contracts on them, he can use them to alter the portfolio beta. For example, if a high beta stock within his portfolio has an SSF contract, he can increase portfolio beta by going long the SSF contract. On the other hand, he can reduce his portfolio beta by going short the SSF contract.

(iv) Similar to changing portfolio beta by use of SSF contracts, one can change a portfolio's exposure to a sector or industry using SSF contracts. This is fairly obvious. For example, by going long SSF contracts on Gamuda Bhd., one gets additional exposure to the construction sector until the maturity date of the SSF contracts. Similarly, if one already owns banking stocks, and then shorts CIMB Group Holding SSF contracts, exposure to the banking sector is effectively being reduced.

(v) SSF contracts are commonly used for executing what is known as *paired-trading*. Paired-trading is essentially taking simultaneous positions in two stocks. The positions however are opposite to each other, i.e., a long position in one and a short position in the other. An example of a paired-trade would be as follows. Suppose you believe that an impending regulation will hurt fixed line phone providers but help mobile service providers, then an obvious pair-trade would be to long Maxis and short Telekom. The strategy may not be workable with the respective stocks, since short-selling is not possible. However, the paired-trade not only becomes easier using SSF contracts, it is also cheaper since a lower cash outlay is needed.

---

[5] This is similar in objective to the covered call strategy we will examine in Chapter 8.

SUMMARY

This chapter provided an in-depth analysis of stock index futures (SIF) contracts. The chapter described the advent of SIF contracts and examined the FBM KLCI and the SET 50 Index futures contracts. The advantages of using SIFs the computation method of the underlying index and the contract specification was discussed.

The cost of carry model is adjusted for use in pricing an SIF contract. Since dividend patterns are lumpy, SIF contracts could be worth less than the underlying spot value. We examined in-depth the application of SIF contracts in hedging, arbitraging, and in speculating. SIF contracts can be used for hedging systematic risk and immunizing portfolio value. Index arbitrage is a key use of SIF contracts. In addition to the three common applications, hedging, arbitrage, and speculation, SIF contracts can also be used in synthesizing or replicating other financial assets. This ability to synthesize an asset allows SIF contracts to be easily used in asset allocation strategies. Additionally, portfolio managers could also use SIF contracts to manage the systematic risk of their portfolio by adjusting their portfolio beta. Adjusting the portfolio beta, which can be a very tedious and costly process becomes much easier and cheaper with SIF contracts.

Issues like execution risk, transactions and the no-arbitrage bounds were discussed. The impact of SIF introduction and trading on underlying market volatility was explored. Much of the empirical evidence appears to point to no significant impact on underlying market volatility. Other empirical work have shown, systematic U-shaped patterns in intraday futures trading volume and volatility, and the possibility of a lead–lag relationship between index futures and the stock market.

KEY TERMS

- Diversification
- Cash and carry arbitrage
- Time/calendar spread
- Systematic risk
- Reverse cash and carry arbitrage
- Bull time spread
- Unsystematic risk
- Base hedge
- Bear time spread
- Index multiplier
- Asset allocation
- Price weighted index
- Capitalization weighted index
- Portfolio beta
- No-arbitrage bounds
- Replication
- Intraday patterns
- Synthetic/position
- Lead–lag relationship
- Geometrically weighted index
- Index divisor
- Spread trading
- Index arbitrage
- Intermarket spreads

End-of-Chapter Questions

1. a.   State some of the benefits of transacting in SIF over stock market transactions.
    b.   (i)   What is systematic risk and unsystematic risk?
         (ii) What risk do you face when you buy a single stock?
         (iii) What risks do you face when you hold a well-diversified portfolio of stocks?
    c.   If S_o = THB 1,010, rf = 6% and annual dividend yield is 1.75%, what is the correct price of an SIF contract expiring in (i) 3 months and (ii) 6 months?
    d.   What impact would an increase in interest rate (rf) have on SIF prices? Why?
    e.   Why do SIF contracts have an index multiplier? What role does the multiplier play?

2. You are currently holding a portfolio of stocks worth RM 1,750,000. You wish to hedge your portfolio. You have the following information:
    - Portfolio beta   = 0.80
    - Spot Index value   = 700 points
    - Risk-free rate   = 5% per year
    - 3-month SIF contract = 708.60 points
    - Expected dividend yield = 0%

    a.   How many SIF contracts should you use to fully hedge your portfolio?
    b.   Outline the hedge strategy and show the resulting portfolio value assuming the market falls 20% by futures maturity.

3. On June 5, I go long a September SET 50 Index futures contract and short a December contract on the same underlying asset.
    a.   Identify my strategy.
    b.   Why would I undertake such a strategy?
    c.   What is my overall expectation about the direction of the underlying assets' price?
    d.   What must happen to prices for me to profit from this strategy?

4. The 3-month SET 50 SIF is quoted at 696.70. The SET 50 is currently at 680 points. Suppose the rf rate is 4% per year and the dividend yield = 0%.
    a.   Prove that there is mispricing.
    b.   Outline the arbitrage strategy and show the arbitrage profit if the SET 50 is at 710 points at contract maturity.

5. You are a fund manager, managing a portfolio with a current value of RM 10 million. The index is now at 800 points (FBM KLCI). You fear that the market might be headed for short term volatility and wish to hedge for 3 months. You have the following information:
    - 3-month KLIBOR   = 8.5% annualized
    - FBM KLCI dividend yield   = 2.0% per year
    - 3-month FBM KLCI futures = 812.69
    - Your portfolio beta   = 1.20

    a.   How many contracts would you need to be fully hedge?
    b.   Outline the hedging strategy and proof that you are fully hedged even if the FBM KLCI index falls by 20% over the 3-month period.

6. a. An index fund is a mutual fund that attempts to replicate the returns of a stock index such as the SET 50. Assume you are the manager of such a fund and that you are fully invested in stocks. Measured against the SET 50 Index, your portfolio has a beta of 1.0. How could you transform this portfolio into one with a zero beta without trading stocks?
   b. You hold a portfolio consisting of only T-bills. Explain how to trade futures to create a portfolio that behaves like SET 50 stock index.
   c. What is meant by the no-arbitrage bound? In what way would this bound be different for a newly developing market as opposed to a mature one?

7. a. On January 2, 2022, an investor goes long a March SIF contract and shorts the June SIF contract. What kind of strategy is this? Why is the investor undertaking such a strategy? What must happen to prices for him to profit on the combined position?
   b. You now hold a RM 1 million portfolio of government T-bills. Show how you could use SIF contracts to design a portfolio that mimics the FBM KLCI.

8. You are provided the following information:
   - SET 50 value = 1,610
   - Risk free rate = 5% annualized
   - SET 50 dividend yield = 2% annualized
   - SET 50 futures = 1,626
   - SET 50 futures maturity = 90 days
   - SET 50 futures multiplier = THB 200

   Is arbitrage possible? What type of arbitrage? Assuming the index is at 1,640 at futures maturity, show your arbitrage strategy and the profit that would be earned if you transacted in one SIF contract (assume dividends are received and reinvested immediately).

9. As fund manager, you now hold a portfolio with a beta of 1.60. Worried about potentially huge volatility over the short term, you wish to alter the beta of your portfolio to 1.0. Suppose the current value of your portfolio is THB 3.2 million and the spot index is at 1,000 points. Outline how you could use SIF contracts for the purpose (show all computation and clearly state the strategy and number of contracts to be used).

10. You work at the Arbitrage Desk of MC Asset Management (MCAM), a fund management company. Aside from managing stock portfolios, MCAM also does proprietary trading, largely index arbitrage. You now notice the following quotations on your screen.
    - FBM KLCI index = 750 points
    - 3-month SIF = 746.64 points (maturing 90 days)
    - rf rate = 4%
    - Dividend yield = 1.75% (annualized)

    a. Prove that arbitrage is possible.
    b. Outline an appropriate strategy.

c. Determine the arbitrage profit assuming the FBM KLCI is at 775 points in 90 days.
d. To what extent is your arbitrage profit dependent on the FBM KLCI's performance?

11. a. You are currently long on a stock portfolio that has a beta of 1.60. Given recent uncertainties, you intend to reduce the beta to 1.20. Your portfolio is currently worth RM 2.8 million and the FBM KLCI is 800 points. Show how the objective can be achieved using SIF contracts.
   b. Given the following quotes:
      - FBM KLCI spot = 747 pts.
      - rf rate = 4.5% annualized
      - FBM KLCI dividend yield = 1.75% annualized
   (i) If the 90-day FBM KLCI futures contract is priced at 762 points, show that arbitrage is possible.
   (ii) Outline the arbitrage strategy and calculate the profit derived if the FBM KLCI is 10% higher at futures maturity.

12. As the manager of a small equity fund, you are worried that the recent run-up in stock prices has been too fast and a downturn may be due. You are therefore planning to "lock in" the RM 9.6 million value of your portfolio. As a widely diversified portfolio, your beta approximates 1.0. You have gathered the following information:
    - FBM KLCI = 800 points
    - FBM KLCI futures = 816 points
    - Futures maturity = 90 days
    - 3-month KLIBOR = 3.5%
    - Annual dividend yield of FBM KLCI = 1.5%

   a. Outline the appropriate strategy by which you can protect yourself from a downward correction. (Specify the number of contracts.)
   b. Assuming the FBM KLCI is at 760 points in 90 days, determine the value of the hedged portfolio.
   c. How would you account for the change in the portfolio's value from the original RM 9.6 million? Explain.

13. Suppose that you are a portfolio manager. Your portfolio consists of THB 150 million of stocks with a beta of 0.90, and THB 10 million invested in Treasury bills. The spot, SET 50 Index is 1,297, whereas the SET 50 futures is priced at 1,300.
    a. What is the overall beta of your portfolio?
    b. You believe that the probability of a stock market decline has increased, and therefore wish to reduce the beta of your portfolio to 0.60. Outline the right strategy. The index multiplex is 200.
    c. Suppose instead that you wish to reduce the beta of your portfolio to zero. (i) How many futures contracts should you use? (ii) What should the expected return on this portfolio approximate? Why?

14. As fund manager, you have had a tough time this year. Market conditions have been difficult so you have been looking at other avenues besides stock-picking. You think you have identified an arbitrage opportunity. However, since index arbitrage is a new area for your firm, you have to convince your boss that it is riskless. The following information is available.
    - FBM KLCI = 864 points
    - 3-month FBM KLCI futures = 881.5 points
    - r_f rate (3-month KLIBOR) = 5%

    Annual dividend yield for FBM KLCI = 2.5%
    a. Show that there is sufficient mispricing to enable arbitrage.
    b. Outline the appropriate arbitrage strategy.
    c. Assuming you could arbitrage up to 10 SIF contracts equivalent, show the profit attainable.
    d. Briefly explain how you would convince your boss that your strategy is riskless.

15. You are trying to convince a client about a riskless arbitrage opportunity. The following quotations are available today.
    - 3-month FBM KLCI futures = 608 points
    - FBM KLCI spot = 600 points
    - Futures maturity = 90 days
    - 3-month KLIBOR = 4%
    - Dividend yield = 2% annualized

    a. How would you proof to your client that arbitrage is possible?
    b. Show the profit attainable if the index is at 640 points at maturity.
    c. How would you convince your client that the profit derived in part (b) is indeed riskless? (Show computation to prove.)

16. What are SSF? What are some of their common uses? What criteria do you think would be used by exchanges in deciding on whether to introduce SSF contracts on a particular stock?

17. A stock is currently selling for THB 16. The stock normally pays a dividend of THB 2 in March of each year. It is now end February. The risk-free rate is 6%. What should the correct price be for an SSF contract on the stock with a 1-month maturity?

18. An investor has 12 stocks in his portfolio. The stock with the highest beta is Genting Bhd., whereas Telekom has the lowest beta in his portfolio.
    a. If the investor wants to temporarily increase the overall beta of his portfolio without buying/selling stocks, how can he do so with SSFs?
    b. How can the investor use SSFs to reduce the beta of his portfolio?
    c. Suppose the investor goes long 3-month SSF contracts on Telekom while simultaneously shorting Genting Bhd. SSFs, what is the impact of this paired-trade on the beta of his portfolio?

19. Gamuda Bhd. shares just went ex-dividend. The next dividend payment is at least 6 months away. The risk-free rate is 6.5%. You notice the following quotes:
    - Gamuda Bhd. stock price = RM 9.50
    - 3-month SSF contract on Gamuda = RM 9.85

    a. Prove that the SSF contract is mispriced.
    b. Outline the appropriate arbitrage strategy.
    c. If you invest an amount equal to about 10,000 shares, what would your profit be at SSF maturity if Gamuda Bhd. stock is higher by 10%?
    d. What would your profit be if Gamuda Bhd. stock fell 10% instead?
    e. Rework parts (a), (b), and (c) above assuming the 3-month SSF contract is being quoted at RM 9.55.

20. Describe how an SSF contract could be used in each of the following situations.
    a. An investor currently holding Siam Cement stocks believes it has long-term potential but is worried about expected oil price hikes on the stock's performance over the next 6 months.
    b. A fund manager with a large exposure to gaming stocks, believes that impending changes to the entertainment tax will benefit Berjaya Toto but hurt Genting.
    c. A speculator believes palm oil prices have peaked and are likely to experience a steep correction.
    d. A portfolio manager with a large position in Telekom Bhd. stock currently at RM 6.50 intends off-loading half his position if the stock reaches RM 6.80.
    e. Mr Lee has inherited a large amount of shares in CIMB Holdings Bhd. He intends holding on to the shares and passing them to his children. However, he is worried about rumors that CIMB Holdings Bhd. may be subjected to a forced merger within the next 3 months.

CHAPTER · 5

Interest Rate Futures Contracts and Currency Futures Contracts

Objectives

This chapter is designed to provide an in-depth analysis and description of interest rate futures (IRFs) and currency futures contracts. The chapter examines two types of IRF contracts. The first, IRF based on short-term interbank rates, for example the 3-month Kuala Lumpur Interbank Offer Rate (KLIBOR) futures contract of Bursa Malaysia Derivatives Berhad (BMDB) and the 3-month Bangkok Interbank Offer Rate (BIBOR) futures contracts of Thailand Futures Exchange (TFEX). The second type is the long-term bond-based contract, for example, the Singapore Exchange (SGX)-listed 10-year Mini Japanese Government Bond futures contract. The chapter also examines currency futures contracts. An in-depth examination of the Hong Kong Exchanges and Clearing (HKEX)-traded Chinese Renminbi (CNH)/USD futures contract is undertaken. Both IRFs and currency futures have a common determinant of their values — interest rates. On completing this chapter, you should have a good understanding of the applications and underlying valuation of interest rate and currency futures contracts.

Introduction
5.1 Interest Rate Futures Contracts

Interest rate futures (IRF) contracts are yet another financial derivative. The underlying asset is typically an interest rate-linked asset like a treasury bill, bonds, or simply monetary deposits. Just as futures contracts such as commodity futures and stock index futures could be used to "lock in" a buy (entry) or sell (exit) price, IRF can be used for locking in the interest rate at which to borrow or lend. Aside from hedging, by locking in the interest rates, interest futures contracts can also be used in arbitraging and in speculating on rate movements. IRF contracts were first introduced on the International Monetary Market (IMM), a subsidiary of the Chicago Mercantile Exchange (CME) in 1976.

Since its introduction in 1976, IRF contracts have been among the most popular derivative instruments introduced. By the early 1990s, IRF contracts were accounting for close to half the total volume of all futures contracts traded in the United States (US). The first IRF contract had the US Treasury Bill as its underlying asset. As a result of the huge popularity of the contract,

IRF contracts with other underlying assets were introduced. These were on assets such as long-term US treasury notes (2 years, 5 years **tenor**) and short-term Eurodollar deposits. Today, at least two US exchanges (Chicago Board of Trade [CBOT] and CME) trade IRF contracts on different underlying assets. While the CBOT concentrates on longer maturity assets/tenors, the CME emphasizes short-term tenors.

IRF contracts had been extremely popular in developed markets as interest rate exposure is much more pervasive than other types of risks. Most businesses, regardless of their industry/product, would have interest rate exposure by virtue of the fact that most businesses are either net lenders or net borrowers at any one time.

> **Note**
> Any business entity that is a net lender/borrower would be exposed to interest rate risk.

A second and perhaps more important reason for the popularity of IRF is the increased volatility of interest rates. Interest rates have of late become much more volatile. Though there are several underlying factors, the major causes of the increased interest rate volatility are (i) volatility in inflation rates, (ii) floating exchange rates and the increased volatility in currencies, and (iii) shifts in government policy, particularly in interest rate targeting and deregulation. Over the last several years, however, traded volume and overall demand for interest rate derivatives appear to have waned. These are largely attributable to the historically low interest rate regimes seen globally. Several developed nations such as Germany and Switzerland have negative interest rates, many others like Japan have near zero interest rates, whereas US is at historic lows. Central bank policies are at the heart of these repressed interest rates. With interest rates at extremely low levels, interest rate risk becomes much less important, and so the reduced need for interest rate derivatives to manage such risk.

Nominal interest rates, as we know, are directly correlated to inflation. When inflation is not stable, nominal interest rates fluctuate more. We explore this relationship further later in this chapter. Floating exchange rates also impact interest rates. Most exchange rate regimes are not freely floating but managed. In managed systems, interest rates play a key role in exchange rate determination. As central banks attempt to move currencies to desired exchange rates, interest rates are often used as the lever to achieve this. As a result, domestic interest rates become more volatile when central banks are active in exchange rate intervention. This also means that both interest rates and exchange rate movements and confounded and move together.

5.2 What is Interest Rate Risk?

Interest rate risk refers to the risk resulting from changes in the interest rate. This risk can occur in several forms. We will examine four different ways by which interest rate risk occurs. These are the following:

(a) **Change in Cost of Funds**. This leads to either higher cost of funds or lower revenue/earnings depending on whether you are the lender or borrower.

(b) **Change in the Value of Assets**. As we will see later, changes in interest rates can lead to changes in the value of traded assets. Depending on whether one is long or short the asset, such value changes can hurt.

(c) **Refinancing Risk**. This type of risk occurs when a business needs to refinance its funding and interest rates have changed. As we will see later, this type of risk is a common form of interest rate risk faced in banking.

(d) **Reinvestment Risk**. This refers to the risk that one may not be able to earn the same rate of returns as previously. Cash flows earned from an existing investment may not be reinvested to earn the same rate of return because interest rates have changed. This form of interest rate risk is common with bond investments.

> **Note**
> Interest rate risk can impact a business through the cost of funds, change in asset value, refinancing cost, and reinvestment risk.

5.3 Bond Pricing, Yields, and Interest Rate Risk

In this section, we examine the mechanics of bond pricing, yields, and duration in order to better understand interest rate risk and its impact. We do so for several reasons. First, straight bonds are probably the easiest financial asset to value. Second, the impact of an interest rate change on bond valuation is easy to see. Third, bonds experience at least two of the abovementioned four forms of interest rate risk: **change in asset value** and **reinvestment risk**.

Bonds are essentially promissory notes that are market-traded. The issuer is the borrower, whereas the buyer of bonds is the lender. Bonds, therefore, are debt instruments. Being debt instruments, interest is paid either as a fixed, annual, or semiannual coupon payment. Interest or coupon of a bond could also be floating as opposed to being fixed. In a floating rate bond, coupon is determined typically as a premium to a reference interest rate. The reference interest rate could be any market-traded interest rate like the London Interbank Offer Rate (LIBOR), Kuala Lumpur Interbank Offer Rate (KLIBOR), Hong Kong Interbank Offer Rate (HIBOR), or Bangkok Interbank Offer Rate (BIBOR). For example, a bond might have a ***floating interest rate*** quoted as 6-month KLIBOR plus x%. What this means is that the bond will pay a coupon equivalent to whatever the 6-month KLIBOR rate is on the due date for coupon payment plus x%. Thus, if the 6-month KLIBOR is quoted as 10% on the due date, if x is 2% and the face value of the bond is RM 1,000, then the coupon payment would be:

$$(10\% + 2\%) \times RM\ 1{,}000 = RM\ 120$$

On the other hand, if the 6-month KLIBOR rate is quoted as 7%, then the coupon payment would be:

$$(7\% + 2\%) \times RM\ 1{,}000 = RM\ 90$$

Notice, therefore, that the coupon payment received depends entirely on what the 6-month KLIBOR rate turns out to be. This in itself is a form of interest rate risk and would fall in the first of the four categories of interest rate risk discussed earlier.

Although a floating rate bond would have coupon payments that vary with the reference interest rate, a fixed rate bond would have fixed coupon payments. This does not, however, mean that fixed rate bonds do not have interest rate risk. They face the second form of interest rate risk, i.e., changes in interest rates causing changes in asset values. (Although floating rate bonds may also face this type of risk, the fact that the coupon will be reset with interest rate change means that this form of risk is muted.) To understand how bond prices (and most other asset prices) change, we review the mechanics of bond pricing by working through the following example:

Assume ABC Corp. has issued 1,000 ten-year bonds with the following features.

Issuer : ABC Corp.
Face value : RM 1,000 (Total RM 1,000,000)
Interest/coupon : 10% annual
Required yield given risk class: 10%

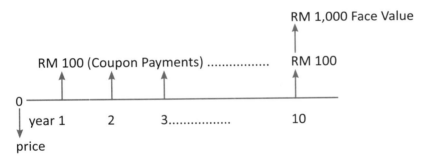

The bond's correct price could be determined by discounting all future cash inflows by the appropriate discount rate (required yield) and aggregating the discounted values. Mathematically,

$$\text{Bond price} = \sum_{t=1}^{n} \frac{C_t}{(1+y)^t} + \frac{FV_n}{(1+y)^n} \qquad (1)$$

where

C_t = annual coupon payments in Ringgit
FV_n = face value received at maturity in year n
y = required yield or required return given the risk class of the bond

Solving the earlier equation gives a value of RM 1,000 as the correct price for ABC Corp.'s bond. Suppose interest rates now rise by 2%, causing the required yield to also rise by 2%.[1] The bond's

---

[1] This assumes a parallel upward shift in the yield curve.

price at the new discount rate of 12% would be RM 887. Notice that the bond's value has fallen as a result of a rise in interest rates. Similarly, a reduction in interest rates causing required yield to fall would cause bond prices to rise. For example, if rates fall 2% and the required yield is now 8%, the bond's price at an 8% discount rate would now be RM 1,134.20.

This simple example essentially shows the inverse relationship between bond prices and interest rates. This inverse relationship is true not just for bond values but is generally true for most other asset prices. Stocks, real estate, and other financial assets are generally inversely related to interest rate movements. This in essence is the second form of interest rate risk defined earlier: change in asset values as a result of a change in interest rates.

Note
Bonds, as with most other assets, are price sensitive to interest rate movements. Asset prices and interest rates are negatively correlated.

5.3.1 Bond Yield and Yield Curves

Notice from Equation 1 that in solving for a bond's price, one needs to define four variables as inputs, these being face value, time to maturity, t, the coupon amount, and the required yield as discount rate. The first three variables are straightforward and can easily be determined. Face value, time to maturity, and coupon amount would be stated as part of a bond's features. The fourth variable, required yield, would have to be determined from the **yield curve**. The yield curve is essentially a locus of points relating the required yield to the time to maturity for a given risk class of bonds. As bonds differ in risk quality and belong to different risk classes, there is typically a "family" of yield curves, with each yield curve representing a certain risk class. As to which yield curve is applicable for a given bond would depend on the bond's rating. The higher the **bond's rating**, the lower the yield curve and the lower the required yield. Figure 5.1 depicts a typical set of yield curves.

C_t = annual coupon payments in Ringgit
FV_n = face value received at maturity in year n
y = required yield or required return given the risk class of the bond

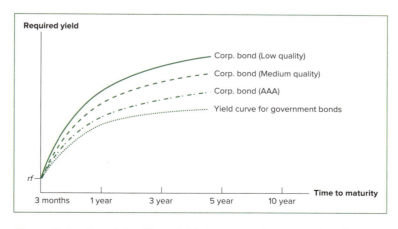

Figure 5.1   Bond Quality, Yield Curve, and Required Yields

For any given maturity, the required yield will be higher for lower quality instruments. In the US, the two exchanges, CME and CBOT, offer different IRF so as to cover the full yield curve. Doing so makes it possible for investors to hedge interest rate risk of different maturities. In Singapore, the introduction of 10-year Mini Japanese Government Bond (JGB) futures contracts also allows for the hedging of longer term interest rate exposures.

> **Note**
> The yield curve is a locus of points relating the required yield to the time to maturity for a given risk class of bonds.

5.3.2 Interest Rate Change, Bond Yields, and Duration

The impact of a change in interest rates on bond prices works through the yield curves. Suppose the government moves to push up interest rates through the central bank. The central bank would usually do this interest rate "intervention" through the interbank money market. The result of such "borrowing" by the central bank would push up interest rates such as the 3-month KLIBOR or 3-month BIBOR rates. With an increase in this base rate, one can visualize an upward shift of all the yield curves. The required yields would increase and, given the higher discount rates, cause bond and other asset prices to fall.

We have thus far established that changes in interest rates are inversely related to bond and asset prices.

Interest Rate	Required Yield	Bond/Asset Values
↑	↑	↓
↓	↓	↑

However, one might want to ask whether the impact is uniform. That is, when interest rates rise, bond prices fall, but would **all** bonds fall equally in value? The answer is no. The extent to which a bond falls in value for a given increase in interest rates will depend on its **duration**. Duration can be thought of as a measure of a bond's **sensitivity** to interest rate changes. The higher the bond or an asset's duration, the more sensitive it is to interest changes. The duration of a bond is calculated as follows:

$$\text{Duration} = \sum t \cdot \left[\left(\frac{CF_t}{(1+y)_t} \right) \Big/ P_o \right] \qquad (2)$$

where

CF_t = coupon and face value received from the bond
y = required yield
P_o = current market price of the bond

For our purpose, there is a more interesting use of duration. In knowing the duration of a bond or asset, we can estimate the likely change in the value of the asset. For example, having calculated the duration, we can estimate the likely impact of a given interest rate increase on the assets value. Equation 3 can be used to estimate this expected change in value/price.

$$\%\Delta \text{ in price} = -D\left[\frac{\Delta i}{(1+i)}\right] \quad (3)$$

where

D = duration of the asset
i = interest rate
Δ = change in variable

We will return to this issue of asset duration and impact on value later in the appendix to this chapter when we examine bank hedging strategies using KLIBOR futures contracts.

> **Note**
> An asset's interest sensitivity is measured by its duration. The higher the duration, the greater the interest rate sensitivity.

5.4 The 3-Month KLIBOR Futures Contract

The 3-month KLIBOR futures contract is Malaysia's oldest and most active IRF contract. The contract was introduced in 1996 by Bursa Malaysia Derivatives Berhad's (BMDB) predecessor, the Malaysian Monetary Exchange (MME). As an IRF contract, the underlying asset is a Ringgit interbank time deposit in the Kuala Lumpur interbank market with a principal value of RM 1,000,000. To reiterate, the underlying asset is a Ringgit deposit, while the contract size is RM 1 million. Thus, when **we go long a 3-month KLIBOR futures contract, we get to borrow RM 1 million** for a period of 3 months beginning from the maturity day of the contract at the futures yield rate. On the other hand, **when we short a 3-month KLIBOR futures contract, we get to lend RM 1 million** for a period of 3 months beginning from the maturity day. The interest we will receive for this lending is the futures yield rate.

> **Note**
> The underlying asset of the 3-month KLIBOR futures contract is a Ringgit deposit of RM 1 million.

One should be able to notice several similarities between the 3-month KLIBOR futures and the earlier contracts, such as the cocoa futures contract we examined in Chapter 3. In the earlier cocoa futures and stock index futures contracts, **we lock in the price** at which we would buy or sell the underlying asset. In the case of the IRF contract, we **lock in the interest rate** at which we will borrow or lend. Just as we locked in the quoted futures price in the earlier contracts, here we lock in the interest rate implied in the futures yield. Furthermore, just as going long cocoa, for example, enables us to take delivery or receive the underlying asset at maturity, here we receive (in borrowing) the underlying asset on maturity day. Similarly, in going short, we make delivery or lend out the underlying asset on the maturity day. In essence, by going long or short, we are making commitments to borrow or lend at a predetermined interest rate. Thus, just as it is obvious how one could hedge cocoa prices by using cocoa futures contracts, one can just as easily use the IRF contracts to hedge interest rate risk. The 3-month

KLIBOR futures contract specifies the delivery or acceptance of RM 1 million of interbank time deposits of 3-month maturity. The underlying spot market, or the market in which the spot asset is traded, is the interbank market. The interbank market can be thought of as the "wholesale" market for loans and deposits. The interbank market is a largely institutional market with banks, merchant banks, discount houses, money brokers, insurance companies, etc., borrowing and lending among themselves. As the wholesale market for loans/deposits, it is also the platform for central bank intervention in executing monetary policy. Rates like the BIBOR, HIBOR, or KLIBOR are the interest rates determined by the borrowing and lending activities of players in the interbank market. Since borrowing/lending is carried out in a range of tenors, there is not one but several interbank rates in the interbank money market. For example, the 1-month KLIBOR would be the interest rate for 1-month borrowing/lending, the 3-month BIBOR and 6-month HIBOR for 3- and 6-month borrowing/lending in the respective money markets.

As is the case with all other spot markets, the quoted rates are for tenors beginning immediately, whereas the futures is always for borrowing/lending beginning on the maturity day of the contract. For example, the 1-month KLIBOR is the quotation for borrowing/lending beginning *today* for a 1 month period. Similarly, the 3-month KLIBOR is the quote for borrowing/lending for 3 months beginning *immediately*. This is different from the 3-month KLIBOR futures which is the quote for borrowing/lending for 3 months but beginning not today but on the maturity day of the futures contract.

Though several tenors are available in the interbank market, the futures exchange, BMDB, has chosen the futures contract to be of 3-month tenor. There are several reasons why this particular tenor and the KLIBOR as opposed to other interest rates (such as base lending rate (BLR)) were chosen. First, the underlying cash market, i.e., the 3-month KLIBOR (spot), is the most liquid in the Kuala Lumpur interbank market. It accounts for almost 80% of the interbank market transactions. Second, the 3-month KLIBOR rates are the benchmark interest rates in the pricing of money market instruments such as banker's acceptances (BAs), T-bills, and repurchase agreements (REPOs). The high correlation between the 3-month KLIBOR rates and these instruments would make the futures contract an ideal hedging tool for those with positions in these instruments. Finally, a futures contract based on the KLIBOR and 3-month tenor would be analogous to other successful IRF contracts elsewhere, such as the Eurodollar contracts and the US 3-month T-bill contracts.

5.5 Contract Specifications — 3-Month KLIBOR and 3-Month BIBOR Futures

Table 5.1(a) outlines the Contract Specifications for the 3-month KLIBOR futures.

TFEX's 3-Month BIBOR Futures Contract

Given the need for Thai financial institutions to manage short-term interest exposure, the TFEX introduced the 3-month BIBOR IRF contract in November 2010. Based on the 3-month

BIBOR, this is Thailand's only short-term IRF contract. Like BMDB, which in addition to the short-term 3-month KLIBOR offers longer-term bond futures based on 3- and 5-year Malaysian government securities, TFEX also offers a 5-year government bond futures contract.

Table 5.1   (a) The 3-Month BIBOR Futures Contract

	Contract Specifications
Underlying Assets	3M BIBOR
Ticker Symbol	BB3
Contract Size	THB 10,000,000
Contract Months	March, June, September, December up to 2 quarters
Price Quotation	In terms of index 100.000 - Yield (on annual basis with 3 decimal points)
Minimum Price Fluctuations	0.005 (or THB 125 per contract)
Price Limit	+ 2.5% of the latest settlement price
Trading Hours	Pre-open: 09:15 a.m.–09:45 a.m. Morning session: 09:45 a.m.–12:30 p.m. Pre-open: 13:45 a.m.–14:15 p.m. Afternoon session: 14:15 a.m.–16:00 p.m.
Speculative Position Limit	Net 2,000 contracts of 3M BIBOR futures on one side of the market in any contract month or all contract months combined
Last Trading Day	The third Wednesday of the contract month and the trading of expiring contract will be ceased after 11:00 a.m. on the last trading day
Final Settlement Price	Calculated from 3M BIBOR fixed at 11:00 a.m. (BKK time) as announced by the Bank of Thailand on the last trading day (4 decimal points)
Settlement Method	Cash Settlement
Exchange Fee	Maximum of THB 20 per contract per side.

Source: TFX website.

Tables 5.1 (a) and (b) show the contract specifications for BMDB's 3-month KLIBOR futures and TFEX's 3-month BIBOR futures contracts. A number of features from the contract specifications are worth noting. First, the delivery months are the usual calendar quarterlies up to 5 years ahead for the KLIBOR and 2 quarters for the BIBOR. In addition to the quarterly months, BMDB also has two serial month contracts. It is also worth noting that the tick size in percent is equivalent to one basis point (one basis point is one-hundredth of one percent) or RM 25 for the KLIBOR but 5 basis points or THB 125 for the BIBOR. The contract size is RM 1 million for the 3-month KLIBOR and THB 10 million for the 3-month BIBOR. Speculative position limits are intended to check excessive speculative play. As a financial derivative, the contract is cash-settled. Notice the similarity in how the final settlement value is determined on maturity day: both are based on the respective quoted rates at 11:00 a.m. on maturity date. This value determination is important since the final settlement value will determine the extent of a position's gain or loss at maturity.

As is the case with the 3-month KLIBOR futures contract described earlier, when **we go long a 3-month BIBOR futures contract, we get to borrow THB 10 million** for a period of 3 months beginning from the maturity day of the contract at the futures yield rate. On the other hand, when we **short a 3-month BIBOR futures contract, we get to lend THB 10 million** for a period of 3 months beginning from the maturity day. The interest we will receive for this lending is the futures yield rate.

Table 5.1 (b) BMDB's 3-Month KLIBOR Futures — Contract Specifications

Contract Code	FKB3
Underlying Shares	Ringgit interbank time deposit in the Kuala Lumpur Wholesale Money Market with a 3-month maturity on a 360-day year
Contract Size	RM 1,000,000 Quoted in index terms (100 minus yield)
Minimum Price Fluctuation	0.01% or 1 tick which is equivalent to RM 25 (RM 1,000,000 × 3/12 × 0.01%)
Contract Months	Quarterly cycle months of March, June, September, and December up to 5 years ahead and 2 serial months
Trading Hours	First trading session: Malaysian time 9:00 a.m. to 12:30 p.m. Second trading session: Malaysian time 2:30 p.m. to 5:00 p.m.
Final Trading Day Maturity Date	Trading ceases at 11:00 a.m. (Malaysian time) on the third Wednesday of the delivery month or the first business day immediately following the third Wednesday of the delivery month if the third Wednesday of the delivery month is not a business day
Final Settlement	Cash settlement based on the cash settlement value
Final Settlement Value	i. Calculated as 100 minus the 3-month KLIBOR as published by Reuters Ltd. on the reference page "KLIBOR" at 11:00 hours (Malaysian time) on the final trading day ii. In the event that the abovementioned calculation (i) cannot be made, the final settlement value shall be calculated as 100 minus the 3-month KLIBOR as published by Dow Jones Telerate Ltd. on page number 46,387 at 11:00 hours (Malaysian time) on the final trading day iii. In the event that the abovementioned calculation (ii) cannot be made, the final settlement value shall be calculated as 100 minus the 3-month KLIBOR as obtained from Bank Negara Malaysia at 11.00 hours (Malaysian time) on the final trading day In the event that none of the above three calculations can be made, the final settlement value shall be determined by the Exchange
Speculative Position Limits	Maximum number of net long or net short positions to be held: • 5,000 contracts for all months combined

Source: Bursa Malaysia website.

5.5.1 Pricing IRF Contracts

Notice that the price of both the 3-month KLIBOR futures and the 3-month BIBOR futures contracts are quoted in terms of an index. You should also realize at this point that different derivative instruments follow different pricing conventions. For example, cocoa futures are quoted in dollars and cents, whereas stock index futures are quoted in terms of index points. IRF contracts are quoted in terms of an index. This index is essentially 100 minus the annual percentage yield to two or three decimal places. For example, if the required yield or going interest rate on the KLIBOR futures is 7.5%, the price will be quoted as 92.50 which is:

$$100 - 7.5 = 92.50$$

Given such an index quotation, the index will increase as the required yield falls and fall when the yield rises. For example:

Interest rate (yield) of 5.5%
Price = 100 − 5.5
     = 94.50

Interest rate (yield) of 8.5%
Price = 100 − 8.5
     = 91.50

> **Note**
> KLIBOR IRF contracts are priced in terms of an index. The index is essentially 100 minus the annual percentage yield.

The use of such a pricing convention is really in keeping with the inverse relationship that we saw between interest rates and bond/asset prices.

5.6 Determining the Equilibrium Price: The Implied Forward Rate

Suppose you called your futures broker and asked for the current price of the 3-month KLIBOR futures contract, and he quotes a price of, let us say, 92.50. How can you tell whether this is the "correct" price or equilibrium price? If you were an arbitrageur, you would certainly want to know whether there is mispricing and therefore an arbitrage opportunity. How can one determine the fair/correct price of an IRF contract? The cost of carry model as we had seen in the case of cocoa futures and stock index futures would not be helpful here. This has to do partly with the fact that the interest rate will appear on both sides of the equation. In a way, a simultaneity problem.

To determine the correct price of an IRF contract, a slightly more circuitous but intuitively logical method known as the ***implied forward rate (IFR)*** is used. The IFR technique makes use of the available spot price of different tenors to solve for the price of the 3-month futures.

> **Note**
> The equilibrium price of an IRF contract is determined using the implied forward rate.

The basic logic of IFR is that a futures price is an expected future spot price. For example, if the current spot price for a ton of crude palm oil (CPO) is quoted at say $1,400, what should the price of a 3-month futures contract on CPO be? Since, the purchase of a 3-month futures contract means delivery in 3 months, the price of the futures contract would depend on the expected price per ton of CPO in 3 months' time! If CPO prices are expected to go up, then the futures could be perhaps $1,500 per ton. On the other hand, if it is expected to go down, then the futures price would be lower than the current spot price. By this logic, the 3-month KLIBOR futures price would not reflect the current KLIBOR 3-month rate, but the 3-month interest rate *expected to prevail* at the maturity of the futures contract. Thus, the 3-month KLIBOR futures prices reflect the 3-month interest rate *expected to prevail in 3 months!* In fact, the yield (given the settlement price) of the KLIBOR at maturity is for money borrowed/lent at the time of contract expiration. This implies that in order to determine the correct price of the 3-month KLIBOR futures, we must know what interest rates would be 3 months from now.

But how can we possibly know this? The answer lies in determining the **IFRs**. To understand what an IFR is and how it determines the price of IRF contract, we work through the following example.

Suppose in the interbank market, the following rates are quoted. (*Note: This is the "spot" market.*)

3-month KLIBOR = 6% (Maturing March 30)
6-month KLIBOR = 7% (Maturing June 30)

For simplicity, assume today's date is January 1.

The 3-month KLIBOR has a tenor = 90 days
The 6-month KLIBOR has a tenor = 180 days
(*Note: February = 28 days, January, March, and May = 31 days*)

Question: Given the earlier information, what is the correct price of a 3-month KLIBOR futures contract?

Since the interest rate implied in the price quoted for a futures contract is for money borrowed for 3 months from the maturity date, the price today would be the **expected 3-month interest rate between March and June**.

That is, the expected 3-month interest rate for 3 months from now. In terms of a timeline:

How do we determine this expected 3-month interest rate? By computing the implied 3-month rate (for the second 3-month period) given the two KLIBOR spot rates. This computed rate is known as the IFR.

IFR can be computed as:

$$[1+\text{IFR}\times(\text{Tenor}/360)] = \frac{[1+\text{Long rate}\times(\text{Long tenor}/360)]}{[1+\text{Short rate}\times(\text{Short tenor}/360)]}$$

So we have:

$$[1+\text{IFR}\times(90/360)] = \frac{1+0.07\times(180/360)}{[1+0.06\times(90/360)]}$$

$[1 + \text{IFR} \times (90/360)] = 1.035/1.015$
$[1 + \text{IFR} \times (90/360)] = 1.0197$
IFR $= 0.0197 \times (360/90)$
IFR $= 0.0788$ or 7.88%

> **Check**
> Given the earlier equation, $(1 + \text{IFR})(1 + \text{short rate})$ should equal $(1 + \text{long rate})$ all adjusted for tenors.
> $[1+0.0788(90/360)][1+0.06\times(90/360)] = [1+0.07(180/360)]$
> $(1 + 0.0197)(1 + 0.015) \qquad = (1.035)$
> (*Note*: $[(1.035) - 1] \times 2 = 0.07$, which is 7%, the 6-month rate.)

Since the IFR is 7.88%, the correct price quotation for the 3-month KLIBOR futures contract should be:

$$100 - 7.88 = 92.12$$

If the price for the futures contract is anything other than 92.12, there is mispricing and arbitrage would be possible.

Note that the same logic of IFR in determining the equilibrium price is equally applicable to the 3-month BIBOR futures though the example used the 3-month KLIBOR futures.

5.7 3-Month IRF: Applications

In this section, we examine the use of the KLIBOR/BIBOR futures contracts in the three common applications of derivative instruments: hedging, arbitrage, and speculation. We work through numerical examples of how each of these applications would work. Though we use the 3-month KLIBOR for illustration, all the applications shown here can be applied equally with the 3-month BIBOR futures contracts. The only needed adjustments would be regulatory/market differences.

(i) Hedging Interest Rate Risk

Managing interest rate risk is obviously an important application for IRF contracts. We examine two situations by which interest movements can hurt. The first looks at how a borrower could hedge against rising interest cost using KLIBOR futures, whereas the second examines how a banker could protect his profit margin from eroding when interest rates fall.

Note
IRF contracts can be used by borrowers to hedge their costs and lenders to hedge their profit margin.

5.7.1 Locking in the Cost of Borrowing

Your company has just signed an agreement with a foreign supplier. The agreement calls for your company to pay RM 10 million in 3 months for goods from the supplier. As you do not have the needed funds, you have arranged with your banker for a 3-month RM 10 million loan. Your banker has agreed to provide the loan at an interest rate of KLIBOR + 2%. You now fear that an increase in interest rates between now and when the loan is taken might increase your cost of funds and thereby erode your profits. Is there any way by which you could use KLIBOR futures to lock in the interest rate on your forthcoming loan?

Assume it is now June 25. Loan will be taken in September (exactly 90 days from June 25). The following quotations are available on June 25.

- 3-month KLIBOR = 7%
- September KLIBOR futures = 92

Given the earlier quotes, the target interest cost you would want to "lock in" is the yield (June 25) on the KLIBOR futures + the 2% premium, i.e., 10% since the KLIBOR futures is yielding 8% (8% + 2% = 10%).

What should the right strategy be? Should we go long or short the KLIBOR futures contract? One could arrive at the right hedge strategy by thinking in terms of the directional movement in interest rates that would hurt you. Clearly a rise in interest rates would hurt, since you are borrowing. Thus, you need to create a futures position that will profit if rates rise. We saw in the earlier section that interest rates and futures prices are inversely related. This means that a rise in interest rates will cause KLIBOR futures prices to fall. To profit from falling futures prices, the right strategy is to go short. Since you need to hedge RM 10 million of borrowings, you need 10 contracts.

Hedge strategy: *Short 10 September KLIBOR futures contracts*

To see whether the hedge strategy does indeed "lock in" the cost, we examine two interest rate scenarios.

Scenario 1: Interest Rates Rise Over the Period by 1.5%

As such, on September 25 the quotes would be:

3-month KLIBOR	= 8.5% (higher by 1.5%)
September KLIBOR futures	= 91.50 *(since the futures matures on that day, the implied rate is 8.5%; same as spot due to convergence)*

Result of Hedge

Profit from futures	= [(92.00 − 91.50) × (RM 25 × 100)] × 10 contracts
	= RM 12,500
Interest on loan	= [8.5% + 2%] × 90/360 × RM 10 million
	= [10.5%] × 1/4 × RM 10 million
	= RM 262,500
Net interest cost	= RM 262,500 − RM 12,500
	= RM 250,000
Effective interest rate with hedge	= RM 250,000 for 3 months, **which is 2.5% of RM 10 million**
Annualized interest rate	= 2.5% × 4 = 10%

This equals exactly 8% + 2%. (KLIBOR futures was 8% in June.) As a result of the hedge, you were able to borrow at the futures rate in June of 8% + 2% instead of 8.5% + 2% which you would have had to pay in September if you had not hedged. Thus, you saved 0.5%.

Note:
(1) The saving came from the profit of RM 12,500 from futures.
(2) The price at maturity of the KLIBOR September futures must be 91.50 because of convergence.
(3) In determining profit from futures, we multiply the net of the entry minus exit prices by RM 25 since that is the value per tick, which is in turn multiplied by 100 since each tick is one basis point which is 1/100 of 1%.

Scenario 2: Interest Rates Fall by 1.5%

With the fall in interest rates, the quotes on September 25 would be:

3-month KLIBOR	= 5.50% (lower by 1.5%)
September KLIBOR futures	= 94.50 (same as spot since it is maturity day for futures; convergence)

Result of Hedge

Loss on futures	= [(92 − 94.50) × (100 × RM 25)] × 10 contracts
	= RM 62,500
Interest on loan	= [5.50% + 2%] × 90/360 × RM 10 million
	= 7.50% × 1/4 × RM 10 million
	= RM 187,500
Net interest cost	= RM 187,500 + RM 62,500
	= RM 250,000

$$\text{Effective interest rate with hedge} = \frac{\text{RM } 250{,}000}{\text{RM } 10 \text{ million}} \times 100$$
$$= 2.5\% \text{ for 3 months}$$
$$= 2.5\% \times 4$$
$$= 10\%$$

Once again, the effective interest rate has been locked in at 8% + 2%. Notice that regardless of whether interest rates go up or down, you have locked in the 10% cost of borrowing.

5.7.2 Hedging: Protecting Interest Income/Revenue

We now examine the hedge strategy from the viewpoint of a banker financier. In the earlier example, the banker quotes a floating interest rate KLIBOR + 2%. In doing so, the banker is passing on the interest rate risk to the borrower. The banker faces no risk but the borrower does. We then saw how the borrower could hedge this risk. What if the banker has to quote a fixed interest rate but his cost of funds is floating? In this case, the customer/borrower faces no risk but the banker does.

Example

As a credit officer of a large Malaysian bank, you have agreed to provide an important institutional customer with a fixed rate, 3-month, RM 20 million loan 90 days from today. You had priced the loan at 12% annual interest rate. Assuming your cost of funds is the KLIBOR rate and the following quotes are now available.

3-month KLIBOR = 9%
3-month KLIBOR futures = 90 (matures in 90 days)

Note that the KLIBOR futures priced at 90 is yielding 10%. Since you priced the loan at 12%, you have essentially priced in a 2% profit margin.

How would you protect yourself from a rise in interest rates? Once again, since a rise in interest rates will hurt by squeezing the profit margin, the appropriate hedge strategy would be to short the KLIBOR futures.

Hedge strategy: *Short 20 three-month KLIBOR futures contracts*

To see whether the abovementioned hedge strategy would indeed enable you to lock in the 2% *interest spread*, let us assume that interest rates rise 2% over the next 90 days. Would your interest spread be protected?

Interest Rate ↑ by 2%
At maturity,
3-month KLIBOR = 11% (↑ 2%)
3-month KLIBOR futures = 89 (convergence implies 11% yield)

Without hedging, with spot rate at 11%, your profit spread would have reduced from 2% to 1% (12% − 11%).

Result of Hedge

Profit from futures = (90 − 89) × (RM 25 × 100) × 20 contracts
= RM 50,000

Interest spread = (0.12 − 0.11)
(Price − Cost)

Interest earned = [(0.01) × RM 20,000,000] × 3/12
= RM 50,000

Total earning = RM 50,000 + RM 50,000
= RM 100,000

% earning = $\frac{RM\ 100,000}{RM\ 20,000,000} \times 100$
= 0.50% for 3 months

Annualized % = 0.50% × 4
= 2%

As a result of the hedge, you have earned a 2% profit margin even though interest rates moved against you. Had the position not been hedged, the profit spread would have narrowed to 1%, while the Ringgit earnings would have been RM 50,000 and not RM 100,000.

5.7.3 Speculating on Interest Rate Movements

Scenario 1: Your analysis of economic conditions leads you to believe that interest rates are likely to fall over the next few months. Can you use KLIBOR futures to take advantage of your analysis?

Today's date: January 10

Quotations:
3-month KLIBOR = 8%
March KLIBOR futures = 91 (tenor = 90 days)

Strategy: Long (Buy) 1 March KLIBOR futures

(Going long would be the right strategy since falling interest rates would mean rising KLIBOR futures prices. To take the advantage of rising KLIBOR prices, you go long.)

Suppose your analysis was correct and interest rates go down by 2%. Then, the March 25 quote:

3-month KLIBOR = 6% (↓ 2%)
March KLIBOR futures = 94 (since it matures; convergence)
Profit on futures = (94 − 91) × (RM 25 × 100)
= RM 7,500 per contract

Since your expectation came true, you profit from the speculative position. If interest rates had gone up instead, you would have made losses.

Scenario 2: Your friend, a technical analyst, tells you that interest rates are going to increase. Since he has made several accurate calls previously, you have confidence in his forecast. How can you profit from your friend's projection?

Today's date: April 1

Quotations:
3-month KLIBOR   = 6%
June KLIBOR futures = 93

Strategy: Short 1 June KLIBOR futures

Suppose your friend was right and interest rates go up by 1.5%. Then on June 25:

3-month KLIBOR   = 7.50% (↑ 1.5%)
June KLIBOR futures = 92.50 (convergence)
Profit on futures   = (93 − 92.50) × 100 × RM 25
                    = RM 1,250 per contract

5.7.4 Arbitraging with IRF

We now examine the third application for IRF contracts: arbitrage. We again examine two types of arbitrage strategies: cash and carry and reverse cash and carry. The cash and carry strategy would be appropriate when the futures contract is overpriced relative to the 3-month and 6-month spot KLIBOR rates. The reverse cash and carry applies when the IRF contract is underpriced.

> **Note**
> When the quoted futures price has a yield different from that of the IFR, there is mispricing and arbitrage is possible.

Example: Cash and Carry Arbitrage

Suppose today's date is June 23 and you observe the following spot rates and futures price.

3-month KLIBOR   = 7% [90 days till September 24]
6-month KLIBOR   = 8% [180 days till December 23]
3-month KLIBOR futures = 92.50 [maturing September 23]

Given these quotations, in order to determine whether arbitrage is possible, we first check for mispricing by computing the IFR.

$$[1+\text{IFR}\times(\text{IFR tenor}/360)] = \frac{[1+\text{Long rate}\times(\text{Long tenor}/360)]}{[1+\text{Short rate}\times(\text{Short tenor}/360)]}$$

$$[1+\text{IFR}\times(90/360)] = \frac{[1+0.08\times(180/360)]}{[1+.07\times(90/360)]}$$

$[1 + \text{IFR} \times (90/360)] = \dfrac{1.04}{1.0175}$

IFR $= 0.0884$

% IFR $= 8.84\%$

Given IFR of 8.84%, the correct 3-month KLIBOR futures price should be:

$$100 - 8.84 = 91.16$$

Since the 3-month KLIBOR futures is quoted at 92.50, the futures is **overpriced**.

To arbitrage this, the appropriate strategy would be:

- Long 6-month KLIBOR (spot) of RM 1 million face value
- Short 1 three-month KLIBOR futures contract

There are two points to note about this strategy. First, notice that we go long the 6-month spot and not the 3-month KLIBOR spot. This has to do with the fact that the futures contract is for borrowing/lending for 3 months beginning from its maturity day. This would exactly coincide with the 6-month KLIBOR today, which would have 3 months left to maturity on September 23 when the KLIBOR futures matures. Since the 6-month KLIBOR of June 23 would have 3 months left on September 23, it is essentially a 3-month rate which is exactly the tenor of the KLIBOR futures on its maturity day of September 23. Since both are for 3-month borrowing/lending, there will be convergence.

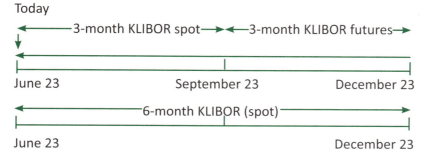

The second point to note is that the abovementioned strategy is consistent with the arbitrage rule: buy low, sell high. Since the futures is overpriced, we short (sell) the futures and long (buy) the relatively underpriced 6-month KLIBOR spot.

Since our arbitrage strategy is based on mispricing, we should make a profit regardless of interest rate movements between June 23 and September 23. To see whether this is true, we examine two scenarios: first, if interest rates rose over the interim period and second, if rates fell. For the first case, let us assume that the 3-month KLIBOR rose by 2% to 9% on September 23.

Scenario 1: Interest Rate ↑ by 2%
The 3-month KLIBOR will be 9%, whereas the September KLIBOR futures that is maturing on that day will be priced at 91.0 due to convergence.

Arbitrage Payoff

Profit on futures = [(92.50 − 91.0) × (RM 25 × 100)]
= RM 3,750

Loss on spot = [(0.08 − 0.09) × RM 1 million] × 90/360
= (RM 2,500)

Arbitrage profit = RM 3,750 − RM 2,500
= RM 1,250

Scenario 2: Interest Rate ↓ by 2%

At maturity on September 23, the spot and futures quote would be:

3-month KLIBOR = 5%
3-month KLIBOR futures = 95 (convergence)

Arbitrage Payoff

Loss on futures = (92.5 − 95) × RM 25 × 100
= (RM 6,250)

Profit on spot = [(0.08 − 0.05) × RM 1 million] × 90/360
= RM 7,500

Arbitrage profit = (RM 6,250) + RM 7,500
= RM 1,250

Notice that regardless of which way interest rates move, you make the same amount of arbitrage profit. As mentioned earlier, this profit results from mispricing. The larger the extent of mispricing, the larger the arbitrage profit.

5.7.5 The Reverse Cash and Carry Arbitrage

While a cash and carry arbitrage would be applicable when the futures contract is overpriced relative to spot, we do a reverse cash and carry arbitrage when the futures is underpriced relative to spot.

In the earlier example, the 3-month KLIBOR is quoted on June 23 at 90 while the 3-month and 6-month spot rates are unchanged. Since the correct yield on the 3-month KLIBOR futures as computed earlier was 8.84% and its correct price 91.16, the futures contract is now underpriced, relative to spot. To execute the reverse cash and carry strategy, we would:

- Long 1 three-month KLIBOR futures contract
- Short 6-month KLIBOR (spot) of RM 1 million face value

To examine whether we will indeed make a profit on the arbitrage and whether it will be independent of interest rate movements, we look at the same two interest rate scenarios.

Scenario 1: Interest Rate ↑ by 2%
At maturity on September 23, the quotes would be:

3-month KLIBOR = 9%
3-month KLIBOR futures = 91 (convergence)

Arbitrage Payoff

Profit on futures	= [(91 − 90) × RM 25 × 100]
	= RM 2,500
Profit on spot	= [(0.09 − 0.08) × RM 1 million] × 90/360
	= RM 2,500
Arbitrage profit	= RM 2,500 + RM 2,500
	= RM 5,000

Scenario 2: Interest Rate ↓ by 2%
At maturity on September 23, the quotes would be:

3-month KLIBOR = 5%
3-month KLIBOR futures = 95 (convergence)

Arbitrage Payoff

Profit on futures	= [(95 − 90) × (RM 25 × 100)]
	= RM 12,500
Loss on spot	= [(0.05 − 0.08) × RM 1 million] × 90/360
	= (RM 7,500)
Arbitrage profit	= RM 12,500 + (RM 7,500)
	= RM 5,000

Notice once again that regardless of interest rate movement, you make a profit of RM 5,000. This is pure arbitrage profit and arises solely from the inherent mispricing. You would have noted in Scenario 1 that with a rise in interest rate, the arbitrage provides a profit in both the spot and futures. Though uncommon, such a profit scenario is the result of mispricing combined with interest rate movement. The key is that in both scenarios, the same RM 5,000 profit from mispricing is made. Finally, it should be noted that the reverse cash and carry arbitrage gave a higher profit relative to the earlier cash and carry arbitrage (RM 5,000 versus RM 1,250). This is solely due to the fact that the mispricing or percentage deviation was larger.

5.8 Singapore Exchange's IRF Contract: The 10-Year Mini Japanese Government Bond Futures Contract

The 10-year Mini Japanese Government Bond (JGB) futures contract was introduced in March 1993 by the then Singapore International Monetary Exchange (SIMEX), the predecessor to the current Singapore Exchange (SGX). It is one of the most liquid, 10-year Mini JGB futures contract, as it references one of the world's largest bond markets.[2] The SGX Mini JGB futures allows investors to establish positions in interest rate markets. It also allows investors to manage their margins and positions in the full-sized JGB futures.

The underlying asset of the SGX Mini JGB futures is the 10-year JGB with 6% coupon with a principal value of ¥en 10,000,000. In addition to this Mini JGB futures, SGX also offers a full-size JGB futures contract that has as underlying a ¥en 100,000,000 notional 10-year JGB with 6% coupon. There is also an option contract on the same underlying.

When we take a long position in the SGX Mini JGB futures contract, we stand ready to take the delivery of a given amount of the 10-year JGB at maturity. For example, if we went long five contracts, it means that we stand ready to (take delivery) purchase ¥en 50,000,000 worth of the 10 year 6% coupon JGB bond at the agreed futures price on maturity. One the other hand, when we short an SGX Mini JGB futures, we agree to deliver a given amount of the 10-year JGB at the predetermined price on the maturity date. The price at which we long or short the JGB futures contract effectively locks in the implied yield. Thus, as is the case with other futures contracts, trading the SGX Mini JGB futures enables one to lock in the interest rate at which we will borrow or lend.

Table 5.2 shows the contract specifications for the SGX Mini JGB futures contract extracted from the SGX's website.

Table 5.2   Contract Specifications: SGX Mini JGB Futures

Contract Code	JB
Underlying asset	Japanese government bond with a 10-year maturity bearing a 6% coupon
Contract size	¥en 10,000,000
Minimum price fluctuation	¥en 0.01 per ¥en 100 face value (¥en 1,000)
Contract months	5 quarterly months in the March, June, September, and December cycle
Trading hours	(T): Singapore time 7:25 a.m.–5:10 p.m. (T + 1): Singapore time 5:30 p.m.–5:15 a.m.
Last trading day	One business day preceding the Tokyo Stock Exchange's (TSE) 10-Year JGB futures' last trading day of the expiring contract month
Final settlement	Cash settlement based on the final settlement price
Final settlement price	Based on tradable Tokyo contract prices

Source: SGX website.

[2] www.sgx.com.

We now examine some of the key features from the contract specifications. First, the contract size is ¥en 10,000,000. Given this standard size, hedgers, for example, would long/short as many contracts as needed based on their underlying exposure. This is the face value of a notional 10-year JGB with a 6% coupon. The SGX Mini JGB futures price is quoted and traded in units with each unit having a monetary value of ¥en 100,000. The minimum price fluctuation or tick size of the Mini JGB futures contract in percent is equivalent to one basis point which in monetary terms equals ¥en 1,000 (one basis point of ¥en 10,000,000). So, price quotations have to be higher or lower by multiples of ¥en 1,000. Contract months of the Mini JGB futures are five quarterly months in the March, June, September, and December cycle. For example, in December of a given year, there would be the December contracts of that year, and the March, June, September, and December contracts of the following year available for traders to buy or sell. As with other financial derivatives, the contract is cash-settled. Final settlement price of the contract at maturity is based on tradable Tokyo contract prices to determine the final settlement value. This is important because the final settlement price will determine the extent of a position's gain or loss at maturity.

5.8.1 SGX Mini JGB Futures: Applications

In this section, we examine the use of SGX Mini JGB futures contracts in the three applications of derivative instruments: hedging, arbitrage, and speculation. The following numerical examples demonstrate how these applications would work with the SGX Mini JGB futures contracts.

(i) Hedging Interest Rate Risk

Portfolio managers, especially bond fund managers, are often faced with interest rate uncertainty. If the interest rates move against an established position, the portfolio value could be affected negatively. For example, if interest rates rise sharply, a portfolio consisting of bonds and other fixed-income securities would experience a sharp fall in value. IRF contracts provide the means for portfolio managers to manage the interest rate risk and preserve underlying portfolio values. Similarly, borrowers faced with higher costs if rates rise and lenders with shrinking incomes if rates fall can use these contracts to protect themselves. In the following illustration, we examine two scenarios under which interest rate movements can result in an undesirable outcome. First, we look at how a bond fund manager could hedge against rising interest rate using the SGX Mini JGB futures contracts.

Hedging: Protecting the Value of a Fixed-Income Portfolio

You are a bond fund manager with a ¥en 1 billion position in Japanese government bonds/securities. The duration of your bond portfolio is 4 years. You are concerned that though interest rates are low currently, there is a very high probability that the interest rates could rise over the next 6 months. As with all fixed-income securities, your bond portfolio's value has an inverse relationship with the interest rate movements. If the interest rates rise, the bond portfolio value will decline, causing negative returns to your investors. How can you manage this exposure? Since your portfolio constitutes Japanese government securities, using the SGX 10-year Mini JGB futures would be logical.

Hedge Strategy
Since you have a long position in Japanese government bonds and rising interest rates will hurt, the appropriate hedge strategy would be to short the JGB futures contracts. A short position in the futures will profit from falling bond values as interest rates rise.

Number of Contracts
Having established that the appropriate strategy is to short the futures contracts, the next question is how many contracts to short? Since the risk class of the underlying and futures is the same, the hedge ratio will depend on the difference between the duration of your portfolio and that of the JGB futures contract. If the duration of your portfolio equals that of the futures, then the hedge ratio is simply 1. You would need to short futures contracts of equal value to that of your portfolio. In this case, you would need to short ¥en 1 billion worth of futures. However, suppose you have calculated the duration of the 10-year Mini JGB futures contract to be 8 years. This has to be compared to your portfolio duration which is 4 years as stated earlier. Since your portfolio duration is half, it implies that the fall or change in the value of your portfolio will be half that of the futures. As such, the number of futures contracts to be shorted should be equal to half the value of your portfolio.

Number of contracts to hedge can be determined as follows:

{(1 − (duration of portfolio/duration of futures)) × Value of Portfolio}/Value per futures contract
{(1 − (4/8) × ¥en 1,000,000,000}/¥en 10,000,000 = 50 contracts

Hedge strategy: *Short 50 June SGX Mini JGB futures contracts*

Assume it is now January. Suppose the quoted price of the SGX 10-year Mini JGB futures that will mature in June is 100. Note that the SGX Mini JGB futures price is quoted in units with each unit having a monetary value of ¥en 100,000.

To see how the hedge strategy will protect against interest rate fluctuation, we examine the two following scenarios, one where interest rates rise over the next 6 and another where rates fall.

Scenario 1: Interest Rates Rise Over the Next 6 Months
Suppose interest rates rise in Japan causing the required yield for the 10-year government bond to rise from **2%** currently to **2.5%** in 6 months.

Using Equation 3 from earlier in the chapter, the impact on the value of your portfolio and on the 10-year JGB would be as follows:

$$\% \Delta \text{ in price} = -D (\Delta i / 1 + i) \times 100$$

Impact on Your Portfolio

% change in value = {−4 (0.005/1.02)} ×100
= −1.96%

Thus, loss in portfolio value = ¥en 1,000,000,000 × (0.0196)
= **¥en 19,600,000**

Impact on 10-Year JGB Bond

% change in value = {−8 (0.005/1.02)} ×100
= −3.92%

Since prices are inversely related to interest rates, rising rates would cause the futures price to be lower, thus

$$100 - 3.92 = 96.08$$

June SGX 10-year Mini JGB futures = 96.08

Result of Hedge

Loss on bond portfolio = (¥en 19,600.000)
Profit from futures = [(100 − 96.08) × ¥en 100,000] × 50 contracts
= ¥ 19,600,000
Payoff to hedged position = 0

Although an unhedged position would have led to losses of ¥en 19.6 million, the fully hedged position has not net losses. We have obviously ignored transaction costs. The transaction costs incurred in the hedging should be treated as the cost of "insurance."

Scenario 2: Interest Rates Fall Over the Next 6 Months

Suppose interest rates fall in Japan, causing the required yield for the 10-year government bond to fall from **2%** currently to **1.6%** in 6 months.

Impact on Your Portfolio:

% change in value = {−4 (0.004/1.02)} ×100
= −0.57%

Since rates fell, the gain in portfolio value = ¥en 1,000,000,000 × (0.0157)
= **¥en 15,700,000**

Impact on 10-Year JGB Bond

% change in value = {−8 (−0.004/1.02)} ×100
= −3.14%

Since prices are inversely related to interest rates, falling rates would cause the futures price to be higher, thus

$$100 + 3.14 = 103.14$$

June SGX 10-year Mini JGB futures = 103.14

Result of Hedge

Gain on bond portfolio = ¥en 15,700.000
Loss on futures = [(100 − 103.14) × ¥en 100,000] × 50 contracts
= (¥en 15,700,000)

Payoff to hedged position = 0

Notice that regardless of whether interest rates rose or fell, the fully hedged position locks in your portfolio value at ¥en 1 billion, less transaction costs.

5.8.2 Speculating on Interest Rate Movements

Scenario 1: Expectation: Falling Interest Rates

You anticipate that the interest rate will fall in the next few months. Can SGX Mini JGB futures be used to take an advantage of this expectation? The answer is Yes. Given the inverse relationship between interest rates and bond prices, the appropriate strategy to benefit from falling interest rates would be: Long the SGX 10-year Mini JGB futures.

Today's date: March 10

Quotations:
Current 10-year yield (interest rate) JGB = 3%
June SGX Mini JGB futures = 151 (tenor = 90 days)

Strategy: Long (Buy) 1 June SGX Mini JGB futures

Assume that your forecast was correct and interest rates decline by 1%. Then, the June 15 quote:

Interest rates = 2%
June SGX Mini JGB futures = 153
Profit on futures = (Sell price − Buy price) × ¥en 100,000
= (153 − 151) × ¥en100,000
= ¥en 200,000 per contract

Because you were correct about the expected interest rates increase, you make a profit from your speculative strategy. However, if you were wrong, you would incur losses.

Scenario 2: Your analysis suggests that the central banks, including the Bank of Japan (BOJ), might hike interest rates in the next few months. How can you use the SGX Mini JGB futures contracts to take advantage of your analysis? Since a rise in rates will cause futures prices to fall, you should short SGX 10-year Mini JGB futures.

Today's date: July 1

Quotations
Interest rates: = 4%
June SGX Mini JGB futures = 154 (tenor = 90 days)

Strategy: Short (sell) 1 June SGX Mini JGB futures

Assume that your analysis was correct and interest rates increase by 1.50%. Then, the September 15 quote:

Interest rates: $\quad\quad\quad = 5.50\%$
June SGX Mini JGB futures $= 151$
Profit on futures $\quad\quad = (154 - 151) \times$ ¥en 100,000
$\quad\quad\quad\quad\quad\quad\quad = $ ¥en 300,000 per contract

5.8.3 Arbitraging with SGX Mini JGB Futures

As with all bond futures contracts, arbitrage trading with SGX Mini JGB futures is possible. Although SGX Mini JGB futures is relatively liquid compared to other interest rates futures traded on SGX, execution risk is still a concern due to the patchy level of liquidity in the market. However, the same principle of arbitrage still applies. If there is a mispricing, either in the futures or spot markets, arbitrageurs can long the relatively cheap security and short the overpriced assets. To do this, we compare the price of SGX 10-year Mini JGB futures with the value of the deliverable bond's **forward** price. The forward price is the bond's spot price plus the cost of carry. Intuitively, *if SGX 10-year Mini JGB futures price > spot price of deliverable bond + net carry cost*, then the SGX 10-year Mini JGB futures is overpriced.

Short SGX 10-year Mini JGB futures and long spot deliverable bond.

On the other hand, *if SGX 10-year Mini JGB < spot price of deliverable bond + net carry cost*, then the SGX 10-year Mini JGB futures is underpriced.

Long 10-year SGX Mini JGB futures and short spot deliverable bond.

5.9 Determinants of IRF Prices

Since the price/value of IRF contracts is linked to interest rates (inversely related), participants have always tried to predict interest rate movements. Although some use "gut feelings" and a sense of timing, most analysts/investors use either technical analysis and/or fundamental analysis. We discuss below some of the key determinants of IRF prices.

(1) Interest Rate Changes

The most important determinant would of course be changes in interest rates. Changes in interest rates lead to changes in yields (required returns) and thereby cause changes in futures contract values.

Interest Rate ⇑ = Yield ⇑; Futures Price ⇓
Interest Rate ⇓ = Yield ⇓; Futures Price ⇑

We have examined these relationships under bond pricing mechanics.

(2) Economic Cycles and Demand and Supply of Credit

Since an interest rate is simply the price of money, interest rates would be affected by the demand and supply of money (or credit). This is no different from the fact that the price of a product changes with changes in its demand and supply. The demand and supply of credit, however, is cyclical. In that, it depends on economic cycles. This is especially true of demand. Though supply is often treated by economists as being exogenous since the government is the main "supplier" of credit, it still is cyclical. During times of economic expansion (boom), the demand for credit, for the purpose of consumption and investment, increases.

At such times, government monetary policy tends to be either neutral or restrictionary. The result would be an increase in the demand for credit but supply has little net increase. Thus, during a boom cycle, interest rates tend to rise. The opposite is true during a down cycle. Interest rates tend to fall because demand is lower but government monetary policy is usually expansionary. Any prediction of interest rates would therefore have to consider where the economy is on the economic cycle and where it is headed.

(3) The Role of the Government

As should be evident from the earlier discussion, the role of government would be a key determinant of interest rate movements. A government's goal in economic management is to reduce cyclicality, that is, reduce the impact of economic cycles. As such, governments often use counter-cyclical measures to reduce the fluctuations that otherwise would be. These measures take the form of either fiscal or monetary policy. It is through monetary policy that governments influence interest rates. Aside from action to change interest rates, for example by announcing a rise or a cut in interest rates, governments can also influence interest rates indirectly, e.g., by changing the statutory reserve ratio of banks or even by imposing credit controls, etc.

Reserve Ratio ⇑ ⇒ Money Supply ⇓ ⇒ Interest Rates ⇑

In addition to counter-cyclical measures, other forms of government action could also affect interest rates. A good example of such action would be intervention in foreign exchange markets. When a government feels that its home currency has depreciated or appreciated too much against a foreign currency, it might choose to intervene in order to affect a desired change in the exchange rate. Such action will cause changes in the money supply (the outstanding amount of home currency in circulation). Given this change in supply of money, the interest rate, being the price of money, will change in reverse order.

(4) The Rate of Inflation

The rate of inflation is directly related to interest rates (nominal interest rates). In financial economics, the relationship between the interest rate and the inflation rate is formalized as the "Fisherian Equation." The equation is as follows:

$$\text{Nominal interest rate} = (1 + \text{Real interest rate})(1 + \text{Inflation rate}) - 1$$

According to this equation, the nominal interest rate is made up of two parts: the real rate and the rate of inflation. Thus, when an economy experiences inflation, the nominal interest rate **will be higher** than the **real interest rate**. The difference between the two interest rates is known as the inflation premium. The higher the prevailing inflation rate, the higher the premium and therefore the nominal interest rate. (The real interest rate is and has been shown in empirical studies to be relatively stable.)

Example: Suppose the real interest rate is 5%; then nominal interest rate that will prevail under different inflation rates is as follows:

Scenario 1
Inflation rate = 10% per year
Nominal interest rate = [(1.05) (1.10)] − 1
= 0.155

Thus, the interest charged on a 1-year loan would be 15.5%.

Scenario 2
Inflation rate = 20% per year
Nominal interest rate = (1.05) (1.20) − 1
= 0.26

The interest charged on a 1-year loan would be 26%.

Scenario 3
Inflation rate = 5% per year
Nominal interest rate = (1.05) (1.05) − 1
= 0.1025 or 10.25%

Notice that the nominal interest rate changes in tandem with the inflation rate. The conclusion that we make from the three scenarios is that nominal interest rates and inflation rates are *positively correlated*.

(5) Expectations

Expectations are simply perceptions formed by market participants regarding potential economic performance. Economists have long believed that expectations play an important role in economic decision-making of participants. For example, if the market/participants have good expectations of future economic performance, they would be more likely to make investments. Increases in investment increases the demand for credit and thereby puts an upward pressure on interest rates. The opposite is true when expectations are poor. Additionally, expectations about future inflation rates can also affect prevailing interest rates. Expectations are formed through the interpretation/reading of several economic indicators. Indicators such as money supply, unemployment rate, capacity utilization, foreign reserves, balance of payments, and the current account balance often provide a picture about where the economy is headed and what the government's response would be. Often times, these expectations can be self-fulfilling and can dictate what governments may have to do (rational expectations hypothesis).

5.10 Contract Performance

As mentioned earlier, interest rate derivatives across the world have seen a drop in trading activity in recent years. According to the World Federation of Exchanges (WFE) Derivatives Report 2020, overall interest rate derivatives volume fell 11.9% in 2020 relative to the prior year. This decline in trading activity was evident in both the short-term and long-term interest rate products. Short-term IRF fell 63.4%, whereas long-term IRF fell by 12.3%.

The sharp decline in activity is the direct result of the global interest rate environment. As argued in Box 5.1 and shown in Figures 5.2 and 5.3, interest rate derivatives have shown reduced activity across the world over the last few years. The reduced activity is a direct consequence of the sharp interest rate cuts in the major economies, following the US subprime crisis and the global financial crisis. Just as interest rates were beginning to rise, especially in the US, the COVID-19 pandemic struck in early 2020. As evident in Figure 5.2, governments reacted to the outbreak of the pandemic with even more aggressive rate cuts. In several developed economies such as Germany, Switzerland, and Japan, short-term interest

> ### Box 5.1
> **Waning Interest in Interest Rate Derivatives?**
>
> IRFs and interest rate derivatives, which were the most popularly traded contracts in the 1990s and early 2000s, have now seen their volumes fall. According to the WFE Derivatives Report 2020, aggregate worldwide traded volume of interest rate derivatives (both futures and options) fell by 11.9% in 2020. Both short-term and long-term interest rate derivatives fell. Short-term interest rate futures fell 63.4%, whereas long-term futures contracts fell by 12.3%.
>
> All three regions covered in the global report, Americas, Asia-Pacific (APAC), and Europe, the Middle-East and Africa (EMEA), saw reduced trading activity in 2020 of 14%, 9.1%, and 6.4%, respectively. One of the most actively traded contract was the CME group's Eurodollar futures contracts, which is directly impacted by interest rate changes, being a currency futures contract.
>
> The decline in IRF trading appears to be a global phenomenon. Why is this so? There may be two reasons for this. The first and most important is the fact that interest rates are currently at historic lows. While rates have been falling since the years of Alan Greenspan as US Federal Reserve Chairman, in the name of pro-growth policies, the

(Continued)

Box 5.1
(*Continued*)

sharpest falls have been since the outbreak of the US subprime crisis of 2007/2008. Today, short-term interest rates like the 3-month rate is below 25 basis points in the US and UK and negative in both Germany and Japan. With interest rates at such low levels, interest rate exposure becomes a lot less important. For a given principal amount, volatility around a 3% interest rate implies much lower risk than at a 6% level. A second important reason for the reduced interest rate risk environment is the near absence of inflation. As we had discussed in the introduction to the chapter, volatility or changes in inflation rates have a direct impact on nominal interest rates. Inflation, however, appears to be a nonissue. Perhaps due to changes in technology, increased productivity, and the advent of China as a low-cost producer of goods for the world, inflation appears to be subdued globally speaking. Though there are isolated countries with rampant inflation, the major countries have little or no inflation. In fact, the constant fear over the last decade in countries like Japan is deflation, not inflation. With low real interest rates and near-zero inflation, nominal interest rates are so low that interest rate risk is a lot more muted today than previously. Figures 5.2 and 5.3 provide more evidence of this. Since early 2021, inflation appears to be making a comeback, though still muted by historical standards. Inflationary expectations have increased the volatility of interest rates, as clearly evident in Figure 5.3.

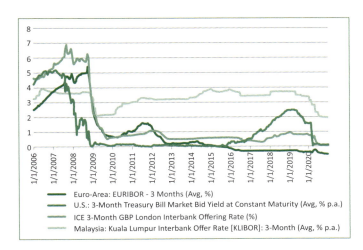

Figure 5.2   15-Year Global Interest Rate Movement (2006–2020)

rates were in negative territory. In the US, the 3-month rate was a mere 25 basis points. Inflation-adjusted real interest rates turned negative even in the US, though the nominal rates were still positive. At these low or near-zero rates, interest rate risk is not substantive and so the reduced need to hedge interest rate risks.

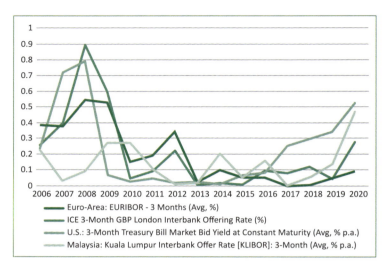

Figure 5.3   Volatility of Global Interest Rates (2006–2020)

Figure 5.2 shows 3-month interest rate movement over the 15-year period 2006–2020. The rates shown are the KLIBOR, LIBOR, European Interbank Offer Rate (EURIBOR), and the 3-month US T-bill rate. The three interest rates other than KLIBOR are used in the pricing of most of the credit issued and traded globally. Notice that the rates were steady or on a rising mode until 2007. Following the onset of the US subprime crisis in late 2007 and its subsequent evolvement as the global financial crisis in 2008, all four interest rates show sharp falls. This was the result of central banks cutting interest rates as part of monetary accommodation to check the impact of the crisis. By 2009/2010, rates had fallen several percentage points from where they were in 2007. The EURIBOR, reflective of German **bond yields**, had gone into negative territory from late 2014. The US 3-month T-bill rate has hovered around 25 basis points for about 6 years, then risen for about 3 years before coming down sharply to near 0.10%. This was due to the Fed's reaction to the onset of the pandemic. The marked decline in interest rates has huge implications on interest rate risk and the magnitude of exposure arising from interest rates. As rates decline, so does the magnitude of risk for a given principal amount. The decline in traded volume of interest rate derivatives, over recent years, should not be a surprise.

Figure 5.3 shows the volatility of the four interest rates for the 15-year period 2006–2020. Volatility was measured simply as the standard deviation of weekly observations over a given year. Rate volatility peaks in 2008 for the three global interest rates. From 2009, volatility reduces substantially and is consistent with the leveling off seen in late 2009, as shown in Figure 5.2. Although the 3-month KLIBOR appears to have its own trajectory, it should be noted that it has the lowest magnitude, i.e., even at its highest point in 2009, its volatility is only a third of LIBOR or US T-bill rates. The decline in the volatility of interest rates coincides with the decline in the rates. As mentioned earlier, the sharp interest rate declines were a policy reaction to the outbreak of the US subprime crisis. The reduction in the traded volume of the 3-month KLIBOR futures and the other IRF contracts are by no means unique. As stated in Box 5.1, globally, interest rate derivatives have gone through a relatively sharp fall in activity over the last few years. This reduction can be attributed to both the reduction in the interest rates and in their volatility. Interest rate exposure reduces when rates fall and remain stable. Notice that interest rate volatility has increased since 2020. This has to do with both inflationary expectations and increased economic uncertainties with the evolution of the pandemic.

5.11 Currency Forward and Futures Contracts

Currency derivatives, forwards, futures, options, and swaps are among the most heavily traded derivative contracts. While a huge portion of currency derivatives are traded on over-the-counter (OTC) markets, several currency futures and option contracts are listed and traded on exchanges in different parts of the world. There are several reasons for the popularity of currency derivatives. The collapse of the Bretton Woods system in August 1971 effectively ended the fixed exchange rate system that was in place till then. The Bretton Woods was a fixed exchange rate regime under which the exchange rate of currencies was fixed to each other according to their gold parity. The gold parity or gold "backing" that a currency had depended on the amount of gold reserves that the country holds and its outstanding money supply. Under a fixed exchange rate regime, exchange rate risk was minimal and so there was little need currency derivatives. However, with collapse of the Bretton Woods system, exchange rates came to be determined not by gold parity but by market forces, i.e., demand and supply. So, post-Bretton Woods, exchange rate exposure became a new risk that businesses had to contend with. A second important reason for the popularity of currency derivatives was the increase in international trade post-WWII. As global trade increased, currency exposure increased, and so the need for currency derivatives. Many multinational firms have sourcing and production across many countries. Many products have value chains that span the globe as firms seek the lowest costs for their operations. A third key factor is the multifold increase in capital flows across countries. Funds flow across countries to finance trade, investments, or simply to take advantage of higher potential returns.

While any number of factors can influence the demand for and supply of a currency, the one key factor is the prevailing nominal interest rate. Nominal interest rates at a given point reflect the many factors at play: the nation's inflation rate, monetary policy stance, demand and supply of credit, business conditions, and even political risks. And since the exchange rate is the price of one currency in terms of another, what matters in determining the exchange rate between two currencies is the relative interest rate differential. There are several equilibrium conditions, or parity conditions, in international finance. One of these is interest rate parity (IRP), which states that nominal interest rate differentials reflect inflation differentials, and so, the currency with the higher nominal interest rate ought to depreciate by the level of the interest differential. Since the nominal interest rate is the return or "yield" that one gets from holding deposits in the currency, we can use the logic of the cost of carry model to price a currency forward/futures contract.

Recall that the cost-of-carry model is

$$F_{t,T} = S_o(1 + rf + c - y)^{t,T}$$

where

$F_{t,T}$ = futures price for a contract with maturity from t to T (t = today, T = maturity)
S_o = current spot price of the underlying asset
rf = annualized risk-free interest rate (being the proxy for the opportunity cost of later payment)
c = annualized storage cost in percent (inclusive of shipping handing, shrinkage, spoilage, etc.)
y = convenience yield (annualized percentage)

Since there is no cost of storage involved nor convenience yield, the variables c and y drop off, r_f being the nominal short term interest rate remains, but we need to bring in the equivalent foreign interest rate as we are interested in the interest rate differential. Thus, the cost of carry model for currency futures can be written as:

$$F_{t,T} = S_o(1 + i^d) / (1 + i^f)^{t,T} \tag{4}$$

where

$F_{t,T}$ = futures quote of exchange rate as home currency per unit foreign currency with maturity from t to T (t = today, T = maturity)
S_o = spot quote of exchange rate as home currency per unit foreign currency
i^d = domestic interest rate of appropriate tenor given futures maturity
i^f = foreign interest rate of appropriate tenor given futures maturity

Students of international finance would identify Equation (4) as a form of the interest rate parity (IRP) equation.

5.11.1 Illustration — Computing Currency Forward/Futures Prices

Suppose we want to determine the correct price of the Hong Kong Exchanges and Clearing (HKEX)-traded Chinese Renminbi (CNH)/US$ futures contract. We could use the cost of carry model in Equation (4). Assume we are provided the following information:

Spot Exchange Rate
— Today's spot quote = US$ 0.1550 per CNH or in CNH (Renminbi) terms taking reciprocal
= 1/0.1550
= 6.4516
= 6.4516 CNH per US$

Interest Rates
US Interest rate — annualized T-bill rate

— 6 months = 0.05%
— 3 months = 0.05% (same due to rounding and the historically low interest rates in US)

China Interest Rates — Shanghai Interbank Offer Rate (SHIBOR)

— 6 month (SHIBOR) = 2.4680
— 3 month (SHIBOR) = 2.3570

3-Month or 90-Day Futures Contract

Given this information, the correct price of a 3-month forward/futures contract would be:

$F_{90} = 0.1550 [(1 + 0.0005)/(1 + 0.02357)]^{0.25}$
$= 0.1550 [(0.9775)]^{0.25}$
$= 0.1550 (0.9943)$
$= 0.1541$

So the correct price of 3-month or 90-day futures contract is **US$ 0.1541 per CNH.** Since the contract size is US$ 100,000, the price per 3-month contract in US$ will be US$ 15,410.00.

6-Month or 180-Day Futures Contract

The 6-month currency futures should have a value as follows:

$F_{180} = 0.1550 [(1 + 0.0005)/(1 + 0.02468)]^{50}$
$= 0.1550 [(0.9764)]^{50}$
$= 0.1550 (0.9881)$
$= 0.1532$

So the correct price of the 6-month futures contract is **US$ 0.1532 per CNH.** The value per contract in US$ given the contract size of US$100,000 will be US$15,320.

Notice that the abovementioned futures quotations were in US$ terms. We can easily derive the equivalent CNH quotes by simply taking the reciprocal of US$ quotes as stated earlier or by rewriting Equation (4), with CNH or CNY (or RMB) as the home currency.

$$F_{t,T} = S_o(1 + i^d) / (1 + i^f)^{t,T}$$

$F_{90} = 6.4516 (1 + 0.02357)/(1 + 0.0005)^{0.25}$
$= 6.4516 (1.0231)^{0.25}$
$= 6.4516 (1.0057)$
$= 6.4885$

Notice that taking the reciprocal of 6.4885: (1/6.4885) = 0.1541, which is the 90-day futures quote in US$ earlier.

Reworking the same for 6-month futures would be:

$F_{180} = 6.4516 (1 + 0.02468)/(1 + 0.0005)^{0.50}$
$= 6.4516 (1.0242)^{0.50}$
$= 6.4516 (1.0120)$
$= 6.5291$

Again taking the reciprocal of 6.5291: (1/6.5291) = 0.1532 which is the 6-month futures quote in US$ earlier.

Given the spot and forward/futures rates, it is obvious that the CNH is at a forward discount against the US$. The 6-month rate of the CNH is at an even higher discount than the 3-month rate. What these rates imply is that the market expects the CNH or Renminbi to depreciate against the US$ over the near future. These prices and expectations reflect currently available information. Asset markets, especially currency markets, are deep and highly efficient from an information viewpoint. The arrival of new information can quickly change prices and expectations.

It is also worth noting that IRP is holding in this case. IRP states that the currency with the lower nominal interest rate should be at a forward premium. The currency with the lower nominal interest rate in this case is the US$, and indeed the US$ is at a forward premium against CNH since it takes more CNH to buy per unit of US$ as we go from spot to 3-month futures and to 6-month futures. However, that IRP is holding in this case should be taken with a pinch of salt, since US interest rates, in particular, are at artificially depressed rates given the Federal Reserve's highly accommodative monetary policy. As discussed elsewhere in the chapter, interest rates are globally at historic lows with many developed markets having near zero or negative interest rates.

5.12 The HKEX's US$/CNH Currency Futures Contract

The HKEX has currency futures contracts on the Chinese currency. Known as the US$/CNH futures contract, it is a US$ quoted futures contract on the CNH, which is the offshore version of the Chinese Yuan (CNY). The CNY, which is alternatively also known as the Renminbi, is the domestic or onshore currency. Thus, the CNH is the international, offshore version of the CNY, which is still not fully convertible or tradeable given currency controls. Today, the CNH is traded mainly in Hong Kong but also in Singapore, London, and Luxembourg.

In earlier years, China had two exchange rates for the CNY: an official rate and a market rate for international transactions. Until quite recently, this was not unusual for many developing countries. Many countries, especially those in the socialist mold, including the likes of India, Egypt, Myanmar, etc., used to have multiple exchange rates. These differential rates for different purposes was unwieldy and often caused serious distortions within the economy. The official rate was usually out of line with market (or black market) rates, which were usually more reflective of the country's economic fundamentals.

Until 1994, China had dual exchange rates with quite a substantial spread between the official and market rates. In January 1994, they were merged into a single rate and pegged to the US$ at about CNY 8 to the US$. The CNY was de-pegged from the US$ in 2005 (the same time when Malaysia de-pegged its Ringgit from the US$) and a series of liberalization efforts

Table 5.3 Contract Specifications — US$/CNH Currency Futures

Contract	US$/CNH Futures (US$ = US dollar/CNH = RMB traded in Hong Kong)
Trading symbol	CUS
Contract month	Spot month, the next three calendar months, and the next six calendar quarter months
Contract size	US$ 100,000
Price quotation	RMB per US$ (e.g., RMB 6.2486 per US$)
Minimum fluctuation	RMB 0.0001 (4 decimal places)
Tick value	RMB 10
Trading hours	8:30 a.m.–4:30 p.m. (day session) 5:15 p.m.–3:00 a.m. (after-hours trading (AHT) session) (expiring contract month closes at 11:00 a.m. on the last trading day)
Final settlement day	The third Wednesday of the contract month
Last trading day	Two Hong Kong business days prior to the final settlement day
Final settlement price	US$/CNY(HK) spot rate published by the Treasury Markets Association (TMA) of Hong Kong at or around 11:30 a.m. on the last trading day
Settlement method	Delivery of US$ by the seller and payment of the final settlement value in RMB by the buyer
Exchange fee	RMB 8

Source: HKEX website.

were undertaken. In mid-2010, the Chinese central bank, the People's Bank of China (PBOC), and the Hong Kong Monetary Authority (HKMA) began initiatives that would allow a new version of the CNY, denoted CNH, to be traded in Hong Kong as an offshore currency. Following this in September 2012, the HKEX launched the world's first currency derivative on the Chinese currency. The US$/CNH futures contract has since then grown substantially to become one of HKEX's most popular currency futures. Subsequently, in addition to the original US$/CNH futures, HKEX also introduced the EUR/CNH, JPY/CNH, AUD/CNH, INR/CNH, and US$/CNH currency option contract. A mini version of the US$/CNH with a smaller contract size of US$ 20,000 is also offered. Table 5.3 shows a summary of the US$/CNH futures contract.

5.12.1 Currency Futures — Applications for Hedging, Speculation, and Arbitrage

In this section, we examine the three common applications of currency futures contracts. As is the case with other derivatives, they can be used for hedging, speculation, and arbitrage. Hedging, as we know from earlier, is risk management that is reducing the risks that arise as a result of an underlying transaction. Speculation seeks to take advantage of expectations, it typically involves only one position. Unlike hedgers who have an underlying position arising from a business transaction and use derivatives to offset the risk, speculators have no underlying as they use derivatives to profit from their expected price movement. Arbitrageurs use derivatives to take advantage of mispricing. When the price of a derivative is not as it should be given its underlying asset's price, mispricing occurs, giving rise to arbitrage opportunity.

(i) Hedging with Currency Futures Contracts

Dalian Electronics Corporation (DEC) is a China-based manufacturer of computer peripherals including memory cards. It exports its products to several countries. DEC has just completed a shipment of products to its main American customer, Compu-land, a nationwide retailer of computers and related appliances. As has been the practice with this customer, DEC has invoiced in US$ and given a 90-day credit period. The total amount of the latest shipment is US$ 6 million. Given the large amount, DEC wants to hedge the currency exposure using its brokers in HKEX. DEC has just been provided the following information by its brokers at HKEX:

— US$/CNH spot rate   = 0.1550 (or CNH 6.4516 per US$)
— US$/CNH 90-day futures = 0.1559 (or CNH 6.4143 per US$)

Given the spot and futures rates, it is quite obvious that the market expects the US$ to depreciate against the Yuan over the near future. To avoid any losses to itself, it is important that DEC hedge its currency risk. What is the right hedging strategy?

There are two equivalent ways to determine the right strategy. The first is to recognize that the derivative position in a hedge should be the opposite of the underlying position/exposure. Here, since DEC has exported and stands to receive payment in US$, the underlying transaction has it to have a **long position** in US$. As such, the hedge would require a derivative position that creates an equal **short position** in US$. An exposure is fully hedged if the derivative position is equal in amount and maturity. A second way to arrive at the right hedge strategy is to think of the direction of price movement that one needs to be protected from. Here, since DEC is going to be receiving US$, their fear is only that the US$ could depreciate and lead to lower proceeds in Yuan. DEC would not fear an appreciation of the US$ as it would be beneficial to them. The correct hedge strategy would therefore be to establish a derivative position which would benefit from a depreciation of the US$ such that it offsets the negative impact. As we know from Chapter 3, a short position benefits from falling prices/values. So, once again, the correct hedge strategy would be to take a short position in the currency futures contract. But how many US$/CNH futures contracts to short? Since contract size as shown in the contract specifications earlier is US$ 100,000 per contract, DEC would need to short 60 contracts to be fully hedged.

Appropriate Hedge Strategy: Short 60 Three-Month US$/CNH Futures Contracts

To see how this hedge strategy will protect DEC, we examine two potential scenarios at contract maturity on day 90: first, if the US$ depreciates to 0.1659 per CNH at maturity and a second scenario where the US$ appreciates to 0.1459 at maturity. For simplicity and to avoid clutter, we ignore brokerage commissions, margin costs, and other transaction costs.

Table 5.4(a)   Scenario 1: US$ Depreciates to 0.1659 per CNH at Maturity

Action	Position Today	Position at Maturity	Profit/Loss
Receivable amount from Compu-land	CNY 38,485,800[1]	CNY 36,166,200	(CNY 2,319,600)
Short 60 US$/CNH futures	(CNY 38,485,800)[2]	(CNY 36,166,200)[3]	CNY 2,319,600[4]
Gain/Loss	0	0	0

Note: Receivable position today in CNY is determined as invoice amount × reciprocal of futures price (6,000,000 × (1/0.1559)).
CNY is analogous to CNH as the onshore Yuan is denoted.

Table 5.4(b)   Scenario 2: US$ Appreciates to 0.1459 per CNH at Maturity

Action	Position Today	Position at Maturity	Profit/Loss
Receivable amount from Compu-land	CNY 38,485,800	CNY 41,124,000	CNY 2,638,200[5]
Short 60 US$/CNH futures	(CNY 38,485,800)[1]	(CNY 41,124,000)[2]	(CNY 2,638,200)[6]
Gain/Loss	0	0	0

[1]   Determined based on the futures rate and not spot as the spot rate has no relevance in the future.
[2]   Shown as negative as it constitutes the deliverable amount or obligation in CNY equivalent.
[3]   The CNY amount of US$ equivalent delivered at maturity.
[4]   Profit amount since the actual delivered was less than the earlier obligation to deliver.
[5]   An implied gain since the value of the receivable in CNY is higher than original.
[6]   Constitutes a loss since amount delivered at maturity was higher than the original obligation to deliver.

Table 5.4(a) shows the hedged outcome if the US$ depreciates. Notice that if DEC had not hedged, the depreciation would have caused DEC to lose CNY 2,319,600. However, by having fully hedged the position, DEC gets to lock in the amount of CNY 38,485,800 for its US$ 6 million receivable.

As shown in Tables 5.4(a) and (b), DEC locks in the amount of CNY 38,485,800 by having hedged with futures effectively. DEC does not benefit from the appreciation of the US$ since implied gains are exactly offset by the actual losses on the short futures position.

Under both abovementioned scenarios, DEC having fully hedged itself has eliminated currency risk arising from its transaction with Compu-Land, having fully hedged itself. DEC effectively locks in its home currency value today and will be unaffected by any subsequent exchange rate movements.

Handling Mismatches between Underlying Exposure and Futures Specifications

In the earlier example, there were no mismatches. The receivable amount of US$ 6 million meant that 60 contracts fully covered the amount. Further, the 90-day credit period given by DEC to its customer matched the 90-day maturity of the contract. In the real business environment, these features need not automatically match. Mismatches are often the case. Mismatches can happen in three areas.

The first is maturity mismatch, where the number of days on which the foreign currency denominated cash flow is due to happen does not match maturity dates of the derivative contract. For example, if a payment will be received 97 days from now, do we use a 90-day contract and leave unhedged the last few days, or do we take position in the 180-day contract and get out on day 97? Either way, we are not fully hedged. There will be residual risks or basis risk.

The second mismatch can occur when the foreign currency amount does not exactly match the contract size of the futures. For example, if DEC was to receive US$ 6.05 million, then do we hedge with 60 contracts and leave the remaining US$ 50,000 unhedged? Or do we short 61 contracts and be "over hedged"? The transaction costs of hedging, the risk averseness of the firm's management, and the materiality of the basis risk would all be considerations in the decision. Suppose if there is a mismatch in both the quantity and maturity, what should the firm do? It is typically in situations like this that the firm might decide to use forwards instead of futures contracts. Being an OTC instrument, forwards are customizable and so can be structured to fit one's exact needs. The trade-off is that forwards are typically more expensive and offer none of liquidity that enables one to reverse out positions in futures contracts.

A final type of mismatch is an asset mismatch, that is, the underlying asset of the derivative, which is available for hedging, is different from the asset from which one's exposure arises. Such asset mismatches are very common where currency risk management is concerned. Except for the major currencies where an array of derivatives, forwards, futures, options, and swaps may be readily available, most currencies, especially emerging market currencies, do not. So, suppose DEC in the earlier example also exports to Vietnam and has a Vietnamese Dong exposure, how can DEC hedge? If DEC can negotiate a customized forward contract with a Vietnamese bank, the problem is solved. But issues of pricing, transparency, even counterparty risk remain. One alternative for DEC to consider would be to cross hedge its Vietnamese Dong exposure with another derivative-based currency that has a high correlation with the Vietnamese Dong. For example, suppose the Singapore Dollar is found to have a sufficiently high correlation with the Vietnamese Dong. DEC can hedge its Dong exposure with available Singapore Dollar futures contracts. However, based on the size of the correlation, a hedge ratio has to be estimated and the contract size adjusted accordingly. Even so, since correlations are based on historical trends that need not hold in the future, cross hedging invariably involves some amount of basis risk.

5.12.2 Speculating with Currency Futures

Speculators, as we have discussed earlier, use derivatives to profit from their expectations. As such, the majority of speculative positions are single positions with no offsetting positions in the spot asset. These *naked positions* can be profitable if the speculator's expectation comes true but would be loss making otherwise. Speculators like using derivatives instead of the spot asset in taking positions since derivatives provide automatic *inbuilt* leverage and ease of entry and exit. Futures contracts, for example, only require the placement of an initial margin, which is a small percentage of the contract value. A 10% initial margin implies a leverage factor of 10 times, an 8% margin a leverage factor of 12.5 times. Since full payment is needed in the spot asset, there is no inbuilt leverage. A speculator with a million dollars to invest could take a futures position in the underlying asset of $10 million if the initial margin is 10%. This larger exposure simply increases the potential for profit by an equal number of times. For example, a 12% increase in the price of the underlying asset will lead to a 12% profit rate if the speculator invests all $1 million in the spot asset. However, a $1 million position in futures would provide a 120% profit, since the position was 10 times larger. This is the magnifying power of leverage. However, leverage can be a double-edged sword. Should the underlying asset's price go down 12%, the speculator's entire position in futures could be wiped out if he has no additional funds for margins. We examine below two speculative positions with US$/CNH currency futures.

(i) A Speculator Expects US$ to Appreciate Against CNH in the Near Future
— The US$/CNH 3-month futures is = 0.1558 or CNH 6.4150 per US$.
— Amount available for investment US$ 100,000 or 1 contract.

Since he is bullish about the US$, his strategy should be: ***long 1 three-month futures contract.***

Scenario 1: US$ Appreciates 5%
Assume his expectation was correct and the spot exchange rate at futures maturity is 0.1480.

Convergence will mean that the futures will also expire at 0.1480 or CNH 6.7567 per US$.

The profit can be determined as (Sell Price − Buy Price) × Contract Size.
At this rate his profit will be [(1/0.1480) − (1/0.1558)] × 100.000 = [6.7567 − 6.4150] × 100.000
$$= \textbf{CNH 34,170}$$

Scenario 2: US$ Depreciates 5%
In this case, suppose the spot price at futures maturity is 0.1635 or CNH 6.1162 per US$. Since he had gone long, his losses will be

$$[6.1162 - 6.4150] \times 100{,}000 = \textbf{(CNH 29,880)}$$

(ii) Speculator Expects US$ to Depreciate Against CNH in the Near Future
Since he is now bearish about the US$, his strategy should now be: ***short 1 three-month futures contract.*** Using the earlier information,

Scenario 1: US$ Depreciates 5%

In this case, the spot price at futures maturity will be 0.1635 or CNH 6.1162 per US$. Since he had gone short and sold at the earlier futures price and buys back to deliver at the lower spot price at maturity, his profit will be:

$$[(6.4150 - 6.1162)] \times 100{,}000 = \textbf{CNH 29{,}880}$$

Scenario 2: US$ Appreciates 5%

As the speculator had shorted the futures contract expecting that to take advantage of a depreciating dollar, the US$'s appreciation will lead to losses. At 5% appreciation, the spot rate at maturity will be 0.1480 or CNH 6.7567 per US$. Thus, his losses will be:

$$[(6.4150 - 6.7567)] \times 100{,}000 = \textbf{(CNH 34{,}170)}$$

As the earlier examples show, speculation has no offsetting positions and so, the profit or loss depends entirely on whether the rates moved according to the direction expected and the size of the move. If exchange rates moved in a direction opposite to what was expected and the size of the move was large, the losses can be substantial. As discussed in chapter, exchanges protect themselves from the counterparty risk of speculators by way of the margining process and daily marking to market. A speculator in a losing position will be forced to fork out margins as the losses increase (price moves in the opposite direction) and inability to pay margins will mean forfeiting all posted margins and taking the losses.

5.12.3 Arbitraging with Currency Futures

The third common use of derivatives are for arbitraging when there is mispricing. Although the profits from arbitrage accrue only to the arbitrageurs, society benefits as arbitrage activity brings prices back in line and thereby improves pricing efficiency. In currency markets, program-trading that involves the use of high-speed computers to track exchange rates in real time across the major money centers of the world, and arbitrage any relative deviations across these markets has meant that global currency markets are highly price efficient.

To understand how arbitrage can be executed with currency futures, we use the background information provided for the US$/CNH futures above and make additional assumptions. Recall from earlier that the spot, 3-month futures and the interest rates were the following:

Spot Exchange Rate
— Spot Quote = US$ 0.1550 per CNH
              = 6.4512 CNH per US$

Interest Rates
US Interest rate — annualized T-bill rate

— 3 months = 0.05%

China Interest Rates — Shanghai Interbank Offer Rate (SHIBOR)

— 3 month (SHIBOR) = 2.3570

Based on these, using Equation 4 from earlier, we determined the correct price of the 3-month futures contract to be;

$$F_{90} = 6.4516 \,[(1 + 0.02357)/(1 + 0.0005)]^{0.25} = 6.4885$$

(i) Futures Mispricing — US$ Overpriced Against CNH or CNH Underpriced Against US$

What if the quoted 3-month/90-day USD/CNH futures price on HKEX is 7.1275 and not 6.4885 as it should be. Clearly the futures contract is mispriced relative to its spot and interest rates. This mispricing gives rise to a riskless or pure arbitrage opportunity. To illustrate the arbitrage strategy and the profit that can be made, we assume the arbitrageur has US$ 1 million to invest in the arbitrage. We again ignore costs of margins, bid-ask spreads, brokerage costs, etc.

To understand the steps below, note that at the futures price of 7.1275, the US$ is overpriced or overvalued relative to the CNH. The arbitrage rule is always to short the overpriced asset and long the underpriced one. So, we need to short the futures contract and go long the Chinese currency at the spot rate. Table 5.5(a) outlines the arbitrage strategy and the resulting profit.

In the first step, 10 USD/CNH futures contracts are shorted. Ten contracts because each contract has a size US$ 100,000 and the arbitrage amount is US$ 1 million. That first action has no cash flow impact today (recall, we ignore margins and transaction costs) but has two cash flow implications at maturity. At maturity, the US$ 1 million has to be delivered and so it is an outflow (negative). In exchange for delivering the US$ 1 million, we receive the CNH amount of 7,127,584, which based on the futures rate.

In step two, we borrow an amount (present value) of CNY which with compounded interest will equal the CNY amount we receive on futures maturity in 3 months. The interest rate is the Chinese 3-month annualized interest rate which is quoted at 2.3570%. Note that this annualized rate has to be divided by 4 since the borrowing is only for 3 months. Next, in step 3, we convert the CNY borrowed to US$ at the quoted spot rate of 0.1550. Since conversion requires the payment (outflow) of CNY, it is negative, while the US$ is received, inflow (positive). In the final step 4, we immediately place an amount of the US$ in hand, as a 3-month deposit in the US at the quoted interest rate of 0.05%. Again the 0.05% annualized rate has to be divided by 4. Given the US interest rate, we need to place US$ 999, 875 in order to have US$ 1 million in 3 months, to coincide with the futures maturity. The US$ 1 million that has accrued at the US bank is used to deliver on the futures contract in step 1. Note that all the steps are done today, and an arbitrage profit of US$ 98,412 is earned immediately. This profit amount is directly dependent on the size of the mispricing. If we work out the percentage mispricing of the futures:

$$[(7.1275 - 6.4885)/6.4885] \times 100 = 9.84\%$$

Table 5.5(a)   Arbitrage Strategy — US$ Overpriced Against CNH in Futures Contract

Action	Cash Flow Today	Cash Flow at Maturity
Short 10 three-month USD/CNH futures	–	(US$ 1,000,000) CNY 7,127,584
Borrow PV of CNY 7,127,584 for 3 months in China at 2.3570% annualized	CNY 7,085,778*	(CNY 7,127,584)**
Convert the CNY to US$ at spot rate	(CNY 7.085,778) US$ 1,098,296	–
Deposit PV of $1 million for 3 months in US at 0.05% annualized	(US$ 999,875)***	US$ 1,000,000
Net Cash Flow	US$ 98,421	0

*Determined as CNY 7,127,584/(1.0059).
**CNY 7,085,778 (1.0059).
*** S$ 1,000,000/(1.000125).

Notice that the 9.84% equals the profit earned in the arbitrage above in percentages terms, since the investment size was US$ 1,000,000:

$$[US\$\ 98{,}421/\$1{,}000{,}000] \times 100 = 9.84\%$$

(ii) Futures Mispricing — US$ Underpriced Against CNH or CNH Overpriced Against US$
We now examine another scenario of futures mispricing. Suppose now the 3-month futures is being quoted at CNH 6.0000 per US$. Once again, the futures is mispriced, since the correct price should be CNH 6.4885 per US$. At 6.0000, the futures is now underpriced. In currency terms, the US$ is now overpriced while the CNH is overpriced. Thus, the arbitrage strategy now should be the exact opposite of the earlier strategy. Table 5.5(b) outlines the arbitrage strategy and the resulting profit for a US$ 1 million equivalent investment.

The arbitrage earns a riskless profit of US$ 75,330. This profit is riskless because as is evident the cash flows net off leaving the profit as residue. This profit is earned immediately (today) upon execution with no subsequent risk. The size of the profit in this second case is lower than earlier simply because the size of the futures mispricing is smaller; 7.5% versus 9.4% in the earlier case.

$$[(6.0000 - 6.4885)/6.4885] \times 100 = 7.52\%$$

Notice that the 7.52% equals the profit earned in the arbitrage above in percentages terms, since the investment size was US$ 1,000,000: [US$ 75,330/$1,000,000] × 100 = 7.53%, the slight difference being due to rounding.

Arbitrage is always profitable provided the magnitude of the mispricing is larger than the transaction costs. Recall from Chapter 3, the discussion of no-arbitrage bounds. As long as the deviation places the mispricing outside the no arbitrage bounds, the arbitrage will be profitable even after accounting for all transaction costs. Where the mispricing is so small that it falls within the arbitrage bounds, the implication is that the potential arbitrage profits will be lower than the transaction costs.

Table 5.5(b)   Arbitrage Strategy — US$ Underpriced Against CNH in Futures Contract

Action	Cash Flow Today	Cash Flow at Maturity
Long 10 three-month USD/CNH futures	–	US$ 1,000,000 (CNY 6,000,000)
Borrow PV of US$ 1 million for 3 months in US at 0.05% annualized	US$ 999,875	(US$ 1,000,000)
Using the borrowed US$, buy CNY equivalent to PV of 6 million in 3 months	(US$ 924,545) CNY 5,964,808	–
Deposit PV of CNY 6,000,000 in China for 3 months at 2.3570% annualized	(CNY 5,964,808)	CNY 6,000,000
Net Cash Flow	US$ 75,330	0

Box 5.2
Capital Flows, Currency Derivatives, and Regulatory Arbitrage

Recent events in Australia show the extent to which cross border capital flows can arbitrage regulatory hurdles. It appears that in an effort to rein in a burgeoning housing bubble, the Australian central bank, The Reserve Bank of Australia (RBA) had placed caps on bank lending to real estate developers. The policy, aimed largely at curbing purchases of Australian homes by foreigners through domestic borrowing, had initially been effective. In addition to foreign speculators, domestic housing developers too were hit hard. Such regulation would have essentially taken the wind out of a domestic housing bubble, had it not been for foreign hedge funds and private equity. Given free capital flows, these foreign entities which are really shadow banks stepped in to provide the needed funding, obviously at higher interest rates. At least for now, the foreign lenders, appear to be making huge profits from the large interest spreads. Their currency exposure can be hedged using currency derivatives. For both the foreign lenders and the foreign speculators of Australian property, the ability to side step the regulation

Box 5.2
(Continued)

appears to be a win-win. The obvious loser is the Australian central bank, the RBA. Not only has its initiative to curb the housing bubble been rendered ineffective, its policy has given rise to profitable regulatory arbitrage. Interest rates on home financing which were at about 6% prior to the RBA policy, were now being funded at 12%. A highly profitable 6% spread to the foreign capital providers with their currency exposure hedged. Thus, despite the fact that the underlying project risk was in no way any different post regulation, the foreign shadow banks were earning equity-like returns from low risk home financing.

This episode amply illustrates the limits of regulation and policy making in a globalized world with free capital flows. For central banks in particular, domestic monetary policy becomes less effective if not impotent. And it arises from the classic "trilemma" in International finance, which argues that domestic monetary policy independence is not possible in the face of free capital flows and/or fixed exchange rates. Although Australia certainly does not have fixed exchange rates nor was the regulatory change above one of broad monetary policy but a targeted attempt at curbing excesses within a sector, it nevertheless resulted in regulation giving rise to arbitrage opportunity. Arbitrage opportunity arises whenever regulation tries to create artificial barriers. As implied by the "trilemma," an independent rate decision even for a specific sector is not possible with free capital flows. While domestic banks are subject to RBA requirements, foreign hedge funds are not. In the absence of capital controls there is nothing to prevent them from stepping in to fill a vacuum created by regulation. The RBA may be the most obvious loser but there is more. Domestic banks that could not benefit from the enlarged spreads are losers too. So, too the Australian family looking to purchase a home of their own.

There are important lessons from the Australian episode for policymakers, particularly of emerging economies. The first and obvious lesson is the fact that in the globalized world that we now live in, regulation that seeks to distort or puts up barriers can be arbitraged away. Aside from eroding policy effectiveness, the outcomes may be diametrically opposite to what was intended. Second, policy options may not be as clear cut as they once were. The trade-offs are increasingly complex and their outcomes increasingly uncertain. The third key lesson is that with the advances in information technology, financial borders have become highly porous. Money and capital can be moved across borders in so many ways and with easy to derivatives, the resulting currency exposure can be hedged. Regulation by way of licensing which by creating

(Continued)

Box 5.2
(*Continued*)

barriers increased the franchise values can now be arbitraged. Entire industries/sectors can be "uberized." Where the profit potential is large and some of the risks can be hedged using currency derivatives, speculative capital will seek out opportunities. The solution lies not in capital controls which can be hugely distortionary but in smart regulation that takes advantage of, rather than go against the grain of technological changes. Enlightened governments and clever policymakers should be able to see the writing on the wall.

Source: Adapted from author's op-ed piece — February 2018.

SUMMARY

This chapter provided an in-depth analysis and description of interest rate futures and currency futures contracts. The interest rate futures contracts examined were the 3-month KLIBOR futures traded on BMDB, the 3-month BIBOR futures traded on TFEX, and a bond futures contract, the 10-year Mini JGB futures contract traded on SGX. The currency futures contract studied was the HKEX's CNH/US$ currency futures. The trading and application of these contracts were examined. The chapter began with a discussion of the mechanics and pricing of interest rate futures contracts. In determining the equilibrium or "correct" futures price, one determines the implied forward rate (IFR). Given the IFR, we can easily determine what the correct futures price should be. The IFR is computed using two other available spot rates.

This was followed by a discussion of interest rate risk. Interest rate risk can occur in four common ways. It can cause a change in the cost of funds, a change in asset values, and induce refinancing risk and reinvestment risk. The impact of a change in interest rates on bond assets and the impact duration on rate sensitivity were also examined. Interest rate futures contracts are priced in terms of an index. The JGB bond futures are priced in units. The pricing convention is such that prices are inversely correlated to interest rates.

As with other derivative instruments, interest rate and currency futures contracts can be used for hedging, arbitraging, and speculation. In using interest rate futures for hedging, borrowers can use it to lock-in the cost of borrowing whereas lenders/bankers can lock-in the interest spreads to protect their profit margins. Currency futures enable users to hedge by locking-in the home currency revenue arising from foreign currency receivables, or the home currency cost arising from foreign currency payables. Currency futures enable the management of exchange rate risks. As with interest rate futures, the value of a currency futures contract is also dependent on interest rates, in this case the relative interest rates of the two currencies in an exchange rate.

The chapter also examined the key determinants of interest rate movements. The role of the government, in particular the monetary policy stance, the rate of inflation, the growth cycle, and expectations are key determinants.

KEY TERMS

- Interest rate risk
- Refinancing risk
- Reinvestment risk
- Floating interest rates
- Bond yields
- Yield curve
- Bond ratings
- Bond futures
- Currency exposure
- Currency futures

- Duration analysis
- Price sensitivity
- KLIBOR rates
- Implied forward rate
- Tenor
- Interest spreads
- Nominal vs real rates
- Fixed vs floating exchange rates

End-of-Chapter Questions

1. a. Describe the relationship between interest rates, required yields, and bond prices.
   b. Define what is meant by interest rate risk.
   c. What is the justification for the 3-month tenor for short-term IRF contracts?
   d. For the following quotes, state the yields in percent.
      (i) 93.65
      (ii) 91.28
      (iii) 94.60
      (iv) 92.30
   e. If the real interest rate is 3.5% and the inflation rate is 8%, what should the prevailing nominal interest rate be?

2. You have just received the following information from your broker regarding spot rates.
   - 3-month KLIBOR = 6.5% (90 days maturity)
   - 6-month KLIBOR = 8.5% (180 days maturity)

   Given these rates,
   a. What is the IFR?
   b. What would be the correct price of a 3-month KLIBOR futures contract?
   c. Rework (a) and (b) assuming all information is for the 3-month BIBOR. Are there any differences?

3. As Treasurer of Gombak Finance Corp. you are worried about the potential interest rate risk on a fixed rate 3-month RM 12 million loan you have promised a customer. The loan will be taken 90 days from today and you had priced the loan at 11% per annum. Your company's cost of funds is the KLIBOR rate. Today's quotations are as follows:
   - 3-month KLIBOR   = 8%
   - 3-month KLIBOR futures = 91

   a. Outline the appropriate hedging strategy to protect your company from interest rate risk.
   b. Suppose interest rates rise by 1.5% over the next 3 months, prove that your hedge strategy above would have protected your interest spread or total earnings.

4. a. Your money market broker quotes you the following spot rates.
   - 3-month KLIBOR = 8%
   - 6-month KLIBOR = 9.5%

   What should the correct price of a 3-month KLIBOR futures contract be?
   b. Your friend, a prominent economist, forecasts that interest rates will increase over the next 90 days. If 3-month KLIBOR futures is being quoted at 90.00 and you are willing to risk RM 2 million, how can you take advantage of your friend's forecast if interest rates indeed go up 1% over the 90 days? What would your profit or loss be?

5. As credit officer of a large bank, you have agreed to provide an important institutional customer with a fixed rate 3-month RM 20 million loan 90 days from today. You had priced the loan at 12% annual interest rate. Assuming your cost of funds is the KLIBOR rate and the following quotes are now available.
   - 3-month KLIBOR = 9%
   - 3-month KLIBOR futures = 90.0 (matures in 90 days)

   a. How would you protect yourself from a rise in interest rates? (Outline the strategy.)
   b. Assuming interest rates rise by 2% over the next 3 months, show using computation that you would have locked in the interest spread.

6. Mr. Tan, the Treasurer of City Finance Corp., has just determined that there will be a THB 180 million "shortfall" (negative gap) for City Finance, 3 months from now. That amount will have to be raised in the interbank market. City's cost of funds is the BIBOR rate. City has priced its medium/longer term loans to yield a 2% spread (profit margin) based on expected 3-month rates. The loans are at fixed rate. Mr. Tan is, however, worried about the interest exposure. Assuming the following quotes are available now.
   - 1-month BIBOR = 6.8%
   - 3-month BIBOR = 7.0%
   - Spot-month BIBOR futures = 93.00
   - 3-month BIBOR futures = 92.00

   a. What is the interest rate that Mr. Tan should aim to "lock in"?
   b. Outline the hedge strategy (specify clearly).
   c. Assuming the spot 3-month BIBOR is the higher by 1.5%, 3 months later, analyze the hedge, and proof that using your strategy, the intended interest rate or spread has indeed been locked in.

7. Mr Amir, Treasurer of Gombak Finance Berhad, has just completed a Maturity Bucket Analysis based on a 6-month horizon. *(This question requires material discussed in Appendix 1.)*

Month	1	2	3	4	5	6	Total
RSA (RM million)	22	84	80	60	72	120	438
RSL (RM million)	26	80	160	60	64	50	440
GAP (RM million)	−4	+4	−80	0	+8	+70	−2

   a. If the market expectation is an increase in interest rates, which maturity bucket should Encik Amir worry most about? Explain why the particular bucket matters.
   b. Outline an appropriate hedge strategy for Encik Amir.
   c. Suppose the following quotes are available.

   Spot
   1-month KLIBOR = 4.0%
   3-month KLIBOR = 5.0%
   6-month KLIBOR = 5.5%

   Futures
   Maturing in 1-month KLIBOR futures = 95.5
   3-month KLIBOR futures = 94.0
   Maturing in 6-month KLIBOR futures = 93.0

What interest rate can Mr Amir "lock in" using your strategy in (b)? Assuming the 3-month KLIBOR is up 2% over the period of your strategy, prove mathematically that Encik Amir is hedged and has locked in his cost of funds.

8. You work at the arbitrage desk of a large insurance firm. Your job is to identify and exploit arbitrage opportunities. You notice the following quotes.
   - 3-month KLIBOR = 7.2%
   - 6-month KLIBOR = 8.5%
   - 3-month KLIBOR futures = 92.50

   a. Proof that arbitrage is possible.
   b. Outline the appropriate arbitrage strategy.
   c. Assuming you can invest/risk up to RM 10 million, determine the profit you would make if the 3-month KLIBOR is at 9.0% on futures maturity.

9. You are the CFO of Gombak Enterprises Berhad (GEB). Your company has just received a shipment of raw materials. Payment on these goods of RM 30 million will be due in 90 days. Your banker, Maybank, has agreed to provide you a 3-month RM 30 million loan at KLIBOR + 2%. The spot 3-month KLIBOR is now quoted at 6%, whereas the KLIBOR futures is priced at 93.00.
   a. What risk is the company exposed to? State three different instruments that could be used by GEB to hedge the risk.
   b. Using KLIBOR futures, proof mathematically, that regardless of whether the interest rate goes up or down by 2% over the next 90 days, GEB's cost is locked in.

10. It is March 24, you notice the following spot market quotations.
    - 3-month BIBOR = 6.75%
    - 6-month BIBOR = 8%

    The 3-month BIBOR futures is priced at 93.00 (maturing June 24).

    a. Is there mispricing?
    b. How would you arbitrage?
    c. Assuming the 3-month BIBOR rate on June 24 is 9%, show the profit you would make per contract.

11. Your company has just completed the structuring of a short term 3-month loan. The financier will provide the RM 50 million loan in 3 months at KLIBOR + 0.5%. At present, the KLIBOR spot and futures are as follows:
    - 3-month KLIBOR = 4.5%
    - 3-month KLIBOR futures = 5.5%

    a. Identify the risk faced. Show how you would manage the risk using KLIBOR futures; outline your strategy.
    b. Prove mathematically that given your strategy in (a), your cost of funds is constant regardless of a 2% change in rates in either direction.

Questions 12–15 require material discussed in the Appendix that follows.

12. The treasurer of Jardine Finance Bhd. has just received the following maturity statement from his subordinate (all amounts are in RM million).

Maturing in Month	Maturing Rate-Sensitive Assets	Maturing Rate-Sensitive Liabilities
1	36	34
2	48	44
3	76	24
4	64	66
5	96	93
6	60	96
Total	380	357

    a. For the full 6-month horizon (basic gap), should the treasurer be worried about a rise or fall in interest rates? Why?
    b. If the treasurer is expecting a fall in interest rates, which monthly maturity bucket should he worry about? Which should he worry about if the expectation is a rise in interest rates?
    c. Assume the treasurer is worried about falling interest rates. The KLIBOR spot and futures prices are as follows:
       - 3-month KLIBOR = 4.5%
       - 6-month KLIBOR = 5.0%
       - KLIBOR futures (maturing 3 months) = 96.00
       - KLIBOR futures (maturing 6 months) = 95.50

       Outline the strategy by which the treasurer can protect his firm from falling interest rates. Prove that even if rates fell by 2.0% over the period you have chosen to hedge, the treasurer will still be able to lock-in a predetermined rate.

13. a. Describe at least four ways by which an increase in interest rates could affect banks.
    b. Why is it that duration mismatches are inherent to banks?
    c. Which is better for banks, a positively sloped yield curve, a flat yield curve, or an inverted one? Briefly explain why.

14. a. Compare and contrast an income gap, basic gap, and maturity bucket approach. What are the gaps measuring? How is the basic gap analysis different from the maturity bucket approach?
    b. Differentiate between the income gap analysis and the duration gap analysis. What are they measuring? When should you use each method?

15. Bank A has asset side duration of 8 years and liability side duration of 2 years.
    a. How will rising interest rates affect the bank? Positively or negatively?
    b. How will falling interest rates affect it?
    c. If interest rates were to rise by 5%, what would be the extent of change in asset and liability values?
    d. What would the impact be on the bank's net worth?

16. a. Determine the correct price of a 10-year Mini JGB futures contract with an indicative annual coupon of 6% paid semiannually, if your required return is 4%.
    b. What will the coupon rate have to be if the 10-year Mini JGB futures contract is to be sold at par?
17. The 10-year Mini JGB futures with a 6% annual coupon is currently priced to yield a 3% return. Suppose a speculator is expecting interest rates to fall over the next 6 months.
    a. Outline the appropriate speculative strategy.
    b. If rates indeed fall by 1% 6 months later, determine the profit/loss, assuming he invests in one contract.
18. Why has there been a visible decline in the traded volume of Interest rate derivatives? Why is the decline a global trend?
19. The annualized 3-month interest rate in the US and China are 1.5% and 2.8%, respectively. Suppose the spot rate is 6.80 CNH per US$.
    (i) Determine the correct price of the 3-month CNH/US$ currency futures contract.
    (ii) If the 3-month currency futures is being quoted at 6.82, is the futures correctly priced?
    (iii) Which currency is overvalued/undervalued in the futures contract?
    (iv) If a speculator expects the CNH which is currently at 6.80 to the US$, to be 6.70 in 3 months, outline the appropriate strategy for the speculator.
    (v) Suppose the speculator goes short two futures contracts at 6.80 CNH per US$ and spot rate at maturity is 6.735 CNH per US$, what is his profit or loss?
20. A Shenzhen, China-based producer of food condiments has just completed a shipment to a US food retail chain. The invoice amount of US$ 12 million will be due in 90 days. The current spot rate is 6.46 CNH per US$. The 90-day currency futures on the HKEX is quoted at 6.435 CNH per US$.
    (i) Outline an appropriate hedge strategy for the Chinese exporter.
    (ii) Ignoring transaction and margin costs, what Renminbi amount can the Chinese exporter lock-in using futures?
    (iii) Proof that the hedge will protect even if the US$ depreciates to 6.30 on day 90.

Appendix

This appendix extends our examination of interest rate risk from a bank's viewpoint. We see how banks can estimate their interest exposure and manage them. From a bank's point of view, interest rate risk can be defined broadly as the impact of an interest rate change on a bank's profits, cash flows and net worth. Since banks are intermediaries between depositors (surplus units) and borrowers (deficit units) and earn their income largely from the interest differential or spread between the two units, banks are inherently exposed to interest rate risk. This risk has been made worse by the fact that banks have little influence over the composition of their liabilities, i.e., their deposit structure. Though interest rate risk had always been present, its relevance has become important since the 1980s in the developed economies. Since the early 1980s, interest rates have been much more volatile. This had to do with the increased inflationary environment of the early/mid-1980s, the movement to a floating exchange rate regime and the deregulation — particularly in the US. If interest rates are stable with the term structure (yield curve) positively sloped, then short-term rates are generally lower than long-term rates. ($< i_L$.) In such an interest rate environment, banks need merely pay short-term rates on deposits and charge long-term rates on loans. The stable spreads ensure stable earnings and a consistent increase in net worth. This cozy situation began to change with interest rate volatility.

Why Interest Rate Risk Matters

When interest rates rise — especially if the rise is consistent — banks face a number of problems:

(a) Cost of funds increase — since a bank would have to pay higher rates in order to attract new deposits.
(b) In competitive environments, the bank would have to pay higher rates even on existing deposits (e.g., savings accounts). Failing which the bank could see outflows on the deposit side (withdrawals, non-renewals, etc.).
(c) The deposit profile could change, i.e., the proportions in current accounts could reduce, whereas that of short-term FDs, savings, etc., could increase. This results from depositors switching accounts.
(d) Although the bank faces higher costs on the liabilities side, its earnings from assets would most likely not keep pace with the rate of increase. *As a result, the bank's income margin gets squeezed.*
(e) Given the typically longer maturity structure (duration) of the asset side compared to liabilities, there will be a differential impact in terms of *market values*. That is, the value of the assets would fall *more* than the fall in liability value. *As a result, the bank's net worth gets squeezed.*

We can summarize the impact of rising interest rates as (i) a potential reduction in income and (ii) reduction in net worth. Both of these would be undesirable. (Note: A steady and consistent fall in interest rates would have the opposite effect.) We now turn to examining each of these two overall problems and analyze how a bank could "manage" or hedge the risk.

Managing Interest Rate Risk

Gap analysis or "Gapping" is a common technique used in managing interest rate risk. Gap analysis is often used by banks in two common forms, i.e., *income gap analysis (IGA)* and *duration gap analysis*. IGA focuses solely on the impact of an interest rate change on a bank's *income*. Duration gap analysis, on the other hand, analyzes the impact of an interest rate change on a bank's *net worth*.

(I) Income Gap Analysis

The simplest form of an IGA is the basic gap analysis. Here, a bank treasurer takes a given time horizon, e.g., the current year, and examines the impact of interest rate change on current annual income/earnings. The first step in this analysis would be to determine the total Ringgit amounts of *rate-sensitive assets (RSA)* and *rate-sensitive liabilities (RSL)* for the 1-year horizon. The treasurer does this by examining the bank's current balance sheet and identifying which asset and liability items are rate sensitive. Given his 1-year time horizon, he examines each balance sheet item to identify those that have to be *repriced* or interest *reset within the year*. By this logic, items like floating rate loans (assets), variable rate deposits (liabilities), loans maturing within the year, marketable securities maturing within the year and money market deposits accounts would all be considered rate sensitive.

Although there are some obvious RSAs and liabilities such as those earlier, there are also some obviously *non-RSAs* and liabilities. Assets such as cash, liquidity reserves, physical assets, and liabilities like shareholders equity and long-term borrowings would fall in this category. In between these obviously rate-sensitive and nonsensitive items are items where the treasurer may have to make a judgment call. For example, medium- and long-term loans provided by the bank on fixed rates clearly do not involve a reset, yet some amount of this may be prepaid. Similarly, current accounts pay no interest and are not rate sensitive; however, in a rising interest rate environment, switching could occur. Given these realities, the treasurer would have to make an estimate of the likely percentage of prepayment and account switching. Examining the bank's past experience with prepayment, etc., should give the treasurer a reasonable estimate. Once this first step is done (determining the total amount of RSAs and liabilities), the next two steps are straight forward. The second step involves determining the gap between rate-sensitive assets and liabilities. With the gap estimate, the treasurer can determine the Ringgit impact on earnings as a result of his forecast change in interest rate.

Basic Gap Analysis — An Illustration

Suppose a treasurer on examining his bank balance sheet identifies the following items as having *less than 1-year maturity*.

Assets
- Marketable securities   RM 60 million
- Overdrafts   RM 120 million
- Variable rate housing loans   RM 100 million
- Variable rate term loans   RM 120 million
- Loans and advances (fixed < 1 year)   <u>RM 140 million</u>

Total   RM 540 million

Liabilities
- NCDs/NIDs   RM 160 million
- Short-term deposits (< 1 year) RM 200 million
- Other variable rate borrowings <u>RM 260 million</u>

Total   RM 620 million

In addition, to these obvious items, let us say the treasurer considers that 3% of fixed rate loans (RM 40 million) on the asset side and 6% of fixed deposits with greater than 1 year maturity (RM 80 million) can be considered rate sensitive based on prior experience.

Thus,

RSA = RM 540 + RM 40
    = RM 580
RSL = RM 620 + RM 80
    = RM 700

Based on these amounts, the gap is
Gap = RSA − RSL
    = RM 580 − RM 700
    = −RM 120 million

If the treasurer expects interest rates to rise an average 5% this year, the impact on the banks income/earnings for the year can be determined as follows:

Δ Income = Gap × Δi
        = −RM 120 million × 5%
        = −RM 6 million

Thus, given the bank's current situation and interest rate outlook, the bank's earnings for the year will be *reduced* by approximately RM 6 million.

Note: The bank had a negative gap since RSA < RSL. Generally, *when interest rates rise,*

+ Gap will mean increased earnings.
− Gap will mean reduced earnings.

when interest rates fall,

+ Gap will mean reduced earnings.
− Gap will mean increased earnings.

The aforementioned analysis which is often known as *basic gap analysis* has two problems. First, the result depends on the time horizon chosen (1 year versus 6 months) and second, the treasurer would not be able to tell *when during* the year does the bank have the most serious gap. A more refined approach is often used by banks. This is known as the *maturity bucket approach.*

The Maturity Bucket Approach

This approach is intended to overcome in particular, the second problem, i.e., to enable one to know when the gap is most acute. Furthermore, by being a multiperiod approach and extending beyond a year, the time horizon restriction is overcome. Though the underlying logic and analytical steps are the same, the maturity bucket approach splits the gap analysis into several interval periods. For example, to determine the gaps on a monthly or quarterly basis.

Maturity Bucket Approach: An Illustration

Mr. Tan, the treasurer of KL Finance Bhd., has just determined based on a 6-month time horizon that the total RSAs and liabilities are RM 480 million and RM 600 million, respectively. He realizes that a 3% increase in average interest rates can have serious consequences on his company's earnings.

Gap = RM 480 − RM 600
= −RM 120 million
Δ Income = −RM 120 × 3%
= −RM 3.60 million

Although he does know what the overall impact would be, he intends to refine the analysis on a monthly basis to examine where the main gaps are. The following table shows the maturity bucket analysis based on an assumed breakdown of assets and liabilities.

Monthly Maturity Bucket KL Finance Berhad

Month	1	2	3	4	5	6	Total
RSA (Maturing) (RM millions)	40	60	80	80	100	120	480
RSL (Maturing) (RM millions)	100	60	280	60	60	40	600
Gap (RM Millions)	−60	0	−200	+20	+40	+80	−120

The earlier basic gap analysis showed that KL Finance could have a problem if interest rates rose. The maturity bucket approach refines the analysis and shows where exactly the problem lies. Clearly KL Finance's serious problems are in the 1-month and 3-month periods (buckets).

This is because it has large negative gaps in those periods. The largest being in the 3-month bucket. Given that the expectation is a *rise* in interest rates, the biggest hit to earnings will come from the negative gaps. The positive gaps in months 4, 5, and 6 will *boost earnings* in that period. This is because the positive gap represents funds that will be "freed" and can therefore be lent at the higher expected interest rates.

Hedging the Interest Rate Risk

Left unhedged, the negative gaps in months 1 and 3 will cause losses should interest rates rise. The risk is essentially one of *refinancing risks*. KL Finance will face a net "outflow" equal to the amount of the gap. Thus, RM 60 million will have to be refinanced in month 1 and RM 200 million in month 3. If rates rise, the cost of funds on these refinancing will increase. However, since the gap amounts would already have been used to finance other assets — nonsensitive assets (this must be the case since total assets must equal to total liabilities in the balance sheet), the company's earnings gets squeezed because while its cost of funds increase, it cannot increase the interest it charges. In protecting KL Finance's income, the treasurer should seek to hedge the refinancing risk.

The most obvious tool that he could use in this situation would be the *KLIBOR IRF contract*. To hedge the two negative gaps, KL Finance would have to short the futures contracts. This is because the negative gap implies that KL Finance would have to refinance or "borrow" amounts equivalent to RM 60 million in month 1 and RM 200 million in month 3. The hedge position should be one that would *profit* when rates increase, such that the treasurer is able to *lock-in* the currently prevailing rates as shown by the futures contracts. To fully hedge the gaps, KL Finance should:

— short 60, spot-month futures contracts
— short 200, 3-month futures contracts

Suppose the treasurer observes the following quotes today.

1-month KLIBOR   = 6.5%
3-month KLIBOR   = 7.0%
Spot-month KLIBOR futures = 93.00
3-month KLIBOR futures   = 92.00

By shorting 60, spot-month futures contracts, and 200, 3-month futures contracts, KL Finance Bhd. would be able to fully offset the impact of any interest rate increase, by being able to *lock in* the current 7% (1-month) and 8% (3-month) yields of the futures contracts. To see how this is possible, we examine below the payoff to the hedged position at the end of 1 month and 3 months (i.e., on the maturity dates) assuming a 1.5% increase in the 1-month rate and 2% increase in the 3-month rate.

Analysis of the Hedged 1-Month Position

Since interest rate increased by 1.5%, the rates on maturity date would be:

1-month KLIBOR = 8%
Spot-month KLIBOR futures = 92.00

Result

Profit from futures position = $(93.00 - 92.00) \times 100 \times 60 \times [RM\ 25 \times 1/3]$
= RM 50,000

Refinancing cost = $8\% \times \dfrac{30}{360} \times RM\ 60\ million$
= RM 400,000

Net cost of funds = RM 400,000 − RM 50,000
= RM 350,000

Effective cost % = $\dfrac{RM\ 350,000}{RM\ 60,000,000} \times 100$
= 0.5833%

Annualized = 0.5833×12
= 7%

Note: This equals the 7.00% refinancing cost that you wanted to "lock in" for the 1-month bucket.

Analysis of the Hedged 3-Month Position

Since interest rate increased by 2% over the 3-month period, the rates on maturity date would be:

3-month KLIBOR = 9.00%
3-month KLIBOR futures = 91.00

Result

Profit from futures position = $(92.00 - 91.00) \times 100 \times 200\ contracts \times RM\ 25$
= RM 500,000

Refinancing cost = $9\% \times \dfrac{90}{360} \times RM\ 200\ million$
= RM 4,500,000

Net cost of funds = RM 4,500,000 − RM 500,000
= RM 4,000,000

Effective cost % = $\dfrac{RM\ 4\ million}{RM\ 200\ million} \times 100$
= 2%

Annualized = $2\% \times 4$
= 8%

Note: This is the 8% refinancing cost that you intended to "lock in" for the 3-month bucket.

(II) Duration Gap Analysis

This second form of gapping analysis is intended to evaluate the impact of an interest rate change on a bank's net worth. The impact on net worth is the result of changes in market values of assets and liabilities. When interest rates change, the market values of assets and liabilities change. The rate of change or sensitivity depends on the asset or liability's *duration*. Duration, as we know, is quite simply the weighted average of the maturities of the asset's (or liability's) component cash flows. It therefore differs from maturity. Since duration is maturity adjusted for interim cash flows, the only situation when duration and maturity would be equal is when there are no interim cash flows, i.e., zero coupon bonds. Thus, duration, and not maturity, is the correct measure of an item's interest rate sensitivity. As in the earlier case of IGA, the impact of interest rate change arises from having a non-zero gap. Duration gap analysis involves the following steps.

(I) Determine the duration of each asset and liability item of the balance sheet on which an interest income is earned or paid by the bank.
(II) Find the weight (proportion) of each item within its category. For example, weight of the asset item to total interest earning assets.
(III) Using the result of steps (I) and (II), determine the weighted duration of assets and liabilities.
Determine the gap — by subtracting the duration of liabilities from the duration of assets.[3]

A simple example of the above steps is shown below.

Simplified Bank Balance Sheet
Assets*

	Amount	Proportion/ Weight	Estimated Average Maturity	Estimated Duration
Short-term Loans	RM 400 million	0.40	1.5 years	1 year
Medium-term Loans	RM 200 million	0.20	4.0 years	3 years
Long-term Loans	RM 400 million	0.40	25 years	20 years
Total Assets	RM 1,000 million			

Liabilities*

	Amount	Proportion/ Weight	Estimated Average Maturity	Estimated Duration
Current Accounts	RM 400 million	0.40	00	
Savings Accounts	RM 200 million	0.20	1.5 years	1 year
Fixed Deposits	RM 400 million	0.40	5 years	4 years
Total Liabilities	RM 1,000 million			

*For the purpose of simplicity, we ignore the nonoperational items of the balance sheet.

---

[3] Where the total amount of interest bearing assets and liabilities are not equal.
Duration Gap = Duration Assets $-\left(\frac{L}{A} \times \text{Duration gap}\right)$.

Given the earlier balance sheet, steps (I) and (II) are complete; thus we determine step (III), the weighted duration of assets and liabilities as follows:

Duration of Assets
= [0.40 × 1 year] + [0.20 × 3 years] + [0.40 × 20 years]
= (0.40) + (0.6) + (8)
= 9.0 years

Duration of Liabilities
= [0.40 × 0] + [0.20 × 1 year] + [0.40 × 4 years]
= 0 + (0.20) + (1.6)
= 1.80 years

Duration Gap for Bank

Duration of assets	= 9.0 years
less Duration of liabilities	= 1.8 years
Positive gap	= 7.2 years

What this means is that the above bank is highly exposed to interest rate risk. Since the duration of assets is five times that of liabilities, the fall in market value of assets as a result of an interest increase will be approximately five times more than the fall in the value of liabilities. This can be seen from the following computation (assuming the current interest rate is 10% and increases by 5% to 15%).

$$\Delta \text{ in value of assets} = \%\Delta P - D \times \left[\frac{\Delta i}{(1+i)} \right]$$

$$\Delta \text{ in value of assets} = -9 \times \left[\frac{0.05}{1.10} \right]$$

$$= -0.40909$$

$$\Delta \text{ in value of liabilities} = -1.8 \times \left[\frac{0.05}{1.10} \right]$$

$$= -0.0818$$

$$= -8.18\%$$

Thus, if interest rates increased 5% from current levels, the above bank's asset value will fall 40.9%, whereas the value of its liabilities by 8.18%. (Notice that the fall in assets is five times the fall in liabilities — 40.9/8.18 = 5.) As a result of this differential fall, the bank's net worth will be squeezed. The impact on the bank's net worth can be determined using the following equation.

$$\%\Delta NW = -D_{GAP} \times \left[\frac{\Delta i}{(1+i)} \right]$$

For the bank in our earlier example, the reduction in net worth as a result of the 5% increase in interest rate will be:

$$\%\Delta NW = -7.2 \times \left[\frac{0.05}{1.10}\right]$$
$$= -0.3273$$
$$= -32.72\%$$

Clearly, the bank is highly exposed since a 5% interest rate rise will reduce net worth by approximately 33%.[4] If we assume that the bank's initial net worth was RM 100 million, a 5% interest rate increase will wipe out RM 32.72 million of the net worth. In the Malaysian banking sector, the risk associated with large duration gaps did not receive due attention until the currency crisis of the late 1990s. In its attempt to fight the speculative attack on the Malaysian Ringgit, Bank Negara Malaysia (BNM) had to raise domestic interest rates substantially.

The sudden and sharp interest rate hikes caused serious problems for many local banks that had large duration gaps/mismatches. The squeeze on net worth was so severe that several domestic banks had to be recapitalized. As the problem was not isolated to one or two banks but quite widespread, the Malaysian government had to establish *Danamodal* in order to provide the needed capital infusion to shore-up the banks. As part of post-crisis policy initiatives, all local banks are now required to establish Asset Liability Committees (ALCO) internally. These committees are tasked with monitoring and managing the bank's duration gaps.

---

[4] The Ringgit amount of this fall in net worth can be determined as total assets $\times$ 0.33.

CHAPTER · 6

Introduction to Options

Objectives

This chapter is designed to provide an overview of options, and introduce readers to option terminologies and lay out the basic functions, mechanics, and use of options. On completing this chapter, you should have a good understanding of options, their payoffs, and features.

What Are Options?

Options, like futures and forward contracts, are derivative securities. A derivative asset is essentially a financial instrument whose value is dependent on the value of its underlying asset. For example, an equity option or option written on a stock will change in value as the underlying stock's price goes up or down. Though this is no different from that of futures or forwards, options differ from forwards and futures in an important way. Options **provide the holder the right but not the obligation to exercise**. This is unlike futures and forwards where unless the position is reversed (offset) before maturity, constitute an obligation to exercise at maturity. As we will see later, this nonobligation constitutes a major advantage for options over other financial instruments.

Exchange-traded options first began trading on the Chicago Board Options Exchange (CBOE) in 1973. Thus, they are very new instruments. Despite the newness, trading volume of options has increased dramatically. Today, several exchanges throughout the world have introduced and successfully trade options. In addition to the exchanges that trade standardized option contracts, there is a thriving market in options in the over-the-counter (OTC) market. Options traded on the OTC tend to be the customized kind. Though the initial option contracts were written on equities, i.e., individual stocks, options are now written on a wide variety of underlying instruments. For example, in developed markets, exchange-traded options are available on **common stocks**, **stock indexes**, **foreign currencies**, **commodities**, and even on other derivatives like **interest rate futures**, **stock index futures,** or **swaps**.

> **Note**
> Call options provide the holder the right but not the obligation to buy the underlying asset at the predetermined exercise price.

6.1 Calls and Puts

All exchange-traded options come in two basic forms: calls and puts. A **call option** *provides the holder the right but not the obligation to buy the underlying asset at a predetermined price.*

A **put option** *provides the holder the right but not the obligation to sell the underlying asset at a predetermined price.* The predetermined price at which the transaction will be carried is known as the **exercise price** or **strike** price. Unlike futures/forwards, options require the payment of a premium on purchase. That is, one pays a premium to acquire a call or a put option.

Note
Put options provide the holder the right but not the obligation to sell the underlying asset at the predetermined exercise price.

Depending on whether the option is **American** or **European style**, this right might be exercised at different times. Although a European-style option is only exercisable at maturity, an American option can be exercised at or any time before maturity. Given this additional flexibility, an American option would be more valuable than a European option assuming all other features are the same.

Note
While a European-style option can be exercised only at maturity, an American-style option can be exercised at or any time before maturity.

An option contract therefore should at the very least specify the following five features:

(a) The type of option, whether call or put
(b) The underlying asset
(c) The exercise price or strike price
(d) The maturity or expiration date
(e) The **exercise style**, whether American or European style

Although the long position (buyer) has a right but not the obligation to exercise, the seller or short position is obliged to fulfill the buyer's wants should he choose to exercise. For example, if the buyer of a call option chooses to exercise, i.e., buy the underlying asset at the exercise price, the seller is obligated to provide him the underlying at that price. The opposite would hold for a put option. If the holder of the put chooses to exercise, i.e., choose to sell the underlying at the exercise price, the seller of the put must stand ready to buy the underlying asset at the exercise price. The following table summarizes this relationship.

Position	Calls	Puts
Buyer (Long)	Has the right but not the obligation to buy underlying asset at exercise price.	Has the right but not the obligation to sell underlying asset at exercise price.
Seller (Short)	Is obliged to sell underlying asset at exercise price.	Is obliged to buy underlying asset at exercise price.

When buyers of options choose to exercise, sellers face potential assignment. Assignment refers to the process by which notification is given to sellers that their obligation is due, i.e., they must now sell if they had shorted call options or buy if they had shorted puts.

Why Use Options

Options like other financial instruments can be used for (i) hedging, (ii) arbitrage, and (iii) speculation. One would be tempted to ask why options are needed if all three tasks could be done with existing instruments. For example, one could just as easily use futures to hedge, arbitrage, or speculate. Options, like any other new product is a result of financial innovation; innovation that responded to new needs. As with all new products, the fact that options have become popular implies that there must be additional value added. Unless a new product can do something that existing instruments cannot or at least do them better, the new innovation cannot succeed.

As will be evident, the fact that options provide a right but not an obligation to the holder gives tremendous advantage. This added flexibility is the source of value-added that options have over other financial instruments. A holder need only exercise if it will be profitable for him to do so. For example, let us say you buy a 3-month **American-style** call option on Maybank stock at an exercise price of RM 20 per share. It means that you can exercise your option, i.e., "call it" at RM 20 per share at any time

Note
The main advantage of options is that they enable the holder to benefit from upside potential while limiting the downside risk.

before or on the maturity date in 90 days. Thus, you would only exercise the option if Maybank stock goes higher than RM 20. If the stock does not reach RM 20 by expiration day, the option would be unexercised, simply let to expire. For this privilege you pay to buy the option; this payment being the **option premium**. So, if you don't exercise because the underlying stock did not go higher than the exercise price, the premium paid is a loss to you but a profit/gain to the seller of the option. Note that the maximum you can lose is the amount of premium; however, the potential profit is technically unlimited.

While an unexercised option will become worthless after maturity, prior to maturity the holder can either exercise it (if profitable to do so) or sell it in the secondary market. The price at which it can be sold would of course depend on the expectation of the underlying stock's price at maturity. It is usual that an option will pass through several owners before reaching maturity.

6.2 Payoffs to Investing in Stocks versus Options

An easy way to fully appreciate the flexibility provided by options is by examining the **payoff** diagrams for investment in options versus other positions. The following six diagrams show the payoffs to alternative investment modes on the same stock, ABC Corp. stock which is currently selling at RM 12 each.

(1) A Long Stock Position

You are **bullish** about ABC Corp. stock. It is currently selling at RM 12. Suppose you take a long position in the stock (buy), what is the payoff given the following possible stock prices over say the next 90 days? Table 6.1 shows the profit or loss payoff to a long stock position.

Figure 6.1 is simply a plot of the prices shown in Table 6.1. As stock prices fall, the position loses but gains when price rises. For example, at a stock price of RM 14, the long position profits RM 2 but loses RM 2 at a stock price of RM 10. Since both the potential profit and loss regions are open ended, we define the **risk profile** of the long stock position as one with unlimited profit/loss potential.

Table 6.1   Stock Price at Maturity and Payoffs

Stock Price	(P/L) Payoff
9.50	(9.50)
10.00	(2.00)
10.50	(1.50)
11.00	(1.00)
11.50	(0.50)
12.00	0
12.50	0.50
13.00	1.00
13.50	1.50
14.00	2.00
14.50	2.50

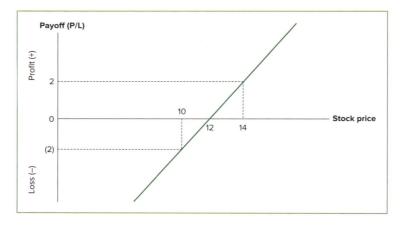

Figure 6.1   Long Stock Position (Outlook: Bullish)

Notice that if you had gone long on a futures or forward contract on the stock at exercise price of RM 12, the payoff would have been exactly as in Figure 6.1. This has to do with the fact that both futures and forwards are obligatory unless reversed out. In this case, the point to the right of RM 12 onwards would constitute "implied" gains, while the area to the left of RM 12 "implied" losses.

(2) A Short Stock Position

Suppose you are **bearish** and decide to short ABC Corp. stock RM 12. The payoff would be as shown in Table 6.2.

Notice that the payoff to the short stock position is the opposite of the long stock position. Here, the short stock position gains when underlying stock price falls and loses when stock price rises. Again, as in the long stock position, the risk profile is one of unlimited profit/loss potential.

Table 6.2 Stock Price at Maturity and Payoffs

Stock Price	(P/L) Payoff
9.50	2.50
10.00	2.00
10.50	1.50
11.00	1.00
11.50	0.50
12.00	0
13.00	(1.00)
13.50	(1.50)
14.00	(2.00)
14.50	(2.50)

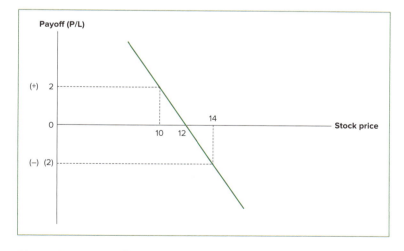

Figure 6.2   Payoff to Short Stock Position (Outlook: Bearish)

That the long stock position gains from rising prices, whereas the short stock position from falling prices, is no different from that of long/short positions in forwards or futures. Had you gone short on a futures contract on the stock at exercise price of RM 12, the payoff would again be the same as that of the short stock position. Now, however, the region to the left of RM 12 would mean implied gains, whereas that to the right implied losses.

(3) A Long Call Position

Suppose you are bullish on ABC Corp. stock but instead of buying (long) the stock, you decide to buy a call option on ABC Corp. stock with an exercise price of RM 12 at 0.20 sen premium. What is the payoff to this long call position? Table 6.3 shows the payoff for a range of underlying stock prices.

As is evident from Figure 6.3, a long call strategy is certainly superior to that of a long stock or long futures position in that the loss potential is now limited to the cost of the premium.

Table 6.3 Stock Price at Maturity and Payoff to Long Call

Stock Price	(P/L) Payoff
9.50	(0.20)
10.00	(0.20)
10.50	(0.20)
11.00	(0.20)
11.50	(0.20)
12.00	(0.20)
12.20	0
12.50	0.30
13.00	0.80
13.50	1.30
14.00	1.80
14.50	2.30

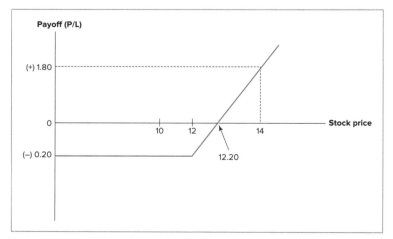

Figure 6.3 Long Call Position (Outlook: Bullish)

At any stock price above RM 12.20, the long call position breaks even. The break-even point for calls is the exercise price *plus* premium. The risk profile is essentially one of unlimited profit potential and limited loss potential. It is for this risk profile that options are said to provide the best of both worlds. They let you benefit from a potential upside rally in the underlying asset but limit your losses if prices move unfavorably.

(4) A Long Put Position

You are bearish about ABC Corp. stock; rather than short the stock, you buy a put with exercise price of RM 12 at a 0.15 sen premium. What is the payoff to this strategy? Table 6.4 and Figure 6.4 show the payoff to a long put position.

Compared to the short stock or short futures position, a long put position limits the loss potential. Once again, if your (bearish) expectation is correct and the underlying stock's price

Table 6.4 Stock Price at Maturity and Payoff to Long Put

Stock Price	(P/L) Payoff
9.50	2.35
10.00	1.85
10.50	1.35
11.00	0.85
11.50	0.35
11.85	0
12.00	(0.15)
12.50	(0.15)
13.00	(0.15)
13.50	(0.15)
14.00	(0.15)
14.50	(0.15)

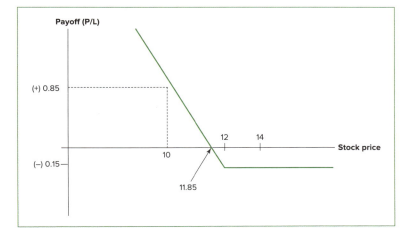

Figure 6.4 Long Put Position (Outlook: Bearish)

falls, you gain but should price move unfavorably (rise), then your potential loss is limited to the amount of the premium. The put breaks even at RM 11.85. The break-even point for puts is the exercise price *minus* put premium.

(5) A Short Call Position

You are bearish to neutral about ABC Corp. stock. A call option on the stock at an exercise price of RM 12 is 0.20 or 20 sen. You decide to short (sell) the call. What is the payoff? Table 6.5 and Figure 6.5 show the payoff to the short call position.

(6) Short Put

You are bullish to neutral about ABC Corp. stock. A put option on the stock at RM 12 is selling for 15 sen. You decide to short the put. What is the payoff to the strategy? Table 6.6 and Figure 6.6 show the payoff to the short put position.

Table 6.5 Stock Price at Maturity and Payoff to Short Call Position

Stock Price	(P/L) Payoff
9.50	0.20
10.00	0.20
10.50	0.20
11.00	0.20
11.50	0.20
12.00	0.20
12.20	0
12.50	(0.30)
13.00	(0.80)
13.50	(1.30)
14.00	(1.80)
14.50	(2.30)

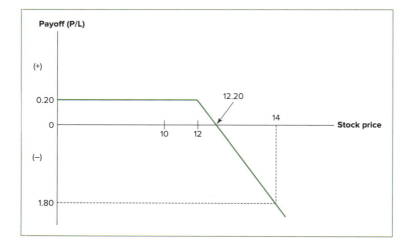

Figure 6.5 Short Call Position (Outlook: Neutral to Bearish)

Table 6.6 Stock Price at Maturity and Payoff to Short Put Position

Stock Price	(P/L) Payoff
9.50	(2.35)
10.00	(1.85)
10.50	(1.35)
11.00	(0.85)
11.50	(0.35)
11.85	0
12.00	0.15
12.50	0.15
13.00	0.15
13.50	0.15
14.00	0.15
14.50	0.15

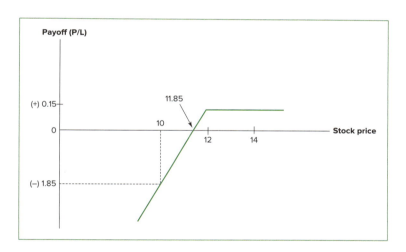

Figure 6.6 Short Put Position (Outlook: Neutral to Bullish)

Note that the short call and short put positions have limited upside potential but unlimited loss potential. This arises from the fact that the seller has obligation and faces assignment should the long position choose to exercise. However, one would only short a call if one were bearish or neutral while short a put, if bullish or neutral.

6.2.1 Stock versus Option Positions

We saw earlier the payoffs to stocks and option positions. Here, we do a direct comparison between the payoffs for stock versus option positions. In order to keep the comparison simple, we return to the example used earlier,

Note
The break-even point for calls is exercise price plus premium. For puts, break-even is at the exercise price minus premium.

i.e., Tables 6.1 to 6.4 and Figures 6.1 to 6.4. We will examine the two possible stock positions, long and short stock, and compare it to the option equipment which is long call and long put.

(1) Long Stock versus Long Call Position

Both the long stock and long call positions are appropriate if one had a bullish expectation. Between the two positions, however, there are some differences. To see these differences, we examine the payoffs taken together. Table 6.7 shows the relative payoffs for a long stock and long call position. Notice that the three columns are really from Tables 6.1 and 6.3. Recall that the two positions are, long stock at RM 12 and long, RM 12 call @ 0.20.

Columns two and three show the payoffs for long stock and the long call position.

Overall, there are three key differences to note. First, the long call position cuts off loses to a maximum of 20 sen. For a stock price below RM 11.80, the stock position loses much more

Table 6.7 Payoff to Long Stock versus Long Call

Stock Price at Maturity	Payoff to Long Stock	Payoff to Long Call
9.50	(2.50)	(0.20)
10.00	(2.00)	(0.20)
10.50	(1.50)	(0.20)
11.00	(1.00)	(0.20)
11.50	(0.50)	(0.20)
12.00	0	(0.20)
12.20	0.20	0
12.50	0.50	0.30
13.00	1.00	0.80
13.50	1.50	1.30
14.00	2.00	1.80
14.50	2.50	2.30

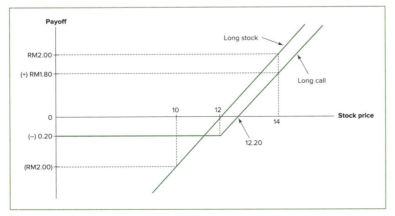

Figure 6.7 Payoff to Long Stock versus Long Call Positions

than a call position. Second, when prices rise, both positions make money, but the call position has a payoff that is always 20 sen lower than that of the stock position. This difference is due to the call premium. The third difference is that the long call position only makes money after the break-even point is reached; in this case, RM 12.20 (exercise price + call premium).

(2) Short Stock versus Long Put Position

Both the short stock and long put positions are consistent with a bearish expectation. Once again, to see the differences between the short stock and the long put positions, we examine the payoffs taken together. Table 6.8, which uses the numbers from Tables 6.2 and 6.4, shows the payoffs taken together. As earlier, the two positions are short stock at RM 12 and long, RM 12 put @ 0.15. Figure 6.8 shows the payoffs in terms of a diagram.

Table 6.8   Payoff to Short Stock versus Long Put

Stock Price at Maturity	Payoff to Short Stock	Payoff to Long Put
9.50	2.50	2.35
10.00	2.00	1.85
10.50	1.50	1.35
11.00	1.00	0.85
11.50	0.50	0.35
11.85	0.15	0
12.00	0	(0.15)
12.50	(0.50)	(0.15)
13.00	(1.00)	(0.15)
13.50	(1.50)	(0.15)
14.00	(2.00)	(0.15)
14.50	(2.50)	(0.15)

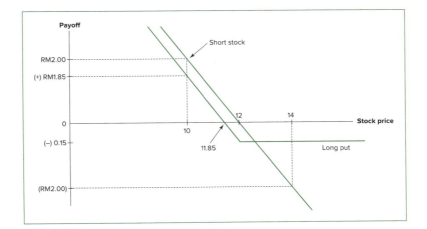

Figure 6.8   Short Stock versus Long Put Position

Again, as in the previous case, we note the three key differences between option and stock positions. First, the long put position cuts off loses to a maximum 15 sen which is the amount of the premium. The short stock position, however, has potentially unlimited losses. Second, when the underlying stock price falls, both positions gain; however, the profit from the long put position is always lower by 15 sen relative to the stock position. This lower profit reflects the premium paid for the put. The final difference is that, although the short stock begins to profit below RM 12, the put position requires a further fall in the underlying stock to at least RM 11.85 before it begins to make money. This RM 11.85 price being the break-even point for the put position (exercise price *minus* put premium).

6.2.2 Forward/Futures versus Option Positions

Comparing the payoffs to a position in forwards/futures with that of options would provide results equivalent to that of the abovementioned stock versus option comparison. Earlier in the chapter, it was alluded that long stock and long forward/futures positions are equivalent in payoff terms as are the respective short positions. This arises from the fact that a forward or futures position is obligatory at maturity. For example, if one holds a long position in a forward or futures contract at maturity, the holder is **obliged** to purchase the underlying asset at the predetermined forward/futures price. If the underlying asset price is lower than the predetermined forward/futures price, then an "implied" loss is made. On the other hand, if the underlying asset price is higher, an "implied" profit is made on the forward/futures position. As such, when viewed at maturity, the long forward/futures position has a payoff equivalent to that of the long stock position. A short forward/futures position and a short stock position have equivalent payoffs. Thus, comparing forward/futures positions with that of options would provide results equivalent to that of comparing stock and options positions.

> **Note**
> The main advantage of options is that they enable the holder to benefit from an upside potential while limiting the downside risk.

The six basic diagrams that we discussed earlier, (i) long call, (ii) short call, (iii) long put, (iv) short put, (v) long futures/stock, and (vi) short futures/stock, are the basics needed for creating a number of trading strategies. As we will see, numerous combinations can be made, resulting in various types of payoffs. Depending on one's needs/desires, a strategy could be designed using the above six basic strategies to get a desired payoff. In conclusion, two points need to be stressed. First, buying options limits the loss potential to a maximum equivalent to the cost of the option's premium. Though loss potential is limited, options enable one to keep the upside potential intact. The potential upside gain from options will be lower than the profit potential of the underlying by the amount of the option premium. Second, investing in options, like all other financial transactions, constitute a zero sum game. That is, a loss to one party would equal the gain to the other. This would be clearly evident from examining Figures 6.3 to 6.6. The fact that options are also a **zero sum game** like any other transaction seems lost these days. If one reads the mass media, one would be led to think that there is something inherently risky about derivatives. This is understandable given the spectacular losses reported. However, as the earlier figures show, for every spectacular loss reported, someone somewhere must have made profits equal to the reported losses. Though all the profits need not have occurred to one party, the total of profits made must equal the losses. What one does not often hear is of the huge profits made!

6.3 Expectations and Option Positions

As we have seen from the earlier payoff diagrams, the payoff to positions at expiry of the options depends on the underlying asset's price performance.

For example, the long call position makes money when the underlying asset moves up in price. On the other hand, the long put position makes money if the underlying asset's price falls. Thus, if one were to take naked[1] or speculative positions with options, the option strategy would clearly depend on the expectation of the underlying asset's performance.

Someone who is bullish about the underlying asset's performance would obviously choose a long call position. Such a position benefits if the expectation is correct. The long call position earns as much as long underlying (stock) position less the premium for prices above the exercise price. Someone who is bearish would long put options. The long put position makes as much profit as the short underlying position less the option premium for prices below the exercise price. That a long call position is undertaken when bullish and a long put when bearish is easy to see. What is harder to visualize is the rationale behind the short call and short put positions, which have limited profit potential but unlimited loss potential; the long positions had the exact opposite risk profile. A question that often arises here is: why would anyone be willing to sell a call or a put when the risk profile to the short position is clearly "disadvantageous." One might argue that in exchange for taking on this "disadvantageous" position, the short position receives the premium. That the premium is the compensation for taking on such a position is only partly true. Keep in mind that the premium is a limited amount, in exchange for receiving it now, the short position faces potential losses several times the premium received. Expectations play a key role. One would be willing to *sell* a call if he or she believes that the underlying asset will likely not move in price or if it does move, the price could go down slightly. Such an expectation is **neutral to bearish**. On the other hand, if someone is **neutral to bullish,** then he would be willing to sell a put. Based on such expectations, the seller of the option expects that the long position will not want to exercise and he gets to keep the premium. For example, someone who is neutral to bearish about the underlying asset's price would be willing to sell a call since an unchanged price (neutral) or a lower price (bearish) at expiry will mean that the option sold will not be exercised. Thus,

---

[1] A naked or uncovered position is a single position with no offsetting positions.

it is expectations that causes someone to be willing to write/short options. As expectations change, so do the option premiums. For example, if most investors are bullish about an underlying asset, few would want to write or sell calls on that asset. Since there will be many buyers but few sellers for the call, the premium rises in order to induce more sellers. The same logic applies when most investors are bearish about an underlying asset; the premiums on the put would rise.

Expectations and Option Premiums				
Expectation of Underlying Asset Price	Demand for Option		Premium	
	Calls	Puts	Calls	Puts
Bullish	Increase	Decrease	Increase	Decrease
Bearish	Decrease	Increase	Decrease	Increase

The Put–Call Ratio

Since the demand for calls and puts represents different expectations, the ratio of outstanding calls versus puts on an optioned asset is a closely watched number. This ratio, which is known as the ***put–call ratio***, is seen as an indicator of the overall market expectation of the underlying asset's performance. If the number of outstanding calls is more than those of puts, it implies a bullish market outlook. A higher number of puts would imply bearishness.

6.4 Options: Uses and Applications

In addition to the fact that options limit downside risk but allow for upside gain, there are several other reasons for the huge popularity of option contracts. We examine some of these advantages and their application.

(1) Options Provide Leverage

As with other derivative instruments, investment in options provides automatic leverage. This arises from the fact that options provide the same exposure to the underlying asset but at a much lower cost. While an investment in the underlying asset, stocks, for example, would require upfront payment of the full cost of the shares, acquiring the options on the stock would require only the payment of the option premium, which is usually a small percentage of the cost of the stock.

(2) Ideal for Risk Management and Arbitrage

As we will see in Chapter 8, options can and are used extensively in risk management, i.e., hedging. To hedge an underlying exposure to rising prices, or to seek protection from rising prices, one would long a call option. The idea as in all previous cases of hedging is the same. If rising prices would hurt our position in the underlying asset, than a long call position would gain from rising prices and so offset the losses. On the other hand, to hedge an underlying exposure to falling prices, one should go long put options. A long position in puts gains from falling prices and so offsets losses on the underlying. We examine the use of options in arbitrage in Chapter 10.

(3) Enhance Portfolio Revenue

Options can also be used to enhance portfolio revenue. Portfolio managers often use options to increase their returns. A common strategy is to sell calls on stocks already owned. This strategy which is known as a **covered call write** will be explored in detail in Chapter 8.

(4) Flexibility and Ease of Use

Options, as we will see, are extremely flexible instruments. Much of their flexibility comes from the fact that options are nonobligatory. Their flexibility makes options a key instrument in financial engineering. Aside from being able to design numerous types of payoffs, options can also be used to create strategies to take advantage of different situations/outcomes. Most of these strategies would not be possible without options.

(5) Managing Information Asymmetries

Options, given their features, come in handy for managing **information asymmetries**. An information asymmetry refers to a situation where both the parties to a transaction may not have access to the same amount/extent of information. Where the information asymmetry is acute, problems of moral hazard could arise. Thus, the party to the transaction who is the financier would be wary of providing funds. Assurances by the other party to the financier may not be sufficient. This is where options come in. To understand how options can be used to overcome the information asymmetry, assume the following: Let's say Syarikat DEF wants to undertake a new project. This new project has very good potential and is likely to be hugely successful. However, Syarikat DEF does not have the funding to undertake the project, and thus wishes to issue additional new shares to raise the needed financing. If Syarikat DEF has not had previous big successes, it may not be able to raise the new financing. A skeptical investing public would not subscribe to the shares offered by the company. How can Syarikat DEF's management convey the information about how good the project is without giving out details that may be used by its competitors? No amount of assurance or announcement about how good the project might work. The information asymmetry here is that management knows how good the project is, given the detailed project information they have. However, potential investors outside would not have the same information.

What companies have done to overcome this type of information asymmetry is to attach put options exercisable at the initial public offer (IPO) price to the new stocks being sold. Such an exercise tells outside investors that management is very confident of the new project and that they are willing to commit themselves to buying back the shares at the original issue price.

(6) Managing Contingent Liabilities/Claims

The management of **contingent liabilities** or **contingent claims** is a key justification for the need for innovation behind options. These are liabilities or claims on a business entity that could arise depending on an uncertain outcome. In other words, contingent claims or liabilities are business situations that involve at least two levels of uncertainties. In an increasingly turbulent world, such situations have become commonplace and their management that much more important. By way of an example, one of the easiest ways to see how a contingent claim/liability could arise would be in international business. Let us say a Malaysian company involved in the manufacturing of a certain electrical component has just submitted a bid in an international tender by a foreign government for supply of the components. Let us assume that payment will be in a foreign currency, that today is the last day for submitting bids, and that the foreign government will choose among several international bidders and will make known its chosen bid and supplier in 1 month's time. For clarity, let us assume further that once the government announces the winning bid, the chosen supplier will supply over the following 5 months and will be paid in full at the end of the 6th month. The following timeline shows the chronology of events.

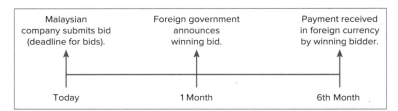

From the viewpoint of the Malaysian company, they will know the outcome in a month and if selected will supply and receive payment in foreign currency 6 months from today. Though simplified, notice that this is by no means a hypothetical situation. In fact, in international business, this is a highly common situation. Clearly the Malaysian company faces risk. If selected, they would be paid in a foreign currency. Since they would have bid a fixed amount in foreign currency, they face the risk that the foreign currency could depreciate against the Ringgit. With production costs in Ringgit, foreign currency depreciation would cause them to make losses. Notice that this currency exposure begins the moment the bid is submitted, yet becomes a reality only if their bid is chosen. There are two simultaneous sets of uncertainties here. First, uncertainty regarding the Ringgit amount that will be received given currency fluctuation and second, uncertainty whether their bid would be chosen.

How could one manage such compound risks? Suppose the company did nothing to hedge, they would face the currency risk if chosen but would have no problem at all if they are not chosen. Clearly there is a need to hedge the currency risk, yet currency futures or forwards would be unsuitable. A forward would be unsuited since if not chosen, a forward contract cannot be easily reversed out. With futures, the company has two choices: (i) take a short position in a 6-month currency futures contract **now** and reverse out in a month if not selected, or (ii) wait until the result is known in a month's time and then if chosen, take a short position in 5-month currency futures.

Although at first glance it may seem appropriate, neither of these alternatives would really be suited. Figure 6.9 shows the alternatives available with using forwards and futures and the problems that could arise.

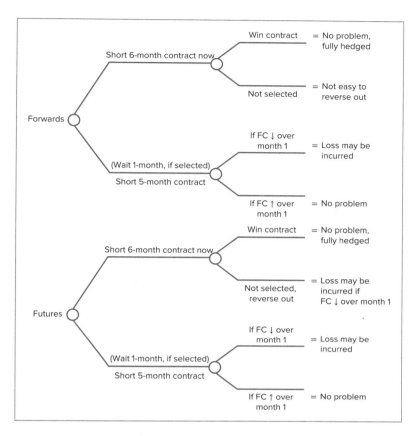

Figure 6.9 Hedging Alternatives Using Forwards or Futures Contracts
Note: FC is foreign currency.

How would options help in managing the compounded risks of the earlier example? The Malaysian company at the time of submitting the bid (today) would simply have to buy (long) 6-month put options on the foreign currency. The number of contracts needed would depend on contract size. Buying the needed number of 6-month put option contracts to equate the amount of foreign currency receivable, the company would **fully hedge both** the currency risk **and** the uncertainty about the outcome of the bid. In the event the company's bid is not chosen, the put options could be left unexpired with losses limited to the cost of the premium; on the other hand, should the company be selected and receive a depreciated foreign currency, the put options purchased become profitable and would be exercised. If properly designed to be fully hedged, the profit payoff from the long put position would equal the losses made on receiving the depreciated currency. Notice that in the absence of options, managing such contingent exposures would be very difficult.

In addition to the abovementioned uses, options may also be used as a means to reduce transaction costs, to avoid tax exposure and to avoid stock market restrictions, such as short-selling.

Box 6.1
Option Trading Volume Overtakes That of Underlying Stocks

The *Wall Street Journal,* on September 27, 2021, carried an article reporting that over the 9 months of 2021, the average notional traded value of equity options on individual stocks exceeded that of the underlying stocks. According to the article, as of end September 2021, total traded volume of stock options was approximately $433 billion, whereas the underlying stocks themselves had total volume of about $404 billion. This appears to be part of a continuing trend from the previous year 2020. The article attributed this to the increased use of options by individual investors. Retail investors in the United States (US) were attracted to options rather than the underlying stock due to the lower initial investment and the inherent leverage that provides for larger potential profits. Retail investors, it appears, were more interested in the bigger bang for the buck that options provided, regardless of the higher risk. Individual investor participation in options trading had increased 400% over the prior 5 years. Based on Options Clearing Corporation data, 2021 saw average daily traded volume of options at 39 million contracts per day, 31% higher than average daily volume in 2020. In addition, 9 of the 10 most active option trading days in history occurred in 2021. Options on certain stocks like, GameStop, Apple, Tesla, and Amazon seem to be investor favorites. The steady rise in US stock markets over 2020 and 2021, fueled by the ultra-loose monetary policies of the Federal Reserve, had undoubtedly attracted individual punters. A steadily rising market provides for easy pickings and profits are manifold higher with options. Whether individual investors would have the same enthusiasm for options when the market turns, is to be seen.

6.5 Option Moneyness

Option moneyness refers to terminologies used to describe whether an option is currently profitable. In describing moneyness, two points need to be kept in mind. First, moneyness is always viewed from that of the long position not from the seller's viewpoint. Second, in describing moneyness, we always compare the exercise price of the option to the current value of the underlying asset. There are three forms of moneyness: (i) in-the-money (ITM), (ii) at-the-money (ATM), and (iii) out-of-the-money (OTM).

(1) In-the-Money
An option is said to be ITM if exercising it now will mean profits. Thus for a call to be ITM, its exercise price must be lower than the current value or spot price of the underlying asset. For a put option to be ITM, its exercise price must be higher than the value of the underlying asset.

- Call: Exercise price < Spot price of underlying
- Put: Exercise price > Spot price of underlying

(2) At-the-Money

An option is said to be ATM if its exercise price equals the spot price of the underlying. Exercising such an option will mean zero profit on exercise and the loss of the premium paid.

- Call: Exercise price = Spot price of underlying asset
- Put: Exercise price = Spot price of underlying asset

(3) Out-of-the-Money

An option is said to be OTM if exercising it will mean losses. A call would be OTM if its exercise price is higher than the current spot price of the underlying asset. A put would be OTM if its exercise price is lower than the underlying asset's spot price.

- Call: Exercise price > Spot price of underlying asset
- Put: Exercise price < Spot price of underlying asset

6.5.1 Option Valuation

We purchase an option by paying the premium stated for it. There are two questions that one might ask here. First, how do we determine what the correct premium should be? Second, what constitutes the value of the premium? In Chapter 9, we address the first question of how to determine the correct price. We will examine two option pricing models, the Binomial Option Pricing Model and the Black–Scholes Option Pricing Model. Here, we focus on the second question, i.e., what constitutes the value of the premium or where does the premium value come from?

The premium of an option, or the option's value, comes from two sources: the ***intrinsic value (IV)*** and ***time value (TV)***.

The premium that is quoted is essentially the sum of these two values.

$$\text{Premium} = \text{IV} + \text{TV}$$

Suppose the premium of a call option on MAS Corp. stock with a RM 5 exercise price is quoted at 25 sen.

$$\text{5 MAS Call @ 0.25}$$

The premium of 25 sen could be the result of 15 sen of IV and 10 sen, TV.

$$0.25 = 0.15 + 0.10$$

Intrinsic Value

The IV of an option can be thought of as the profit that can be attained by the immediate exercise of the option. If it will not be profitable to exercise the option, then the IV equals zero. Yet another way to think of the IV is as the amount by which an option is ITM. The IV equals to the amount by which the option is ITM. If the option is at or OTM, then it is said to have zero IV. Going by this definition, IV for calls and puts is given as:

> **Note**
> IV is the amount by which an option is ITM or the profit that can be attained if exercised immediately.

Call IV = Spot price − Exercise price
Put IV = Exercise price − Spot price

Time Value

Notice from the abovementioned definition that the IV would equal zero if an option is not ITM. Yet it is obvious that the premium of an option cannot be zero. That is, an option that is yet to expire cannot have a zero price. Even if the option is deep OTM, as long as it has time left to maturity, it must have a nonzero price. Such an option derives all its value from TV. In other words, the premium of an ATM or OTM option derives all its value from TV.

TV refers to the value that arises from the probability that an option could become profitable by the time of its maturity. The longer the time left to maturity, the higher the TV will be. As an option approaches maturity, TV reduces. TV equals zero at maturity. Thus, if an option expires ATM or OTM, its premium/value is zero since both the intrinsic and TVs are zero.

Having discussed intrinsic and TVs, we now turn to a graphical analysis of these values and draw some general observations of each of these components of option value. We begin with Figure 6.10 that examines the maximum and minimum bounds for an option's value. Suppose we have a call option on a stock with a zero exercise price and

> **Note**
> TV refers to the value that arises from the probability that an option could become profitable by the time of its maturity.

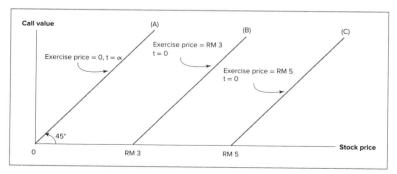

Figure 6.10   Call Option; Maximum and Minimum Value Bounds

infinite maturity, what would its value be? Its value will be equal to the value of the underlying asset. That is, holding the option is just like holding the stock. Graphically the call's value will rise at a 45° angle from the origin.

Line A earlier shows the value of a call with a zero exercise price and infinite time to maturity. (Notice that unlike the earlier payoff graphs, we now have call value and not profit/loss on the vertical axis.) Line A therefore represents the maximum value of the call option. The highest possible value for an option equals to the value of the underlying asset. An option cannot have a value greater than that of the underlying asset. Let us now change the parameters of the call option and see what happens to its value. Suppose the call now has an exercise price of not zero but RM 3 and the time left to maturity is now zero, i.e., the call is exercisable immediately. The value of the call is now given by Line B. Line B begins at RM 3 and is parallel to Line A. What this means is that at any price below RM 3 the call is worthless and has zero value. However, at any price above RM 3, the call has a value equal to the difference between the exercise price and stock price; in other words, IV. For example, at a stock price of RM 3.30, the value of the call will be RM 0.30 or 30 sen. This equals to the IV. Since the call is exercisable immediately, there is no TV, thus the call value equals the IV. Line B can therefore be thought of as the IV of the RM 3 call. Line B also denotes the minimum value of the RM 3 call. If the stock price is below RM 3, the IV is zero and so is the value of the call. At any price above RM 3, the call value equals the IV.

Suppose we now change the exercise price of the call from RM 3 to RM 5. What is the call value if it is again exercisable immediately ($t = 0$)? The new call value will be given by Line C. Notice that Line C represents a parallel shift to the right just as in the case of Line B earlier. Now, Line C which represents the IV equals zero for any stock price below RM 5 but takes off at a 45° angle from RM 5. The 45° angle is significant since it shows that there will be a one-to-one correspondence in the values of the stock and call beyond the RM 5 level. That is, every 1-sen increase in stock price beyond RM 5 will cause a 1-sen increase in the IV and call value.

Let us now make one more change to the parameters of the earlier call. Suppose we keep the exercise price at RM 5 but now extend the time left to maturity from zero to 30 days. Obviously, the value of the call will be more than that represented by Line C. Line C represents the IV which is also the minimum value for the call. Now, however, the call's value must include TV since there is now 30 days left to maturity. Surely the value would be higher than Line C (but lower than Line A which is theoretical maximum value since the call value cannot exceed underlying asset value), but how much higher? To derive the call value now that TV is not equal to zero, an option pricing model has to be used. We will discuss option pricing in Chapter 9, but for now suppose an option pricing model was used to derive call values for the same RM 5 exercise price and 30-day maturity but for **different** underlying stock prices, the value of the call option will be given by the curve shown in Figure 6.11.

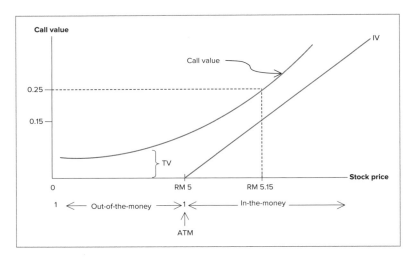

Figure 6.11   Call Value, Intrinsic Value, and Time Value

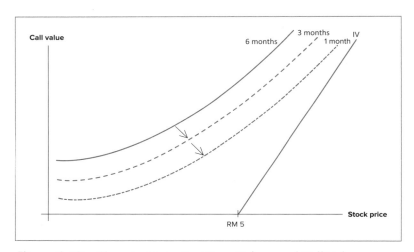

Figure 6.12   Time to Maturity, Time Value, and Call Value

The curve depicting the value of the call is a plot of points for call value at different exercise prices. The IV line denoted IV is Line C from Figure 6.10 earlier. TV is represented by the **area** between the IV line and the call value curve. As such, at a stock price of RM 5.15 for example, the call will have a premium of 25 sen which is made up of an IV of 15 sen and a TV of 10 sen. The figure also shows the region within which the call would be OTM, ATM, and ITM.

In Figure 6.10, we saw how a change in the exercise price causes a change in the IV. When exercise price went from RM 3 to RM 5, the IV line shifted from Line B to Line C. Let us now examine what would happen if the exercise is kept the same but the time to maturity changes. Suppose in the same example, time to maturity is now 90 days or 3 months instead of 30 days, what would happen to the value of the call? Intuitively it is obvious that the value of the call should be higher for any given stock price since TV is now higher. Figure 6.12 shows the impact of higher maturities on call value.

Notice that the IV line is unchanged since exercise price is the same. The curve labeled 1 month is essentially the same curve representing call value in Figure 6.11. The other two curves represent the call values for maturities of 3 months (90 days) and 6 months. Each of these longer maturity curves have higher call value for any given stock price, meaning that TV is higher for any stock price.

Note
Since TV is zero at maturity, an option's value at expiry equals its IV.

Box 6.2
Options Are Everywhere

Although we discuss options in this chapter as formal financial instruments that are usually exchange-traded, the fact of the matter is that options occur everywhere in life. Your choice of taking different majors within a degree program is an option. The ability to retake a course or drop a course midway is also an option that a student can exercise. Universities typically charge a higher course fee if one drops a course late in the semester as opposed to early in the semester. If the fee for dropping a course is the same at any point in the semester, then there is effectively no additional "premium" for dropping a course later. Some universities allow students to retake and replace the grade for a limited number of courses in order to improve their overall grade point average. When a student chooses to do this, he is essentially buying an option to improve his grade. The fee to retake the course is the premium. If the university's policy is to replace the grade if there is an improvement but keep the old grade if the student performs worse on the retake, then, the student is effectively buying a call option when he pays for the retake. In this case, since the grade cannot get worse than what he has received previously but can go higher, the "payoff" is essentially like that of a call option.

Suppose a businessman has borrowed to fund his business, he essentially has a call option on the business. If, at a point in time in the future, the value of the business is less than the total outstanding on the loan (principal + interest accrued), the businessman is effectively "out of the money." He would have an incentive to default on the loan. If, however, the value of the business is more than the outstanding loan amount, the businessman is essentially "in the money," and thus it is worthwhile for him to repay the loan. In repaying the loan and taking over the business, the businessman is effectively exercising the implicit call option. A default on the loan implies that he chooses not to exercise. If the businessman has a call option, then the bank that loaned him the money is effectively in a "short put" position (see Box 6.3).

When a homeowner buys fire insurance on his home, he is essentially buying a "put" option. The insurance premium paid to the insurer is the fee for the put option. If the

(Continued)

Box 6.2
(Continued)

house burns down and is totally damaged, the homeowner can exercise the "put" by claiming the full amount of the insurance. If there is no fire within the insured period, the homeowner has no cause to exercise and simply loses the premium paid.

If a firm undertaking a foreign investment receives a guarantee from the foreign government on its invested capital, it is essentially receiving a put option. Since the firm made no extra payment to receive the guarantee, it is really getting a put option for free. Why would a foreign government give such options for free? They would, in order to attract foreign investment in select industries.

The bottom line here is that embedded options occur everywhere. Framing the choices in option terms and evaluating them could lead to better decision-making.

6.5.2 Time Decay and Options

Options are often also known as a "***wasting asset***." A wasting asset is a financial asset that is subject to ***time decay***. Wastage or time decay happens because options lose their value merely with the passage of time. Even if the underlying asset price is unchanged, the passage of time would mean the loss of time and so reduced option value/premium. In Figure 6.12, time decay is shown by the direction of the arrow. A call option with 6 months to

Note
Options are considered a wasting asset since they are subject to time decay. TV is lost with the passage of time, thereby reducing option value.

maturity would have values corresponding to the top most curve. Three months later, with 3 months left to maturity, the call value would be represented by the lower 3-month curve. With 1 month to maturity, call value corresponds to the lowest curve. This value keeps reducing further with the curve tending closer to the IV line as maturity approaches. At maturity, the curve collapses into the IV line such that at maturity TV is zero.

Time decay in the earlier example is ***negative*** in the sense that it is tending downward. In other words, time decay works against the long position and in favor of the short position. The holder of the call loses as call value reduces. Any loss for the long position represents a gain for the short position. In later chapters, we will see instances of ***positive time decay***.

IV and TV for Puts

The same analysis as that of call values is applicable to put options. The underlying logic is exactly the same. The one difference being that the regions within which the put would be

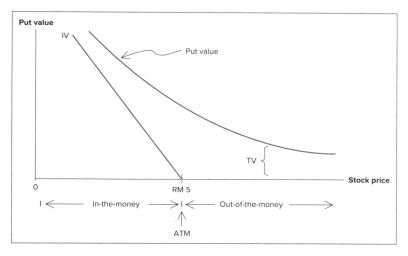

Figure 6.13   Put Value, Intrinsic Value, and Time Value

OTM and ITM is reversed. Figure 6.13 shows the intrinsic and time premium for a put option with an RM 5 exercise price and 30 days to maturity.

We end our discussion of IVs and TVs with the following summary observations.

Intrinsic Value
(a) Lowest value is zero, IV is never negative.
(b) IV is positive for ITM options. IV is zero for ATM options. IV is zero for OTM options.
(c) At maturity, option value equals IV.

Time Value
(a) TV is always positive (> 0) before maturity, even for deep OTM options.
(b) *Ceteris paribus*, the longer the time left to maturity, the greater is the TV.
(c) As the option approaches maturity, TV reduces; this is time decay.
(d) At option maturity, TV = 0.
(e) The more OTM the option is, the lower is its TV and so the lower is its premium/value.
(f) TV is highest when an option is near or ATM and reduces as the option goes deep ITM or deep OTM.

Box 6.3
The Logic of Options and Defaulting Home Loans

The widespread default on home mortgages following the bursting of the housing bubble during the subprime crisis in the US, is easy to understand when seen in the context of options. For most people, a house is usually their most valuable asset. It is

(*Continued*)

Box 6.3
(*Continued*)

usually an investment that has not only taken up a major portion of their earnings/investment, but provides a home for their families. Therefore, defaulting on a home mortgage is usually the last thing one would do. Yet, the widespread default of home mortgages caught policymakers by surprise. Most homeowners chose to default because, morals aside, it was the rational thing to do. The bursting of the housing bubble and the substantial fall in house prices meant that mortgage owners were **effectively long, deep-out-the-money call options**. The principal value of the mortgage plus accumulated interest were in most cases, way above current market values of the houses. The loose lending policies and the many abuses in the lending practice led to this outcome.

The full settlement of a loan can be thought of as a call option on the financed asset. In the case of an outstanding home mortgage, choosing to pay off the loan and taking possession of the house is equivalent to exercising a call option on the house. The exercise price being the outstanding loan amount. Just as it is never rational to exercise an OTM call option, there will be no incentive to settle or service a home mortgage if the outstanding loan value is higher than current market value. Banks try to avoid this incentive to default in a number of ways. For example, banks would require a substantial investment by the borrower by providing financing for perhaps a maximum 90% of the value of the house. Further, they would be examining the borrowers' earnings and his other obligations to determine his capacity to repay. They may also require other forms of guarantees, etc. In the US, these basic rules of prudence were ignored because banks originating the loans securitized and sold them off. Home mortgages were provided to people without the means to pay (subprime), and the margin of financing was often 100%. Such easy financing fueled the housing bubble. When the bubble burst, house prices collapsed. The widespread default was the result of two factors. First, the homeowners were holding deep OTM call options and second, since homeowners had put in little if any of their own money, they had a little to lose by walking away. So, homeowners chose to default because they were holding deep OTM call options for which they had paid little or no premium. If there is any one to be blamed for all of these, it should be the American policymakers who allowed the buildup of these preserve incentives.

In Chapter 11, we examine the use of the logic of options in other contexts.

SUMMARY

This chapter provided an overview of options. Options come in two forms: calls and puts. Call options provide the holder the right but not the obligation to buy the underlying asset at the predetermined exercise price. Put options provide the right but not the obligation to sell the underlying asset at the predetermined exercise price. Each option must have the following five features: option type, the underlying asset, the exercise price, maturity date, and exercise style. There are generally two exercise styles: American and European. While an American-style option can be exercised at any time before maturity, European-style options can only be exercised at maturity. Given the greater flexibility, American-style options would have higher premiums.

Unlike forwards/futures, the long position in options has to pay a premium to the option writer or seller. Depending on which way underlying asset prices move, the premium changes in value. Rising underlying asset prices would raise call premiums but would cause put premiums to reduce. The opposite is true if underlying asset price falls. Differences in expectations play a key role in whether one goes long or short options. Since a long position in options is nonobligatory, the risk profile is one of unlimited upside potential but limited downside risk. The maximum loss possible on a long position is the premium paid.

Aside from a favorable risk profile, options have other advantages. Options provide leverage, are extremely flexible, can be used to manage contingent liabilities, information asymmetries and to enhance portfolio returns. An option's premium or value has two components: IV and TV. IV is simply the amount by which an option iin-the-money. Options that are ATM or OTM have zero IV. TV is value that arises from the probability that an option could become profitable before maturity. TV is greatest when the option is ATM. It reduces as the option moves away from the exercise price in either direction. *Ceteris paribus*, TV is higher, the longer the time left to maturity.

KEY TERMS

- Call option
- Put option
- Exercise price
- American style
- European style
- Option premium
- In-the-money (ITM)
- At-the-money (ATM)
- Bullish
- Bearish
- Neutral to bullish
- Neutral to bearish
- Out-of-the-money (OTM)
- Intrinsic value (IV)
- Time value (TV)
- Contingent claim
- Asymmetric information
- Put–call ratio
- Option moneyness
- Wasting asset
- Time decay
- Positive time decay
- Negative time decay
- Risk profile

End-of-Chapter Questions

1. For a short position in a RM 6.50 put sold for 0.10 to achieve its maximum profit at expiration, what must be the price of the underlying stock?

2. What is the maximum loss potential of the following position: long 50 RM 4 calls purchased for 0.18 each?

3. Assume a stock is trading at RM 7.10 and an RM 7 call is trading at 0.21. How much time premium is there in this call option?

4. You currently have no position. You are neutral to bullish on the market in general and on MTC Bhd. stock in particular. You are willing to buy the stock if the price dips, but you feel no urgency and are willing to wait. Outline an appropriate strategy. Graph the position.

5. You bought an ATM, 3-month call option on Syarikat GEDC 2 months ago. GEDC's stock price has been unchanged since then. State the impact on the call's premium. Would it be higher or lower than the premium you paid? Explain why.
   a. Suppose you had bought an ATM put option instead, would its premium now be higher or lower? Explain.
   b. If you had bought the put option in (a) above, and GEDC had paid a dividend yesterday, would the premium be higher or lower today? Explain why.

6. You think TRI Inc. stock is likely to be neutral over the next 3 months. If it does move, you think a marginal increase is likely. State and graph an appropriate option strategy.

7. A call option with 1 month to maturity is selling at RM 0.25 premium. The exercise price is RM 6. The underlying stock is selling at RM 5.85.
   a. Using a carefully labeled figure, show the IV, TV, and the premium.
   b. Suppose the maturity period for the above option is lengthened but everything else is unchanged.
      (i) State the impact on IV and TV.
      (ii) Show the impact by means of a graph.

8. If futures can be used for hedging, arbitrage, and speculation, what is the need for options?

9. Syarikat MC's stock is now traded at RM 5.30. Its RM 5 exercise price call and put is quoted at RM 0.45 and RM 0.18, respectively. Both options have 2 months to maturity. Graph (separately), the IV, TV, and values of the call and put options. Label all axes carefully.

10. What is a contingent claim? Describe the best instrument for hedging such a claim.

11. XYZ Corp. current stock price = RM 6.
    30-day call   30-day put
    5.50 call = 0.70   5.50 put = 0.09
    6.00 call = 0.30   6.00 put = 0.20
    6.50 call = 0.08   6.50 put = 0.80
    a. Which options are ITM? By what amount?
    b. Which options are ATM?
    c. Would the premium of a 60-day option be higher or lower than the premium above if it were (i) a call option? and (ii) a put option?

12. Compute the IV and time premium for each of the call and put options in Question 11.
13. An option has a time premium of 0.13. Its exercise price is RM 5.50, the underlying stock price is now RM 5.80. What should the option's premium be if it were:
    a. (i) A call option?
        (ii) A put option?
    b. Why are the premiums different?
14. Write short notes on the following.
    a. The no-arbitrage bounds
    b. Convergence principle
    c. Negative time decay
15. A stock is currently selling at RM 10. An ATM call option with 30 days to maturity is being quoted RM 0.90. Assume there are four other 30-day options on the stock. These are an RM 9 put option, an RM 9 call option, and an RM 12 call and put option.
    a. Of the five available options, which is likely to have the highest price? Which is likely to have the lowest price?
    b. Which option(s) will gain in value if the underlying stock rises to RM 11? Rank by order of likely increase.
    c. Which option(s) will gain in value if the underlying stock goes to RM 8? Rank by order of likely increase.
16. Explain why the value of a call option increases as the underlying asset's value increases but the opposite is true for a put option on the same asset. What does this imply about the choice of option to hedge against rising or falling values of the underlying asset?
17. Assume a call and put option on the same underlying, having the same maturity and exercise price. For a given change in the underlying asset's value, would the call and put options have the same change in their premiums? Explain what determines the extent of change in option values.
18. As a result of a month-long lockdown due to the COVID-19 pandemic, a derivatives exchange following reopening, decides to automatically extend by 1 month, all options that were due for expiration during the lockdown.
    a. What is the likely impact on the TV of a call option?
    b. What is the likely impact on the TV of a put option?
    c. Would the IV of the options be impacted?
19. Using information from Question 18, describe the impact, positive or negative, on the following:
    a. The holder of a call that was ITM the money during the lockdown
    b. The holder of a call that was OTM during the lockdown
    c. The writer/seller of a call that was OTM during the lockdown.
    d. Would it be any different for the holder of a put?
20. When an unexpected event like COVID-19 strikes, *ceteris paribus,* who is likely to benefit more,
    a. Holders of calls or puts
    b. Buyers versus sellers of calls
    c. Buyers versus sellers of puts

CHAPTER · 7

Equity, Equity Index, and Currency Options

Objectives

This chapter examines the design and trading of equity options, equity index options, and currency options. The mechanics of their trading and issues related to their application for hedging, arbitrage, and speculation are examined in detail. On completing the chapter, you should have a good understanding and appreciation for the use of these instruments.

Introduction

As seen in Chapter 6, options can have various underlying assets. In this chapter, we examine three of the most commonly traded financial options: equity options which are also known as stock options, equity index options, and currency options. Equity options which we saw in Chapter 6 are essentially options to buy or sell an individual listed stock. Equity index options are options written on an underlying equity index, e.g., the Nikkei 225 Index, the Hang Seng Index, or the SET 50 Index. An index call option would entitle one to buy the underlying index of stocks, whereas an index put option would provide the right to sell the index at the predetermined exercise price. Currency options are options to buy or sell a foreign currency. This chapter examines two index options (the Financial Times Stock Exchange (FTSE) Bursa Malaysia Kuala Lumpur Composite Index (FBM KLCI) and the SET 50 Index), stock options traded on Hong Kong Exchanges and Clearing (HKEX) and the US$/Chinese Renminbi (CNH) currency option which is also traded on HKEX. Singapore Exchange's (SGX) Nikkei 225 Index options are presented in the appendix.

Hong Kong's HKEX and Singapore's SGX were early entrants in the financial options space. Malaysia and Thailand were later entrants. Malaysia's first exchange-traded option contract was introduced only in December 2000. It was an equity index option, known as the FBM KLCI options. It had both call and put options of varying exercise prices on the underlying FBM KLCI. The introduction of index options represented an extension on the only other product, the index futures, which has the same underlying asset. As an index-linked derivative, the FBM KLCI options are heavily dependent on market sentiment and other macro factors for their performance. In May 2012, Bursa Malaysia Derivatives Berhad decided to drop the index options contract and replace it with options on the FBM KLCI futures contract. Thus, where previously the options were based on the FBM KLCI Index, now it is the index futures contract. The apparent reason for this switch was the poor market reception for the index options and the perceived higher demand for options on Index futures. However, despite the change, there appears to have been no improvement in traded volume. The experience in Thailand with the SET 50 Index options appears very different from the Malaysia experience. Though introduced some 7 years later than in October 2007 on Thailand Futures Exchange (TFEX), the Thai index options have been much more successful. From a mere 9,000 contracts traded in 2007 annual volume has reached 1.7 million contracts in 2020, a compounded annual growth rate (CAGR) of 46% over the 14 years since launch.

7.1 Trading Option Contracts

As is the case with other derivative instruments, options may be used for hedging, arbitrage, and speculative purposes. However, unlike other derivatives, options involve no obligation on the part of the buyer. The buyer of a call option on a stock has the right to buy the underlying stock at the exercise price. On exercise, the holder of the call pays the exercise price in return for the stocks from the call writer. In the case of a put, the holder on exercise receives the exercise price in return for his shares. Although such is the case in physical settlement, equity index and the index futures options are cash-settled. As such, there is no delivery of the underlying asset. Holders of index call options merely receive their profits; the difference between the settlement price of the asset and the exercise price forwarded to them by crediting their accounts with their brokers. Similarly, holders of put options who exercise receive their profits which is the excess of the exercise price over the underlying asset's settlement price.

Equity Options

Position	Profit on Exercise	Fund Flow
Long call on stock	Settlement price *minus* Exercise price	Short call position pays the difference.
Long put on stock	Exercise price *minus* Settlement price	Short put position pays the difference.

Equity Index Options

Position	Resulting Position	At Maturity
Long call options on index	Right to buy the underlying index at exercise price on maturity date.	Receive cash equivalent to profit. Index settlement price *minus* exercise price.
Long put options on index	Right to sell the underlying index at exercise price on maturity date.	Receive cash equivalent to profit. Exercise price *minus* index settlement price.

Equity Index Options on Futures

Position	Resulting Position	At Maturity
Long call options on index futures	Right to take a long position in the index futures contract at exercise price on maturity date.	Receive cash equivalent to profit. Futures settlement price *minus* exercise price.
Long put options on index futures	Right to take short position in the index futures contract at exercise price on maturity date.	Receive cash equivalent to profit. Exercise price *minus* Futures settlement price.

Note that as described in Chapter 6, the long position (buyer) will only exercise if it is advantageous (profitable) to do so. The expectations underlying the established positions are the same. Bullish about underlying asset performance — long call options. Bearish about underlying asset — long put options. Regardless of what the underlying asset is, these basic principles apply in all cases of exchange-traded options.

To see how an investor could profit from trading in options, we examine a long call and a long put position. Let us say a trader is bullish about the FBM KLCI and wishes to trade options to benefit from a potential upside rally. Suppose the FBM KLCI futures is now 1,850 points and 30-day at-the-money futures index calls are being quoted as follows:

> **Note**
> Unlike futures, there is no possibility of a loss on exercise for the long position in options.

$$1{,}850 \text{ call @ 4 points}$$

This means that the 30-day index call option exercisable at 1,850 points has a premium of 4 points. The premium in Ringgit will be 4 points × ***index multiplier***. There is no index multiplier for index options; however, since that of index futures is RM 50, to purchase the call the investor pays a premium of:

$$4 \text{ points} \times \text{RM } 50 = \text{RM } 200$$

This premium of RM 200 per call option is paid in full at the time of purchase. Let us now examine what the investor's profit payoff will be under two scenarios: a first scenario, assuming the FBM KLCI rises by 15 points over the next 30 days, and a second scenario, in which the spot index falls 15 points.

Scenario 1: FBM KLCI Rises 15 Points

At maturity, the FBM KLCI will be 1,865 points. The call option is clearly in-the-money and profitable for the holder to exercise. Assuming the ***settlement value*** of the option at maturity is also 1,865 points,[1] the long position stands to profit.

---

[1] We will discuss the settlement procedure under contract specification later in the chapter.

Profit on Exercise for Calls
(Settlement value − Exercise price) × Index multiplier (1,865 points − 1,850 points) × RM 50
= (15 points) × RM 50
= RM 750

Exercise is executed in accordance with the rules of the clearinghouse. For FBM KLCI futures options, clearing rules dictate that options that are in-the-money are automatically exercised at maturity. The investor in our example will see his call options automatically exercised at maturity. Money, equivalent to the amount of his *profit on exercise*, will be credited into his account. This is the essence of *cash settlement*. The RM 750 profit credited into his account is transferred from the margin account of the short position, i.e., the seller of the call. The net payoffs to the long and short call positions are as follow:

Long Call			Short Call		
Pay premium	=	(RM 200)	Receive premium	=	RM 200
Profit on exercise	=	RM 750	Loss from exercise	=	(RM 750)
Net profit/Loss	=	RM 550	Net profit/Loss	=	(RM 550)

Scenario 2: FBM KLCI Falls 15 Points
Suppose the FBM KLCI falls 15 points over the next 30 days; its value will be 1,835 points at maturity, 15 points lower than the original 1,850 points. The call option will now expire out-of-the-money and obviously will not be exercised. Without being exercised, no fund flow will occur. The payoff to the long and short positions will be as follows:

> **Note**
> The maximum loss possible to the long position in options is the amount of premium paid.

Long Call			Short Call		
Pay premium	=	(RM 200)	Receive premium	=	RM 200
Profit/loss on exercise	=	0	Profit/loss on exercise	=	0
Net profit/Loss	=	(RM 200)	Net profit/Loss	=	RM 200

Without being exercised, the original premium paid by the long position becomes the profit of the short position.

7.2 Option Premiums and Underlying Asset Price

The earlier example illustrated the exercise procedure and the net payoffs to the long and short positions upon exercise. The assumption was that the option position is held until maturity. However, an investor taking a position in options need not hold the position to maturity. Returning to our example, the investor went long a 1,850 point index call @ 4 points. The premium paid was RM 200. Although the FBM KLCI options have European-style exercise and so cannot be exercised before maturity, there is nothing to stop the investor from realizing or taking profit by selling off his option. If the investor's original bullish sentiment had been correct and the underlying asset had gone up in value, the call option that was at-the-money during purchase would now be in-the-money. The call would now command a higher premium. For example, suppose 2 weeks after purchase, the FBM KLCI is at 1,854 points, up 4 points. The 1,850 call option may now have a quoted premium of say 9 points. Thus, by selling the call at the current premium of 9 points, the investor will be making a trading profit of:

Trading Profit = (Current Premium Value − Original Premium Value) × Index Multiplier
= (9 points − 4 points) × RM 50
= RM 250

Had the FBM KLCI gone down in value, the call that was bought at-the-money would now be out-of-the-money and have a lower premium. Selling such a call would obviously result in losses. Making trading profits before maturity rather than holding options to maturity is probably a bigger reason and a key contributor to trading volume in options. When the investor in our example initially goes long one call option, his action increases trading volume by one contract that day and increases open interest also by one contract. However, when he reverses out his position at a future date by selling the call, trading volume *increases* on that day by one contract but open interest *reduces* by one contract. This happens because he has now closed out his position.

When options are made available for trading on an exchange, anyone with an account can choose to buy or sell the listed options. This is no different from any other exchange traded asset. However, in the case of options, what changes as a result of the trading is the *premiums*. Since the exercise price, maturity, and contract size are all predetermined, what changes when underlying asset changes in value is the value of the premiums. When the underlying assets spot price/value increases, call premiums will rise, whereas put premiums will fall. When underlying asset's price/value falls, call premiums fall in value but put premiums rise.

Underlying Asset Price	Call Premium	Put Premium
Increase	Increase	Decrease
Decrease	Decrease	Increase

Call premiums are *positively correlated* with underlying asset values, whereas put premiums are *inversely correlated*. This is logical given the fact that a call represents a right to buy at the predetermined exercise price, whereas a put represents the right to sell at the exercise price. Since the exercise price is unchanged, rising underlying asset

Note
Call premiums are positively correlated to underlying asset prices, whereas put premiums are inversely correlated.

prices will be favorable to call holders but unfavorable to put holders. Put another way, a call option will either become *less* out-of-the-money or *more* in-the-money as underlying asset price increases. A put option, on the other hand, will either become *less in-the-money* or *more out-of-the-money* as the underlying asset price increases.

Option premiums therefore act to equalize demand and supply. For example, if the market turns bullish on the underlying asset and given current premiums, there is more demand than supply for call options, then call premiums will rise until the higher premiums attract more sellers. While call premiums rise, put options on the same asset will see their premiums fall, since there will be less demand for puts. Bearish sentiment, on the other hand, would cause increased demand for puts and so raising put premiums. Call options on the same asset will see their premiums fall. As we will see in a later chapter, calls and puts on the same underlying asset and same maturity must have changes in premiums that are inversely related.

7.3 American-Style Options and Early Exercise

We have determined that rising underlying asset prices will cause call premiums to rise while falling asset price would cause put prices to rise. If the option has European-style exercise, the holder has only one way to realize profits before maturity, i.e., by selling the option at the higher prevailing premium. However, if the option is American style, the holder of an in-the-money option has two choices. First, since American-style options can be exercised at or any time before maturity, the holder can choose to exercise immediately in order to realize profits. Alternatively, he can choose not to exercise but sell the option at the higher prevailing premium.

> **Note**
> Early exercise of an option would be inferior to selling the option since exercise captures only the intrinsic value. Selling the option would provide a premium that includes both intrinsic and time value.

Would the two choices provide the holder of the American style the same profit payoff? The answer is no. That the payoffs would be different has to do with the intrinsic and time values discussed in Chapter 6. Recall that an option's premium reflects the sum of its intrinsic and time values. Intrinsic value is the difference between the option's exercise price and the prevailing spot price of the underlying asset. The difference which is the intrinsic value is simply the profit one could derive from immediate exercise. Time value arises from time left to maturity. It should now be clear as to which of the two choices is better. Exercising the option would enable the holder to realize *only* the intrinsic value. However, the second choice of selling the option would provide the holder the premium that will always be higher than intrinsic value before maturity. Recall that time value is always positive before maturity. As such, selling rather than exercising would almost always be the superior choice. Thus, it should not be a surprise that though American-style options allow for **early exercise**, early exercise is uncommon. The only situation in which early exercise is advantageous is just before a large dividend payout by the underlying stock. Since stock price falls post-dividend, in the case of a large dividend payout, the loss in time value due to early exercise will be lower than the reduction in intrinsic value after dividend.

7.4 Intermediation and Margining

When options are listed on an exchange for trading, anyone with an account with a broker can choose to either buy or sell the listed options. A buy or sell order will go through as long as there is a counterparty. As an exchange-traded contract, parties to a transaction need not worry about the integrity of their counterparty. As the intermediary, the exchange, by means of novation, guarantees all transactions registered through its clearinghouse.

It is obvious that in guaranteeing transactions, the exchange is taking on the default risk of participants. As we saw in Chapter 3, derivative exchanges manage this risk by means of margining and the daily marking-to-market process. Unlike futures contracts where both the long and short positions have to post margins, margining for option contracts is somewhat different. In the case of futures, recall that both the long and short futures positions had risk profiles that had unlimited profit and loss potential. Depending on which way prices moved, the long or short futures position could lose, thus the need for margins on both parties. In the case of options, however, the long and short positions do not have the same risk profile. The maximum loss possible to the long call position is the amount of the premium. The investor's counterparty, the short call position, however, has the opposite risk profile. The short call position faces limited profits but unlimited loss potential. Figure 7.1 shows the payoff diagrams.

At maturity, for FBM KLCI index futures level above 1,854 points, the long position makes money but short position loses. At higher levels of the FBM KLCI, the short position loses progressively more. As we saw in Chapter 6, the long and short put positions have risk profiles identical to that of the respective call positions, that is, the long put has limited risk, unlimited profit, whereas the short put, limited profit, unlimited downside. Figures 7.2(a) and (b) shows the risk profit for an FBM KLCI put option exercisable at 1,850 points with a premium of 3 points.

238 CHAPTER 7 Financial Derivatives: Markets and Applications

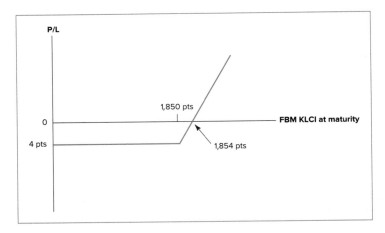

Figure 7.1 (a) Payoff Profile to FBM KLCI Index Call Positions; Long FBM KLCI, 1,850 Call @ 4 Points

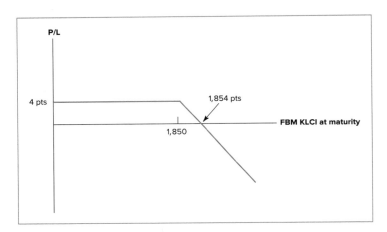

Figure 7.1(b) Short FBM KLCI Index, 1,850 Call @ 4 Points

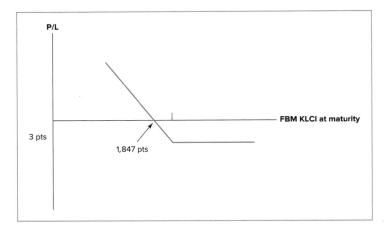

Figure 7.2(a) Payoff Profile to FBM KLCI Index Put Positions; Long FBM KLCI, 1,850 Put @ 3 Points

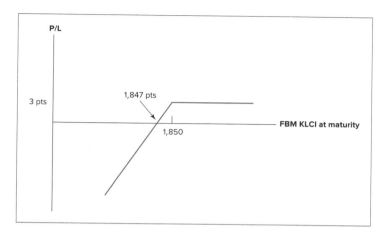

Figure 7.2(b)   Payoff Profile to FBM KLCI Index Put Positions; Short FBM KLCI, 1,850 Put @ 3 Points

Since the long position in options, regardless of whether it is a call or a put, has maximum downside risk equal to the amount of the premium and the premium is fully paid for at the time of purchase, the long position cannot possibly lose anymore. Thus, in the case of options, margins are applicable only to the short position. The short position posts an initial margin and faces daily marking-to-market and margin calls if underlying spot prices move in an unfavorable direction.

Notice that the earlier four payoff diagrams are no different from those seen in Chapter 6 for equity options, which are options on individual stocks. Regardless of underlying asset, the payoffs to calls and puts are the same.

7.5 Option Classes and Series

When options are made available for trading, an exchange typically lists a series of options of the same maturity but at different exercise prices. The idea behind having such a series is to have at least one in-the-money, one at-the-money, and one out-of-the-money option on the same underlying asset. As an example, suppose the FBM KLCI index futures is currently at 1,830 points, the class of index options listed for trading might look as follows:

30-day Index Options	
Calls	Puts
1,810 call @ 45 points	1,810 put @ 2 points
1,830 call @ 24 points	1,830 put @ 23 points
1,850 call @ 3 points	1,850 put @ 44 points

The list shows three 30-day index calls and puts at different exercise prices and hypothetical premiums. Since the FBM KLCI futures is currently assumed to be at 1,830, the 1,830 call and put are both at-the-money. The 1,850 call is out-of-the-money but the 1,850 put is in-the-money. Finally, the 1,810 call is in-the-money, whereas the put of the same exercise price is out-of-the-money.

The entire set of options on an underlying asset (both calls and puts) of various maturities and exercise prices are together known as a **class of options**. Options on the underlying asset with the same maturity and exercise price are known as an **option series**. Thus, in the earlier list, we see three option series, with each series representing an exercise price. When combined with index options of other maturities that may be outstanding, the earlier list would constitute a class of options.

Option moneyness as we know changes as the underlying asset changes in value. For example, suppose in the earlier illustration, the FBM KLCI index futures is at 1,880 points a week later; all the option series would have changed in moneyness. All three of the abovementioned calls would now be in-the-money, whereas all the puts out-of-the-money. As such, exchanges will have to list new option series in order to have at-the-money, in-the-money, and out-of-the-money options. Thus, a new series of calls and puts with exercise prices of 1,880 points, 1,860 points, and 1,900 points would have to be listed in order to have available at-the-money, in-the-money, and out-of-the-money options. The earlier listed options with exercise prices of 1,810, 1,830, and 1,850 points would continue to be available for trading, though at vastly different premiums.

One might be tempted to ask why, if in-the-money options are available, would anyone want to go long, out-of-the-money options? First, an out-of-the-money option may be needed as part of an overall strategy. Additionally, one should keep in mind that in efficient markets, one is no better off buying an in-the-money option relative to someone else who buys an out-of-the-money option. As you would have noticed, in-the-money options have much higher premiums than out-of-the-money options. In efficient markets, premiums would adjust to reflect the different exercise prices. In the absence of such adjustment, the options would be mispriced relative to one another, giving rise to arbitrage opportunity. In Chapter 10, we will examine how such relative mispricing could be arbitraged.

> **Note**
> *Ceteris paribus*, in-the-money options will have higher premiums. In efficient markets, premiums adjust to reflect option moneyness.

7.6 Malaysia's FBM KLCI Options: Contract Specifications

Contract specifications as we know are a key feature of exchange-traded contracts. Contract specifications outline the features and the rules by which trading in the contract is carried out. Table 7.1 is a reproduction of Bursa Malaysia's contract specifications for the FBM KLCI Futures Option.

Table 7.1 FBM KLCI Options: Contract Specifications

Contract Code	OKLI
Underlying Instrument	FBM KLCI Futures (FKLI)
Type	European style
Contract Size	One FKLI contract
Tick Size	0.1 index point valued at RM 5
Contract Months	Spot month, the next month, and the next two calendar quarterly months. The calendar quarterly months are March, June, September, and December.
Trading Hours	• First trading session: Malaysian time 8:45 a.m. to 12:45 p.m. • Second trading session: Malaysian time 2:30 p.m. to 5:15 p.m. Monday to Thursday (Malaysia time) After-hours (T+1) trading session: 9.00 p.m. to 11.30 p.m.
Exercise Price Interval	At least 13 exercise prices (6 are in-the-money, 1 is at-the-money and 6 are out-of-the-money) shall be set at interval of 10 index points for the spot and next month contracts. At least 7 exercise prices (3 are in-the-money, 1 is at-the-money and 3 are out-of-the-money) shall be set at interval of 20 index points for the next 2 quarterly month contracts.
Last Trading Day	The last business day of the contract month.
Settlement of Option Exercise	In the absence of contrary instructions delivered to the clearinghouse, an option that is in-the money at expiration shall be automatically exercised. Exercise results in a long FKLI position, which corresponds with the option's contract month for a call buyer or a put seller, and a short FKLI position for a put buyer or a call seller. The resultant positions in FKLI shall then be cash-settled based on the final settlement value of FKLI.
Speculative Position Limit	10,000 FKLI-equivalent contracts (a combination of OKLI and FKLI contract), net on the same side of the market in all contract months combined.

Source: Bursa Malaysia website.

We now turn to a description of some of the key features of the abovementioned contract specifications. First, the underlying asset is the FBM KLCI futures contracts. Thus, this is essentially an option on a futures contract. Such products are generally termed *futures options*. The minimum price fluctuation is 0.1 index points or RM 5. The minimum price fluctuation means that the futures price quoted as index points must be at least RM 5 higher or lower. Since these are options, the minimum price fluctuation refers to the **premium tick size**. That is, someone willing to sell an option at a lower than current premium must be willing to quote an ask price at least RM 5 lower. The ask price is the price at which someone is willing to sell, whereas the bid price is the price

Note
A futures option is an option on a futures contract. The underlying futures contract could be equity, currency, or commodity futures.

at which someone is willing to buy. Suppose, for example, an index call is currently quoted as follows:

1,850 call @ 4 points

A premium of 4 points would have a Ringgit value of RM 200. This is because the 4 points must be multiplied by the index multiplier of RM 50 for index futures (see Chapter 4). If an investor is willing to sell the call at a lower price/premium, he must reduce his ask price by at least 0.1 point or RM 5 from the current ask price of 4 points. Thus, he could quote 3.9 points or RM 195 as his ask price. Similarly, someone who is willing to buy at a higher price than the current 4 points must quote at 4.1 points or RM 205 as his bid price.

The **contract months** and daily trading hours are exactly as that of index futures. Notice that again as in index futures, the option contracts are traded for 15 minutes beyond the close of the underlying stock market. As explained in Chapter 4, this additional 15-minute window is to enable fund managers and other players to hedge their additional net exposures, if any, for the trading day.

Exercise price interval refers to the option series we had discussed earlier. Recall that exchanges typically list at least three call and put options of the same maturity but at different exercise prices. As shown in Table 7.1, at least 13 options with different exercise prices will be offered for the spot and next month, whereas the next two quarterly contracts will have seven different exercise prices available. The intervals between the exercise prices will be 10 points for the 13 spot and next month contracts. The latter maturing contracts (next two quarterly) will have broader exercise price intervals of 20 points. This is done so that there would be at least one in-the-money, at-the-money, and out-of-the-money options.

The **exercise style** is European. All options that are in-the-money at maturity are automatically exercised. The counter parties (short positions) to these in-the-money options will be assigned. As described earlier, profits made by the long position will be credited to their accounts after having been deducted and transferred from the margin accounts of the short position holders.

Margins on option contracts are subject to what is known as **risk-based margining**. More specifically, the clearinghouse executing the margin requirement, uses a computerized risk-based margining system known as *Theoretical Intermarket Margining* or TIMS. The system takes into consideration four key components: the premium margin, risk margin, spread margin, and delivery margin in addition to underlying market volatility and option sensitivity. Thus, the initial and maintenance margins vary from time to time under this system.

The **position limit** is 10,000 contracts on either the long or the short side. This 10,000 contract limit applies for the combined position in both the FKLI Index futures and the OKLI Index futures options. Recall that these limits are intended to check excessive speculative activity.

Where transaction costs are concerned, relative to the other derivative contracts, options are typically the most expensive. For example, compared with forwards, futures, and options, *ceteris paribus*, futures are usually the cheapest followed by forwards. Options would be the most expensive of the three. Still, options have continued to thrive despite the higher relative costs due to their many advantages.

7.7 Stock Options Traded on Hong Kong's HKEX

Stock options or equity options, as they are commonly known, are a popularly traded option contract in many markets. Table 7.2 shows a summary of HKEX's stock options.

Table 7.2   HKEX Stock Options — Contract Specifications

	Contract Terms
Underlying Stocks and HKATS Codes	Please refer to the list of stock options
Option Types	Puts and calls
Contract Size	Relevant information regarding contract size and tier level of individual stock option classes can be found in the list of stock options
Contracted Value	Option premium multiplied by the contract size
Contract Months	Spot, the next three calendar months, and the next three calendar quarter months (the exchange may introduce any other longer-dated expiry month in selected stock option classes as it deems necessary)
Minimum Fluctuation	HK$ 0.01
Option Premium	Quoted in HK$ on a per share basis
Strike Prices	<table><tr><th colspan="2">Underlying Prices</th><th>Interval</th></tr><tr><th>From</th><th>To</th><th></th></tr><tr><th>(HK$)</th><th>(HK$)</th><th>(HK$)</th></tr><tr><td>0</td><td>2</td><td>0.05</td></tr><tr><td>2</td><td>5</td><td>0.1</td></tr><tr><td>5</td><td>10</td><td>0.25</td></tr><tr><td>10</td><td>20</td><td>0.5</td></tr><tr><td>20</td><td>50</td><td>1</td></tr><tr><td>50</td><td>100</td><td>2.5</td></tr><tr><td>100</td><td>200</td><td>2.5</td></tr><tr><td>200</td><td>300</td><td>5</td></tr><tr><td>300</td><td>500</td><td>10</td></tr></table>
Trading Hours	9:30 a.m. to 12:00 noon and 1:00 p.m. to 4:00 p.m.
Expiry Day	The business day immediately preceding the last business day of the contract month

(*Continued*)

Table 7.2 (*Continued*)

	Contract Terms
Exercise Style (American)	Options can be exercised at any time up to 6:45 p.m. on any business day and including the last trading day
Exercise Fee	HK$ 2
Settlement	Physical delivery of underlying shares on exercise and settlement period are: T + 1 (options premium, payable in full) or T + 2 (stock transfer following exercise)
Trading Tariff	Tier 1 HK$ 3 Tier 2 HK$ 1 Tier 3 HK$ 0.50 Brokerage Commission Negotiable

These are put and call options on individual listed stocks. Currently, a total of 124 stocks listed on HKEX have been selected as eligible for options to be written on them. A full list of these stocks are available on HKEX website. Not surprisingly the most heavily traded options are on stocks of mainland China based companies, the likes of Tencent, China Communications Construction Co. (CCC), and Bank of China (BOC). With regards to contract size, the 124 stocks with options are divided into two categories, 56 stocks have option contracts with more than one underlying board lot of shares. The remaining 68 have option contract sizes equivalent to one board lot. The board lot refers to the number of shares in a listed/traded lot. Though typically 1,000 shares, some high-valued stocks have board lots of 100, 200, or 500 shares.

There are a few key points to note about the HKEX options based on the contract specifications. First notice that the contract size of the option will vary by the underlying stock's board lot. Thus, options on Tencent shares that currently trade at HK$ 454 have a board lot size of 100 shares, BOC trades at HK$ 29.10 and has a board lot size of 500 shares. CCC, which trades at about HK$ 4.57, has a lot size of 1,000 shares. A second point to note is that the interval in strike price series of the options varies with the underlying stock's price. The higher the stock price, the larger the exercise price interval. This is logical since the exchange would want to offer options that are in-, at-, and out-of-the-money at any given point. A third key point to note is that the exercise style is American, which means that the holder can exercise within the business hours of any trading day before maturity. Settlement requires physical delivery of the underlying stock.

Going by convention, suppose BOC stock is currently trading at HK$ 29.10 a 30-day stock option on BOC with an exercise price of HK$ 29 could be quoted as follows:

HK$ 29, 30-day BOC call @ 0.78

The quoted option premium of 78 cents can be attributed to 10 cents of intrinsic value, since it is already in the money by 10 cents, and the remaining 68 cents constitute the time value, as there are still 90 days to maturity.

A second series on the same stock with exercise price of HK$ 30 could be quoted as:

HK$ 30, 30-day BOC call @ 0.08

The premium of the HK$ 30 call is much lower since it is clearly out of the money. Since the intrinsic value is zero, the 8 cent premium is attributable to time value. Suppose the earlier two options on BOC stock were 30-day puts rather than calls, the premiums would obviously be different. The HK$ 29 put is slightly out of the money, whereas the HK$ 30 put is in the money. Thus, if they were puts, the HK$ 30 put would have the higher premium.

Although the American-style exercise of these equity options do indeed provide more flexibility than European-style options that can only be exercised at maturity, recall from our earlier discussion that selling rather exercising may be more profitable since one gets to sell for a premium that includes both the intrinsic and time values. As discussed, early exercise only enables the realization of the intrinsic value alone.

Box 7.1
Exchange-Traded Fund Options

Exchange-traded funds or ETFs are a fairly recent innovation. ETFs are really an outgrowth of the index fund, which is a mutual fund that passively manages a portfolio mimicking a stock index. Like an index fund, it is passively managed and invests in a portfolio that tracks closely an underlying stock index. Of late, there are ETFs that are based on narrow categories like "gold," real estate, or particular sectors of the economy. Gold ETF is one that invests only in stocks of firms involved in the gold business. On the other hand, the DJ Wilshire International Real Estate ETF offers exposure to stocks of real estate firms across a spectrum of countries. The world's best known ETF is probably the SPDR (also known as spider), which tracks the S&P 500 Stock Index of the United States (US).

What makes ETFs an interesting proposition is the exposure they provide to an index or basket of stocks in the form of a single unit or share of the ETF. That is, buying a single share of an ETF is similar to taking a small position in each of the stocks within the underlying index. This is made possible by the fact that an ETF is listed on an exchange and its shares traded like any other shares. Besides the trading flexibility that it allows, ETFs offer instant diversification, access to diverse market segments, transparent pricing, and above all lower transaction costs. The lower transaction costs result from the fact that ETFs are passively managed. Like other listed shares, the value of an ETF share gets a price quote that is dependent on the ETF's NAV. Following the huge success of ETFs, a number of US derivative exchanges, notably the Chicago Board

(*Continued*)

Box 7.1
(Continued)

Options Exchange (CBOE) have introduced options on ETFs. Known simply as ETF options, they offer investors the right to buy or sell a predetermined size of the underlying listed ETF at the exercise price. Operationally, they are like index options. However, many ETF options have American-style exercise and may require physical delivery of the constituent stocks. In addition to ETF options on equity, there are also ETF options on commodities. Some examples of these are Financial Select Sector SPDR (XLF), an ETF of financial sector stocks from the S&P 500 index, iShares MSCI Emerging Markets Index (EEM), an ETF of "stocks from MSCI's Emerging Markets Index" and US Natural Gas Fund ETF (UNG), a commodity ETF.

7.8 Stock Index Options in Thailand — The SET 50 Index Options

Launched on October 29, 2007, the SET 50 Index option was the second derivative product listed on the TFEX. The SET 50 Index option contract is an exchange traded option contract that has the SET 50 Index, a basket of the top 50 stocks listed on the Stock Exchange of Thailand (SET), as its underlying asset. The SET 50 Index option contract gives traders the right, but not the obligation, to buy or sell the underlying asset, which is the SET 50 Index, at a specified exercise price on the maturity date. Since its launch, the SET 50 Index option contract has experienced impressive growth in trading volume. Figure 7.3 illustrates the annual trading volume of SET 50 Index options from 2007 to 2020.

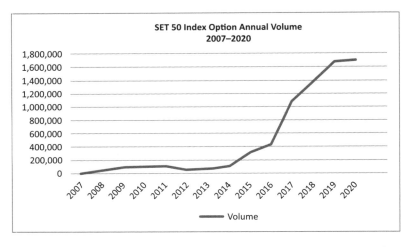

Figure 7.3   SET 50 Index Options — Growth in Annual Trading Volume

The total annual traded volume of the SET 50 Index options which was merely 9,000 contracts in 2007, reached approximately 1.7 million contracts in 2020. This constitutes a highly impressive average CAGR of 46% over the 14 years.

Table 7.3 shows the contract specifications for the SET 50 Index options extracted from the TFEX's website.

The SET 50 Index options are available in both call, with ticker symbol S50C, and put, with ticker symbol S50P, options. The contract multiplier is THB 200. Which means that if the SET 50 Index is at 1,000 points, each option contract would cost 1,000 × THB 200 or THB 200,000. The exercise style of SET 50 Index options are European, which means that they can only be exercised on the maturity date. Like most financial derivatives, they are cash settled. The Final settlement price of the contract at maturity is determined by averaging the value of the index, based on trading during the last 15 minutes and the closing index value. The averaging is done after removing the three highest and lowest values during that period, rounded to the nearest two decimal points.

Table 7.3   Contract Specifications of the SET 50 Index Options

Underlying Asset	SET 50 Index Which is Calculated from the Prices of 50 Selected SET Stocks
Ticker Symbol	S50C: Call Options S50P: Put Options
Contract Multiplier	SET 50 multiplied by THB 200
Minimum Price Fluctuation	0.10 index point
Daily Price Limits	30% of the previous day's SET 50 Index
Exercise Style	European
Contract Months	3 nearest consecutive months plus 1 quarterly month
Trading Hours	Morning preopen: 09:15–09:45 hours. Morning session: 09:45–12:30 hours. Afternoon preopen: 13:45–14.15 hours. Afternoon session: 14:15–16:55 hours
Final Trading Day	The business day immediately preceding the last business day of the contract month
Final Settlement	Cash settlement based on the final settlement price
Final Settlement Price	The final settlement price shall be the numerical value of the SET 50 Index, rounded to the nearest two decimal points as determined by the exchange, and shall be the average value of the SET 50 Index taken during last 15 minutes and the closing index value, after deleting the three highest and three lowest values
Settlement Method	Cash settlement

Source: TFEX website.

7.8.1 SET 50 Index Options: Applications

7.8.1.1 Hedging Equity Exposure with SET 50 Index Options

A highly popular use of index options like the SET 50 Index option is to hedge one's portfolio against market volatility. Popularly known as *portfolio insurance*, the strategy involves combining index put options with an existing broad portfolio of stocks. The objective is to limit potential downside risk while at the same time, benefit from any upside rally. Recall from our discussion in Chapter 6 that options, given their flexibility, enables us to limit downside risk while simultaneously benefitting from potential upside movements.

Assume that you hold a portfolio of Thai stocks that track the SET 50 Index. The beta of your portfolio like that of the index is 1.0. It is obvious that the value of the portfolio is heavily dependent on market movements. If the market rallies, your portfolio's value increases. On the other hand, if the market declines, you experience losses on your position as well. Suppose the current value of your stock portfolio is THB 1 million, and the SET 50 Index is currently at 1,000. If over the next 3 months, the SET 50 Index goes up to 1,100, or a 10% increase, your portfolio, which mimics the SET 50 Index will also go up by 10%. The total value of your portfolio will be THB 1.1 million. On the other hand, if the SET 50 Index declines, e.g., to 900, your portfolio value will also reduce by 10%, and the value of your portfolio will be THB 900,000.

Suppose you now have reasons to believe that the next 3 months could be highly volatile for Thai stocks with potential for sharp downturns. A natural question that arises is, how can we limit the downside risk and hedge the portfolio against a market downturn?

Since you seek protection from falling prices, hedging would require you to combine your stock portfolio position with an option position that benefits from falling prices. Recall that a long put position gains when underlying asset price falls. Thus, the correct strategy here would be long 3-month SET 50 Index put options.

The following information is available to you in January.

SET 50 Index = 1,000 points
Put Option:
    Exercise Price, $K = 1,000$ (at-the-money)
        Maturity, $T =$ March (90 days)
    Put Premium, $P = $ THB 15

The next step is to determine the number of SET 50 Index put option contracts you need to purchase. This will depend on a number of factors like (i) whether you want to fully or partially hedge, (ii) the size of each index option contract, and (iii) adjustment for differences in your portfolio's beta relative to the market portfolio represented by the index option. Since your portfolio mimics the SET 50 Index and has beta = 1.0, the number of contracts needed to fully hedge your portfolio of THB 1 million can be determined as follows:

Value of portfolio/Value per option contract
THB 1,000,000/(1,000 × THB 200) = 5 contracts

Hedge strategy: long 5 March SET 50 Index put option contracts

To see how the SET 50 Index put option will protect your portfolio, we examine the following two scenarios, one where the SET 50 Index falls in March, and another where the index rises.

Scenario 1: SET 50 Index Falls over the Next 3 Months
Suppose the SET 50 Index falls from 1,000 points in January to 800 points at maturity in March.

Impact on Your Portfolio:
Your portfolio value will be THB 800,000.

Impact of the SET 50 Index Put Option:

Profit from exercise of puts	= Max($K - S_T$, 0) × Multiplier × Number of contracts
	= Max(1,000 − 800, 0) × THB 200 × 5
	= THB 200,000
Less premium paid for puts	= (THB 15 × THB 200) × 5 contracts
	= (THB 15,000)
Net Profit from puts	= THB 185,000

Result of Hedge

Value of your stock portfolio	= THB 800,000
Profit from puts	= THB 185,000
Value of hedged portfolio at maturity	**= THB 985,000**

Notice that even though the index fell 200 points and the stock portfolio's value fell by THB 200,000, the puts provided a profit of THB 185,000 effectively reducing the loss of the overall hedged portfolio to THB 15,000. This loss is essentially the cost of the portfolio insurance as reflected in the total premium paid for five index put option contracts. So, the maximum loss possible for a fully hedged portfolio is the total premium paid for the insurance.

Scenario 2: SET 50 Index Rises over the Next 3 Months
Suppose the SET 50 Index rises from 1,000 in January to 1,200 in March.

Impact on Your Portfolio
Your portfolio value will now be THB 1,200,000.

Impact of the SET 50 Index Put Options

Profit from exercise of puts = Max($K - S_T$, 0) × Multiplier × Number of contracts
= Max(1,000 − 1,200, 0) × THB 200 × 5
= THB 0
Less premium paid for puts = (THB 15,000)
Net Profit/loss from puts = (THB 15,000)

Result of Hedge

Value of your stock portfolio = THB 1,200,000
Profit/loss from puts = (THB 15,000)
Value of hedged portfolio at maturity = THB 1,185,000

When the market and underlying stocks rise, the put options will not be exercised and loss from the put position will only be the premium paid when you purchased the put options. Overall, notice that under this strategy, the index put options act as insurance to your stock portfolio. When the market declines, the put options will provide positive payoffs to offset the loss to your stock portfolio. On the other hand, when market rises, the strategy still allows you to benefit from the price increases. Table 7.4 and Figure 7.4 show the value of long

Table 7.4 Payoff to Hedged Long SET 50 Stocks Position

SET 50 Index	Value of Stock Portfolio Position	Profit/Loss to Long Put Position	Value of Combined Position at Maturity
500	500,000	485,000	985,000
600	600,000	385,000	985,000
700	700,000	285,000	985,000
800	800,000	185,000	985,000
900	900,000	85,000	985,000
1,000	1,000,000	(15,000)	985,000
1,100	1,100,000	(15,000)	1,085,000
1,200	1,200,000	(15,000)	1,185,000
1,300	1,300,000	(15,000)	1,285,000
1,400	1,400,000	(15,000)	1,385,000
1,500	1,500,000	(15,000)	1,485,000

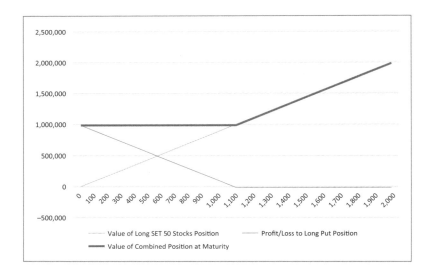

Figure 7.4 Portfolio Insurance with SET 50 Index Put Options

SET 50 stocks positions, the profit/loss from the put options and the value of combined position at maturity.

The overall payoff line in bold shows that the hedged portfolio maintains its original value even as the stock market falls but the hedged portfolio participates in the upside if the market rises. This dual benefit of downside protection and simultaneous upside participation arises from the inherent flexibility of options, that they provide the right but not the obligation.

7.8.1.2 Speculating with SET 50 Index Options

Speculative trading is a commonly used application of index options such as the SET 50 Index option contracts. To see how index options could be used as part of speculative strategies, consider the following. Suppose you expect the Thai equity market to rise over the next few months and wish to take advantage of the expectation. Since you are expecting broad market movement, you need an equity derivative that provides exposure to the overall market, not just individual stocks. The SET 50 Index options would provide the broad market exposure needed to take an advantage of your view. Since you are bullish and call options benefit from upside movement of the underlying, the correct strategy would be to **long SET 50 Index call options.**

Illustration: Speculative Strategy for Bullish Expectation

The following information is available to you in January.

SET 50 Index = 1,000 points
Call Option:
    Exercise Price, K = 1,000 (at-the-money)
    Maturity, T = March (90 days)
    Call Premium, C = THB 20

Table 7.5 illustrates the SET 50 Index call option payoff and profit/loss at maturity for various SET 50 Index values. Notice that if the SET 50 Index remains at 1,000 or below, the call option

Table 7.5 SET 50 Index Call Option Payoff and Profit/Loss

SET 50 Index	Call Option Profit/Loss
500	−20
600	−20
700	−20
800	−20
900	−20
1,000	−20
1,100	80
1,200	180
1,300	280
1,400	380
1,500	480

will be out-of-the money and so, will not be exercised. However, the premium paid constitutes the loss of THB 20. This is because when you purchased the index call option in January, you paid a call premium of THB 20, and when the option is exercised, the profit will always be THB 20 less than the profit from exercise. As we can see from the table, the higher the SET 50 index at maturity, the larger the call option payoff and profit will be.

Table 7.5 shows the payoff without the index multiplier. Taking the multiplier into consideration, since the contract multiplier is THB 200 and the call premium is THB 20, the total cost of buying one SET 50 Index call option contract would be THB 200 × THB 20 = THB 4,000. Thus, if in March, the SET 50 Index rises to 1,100 (i.e., $S_T = 1,100$), you would exercise the call option and the payoff will be $\max(S_T - K, 0) = \max(1,100 - 1,000, 0) = 100$. Since the contract multiplier is 200, your total payoff will be 100 × THB 200 = THB 20,000 for one contract. Net of the premium paid, your profit will be THB 20,000 − THB 4,000 = THB 16,000.

If, on the other hand, the SET 50 Index had gone down in value, for example to 900, the call would not be exercised at maturity. Thus, your loss would be equal to the amount of premium you paid, which would be THB 4,000. Intuitively, if the SET 50 Index is below the exercise price at maturity, the call option will be out of the money. Recall that the maximum loss for a long call option will be the option premium that you paid when you created the position, which in this case would be THB 20 × 200 = THB 4,000 per contract.

Illustration: Speculative Strategy for Bearish Expectation

Suppose you now anticipate a market downturn and expect that the SET 50 Index will decline over the next 3 months, can you use the SET 50 Index options to take advantage of your expectation? The answer is yes. However, in this case, since you want to benefit from falling prices, you use a put option instead. As we discussed in the earlier sections, a (European) put option gives a holder the right to sell the underlying asset at exercise price, and so benefits from falling prices.

The following information is available to you in January.

SET 50 Index = 1,000
Put Option:
    Exercise Price, K = 1,000 (at-the-money)
    Maturity, T = March (90 days)
    Put Premium, P = THB 15

Table 7.6 illustrates the profit/loss payoff to the SET 50 Index put option at maturity for various SET 50 Index values. Notice that if the SET 50 Index remains at 1,000, the put option will have provide zero profit on exercise resulting in a loss of THB 15. This is because when the put option was purchased in January, you paid the put premium of THB 15, and regardless of whether the put option is exercised at maturity, the profit/loss will always be THB 15 less

Table 7.6 SET 50 Index Put Option Payoff and Profit/Loss

SET 50 Index	Put Option Profit/Loss
500	485
600	385
700	285
800	185
900	85
1,000	−15
1,100	−15
1,200	−15
1,300	−15
1,400	−15
1,500	−15

than the profit on exercise. As seen from the table, the lower the SET 50 Index at maturity, the larger the put option's profit payoff.

The put option has the exercise price of 1,000. Since the contract multiplier is THB 200 and the put premium is THB 15, the total cost to buy the SET 50 Index put option will be THB 200 × THB 15 = THB 3,000. If in March, the SET 50 Index declines to 900 (i.e., $S_T = 900$), you would exercise the put option and the payoff will be max($K - S_T$, 0) = max(1,000 − 900, 0) = 100. Since the contract multiplier is THB 200, your total payoff will be 100 × THB 200 = THB 20,000 for 1 contract. Your profit net of premium will be THB 20,000 − THB 3,000 = THB 17,000.

If instead of going down as you had expected, suppose the SET 50 Index had gone up in value, for example to 1,100, the put would now be out-of-the-money and not worthy of being exercised. In this case, your payoff would be a loss equivalent to the amount you paid as premium, which in this case is THB 3,000. Intuitively, for any SET 50 Index value above the exercise price at maturity, the put option will be out of the money. As was the case with call options, the maximum loss for a long put option will be the option premium.

7.8.1.3 Arbitrage Strategy — Arbitraging with Index Options

Yet another application of SET 50 Index options is in executing arbitrage strategies. Arbitrage, as discussed in earlier chapters, is the act of taking advantage of the mispricing of asset or price differentials across markets. In the context of options, when calls and puts are traded on the same underlying asset for the same exercise price and maturity, an equilibrium relative pricing condition known as put–call parity should prevail. The put–call parity condition is described in depth in Chapter 10. In simple terms, if a put option is overpriced, the arbitrage strategy would be to short (sell) the put that is overpriced and long (buy) a *synthetic* put position that can be created using calls and the underlying stock. Such arbitrage will earn a return equivalent to the size of the mispricing. However, as more and more such arbitrage happens, the mispricing will narrow and eventually disappear restoring equilibrium in pricing.

Taking into account, the interest rate and the timing difference in cash outlays, the put–call parity can be written as follows:

$$S - K(1+r)^{-t} = C + -P$$

where

S = stock price
r = annualized interest rate
K = exercise price of the options
t = days to maturity of the options
C = call premium
P = put premium

The put–call parity implies that any deviation from the abovementioned relationship would provide an arbitrage opportunity, and a riskless arbitrage profit can be made because of mispricing. Consider the following example. Suppose the SET 50 Index currently is 1,000. SET 50 Index options, 90 days to maturity, with an exercise price of 1,000 are quoted THB 20, and THB 10 for the call and put, respectively. Assume that the risk-free interest rate is 5%. To see whether there is mispricing, we examine the put–call parity as follows:

$S - K(1+r)^{-t}$ $= C + -P$
$1,000 - 1,000(1.05)^{-0.25}$ $= 20 - 10$
$1,000 - 987.88$ $= 10$
$12.12 > 10$

As is obvious from the earlier analysis, the put–call parity is violated. The mispricing differential is equal to THB 2.12 (THB 12.12 – THB 10) or THB 2,424 (THB 2.12 × multiplier THB 200) of arbitrage profit to be made per contract. What arbitrage strategy should we take to capture this mispricing opportunity? Looking at the earlier analysis, we can see that the left-hand side of the equation is larger than the right side. Thus, to take advantage, we need to short the components on the left side and at the same time long the right-hand side. Thus, our arbitrage strategy should be as follows:

Arbitrage Strategy
— Short SET 50 Index
— Lend an amount equal to the PV of exercise price
— Long call
— Short put

Table 7.7 Payoffs to Arbitrage Strategy with SET 50 Index Options

Strategy	CF_0 (today)	At Maturity	
		SET 50 = 1,200 CF_{90}	SET 50 = 800 CF_{90}
Short SET 50	THB 1,000	(THB 1,200)	(THB 800)
Lend PV of exercise	(THB 987.88)	THB 1,000	THB 1,000
Long call option	(THB 20)	THB 200	0
Short put option	THB 10	0	(THB 200)
Net cash flow	THB 2.12	0	0

Table 7.7 illustrates the needed arbitrage transactions and shows that regardless of market movement the riskless arbitrage profit is locked in at the point of strategy execution. The table shows two scenarios, first when the SET 50 Index rises to 1,200 and a second scenario where the index falls to 800 points. Notice that the strategy yields a positive net cash flow of THB 2.12 when the positions are established. In both scenarios, however, we can see that the cash flows at maturity are equal to 0, suggesting a risk-free arbitrage opportunity.

Box 7.2
Vigilante Capitalism: Should We Cheer It On?

For perhaps the first time, the small guys seem to have turned the tables on the big boys. Retail investors on Reddit used the discussion website to gang up against hedge funds that were shorting Gamestop, a small video games retailer. The small investors had used the commission-free online broker, Robinhood, to take long positions on both Gamestop stock and its call options. In true David versus Goliath form, the retail players were collectively taking the opposite position of the hedge funds. Gamestop stock which was around $6 in September 2020 and $20 in early January this year, ended the month at $347 an approximate 1,600% rise. The traded volume of the puny company's stock exceeded the likes of Tesla and Apple, the latter being more than 200 times its size. As if Gamestop stock wasn't enough, the retail players on the same Reddit forum then targeted Silver, jumping on a Silver ETF, causing a huge spike in spot prices. The foray into Silver, however, seems to have been shorter lived and much less successful than their move on stocks. Like vigilantes, who in the absence of authorized enforcement, take it upon themselves to clean up a neighborhood, these retail investors had chosen to go up against the hedge funds. Hedge funds, as some critics have alleged, have for long been able to rig markets given their size and financial clout. This was probably the first time that retail investors had orchestrated a broad-based push back against hedge

(*Continued*)

Box 7.2
(*Continued*)

funds. As a result, at least one large hedge fund was forced to close out its short position in Gamestop at losses estimated in tens of billions.

Loose regulation on short selling, extensive use of derivatives particularly equity options that make it easy to synthesize short positions, without actually shorting the stock, low trading fees and tax on gains, all give undue advantage to big players with access to borrowed capital. Establishing synthetic short positions using options avoids the need to borrow the underlying stock, thus placing little restriction on how large the short position could be. Ironically, what is tolerated on Wall Street would not be in other asset markets. For example, in commodity futures markets, uptick rules, risk-based margining, and perhaps most importantly, position limits act as constraints. Furthermore, on many occasions derivative exchanges have stepped-in to change delivery requirements when there is clear evidence of a market squeeze or cornering. Such initiatives effectively cause the ill-gotten profits to evaporate. Thus, the derivative markets may have tighter and more effective regulatory control on players than does Wall Street.

Despite the issues, short selling should not be stopped, for it does have an important role especially in arbitrage activity. Well-functioning markets need arbitrageurs to keep prices in line. When prices go out of line to be either artificially depressed or pumped up through speculation, arbitrage activity can move in to take advantage of relative mispricing, effectively killing off the speculation, and restoring "equilibrium" prices. Many hedging strategies too may require the taking of short positions as part of the overall hedge. Thus, a blanket prohibition of short selling would be misplaced.

What the Reddit investors did with Gamestop was by no means an arbitrage. Quite the opposite, they were actually taking naked speculative positions themselves by going long in such a big way, in a stock that had little by way of fundamentals. Their collective action amounts to little more than syndicated ramping to pump up prices. Indeed, Gamestop's stock price movement over the 2-week period January 20 to February 4 shows a classic pump and dump pattern. The stock which was at $39 on January 20, hit its peak of $347 a week later on January 27 before sliding to $53 on February 4. It remained at that price range to end at $52 on February 12. On most exchanges, such action would constitute serious violation. So, while the hedge funds on short side were wrong, so too the retail players. Two wrongs do not make a right.

Although there is no doubt that markets should be sufficiently free in order to operate efficiently, it must be balanced against the need for regulatory oversight to ensure that

> **Box 7.2**
> (*Continued*)
>
> they are free from manipulation. Like everything else there is a trade-off. A huge social cost arises when markets are not credible, unfair, and lack integrity. Disintermediation and reduced investor interest can cause a substantial increase in the cost of funds to all listed firms, this in turn leads to reduced national competitiveness and systemic problems.
>
> *Source*: Adapted from author's op-ed article.

7.9 Currency Options

Currency options, like currency futures, are derivatives that have an exchange rate or spot exchange rate as the underlying asset. Just as a call option on a stock will enable one to buy the underlying stock at the exercise price if one chooses to exercise, a currency call option will enable the purchase of the underlying foreign currency at the exercise price. Similarly, a currency put option would allow the holder to sell the underlying foreign currency at the exercise price, if he chooses to exercise. Though currency options are widely traded on over-the-counter (OTC) markets, there are several exchange traded currency options. The International Monetary Market (IMM), which is part of the Chicago Mercantile Exchange (CME) is the pioneering exchange for currency derivatives, having introduced them in the early 1970s following the collapse of the fixed exchange rate Bretton Woods system in late 1971. Since then a number exchanges worldwide, like the Tokyo International Financial Futures Exchange (TIFFE), the London International Financial Futures and Options Exchange (LIFFE), BM&F (Brazil), MATIF (France), SGX (Singapore), HKEX (Hong Kong), have all introduced currency derivatives. The objective being to provide the means for businesses to hedge their currency risks. Both the SGX in Singapore and HKEX of Hong Kong offer several currency options. According to the World Federation of Exchanges' (WFE) 2019 report, global trading volume for currency derivatives grew 30.9% in 2019 Singapore's SGX which had a 6% volume growth of currency derivatives was in ninth position among the top 10 exchanges for currency derivatives in 2019. We will discuss in depth the US$/CNH Currency Options traded on HKEX.

The US$/CNH Currency Option Contracts

Following the successful launch of the US$/CNH currency futures in September 2012, and the very active market in OTC currency options, the HKEX introduced exchange-traded currency option contracts in March 2017. As we saw in Chapter 6, options, in addition to providing hedging benefits, have the flexibility to be used in a multitude of positions. As the HKEX lists a large series of calls and puts at different exercise prices, bull-call spreads and bear put spreads can be used in addition to outright calls and puts for hedging. The spread strategies enable lower costs of hedging. The lower costs obviously come with a cap on the upside. In addition to spreads, straddles are commonly used to take advantage of expectations about the volatility of the US$/CNH exchange rate. The contract size (or notional principal) is US$ 100,000. The call options would enable the holder to receive US$ 100,000 for each contract on exercise in exchange for payment in CNH. The put holder on the other hand delivers US$ and receives CNH at maturity. Thus, unless the positions are offset before maturity, the positions are physically settled in cash at maturity. Table7.8 shows a summary of the contract specifications.

Table 7.8 HKEX US$/CNH Currency Options — Contract Specifications

HKATS Code	CUS	
Contract Size	US$ 100,000	
Price Quotation	Amount of RMB per US$	
Options Premium	4 decimal places (e.g., 0.0001)	
Tick Value	RMB 10	
Strike Prices	Strike intervals shall be set at intervals of 0.05 ±10% from the at-the-money strike price	
Exercise Style	European	
Settlement on Exercise	Physical delivery on exercise	
	Holder	**Writer**
Call options	Payment of the Final Settlement Value* in RMB	Delivery of US$
Put options	Delivery of US$ Value in RMB	Payment of the final settlement
*Final settlement value is the strike price multiplied by the contract size; applies to both call and put options		
Official Settlement Price	US$/CNY (HK) spot rate published by Hong Kong Treasury Markets Association (TMA) at or around 11:30 a.m. on the expiry day	
Contract Months	Spot month, the next 3 calendar months, and the next 4 calendar quarter months	
Final Settlement Day	Generally the third Wednesday of the contract month	
Trading Hours	9:00 a.m. to 4:30 p.m. on a normal trading day 9:00 a.m. to 11:00 a.m. on the expiry day	
Expiry Day	Two Hong Kong business days prior to the final settlement day	
Large Open Positions	500 open contracts in any one series	

Source: HKEX website.

7.9.1 Applications with Currency Options

7.9.1.1 *Hedging Exchange Rate Risk with Currency Options*

To see how currency options could be used to manage exchange rate risk, we use two examples, one a Chinese exporter with US$ receivable and second a Chinese importer with a US$ payable. Since the nature of the currency risk is different, each Chinese company would have to use a different option to hedge itself.

(i) Hedging a US$ Receivable

Suppose a Chinese producer of apparel has exported to a US retail chain and has a US$ 3 million receivable in 60 days. What is the nature of the currency risk and how should the Chinese firm hedge the risk? Since the firm has a receivable in US$, its fear would be the US$ depreciating against the Renminbi or Yuan. A depreciation of the US$ would mean lower proceeds in home currency terms. Thus, to protect itself, the firm should buy a currency option that will benefit from a fall in the US$. A put option would. Thus, the correct hedge strategy for this firm with a US$ receivable would be

long 30 two-month US$/CNH put options

Going long put options would enable them to sell the US$ at the exercise price on maturity. The firm will only choose to exercise the puts, if the spot exchange rate is ***lower*** than the exercise price. Should the firm choose to exercise, it simply delivers the US$ received from its customer and receives in return CNH. Thirty contracts are needed given the contract size is 100,000 and the total exposure is US$ 3,000,000. Suppose the exercise price of the puts are CNH 6.45 per US$, the firm will be assured of a minimum CNH 19,350,000 proceeds from the US$ receivable, determined as follows:

$$\text{CNH } 6.45 \times 100{,}000 \times 30 \text{ contracts} = \text{CNH } 19{,}350{,}000$$

Note that unlike, forwards and futures where the amount hedged will be "locked-in," here, with options, the above is a revenue floor. Should the spot exchange rate at option maturity be any higher than the exercise rate of CNH 6.45 per US$, the firm would be better off not exercising the puts and simply converting the received US$ 3,000,000 at the higher spot rate. The put option therefore sets a minimum amount in CNH for the US$ receivable.

(ii) Hedging a US$ Payable

Now, suppose a Chinese airline has imported aircraft parts from Boeing and has a US$ 5 million invoice payable in 90 days. What is the nature of the currency risk and how should the Chinese firm hedge the risk? Since the firm has a US$ payable, its fear will be the potential appreciation of the US$ against the Renminbi or Yuan. An appreciation of the US$ will mean higher costs in home currency terms. Thus, to protect itself, the Chinese airline should buy a currency option that will benefit from a rise in US$. Clearly in this case, call options would benefit from rising US$. Thus, the correct hedge strategy for the Chinese airline would be

long 50 three-month US$/CNH call options

Going long the currency call options would enable the firm to buy/receive US$ at the exercise price on option maturity. Should the firm choose to exercise, it pays the CNH amount based on the exercise price and receives the US$ 5,000,000. Clearly, the firm will only choose to exercise if it is beneficial to do so. Here, exercise will happen if the US$ appreciates and the spot rate at option maturity is **higher** than the exercise exchange rate. Assuming the exercise exchange rate is 6.45 CNH per US$, the hedge strategy establishes a ceiling or maximum cost to the firm of CNH 32,250,000. This maximum amount is determined as:

$$CNH\ 6.45 \times 100,000 \times 50\ contracts = CNH\ 32,250,000$$

Should the spot rate at option maturity be any lower than 6.45, it will better for the firm to not exercise the calls, but simply buy the needed US$ at the lower spot rate and pay Boeing. Thus, the use of currency call options in this case, enables the Chinese airline to establish a maximum home currency cost for its imported parts.

7.9.1.2 Speculating with Currency Options

Currency options are often used to speculate on future exchange rate movements. Currency traders may have expectations of the future movement of one currency against another. These expectations may be due to changes in economic fundamentals like interest rates, gross domestic product (GDP) growth rates, inflation rates, or other noneconomic factors like political events, etc. Thus, when a speculator believes based on his assessment that a currency is likely to appreciate or depreciate against another, he might want to establish a position using currency options in order to profit from that expectation. To see how such speculative trading can be undertaken, we use the example of the US$/CNH currency option traded on HKEX. Going by the contract specification in Table 7.7, note the following:

— The call option would provide the right to buy US$ 100,000 at the predetermined CNH (RMB) exercise price on maturity date.
— The put option would provide the right to sell US$ 100,000 at the predetermined CNH (RMB) exercise price on maturity date.

To understand how the US$/CNH currency option contract can be used for speculation, we examine two scenarios, first, where a trader is bullish about the US$ and expects it to appreciate against the CNH. The second scenario is the opposite, a trader is bearish about the US$ and expects it to depreciate against the CNH.

Scenario 1: Expectation — Bullish About US$ Against CNH

A currency trader believes based on his assessment of the latest economic data that the US$ is likely to appreciate against the CNH over the next 3 months. He observes the following quotations on the HKEX:

3-Month Call Option
— Exercise price of RMB 6.35 per US$
— Premium is quoted at RMB 0.0380 per US$

3-Month Put Option
— Exercise price of RMB 6.35 per US$
— Premium is quoted at RMB 0.0320 per US$

Since the trader wants to take advantage of a rising US$, the appropriate position would be to long the 3-month call option. Assuming he goes long one contract and if his expectation was correct and the US$ appreciates to 6.47 at contract maturity, then the profit from his strategy would be:

— Profit on Exercise $= ((6.47 - 6.35) \times 100{,}000)$
  $= $ RMB 12,000
— Less Premium Paid $= $ RMB 0.0380 per US$ $\times 100{,}000$
  $= $ (RMB 3,800)

Net Profit = RMB 8,200

If, however, the trader's expectation did not turn out and the US$ instead depreciated against the CNH (RMB) to say RMB 6.32 per US$ at contract maturity, then the trader would obviously not exercise the call option and he would lose the RMB 3,800 he had paid for the premium. Given the premium of RMB 0.0380 per US$, the break-even exchange rate is RMB 6.3880. At any exchange rate higher than RMB 6.3880 per US$ at maturity, he will make profits on his position.

Scenario 2: Expectation — Bearish About US$ Against CNH

Suppose a Singapore-based currency trader is of the opinion that the CNH or RMB is likely to appreciate against the US$ over the next few weeks. He wants to trade on his expectation of a depreciating US$ against the Chinese currency. He sees the following quotes for at-the-money currency options on HKEX:

Spot Month Call Option
— Exercise price of RMB 6.38 per US$
— Premium is quoted at RMB 0.021 per US$

Spot Month Put Option
— Exercise price of RMB 6.38 per US$
— Premium is quoted at RMB 0.0200 per US$

Since he is bearish about the US$ and a put position benefits from falling values, the appropriate strategy would be to long put options. Suppose he goes long one spot month put option contract and the US$ depreciates to 6.21 at contract maturity, then it is clearly profitable for him to exercise. To exercise, he needs to deliver US$ and receive CNH/RMB in return. Thus, he needs to first buy the US$ at the spot rate of 6.21, then deliver it and receive the exercise price of RMB 6.38. The profit would be:

— Purchase US$ 100,000 at spot of 6.21 = (RMB 621,000)
— Exercise put and receive RMB   = RMB 638,000
— Profit from exercise   = RMB 17,000
— Less premium paid   = (RMB 2,000)
Net Profit   **= RMB 15,000**

Note that this speculative profit of RMB/CNH 15,000 excludes transaction costs as we ignored bid-ask spreads when purchasing the US$ at spot. Note that the break-even exchange rate for his strategy is RMB 6.36 per US$. At any spot rate below 6.36, the strategy becomes profitable.

If, however, the trader's expectation turned out to be wrong and the US$ appreciated, he would not exercise the put and would lose the entire premium of RMB 2,000. It is obvious that given a highly liquid market, the trader can cut losses by selling his put and reversing out his position prior to maturity. So, if the trader sees the US$ appreciating after he had gone long the put option, he can either continue to hold the position if he is convinced of his outlook or choose to cut losses and get out of the position by selling the put. Since the US$ has already moved against him, the put he bought at a premium of RMB 2,000 would already be trading at a lower premium, implying he will still make a loss. This is the reality of naked speculative positions, where unlike a hedge, there is no other position to offset the losses. A naked speculative position either profits or loses depending on whether prices moved according to expectations or otherwise. The size of the profit will depend of the size of the movement in prices or in this exchange rates.

7.9.1.3 Arbitraging with Currency Options

Arbitraging with currency options works on the same principle as with other arbitrage situations. One goes long (buys) the undervalued asset while shorting (selling) the overvalued one. The one complication here is that an exchange rate, which is the basis of currency options, is the price of one currency in terms of another. One should be careful to differentiate between mispricing of the exchange rate, where one currency is misaligned against another versus a mispriced currency option. A currency option is mispriced when its quoted price has deviated from its theoretical value. The theoretical value or correct price of a currency option can be determined using an option pricing model such as the Garman–Kohlhagen model. The Garman–Kohlhagen model is probably the most popularly used currency option model, which we will examine in Chapter 9.

When a currency option's quoted price is different from its model-derived price, the currency option is mispriced. If the percentage deviation in pricing is larger than the potential transactions costs, the mispricing can be arbitraged profitably. But how do we arbitrage a mispriced currency option? If a currency call option is overpriced, we short the call and long a synthesized short call position. The synthetic position is created using puts and the underlying asset, in this case the exchange rate. In the context of options, when calls and puts are traded on the same underlying asset for the same exercise price and maturity, an equilibrium relative pricing condition known as put–call parity should prevail. The put–call parity condition is described in depth in Chapter 10. Such arbitrage will earn a return equivalent to the size of the mispricing. However, as more and more such arbitrage happens, the mispricing will narrow and eventually disappear restoring equilibrium in pricing.

SUMMARY

This chapter examined equity options, equity index options, and currency options. All three are among the most popularly traded option contracts. Equity options are options on individual listed stocks. Equity options being the most basic form were also discussed in Chapter 6. Equity index options are options on an underlying equity index. Currency options have as underlying an exchange rate. The chapter examined the features and trading applications of these option contracts. Their use in hedging, arbitrage, and speculation was examined.

The maximum possible loss to the long position in options is the premium paid. Since the premium is fully paid for at the time of purchase, fund flow at maturity can only be from the short position to long position. Such a fund flow can only happen if the long position chooses to exercise. The long position would only choose to exercise if it is profitable to do so. The profit attainable by the long position at exercise constitutes a loss to the short position.

Index options have premiums quoted in points. The quoted points are multiplied by the index multiplier to determine the monetary value of the premium. Stock options and currency options are generally quoted directly in monetary terms. Stock option premium, however, is quoted on each share of the underlying stock. The premium would thus have to be multiplied by 1,000 (500, 200, or 100) to reflect the fact that the lot sizes of the underlying stocks.

The relationship between underlying asset price and call and put premiums was explored. Call premiums increase when underlying asset price increases; put premiums increase when the underlying asset price decreases. It is also argued in the chapter that though American-style options allow for early exercise, early exercise rarely occurs. This has to do with the fact that it is usually more sensible to sell rather than exercise the option. When selling at the prevailing premium, one realizes both the intrinsic value and time value. Exercising the option will only enable the realization of intrinsic value.

The exchange by means of novation becomes the intermediary to every option trade. Default risk is transferred onto the exchange. Unlike futures where default risk could occur on both the long and short side, in the case of options, default risk is one-sided. Only the short position could potentially default. There is no further potential loss to the long position beyond the premium, which has already been fully paid for. Thus, in margining for options, only the short position faces margins. There is usually a series of options that is made available for trading for the same underlying asset and maturity. The idea is to have options that are in-, at-, and out-of-the-money available for trading. In efficient markets, the premiums will adjust for the moneyness such that one is no better or worse off from buying an in-the-money as opposed to an out-of-the-money option.

KEY TERMS

- Profit on exercise
- Index multiplier
- Positively correlated
- Negatively correlated
- Early exercise option classes
- Option series
- Option moneyness
- Settlement value
- Cash settlement
- Risk-based margining
- Tick size
- Contract month
- Automatic exercise
- Currency exposure
- Exchange rates

End-of-Chapter Questions

1. Consider a stock priced at RM 10 with a standard deviation of 30%. The risk-free rate is 0.05. There are put and call options available at exercise prices of RM 10 and a time to expiration of 6 months. The calls are priced at 89 sen and the puts cost 25 sen. There are no dividends on the stock and the options are European. Assume that all transactions consist of 1,000 shares or one contract (1,000 options). Use this information to answer the following questions:
   a. What is your profit if you buy a call, hold it to expiration and the stock price at expiration is RM 17?
   b. What is the break-even stock price on the transaction?
   c. What is the maximum profit on the transaction described in (a)?
   d. What is the maximum profit that the writer of the call can make?

2. Briefly explain why margins are required only for the seller of options but for both parties in the case of futures.

3. State the difference in the margining process for buyers and sellers in the futures markets as opposed to options. State the reason for this difference.

4. a. TRY Corporation is faced with serious problems as a result of the recent economic turmoil. Suppose call and put options are currently traded on the stock, what is the likely effect on the value of outstanding calls and puts?
   b. A stock's price remains static over a period of time. What is likely to happen to the premium of a call option written on the stock? Explain why.

5. Your company has just exported Crude Palm Oil to a Japanese customer. You will receive ¥en 30 million in 90 days. Do you have exposure? Suppose forwards, futures, and options were available on the currency, which would be the best instrument to hedge? Explain why.

6. Why do derivative markets typically have slightly longer trading hours than underlying stock markets?

7. You observe the following price quotes.
   ATH Corp. stock price = 7.30
   7.00 put on ATH Corp. stock = 0.10
   7.00 call on ATH Corp. stock = 0.50

Assuming the options have 15 days left to maturity, determine the intrinsic and time values of each option. Why is the call priced much higher than the put?

8. Given the same maturity, why does a deep in-the-money call have a higher value than a deep out-of-the-money option? Where does most of its value come from?

9. Why are several options of the same maturity and underlying asset but of different exercise prices traded simultaneously?

10. For each of the following option positions state:
    a. The risk profile
    b. The break-even and effective price
    c. The resulting stock position
        (i) Short 7.00 put @ 0.20
        (ii) Long 7.00 call @ 0.30
        (iii) Short 7.00 call @ 0.30
        (iv) Long 7.00 put @ 0.20

11. a. State and briefly explain two factors that increase the likelihood that an American call will be exercised early.
    b. An American-style put increases in value when time to expiration increases, but a European put may increase or decrease in value as time to expiration lengthens.

12. You work at HHG Stock Brokers. A wealthy foreign client who is bullish about Malaysian stocks wants to establish an exposure in the local equity market. The FBM KLCI is now at 900 points. At-the-money index put and call options are being quoted at 6 points and 8 points, respectively. Assuming the client is willing to invest up to RM 1 million,
    a. State three ways by which the client can get the exposure to Malaysian equities that he wants.
    b. State the size of the exposure, the approximate transaction cost, and outline the strategy for each of the three alternatives.
    c. In determining the best alternative to recommend to your client, what two factors should you consider?

13. You own an American-style call option on a stock. The option has 2 more weeks to maturity but is already in-the-money. Which would be the preferable course of action, exercise the option or selling it? Briefly justify your choice.

14. a. You own an option that is currently out-of-the-money. What is the implication in terms of the margin requirement?
    b. You sold an option that is now in-the-money. What is the consequence to your margin account?
    c. You sold an option that is now out-of-the money. What is the consequence to your margin account?
    d. You sold a call option on a stock which is now selling at the exercise price. What is the consequence to your margin account?

15. a. Differentiate between a stock index futures contract and a stock index option contract.
    b. State and describe instances where the two contracts could be used for the same purpose.

c. State two instances where the use of the index option contract may be better than the index futures contract.

16. A fund manager having had a good year wants to safeguard the profits earned thus far while also participating in any potential market rallies over the next few months. Between the SET 50 Index futures and the SET 50 Index options, which derivative should he choose? Why?

17. An investor is very bearish about Thai equities over the next 3 months. He has no position now but wants to speculate on market direction. He wants to short the SET 50 futures contract. His friend, however, advises him to use the put options of the SET 50 Index options instead.
    (i) Under what circumstance would the put option position be advantageous?
    (ii) What advantage does the index futures have over the index futures options?

18. For the following positions in an index futures option contract,
    a. State the resulting position in the underlying.
        (i) Long call
        (ii) Short call
        (iii) Long put
        (iv) Short put
    b. Assume a call and put at the same exercise price and maturity.
        (i) If the call expires in the money, describe what would happen to the short call and short put holders?
        (ii) If the put expires in the money, what would happen to the short put and long call positions?

19. A Chinese manufacturer of ceramic tiles has just exported a large shipment of tiles to its American customer Homedepot. The invoice amount of US$ 30 million will be due in 90 days. The Chinese firm is now worried about its currency exposure. It fears any depreciation in the US$ against the Yuan could shrink profits or even cause losses. They are considering whether to use the US$/CNH currency futures traded on HKEX or the currency options traded on the same exchange. They have come to you for advice. Explain to the Chinese exporter
    a. the advantages/disadvantages of each currency derivative.
    b. Under what circumstances would you recommend the use of currency options instead of currency futures?

20. Compare and contrast single stock futures (SSF) with stock options.
    a. Which stock derivative would you recommend to an investor who merely wants to lock in a stock's value over the next 1 month? Justify your answer.
    b. Which stock derivative would you recommend to an investor who anticipates a rally in the stock but wants downside protection at the same time? Again justify your answer.

Appendix

Singapore — The SGX Nikkei 225 Stock Index Option Contracts

The Nikkei 225 Index is probably the most widely quoted Japanese equity index in the world. It is a price-weighted equity index, which consists of 225 stocks traded on the first section of the Tokyo Stock Exchange. In 1986, the Singapore International Monetary Exchange (SIMEX), predecessor to the current SGX, introduced the SGX Yen Nikkei 225 futures contract then, the world's first futures contract based on the Japanese stock market. Following the success of the Nikkei Index futures contract, the Nikkei 225 Index option was launched in 1992. As with other equity index options, the SGX Nikkei 225 Index option gives holders a right, but not an obligation, to buy or sell the underlying asset, which, in this case, is the SGX Nikkei 225 Index futures, at a specific price on the maturity date. Thus, like Malaysia's FBM KLCI Index options, the underlying is an index futures contract.

The SGX Nikkei 225 Index options have had very impressive growth in traded volume. Total traded volume, which was about 4 million contracts over the 10 years 2000–2010, increased to about 80 million contracts over the subsequent 10 year period 2011–2020. This constitutes a 20-fold increase in traded volume. Table 7.9 shows the contract specifications for the SGX Nikkei 225 Index options extracted from the SGX's website.

Table 7.9   Contract Specifications — SGX Nikkei 225 Index Options

Product Type	Options
Product Category	Equity index
Ticker Symbol	Calls – CNK , Puts – PNK
Contract Size	1 × Nikkei 225 Index futures contract
Minimum Price Fluctuation	1 index point (500). Trades may occur at a price of 300 whether or not such trades rest of position for both parties to the trade.
Contract Months	6 nearest serial months and 32 nearest quarterly months
Trading Hours (Singapore Time)	T Session: Order Cancellation: 7.15 a.m. – 7.30 a.m. Opening : 7.30 a.m. – 2.30 p.m. T + 1 Session: Order Cancellation : 2.45 p.m. – 2.55 p.m. Opening : 2.55 p.m. – 5.15 a.m.
Last Trading Day	The day before the second Friday of the contract month
Daily Price Limits	N.A.
Settlement Basis	Cash settlement
Final Settlement Price	The Special Nikkei 225 Index quotation based on the opening prices of each compons Nikkei 225 Index on the business day following the last trading day.
Position Accountability/ Position Limit	Position limit is not applicable to this contract. However, a person owning or controlling 10,000 contracts net long or net short in all contract months of SGX Nikkei Stock Ave Options, SGX Mini Nikkei Stock Average Futures, and SGX USD Nikkei Stock Avere combined in position delta, or such position as the Exchange may prescribe from time to time

Source: SGX website.

The SGX Nikkei 225 Index options are available in both call, with ticker symbol CNK, and put, with ticker symbol PNK, options. Contract size is one SGX Nikkei 225 futures contract. Since the contract size of the SGX Nikkei 225 futures is ¥en 500 multiplied by the index futures price, which means if the SGX Nikkei 225 Index futures price is 28,000, one SGX Nikkei Index option contract would have a value of 28,000 × ¥en 500 or ¥en 14,000,000. The exercise style of the SGX Nikkei 225 Index options is European, which means it can only be exercised on the maturity date and are cash-settled.

SGX Nikkei 225 Index Options: Applications

As is the case with all derivative instruments, the Nikkei 225 Index options can be used for (i) managing equity risks through hedging, (ii) arbitraging mispricing relative to underlying asset, and (iii) establishing speculative positions to take advantage of market expectations. The following section provides detailed and fully worked out examples of how these three applications could be executed.

Hedging Equity Risks with SGX Nikkei 225 Index Options

Assume that you hold a well-diversified portfolio of Japanese stocks that mimics the Nikkei 225 Index. The value and performance of your portfolio obviously depends on market movements. If the market rallies, your portfolio's value increases. On the other hand, if the market declines, you would have losses on your position as well. Suppose, your stock portfolio is currently worth ¥en 28 million, and the Nikkei 225 Index is currently trading at 28,000 points. If next month, the Nikkei 225 Index goes up to 30,800, or a 10% increase, your portfolio, which mimics the Nikkei 225 Index, will also go up by 10% as well, and the value of your portfolio will be ¥en 30.8 million. On the other hand, if the Nikkei 225 Index declines, e.g., to 25,200, your portfolio value will also be reduced by 10%, and the value of your portfolio will now be ¥en 25.2 million.

Figure 7.5 illustrates the value of your long stock portfolio that tracks the Nikkei 225 Index.

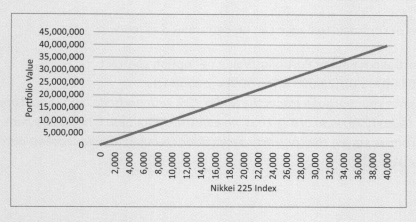

Figure 7.5   Payoff to Long Stock Portfolio

As is clear from the figure, if the Nikkei 225 Index rises above 28,000, your portfolio value should increase. However, if you have reasons to believe that the next one month may be volatile, it would be logical to seek protection. A natural question to ask is, can we limit the downside risk and hedge the portfolio against a market downturn?

SGX Nikkei 225 Index option can also be used to hedge the portfolio against such uncertainty. In this context, combining SGX Nikkei 225 Index put options with your existing stock portfolio will allow you to limit the downside risk while at the same time, keep intact the upside potential. The hedge strategy should therefore be **long (buy) 1-month SGX Nikkei 225 Index put option contracts**. Since the SGX Nikkei 225 Index put option allows you to lock in the selling price of the Nikkei 225 Index futures at maturity, it will provides a positive payoff if the market declines. On the other hand, if the market rises, the put option need not be exercised. The SGX Nikkei 225 Index put option therefore acts as an insurance against downside risk to your stock portfolio.

Hedging Illustration

The following information is available to you in January:

Nikkei 225 Index spot = 28,000 points
Nikkei 225 Index Put Option:
    Exercise Price, K = 28,000
    Maturity, T = February (30 days)
    Quoted Put Premium, P = ¥en 635

Since you have a long position in Japanese stocks and a market decline will hurt, the appropriate hedge strategy would be to long SGX Nikkei 225 Index put option contracts. A long position in the put options will profit from declining Nikkei 225 Index. The obvious question that arises is how many contracts of SGX Nikkei 225 Index put option should you buy? Since your portfolio mimics the Nikkei 225 Index, you would need to long SGX Nikkei 225 Index put option contracts of equal value to that of your portfolio, which is ¥en 28 million. This will fully hedge your portfolio.

The number of contracts to hedge can be determined as follows:

(Value of Portfolio × Beta of Portfolio)/Value per option contract
(¥en 28,000,000 × 1.0)/(28,000 × ¥en 500) = 2 contracts
(*Note that since your portfolio tracks the Nikkei 225, your portfolio beta should approximate the market (Nikkei 225) beta of 1.0. Thus, no adjustment for beta is necessary here. The value per option contract given the contract specifications is equal to index spot value × the index multiplier of ¥en 500.*)

Hedge Strategy: Long 2 February SGX Nikkei 225 Index Put Option Contracts

To see how the SGX Nikkei 225 Index put option will protect your portfolio, we examine the following two scenarios, one where the Nikkei 225 Index falls in February, and another where the index rises.

Scenario 1: Nikkei 225 Index Falls 10% Over the Next Month

Assume that the Nikkei 225 index falls from 28,000 in January to 25,200 in February.

Impact on Your Portfolio:
Your portfolio value will now be ¥en 25,200,000.

Impact of the SGX Nikkei 225 Index Put Option:

$$\text{Proceeds from exercise of puts} = \text{Max}(K - S_T, 0) \times \text{Multiplier} \times \text{Number of contracts}$$
$$= \text{Max}(28{,}000 - 25{,}200, 0) \times ¥en\ 500 \times 2$$
$$= ¥en\ 2{,}800{,}000$$

Less premium paid for puts = (¥en 635 × 500 × 2 = ¥en 635,000)
Profit/loss from puts = ¥en 2,165,000

Result of Hedge

Value of stocks portfolio at maturity = ¥en 25,200,000
Profit/loss from puts = ¥en 2,165,000
Value of combined position at maturity = ¥en **27,365,000**

Notice that even though the market fell 10%, your portfolio value is largely maintained. It is only lower by ¥en 635,000, which is the amount of premium paid. The index put options prevented any losses beyond the amount of premium paid.

In the second scenario, we will examine the impact of the hedge with put options when the index rises.

Scenario 2: Nikkei 225 Index Rises 10% Over the Next 1 Month

Assume that the Nikkei 225 Index rises from 28,000 in January to 30,800 in February.

Impact on Your Portfolio:
Your portfolio value will be ¥en 30,800,000.

Impact on Your SGX Nikkei 225 Index Put Option:

$$\text{Proceeds from exercise of puts} = \text{Max}(K - S_T, 0) \times \text{Multiplier} \times \text{Number of contracts}$$
$$= \text{Max}(28{,}000 - 30{,}800, 0) \times ¥en\ 500 \times 2$$
$$= ¥en\ 0$$

Less premium paid for puts = (¥en 635 × 500 × 2 = ¥en 635,000)
Profit/loss from puts = (¥en 635,000)

Result of Hedge
Value of stock portfolio at maturity = ¥en 30,800,000
Profit/loss from puts = (¥en 635,000)
Value of combined position at maturity = **¥en 30,165,000**

Notice now that when the underlying Nikkei 225 Index rises, the put options will not be worth exercising and the loss from the put position will be the premium paid. In essence, the put options act as an insurance to your stock portfolio. If the market declines, the put options will provide positive payoffs to offset the loss on your stock portfolio, however, when market rises, the option strategy enables you to benefit from the rise. Table 7.10 and Figure 7.6 show the value of long stock positions, the profit/loss from the put options, and the value of combined position at maturity.

Speculating with SGX Nikkei 225 Index Options
Suppose you expect the Japanese equity market to rise over the next few months, how can you use SGX Nikkei Index options to take an advantage of your view? Since call options give investors the right to buy the underlying, which in this case is an index futures contract at the predetermined exercise price, you should long (buy) SGX Nikkei 225 Index option.

Illustration — Bullish Expectation
The following information is available to you in January.

SGX Nikkei 225 Index futures = 28,000
Call Option:
    Exercise Price, K = 28,000
    Maturity, T = February (30 days)
    Call Premium, C = ¥en 920

Table 7.10 Payoff to Hedged Long Stock Portfolio Position

Nikkei 225 Index	Value of Stock Portfolio (in ¥)	Profit/Loss to Long Put Position (in ¥)	Value of Combined Position at Maturity (in ¥)
20,000	20,000,000	7,365,000	27,365,000
22,000	22,000,000	5,365,000	27,365,000
24,000	24,000,000	3,365,000	27,365,000
26,000	26,000,000	1,365,000	27,365,000
28,000	28,000,000	(635,000)	27,365,000
30,000	30,000,000	(635,000)	29,365,000
32,000	32,000,000	(635,000)	31,365,000
34,000	34,000,000	(635,000)	33,365,000
36,000	36,000,000	(635,000)	35,365,000
38,000	38,000,000	(635,000)	37,365,000
40,000	40,000,000	(635,000)	39,365,000

Equity, Equity Index, and Currency Options

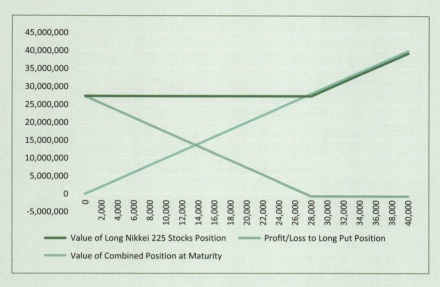

Figure 7.6   Portfolio Insurance with SGX Nikkei 225 Index Put Option

Table 7.11   SGX Nikkei Index Call Option Payoff and Profit/Loss

SGX Nikkei 225 Index Futures at Maturity	Call Option Profit on Exercise	Call Option Profit/Loss
2,000	0	−920
4,000	0	−920
8,000	0	−920
12,000	0	−920
16,000	0	−920
20,000	0	−920
24,000	0	−920
28,000	0	−920
32,000	4,000	3,080
36,000	8,000	7,080
40,000	12,000	11,080
44,000	16,000	15,080
48,000	20,000	19,080
52,000	24,000	23,080
56,000	28,000	27,080

Table 7.11 illustrates the SGX Nikkei 225 Index call option's profit on exercise and profit/loss (net of premium) at maturity for various SGX Nikkei 225 Index futures values. Notice that if SGX Nikkei 225 Index futures remains at or below 28,000, the call option will have a zero profit on exercise, with a loss of ¥en 920. This is because when you purchased the call option in

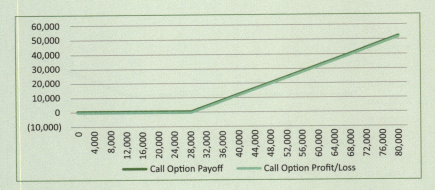

Figure 7.7 SGX Nikkei 225 Index Call Option Payoff at Exercise and Net Profit/Loss

January, you paid a call premium of ¥en 920, and regardless of whether the option will be exercised at maturity or not, the profit/loss will always be ¥en 920 less than the option's profit on exercise. As seen from the table, the higher the SGX Nikkei 225 Index futures at maturity, the larger the call option payoff and profit will be. Figure 7.7 shows the plot of the SGX Nikkei 225 Index call option's payoff at exercise and profit/loss from Table 7.11.

More specifically, if you expect that the SGX Nikkei 225 Index futures will rise over the next 1 month, you will buy one call option contract on the SGX Nikkei 225 Index futures. The call option has the exercise price of 28,000. Since the contract size of the SGX Nikkei 225 Index futures contract is ¥en 500 multiplied by the index price, and the call premium is ¥en 920, the total cost of buying the SGX Nikkei 225 Index call option will be $500 \times 920 = $ ¥en 460,000. If in February, the SGX Nikkei 225 Index futures rises to 30,000 (i.e., $S_T = 30,000$), you would exercise the call option and the payoff will be $\max(S_T - K, 0) = \max(30,000 - 28,000) = 2,000$. Since the contract multiplier is 500, your total payoff will be $500 \times 2,000 = $ ¥en 1,000,000 for one contract. Your profit net of premium will be $1,000,000 - 460,000 = $ ¥en 540,000.

On the other hand, if the SGX Nikkei 225 Index and index futures had gone down in value, e.g., to 25,000, the call would not be exercised at maturity. Your profit on exercise would be zero, and your loss would be equal to the amount of premium you paid, which would be ¥en 460,000. Intuitively, if the SGX Nikkei 225 Index futures is below the exercise price at maturity, the call option will be out of the money. The maximum loss for a long call option will be the option premium that you paid when you created the position, which in this case would be ¥en $920 \times 500 = $ ¥en 460,000 per contract.

What if you anticipate a market downturn and expect that the SGX Nikkei 225 Index futures will decline over the next month, can you use SGX Nikkei 225 Index options to profit from your expectation? The answer is yes. But in this case, you will use a put option instead. As we discussed in the earlier sections, a (European) put option gives a holder the right to sell the underlying asset, at the exercise price, on the maturity date.

Illustration — Bearish Expectation

The following information is available to you in January.

SGX Nikkei 225 Futures = 28,000
Put Option:
    Exercise Price, K = 28,000
    Maturity, T = February (30 days)
    Put Premium, P = ¥en 635

Table 7.12 illustrates the SGX Nikkei 225 Index put option profit on exercise and net profit/loss at maturity for various SGX Nikkei 225 Index futures values. Notice that if the SGX Nikkei 225 Index futures is at 28,000 or higher, the put option will not be exercised and the position nets a loss of ¥en 635. This is because when you purchased the put option in January, you paid a put premium of ¥en 635, and regardless of whether the put option will be exercised at maturity or not, the profit/loss will always be ¥en 635 less than the option's profit on exercise. As we can see from the table, the lower the SGX Nikkei 225 Index futures at maturity, the larger the put option's profit will be. Figure 7.8 shows the SGX Nikkei 225 Index put option's payoff on exercise and profit/loss net of premium from Table 7.12.

The put option has an exercise price of 28,000. Since the contract size of the SGX Nikkei 225 Index futures contract is ¥en 500 multiplied by the index price, and the put premium is ¥en 635, the total cost to buy the SGX Nikkei 225 Index call option will be $500 \times 635 = $ ¥en 317,500. If at maturity in February, the SGX Nikkei 225 Index futures declines to 26,000 (i.e., $S_T = 26{,}000$), you would exercise the put option that you purchased earlier and the payoff on exercise will be $\max(K - S_T, 0) = \max(28{,}000 - 26{,}000, 0) = 2{,}000$. Since the contract multiplier is 500, your

Table 7.12   SGX Nikkei 225 Index Put Option Payoff and Profit/Loss

SGX Nikkei Index Futures	Put Option Profit on Exercise	Put Option Profit/Loss
0	28,000	27,365
4,000	24,000	23,365
8,000	20,000	19,365
12,000	16,000	15,365
16,000	12,000	11,365
20,000	8,000	7,365
24,000	4,000	3,365
28,000	0	−635
32,000	0	−635
36,000	0	−635
40,000	0	−635
44,000	0	−635
48,000	0	−635
52,000	0	−635
56,000	0	−635

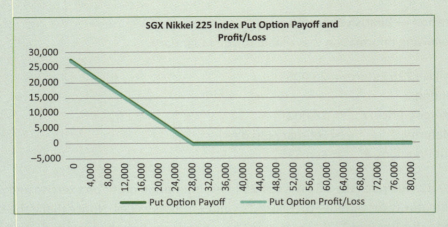

Figure 7.8 SGX Nikkei 225 Index Call Option Payoff at Exercise and Net Profit/Loss

total exercise payoff will be 500 × 2,000 = ¥en 1,000,000 for one contract. Your profit net of premium will be 1,000,000 − 317,500 = ¥en 682,500.

Alternatively, if the Nikkei 225 Index had gone up in value, for example to 30,000, the put would not be exercised at maturity. Your payoff on exercise would be zero, and your loss would be equal to the amount of premium you paid, which would be ¥en 317,500. Intuitively, if the Nikkei 225 Index is above the exercise price at maturity, the put option will be out of the money. The maximum loss for a long put option will be the option premium that you paid when you created the position, which in this case would be ¥en 500 × 635 = ¥en 317,500 per contract.

Arbitrage Strategy

The third common application of SGX Nikkei 225 Index options is arbitrage. As discussed in depth in Chapter 10, the put–call parity describes an equilibrium pricing relationship between calls and puts written on the same underlying asset, of the same exercise price and maturity. Taking into account, the interest rate and the timing difference in cash outlays, the put–call parity for futures options such as the SGX Nikkei 225 Index option can be written as follows:

$$F(1+r)^{-t} - K(1+r)^{-t} = C + -P$$

where

F = futures price
r = annualized interest rate
K = exercise price of the options
t = days to maturity of the options
C = call premium
P = put premium

The put–call parity condition implies that any deviation from the earlier relationship would provide an arbitrage opportunity, and a riskless arbitrage profit can be made from the mispricing. Consider the following example. Suppose the Nikkei 225 Index futures is currently at 28,000. SGX Nikkei 225 Index options of 30 days to maturity, with an exercise price of 27,000 are quoted at ¥en 1800, and ¥en 200 for the call and put, respectively. Assume that the risk-free interest rate is 5%. To see whether there is mispricing, we check the put–call parity as follows:

$$F(1+r)^{-t} - K(1+r)^{-t} = C + -P$$
$$28{,}000(1.05)^{-0.083} - 27{,}000(1.05)^{-0.083} = 1{,}800 - 200$$
$$27{,}886.84 - 26{,}890.88 = 1{,}800 - 200$$
$$995.96 < 1600$$

Clearly, the put–call parity is violated. The mispricing differential is equal to ¥en 604.06 (¥en 1,600 − ¥en 995.96) or ¥en 302,029 of arbitrage profit to be made per contract. What action should be taken to profit from this arbitrage opportunity? Looking at the abovementioned analysis, we can see that the right side is larger than the left side. Thus, to take advantage, we will short the right side and at the same time long the left side. Our arbitrage strategy should therefore be as follows:

— Long SGX Nikkei 225 Index futures
— Lend an amount equal to the PV of SGX Nikkei 225 Index futures price
— Borrow an amount equal to the PV of exercise price
— Short index call
— Long index put

Table 7.13 illustrates the arbitrage transactions and resulting payoffs under two scenarios. One where the SGX Nikkei 225 Index futures increases to 30,000 at maturity, and another one where the futures index declines to 20,000. The strategy yields a positive net cash flow of ¥en 604.06 when the positions are established. In both subsequent scenarios at maturity, however, the cash flows net off to equal 0, implying no further obligations and therefore a risk-free arbitrage opportunity.

Table 7.13   Payoffs to Arbitrage Strategy with SGX Nikkei 225 Index Options

Strategy	CF$_0$ (Today)	At Maturity	
		SGX Nikkei 225 futures = 30,000 CF$_{30}$	SGX Nikkei 225 futures = 20,000 CF$_{30}$
Long SGX Nikkei 225 Index futures	0	¥en 2,000	(¥en 8,000)
Lend amount equal to the difference between PV of SGX Nikkei 225 futures price and PV of exercise	(¥en 995.94)	¥en 1,000	¥en 1,000
Short call option	¥en 1,800	(¥en 3,000)	0
Long put option	(¥en 200)	0	¥en 7,000
Net cash flow	¥604.06	0	0

CHAPTER · 8

Option Strategies and Payoffs

Objectives

This chapter provides an in-depth exposition of the many popularly used option strategies and their payoffs. Strategies, commonly used for hedging, arbitrage, and speculation are described and the efficacy evaluated.

On completing the chapter, readers should have a good appreciation of the flexibility of options and be able to recommend/design appropriate option strategies for a given market outlook or objective.

Introduction

One of the main advantages of options over other financial assets/instruments is their flexibility. This flexibility arises from the fact that options may or may not be exercised. This enables an investor to establish option positions now, with a view to exercising them only under certain states of outcomes in the future. As we will see later, options allow for the establishment of positions that may not be possible with other derivatives. The flexibility inherent in options also enables options to be combined with positions in the underlying asset (long or short stock) and positions in other derivative instruments such as forwards, futures, etc. As one can imagine, the number of different ways or permutations in which one could combine options with other instruments would be numerous. Furthermore, options may also be combined in different ratios, for example, one long call of a certain exercise price combined with say, two short calls of another exercise price. Thus, the number of possible option strategies can be infinite. In this chapter, we examine some of the commonly used option strategies and their payoffs.

As is the case with any investment, an investor establishes an option strategy with an objective in mind or for a given market outlook. For example, an investor might establish an option position with the sole objective of taking advantage of market or underlying asset volatility. He may not necessarily have a market outlook that is either bullish or bearish. On the other hand, another investor might undertake an option position based on market outlook alone. He applies a certain strategy if he has a bullish outlook and another if he is bearish.

Though numerous, for ease of clarity we can categorize the strategies into four broad categories:

(a) Uncovered/naked positions
(b) Hedge positions
(c) Spreads
(d) Combination strategies

While this is categorization by the structure of the strategy, one could also categorize the strategies by market outlook. For example, strategies for a bull market outlook, bear market outlook, a neutral outlook, etc. In the rest of this chapter, we examine the strategies grouped by the first categorization. Again, for ease of understanding and clarity, we use the example of stock option, i.e., the underlying asset is an individual listed stock.

8.1 Uncovered/Naked Positions

An uncovered or "naked" position is where one takes a position in an asset without establishing an offsetting position. Since they are by definition single positions, the payoff diagrams are straightforward. Using calls, put, and stocks (underlying asset), there are a total of *six* uncovered positions that are possible. These are the following:

(a) Long call
(b) Short call
(c) Long put
(d) Short put
(e) Long stock
(f) Short stock

These six positions are the basis of the more complex strategies that follow. They can also be thought of as the basis of financial engineering techniques. Since these six basic positions have been discussed in depth in Chapter 6, we now move on to the next category of strategies: hedge strategies. One should, however, note that naked positions are generally considered risky positions in the sense that four of the abovementioned six positions have potentially unlimited downside exposure, the exceptions being long call and long put positions. Although both these positions have limited downside risk, the fact remains that one could lose the entire investment (premiums) in these two positions if the expectation underlying the strategy does not come through.

8.2 Hedge Strategies

A hedge position combines an option with the underlying asset in such a way that the overall position either reduces or eliminates risk. A fully hedged position would be riskless. The combination would be such that price movements offset each other. For example, a loss on the underlying asset would be offset by a gain in the option position and vice versa. Although the total elimination of risk is good, one has to keep in mind that except where there is mispricing, a strategy that is riskless will mean only a risk-free rate of return. With options, one can eliminate unwanted risk but at a cost; the cost being the option premium. We will examine three common hedge strategies: hedging exposure to a long stock position, hedging exposure to a short stock position, and "locking-in" a fixed underlying asset value even in turbulent environments.

8.2.1 Hedging a Long Stock Position (Portfolio Insurance)

The most obvious need for a hedge arises when one has a long stock or long underlying position. With a long stock position, one is exposed to downward movements in the stock's price. Increases in the stock's price are favorable. Thus an investor with a long stock position would want to protect downside risk while keeping as much as possible the upside profit potential. In order to achieve this, the investor should combine the long stock position with an option position that would profit if the stock goes down in

> **Note**
> A hedge strategy combines an option position with a position in the underlying asset in such a way that the overall position either reduces or eliminates risk.

value. The idea being that should the stock fall in value, the losses on the stock will be offset by the gains on the option position. On the other hand, should the stock rise in value, the option which would be out-of-the-money would be left unexercised. Such a strategy gives the investor the best of both worlds; he is protected from price falls but keeps intact the upside profit potential.

In determining the appropriate option position, the investor begins by asking, what option position would make money if the underlying asset goes down in value? Recall from Chapter 6 that there are two option positions that would gain when the underlying asset goes down in value: the short call position and the long put position. Clearly the short call position will only provide downside protection to the extent of the premium received. Furthermore, the short call will mean that the upside potential on the stock cannot be realized by the investor, since a rise in the underlying stock price would mean that the purchaser of the call would exercise, and the investor, once assigned, will have to give up the stock at the exercise price of the call option he sold/shorted. Therefore, the logical hedge choice would be to use the long put position. This strategy of hedging stock positions with put options is a popular strategy. Portfolio managers quite routinely use this strategy to protect their portfolio of stocks from short-term fluctuation by going long index put options. Thus, this strategy is often commonly referred to as ***portfolio insurance***. We examine below a numerical example of this strategy.

Portfolio Insurance: Illustration

Suppose you had just gone long (purchased) one lot of XYZ Inc. stock at a price of RM 15 each, for a total investment of RM 15,000. You believe this stock has long-term potential but wish to protect yourself from any short-term downside movement in price. Suppose 3-month, at-the-money put options on XYZ Inc. stock are being quoted at RM 0.15 or 15 sen each or RM 150 per lot (RM 0.15 × 1,000). The appropriate option strategy to hedge the long stock position would be:

Long 1, 3-month XYZ Inc. put @ RM 0.15
Combined position: • Long 1 lot XYZ Inc. stock @ RM 15
 • Long 1, 3-month XYZ Inc. put @ RM 0.15

Table 8.1 shows the payoff to the long stock, long put, and the combined position for a given range of stock prices at option maturity in 3 months.

Table 8.1 Payoff to Hedged Long Stock Position

Stock Price at Maturity	Value of Long Stock Position	Profit/Loss to Long Put Position @ 0.15	Value of Combined Position at Maturity
8.00	8,000	6,850	14,850
12.00	12,000	2,850	14,850
15.00	15,000	(150)	14,850
18.00	18,000	(150)	17,850
20.00	20,000	(150)	19,850

Notice that at prices below RM 15, the long put becomes profitable and offsets the loss in the long stock position. For example, at a stock price of RM 8, the long stock position is worth RM 8,000; a loss of RM 7,000 from the original stock value of RM 15,000. However, this loss is almost fully offset by the gain from the put options. The profit of RM 6,850 from the put is arrived at as follows:

Proceeds from exercise of puts = RM 15,000
Less cost of stock delivered on exercise = (RM 8,000)
Less premium paid for puts = (RM 150)
Profit from puts = **RM 6,850**

For any stock price at or above RM 15.00, the puts would obviously not be exercised. Thus, the RM 150 loss in the third column. The fourth column that sums columns 2 and 3 shows the payoff to the overall hedged position. Notice that the minimum value of the hedge position is RM 14,850, this being the exercisable value of the puts less the cost of the puts. Figure 8.1 shows the payoff profile of the long stock and long RM 15 put positions. The overall payoff profile is shown in bold.

The dotted line represents the payoff to the long stock position, the dashed line shows the payoff of the long put, whereas the bold line represents the payoff of the overall hedged position. (These lines when multiplied by 1,000 for one lot of stocks would represent columns 2, 3, and 4, respectively, of Table 8.1.)

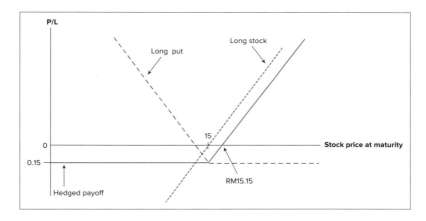

Figure 8.1 Payoff Profile to Portfolio Insurance

Notice that the risk profile of the combined hedge position is identical to that of a call option, i.e., an RM 15 call @ RM 0.15 would have the same payoff profile. We address this issue of a synthetic call in Chapter 10. *[Note: One could derive the call payoff by subtracting RM 15,000 which is the current value of the one lot of stocks from column (4) of Table 8.1.]*

Portfolio Insurance Strategy

When to use: When one needs protection against falling value of the underlying asset in which one has a long position.

Risk profile: Limited downside risk, unlimited upside potential.

Break-even point: Since overall position is that of a long call; exercise price + premium = RM 15 + 0.15 = RM 15.15.

Desired objective: To gain from potential upside rally while limiting downside risk.

Note
A portfolio insurance strategy combines a long put option with the long stock position in order to limit downside risk while maintaining the upside potential.

8.2.2 Hedging a Short Stock Position

With a short stock position, one needs protection not from falling prices but from a rise in the underlying stock price. One establishes a short stock position when one is bearish and expects the stock to fall in value. Since the short stock position gains in value from falling prices but loses when the price increases, the hedge position would mean combining the short stock position with an option that *rises* when the underlying stock price increases. The idea of the hedge being to offset the losses of the short stock position with the gains from the option position when underlying stock price rises. Thus, an investor who wishes to hedge his short stock position begins by asking, which option position would gain when the underlying stock price rises. The logical answer to this question would be to long a call option on the stock. If he wants to protect his current short stock value, then going long an at-the-money call option would be most appropriate. We now examine a numerical example of the strategy.

Hedging a Short Stock Position: Illustration

Suppose you shorted ABC Corp. stock at RM 12. You subsequently hear rumors that ABC Corp. has landed a huge government contract. You don't know if there is any truth to this rumor. You still feel you were right in shorting the stock but would like to hedge yourself from potential large losses if the stock price rises. How can you hedge?

- Suppose a 3-month RM 12 call option on the stock is being sold at a premium of RM 0.10 or 10 sen, then you insure/hedge your position by going long the RM 12 call. The cost of the hedge would be RM 0.10 × 1,000 shares = RM 100 per contract. The combined position is now:

    (i) Short 1 lot of ABC Corp. stock at RM 12
    (ii) Long 1 three-month RM 12 call @ RM 0.10

Table 8.2 shows the payoff to the short stock, long call and the combined position for a given range of stock prices at option maturity in 3 months.

Table 8.2 Payoff to Hedged Short Stock Position

Stock Price at Maturity	Value of Short Stock Position	Profit/Loss to Long Put Position @ 0.10	Value of Combined Position at Maturity
8.00	4,000	(100)	3,900
10.00	2,000	(100)	1,900
12.00	0	(100)	(100)
14.00	(2,000)	1,900	(100)
16.00	(4,000)	3,900	(100)

Figure 8.2 shows the payoffs in Table 8.2 on a per share basis.

Notice that when the stock price falls, the short stock position gains while the call would be out-of-the-money and would not be exercised. For example, if ABC Corp.'s stock price at the time of option maturity is RM 8, the short stock position makes a profit of RM 4,000 [(RM 12 − RM 8) × 1,000]. The call, however, is not exercised and so loses the RM 100 premium paid for it. However, when the underlying stock price rises above RM 12, the opposite happens. For example, at a stock price of RM 14 at option maturity, the short stock position loses RM 2,000 [(RM 12 − RM 14) × 1,000]. The long call position, however, makes money since the call is in-the-money and would be exercised. The profit from the call offsets almost all the losses incurred on the short stock position. The value of the hedged position in column (4) is arrived as follows:

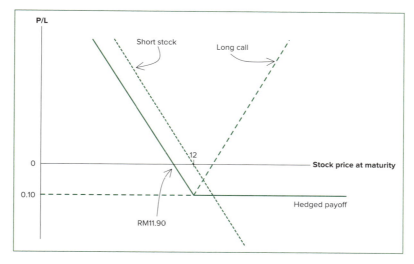

Figure 8.2   Payoff Profile to Hedged Short Stock Position

At Stock Price of RM 14 at Maturity

Exercise the call and pay (RM 12 × 1,000)	= (RM 12,000)
Value of the stock received (RM 14 × 1,000)	= RM 14,000
Less premium paid for call (RM 0.10 × 1,000)	= (RM 100)
Net profit from exercise of call	= RM 1,900

(Note: The value of the stock received on exercising the call of RM 14,000 can be realized by immediately selling the stock at the prevailing market price of RM 14 each.)

Note
A short stock position can be hedged against rising prices by combining it with a long call position. This protects the downside while maintaining upside potential.

Note that the risk profile is, limited downside, unlimited upside potential. The hedged payoff that combines the short stock position with that of a long call resembles that of a long put position.

Hedged Short Stock Position

When to use: When one needs protection against rising values of the underlying asset of which one is short.

Risk profile: Limited downside, unlimited upside potential.

Break-even point: Since overall position is that of a long put; exercise price − premium = RM 12 − RM 0.10 = RM 11.90.

Desired objective: To gain from falling prices while limiting risk associated with rising prices.

8.2.3 Conversion Strategy (Locking-in a Fixed Value of Underlying Asset)

A *conversion strategy* involves the use of both call and put options to "lock in" the value of the underlying stock. Though the conversion strategy is often used in the context of an arbitrage proof (as we will see in Chapter 10), the strategy can also be considered a hedge strategy in that it assures a fixed value of the underlying asset/portfolio. However, unlike the earlier two strategies that provided downside protection while also allowing for profits from favorable price movement, the conversion strategy locks in the value either way. Thus, the strategy while protecting against unfavorable price movement, does not allow one to benefit from upside movement. As such, this strategy is intended solely for protection from *any* price movement, i.e., all volatility. A conversion strategy could be used to hedge a long stock position while a short stock position could be hedged with a reverse conversion. One might wonder why a conversion strategy should be used when it locks in the value and does not allow for profiting from rising prices, whereas a portfolio insurance strategy, in also providing upside potential, is clearly superior. The answer lies in the fact that the conversion strategy would be cheaper to establish.

Conversion Strategy: Illustration

An investor just bought one lot of DEF Corp. stock at RM 15 for an investment of RM 15,000. He subsequently hears that the stock is likely to undergo serious turbulence over the next 2–3 months. The investor intends keeping the stock over the longer term and wants to profit from long-term capital appreciation. His objective now is to avoid/eliminate the impact of short-term volatility on his investment. Three-month at-the-money call and put options are priced as follows:

DEF Corp., 3-month, RM 15 call @ RM 0.13
DEF Corp., 3-month, RM 15 put @ RM 0.15

In order to establish the conversion strategy, he combines his current long stock position with option positions as follows:

Conversion Strategy
- Long stock at RM 15
- Long 1 three-month, RM 15 put @ 0.15
- Short 1 three-month, RM 15 call @ 0.13

Table 8.3 shows the payoff to the strategy for a given range of stock prices at option maturity in 3 months.

Notice that regardless of the stock's price in 3 months, the value of the investment as seen in the last column remains fixed at RM 14,980. The investor has essentially locked in the

Table 8.3 Payoff to Conversion Strategy

Stock Price at Maturity	Value of Long Stock Position	Profit/Loss to Long Put @ 0.15	Profit/Loss to Short Call @ 0.13	Value of Combined Position
8.00	8,000	6,850	130	14,980
12.00	12,000	2,850	130	14,980
15.00	15,000	(150)	130	14,980
18.00	18,000	(150)	(2,870)	14,980
20.00	20,000	(150)	(4,870)	14,980

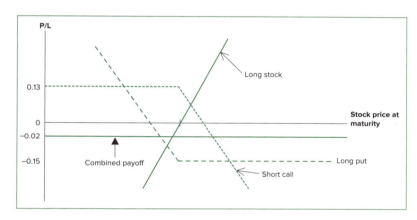

Figure 8.3 Payoff Profile of Conversion Strategy

current RM 15,000 value of his investment at a cost of RM 20. The net cost to him is RM 20 which is:

Premium received for call shorted : RM 0.13 × 1,000 = RM 130
Premium paid for put bought   : RM 0.15 × 1,000 = (RM 150)
Net cost of strategy   = (RM 20)

The RM 14,980 value that is the resulting payoff is simply the portfolio value net of the RM 20 cost. Although the disadvantage of this strategy relative to portfolio insurance is that upside movement cannot benefit the investor, keep in mind that the transaction cost is much lower, RM 20 versus RM 150, that would have been the cost for portfolio insurance. In any case, one does not use this strategy for a stock with potential upside rally in the short term. Figure 8.3 graphs the payoff profile.

Note the overall payoff is a horizontal line at −0.02. What this means is that the cost of the strategy is always 2 sen per share or RM 20. Thus, regardless of price movement the value of the investment will always be RM 15,000 less RM 20 which equals RM 14,980.

Note
A conversion strategy combines a long stock position with a short call and long put, in order to lock in a fixed value of the underlying stock.

> **Conversion Strategy**
> *When to use:* When one wants to avoid/eliminate all temporary volatility.
> *Risk profile:* Risk limited to transaction cost, neither upside nor downside potential.
> *Desired objective:* To lock in the value of portfolio regardless of underlying volatility.

8.3 Spread Strategies

A **spread strategy** can be thought of as a speculative position with a safety net. A spread position typically involves the establishment of offsetting positions in the same asset but across different markets, at different maturities or different exercise prices. In Chapter 4, we saw an example of a spread where the investor took opposite positions (long/short) in the same underlying asset but of different maturities. Such a spread is known as a time or calendar spread. When one takes opposite positions across two different commodities, it is a **commodity spread**; across markets, they are **intermarket spreads**. Here, we will examine spread positions established using options. These involve establishing offsetting positions in the same options. The strategies we examine involve the use of the same type of option but at different exercise prices.

We begin by examining two types of spreads: **bull spreads** and **bear spreads**. Both these spreads can be established using calls alone or only puts. That is, you establish the spread using either calls or puts, not both. When a bull spread is established using calls, it is referred to a a **bull call spread**. A bear spread setup using puts would be a **bear put spread**.

In establishing a bull call spread, for example, one goes long a call option at a certain exercise price while simultaneously shorting the same call at a higher exercise price. Since one call position offsets the other, both the up and downside are limited. The idea is to gain a little on an expected underlying asset price movement without taking on too much risk. Thus, spread positions are typically established when one is only moderately confident of the forecast underlying asset price movement or when one is only mildly bullish or mildly bearish, i.e., neutral to bullish or neutral to bearish.

> **Note**
> Spread positions are established to profit from expected marginal price movements while protecting downside risk.

8.3.1 A Bull Call Spread: Illustration

Suppose you are moderately bullish about the performance of GET Ltd. stock over the next 30 days. You think there is a likelihood of a moderate increase in the stock price. You do not want to go long the stock since any price reduction would hurt you. You want to use options to benefit from the expected moderate stock price appreciation while minimizing your downside risk. The appropriate option strategy would be to establish a bull spread which could be set up using either calls or puts. We first examine the bull call spread. Assume the following two 30-day calls are available.

GET Ltd., RM 9.50 call @ RM 0.15
GET Ltd., RM 10.50 call @ RM 0.05

The bull call spread would require the purchase of the call with the lower exercise price and sale of the call with the higher exercise price. Therefore, the strategy here would be:

Long RM 9.50 call @ RM 0.15
Short RM 10.50 call @ RM 0.05

Table 8.4 shows the payoff to the two call positions and the overall strategy for a range of underlying stock prices at option maturity.

Notice that at any stock price below RM 9.50, the loss to strategy is limited 10 sen per stock or RM 100 per contract. At any stock price above RM 9.60, the strategy makes money; however, the maximum profitable achievable is 90 sen per share or RM 900 (0.90 × 1,000) per contract. In exchange for limiting the downside, we trade-off any potential profit beyond 90 sen per share. One might wonder why a bull spread is used when downside risk can be limited while keeping unlimited upside potential on the stock with a long call. It is usually a transaction cost argument. A long call position at RM 9.50 exercise price costs more than the above spread. Though an RM 10.50 exercise call would be cheaper, the position would require a much larger upward price movement to break even. Since you are not very bullish

Table 8.4 Payoff to Bull Call Spread

Stock Price at Maturity	Profit/Loss to Long 9.50 Call @ 0.15	Profit/Loss to Short 10.50 Call @ 0.05	Value of Combined Position
8.00	(0.15)	0.05	(0.10)
9.00	(0.15)	0.05	(0.10)
9.50	(0.15)	0.05	(0.10)
9.60	(0.05)	0.05	0
10.00	0.35	0.05	0.40
10.50	0.85	0.05	0.90
11.00	1.35	(0.45)	0.90
11.50	1.85	(0.95)	0.90

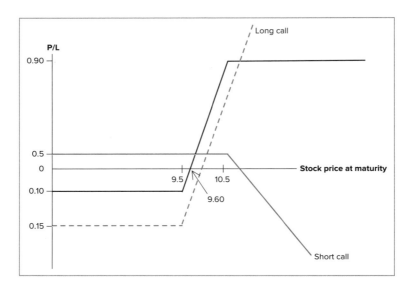

Figure 8.4 Payoff Profile of Bull Call Spread

on the stock, the RM 10.50 exercise price may simply not be achievable. Thus, the bull spread is still sensible. Figure 8.4 shows the graphical payoff profile.

8.3.2 A Bull Put Spread

A **bull put spread** is the use of put options instead of calls to establish the spread. The market outlook, rationale, and payoff profile are the same as that of a bull call spread. As in the case of bull call spreads, the investor goes long the lower exercise put and shorts the higher exercise put.

Bull Put Spread: Illustration

Suppose the investor in the earlier example wishes to create a bull put spread on GET Ltd. stock. The following 30-day put options are available.

GET Ltd., RM 9.50 put @ RM 0.10
GET Ltd., RM 10 put @ RM 0.58

To establish the spread, the investor does the following:

Long RM 9.50 put @ RM 0.10
Short RM 10 put @ RM 0.58

Table 8.5 shows the payoff to the two put positions and the overall strategy for a range of underlying stock prices at maturity.

For any stock price at or below RM 9.50, the spread loses 2 sen per stock. However, as prices rise above RM 9.52, the position begins to profit. The maximum profit, however, is capped

Table 8.5 Payoff to Bull Put Spread

Stock Price at Maturity	Profit/Loss to Long 9.50 Put @ 0.10	Profit/Loss to Short 10.00 Put @ 0.58	Value of Combined Position
8.00	1.40	(1.42)	(0.02)
9.00	0.40	(0.42)	(0.02)
9.50	(0.10)	0.08	(0.02)
9.52	(0.10)	0.10	0
10.00	(0.10)	0.58	0.48
10.50	(0.10)	0.58	0.48
11.00	(0.10)	0.58	0.48
11.50	(0.10)	0.58	0.48

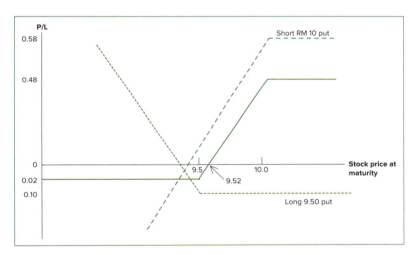

Figure 8.5 Payoff Profile to Bull Put Spread

at 48 sen per stock or RM 480 per contract (RM 0.48 × 1,000 shares). Figure 8.5 plots the payoff profile.

Though the overall payoff, risk profile, price expectation, and objective of use is the same, there are some differences between the bull call and bull put spreads. These differences arise from the way we determine the break-even points, maximum loss and maximum profit.

Note
Bull call/put spreads are established to profit from expected marginal rise in underlying asset price while limiting downside risk.

Strategy	Break-even Point	Maximum Loss	Maximum Profit
Bull Call Spread	Lower exercise price + Difference in premium	Difference in premium	Difference in exercise price − Difference in premium

(Continued)

(Continued)

Strategy	Break-even Point	Maximum Loss	Maximum Profit
Bull Put Spread	Higher exercise price – Difference in premium	Difference in exercise price – Difference in premium	Difference in premium

(Note that the maximum profit and loss to the two strategies are diagonally opposite.)

Bull Call/Bull Put Spread
When to use: When one is neutral to bullish or moderately bullish about the underlying asset price.
Risk profile: Limited downside, limited upside.
Break-even point: As described earlier.
Desired objective: To take advantage of expected marginal upmovement while also limiting downside risk.

8.3.3 A Bear Call Spread

A bear spread is an appropriate strategy when one is mildly bearish or neutral to bearish. Since one is not outright bearish, a long put or short stock position would not be appropriate. Bear spreads can be established with either calls or puts. A ***bear call spread*** is a spread position established using calls alone. The key difference between the bear and bull call spreads is that in a bull call spread, we long the lower exercise call and short the exercise call. In a bear call spread, we do the opposite, i.e., we long the higher exercise price call and short the lower exercise call. The position is used to take advantage of the expected marginal fall in the price of the underlying stock while also protecting against any upward price movement. Like the bull spreads, the risk profile is one of limited upside and limited downside potential.

Bear Call Spread: Illustration
Suppose you are neutral to bearish about TEG Corporation stock. You think it could go down in price but not by much. You want to make some money without exposing yourself to large potential losses if the stock price in fact goes up. Clearly neither a short stock nor short call position would be appropriate since both positions could incur large losses if the price goes up. The following 90-day call options on TEG Corporation stock are available.

TEG Corporation, RM 6.50 call @ RM 0.87
TEG Corporation, RM 7.50 call @ RM 0.12

Using these calls, you could establish the bear call spread as follows:

Short RM 6.50 call @ RM 0.87
Long RM 7.50 call @ RM 0.12

Table 8.6 shows the payoff to the option positions and the overall payoff.

Thus, if your expectation is indeed correct, you make a profit of 75 sen per stock or RM 750 (RM 0.75 × 1,000) from the spread; if, however, the stock price rises, your losses are capped at a maximum RM 250 (RM 0.25 × 1,000). Figure 8.6 graphs the payoff.

Table 8.6 Payoff to Bear Call Spread

Stock Price at Maturity	Profit/Loss to Short 6.50 Call @ 0.87	Profit/Loss to Long 7.50 Call @ 0.12	Value of Combined Position
6.00	0.87	(0.12)	0.75
6.50	0.87	(0.12)	0.75
7.00	0.37	(0.12)	0.25
7.25	0.12	(0.12)	0
7.50	(0.13)	(0.12)	(0.25)
8.00	(0.63)	0.38	(0.25)
8.50	(1.13)	0.88	(0.25)

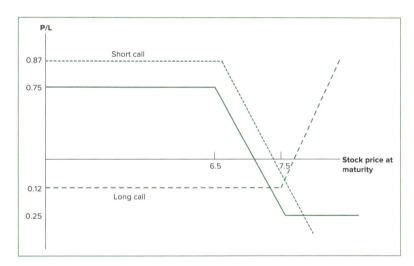

Figure 8.6 Payoff Profile to Bear Call Spread

8.3.4 Bear Put Spread

The **bear put spread** which has a payoff profile similar to that of the bear call spread is used for the same underlying stock price expectation, i.e., for a mildly bearish price outlook. The strategy is established by going long the higher exercise put and shorting the lower exercise one.

Bear Put Spread: Illustration

Using the same earlier example of TEG Corporation stock, suppose the following puts are available.

TEG Corporation, RM 6.50 put @ RM 0.35
TEG Corporation, RM 7.50 put @ RM 0.75

The bear put spread would be established as follows:

Short RM 6.50 put @ RM 0.35
Long RM 7.50 put @ RM 0.75

Table 8.7 shows the profit payoff. Should TEG Corporation stock price fall below RM 7.10, the strategy makes money. Profits are maximized at 60 sen per share or RM 600 (RM 0.60×1,000). Similarly, losses too are limited to a maximum 40 sen or RM 400. Figure 8.7 graphs the payoff profile.

Note
Bear call/put spreads are established to profit from expected marginal fall in underlying asset price while limiting downside risk.

Table 8.7   Payoff to Bear Put Spread

Stock Price at Maturity	Profit/Loss to Short 6.50 Put @ 0.35	Profit/Loss to Long 7.50 Put @ 0.75	Value of Combined Position
6.00	(0.15)	0.75	0.60
6.50	0.35	0.25	0.60
7.00	0.35	(0.25)	0.10
7.10	0.35	(0.35)	0
7.50	0.35	(0.75)	0.40
8.00	0.35	(0.75)	0.40
8.50	0.35	(0.75)	0.40

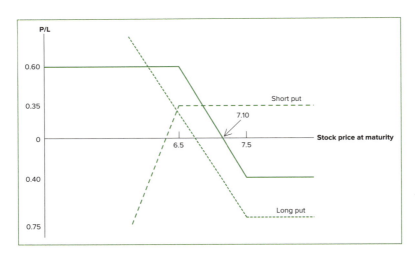

Figure 8.7   Payoff Profile to Bear Put Strategy

The break-even point and maximum profit and loss to the bear call and bear put spreads can be determined as follows:

Strategy	Break-Even Point	Maximum Loss	Maximum Profit
Bear Call Spread	Lower exercise price + Difference in premium	Difference in exercise prices – Difference in premium	Difference in premium
Bear Put Spread	Higher exercise price – Difference in premium	Difference in premium	Difference in exercise prices – Difference in premium

(Note: The maximum profit and loss of the two strategies are diagonally opposite.)

Bear Call/Bear Put Spread
When to use: When one is neutral to bearish or moderately bearish about underlying asset price.
Risk profile: Limited downside, limited upside.
Break-even point: As described earlier.
Desired objective: To take advantage of expected marginal fall in underlying asset price while limiting loss potential

8.4 Combination Strategies

A combination involves the use of **both** types of options, calls and puts as part of the strategy. These options are either both bought or sold. The difference between the spread and a combination is that a spread uses only one type of options, **either** a call or a put, whereas combinations use both. Though combinations can be in several variants, the two most common combination strategies are the following:

(a) The straddle
(b) The strangle

Both these strategies are intended for extremes of volatility. That is either very high volatility or no volatility at all of the underlying asset's price. Though the straddle and strangle are used for similar underlying asset price expectations, as we will see, there is a subtle difference between the two strategies.

Note
A long straddle strategy is designed to profit from extreme volatility, whereas the short straddle to profit from minimal volatility.

8.4.1 Straddle Strategy

The straddle strategy comes in two variants: the **long straddle** and short straddle. The long straddle involves the **purchase** of both a call and a put option on the same underlying asset, at the same exercise price and of the same maturity. The short straddle, on the other hand, involves shorting a call and a put of the same underlying asset, exercise price, and maturity. Why and when would such a strategy be useful? The long straddle is essentially a strategy designed to benefit from extreme volatility of the underlying asset's price. Thus, the strategy would be most appropriate when the underlying asset is subject to serious uncertainty. For example, when a company is faced with an impending court decision that could go either way or when a company is in merger negotiations that could either succeed or fail.

8.4.2 Long Straddle: Illustration

PMC Bhd., the country's largest oil refiner, has just been subject to a hostile takeover by Sime Darby Bhd. Its current owners have pledged to fight off the takeover attempt. You realize that this is a potentially volatile situation. PMC's stock price had already rallied. If a bidding war ensues, the stock price could rise substantially; on the other hand, if the hostile takeover is fought off, PMC stock could fall back to previous lows. Suppose 90-day at-the-money calls and puts are priced as follows:

PMC Bhd., RM 7 call @ RM 0.12
PMC Bhd., RM 7 put @ RM 0.08

To benefit from the underlying stock volatility, you could establish a long straddle position as follows:

Long RM 7 call @ RM 0.12
Long RM 7 put @ RM 0.08

Table 8.8 and Figure 8.8 show the payoff profile of the strategy.

Notice that the strategy benefits from large movements on both sides. A rise in the stock price above RM 7.20 or a fall below RM 6.80 would mean profits for the strategy. As such, regardless of whether the takeover succeeds or not, the long straddle makes money. The

Table 8.8 Payoff to Long Straddle Position

Stock Price	Profit/Loss to Long RM 7 Call @ 0.12	Profit/Loss to Long RM 7 Put @ 0.08	Value of Combined Position
5.00	(0.12)	1.92	1.80
6.00	(0.12)	0.92	0.80
6.50	(0.12)	0.42	0.30
7.00	(0.12)	(0.08)	(0.20)
7.20	0.08	(0.08)	0
7.50	0.38	(0.08)	0.30
8.00	0.88	(0.08)	0.80
8.50	1.38	(0.08)	1.30
9.00	1.88	(0.08)	1.80

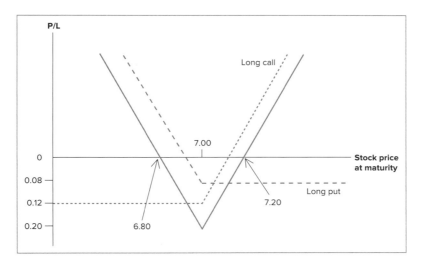

Figure 8.8 Payoff Profile to Long Straddle Position

profit to the position gets larger as the stock price movement gets larger. Note that there is no way one could benefit from a potentially highly volatile situation such as this without the use of options.

Long Straddle Strategy
When to use: Underlying asset likely to undergo extreme volatility.
Risk profile: Limited downside, unlimited upside.
Break-even points: Call exercise + Total premium;
                     Put exercise − Total premium
Desired objective: To take advantage of potential large price swings.

8.4.3 Short Straddle: Illustration

If the long straddle is intended to profit from extreme volatility, the short straddle position is designed to profit from minimal or zero volatility. The short straddle position is established by selling both the call and put options of the same underlying asset and maturity at the same exercise price.

Suppose you are neutral on MTC Inc. stock. The stock is currently traded at RM 8. You think MTC stock is likely to remain unchanged at this level over the next 30 days.

At-the-money options of 30-day maturity on MTC Inc. stock is quoted as follows:

MTC Inc., RM 8 call @ RM 0.22
MTC Inc., RM 8 put @ RM 0.18

To benefit from your expectation of minimal volatility in the stock's price, you establish a short straddle position as follows:

Table 8.9 Payoff to Short Straddle Position

Stock Price	Profit/Loss on Short RM 8 Call @ 0.22	Profit/Loss on Short RM 8 Put @ 0.18	Value of Combined Position
6.00	0.22	(1.82)	(1.60)
7.00	0.22	(0.82)	(0.60)
7.60	0.22	(0.22)	0
8.00	0.22	0.18	0.40
8.40	(0.18)	0.18	0
9.00	(0.78)	0.18	(0.60)
10.00	(1.78)	0.18	(1.60)

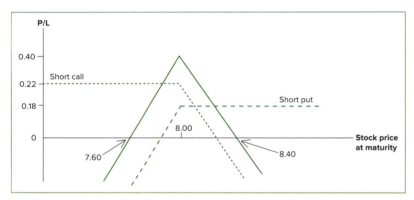

Figure 8.9 Payoff Profile to Short Straddle Position

Short RM 8 call @ RM 0.22
Short RM 8 put @ RM 0.18

Table 8.9 and Figure 8.9 show the payoff profile of the strategy.

Notice that the strategy makes the largest profit of RM 400 [(RM 0.22 + RM 0.18) × 1,000)] which is the sum of both premiums received when the stock price remains unchanged at maturity. The strategy is profitable as long as the stock price remains between the two break-even points: RM 7.60 and RM 8.40. Note, however, that from a risk profile viewpoint, the strategy has potential for large losses. Losses could occur if the underlying asset price moves substantially in either direction. The larger the price move, the larger the potential loss.

8.4.4 Strangle Strategy

As mentioned earlier, **strangles** are used for largely the same objective and market/asset price expectation as **straddles**. That is, a **long strangle** would be used to profit from volatility just as a long straddle would. Likewise, a

> **Note**
> A long strangle strategy is appropriate when extreme volatility is expected to cause the underlying asset to break out of its trading range. A short strangle is appropriate when minimal volatility would mean continued range trading.

Short Straddle Position

When to use: When minimal price movement is expected. Risk profile: Limited upside, unlimited downside.

Break-even points: Call exercise + Total premium; Put exercise Total premium

Desired objective: To profit from unchanged underlying asset price.

Box 8.1
Long-Term Capital Management Strangles Itself with Straddles

Long-Term Capital Management (LTCM) was the hedge fund that blew up spectacularly in 1998 following Russia's announcement of a moratorium on its debt. Though LTCM's ultimate failure was due to its huge bet on the spread between US Treasuries and Russian bonds converging to normal levels. (LTCM had short US treasuries and gone long Russia bonds.) The hedge fund had also bet on equity derivatives. It appears that in late 1997, LTCM, noticing that the premiums for S&P 500 equity index options were unusually large, began shorting (selling) index call and puts. The options they shorted were 5-year S&P 500 index calls and puts.

If the exercise prices of the calls and puts sold were the same, LTCM would effectively be a **short strangle**. If the exercise prices were not the same, the net position would have been a **short straddle**. Either way, the hedge fund was betting that stock market volatility will be minimal. LTCM had betted so aggressively in the strategy, that a 1% point in underlying market volatility would have cost it US$ 40 million. As luck would have it, the S&P 500 index's annual volatility which had averaged 10%–13% over the 1990s, jumped to 19% in May 1998 and then to 26% a few weeks later. The result was that LTCM's bet went horribly wrong, incurring losses way beyond what its mathematical models had predicted.

Source: Mallaby, S. (2011), *More Money than God: Hedge Funds and the Making of a New Elite*, Bloomsbury, London.

short strangle would profit from stable prices just as a short straddle would. The difference between a straddle and strangle is that in a strangle, the options are bought (sold) at different exercise prices. The call has an exercise price higher than that of the put. One would use a strangle rather than a straddle when the underlying asset trades within a price range.

8.4.5 Long Strangle: Illustration

Ropel Corp. is a large plantation firm whose stock has traditionally been trading in the RM 6.50–RM 7.50 range. You believe that given the company's problems with its plantations in Sumatra, Indonesia, the stock price could come under turbulence. The Indonesian government's arbitration committee is likely to rule on Ropel Corp.'s claims in Sumatra. The judgment is likely to be announced within the next 30 days. A favorable judgment would likely see a huge upmovement in stock price while an unfavorable one could see slumping stock price. In either case, you think the current trading range will be broken. How can you use options to take advantage? Suppose the 30-day RM 7.50 and RM 6.50 calls and puts are quoted as follows:

Ropel Corp., RM 7.50 call @ RM 0.15
Ropel Corp., RM 6.50 put @ RM 0.20

The long strangle position is established by going long both the call and the put.

Long RM 7.50 call @ RM 0.15
Long RM 6.50 put @ RM 0.20

Table 8.10 and Figure 8.10 show the payoff profile to the long strangle strategy.

Table 8.10 Payoff to Long Strangle Strategy

Stock Price at Maturity	Profit/Loss on Long RM 7.50 Call @ 0.15	Profit/Loss on Long RM 6.50 Put @ 0.20	Value of Combined Position
4.00	(0.15)	2.30	2.15
5.50	(0.15)	0.80	0.65
6.15	(0.15)	0.15	0
6.50	(0.15)	(0.20)	(0.35)
7.00	(0.15)	(0.20)	(0.35)
7.50	(0.15)	(0.20)	(0.35)
7.85	0.20	(0.20)	0
8.50	0.85	(0.20)	0.65
10.00	2.35	(0.20)	2.15

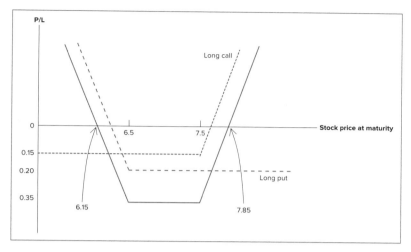

Figure 8.10   Payoff Profile of Long Strangle Strategy

Long Strangle Strategy
When to use: Underlying asset price expected to breakout of current trading range.
Risk profit: Limited downside, unlimited upside.
Break-even points: Call exercise + Total premium; Put exercise − Total premium
Desired objective: To take advantage of extreme volatility causing a price breakout from range.

8.4.6 Short Strangle Strategy

Where the long strangle strategy is designed to profit from volatility causing the underlying asset to break out of its trading range, the short strangle is intended to benefit from minimal volatility. That is, the short strangle benefits when the underlying asset continues trading within its range.

Short Strangle: Illustration

You have just read that given current inventory, expected supply and demand, palm oil prices are expected to remain stable over at least the next 3 months. Given this outlook, you expect the stock of The Kuala Lumpur — Kepong Group (KLK), a large oil palm plantation, to continue trading in its current RM 6.50–RM 7.50 range. The 30-day RM 6.50 put and RM 7.50 call are quoted as follows:

KLK, RM 7.50 call @ RM 0.15
KLK, RM 6.50 put @ RM 0.20

The short strangle is established by shorting both the earlier options. Notice once again that the exercise price of the call is higher than that of the put.

The strategy is set up as follows:

Short RM 7.50 call @ RM 0.15
Short RM 6.50 put @ RM 0.20

Table 8.11 shows the payoff to strategy. Figure 8.11 plots the payoff.

Note that the strategy profits RM 350 [(RM 0.20 + RM 0.15) × 1,000] when the underlying stock trades within the RM 6.50–RM 7.50 range. For stock prices beyond the break-even points

Table 8.11 Payoff to Short Strangle Strategy

Stock Price	Profit/Loss to Short RM 7.50 Call @ 0.15	Profit/Loss to Short RM 6.50 Put @ 0.20	Value of Combined Position
4.00	0.15	(2.30)	(2.15)
5.00	0.15	(1.30)	(1.15)
6.15	0.15	(0.15)	0
6.50	0.15	0.20	0.35
7.00	0.15	0.20	0.35
7.50	0.15	0.20	0.35
7.85	(0.20)	0.20	0
9.00	(1.35)	0.20	(1.15)
10.00	(2.35)	0.20	(2.15)

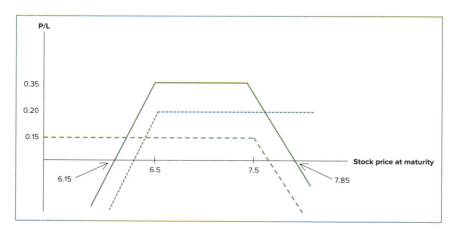

Figure 8.11 Payoff Profile to Short Strangle Strategy

of RM 6.15 or RM 7.85, the strategy makes losses. The larger the price movement beyond the break-even points, the larger the losses.

> **Short Strangle Strategy**
> When to use: Underlying asset expected to continue trading in its current range.
> Risk profile: Limited upside, unlimited downside.
> Break-even points: Call exercise + Total premium; Put exercise − Total premium
> Desired objective: To take advantage of underlying asset price remaining within range.

8.5 Covered Call Strategy

A covered call strategy (also known as a **covered call write**) is a highly popular strategy particularly among fund managers. The strategy involves selling a call option on a stock already owned. Typically, the call sold is at an exercise price higher than the stock's current price, i.e., out-of-the-money. There are usually two key objectives behind the covered call strategy, i.e.,

(a) revenue enhancement; and
(b) to lock in a target sell price.

The first objective, revenue enhancement, is the more important of the two and the reason for the popularity of the strategy. Fund managers use the strategy to increase or enhance their returns. Fund managers would typically have to hold so-called "defensive stocks" as part of their portfolio. These are usually stocks of companies with good fundamentals, a stable business and a low-leveraged balance sheet. Such stocks are considered defensive because they have low betas and hold their values well even during market downturns. Although these defensive stocks hold their value well, they often do not provide large returns since their capital gains tend to be small. Essentially, such stocks do not go up or down much. The problem for fund managers is that while they need to invest a portion of their funds in such defensive stocks in order to attain a well-balanced portfolio, the returns from such investment are usually very low. As such, fund managers hold defensive stocks and try to enhance the revenue of such holdings by executing a covered call strategy. Since the stocks do not move much, selling out-of-the-money calls would mean receiving premiums and a low probability of assignment. Even if the stock price rises beyond the exercise price of the call sold, the fund manager still profits from both the capital gains realized on price movement between the stock's current price and call exercise and from the premium he receives. The percentage returns from these two possibilities are computed as follows:

(a) **Unassigned returns** (if call sold expires unexercised)

$$= \frac{\text{Premium received}}{\text{Purchased price of stock} - \text{Premium received}}$$

(b) **Returns with assignment** (if call sold is exercised)

$$= \frac{\text{Premium received} + \text{Capital gain}^*}{\text{Purchased price of stock} - \text{Premium received}}$$

(*Capital gain is the difference between the stock price at purchase and exercise price of call.)

The covered call strategy therefore enables fund managers to hold defensive stocks while earning a little extra on the otherwise meager returns of such stocks.

The second objective of covered calls is to lock in a target sell price. This is usually intended as part of investment discipline, i.e., to force a fund manager to get rid of a stock he has purchased once it reaches the intended target sell price. Often times, investors might have an intended sell price when acquiring a stock. However, when the stock has reached the target price, one often hesitates to sell, hoping for more profits from a further run up in prices. The problem here is that after a brief rally, the stock might fall substantially, often below the original purchase price. The result is losses. Had the stock been sold when it reached the target sell price, profits would have been made. It is to avoid temptations such as these and to enforce investment discipline that a covered call strategy is used. Having sold a call, one will have to deliver (sell) the stock if the stock price exceeds the exercise price at maturity. When the call sold gets exercised, one is forced to sell at the exercise price.

Covered Call Strategy: Illustration

You own one lot of MOX Bhd. stock as part of your portfolio. You like the stock as part of your portfolio. However, given the price stability, there is hardly any capital gains. Your only returns on the stock is the small dividend yield. The stock is currently traded at RM 7. A 30-day RM 7.50 call is being quoted RM 0.10 or 10 sen. You decide to use the covered call strategy to enhance your returns from the stock. Thus, you

> **Note**
> A covered call strategy is intended to enhance revenue from holding defensive low-beta stocks and/or to lock in a target sell price.

Short 1 MOX Bhd. RM 7.50 call @ RM 0.10

Table 8.12 shows the payoff to the covered call strategy. Figure 8.12 plots the payoff.

Note that at any price above RM 7.50, the short call will be assigned. You would then have sold the stock at an effective price of RM 7.60 (RM 7.50 + premium, RM 0.10). Should the price fall below the current RM 7, then you lose; however, you are still better off with a covered call, since you get to keep the premium. The fact that you receive the premium is

Table 8.12 Payoff to Covered Call Strategy

Stock Price at Maturity	Payoff to Long Stock	Profit/Loss to Short 7.50 @ 0.10	Value of Combined Position
6.00	(1.00)	0.10	(0.90)
6.50	(0.50)	0.10	(0.40)
6.90	(0.10)	0.10	0
7.00	0	0.10	0.10
7.20	0.20	0.10	0.30
7.40	0.40	0.10	0.50
7.50	0.50	0.10	0.60
8.00	1.00	(0.40)	0.60
9.00	2.00	(1.40)	0.60

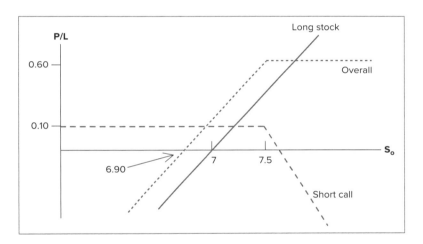

Figure 8.12 Payoff Profile to Covered Call Strategy

the revenue enhancement. The value of a covered write here is always RM 0.10 higher than the value of the underlying. When the covered calls are written on **stocks bought on margin**, a handsome rate of return on investment may be earned. Furthermore, by repeating this strategy over every 30 days (using 30-day options), a good annualized return can be earned.

Using the two earlier mentioned equations, the annualized percentage returns under the two possible scenarios: (i) if the call is assigned, and (ii) if the call expires unexercised, would be as follows:

(a) Unassigned returns *(Call expires unexercised)*

$$\text{Assigned \% return} = \frac{\text{RM } 0.10}{\text{RM } 6.90} \times \frac{360}{30}$$
$$= 0.014493 \times 12$$
$$= 0.1739$$
$$= 17.39\%$$

(b) Returns with assignment *(Call shorted is assigned)*

$$= \frac{0.10 + 0.50}{RM\ 6.90}$$

$$= 0.08696$$

$$= 8.696\ or\ 8.7\%$$

> **Covered Call Strategy**
> *When to use:* To enhance revenue or lock in target sell price. Risk profile: Limited upside, unlimited downside.
> *Break-even points:* Since overall resembles short put, exercise price – premium.
> *Desired objective:* To earn extra revenue on defensive stocks held or to lock in a target sell price on underlying stock held.

Box 8.2
Equity Option Strategies: Can the Tail Wag the Dog?

In recent weeks, the financial markets were rattled by news that Softbank, a Japanese investment holding firm, had huge exposures in equity derivatives. The *Financial Times* (*FT*) which broke the news identified Softbank as the "Nasdaq Whale," as the exposure was mainly on United States (US) tech stocks listed on Nasdaq. What followed was a steep fall in Softbank's Tokyo listed stock price. Investors spooked by the news, dumped the stock causing Softbank's market capitalization to fall 5.4% or US$ 9 billion on the day following the news. The Nasdaq Composite index meanwhile is reported to have shed some US$ 1.9 trillion in value in just 3 days surrounding the news. Note that the initial report of the *FT* was simply that Softbank had exposure in equity derivatives, not that they had suffered losses. Yet, the initial market reaction was grossly negative.

When *FT* later reported that Softbank may be sitting on large unrealized profits of about US$ 4 billion from the equity derivatives, Softbank's stock price which had fallen some 17% within a week, recouped almost all the losses the following week. The misstep is clear. Reports that a company was involved in derivatives was enough to not just send its investors running but also cause a near market rout.

Softbank, it appears, had established what is known as a bull call spread using equity call options on stocks of a very select group of tech companies. These were the likes of Amazon, Microsoft, Netflix, Facebook, Adobe, and such. A spread, though speculative in nature, involves offsetting positions such that the downside is limited. Thus the risk

Box 8.2
(*Continued*)

profile is far different from naked speculative positions, which can have an unlimited downside. In establishing the bull call spread, Softbank had bought out-of-the-money calls and sold call options with even higher exercise prices. The premium received from the options sold helps to reduce the overall cost of the strategy but imposes a cap on the upside. In essence, the spread position has both a limited upside and downside effectively capping the potential gains and losses.

A bull call spread is used to profit from a potential rise in the underlying stock price while simultaneously protecting against any fall in value. As the underlying stock rises in value, the call option bought, makes profits but the rising profits get capped when the underlying stock position has to be assigned to the party to whom the higher priced call was sold. The size of the profit therefore depends on the difference between the two exercise prices. Outright losses, though limited are possible if the underlying stock price never rises above the lower of the two exercise prices.

A spread, therefore, is nothing but a speculative strategy but one with a safety net below. Softbank's overall strategy was relatively "safe," except that in this case their aggregate position was reportedly large and focused on a few underlying stocks. Note that they were using single stock options. Such large and concentrated positions can indeed move markets. The fact that derivatives have in-built leverage enables large positions to be taken at very low net investment. When there is herding and similar strategies are also used by other investors, underlying asset prices can seriously deviate from fundamentals. Changes in option values invariably impact underlying stock prices because of the need for dynamic hedging. For example, sellers of call options have to cover their short position by buying the underlying stock (see Chapter 9). Delta hedging, as the process is called, requires the maintenance of a hedge ratio, by purchasing a proportion of the underlying stock as the option value increases. The proportion of stock needed to be purchased increases "exponentially" as the option becomes increasingly in-the-money. The result is a feedback loop causing higher stock prices as shorts chase the stock to avoid losses on the calls they sold. Thus, large and concentrated derivative positions can move asset prices and when other retail players piggy back on the trade, markets can take a life of its own. The tail can indeed wag the dog.

The initial stock price reaction to Softbank's derivatives position points to deepseated misperception about derivatives. The fact that derivatives, forwards, futures, options, and swaps can be very effective in risk management is often lost. The long history of

(*Continued*)

Box 8.2
(Continued)

financial scandals involving derivatives has obviously colored perception. It should be noted that no money has ever been lost when derivatives were used appropriately for risk management. A well-designed hedge position cannot lose money. Softbank's spread position was in no way a hedge. They were trying to make quick money, albeit with limited downside. This, however, is far different from the actions of Barings PLC or Orange County which were driven by greed and a huge dose of ignorance if not stupidity. But as another case, that of Germany's Metallgesellschaft shows, with highly levered instruments like derivatives, even an intended hedge can go wrong if factors like differences in accounting regimes, disclosure requirements, and liquidity mismatches arising from margin requirements are not well considered in designing the strategy.

Source: Reproduction of author's op-ed piece.

8.6 Butterfly, Condor, Ratio, and Box Spreads

In this section, we examine some additional strategies. These strategies are somewhat more complicated relative to the earlier strategies. We will examine four strategies all of which belong to the category of spread strategies.

(I) The Butterfly Spread

As with all spread positions, one could be either long or short a butterfly spread. A long butterfly spread is designed to profit from a neutral or unchanged underlying asset price. The short butterfly, on the other hand, profits from movements away from the current trading price of the underlying asset. Again, as in the case of bull and bear spreads, the butterfly can be established using call options or with put options.

A long butterfly spread is established by taking positions in a total of four option contracts of three different exercise prices but with the same maturity. The long butterfly spread with calls and the same position established using puts would be as follows:

Long Butterfly Spread with Calls

This position would be established by going long a call with a "low" exercise price (X_1), then going short two calls of a higher exercise price (X_2) and long another call with an even higher exercise price (X_3). Thus, four calls with three exercise prices are used. Using X_t to determine exercise price, the exercise prices are as follows: $X_1 < X_2 < X_3$. The strategy therefore is

- Long 1, call with exercise price $= X_1$
- Short 2, calls with exercise price $= X_2$
- Long 1, call with exercise price $= X_3$

where $X_1 < X_2 < X_3$.

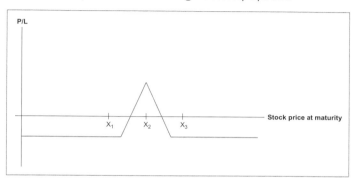

Payoff Profile to Long Butterfly Spread

Regardless of whether the long butterfly is established using calls or puts, the overall payoff and risk profile is the same.

Note that the strategy provides the highest profits when the stock price at maturity is at X_2. (X_2 was the exercise price of the two shorted calls/puts.) The risk profile of the strategy is one of limited profits and limited downside. Note that this strategy would have a market outlook or expectation of underlying asset performance, which is the same as that of the short straddle. However, while the short straddle has unlimited downside risk, the long butterfly has limited downside.

The Short Butterfly Strategy

The short butterfly strategy aims to profit from price movements away from the current trading price of the underlying asset. In terms of market outlook or expected underlying price movement, it is similar to the long straddle. The position can be established with calls or puts as follows:

Short butterfly with calls

- Short 1, call with exercise price $= X_1$
- Long 2, calls with exercise price $= X_2$
- Short 1, call with exercise price $= X_3$

where $X_1 < X_2 < X_3$.

Short butterfly with puts

- Short 1, put with exercise price $= X_1$
- Long 2, puts with exercise price $= X_2$
- Short 1, put with exercise price $= X_3$

where $X_1 < X_2 < X_3$.

Like the long straddle, the short butterfly position gains with large price swings. However, as is evident from the following payoff diagram, the profit potential is limited — as is the downside.

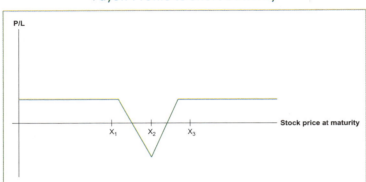

Payoff Profile to Short Butterfly

(II) The Condor Strategy

The condor is a variant of the butterfly strategy, just as the strangle was a variant of the straddle. Again as with the butterfly strategy, the condor can be constructed using calls or by using puts. In terms of category, the condor would belong to spreads. The long condor is designed to benefit from the underlying asset's price remaining within its current range. The short condor, on the other hand, benefits when the underlying asset breaks out of its price range. If the butterfly spread strategy is comparable to straddles, the condor is a spread strategy comparable to strangles. The difference being that, as a spread, the condor (like the butterfly and all other spreads) is limited on both the profit and loss sides.

Long Condor

The long condor is established using four options on an underlying asset (either calls or puts) of the same maturity but at four different exercise prices. Regardless of whether calls or puts are used, the steps and risk profile are the same.

Long condor with calls

- Long 1 call with exercise price $= X_1$
- Short 1 call with exercise price $= X_2$
- Long 1 call with exercise price $= X_3$
- Long 1 call with exercise price $= X_4$

where $X_1 < X_2 < X_3 < X_4$.

Long condor with puts

- Long 1 put with exercise price $= X_1$
- Short 1 put with exercise price $= X_2$
- Long 1 put with exercise price $= X_3$
- Long 1 put with exercise price $= X_4$

where $X_1 < X_2 < X_3 < X_4$.

The long condor has a payoff profile that benefits from the underlying asset continuing to trade within its price range.

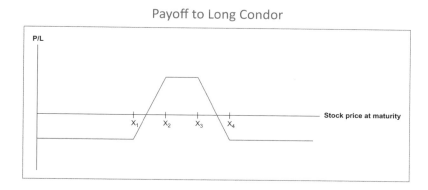

Payoff to Long Condor

Short Condor

The short condor position is established by doing the opposite of what was done to establish the long condor. Using either calls or puts, the position would be established as follows:

Short condor with calls

- Short 1 call with exercise price $= X_1$
- Long 1 call with exercise price $= X_2$
- Long 1 call with exercise price $= X_3$
- Short 1 call with exercise price $= X_4$

where $X_1 < X_2 < X_3 < X_4$.

Short condor with puts

- Short 1 put with exercise price $= X_1$
- Long 1 put with exercise price $= X_2$
- Long 1 put with exercise price $= X_3$
- Short 1 put with exercise price $= X_4$

where $X_1 < X_2 < X_3 < X_4$.

Note that the key difference between the butterfly and the condor is that, the butterfly used two options at the *same* intermediate exercise price, whereas in the condor, the exercise prices are different. As with the long strangle, the short condor position is intended to gain from the underlying asset's price breaking out of its trading price range. However, as a spread position, the profits are not potentially unlimited, but capped.

Payoff to Short Condor

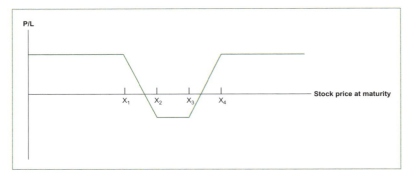

(III) Ratio Spreads

A ratio spread is a spread position established using different ratios of long or short positions in an option. For example, a call ratio spread might be established by going long two calls of a certain exercise price and going short one call of another exercise price or vice versa of the same underlying asset and maturity. Since the ratio of options bought versus shorted can be in any ratio, e.g., 2:1, 3:2, 2:4, and so on, the number of possible payoffs can be numerous. Again, as with other spreads, the ratio spread can be constructed using calls, in which case it would be known as a call ratio spread or with puts, put ratio spreads. We examine below an example of a call ratio spread.

A Call Ratio Spread

In its simple form, a call ratio spread can be thought of as a variant of, say, the bull spread. Recall that in establishing the bull spread with calls, the investor went long a call with the lower exercise price and shorted a call with the higher exercise price. Specifically, in our example of a bull call spread, the investor had gone long an RM 9.50 call and shorted a RM 10.50 call. What if instead the proportions were not equal? That is, the number of options shorted is not equal to the number bought (long)? Then we have a ratio spread. For example, suppose our investor went long *two* RM 9.50 calls and shorted one RM 10.50 call. We would have a 2:1 ratio call spread. The rationale of such a ratio spread would be to alter the payoff from that of the normal bull spread. Using the same options as that used in our bull spread example, the 2:1 ratio call spread would have a payoff as follows:

- Long 2 RM 9.50 call @ RM 0.15 each
- Short 1 RM 10.50 call @ RM 0.05

The payoff to the bull call we saw in Section 8.4 (Figure 8.4) is reproduced for comparison. Notice that on the downside, the potential loss is more than that of the bull call spread; this is because the investor is long two calls at 0.15 each. The total downside is limited to 0.25 (0.15 × 2 − 0.05). For this larger downside, the investor is compensated on the upside, in the sense that the upside is not limited to 0.90 but is now potentially unlimited. For example, at a stock price above RM 10.50, the ratio spread earns more than the bull call spread. At a stock price below RM 9.50, however, the ratio spread makes larger though limited losses. The advantage of the ratio spread over the bull call spread clearly lies on the upside.

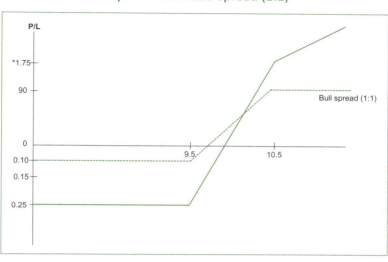

Payoff to Call Ratio Spread (2:1)

*(2 × RM 0.90 − 0.05)

(IV) Box Spread

The box spread can be considered an all option variant of the conversion strategy. The desired objective in creating a box spread is often to arbitrage relative mispricing among option premiums. As we will see in Chapter 10, the same can be said of the conversion strategy, i.e., the conversion can be used as an arbitrage strategy. The box spread is established by combining a bull spread with calls and a bear spread with puts. All options are on the same underlying asset, and have the same maturity. Each pair of options that make up the bull spread and bear spread have the same exercise prices. Thus the box spread is established as follows:

- Long 1 call at exercise price $= X_1$
- Short 1 call at exercise price $= X_2$
- Short 1 put at exercise price $= X_1$
- Long 1 put at exercise price $= X_2$

where $X_1 < X_2$.

Note that the first two call options make up the bull spread with calls, whereas the latter two put options, the bear spread. The payoff profile to the box spread is as follows:

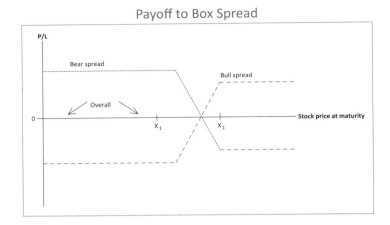

Should the relative premiums not be in line, the overall payoff would be at non-zero, thereby leading to arbitrage opportunity. The box spread can therefore be established to take advantage of relative mispricing between option premiums.

8.7 Summary of Strategies by Market Outlook

The following is a categorization of the abovementioned strategies according to the expected market price performance of the underlying asset.

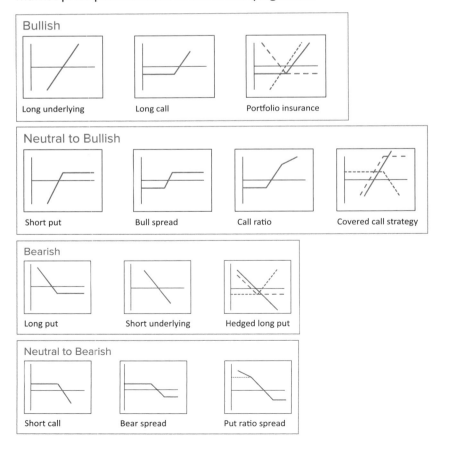

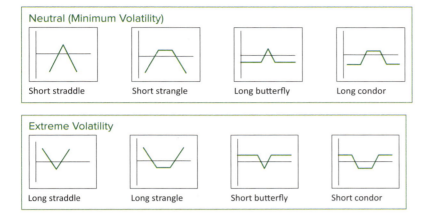

Box 8.3
Options Strategies: The Long and Short of It

It should be clear from this chapter that there are numerous ways of using or combining options to achieve desired payoffs. Obviously, the appropriate option strategy would depend on expectations. There are strategies to take advantage of bullish expectations, yet others for bearish conditions, extremes in underlying volatility and so on. As the diagrams in Section 8.7 show, there may be more than one appropriate strategy for a given expectation. Yet, from the diagrams it is obvious that the strategies for a given expectation can be vastly different from a risk profile perspective. To take a simple example, when one is bullish one can either take a long underlying position, a long call on the same underlying, or create a synthetic call by way of portfolio insurance. All three strategies allow an investor to participate in an upside rally. However, their risk profiles are different. The long underlying strategy has unlimited downside whereas the long call and portfolio insurance have limited downside. So, why would anyone bullish opt for a long underlying strategy instead of the other two, when it is clearly disadvantageous? The answer lies in cost. Clearly, the long underlying is cheaper than long call. There are no call premiums to be paid. So, the long underlying position is relatively riskier but much cheaper. Between the latter two positions, long call and portfolio insurance, in well-functioning markets the cost of the two ought to be the same, so the difference lies in underlying position. If one is already holding the underlying asset, then the best way to participate in a potential upside while limiting downside exposure is through portfolio insurance. If one does not have the underlying, then the long call is the only way to take advantage of a potential upside while also protecting downside exposure.

The bottom line in pinning down the right option strategy is balancing cost, risk current position with expectation. Thus, if the potential profit of a strategy is lower than another, its cost must also be lower. Unless there is mispricing, one would not be able to establish a relatively more profitable or lower risk position at a lower relative cost.

SUMMARY

This chapter examined common option strategies and their payoffs. An option strategy is usually established to achieve an investment objective or to take advantage of a given market outlook about the underlying asset's price. Given the flexibility of options, there are numerous possible strategies. These can be categorized into four large categories: (i) naked or uncovered positions, (ii) hedge strategies, (iii) spreads, and (iv) combinations. Uncovered positions are largely speculative strategies. Hedge strategies are intended to minimize or eliminate price exposure related to an underlying asset position. Portfolio insurance is an option strategy that seeks to hedge a long underlying position. It involves combining a long put position with the long stock position. Portfolio insurance provides downside protection while also enabling the realization of potential profits from upmovements. A short underlying position can be hedged by the use of call options, essentially, combining a long call position with the short underlying. Conversion strategies enable one to lock in a fixed value for the underlying asset in the midst of market turbulence.

Spread strategies are used to profit from marginal price movements while limiting downside risk. A bull spread is used when upmovements are expected; a bear spread to profit from down movements. Spreads can be established using only calls or puts. Combination strategies use both calls and puts to establish the position. The long straddle and long strangle positions gain from extreme volatility, whereas the short straddle and short strangle positions from minimal or zero volatility. The difference between the straddle and strangle is that the latter is used where there is range trading. The covered call strategy is a common strategy used by fund managers to enhance revenue and/or to lock in a target sell price.

KEY TERMS

- Naked/uncovered positions
- Portfolio insurance
- Conversion strategy
- Spread strategy
- Bull call spread
- Bull put spread
- Bear call spread
- Bear put spread
- Straddles
- Strangles
- Long straddle
- Short straddle
- Long strangle
- Short strangle
- Covered call write

End-of-Chapter Questions

1. You just heard on CNN that war in the Gulf could break out at any moment. The thinking on Wall Street appears to be that while a short and quick war that ends within a month would be bullish for United States (US) stocks, a long dragged out one could be hugely detrimental. As a savvy investor of options, you are thinking of an appropriate strategy. The website of your US broker has the following quotes.
   - DJIA = 7,960 points
   - S&P 500 = 950 points
   - 90-day US Treasury Bill rate = 5.6%
   - 90-day S&P 500, 950 call @ 14 points
   - 90-day S&P 500, 950 put @ 10 points
   - Spot month S&P 500, 940 put @ 3 points (expiring next week)

   a. State and outline the appropriate option strategy.
   b. Graph the strategy. Show the overall payoff (carefully label the graph).
   c. Briefly explain why this is the best strategy.

2. Crude Palm Oil (CPO) has been trading in the RM 900–950 range over the last several months. The Commodity Research Bureau (CRB) of the US is expected to release its report on US Soy Bean Oil production next week. Given "wild" weather in the US, the report is expected to forecast either a big increase or decrease in US Soy Bean Oil production over the next 3-month period. Suppose options were available on CPO at BMDB.
   a. Outline an appropriate option strategy. Briefly explain why your strategy is appropriate.
   b. Graph your position (label all axes/points).
   c. State the risk profile of your strategy.

3. An option has a time premium of 18 sen. Suppose the exercise price is RM 12 and the underlying stock is currently selling at RM 12.40. Determine the correct premium if the option is
   a. A call option
   b. A put option
   c. An RM 12 straddle

4. You own a portfolio currently worth THB 4.5 million and beta = 1.0. You foresee the next 3 months being volatile and wish to avoid potential losses. The SET 50 Index is now at 900 points. Three-month 900 calls are at 4.50 points while 900 puts are 3 points.
   (i) Describe the hedge strategy.
   (ii) How many options are needed to fully hedge?
   (iii) What is the cost of this insurance?
   (iv) State the net value of your portfolio if the SET 50 Index is at 750 points at maturity.
   (v) Graph the position and describe the risk profile.

5. A speculator does the following transactions on Day 1 and Day 2. Assume all options have the same underlying and maturity.
   Day 1: Sell 1 RM 6 call @ RM 0.20 and sell 1 RM 6 put @ RM 0.20
   Day 2: Buy 1 RM 6 put @ RM 0.35 and sell 1 RM 5.50 put @ RM 0.15

a. What is the final position?
b. What is the maximum profit potential of the final position?
c. What is the break-even point(s) of the final position?
d. What happened to the stock price between Day 1 and Day 2? Briefly explain why.

6. You expect a stock to continue trading within an RM 1 price range. The following options are available.
   - RM 6 call @ RM 0.20
   - RM 5.50 call @ RM 0.70
   - RM 5 put @ RM 0.08
   - RM 5.50 put @ RM 0.50

   a. State the appropriate strategy. Specify the option and whether to long or short.
   b. Graph the strategy you have recommended above (label all axes and intersections).

7. A trader undertakes the following trades on 30-day stock options.
   - Short RM 7 put @ RM 0.30
   - Long RM 8 put @ RM 0.60

   a. Graph the position and state the name of the strategy.
   b. What is the maximum profit, maximum loss, and break-even point(s) for the strategy?
   c. What is the trader's outlook to justify this strategy?
   d. What is the payoff to the strategy if the underlying stock is at RM 5.50 at maturity? (Profit per contract)
   e. What is the resulting stock position if the stock price at maturity is RM 8.60?

8. Mr. Ahmad is a fund manager at ST Asset Management. He does not own any shares in MAS but is relatively bullish on its outlook. Still he is worried about the rise in oil prices and the potential damage on MAS's profits. Outline an appropriate option strategy given Mr. Ahmad's outlook and skepticism. The following options are available (plot the position, label all axes, maximum and minimum points, specify the option and state long or short position). MAS stock is currently traded at RM 7.

   90-day calls   **90-day puts**
   RM 6.50 call @ RM 0.48   RM 6.50 put @ RM 0.08
   RM 7.50 call @ RM 0.08   RM 7.50 put @ RM 0.70

9. Assume you work for a foreign fund management company. Your company has a small portion of its funds in Thai stocks. Just about all the stocks your company holds are index stocks. Though small, the portfolio is very well diversified. Following steep falls, the SET 50 Index is now at 680 points. Your company wants to "lock in" current values. The following index options are available.

   90-day calls   **90-day puts**
   660 call @ 22 pts   660 put @ 1 pt
   680 call @ 9 pts   680 put @ 7 pt
   700 call @ 2 pt   700 put @ 23 pts

   a. Outline the appropriate hedge strategy. [State the option(s) used.]
   b. What is the cost of the insurance?
   c. What is the maximum possible loss?

10. You think MBB stock has potential for an upward move in price. You have no position whatsoever in the stock now. You would like to take opportunity of any upmovement in price but want to strictly limit your downside risk. MBB Stock price now = RM 12.
   a. Given the following information, outline three possible appropriate strategies. For each strategy
      (i) State the position
      (ii) Graph the strategy
      (iii) Outline the risk profile
      (iv) State the maximum profit, maximum loss, and break-even point(s).

30-day calls	30-day puts
RM 11 call @ RM 1.55	RM 11 put @ RM 0.25
RM 12 call @ RM 0.70	RM 12 put @ RM 0.45
RM 13 call @ RM 0.22	RM 13 put @ RM 1.40

   b. From a cost viewpoint, which is the best strategy?

11. You own five lots of CNB stocks; its current price is $7.20, which is what it was several months ago. This is a stable stock. Though you like the stability, you wish to enhance your returns. You will not be satisfied with the mere 2% dividend return. You notice the following quotes.
    - $7.50 call = $0.30
    - $7.50 put = $0.60

    Outline an appropriate strategy and graph the position.

12. You have examined BAT Bhd. stock and you are convinced the stock will continue trading in an RM 6.50–RM 7 price range. You see the following quotes.
    - RM 7 call @ RM 0.15
    - RM 7.50 call @ RM 0.80
    - RM 6.50 put @ RM 0.20
    - RM 7 put @ RM 0.10

    What would be an appropriate strategy given your conviction of stock price movement? Graph the strategy.

13. You just shorted Promet Ltd. stock at RM 3.50. You now hear that Promet had landed a large government project. You don't know whether this is reliable information, yet feel uneasy. Is there any option strategy to protect you from a countermove?

14. The spot price of MOX stock is now RM 8.10. You observe the following prices for the 30-day options.
    - RM 8 put   = RM 0.16
    - RM 8 call   = RM 0.42
    - RM 8.50 put = RM 0.61
    - RM 8.50 call = RM 0.20

    Suppose you long one RM 8 call and short two RM 8.50 calls.
    a. Graph the position, label all axes, maximum and minimum profit/loss points.
    b. What are the break-even points and the risk profile of this strategy?
    c. What must your expectation be to justify this strategy?
    d. State one other strategy that has a similar risk profile and state one advantage of the strategy in (a) over the stated strategy.

15. A large Malaysian conglomerate which had experienced a serious hit during the currency crisis appears headed for imminent failure. You have been closely watching this company. The company has approached the government for a financial rescue. If the firm receives the rescue, its stock price is likely to increase substantially, otherwise a huge fall in stock price is likely. Using the following information, outline *two* appropriate option strategies. The stock is currently trading at RM 7.

    90-day call
    RM 7 call @ RM 0.26
    RM 7.50 call @ RM 0.09

    90-day put
    RM 7 put @ RM 0.18
    RM 7.50 put @ RM 0.34

16. You expect NTC Inc. stock to make a big move over the next few weeks. You are however unsure about the direction of the move. You want limited downside risk. Outline and graph *four* appropriate strategies. Which one strategy would you choose? Explain why.

17. You own 15 lots of PBB Bhd. stock currently selling at RM 4.20. In 30 days, you need to RM 60,000 as deposit for a shop house you have arranged to purchase. You think PBB is likely to rally over the next few weeks, yet you cannot risk losing too much. You want to participate in a potential rally without exposing yourself to too much risk.
    The following quotes are available.

    - 30-day PBB Bhd. RM 4.25 call @ RM 0.25
    - 30-day PBB Bhd. RM 4.25 put @ RM 0.15

    Suggest a strategy using options that would be appropriate.

18. ERB Inc. is one of three telecoms companies in the country. All three companies had bid for a large nationwide telecom project. The winning company could go on to substantially increase its market share. ERB stock is the only one with options traded on it. ERB is now selling at RM 7 per stock and the government will announce the winning bid in 2 weeks. You do not own any ERB stock. Outline an appropriate option strategy. At-the-money calls and puts are quoted at RM 0.20.

19. You own 10 lots of Utusan stock that you bought 2 years ago. It is now selling at RM 3.50 and as has been very stable at this price. You have been receiving a 2.5% dividend over the last 2 years. You do not intend selling the stock now but would not mind letting it go at an RM 3.80 price range. A 30-day at-the-money call is quoted at RM 0.30. Outline a strategy that will let you either earn a higher returns or sell the stock at RM 3.80. Graph the position.

20. You expect CPO to trade in the RM 1,300 to RM 1,350 per ton price range over the next few months. Assuming 3-month options on CPO were available, outline an appropriate strategy. Graph the position using assumed option premiums.
    (i) Using your own set of prices, outline and graph a "Covered Call" position.
    (ii) State two reasons why fund managers might want to use such a strategy.

21. a. Your company's CFO appears to be highly confused. In order to hedge a recently received £20 million payment from a British customer, which is still being held in your company's bank account in London, he went long, 3-month forward contracts on the pound for £20 million. Realizing that this may not be appropriate, he quickly shorts 3-month futures contracts for £20 million. Determine/describe

the company's net exposure to movements in the British pound sterling. (Graph the positions, and show the overall.)

b. Suppose a trader goes long the 3-month CPO futures contract and shorts the 6-month contract. Name his strategy; what must be his expectation? What must happen to CPO prices for him to profit?

22. Your boss at the Fund Management Company you work for has just examined your portfolio. He instructs you to reduce your holdings of cash and to reduce the overall beta of your portfolio. In order to do both, you just bought a huge position on Nestle stock. Given the stock's stable nature, it has very low beta. Now you are worried that this new investment could drag down the overall returns of your portfolio. You want to have the defensive stock in your portfolio but need to have higher returns than a passive buy and hold strategy. Assuming options on Nestle stock is available, outline an appropriate strategy. (Graph the strategy, show the overall payoff, use assumed stock and exercise prices.)

23. Suppose that on an airplane flight you overhear one businessman talking excitedly to another about Dell. You also think that you hear the terms "financial distress" and "takeover candidate." Finally, you hear one of the businessmen say, "Dell's stock price will really move when this becomes public." However, because the pilot rudely interrupted your eavesdropping, you do not know whether your unwitting informant expects Dell's stock price to move up or move down. State *at least three* appropriate option strategies.

24. a. A Thai company has submitted a tender to supply parts for a foreign project. The outcome of the bid will be known in a month's time. If accepted, payment in foreign currency will occur 2 months later. Assuming forwards, futures, options, and swaps are available for the foreign currency, state your best recommended strategy. Justify your answer.

b. The country's three mobile phone operators, Celcom, Maxis, and Digi, have all applied for 5G license. The government has made it clear that only two licenses will be awarded. Winning a 5G license is seen as being very advantageous, whereas the one company not chosen is likely to be sidelined. An announcement on the license is due within the next 90 days. Celcom is not listed while the other two are. Assuming Maxis is the only listed one with stock options available, outline an options strategy appropriate for the situation. (Use your own estimates for premium, maturity, and exercise price; graph the position and clearly show the overall payoff).

c. A trader believes the FBM KLCI is likely to trade within its current channel between the 880 points support and 910 points resistance levels. State and outline (be specific) an appropriate option strategy to take advantage of that outlook. Graph the position and show the overall payoff.

25. An options trader undertakes the following trades on stock options.
- Long RM 9.50 call @ RM 0.40
- Short RM 10.50 call @ RM 0.10
- Short RM 9.50 put @ RM 0.15
- Long RM 10.50 put @ RM 0.45

   a. Graph his position and determine the overall payoff. Identify the strategy (name) and the risk profile.
   b. What is the maximum profit/loss to the overall strategy?

CHAPTER · 9

Option Pricing

Objectives

This chapter examines the pricing of options. Two option pricing models, the Binomial (BOPM) and Black–Scholes option pricing models (BSOPM), are examined in detail. The chapter also analyzes the determinants of option values and explores the relationship among these determinants. Issues related to option pricing are also discussed. In addition to the pricing of options on single stocks, the valuation of stock index options and options on currencies are examined. On completing this chapter, readers should have a good understanding of the logic of the two option pricing models, pricing mechanics, and the determinants of option values.

Introduction

The pricing of options, unlike that of other financial assets can be complicated. This has to do with the fact that options, being derivatives and nonobligatory, have values that are dependent on certain outcomes. An options value at maturity is very easily determined. Option value at expiration can only take one of the following two values.

Value/price = 0 if the option is out-of-the-money at maturity
Value/price = Intrinsic value (IV) if the option is in-the-money at maturity

This comes directly from the following equation:
Call value at maturity: MAX {0, $S_T - X$}

Put value at maturity: MAX {0, $X - S_T$}

where

X = exercise price
S_T = underlying asset price at maturity, T

Regardless of whether the option is a call or a put, value at maturity is either zero or the IV. Thus, determining option values at maturity is straight forward and requires no pricing model. Determining an option's price/value before maturity is much more challenging. In particular, because the option's price before maturity arises from two sources: IV and time value. While IV is either zero or the difference between the exercise and underlying asset price, determining time value,

Note
An option's value at maturity is simply its IV. If the option expires at or out-of-the-money, its IV is zero and the option is worthless. If the option expires in-the-money, then its value at maturity equals its IV.

is more complex. As option value before maturity is a combination of both intrinsic and time values, mathematical models are needed to value options before maturity.

In this chapter, we examine two key models of option pricing. These are (i) the binomial option pricing model (BOPM), and (ii) the **Black–Scholes option pricing model (BSOPM)**. While the first is a discrete time model, the latter is of continuous time. A brief examination of other continuous time models is done in the appendix of this chapter. In addition to the valuation of options on individual stocks, the chapter examines the valuation of stock index options, index options with stock index futures as underlying and the valuation of options on currencies.

9.1 Asset Valuation in Finance

The underlying logic of asset pricing in finance is that the value of an asset is equivalent to the present value (PV) of future cash flows that could be derived from the asset. Mathematically,

$$\text{Price} = PV = \sum_{t=1}^{n} \frac{CF_t}{(1+K)^t}$$

where

CF = futures cash flow
K = discount rate

This underlying logic is applied as variations in valuing financial assets such as bonds and stocks. Thus, a simple financial asset like a straight bond (coupon, noncallable) can be valued as:

$$\text{Bond price} = \sum_{t=1}^{n} \frac{C_t}{(1+K)^t} + \frac{FV_n}{(1+K)^n}$$

where

C_t = coupon in year t
FV_n = face value received at maturity in year n

Such an asset valuation is easy when the future cash flows are either predetermined, as in the case of bonds, or fairly easy to estimate as in the case of future stock dividends, etc. Dividend discount models of stock valuation, e.g., value stocks by using estimated future dividends. Though options too are a financial asset, future cash flows from options are unpredictable and depend entirely on certain states of outcome. Under some states of outcome the option would be worthless, in other states highly profitable. In essence, whether an option will be worth anything depends on what the exercise price is and what the underlying asset's price turns out to be.

Before maturity, since the exercise price is known, the option value will depend on **the expected price** of the underlying asset at option maturity. This expected price would clearly depend on the underlying asset's **current price** (S_0) and the volatility of its price (σ). **Ceterus paribus**, an underlying asset with a higher price **volatility** has a higher probability of being profitable at maturity. For example, a higher probability of upmovement would make calls on the asset more valuable, whereas higher probability of downmovement would make put options on the asset more valuable.

We have thus far established that the expected price of the underlying asset is key. This expected price in turn depends on the current price, volatility, and the probability of directional movements. This is the logic of the two option pricing models that we examine. For purposes of clarity, we examine both models only in the context of European-style options. The two pricing models are the following:

(i) The BOPM
(ii) The BSOPM

9.2 The Binomial Option Pricing Model

The underlying logic of the BOPM is that the current value of an option must equal the PV of the possible **payoffs** to the option at maturity. In the case of a call option, e.g., current value is determined by identifying the different possible outcomes under which the call will be profitable, estimating the probability of each of these outcomes occurring and then finding the PV of these payoffs adjusted for probability.

Note
The BOPM is based on the logic that the current value of the option must equal the PV of the possible payoffs to the option at maturity.

The BOPM is a discrete time model, in that underlying asset price changes at a given fixed time interval. As with other models, one uses the BOPM to determine the value given a set of assumptions. To see how the model works, let us work through a series of examples for different time intervals. We begin with a highly simplified single period version of the model.

Suppose, we want to find the value of a European-style call option on an underlying stock that is currently selling at RM 10. We assume the following: (i) the call option on the stock has an RM 10 exercise price and 1 year maturity; (ii) the price of the underlying stock can only change in price once during the one year; (iii) the percentage change in the stock's price is 10%, i.e., it can either go up or down by a fixed 10%; (iv) the probability of an up- or downmovement is an equal 50%; and (v) the risk-free interest rate is 8% per annum. Under these assumptions, the possible stock and call values at maturity in 1 year would be as follows:

At maturity in 1 year, the stock's price could either be RM 11 (10% higher) or RM 9 (10% lower). The probabilities of each outcome occurring is 50% or 0.6. Given these possible stock price movement, the call, denoted C_t now, would have a payoff of RM 1 (Stock price – Exercise price) or RM 0. The payoff of RM 1 for the call is denoted C_u to signify that value occurs if the underlying stock price goes up. On the other hand, if the stock value goes down, call value is denoted C_d and expires out-of-the-money. Clearly, the call is only valuable if it ends in-the-money. Since the probability of the stock going up is 50%, the RM 1 payoff from the call has a 50% probability. Thus, adjusting for probability and the fact that the payoff occurs 1 year from now, the current value of the call can be determined as:

$$C_t = \frac{p_u \cdot C_u + p_d \cdot C_d}{(1+r)^t} \qquad (1)$$

where

t = time to maturity of call
r = risk-free interest rate
p_u = probability of upmovement
p_d = probability of downmovement

Equation 1 is essentially the **Single Period BOPM**. Using Equation 1, the call should have a current value:

$$C_{1yr} = \frac{[(0.5)(RM\ 1.00)] + [(0.5)(0)]}{(1.08)^1}$$
$$= RM\ 0.46$$

The value of the call using the single period model is 46 sen.

Holding all other assumptions constant, suppose we now allow the stock's price to change twice within a year, i.e., once every 6 months. The stock price movement and corresponding payoff would be:

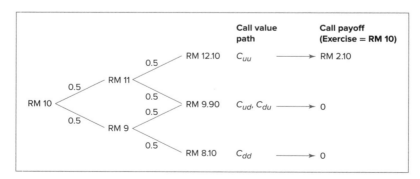

As earlier, the stock price can be either RM 11 or RM 9 at the end of the first 6-month period. In the second 6-month period, the stock can have three possible ending values. Since a call derives its value directly from the stock, the corresponding call value at RM 12.10 stock price is RM 2.10 (stock price − exercise price). There is only one price path that could give the RM 2.10 call payoff. This is denoted C_{uu}, meaning the underlying stock price must go up in first 6 months and again in the second 6-month period. The second stock ending value of RM 9.90,[1] however, has two possible paths: C_{ud}, and C_{du}; i.e., the stock price could reach RM 9.90 from the current RM 10 by following two possible paths. First, by going up 10% from RM 11 in the second period. The final stock price of RM 8.10 has only one possible path, i.e., falling in both periods. The point to note here is that with two periods over which price can change, there are three end nodes (ending prices) and four possible price paths to these three end nodes. The value of call using BOPM would be:

$$C_t = \frac{\rho_{uu} \cdot C_{uu} + \rho_{ud} \cdot C_{ud} + \rho_{du} \cdot C_{du} + \rho_{dd} \cdot C_{dd}}{\left(1 + \frac{r}{2}\right)^2} \qquad (2)$$

Equation 2 is the two-period model of the BOPM.

$$C_2 = \frac{[(0.25)(2.10)] + [(0.25)(0)] + [(0.25)(0)] + [(0.25)(0)]}{(1.04)^2}$$

C = RM 0.485 or 48.5 sen

Notice that the value of the call is now different: 48.5 sen versus 46 sen earlier. Suppose we now relax the periodic price change assumption and allow the stock price to change at shorter intervals, first three times a year or once every 4 months and then four times a year or once every 3 months, what will happen to call value? Figures 9.1 and 9.2 show the **decision tree** diagram that plots the price paths for each of these periods.

Examining Figure 9.1, note that with three periods we have four end nodes or four ending prices. Additionally, there are a total of eight alternative paths leading to these ending prices. Although the extreme end values of RM 13.31 and RM 7.29 have only possible path from the

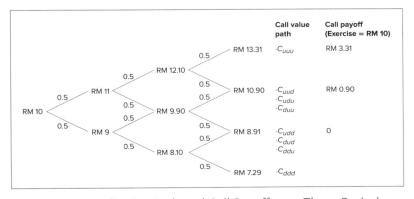

Figure 9.1 Stock Price Path and Call Payoff over Three Periods

---

[1] The RM 9.90 price is essentially an unchanged value from the RM 10 current stock price. The RM 9.90 represents 10% movements (rounded) from RM 11 or RM 9.

RM 10.00 current stock price (C_{uuu} and C_{ddd}, respectively), the intermediate stock prices of RM 10.90 and RM 8.91 have three alternatives paths each. The **cumulative probability** of each path is $0.5 \times 0.5 \times 0.5 = 0.125$. Rewriting Equation 2 for the three-period version, we get:

$$C_t = \frac{\left\{\begin{array}{l} \rho_{uuu} \cdot C_{uuu} + \rho_{uud} \cdot C_{uud} + \rho_{udu} \cdot C_{udu} + \rho_{duu} \cdot C_{duu} \\ +\rho_{udd} \cdot C_{udd} + \rho_{dud} \cdot C_{dud} + \rho_{ddu} \cdot C_{ddu} + \rho_{ddd} \cdot C_{ddd} \end{array}\right\}}{\left(1+\dfrac{r}{3}\right)^3}$$

$$C_3 = \frac{[(0.125)(\text{RM } 3.31)] + [(0.125\ 3)(0.90)] + [0] \cdots + [10]}{\left(1+\dfrac{0.08}{3}\right)^3}$$

$$= \frac{\text{RM } 0.414 + \text{RM } 0.34}{(1.0267)^3}$$

$$= 0.697 \text{ or } 70 \text{ sen}$$

There are two points to note here. First, the call value is now 70 sen. This value change was simply due to the shorter time interval for price change. The second point to note is that Equation 2 rewritten for the three periods has become much more complicated. This is because of the fact that the number of price paths has doubled from four to eight when we go from two periods to three periods. Generally, the number of price paths for a given number of periods (n) is determined as 2^n.

Figure 9.2 shows the stock price paths and call option payoff when we allow for four periods of price over a year, i.e., stock price is allowed to change once every 3 months. We now have five nodes or ending stock values. The range of ending stock price is obviously broader with prices ranging from RM 14.64 to RM 6.56. Of these five ending stock values, there are two values at which the call would be in-the-money, these being the highest two ending stock prices. Notice that there are now a total 16 alternative price paths (2^4) leading the five end points. The ending stock price of RM 9.80 has six alternative paths leading to it. Each price path has a probability of $0.0625.5 \times 0.5 \times 0.5 \times 0.5$.

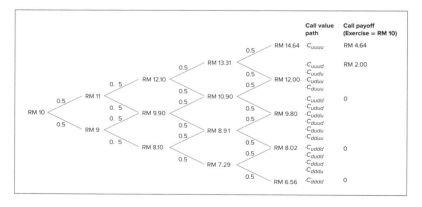

Figure 9.2   Stock Price Path and Call Payoff over Four Periods

Working through an extended version of Equation 2 for the four periods gives a call value = 73 sen. It should be evident that working through Equation 2 with 16 alternative price paths is clearly very cumbersome. It becomes even more so as we allow the stock price to change over shorter periods. For example, shortening the price change period from the current 3 months to 2 months would mean an increase in total alternative price paths from 16 to 64! Table 9.1 shows the relationship.

Table 9.1 Price Change Intervals and Number of Price Paths

Number of Stock Price Movements (Per Year)	Number of Nodes/End Prices	Total Number of Price Paths (2^n)
1	2	2
2 (semiannually)	3	4
3	4	8
4 (quarterly)	5	16
6	7	64
12 (monthly)	13	4,096
24 (fortnightly)	25	16,777,216

It is obvious that even allowing for stock price to change six times a year or once every 2 months, the BOPM becomes very tedious to work with. Allowing monthly price changes becomes impossible to work with manually. Generally, when there are several periods of price change, each of a fixed discrete time, the Multiperiod BOPM is used. The **Multiperiod BOPM** (and its continuous form version) is described in the appendix to this chapter.

Note
Shortening the time interval between price changes makes the binomial model increasingly tedious to work with. However, since shorter price change intervals reflect reality we get more accurate option value estimates.

Two factors should have been obvious thus far. As we shorten the time interval over which stock prices can change, (i) the call value changes and tends to a higher value, and (ii) the model becomes increasingly tedious/complicated. Since we know that stock prices change numerous times over a year, shortening the time interval between prices changes (or allowing for more number of periods of price change) **increases the accuracy** of our option value estimate. In essence, when one uses the BOPM (without the help of specialized software), one may be trading off accuracy for tedium. The more accurate one wants to be, the more tedious/complicated the price paths. As one progressively reduces the time interval of stock price change, one gets progressively more accurate option value estimates. If one imagines a "true value" of an option, then using the BOPM with smaller and smaller price change intervals provides option value estimates that get closer and closer to this "true value." Thus, the model does not provide a **closed-form solution**. Still, this was the only option pricing model being used until 1972, when Fischer Black and Myron Scholes came out with their now famous BSOPM.

9.2.1 Binomial Option Pricing: Probabilities and Volatility

In this section, we examine the role of probabilities and underlying stock volatility on BOPM valuation. For ease of clarity, we treat each of these two items separately. We begin with probabilities. We have assumed thus far that there is equal probability of the underlying stock price going up or down. Although this is a risk-neutral situation, it need not be the case. For example, one might be bullish on the stock and so assign a higher probability for upmovements. On the other hand, if a stock is expected to go down over the future, one might assign higher probabilities to downward movements. It is obvious that a change in the probabilities will impact option valuation. Using the example from earlier, we examine the impact of a change in probability.

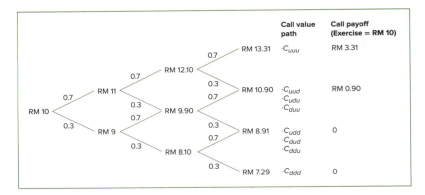

Figure 9.3 Impact of Probabilities on Call Value Stock Price Path and Call Payoff over Three Periods

Suppose you are bullish about the underlying stock's performance over the next year. You believe the probability of an upmovement should be 70%. You now wish to determine the value of the call option on the stock. Again, for the sake of clarity, we stick to the three-period BOPM as in Figure 9.1. Note that except for the change in probability, all other factors are held constant. Figure 9.3 is a reproduction of Figure 9.1 with the new probabilities.

Note that now, the probability for the alternative paths are not equal anymore. Earlier, each path had a probability of (0.125) since each branch, regardless of up or down, had 0.50 probability. Now, the probability for each alternative path would depend on whether there are more up or down branches within the path. For example, C_{uuu}, C_{ddd}, C_{udd}, and C_{ddu}, would all have different probabilities. Using only the two ending values at which the call is in-the-money, RM 13.31 and RM 10.90, the value of the call is now:

$$C_t = \frac{p_{uuu} \cdot C_{uuu} + p_{uud} \cdot C_{uud} + p_{udu} \cdot C_{udu} + p_{duu} \cdot C_{duu} + 0}{\left(1 + \dfrac{r}{3}\right)^3}$$

(Note: C_{uud}, C_{udu} and C_{duu} all have equal cumulative probability of 0.147.)

$$C_3 = \frac{[(0.343)(RM\ 3.31)] + [(0.147 \times 3)(0.90)] + [0] \cdots [0]}{(1.0267)^3}$$

$$C_3 = \frac{RM\ 1.1353 + RM\ 0.3969}{1.0823}$$

$$= RM\ 1.42$$

The new call value holding all other factors constant is RM 1.42. At this value, a change in upward probability from 0.50 to 0.70 has led to a doubling of call value.

9.2.2 Volatility and BOPM Option Value

Having seen the impact of changed probabilities, we now turn to the impact of a different volatility estimate. Again, we hold all other assumptions the same and change only the volatility. Recall that we had earlier assumed that the underlying stock price would change by only 10%. Suppose, we now increase the volatility by doubling the rate of price change from 10% to 20%, how would the call value change? Figure 9.4 shows the revised decision tree from Figure 9.1.

Since the probabilities are unchanged from Figure 9.1 but end values have, we rework the call value as:

$$C_3 = \frac{[(0.125)(RM\ 7.28)] + [(0.125 \times 3)(RM\ 1.52)] + [0] \cdots [0]}{\left(1 + \frac{0.08}{3}\right)^3}$$

$$C_3 = \frac{RM\ 0.91 + RM\ 0.57}{(1.0267)^3}$$

$$= RM\ 1.37$$

We now see the impact of increased volatility on the call option value. With a doubling of volatility, the call option value goes from 70 sen (Figure 9.1) to RM 1.37, which is almost double. This relationship between volatility and option value is discussed further, later in this chapter.

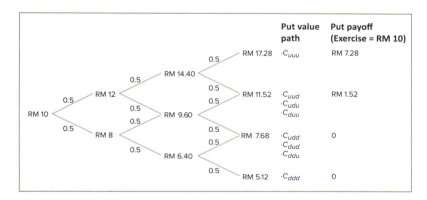

Figure 9.4 Impact of Volatility Change on Call Value

9.2.3 Pricing Put Options with BOPM

This section discusses the use of the BOPM in valuing put options. The logic of pricing put options is exactly the same as that of the valuation of calls. The stock ending values of the decision tree where the call option is out-of-the-money would be the ones where a put option of the same exercise price would be in-the-money. Thus, the end values where the call option had zero payoff would be the values of interest to us in pricing put options. We illustrate this by examining a put option of the same exercise price and maturity on the stock we examined in Figure 9.1. Recall that it was a one year call option on a stock with a current value of RM 10. We use the same assumptions in valuing this RM 10 put options. Again for purposes of clarity, we keep to the three-period model where the underlying stock price only changes in price three times.

Rewriting Equation 2 for three periods and for the put option, we get:

$$P_t = \frac{\left\{ \begin{array}{l} \rho_{uuu} \cdot P_{uuu} + \rho_{uud} \cdot P_{uud} + \rho_{udu} \cdot P_{udu} + \rho_{duu} \cdot P_{duu} \\ + \rho_{udd} \cdot P_{udd} + \rho_{dud} \cdot P_{dud} + \rho_{ddu} \cdot P_{ddu} + \rho_{ddd} \cdot P_{ddd} \end{array} \right\}}{\left(1 + \frac{r}{3}\right)^t}$$

$$P_3 = \frac{[(0) + \cdots [0], + [(0.125\ 3)(RM\ 1.09)] + [(0.125)(RM\ 2.710)]}{\left(1 + \frac{0.08}{3}\right)^3}$$

$$= \frac{RM\ 0.409 + RM\ 0.34}{(1.0267)^3}$$

$$= RM\ 0.69$$

The value of an at-the-money put of RM 10 exercise price is 69 sen. The closeness in the price of the call at 70 sen and of the put at 69 sen have to do with the fact that they are both at-the-money (RM 10 exercise price, current stock price = RM 10).

As in the case of call options, a change in probabilities or underlying stock price volatility would also affect put option prices. For example, given the same probabilities and end value as in Figure 9.3, the value of the put would be computed by the same logic. Since the ending stock value of RM 8.91 has three alternative paths and the cumulative probability for each path is 0.063 (note that each of the three paths have one up movement and two down movements) while the probability for the single path to the RM 7.29 stock price is 0.027 (0.3 × 0.3 × 0.3), we use these probabilities to compute the adjust put price.

$$P_3 = \frac{[0] + \cdots [0] + [(0.063 \times 3)(RM\ 1.09)] + [(0.027)(RM\ 2.71)]}{\left(1 + \frac{0.08}{3}\right)^3}$$

$$= \frac{RM\ 0.206 + RM\ 0.0732}{(1.0267)^3}$$

$$= RM\ 0.26$$

With the changed probabilities, the value of the put option goes from 75 sen in the earlier case to 26 sen. The large drop in put option value has to do with the fact that with lower downward probability, the put becomes less valuable since puts profit from downward movement in underlying asset price. Since the revised probabilities of Figure 9.3 reflect bullishness of the underlying stock, it favors the long call position and works to reduce the value of a long put position.

Although the revised probabilities had the opposite effect on the call and put, increased volatility impacts both options favorably. Doubling underlying asset volatility to 20% as in Figure 9.4 and holding all other assumptions, the same the **put option value/payoff** would be:

$$P_3 = \frac{[0] + \cdots [0] + [(0.125 \times 3)(RM\ 2.32)] + [(0.125)(RM\ 4.88)]}{\left(1 + \dfrac{0.08}{3}\right)^3}$$

$$= \frac{RM\ 0.87 + RM\ 0.61}{(1.0267)^3}$$

$$= RM\ 1.37$$

With a doubling of stock price volatility, the value of the put increases from 69 sen in the base case (Figure 9.5) to RM 1.37. (Note that both the call and put price at the higher volatility

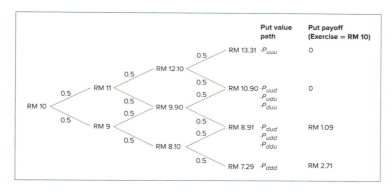

Figure 9.5   Stock Price Path and Payoff to Put Option

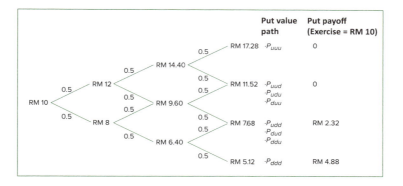

Figure 9.6   Impact of Volatility Change on Put Value

of RM 1.37 is coincidental and has no significance.) What is significant is the fact that both the call and the put rose in value with an increase in volatility.

Despite the fact that the BOPM can be cumbersome to work with and does not provide a closed-form solution, the binomial model has an advantage over the Black–Scholes model when it comes to valuing American-style options. Since an American-style option can be exercised at any time, the binomial model that involves a step-by-step process allows for the option value to be determined at any intermediate point before maturity.

9.3 The Black–Scholes Option Pricing Model

The BSOPM is arguably one of the most elegant models in finance. As a model, the BSOPM has applications in various areas beyond option pricing alone. It is for this diverse applicability and the huge contribution to the area of finance that its authors were awarded the Nobel Prize for Economics in 1997. (As Fischer Black had died in 1995, the award went to his co-authors Robert Merton and Myron Scholes instead.) The biggest advantage of the BSOPM over the earlier BOPM is that the BSOPM provides a closed-form solution to option pricing. Thus, unlike the binomial model where progressive shortening of the discrete time interval provides increasingly accurate prices that converge toward "true-value," this model is in continuous time form, meaning, the time interval between underlying asset price change is so small as to approach zero (Δt, $\ell im \to 0$). The BSOPM was the result of several years of work by its authors. Black, a mathematician, and Scholes, a teacher of finance, had set out to develop a valuation model for stock warrants. (Stock warrants which we will see in Chapter 11 can be thought of as long dated call options on stocks.) The result they found had a close resemblance to a well-known heat transfer equation in physics, and solved the mystery of option pricing.

The popularity of the model arises from the ease of its use and the fact that most of the parameters needed are easily available. Before using the BSOPM to compute option values, we first discuss the underlying logic of the model.

9.3.1 The Underlying Logic of BSOPM
Determining Option Pricing by Means of the Riskless Hedge Portfolio

Recall that a derivative instrument is a financial instrument whose value depends on the value of an underlying asset. Since an option value would depend on the future value of the underlying asset, it would appear that in order to value an option, one would have to value the underlying asset! Or that, in valuing the option, the **distribution** of the asset prices and the appropriate discount rate to use would be needed. Note from the earlier mentioned valuation models that they each need estimates of cash flow (which depends on the distribution of prices) and the appropriate discount rate. It is the attempted estimation of these two variables that acted as a stumbling block to option valuation until Fischer Black and Myron Scholes came into the picture. Black and Scholes showed that one need not get into price distribution nor discount rate estimation. Theirs was a model that cleverly sidestepped the problems associated with these two estimates. Their underlying logic was to estimate option prices using arbitrage pricing logic. They showed that an option payoff can be replicated using simple available instruments and that since replication is possible, it would be possible to create a riskless hedged portfolio with options.

We discuss below how this can be done, and its implications.

Scenario: Assume ABC Corp.'s stock is currently selling at RM 50. No dividends are expected on the stock over the next 6 months. The risk-free rate (3-month Kuala Lumpur Interbank Offered Rate [KLIBOR]) is at 6%. A European-style call option on the stock is available. For simplicity, assume the exercise price of the option is RM 50 (i.e., it is at-the-money). Ignoring transaction costs, determine the payoff to the following investment alternatives if (a) ABC Corp.'s stock is at RM 55 at option expiration, (b) ABC Corp.'s stock is at RM 45 at option expiration.

Investment Alternative 1: Leveraged Long Stock Position

Portfolio 1: Long 1 ABC Corp. stock at RM 50 by borrowing the PV of RM 45 at 6% *rf* rate. (We borrow the lower of the two possible prices. Note, we are assuming that the stock can only take on one of the two prices at expiration.)

Investment Alternative 2: Long Call Position

Portfolio 2: Long 2 six-month RM 50 call options on ABC Corp. stock.

Payoff to Portfolio 1: At Maturity

(1) S_o at Maturity	(2) Loan Repayment Amount	Net Cash Flow (1) – (2)
55	45	10
45	45	0

[Note: At 6% annual rf rate, the PV of your borrowing for 6 months would have been RM 43.70; thus, your net investment (out of pocket) in Portfolio 1 is RM 50 – RM 43.70 = RM 6.30.]

Payoff to Portfolio 2: At Maturity

(1) S_o at Maturity	(2) Payoff to Long Calls IV = (S_o – Exercise Price) × 2
55	10
45	0

Notice that the payoff to both investment alternatives is exactly the same. This has a number of important implications as follows:

(1) If both alternatives have the same payoff, then in efficient markets they must have the same cost, i.e., the net investment in each must be equal.

(2) Since both portfolios provide the same payoff, it implies that the portfolios themselves must be similar.
(3) Given Implication 2, we should be able to construct a **riskless hedge** portfolio by combining the two alternative investments in an appropriate way.

Going by Implication 1, we can determine the value or correct price of the call option. Since both investment alternatives provide the same payoff, the net investment in Portfolio 1 must equal the cost of buying the two call options in Portfolio 2. What is the net investment? The investor paid RM 50 for the stock but borrowed the PV of RM 45, which is RM 43.70, thus the net investment (out of pocket cost) he made is RM 50 – RM 43.70 = RM 6.30. This means that the cost of establishing Portfolio 2 should also be RM 6.30. The correct price per call option should therefore be RM 6.30/2 = RM 3.15. Should the price of the call be anything other than RM 3.15 each, riskless arbitrage profits could be made. (This will be proven as follows.)

The Risk-Free Rate and Option Prices

We arrived at the call option price by determining the net investment needed in Portfolio 1. The net investment needed was RM 6.30 given rf of 6%. But what if the rf rate changed? Obviously, the net investment needed to Portfolio 1 would be different. Suppose the rf rate is 9%, then the net investment need for Portfolio 1 would now be RM 50 – RM 43.10 = RM 6.90. This means that the cost of establishing Portfolio 2, buying 2 calls would also be RM 6.90. The price of each call option is now = RM 3.45 which is 30 sen higher than previously. Once again, given the new rf rate, the call price must be RM 3.45 given arbitrage relationships. The following table shows what the equilibrium call prices would have to be for different risk-free rates. Notice the positive correlation between interest rates and call option prices.

Risk-Free Interest Rate	PV of RM 45 for 6 Months	Net Investment Needed for Portfolio 1	Equilibrium Call Price to Equalize Net Investment for Portfolio 2
3%	RM 44.34	RM 5.66	RM 2.83
6%	RM 43.70	RM 6.30	RM 3.15
9%	RM 43.10	RM 6.90	RM 3.45
12%	RM 42.52	RM 7.48	RM 3.74

Implication 2 is harder to visualize. It states that since both portfolios provide the same payoff, they must be essentially the same. Recall that Portfolio 2 is essentially a long call position, whereas Portfolio 1 is a long stock position financed by borrowings. Thus, it means that a long call position is really equivalent to a levered equity position. That is, going long or owning a call option is the equivalent of buying equity by financing most of the purchase with debt.

Implication 3 states that if a long call position (Portfolio 2) is equivalent to levered stock position (Portfolio 1), then a riskless hedged portfolio can be created by combining the two

Table 9.2 Creating a Riskless Hedged Portfolio

	CF_o	S = 55		S = 45	
		CF (At Maturity)	Net Profit	CF (At Maturity)	Net Profit
Long stock	(50)	55	5	45	(5)
Borrow PV of 45 @ 6% for 6 months	43.70	(45)	(1.30)	(45)	(1.30)
Sell 2 calls @ RM 3.15 each	6.30	(10)	(3.70)	0	6.30
Net cash flow (CF)	0	0	0	0	0

Table 9.3 Mispricing and Arbitrage Profits

	CF_o	S = 55		S = 45	
		CF (At Maturity)	Net Profit	CF (At Maturity)	Net Profit
Long stock	(50)	55	5	45	(5)
Borrow PV of 45 @ 6% for 6 months	43.70	(45)	(1.30)	(45)	(1.30)
Sell 2 calls @ RM 3.50 each	7.00	(10)	(3.00)	0	7.00
Net cash flow (CF)	.70	0	.70	0	.70

portfolios in an appropriate way. Indeed, Table 9.2 shows how a riskless hedged portfolio can be created by combining Portfolio 1 with a short call position (i.e., reversing the original long call position of Portfolio 2).

Why is the above a riskless hedged portfolio? Notice that whether the underlying stock price increases (to RM 55) or decreases (to RM 45), the cash flows all balance out.

The fact that one could create a riskless hedged portfolio as earlier has a powerful meaning. That is, the price of the call option given the underlying stock price, time to maturity and a risk-free rate must equal to the RM 3.15 price calculated earlier. Should the price be anything other than RM 3.15, riskless arbitrage profits can be made. When such profits are available, rational investors will take advantage of the "mispricing" through arbitrage, thereby causing the option's price to converge to its equilibrium RM 3.15 price. Table 9.3 shows how riskless arbitrage profits could be made if the call price was RM 3.50 instead of RM 3.15. Notice that a riskless profit of 70 sen can be made. This is pure arbitrage profit.

It is the riskless hedged portfolio and the implications outlined earlier that became the cornerstone of the BSOPM. The two stumbling blocks to option valuation estimations: (i) the price distribution of the underlying asset, and (ii) the appropriate discount rate, were both shown by Black–Scholes to be irrelevant. Notice from Table 9.2 that Portfolio 2 exactly tracks Portfolio 1 payoffs. Thus, no matter what price the underlying stock takes, Portfolio 2 would offset it. So, determining expected stock prices is irrelevant to determining the value of the option.

Furthermore, it is clearly evident from Implication 1 and subsequent table that the only relevant discount rate is the risk-free rate. One need not have to adjust the discount rate for the underlying stock risk (stock beta) since it can be combined with options to create a riskless portfolio. A riskless portfolio would earn a riskless rate of return.

Note
The BSOPM is built on several assumptions. Of these, the assumptions of unchanged interest rates and constant volatility of the underlying asset until option maturity are considered the most restrictive.

9.3.2 Underlying Assumptions of the BSOPM

As is the case with all other mathematical models in financial economics, the BSOPM is built of a set of underlying assumptions. Although some of these assumptions are fairly standard in most finance models, i.e., frictionless/efficient markets, no trading costs, etc., others may be more binding and have a direct consequence on pricing. The following are the seven key assumptions of the BSOPM:

(i) Efficient markets with frictionless trading
(ii) No transaction costs *(the model ignores bid-ask spread, commissions, etc.)*
(iii) Option has European-style exercise
(iv) The underlying stock will pay no dividends during the maturity of the option
(v) Underlying stock returns are log normally distributed *(this means that the logarithmic stock returns are normally distributed)*
(vi) The risk-free interest rate remains unchanged over option maturity
(vii) Underlying stock volatility is constant over option maturity

Of these assumptions, the last two about constant interest rates and volatility have been the most controversial and somewhat unrealistic. If the BSOPM has a weakness, it has to do with these two assumptions, in particular, the assumption of constant volatility. A change in these assumptions would of course require recomputation of the model.

The BSOPM for a call option is as follows:

$$C = S \cdot N(d_1) - Ke^{-rt} \cdot N(d_2)$$
$$d_1 = \frac{\ln(S/K) + [r + (\sigma^2/2)]T}{\sigma\sqrt{T}}$$
$$d_2 = d_1 - \sigma\sqrt{T}$$

where

S = spot price of underlying asset
K = exercise price of call option
T = time to expiration (as % of year)
r = rf interest rate
e^{rt} = exponential function of rf and T
N(.) = cumulative standard normal distribution function
σ = volatility of underlying asset as measured by standard deviation
ln (S/K) = natural logarithm of S/K

One of the strengths of the Black–Scholes model is that it is very user friendly and easily programmable. As such, it has over time become the model of choice for option traders.

Notice that the equation can be divided into two parts; $S \cdot N(d_1)$ and $-Ke^{-rt} \cdot N(d_2)$. Since it has been shown earlier that a call option is equivalent in payoff to a leveraged stock position, where the leveraged stock position constitutes a long position in stock financed by borrowing. The first part, $S \cdot N(d_1)$ can be thought of as the proportion of stock to held (long), whereas the second part, $-Ke^{-rt} \cdot N(d_2)$, can be thought of as the proportion of a bond to be shorted. A short position in a bond is equivalent to having borrowed. The proportion of stock and bond to be long/short is determined by $N(d_1)$ and $N(d_2)$. Both these variables, $N(d_1)$ and $N(d_2)$, are table values of the computed d_1 and d_2. Thus, the table used is the cumulative standard normal distribution function. The values derived for $N(d_1)$ and $N(d_2)$ would constitute the area under curve (or probability) for the computed d_1, d_2 values. In a way, $N(d_1)$ and $N(d_2)$ can also be thought of as playing the same role as probabilities in the binomial model.

Calculating option prices with the BSOPM is a three-step process.

(i) Calculate d_1 and d_2.
(ii) Using the cumulative normal distribution table, find the values of $N(d_1)$ and $N(d_2)$.
(iii) Plug the values into the model and solve.

Illustration: Calculating Call Value Using Black–Scholes

Suppose: Stock price, S_0 = RM 11
Exercise price, k = RM 10
Interest rate, r = 0.10
Maturity, T = 90 days = 0.25
Standard deviation, σ = 0.5

What is the correct price of the call?

Step 1: Calculate d_1, d_2

$$d_1 = \frac{ln(11/10) + \left[0.10 + (0.5^2/2)\right] \times 0.25}{0.5\sqrt{0.25}}$$

$$d_1 = \frac{0.0953 + (0.225 \times 0.25)}{0.25}$$

$$= \frac{0.15155}{0.25}$$

$$= 0.61$$

$$d_2 = d_1 - \sigma\sqrt{T}$$

$$= 0.61 - 0.25$$

$$= 0.36$$

Step 2: Find $N(d_1)$ and $N(d_2)$ using the table.
$N(d_1) = 0.7291$
$N(d_2) = 0.6406$

Step 3: Plug values into model and solve.
$C = $ RM $11(0.7291) - $ RM $10^{(-0.10 \times 0.25)} \cdot (0.6406)$
$ = $ RM $8.02 - $ RM $9.75 \cdot (0.6406)$
$ = $ RM $8.02 - $ RM 6.25
$ = $ RM 1.77

Decomposing the abovementioned call value of RM 1.77 into intrinsic and time values, the IV here is RM 1 while the remainder 77 sen would constitute time value.

9.3.3 Pricing Put Options

Black–Scholes Option Pricing Model

Though the Black–Scholes model was developed for pricing European call options, the model can just as easily be used in valuing a European-style put option. Without getting into the derivations but using the logic of replication, it should be obvious that a put can be replicated using a portfolio opposite to that of the call. (This assumes that the underlying asset, exercise price, and maturity is the same.) If a call payoff as we saw earlier can be created by going long a proportion of stock and shorting bonds, then a put would have a payoff equivalent to going long bonds and shorting stock. Thus, it should not be surprising that the BSOPM for put valuation is a revised format of the call valuation model as follows:

$$P = Ke^{-rt} \cdot N(-d_2) - S \cdot N(-d_1)$$

The steps involved in valuation are much the same as earlier. The negative sign before d_1 and d_2 is explained later.

Pricing Put Options — An Illustration

To see how the BSOPM is used in pricing put options, we work through the same previous example. We computed the price of the call option in earlier example to be RM 1.77. To see the equivalence in pricing put options with that of a call, we value a put option using the same features. The first two steps, (i) calculating d_1, d_2, and (ii) finding $N(d_1)$ and $N(d_2)$ are the same. However, a small adjustment has to be made before we plug in and solve for option value in step (iii). The small adjustment is to convert $N(d_1)$ and $N(d_2)$ to $N(-d_1)$ and $N(-d_2)$; since $N(-d_1)$ is simply $1 - N(d_1)$, as $N(d_1)$ was determined earlier for the call to be 0.7291,

$N(-d_1) = 1 - N(d_1) \Rightarrow 1 - 0.7291 = 0.2709$

Similarly, since $N(-d_2)$ was 0.6406,
$N(-d_2) = 1 - N(-d_2) \Rightarrow 1 - 0.6406 = 0.3594$

We now plug in this values to solve for the put value.
$P = Ke^{-rt} \cdot N(-d_2) - S \cdot N(-d_1)$
   $=$ RM 9.75(0.3594) $-$ RM 11(0.2709)
   $=$ RM 3.5042 $-$ RM 2.98
   $=$ RM 0.52

The value of the put with the same features as that of the earlier call is RM 0.52 or 52 sen. The reason for the much lower value for put is obviously due to the fact that the put is out-of-the-money, whereas the call was in-the-money. The put, being out-of-the-money, has zero IV. Its premium of 52 sen comes entirely from time value.

9.4 Determinants of Option Prices

As is evident from the BSOPM, there are five input variables or parameters that go into the model. These five input variables are the following:

(a) Stock price S_o
(b) Exercise price K
(c) Maturity T
(d) Interest rate r
(e) Volatility σ

We now examine the nature of the relationship between each of these five input variables and option prices. At least four of these relationships are commonly referred to by names denoted by Greek letters such as delta and theta. Thus, these relationships are often simply referred to as option greeks. These relationships are essentially partial derivatives. The big advantage of having a closed-form solution as the BSOPM is that the values of these parameters (partial derivatives) are easily determined in addition to whether their impact is positive or negative. Though these relationships are described here, their dynamics are explored in the appendix to this chapter.

(1) Stock/Underlying Asset Price

The change in stock or underlying asset price is positively correlated to call values and negatively to puts. The logic is straightforward. Since a call represents a right to buy the underlying stock/asset at a predetermined price, subsequent increases in underlying price benefits calls. Going by this logic, a fall in underlying stock price reduces call value.

> **Note**
> Delta describes the relationship between the underlying stock price and option values. The change in underlying asset price is positively correlated to call value and negatively to puts.

Put option values on the other hand are negatively correlated to underlying asset price movements. Since a put represents a right to sell the underlying at a predetermined price, falling underlying asset prices are beneficial to puts while price increases are detrimental.

This relationship between underlying asset price and option values are known as **deltas**. Mathematically,

$$\text{Delta} = \frac{\partial C}{\partial S}$$

$$= \frac{\text{Change in value of option}}{\text{Change in underlying asset value}}$$

As delta has other important implications, it is further described in the next section.

(2) Exercise Price

The exercise price has a negative correlation with call options and a positive one with put options. This relationship should be easy to see. Since a call is a right to buy at the exercise price, an increase in the exercise price implies the call holder has to pay more. The put holder in exercising the right to sell receives more if the exercise price is increased. Raising the exercise price clearly benefits put options but works against calls.

> **Note**
> Higher exercise prices reduce the value of calls but increase the value of puts. Thus, exercise price is negatively correlated to call values but positively to put.

(3) Volatility

Underlying asset price volatility has a positive correlation with both option prices. Increased volatility of the underlying asset increases the value of the call and put. Option values fall when volatility reduces. Although it may seem counter intuitive since most asset prices generally fall when volatility increases, the logic is as follows. Recall that what differentiates options from other assets is that options limit downside. Thus, if the underlying asset price moves unfavorably, we can choose to simply not exercise. Since volatility is price movement both ways, the fact that with options unfavorable price moves have no (or muted) impact, implies that higher volatility allows for higher profit potential. Volatility can only help and not hurt in the case of options. The relationship between option value and underlying asset volatility known as **vega**.

$$\text{Vega} = \frac{\partial C}{\partial \sigma}$$

$$= \frac{\text{Change in option value}}{\text{Change in underlying asset price volatility}}$$

To better understand the impact of the next two input variables, time to maturity and interest rates, it should be useful to revisit our Chapter 6 discussion of intrinsic and time values. Recall that an option value constitutes IV and time value. The call and put option IVs were determined earlier as:

> **Note**
> The relationship between option values and underlying asset volatility is known as vega. The underlying asset's price volatility is positively correlated with call and put values.

Call IV = S − exercise price
Put IV = exercise price − S

where S is the current underlying asset or stock price.

Although the above definition of IV is correct, it ignores the time difference between the stock price and the exercise price. Notice that the stock price is the current stock price, whereas the exercise price is the price to be paid (for calls) or received (for puts) at maturity. Thus, in determining IV, one should really use the PV of the exercise price. Taking into account this time difference we get:

$$\text{Call IV} = S - \frac{\text{exercise price}}{(1+r)^t}$$

$$\text{Put IV} = \frac{\text{exercise price}}{(1+r)^t} - S$$

where
r = annualized *rf* interest rate
t = time to maturity of option as proportion of year

Time value, as earlier mentioned, is essentially the difference between the option premium and IV.

(4) Interest Rates

The impact of interest rates on option values can be seen directly from the above IV equations. An increase in interest rates would increase call IV since the PV of the exercise price would be lower. Holding time value constant, call value increases as call IV increases. The same result will be seen by inputing a higher interest rate in the BSOPM. In the case of put options, the effect is opposite; higher interest rates reduce the PV of exercise price. Since Put IV is the net of the PV of exercise price less stock price, rising interest rates would provide lower Put IVs for the same stock price. This relationship between interest rates and option values is termed **rho**.

Table 9.4 Input Variables and Option Values

Impact of an Increase in	Call Value	Put Value
Stock price	↑(higher)	↓(lower)
Exercise price	↓(lower)	↑(higher)
Volatility	↑(higher)	↑(higher)
Interest rate	↑(higher)	↓(lower)
Maturity	↑(higher)	? ambiguous

$$\text{Rho} = \frac{\partial C}{\partial r}$$

$$= \frac{\text{Change in option value}}{\text{Change in interest rate}}$$

(5) Time to Maturity

Lengthening time to maturity has a positive effect on call values. Both the time value and IV of the call option increases with lengthened maturity. As we saw in Chapter 6, time value is higher the longer the time left to maturity. From the IV equation for call options above, a longer time to maturity reduces the PV of exercise price, thereby also increasing call IV. For put options, however, the impact is somewhat ambiguous. This is because lengthening time to maturity has an opposite effect on put intrinsic and time values. While the time value increases with longer maturity, the put option IV reduces with longer maturity (as evident from the earlier equation for put IV) by reducing the PV of the exercise price. Thus, in the case of put options, the overall impact would depend on whether the time value increases more than the fall in IV. This relationship between option values and time to maturity is known as **option theta**.

Note
The relationship between time to maturity and option values is termed theta. Time to maturity is positively correlated with calls but has an ambiguous relationship to put values. This is due to the opposite impact of time to maturity on the put intrinsic and time values.

$$\text{Theta} = \frac{\partial C}{\partial t}$$

$$= \frac{\text{Change in option value}}{\text{Change in time to maturity}}$$

Table 9.4 summarizes the impact of these five input variables on call and put prices.

Except for put values and maturity, which would remain ambiguous, a **decrease** in each of these input variables would have the **opposite** of the effect shown earlier.

Table 9.5(a) Impact on Call Value of Input Variable

Spot	Exercise Price				Volatility %				Days to Maturity				Interest Rate %			
Value	680	700	720	740	15	20	25	30	0	10	30	60	5	6	7	8
760	90.0	73.5	58.4	45.3	49.6	53.7	58.4	63.6	40.0	42.3	49.3	58.4	58.4	59.2	60.2	61.0
740	72.8	57.7	44.4	33.2	33.7	38.9	44.4	50.0	20.0	25.4	34.4	44.4	44.4	45.1	45.9	46.6
720	56.9	43.5	32.3	23.2	20.7	26.5	32.3	38.1	0.0	12.5	22.2	32.3	32.3	32.9	33.5	34.1
700	42.7	31.4	22.3	15.3	11.2	16.7	22.3	28.0	0.0	4.6	13.0	22.3	22.3	22.8	23.3	23.8
680	30.5	21.5	14.6	9.5	5.2	9.6	14.6	19.7	0.0	1.2	6.8	14.5	14.6	14.9	15.3	15.7

Table 9.5(b) Impact on Put Value of Input Variable

Spot	Exercise Price				Volatility %				Days to Maturity				Interest Rate %			
Value	680	700	720	740	15	20	25	30	0	10	30	60	5	6	7	8
760	4.3	7.6	12.4	19.1	3.6	7.7	12.4	17.6	0.0	1.3	6.3	12.4	12.4	12.1	11.8	11.4
740	7.1	11.8	18.4	27.0	7.7	12.9	18.4	24.0	0.0	4.4	11.5	18.4	18.4	17.9	17.5	17.1
720	11.9	17.7	26.3	37.0	14.7	20.5	26.3	32.1	0.0	11.5	19.2	26.3	26.3	25.7	25.1	24.6
700	17.0	25.6	36.3	49.2	25.2	30.7	36.3	42.0	20.0	23.7	30.0	36.3	36.3	35.6	34.9	34.3
680	24.8	35.6	48.6	63.4	39.2	43.7	48.6	53.7	40.0	40.2	43.8	48.6	48.6	47.7	46.9	46.1

9.5 Illustration of Price Dynamics — Changing Call and Put Values

The aforementioned relationships are proven in Tables 9.5(a) and (b). The tables show the computed Black–Scholes values for call and put options on a nondividend paying equity portfolio. One could also think of it as a single nondividend paying stock. The base case inputs for both the call and put options were as follows:

Exercise price, k = RM 720
Volatility   = 25%
rf interest rate = 5%
Maturity   = 60 days

Each input variable was changed individually, holding all the other variables the same as the base case. The tables show the earlier mentioned relationships. For example, given the same spot value, call value decreases as exercise price increases but put values increase. Similarly, for a given spot value, increasing volatility increases both and the call and put values. Rising interest rates (last panel) increase call values but reduce put values for the same spot value. Finally, increasing maturity increases call and put value. While rising call value is consistent with our earlier discussion, put values also rise, though we had concluded that the impact is ambiguous. Although that is indeed the case, it turns out that in this example, put values too rise with rising maturity. Finally, one might wonder why the impact of changes in the underlying spot is not specified as an input variable in the tables. In fact the impact of spot price change is shown throughout. For example, reading any column downward shows the impact of an underlying asset price change. Examining the first panel, for a given exercise price, call values decrease but put value increases. This clearly shows the positive and negative correlations between underlying asset price and values of calls and puts, respectively.

9.6 Issues in Option Pricing

In this section, we examine issues related to the use of the Black–Scholes model in the pricing of options. Specifically, we examine four issues: (i) the adjustment for dividends, (ii) option deltas, (iii) **hedge ratios** (HR) and (iv) estimating the volatility input and implied volatility.

(I) Dividends

As mentioned earlier, the BSOPM assumes no dividend payment by the underlying stock. Yet dividends are a reality. Since dividend payments do affect the value of the underlying stock, dividends affect option values. Fortunately, the adjustment needed for expected dividends is fairly straight forward in the BSOPM. Since a dividend constitutes a payment by the firm issuing the stock and dividends reduce ex dividend stock values, we adjust **by reducing the stock price used as input by the PV of the expected dividend**. Only dividends expected during the life of the option need to be adjusted for. Should there be more than one expected dividend, the cumulative PVs of all dividends during option life should be deducted.

Dividend Adjustment: Illustration

Suppose you are trying to value an option with 6 months to maturity. The underlying stock that is currently selling for RM 12 is expected to pay a dividend of RM 0.50 or 50 sen per share 4 months from now (120 days). Assume the current risk-free interest rate is 8% per year. The PV of the dividend is:

$$PV = \frac{Dividend}{(1+rf)t}$$

$$= \frac{RM\ 0.50}{(1.08)^{0.333}}$$

PV of expected dividend = RM 0.487 or 49 sen

Regardless of whether we are valuing a call or put option, the input variable for stock price in the BSOPM will be RM 12 − RM 0.49 = RM 11.51. We use RM 11.51 and not the RM 12 current stock price in the model. The impact of such an adjustment on the value of the call and put option would be as follows:

As dividends ↑ ; Call Value ↓ ; Put Value ↑

This is logical since dividends reduce stock price and falling stock price reduces call values but increase put values.

(II) Option Deltas

We have established that when the price of the underlying asset changes, option values change with the relationship being known as **option delta**. Delta is probably the most commonly referred to of the earlier relationships (greeks). An option delta has two common uses. First, deltas can be used to determine the likely new price of an option given an expected finite change in the underlying asset price. This is logical since delta describes the pricing relationship between the two assets. The second important use of deltas is in determining HRs. That is, the number of options needed to hedge the underlying asset/stock. We explore this in the next section.

Diagrammatically, option deltas are really the slope of the curve representing option value. Figures 9.7 and 9.8 show the call value and put value curves and the respective deltas.

There are two important factors to be noted from Figure 9.7. First, as the call option has a positive slope, call deltas are always positive. The put option, however, has a negative slope, thus put deltas are always negative. Second, since the option values are curved, the slope is obviously different at different points of the curve. Generally, deltas have values approximating 0.50 in the region when the option is at-the-money. As the option gets to be in-the-money, the delta increases. Delta approaches 1.0 when the option is deep in-the-money. The opposite is true when one moves into the region where the option is out-of-the-money. As the option gets to be more and more out-of-the-money, deltas become progressively lower and approach 0.

Note
Though the BSOPM assumes no dividend payments by the underlying stock, expected dividend payments during the option's life can be adjusted for by reducing the stock price used as input by the PV of the expected dividend.

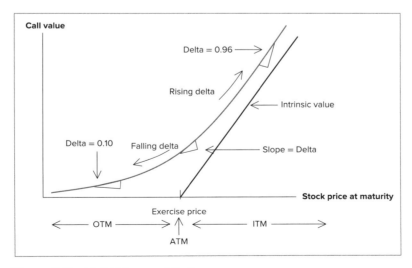

Figure 9.7   Call Value and Delta

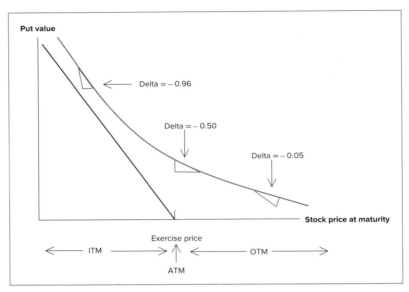

Figure 9.8 Put Value and Delta

To summarize:
Call delta has a value between 0 and 1; thus > 0, always positive.
Put delta has a value between −1 and 0; thus − < 0, always negative.

For the BSOPM, it can be shown that the call and put deltas are given by the $N(d_1)$ values as follows:

$$\text{Call delta} = \frac{\partial C}{\partial S} = N(d_1)$$

$$\text{Put delta} = \frac{\partial P}{\partial S} = N(d_1) - 1$$

> **Note**
> Calls have deltas between 0 and 1 and are always positive. Puts have negative deltas ranging between −1 and 0. Given the same underlying asset, maturity and exercise price, the call delta minus put delta equals 1.0.

Thus, for a call and put option on the same underlying asset, exercise price and maturity, the relationship between a call and put delta is as follows:

$$\text{Call delta} - \text{Put delta} = 1.0$$

Exact call and put deltas can be derived directly from the $N(d_1)$ values in the BSOPM.

(III) Hedge Ratios

The HR refers to the number of options needed to hedge each unit of the underlying asset. For example, suppose an investor is long one lot of an underlying stock and wishes to hedge using put options, how many put options should he go long? Similarly, if someone wants to hedge a short stock position, how many call options should he go long? This is a very practical issue. It should be evident that the HR is directly linked to option deltas since deltas show the extent of a change in option price/value resulting from a change in the underlying assets value. Since the absolute and percentage change in the price of the underlying and the option is different, to fully hedge a position, a "correct" proportion of options to the underlying asset will be needed to equalize the rates of price changes; this right proportion is the HR.

Before elaborating further on the HR, it would be useful to keep in mind that HRs are relevant when the investment horizon in the underlying asset is different from that of the maturity of the option. For example, suppose an investor intends to hold a long position in one lot of Syarikat ABC stock for the next 90 days. To protect himself from a fall in Syarikat ABC stock price he wishes to go long on at-the-money put option with exactly 90 days to maturity. Each put option has a contract size equal to one lot of the underlying stock. In this case, since the option maturity matches the investment horizon, the HR would simply equal 1.0. That is, the investor should just long one put option contract to fully hedge the one lot of stocks he has for the next 90 days. By holding the position all the way to maturity, the investor locks-in a minimum value equivalent to the exercise price of the put option.

If, however, there was a maturity mismatch, then the right proportion of options needed will have to be determined based on the option current delta. Here, there is a maturity mismatch; you are going to unwind the position before maturity. You would be selling off the stock and the put option 15 days from now. Since the put has not matured (European style), you merely sell the put option hoping to gain from the higher put price if the stock had fallen. If the stock had gone down in price, then your protection would be the higher price at which you would sell the puts. But would the rise in put price equal the fall in stock price? The answer is no! Since the stock was at RM 10 and the exercise price of the put was also RM 10, the puts would have been at-the-money when you established the position. Assuming the option delta was 0.50 at that point, if the stock price is RM 9 on the 15th day, the put price would have increased by 50 cents. (Δ in put price $\approx \Delta$ in stock price $\times$ put delta.) Thus, buying 10 puts to protect the 10 lots of shares would have only "half protected" you. Since the option delta at the time of establishing the position is 0.5, you should use 20 put option contracts to hedge the 10 lots of underlying stock. The HR can be generalized as HR = 1/delta.

Dynamic Hedging

As mentioned earlier, delta provides estimates of the potential change in option value for small (finite) changes in underlying stock price. However, delta itself, as we know, changes at different underlying stock prices. Thus, the HR changes as underlying asset price changes. The number of options needed to hedge the underlying asset changes as the asset price changes. This implies that hedging in a situation of timing mismatch must necessarily be dynamic in nature. Risk managers of asset management firms use dynamic hedging to manage their exposures. Dynamic hedging refers to the continual rebalancing of portfolios to minimize exposure.

(IV) Estimating Volatility

Of the five input variables that go into the BSOPM, four are easily determined. Variables such as K (exercise price) and T (time to maturity) would be directly observable from the option contract. S (Stock/underlying asset price) and r (risk-free interest rate) would also be easily obtainable. The fifth input, which is the volatility of the underlying asset price would not be readily available. It has to be estimated. Estimating the volatility input using past underlying price data gives us **historical volatility**. It is common to use this historical volatility as the input variable. Using historical volatility implies that we are assuming that the underlying asset's volatility over the future period until option maturity will be the same as in the previous period.

In addition to historical volatility, there are at least two other commonly used volatility definitions, these are **expected** or **future volatility** and **implied volatility.** Expected volatility is quite simply the volatility expected to prevail over a future period. Expected volatility may be a more sensible estimate to use if we know that the underlying will be subject to certain events/outcomes over the immediate future. For example, suppose the underlying stock is a firm that is currently in merger negotiations or is the subject of a hostile takeover bid, then it is obvious that future volatility is likely to be very different from its historical volatility. In this case, one would use the historical volatility as the base and add an estimated additional volatility to arrive at the expected volatility. This is clearly a judgment call and subjective.

9.7 Implied Volatility

Implied volatility is essentially the volatility implied in an option price. Since five parameters go into the BSOPM to determine the sixth item which is the option value, it is possible to work out the sixth variable given any five variables. Thus, given the four other input variables (s, k, r, and T) and the call value, we can derive the volatility estimate that justifies the given call value. This would be the implied volatility. Since the volatility estimate is used in the BSOPM through d_1 and d_2 estimates, which are then used to determine the delta $N(d_1)$ and $N(d_2)$, trying to work out implied volatility by hand is very difficult. However, just about all option software can handle the iterative process needed to compute volatility implied in an option price.

Implied volatility is a popular item heavily used by option traders. There are two common uses of implied volatility in option trading. First, traders can use implied volatility estimates to determine the "expensiveness" of an option relative to other options. An easy way to see this would be to consider two options on the same underlying asset but with maturities a month apart. If the option with the closer maturity has a higher implied volatility, it is obviously more expensive in price relative to the other option. A second common use of implied volatility is in determining option mispricing. A rule of thumb use by traders is to compare implied volatility with actual or historical volatility. Generally, if the implied volatility is much higher than historical or actual current volatility, then the option is deemed to be overpriced. The opposite is true if implied volatility is lower than historical volatility, the option would be considered underpriced.

Estimating Historical Volatility

Having discussed the different types of volatilities, we now turn to a discussion of how to estimate the volatility input to be used in a model like the BSOPM. Volatility, which is really dispersion around an expected/mean return, is measured using standard deviation (σ). Computing standard deviation is a common statistical procedure. We begin by identifying the window period (N) (e.g., the last 30 trading days) over which we will estimate the historical volatility. Since we are trying to estimate the volatility of the underlying asset/stock, we collect the daily prices (closing prices for stocks) over the window period. Next, we go through the following steps. First, we determine the daily price relative given the daily prices. The daily price relative is determined as S_t/S_{t-1}, i.e., dividing a given day's closing price with that of the previous day. Second, we determine the logarithmic price relative, which is simply taking the natural log of each day's price relative. Using these logarithmic price relatives, we determine the mean or average price relative.

$$\text{Mean } PR = \frac{1}{N} \cdot \sum_{n=1}^{N} \ln PR_t$$

Third, using the mean PR, we compute the square of the difference from the mean on a daily basis, i.e.,

$$[\ln PR_t - \text{Mean } PR]^2$$

The sum of these when divided by the number of observations less the degree of freedoms (in this case only one, mean) gives us the variance:

$$\text{Var} = \sum_{n=1}^{N} (\ln PR_t - \text{Mean } PR)^2 \Big/ N - 1$$

Finally, by taking the square root of the variance we get the daily standard deviation estimate. This daily standard deviation can be adjusted for the period need by multiplying by the square root of the needed period. For example, to get the annualized given, say 240 trading days in a calendar year, we do the following.

Annualized volatility = Daily volatility (σ) × $\sqrt{240}$
Annualized σ = Daily (σ) × $\sqrt{240}$

Table 9.6 Volatility Estimation for Telekom Malaysia Shares

Day (N)	Close Price (P_t)	Price Relative (PR_t) ($PR_t = P_t/P_{t-1}$)	ln (PR_t)	[ln PR_t − Mean PR]$_2$
0	9.65	–	–	–
1	9.60	0.9948	−0.0052	0.00024
2	9.60	1.000	0	0.00011
3	9.55	0.9948	−0.0052	0.00024
4	9.65	1.0105	0.0104	0.0000
5	10.2	1.0570	0.0554	0.00203
6	10.6	1.0392	0.0385	0.00080
7	11	1.0378	0.0371	0.00072
8	11	1.000	0	0.00011
9	10.9	0.9909	−0.0091	0.00038
10	10.7	0.9817	−0.0185	0.00083
			(sum) Σ = 0.1034	0.00546

Mean = 0.1034 ÷ 10 = **0.01034**

Estimating Volatility: Illustration

We now use the earlier description to work out an estimate of volatility for the shares of Telekom Malaysia Bhd. For want of space we limit the observations to 10 trading days, i.e., two calendar weeks. (For simplicity, we ignore the two weekends in between). Table 9.6 shows the daily closing prices, the price relative and the log of price relative.

$$\sum_{t=1}^{T}[ln\ PRt - Mean\ PR_t]^2$$

$$Var = \sum_{t=1}^{T} \frac{[ln\ PRt - Mean\ PR_t]^2}{N-1}$$

$$Var = \frac{0.00546}{9}$$

$$= 0.000607$$

Standard deviation (σ) = $\sqrt{0.000607}$

$$= 0.02464$$

Thus, the estimated daily volatility for Telekom Malaysia shares is 0.02464. Assuming 240 trading days in a calendar year.

Annualized standard deviation (σ) = $0.02464 \times \sqrt{240}$

$$= 0.3817$$

Thus, based on our 10-day observation, we would estimate Telekom Malaysia share to have an estimated annual volatility of **38.17%**.

Tradeoff in Volatility Estimation

It should be obvious that, had we used a different 10-day period or a longer period, we might have gotten a different volatility estimate. This is indeed the case. Statistically, we get better estimates when we use a long observation period. For example, using a 1-year period or 240 trading days/observations would provide a highly dependable volatility estimate. Although this will be statistically more accurate, there is indeed a tradeoff. Suppose, we were trying to value an option using BSOPM, with 30 days left to maturity, volatility estimated using the most recent price data may be more accurate than one based on the last 1 year's data. This is especially so since the BSOPM assumes the input volatility will prevail unchanged over the life of the option. A compromise between length of observation and currency of data may be to use perhaps the most recent 60 or 90 trading days. Still, the issue of estimated volatility is the only "subjective" input variable in the BSOPM. Thus, differences in option valuation using BSOPM on a nondividend paying stock can only arise from the use of different volatility estimates.

9.8 Valuing Equity Index Options

In this section, we examine the valuation of equity index options. Equity index options traded on derivative exchanges may have two slightly different underlying assets, either a stock index or a stock index futures contract. In Chapter 7, we saw that the index option contracts listed on Bursa Malaysia and that of the Nikkei 225 listed on the Singapore Exchange (SGX), have the stock index futures contracts as their underlying. However, Thailand's SET 50 Index options has the SET 50 stock index as its underlying. Although they are all equity index options, the difference in their underlying asset requires adjustment in valuation. Accordingly, we separate the valuation. We first examine the valuation for SET 50-type index options and then the valuation for an index options with a stock futures contract as underlying.

9.8.1 Pricing Stock Index Options

As we saw in Chapter 7, stock index options are an increasingly popular means by which fund managers undertake portfolio insurance strategies. Since stock indexes represent the broad underlying stock market, index options are ideal for hedging the broad market exposure typical of well diversified portfolios. In addition, index options can also offer a quick and efficient way to establish speculative positions that will enable one to get broad market exposure. Since an index option, like the SET 50 stock index option, is simply a collection of 50 listed stocks, the pricing of a stock index option contract, therefore, follows the logic of stock options described earlier. Even so, some adjustments are necessary, the main one being for dividend payments. As we saw in Section 9.6, the treatment of dividends in the case of options on an individual stock is fairly straightforward. Individual stocks are unlikely to have more than one dividend payment over, say, the life of a 3-month option. But an index option has many constituent stocks each with dividend payments at different times. Thus, it is very likely for a 3-month index option to have several dividend payments over its tenor.

Dividends as we saw in Chapter 4, tend to be lumpy with concentration in some months like March and September. This is further complicated by the fact that firms do not pay their annual dividends in one go, but typically split them as interim and final dividends. Firms also do not fix their dividend payment date to a fixed date each year. To overcome these complications and since the dividend amount is typically small relative to stock value, it is common to treat the many discrete dividend payments (or yields) to be in continuous form. Thus, in valuing index options, the expected dividend yields are discounted from the current index value (S) in continuous form. Using q to denote the expected dividend yield, the BSOPM for stock index call options can be written as:

$$C = Se^{-qt} N(d_1) - Ke^{-rt} \cdot N(d_2)$$

Accordingly,

$$d_1 = \frac{\ln(S/K) + [(r-q) + (\sigma^2/2)]T}{\sigma\sqrt{T}}$$

$$d_2 = d_1 - \sigma\sqrt{T}$$

For stock index put options,

$$P = Ke^{-rt} N(-d_2) - Se^{-qt} N(-d_1)$$

where

S = current value of the stock index
K = exercise price
q = expected dividend yield
σ = estimate of index volatility
r = risk-free rate
T = time to maturity of option

Illustration: Valuing an Index Call Option

It is January 202X, you want to determine the correct value of a SET 50 Index call option, the following information is available:

SET 50 Index	(S)	= 1,004 points
Call exercise Price	(K)	= 1,000
Maturity	(T)	= March (90 days)
Risk-free rate (annualized)	(rf)	= 3%
Estimated volatility of index	(σ)	= 20%
Expected annualized div yield	(q)	= 2%

Step 1: Compute d_1 and d_2

$$d_1 = \frac{\ln(S/K) + [(r-q) + (\sigma^2/2)]T}{\sigma\sqrt{T}}$$

$$= \frac{\ln(1{,}004/1{,}000) + [(0.03 - 0.02) + 0.20^2/2]\,0.25}{0.20\sqrt{0.25}}$$

$$= \frac{0.0040 + [0.01 + 0.02]\,0.25}{0.20(0.50)}$$

$$= \frac{0.0115}{0.10}$$

$$= 0.1150$$

$d_2 = 0.1150 - 0.10$

$ = 0.0150$

$N(d_1) = 0.5438 \qquad N(d_2) = 0.5040$

Thus, the value of the call option will be:

$C = S e^{-qt} N(d_1) - K e^{-rt} N(d_2)$

$ = 1{,}004 e^{-(0.02 \times 0.25)} (0.5438) - 1{,}000 e^{-(0.03 \times 0.25)} (0.5040)$

$ = 999 (0.5438) - 992.53 (0.5040)$

$ = 543.26 - 500.24$

$ = 43.02$

Since the contract multiplier for the SET 50 Index option is THB 200, each contract has a price of $43.02 \times 200 =$ **THB 8,604**

9.8.2 Valuing Call Options on Stock Index Futures

The BSOPM can be used to value a European-style call option on an Index futures contract like options on the FBM KLCI Futures. In valuing options on futures contracts, one has to account for the fact that the positive net carry of a futures contract reduces over time to reach zero at maturity. This certain diminution in value should be estimated and adjusted for. Recall from Chapter 4 that we had determined the value of a stock index futures (SIF) contract as:

$$F_T = S_o (1 + rf - d)^{t,T}$$

where

F_T = the correct price of a SIF contract with maturity t to T
S_o = current value of the underlying index
rf = risk-free interest rate
d = the dividend yield of the underlying index

Since the BSOPM is in continuous time form, we can rewrite the earlier equation as:

$$F_T = S_o \times e^{(rf - d)(t - T)}$$

What this tells us is that the futures price that is typically higher than S_o by the amount of net carry shown as, $e^{(rf-d)(t-T)}$ will see its premium reduced as maturity is reached such that at maturity $F_t = S_o$. If one can be sure that the quoted futures price is the theoretical price and there is no mispricing, then S_o can be taken as the underlying asset value in the valuing the option. If such an assumption cannot hold, the underlying asset value (Ω) that goes into the equation would be:

$$\Omega = F_T \times e^{-(rf-d)(t-T)}$$

The BSOPM for a European-style call option on a stock index futures contract can be written as:

$$C = \Omega \cdot N(d_1) - Ke^{-rt} \cdot N(d_2)$$

where, Ω is the underlying asset value and all the other input variables of the BSOPM (K, r, t, and σ) are the same. Thus,

$$C = \Omega \times N(d_1) - Ke^{-rt} \times N(d_2)$$

$$d_1 = \frac{\ln(\Omega/K) + [r + (\sigma^2/2)]T}{\sigma\sqrt{T}}$$

$$d_2 = d_1 - \sigma\sqrt{T}$$

Illustration: Determining the Value of a Call Option on an Index Futures Contract

To understand the valuation of options on an index futures contract, we work through the following example. Suppose the FBM KLCI futures is being quoted at 1,830 points. Dividend yield over the period is expected to be 7%, the risk-free rate is 3% and volatility is estimated at 20%. What would be the correct value of a 30-day call option with a strike price of 1,800 points?

We begin by determining Ω.

$$\begin{aligned}\Omega &= 1{,}830 \times e^{-(rf-d)(t,T)} \\ &= 1{,}830 \times e^{-(0.03-0.07)(0.0833)} \\ &= 1{,}830 \times 0.9917 \\ &= 1{,}814.8 \\ &= 1{,}815\end{aligned}$$

$$\begin{aligned}d_1 &= \{\ln(1{,}815/1{,}800) + [(0.03 + (0.20^2/2)] \cdot 0.833\}/0.0577 \\ &= [(0.0083) + (0.0042)]/0.0577 \\ &= 0.22\end{aligned}$$

$$\begin{aligned}d_2 &= 0.22 - 0.0577 \\ &= 0.16\end{aligned}$$

$$N(d_1) = 0.59 \quad N(d_2) = 0.57$$

$$\begin{aligned}C &= 1{,}815\,(0.59) - 1{,}800\,e^{-(0.03-0.07)(0.0833)}\,(0.57) \\ &= 1{,}071 - 1{,}786\,(0.57) \\ &= 1{,}071 - 1{,}018 \\ &= 53\end{aligned}$$

Since the quotes have been entered as points, the value of the call option on the index futures would be 53 points. In Ringgit terms, it would be 53 points × RM 50 = RM 2,650. The RM 50 being the index multiplier for futures. In terms of value composition, the IV is 15 points × RM 50 = RM 750, while the time value is RM 1,900.

Note that the Ringgit value of the contract is 1,830 points × RM 50 = RM 91,500. An investor buying the 30-day call option pays RM 2,650 for the right to take a long position (buy) the underlying futures contract on maturity day for RM 90,000. Suppose the index futures contract on maturity day is at 1,860 points. Since, the investor's call option is in the money it will be automatically exercised by the exchange and the profit of RM 3,000 [(1,860 points − 1,800 points) × RM 50] will be credited to his account. The same amount will be debited from the option seller's margin account. Alternatively, if the option expires out of the money, i.e., if the futures at maturity has a value below 1,800 points, then investor gets nothing and so loses the RM 2,650 that he had paid for the option. Note again that since this is a long call position, the maximum loss possible is the premium paid.

9.9 Valuing Currency Options

The Garman–Kohlhagen Currency Option Model

A key challenge in valuing a currency option was the presence of two risk-free interest rates. That of the home currency and the foreign currency. Since the underlying spot exchange rate is the price of a foreign currency in terms of home currency, and as the spot rate itself is determined mainly by the interest rates, both interest rates have to be considered. It was Garman and Kohlhagen who in 1983 showed that if exchange rates are assumed to follow a Brownian motion, then a currency option is similar to an equity option with a known dividend yield. Since holding a foreign currency earns one the foreign risk-free interest rate, it is analogous to an equity holder earning the dividend yield. Based on this logic, Garman and Kohlhagen modified the BSOPM used for equities to handle the dual risk-free interest rates. Accordingly, the Garman–Kohlhagen (GK) Model is written as:

$$C = S_o e^{-r_f T} \times N(d_1) - K e^{-r_d T} \times N(d_2)$$

$$d_1 = \frac{\ln(S_o/K) + [(r_d - r_f) + \sigma^2/2]T}{\sigma \sqrt{T}}$$

$$d_2 = d_1 - \sigma \sqrt{T}$$

where

S_o	= current (spot) underlying exchange rate
K	= exercise exchange rate
$N(.)$	= cumulative standard normal distribution function
T	= time to maturity of option
σ	= volatility of the exchange rate

r_d = domestic risk-free interest rate
r_f = foreign risk-free interest rate
$ln(S_o/K)$ = natural logarithm of S/K

The GK model is meant for currency options with European-style exercise. Like the BSOPM, the GK model assumes there are no taxes, ignores transaction costs, that there are no arbitrage opportunities and that exchange rate markets are continuous with returns being lognormally distributed. The domestic and foreign interest rates and exchange rate volatility are assumed to hold constant over the life of the option contract.

To understand how currency option pricing is determined using the aforementioned GK model, we work through an example of a 3-month US$/Chinese Renminbi (CNH) currency option traded on Hong Kong Exchanges and Clearing (HKEX) (see Chapter 7 for contract details). Note that the call option of this contract, enables the holder to buy US$ using CNH or Renminbi at the predetermined exercise price. The contract size is US$ 100,000. Suppose you have the following information today:

S_o = 6.50 CNH per $
K = 6.45 CNH per $
T = 90 days or (T = 0.25)
σ = 8% annualized
r_d = 3-month (SHIBOR) = 2.3570%
r_f = 3-month T-bill rate 0.05%

$$d_1 = \frac{ln(6.50/6.45) + [(0.0236 - 0.0005) + (0.08^2/2)]0.25}{0.08\sqrt{0.25}}$$

$$= \frac{0.0077 + 0.0066}{0.0400}$$

$$= \frac{0.0143}{0.0400}$$

$$= \mathbf{0.3575}$$

d_2 = 0.3575 − 0.0400
= **0.3175**

$N(d_1)$ = **0.6406** $N(d_2)$ = **0.6255**

$C = 6.50\ e^{-(0.0005)(0.25)} \times (0.6406) - 6.45 e^{-(0.0236)(0.25)} \times (0.6255)$
= 6.4992(0.6406) − 6.4492(0.6255)
= 4.1634 − 4.0340
= 0.1294

The value of one option contract would be 0.1294 × 100,000 = CNH 12,940

Should there be exercise, the call option contract will enable the holder to receive US$ 100,000 in exchange for a CNH 645,000. His break-even, inclusive of premium paid would be CNH 657,940. Given the exercise exchange rate, the currency option is slightly in the money. As the Chinese currency is "pegged" within a tight band of the US$, the volatility is rather low relative to other currencies. As we know from earlier, volatility is positively correlated with option value.

The value of a currency put option can be determined as:

$$P = Ke^{-r_dT} \times N(-d_2) - S_o e^{-r_fT} \times N(-d_1)$$

Using the earlier example, we can determine the value of a put option on the US$/CNH contract as follows:

Since $N(d_1)$ and $N(d_2)$ above were 0.6406 and 0.6255,
$N(-d_1) = 1 - N(d_1)$
$= 1 - 0.6406$
$= \mathbf{0.3594}$
$N(-d_2) = 1 - N(d_2)$
$= 1 - 0.6255$
$= \mathbf{0.3745}$

Plugging these values into the earlier equation and solving,

$P = 6.4492\,(0.3745) - 6.4992(0.3594)$
$= 2.4152 - 2.3358$
$= 0.0794$

Thus, one put option contract will be worth $0.0794 \times 100,000 = $ CNH 7,940

Box 9.1
The Binomial Model, the BSOPM, and the Valuation of Employee Stock Options

The binomial model as we have seen, builds a lattice (or tree) to determine the different end values that the option's underlying asset (stock) could take at maturity. The potential number of ending stock values will depend on the number of times the stock's price is assumed to change. Beginning with the potential stock values at maturity, the binomial model works backward by discounting the end values to find an aggregate present value, which is then the value of the option. Since the estimated option value depends on the number of end values of the stock, which in turn depends on how many times we have allowed stock price to change, the binomial model is said to be "open ended."

Box 9.1
(*Continued*)

It should be evident that the binomial model is more of a numerical approach to pricing options rather than a model. The BSOPM, on the other hand, is a "closed-form" analytical solution to the only possible value of an option under no arbitrage conditions. Though more cumbersome, the binomial model does have some advantages over the BSOPM in some real world applications. One such case is the pricing of employee stock options (ESOs).

An ESOs is essentially an option given by a company to its employees, enabling them to buy the company's shares at predetermined exercise price(s) in the future. Since ESOs are part of incentive schemes, the exercise price is typically at a discount to market values. The total number of shares eligible for an employee may differ and the number of stocks that could be purchased may be staggered over two or more future dates. The objective of ESOs is to incentivize employees by making them shareholders. Since an ESOs is essentially share-based employee compensation, the International Accounting Standards Board (IASB) requires the valuation and reporting of ESOs in financial statements. The requirement comes under International Financial Reporting Standards (IFRS2). In valuing ESOs, there are a number of features that make the BSOPM less effective. Among these are the following:

(a) The long tenure of ESOs, often more than 5 years
(b) The nontransferable nature of the grants
(c) Subject to blackout periods, over which an employee cannot sell the shares he has bought under the ESOs
(d) Term truncation, i.e., an eligible employee who is terminated, may only be able to exercise the ESOs within, say 30 days of termination

Given the constant volatility, unchanged interest rates and dividend assumptions of the BSOPM, the model is unsuited to handle this complication. In the case of the binomial model, since one can build in the needed variations, it is that much more flexible than the BSOPM. Thus, in valuing ESOs, for financial reporting, the binomial model is the preferred model.

SUMMARY

This chapter examined the pricing of options. The pricing of options on individual stocks, options on equity indices and currency options were examined. Two option pricing models, BOPM and the BSOPM, were examined in detail. The five determinants/input variables in the Black–Scholes model and the nature of their relationship to option value were discussed. Issues related to option pricing, the adjustment for dividend payments, option deltas, HRs, and volatility estimation were explored.

The BOPM is built on the logic that the current value of an option must equal the present value of the possible payoffs to the option at maturity. As a discrete time model, it assumes that the underlying asset price changes at a given fixed time interval. Reducing this time interval and allowing for more price change enhances the accuracy of valuation but makes the model more cumbersome. Anything more than three or four price changes before maturity makes the model difficult to work with by hand. Since the option value can be determined at every time interval, the BOPM has the advantage over the Black–Scholes model when it comes to valuing American-style options. The main weakness of the binomial model is that it does not provide a closed-form solution. Progressively smaller time intervals between asset price change provides better accuracy with the estimated option price converging toward its "true" price.

The BSOPM overcomes the problems associated with the binomial model. Its main advantage is that it provides a closed from solution. The BSOPM uses five input variables: S_o (underlying asset/stock price), K (the exercise price), T (time to maturity of option), r (the risk-free interest rate), and σ (the standard deviation or volatility of the underlying asset price). The BSOPM is built on the logic that an option payoff can be replicated by a portfolio consisting of stocks and bonds. A call option payoff can be replicated with a long position in a proportion of stock and a short position in a proportion of bonds. If there are weaknesses with the model, they arise from some of the assumptions made, in particular the assumption that the underlying asset volatility remains unchanged over the life of the option. Still, given the ease with the model could be used and the fact that it is easily programmable has meant that the BSOPM is the model of choice for option traders.

A key advantage of having a closed-form solution as the BSOPM is that the values of the input parameters and their partial derivatives can be easily determined. This would enable one to estimate (or have an intuitive feel for) the impact of a change in any one of these parameters on option value. The impact of a change in the underlying stock price on call value is positive while that of put value, negative. This relationship is commonly known as *delta*. The exercise price, K, is negatively correlated to call values but positively to put values. Volatility, however, is positively related to both option values. The relationship being known as *vega*. The relationship between interest rates and option values is termed *rho*. Rho is positive for call options but negative for puts. *Theta* denotes the relationship between time to maturity and option values. While theta is positively correlated with call values, its impact on put values is ambiguous. The ambiguity arises from the fact that time to maturity has a differential impact on a put's intrinsic and time value. The chapter also examined the pricing of equity index options and of currency options.

KEY TERMS

- Binomial option pricing
- Call/put value path
- Call/put payoff
- Decision tree
- Volatility
- Lognormal distribution
- Cumulative probability
- Black–Scholes option pricing model
- Closed-form solution
- Logarithmic stock returns

- Option delta
- Option vega
- Option theta
- Rho
- Hedge ratio
- Historical volatility
- Implied volatility
- Expected/future volatility
- Stock index options
- Currency options

End-of-Chapter Questions

1. You wish to hedge a position equivalent to 400 MBB stocks. The call delta is 0.60. How many calls would you need to fully hedge the position?

2. How many puts would you need to fully hedge the position in Question 1?

3. Calculate the fair value of a call option using BSOPM and the following information.
   Stock price   = RM 40
   Exercise price   = RM 35
   Interest rate   = 12%
   Maturity   = 180 days
   Standard deviation = 30%
   Dividends   = 0

4. a. A stock has a current price of RM 50. Assuming it has a 10% volatility, changes price three times over maturity and an equal probability of an up or down movement, use the BOPM to calculate the value of a call option with RM 50 exercise price. Assume the call has a maturity of 6 months and the risk-free interest rate is 12% per annum.
   b. Redo part (a) assuming the option is a put.

5. You own four lots (each lot is 1,000 shares) of Syarikat ABC stock currently selling at RM 5.25. The following options are available.
   - RM 5 call @ 0.45
   - RM 5 put @ 0.10

Assume the RM 5 call has a delta of 0.80.

State how you would hedge your stock portfolio. How many of the options would you use?

6. ANZAC stock is now trading at RM 19. The stock has a price volatility (standard deviation) of 30%, and is expected to pay a dividend of RM 3 in 30 days. Determine the correct value of a call option on the stock given the following information.
   - Maturity = 90 days
   - Interest rate (rf) = 12%
   - Exercise price = RM 15

7. Redo Question 5 assuming the option is a put option. What is its value? Briefly explain why the put value is lower than that of the call option in Question 5.

8. Would it be possible for two calls written on the same underlying asset to have different
   a. implied volatilities?
   b. historical volatilities?

9. The exercise price and interest rates have an opposite impact on calls and puts. Explain why interest rates have a differential impact on calls versus puts.

10. a. Briefly describe the following; and state the nature of relationship with call and put prices.
      (i) Delta
      (ii) Vega
      (iii) Rho
      (iv) Theta
    b. Graphically, plot delta for a call and put option. Label the points at which delta approximates 0.5, approaches 0, and approaches 1.0.

11. a. OYL Industries stock is currently RM 19.60. Assuming an rf rate of 8%, stock price volatility (standard deviation) of 40%, both annualized and zero dividends, determine using the BSOPM
      (i) fair value for an RM 20 call option with 90 days to maturity, and
      (ii) fair value for an RM 20 put option with 90 days to maturity.
    b. What has been the key criticism against the BSOPM? Explain why the criticism may be valid.

12. a. You are in charge of risk management at FMA Asset Management Bhd. The company has an RM 28 million portfolio of diversified Malaysian stocks. You intend to hedge the position using index futures options. You do not plan to hold the options to maturity but trade them for profit. Three-month, at-the-money index futures calls and puts are quoted as follows:
      - FBM KLCI 800 calls @ 16 points
      - FBM KLCI 800 puts @ 14 points
      - The call delta is 0.52

      (i) Outline your hedge strategy.
      (ii) What is the cost of your hedge strategy?
    b. What is meant by dynamic hedging? What necessitates hedging to be dynamic?

13. a. Use the multiperiod BOPM to estimate the value of a call that has 3 months to expiration and a strike price of RM 30. The stock now sells for RM 35.50/share. Volatility is 10% with 70% upward probability. The riskless interest rate is 2% per month. (Assume price changes three times over the period.)
    b. What would the value be if the earlier option is a put?
    c. State and briefly explain two reasons why there is a huge difference between the value of the call and put.

14. This question requires the use of the put–call parity equation shown in Chapter 10.
    a. A stock is currently selling at RM 8.50. An RM 8 call on the stock with 90 days to maturity is selling at RM 0.76. If the rf rate is 8%, what should the correct price be for an RM 8 put option on the stock for the same maturity?
    b. Suppose the put above mentioned is being quoted at RM 0.34, outline the arbitrage strategy.
    c. Compute the arbitrage profit per contract.
    d. By means of a graph, show the strategy and the overall payoff.

15. A stock is currently selling at RM 10. It has both calls and puts available. Assume the options will expire at a future period X, and that stock price will change three times until maturity period X. Assume further that the probability of a price increase is 60%, whereas that of a decline is 40%. The annualized rf rate between now and period X is 8% and the stock has 10% price volatility.
    a. Plot the tree diagram to show the price path and end values for an RM 10 call expiring at period X. What is the value of the call option using the BOPM?
    b. What would the BOPM value be for a put option with the same features? Briefly explain why the put has a value higher/lower relative to the call above.
    c. Using the BSOPM, you have just determined the price of a call option to be RM 0.76. However, your broker tells you that the option is currently being traded at RM 0.94. Given the price discrepancy, how does the implied volatility at the quoted price compare to your volatility estimate?

16. Fill in the blanks to show the impact on option price. (+) to show an increase in option value, (−) for decrease, and (0) for unchanged value.

		Value of Option	
		Call	Put
a.	A company announces a cut in forthcoming dividends.	_____	_____
b.	Given rumors of an impending merger, a company's underlying stock becomes more volatile.	_____	_____
c.	Bank Negara announces a cut in interest rates.	_____	_____
d.	In line with the current bearish trend, the stock falls in value.	_____	_____
e.	The Securities Commission allows a company to extend the maturity period on its outstanding stock options.	_____	_____

Option Pricing

17. Explain why a call delta is always positive, whereas that of a put always negative.

18. Using (+) to denote an increase, (−) to denote a decrease, and (0) to denote indeterminate impact, fill in the following table.

For a *Decrease* in	Call Value	Put Value
Expected dividends		
Interest rates		
Stock price		
Exercise price		
Volatility		

19. Given the following information, determine the value of a call option on an index futures contract.
- Futures price = 1,680
- Call exercise price = 1,650
- Dividend yield = 6%
- Maturity = 30 days
- rf interest rate = 4%
- Estimated volatility = 25%

20. Determine the profit/loss to the long and short position if at maturity the futures is at the following:
   (i) 1,635
   (ii) 1,650
   (iii) 1,682

21. It is March 202X, the following information is available from TFEX:
- SET 50 Index $(S) = 1,126$ points
- Call exercise price $(K) = 1,120$
- Maturity $(T) =$ June (90 days)
- Risk-free rate (annualized) $(rf) = 3\%$
- Estimated volatility of index $(\sigma) = 30\%$
- Expected annualized div yield $(q) = 2\%$

  (i) Determine the correct value of the SET 50 Index call option expiring in June.
  (ii) Explain the likely impact on the value of the option if Thai stock market volatility increased substantially from the end of March onward.
  (iii) Explain how an investors' payoff profile would differ between a long position in a stock index futures and long position in an index call option. Assume the positions are held to maturity.

22. An American producer of cosmetics has just completed a large shipment to a Chinese retail chain. The invoice amount of RMB/CNH 25.2 million is due in 90 days. The American firm wants to hedge its currency exposure using the 3-month US$/CNH currency option traded on HKEX. The following information is available for at-the-money options:
    - S_o = 6.30 CNH per $
    - K = 6.30 CNH per $
    - σ = 6% annualized
    - r_d = 3-month (SHIBOR) = 2.3%
    - r_f = 3-month T-bill rate 0.05%
    - Contract size = US$ 100,000

    (i) Outline the correct hedge strategy using HKEX's US$/CNH currency option.
    (ii) Using the GK Model, determine the total premium the American firm would have to pay to fully hedge its currency exposure.

Appendix 1

Option Greeks and Comparative Statics

This appendix extends our earlier discussion of option greeks and shows how these variables can be useful in risk management. Options greeks is the term used to describe the partially differentiated result of each of the five parameters that go into option valuation using BSOPM. Since four of the variables have names from the Greek alphabet, *delta, theta, rho*, and *vega*, they are collectively termed option greeks. Option greeks being partial differentials are really sensitivities or a measure of how sensitive an option is to changes in the input variable. We begin our discussion with an examination of the dynamics of these option greeks based on Tables 9.5(a) and 9.5(b) in the chapter. This is followed by a description of comparative statics and the computation of their values for a stock option. We estimate the value of each option greek using formula derived from the BSOPM. Finally, we examine how the ability to estimate the value helps in risk management.

Option Greeks — Dynamics

In Tables 9.5(a) and 9.5(b), we saw in tabular form the impact of a change in the input variables on call and put option values. The following figures show the graphical representation of the impact of the four parameters on the same call option. The graphs are based on a broader range of underlying asset values and input parameters.

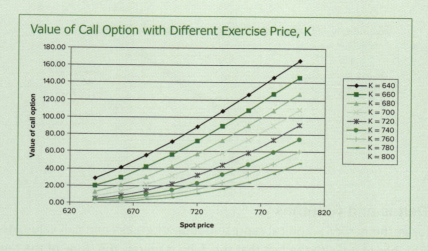

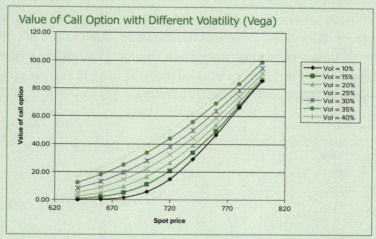

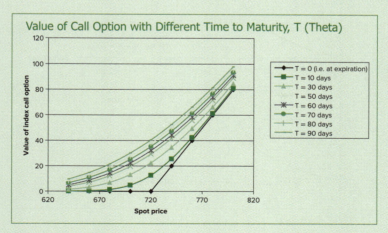

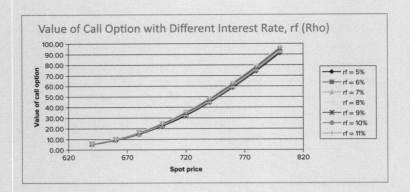

Option Deltas and Gammas

Notice that in the earlier graphical representation of greeks and call value, delta is not graphed. This has to do with the fact that the delta is merely the slope of the option value curve. From a calculus viewpoint, delta would be the first derivative of option value with respect to changes in stock value. Delta which is the slope, changes and has different values at different points. Deltas change as stock price changes. Call deltas range from 0 to 1, whereas put deltas from −1 to 0. The variation in the delta of a call and put option to changes in the underlying stock/asset price is typically as follows:

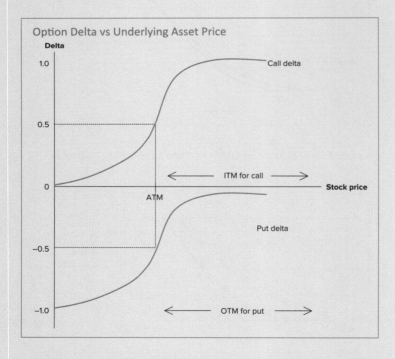

(ATM – at-the-money; OTM – out-of-the-money; ITM – in-the-money)

The graph is constructed with delta on a vertical axis and underlying stock price on the horizontal axis. Put delta plots are in the negative region. Notice that in the region to the right of the point denoted at-the-money, the call is in-the-money and has delta approaching 1, the put on the other hand is out-of-the-money in that region and has delta approaching

Table 1 Input Parameters and Comparative Statics for Calls and Puts

Input	Calls Formula		Sign	Puts Formula		Sign
Exercise price, K	$\dfrac{\partial C}{\partial K}$	$-e^{-rt}N(d_2)$	(−)	$\dfrac{\partial P}{\partial K}$	$\dfrac{\partial C}{\partial K}+e^{-rt}$	+
Volatility (vega)	$\dfrac{\partial C}{\partial \sigma}$	$S\sqrt{T}\cdot N'(d_1)$	(+)	$\dfrac{\partial P}{\partial K}$	$S\sqrt{T}\cdot N'(d_1)$	+
Interest Rate (rho)	$\dfrac{\partial C}{\partial r}$	$TKe^{-rt}\cdot N(d_2)$	(+)	$\dfrac{\partial P}{\partial r}$	$\dfrac{\partial C}{\partial r}-Tke^{-rt}$	−
Time (theta)	$\dfrac{\partial C}{\partial T}$	$Ke^{-rt}\left[\dfrac{\sigma N'(d_2)}{2\sqrt{T}}\right]+rN(d_2)$	(+)	$\dfrac{\partial P}{\partial T}$	$\dfrac{\partial C}{\partial T}-rke^{-rt}$	−/+
Stock Price (delta)	$\dfrac{\partial C}{\partial S}$	$N'(d_1)$	(+)	$\dfrac{\partial P}{\partial S}$	$\dfrac{\partial C}{\partial S}-1 = N(d_1)-1$	−
Gamma	$\dfrac{\partial^2 C}{\partial S^2}$	$\dfrac{N'(d_1)}{S\sigma\sqrt{T}}$	(+)	$\dfrac{\partial^2 P}{\partial S^2}$	$\dfrac{N'(d_1)}{S\sigma\sqrt{T}}$	+

Note: (1) The sign (+) or (−) shows the nature of the correlation positive or inverse to option value.

(2) $N'(d)$ is determined $\dfrac{e^{-d_1^2/2}}{\sqrt{2\pi}}$; where π is mathematical constant with value = 3.1416.

zero. It is obvious from the graph that delta is sensitive to changes in underlying stock price. The sensitivity of delta (and HR) to changes in the underlying stock price is known as *gamma*.

Gamma, from a calculus viewpoint, is the second derivative of call value to changes in underlying stock value. Gamma measures how delta changes when the underlying asset price changes.

$$Gamma = \frac{\partial^2 C}{\partial S^2} = \frac{\text{Change in option delta}}{\text{Change in underlying stock price}}$$

Estimating Sensitivity: Comparative Statics

The *extent* to which a change in any of the five input parameters will cause a change in option values can be determined by partially differentiating the BSOPM value of the option with respect to *each* of the five variables. Such an exercise is termed *comparative statics* since only one variable is allowed to change. Since all other input variables are held constant, the result tells us how sensitive the option value will be for a given change in the variable. A key advantage of the BSOPM closed-form solution is that a formula can be derived for each option greek in order to estimate the size/extent of its impact on the option. Table 1 shows the formulae to estimate sensitivity of a stock option, for each of the five input parameters.

Comparative Statics: Illustration

We now turn to an illustration of how to determine sensitivity using the given formulae. We use the example of a European-style call option on MAS stock. Assume MAS stock price is now RM 6. If there is a 30-day RM 5 call option on the stock, what should its price be, if the 3-month KLIBOR is 4% annualized and stock price volatility is 40%?

The value of the call using BSOPM is RM 1.04, derived as follows:

$$d_1 = \frac{\ln(6/5) + [0.04 + (0.40^2/2)]0.083}{0.40\sqrt{0.083}}$$

$$= \frac{0.1823 + 0.0100}{0.1152}$$

$$= \frac{0.1923}{0.1152}$$

$$= 1.67$$

$$d_2 = 1.67 - 0.1152$$

$$= 1.55$$

$N(d_1) = 0.9525 \qquad N(d_2) = 0.9394$

$C = 6.00(0.9525) - 5.00e^{(-0.04 \times 0.083)}(0.9394)$

$= 5.72 - 4.68$

$= RM\ 1.04$

The IV being RM 1 while time value would be the remaining RM 0.04.

Sensitivity to change in exercise price

(1) $\dfrac{\partial C}{\partial K} \Rightarrow -e^{-rt} \cdot N(d_2)$

$= -[e^{(-0.04 \times 0.083)}](0.9343)$

$= -(0.9966)(0.9394)$

$= -0.9363$

What this implies is that for the above call, if the exercise price is increased by RM 1, the value of the call will fall by RM 0.93 or fall 93 sen.

To put it another way, if there was another call option on MAS stock with exactly the same features but an exercise price RM 1 higher, i.e., RM 6 exercise price (at-the-money), its value will be approximately 10 sen (RM 1.04 − RM 0.9363).

Sensitivity to change in underlying stock price

(2) Delta $\dfrac{\partial C}{\partial K} \Rightarrow N(d_1)$

From our earlier computation, $N(d_1)$ for the MAS call option was $N(d_1) = 0.9525$.

What this implies is that if MAS stock price were to increase to RM 6.10 (10 sen higher); the value of call will rise to RM 1.135. That is, the call value rises by 9.5 sen (RM 1.04 + 0.095). As we saw in the chapter, a delta of 0.95 means option value will effect at 95% rate of change in underlying stock price. Similarly, if MAS stock were to fall to RM 5.90, the value of the call will fall to 94.5 sen (stock price Δ – 10 sen; option value Δ – 9.5 sen).

Sensitivity to change in delta

(3) Gamma $\dfrac{\partial^2 C}{\partial S^2} \Rightarrow \dfrac{N'(d_1)}{S\sigma \sqrt{T}}$

where $N'(d_1) = \dfrac{e^{-d_1^2/2}}{\sqrt{2\pi}}$

$N(d_1) = \dfrac{e^{-(1.67^2/2)}}{\sqrt{2(3.1416)}} = \dfrac{0.247969}{2.506631} = 0.09893$

$= \dfrac{0.09893}{S\sigma \sqrt{T}} = \dfrac{0.09893}{RM\ 6(0.4)\sqrt{0.83}} = \dfrac{0.09893}{RM\ 6(0.1152)}$

$= \dfrac{0.09893}{0.6912} = 0.1431$

Gamma, as we saw earlier, is a second order derivative that stands for the change in delta for a given change in the underlying stock price. A gamma of 0.14 means that a 1% change in the underlying stock price will cause 0.14% change in delta. Since the delta of a put and call with the same features are related, it should be obvious that their differentiated value, gamma, should be related too. Indeed, the gamma of a put and that of a call are equal. Both gammas are maximized when the call and put are at-the-money, i.e., when delta is 0.50. Gamma reduces as the option either goes in-the-money or out-of-the-money. Gammas are smallest for options that are either deep in or out-of-the-money. Finally, gammas, though always positive (even for puts), increase rapidly as the maturity approaches.

Sensitivity to change in volatility

(4) Vega $\dfrac{\partial C}{\partial \sigma} \Rightarrow S \sqrt{T} \cdot N'(d_1)$

$= RM\ 6(\sqrt{0.083})(0.09893)$
$= RM\ 6(0.028501)$
$= 0.17$

What is implied here is that a 1% change in volatility will cause a 0.17% change in call value. For example, if the volatility of MAS stock price were to increase by 1% to 41%, the value of call would rise from the current RM 1.04 to RM 1.04177.

A put option with the same features as the call will have the same vega value. Where price change (Ringgit value) is concerned, changes in volatility have the greatest impact when the option is at-the-money. As such, an investor who believes that stock volatility is likely rise and wants to "trade volatility" would benefit most from positions in at-the-money options.

Sensitivity to change in interest rate

(5) Rho; $\dfrac{\partial C}{\partial r} \Rightarrow TKe^{-rt}N'(d_1)$

$= (0.083)[5.00e^{(-0.04 \times 0.083)}(0.9394)]$
$= (0.083)(4.68)$
$= 0.388$

With a value of 0.388, the implication is that a 1% increase in the risk-free rate will cause a 0.388% increase in call value. Thus, if the risk-free interest rate were to rise by 1% from 4% currently to 5%, the call value will increase from RM 1.04 to RM 1.04404 (a change of 0.388%).

Sensitivity to change in time to maturity

(6) Theta $\dfrac{\partial C}{\partial r} \Rightarrow Ke^{-rt}\left[\dfrac{\sigma N'(d_2)}{2\sqrt{T}} + rN(d_2)\right]$

where $N'(d_2) = \dfrac{e^{-d_2^{\,2}/2}}{\sqrt{2\pi}}$

$N'(d_2) = \dfrac{e^{-(1.552/2)}}{\sqrt{2(3.1416)}}$

$= \dfrac{0.3008}{2.506631}$

$= 0.1200$

$Ke^{-rt} = RM\ 5.00e^{(-0.04 \times 0.083)}$

$= RM\ 4.98$

Thus,

$4.98 = \left[\dfrac{(0.40)(0.1200)}{2\sqrt{.083}} + (0.04)(0.9394)\right]$

$= 4.98\left[\dfrac{0.0480}{0.57619} + (0.037576)\right]$

$= 4.98(0.120882)$

$= 0.602$

A theta value of 0.602 here implies that a one-unit increase in time to maturity will cause the call option value to increase by RM 0.60 or 60 sen.

Since time to maturity is input into BSOPM as a fraction of a year (0.083 in this case), a one-unit increase in time here implies a *1-year* increase in time to maturity. Thus, if time to maturity is increased from the current 30 days to 1 year and 30 days or 395 days, which would be entered into BSOPM as 1.083, then value of the call will increase by 60 sen. Reworking call value using 1.083 as time to maturity will give a call value of RM 1.61, which represents a 60 sen in call value.

Since theta is really a measure of time decay, the thetas are negative for long option positions and positive for short positions. This is logical since time decay is favorable to sellers but works to the disadvantage of option buyers.

Option Greeks and Trading/Investment Strategies

The information that option greeks provide can be used to establish trading strategies. The strategies may be established with the objective of profiting from expected value changes or for the purpose of risk management, or a combination of both. The delta-neutral strategy we saw in the chapter is an example of a trading strategy that minimizes risk. In Chapter 10, we will see how mispricing can be arbitraged using synthesized positions. When a conversion or reverse-conversion strategy is used to arbitrage mispriced values, or violations of the put–call parity, it would constitute a delta-neutral trading position. The objective being to profit from the mispricing while minimizing risk. Since delta values change as underlying asset price changes, delta-neutral strategies require constant "rebalancing," thus the need for dynamic hedging.

In addition to delta-neutral positions, there are other delta based trading strategies. In fact, option traders often create very specific option positions with particular delta, gamma, theta, vega or rho values in order to meet specific expectations. For example, if one is bullish, which of several available series of call options should one buy? We know that stock options with several exercise prices (series of options) are available simultaneously. Since in, at and out-of-the-money options are all available, which one should you buy if you are bullish about the underlying stock. We know that premiums will reflect moneynesses. In-the-money options will have higher premiums while out-of-the-money options would be cheap. Similarly, the delta of the in-the-money option would be high while that of the out-of-the-money option would be low. Delta therefore is related to option moneyness. There is an implicit tradeoff that an investor faces as a result of this relationship. Essentially, buying an out-of-the-money option while cheaper would have a lower delta. In-the-money options, on the other hand, though expensive would have high deltas.

Unless one is very bullish about the underlying stock, buying an out-of-the-money option is not appropriate if one intends to profit from trading options. When delta is low, a substantial increase in underlying stock value is needed for a meaningful increase in the option value.

For example, suppose a stock is selling for RM 5, an RM 10 call on the stock is selling for RM 0.20 (20 sen). Assume the delta of the option is 0.05. If two weeks later, the stock price is RM 6, the option value ought to be 25 sen, an increase of 5 sen, (RM 1 × 0.05); however, this ignores the negative impact of theta, time value. With two weeks gone by, time decay would have reduced, if not eliminated, the 5 sen increase due to delta. Thus, if one is mildly bullish, the appropriate delta based strategy would be too long a deep in-the-money option. The high delta of such an option would cause meaningful increase in option value, even for a marginal increase in the underlying stock price. Thus, the appropriate delta position to take would depend on the extent/degree of one's bullishness. In the earlier example of mildly bullish expectation, going long a high delta, low theta call option would be the most appropriate.

Trading Volatility

Recall from our discussion in the chapter that *implied volatility* can be an indicator of potential mispricing. Option traders often compare implied volatility with historical volatility. If an option's implied volatility is deemed to be lower than its historical volatility, traders would consider the option to be undervalued. They would long the option and short the replicating position. The opposite would be done if the implied volatility is higher than their estimate of historical volatility.

Based on the same logic, if a trader believes that an option's expected (future) volatility is likely to be higher than implied volatility, he would typically establish a *positive vega position*, i.e., establish a net long position in the option. Usually, future volatility of an option would be expected to increase if the firm issuing the underlying stock experiences or is expected to experience some uncertainty. If option volatility is expected to fall in future, a negative vega position, essentially shorting the option would be appropriate. Finally, where volatility is expected to increase but the direction of the underlying stock price movement is unknown, the logical strategy would be a *positive vega* but *neutral delta* position. The *long straddle* position we saw in Chapter 8 would fit this requirement. The long straddle is positive vega but delta-neutral.

Position Deltas and Gammas

Position deltas and gammas are essentially the overall or "net" delta or gamma of a portfolio. The portfolio may consist of several different stocks and options, both calls and puts written on the stock.

The position in the stocks, calls and puts may also be a combination of long and short positions. We know from earlier that long call positions have positive deltas, long put positions, negative deltas. The opposite would be the case for short call and short put positions. The size of the option deltas would of course depend on option moneyness. As mentioned in the chapter, a long stock position has a delta = +1.0, whereas the delta of a short stock position would be −1.0.

Position	Delta	Size of Delta
Long stock	Positive	1.0
Short stock	Negative	1.0
Long call	Positive	Depends on moneyness
Short call	Negative	Depends on moneyness
Long put	Negative	Depends on moneyness
Short put	Positive	Depends on moneyness

A trader who has a combined stocks and options portfolio would be interested in the overall net delta of his portfolio. This overall delta is known as *position delta*. The position delta essentially measures the sensitivity of the portfolio to (small) changes in stock prices. If the lot size of stocks and options are equal, then the position delta of a portfolio would simply be the sum of individual stock/option deltas in the portfolio. This is very similar in logic to portfolio betas which are simply the weighted average of individual stocks within the portfolio. The position delta for a portfolio can be computed as:

$$\text{Portfolio delta} = \sum_{i=1}^{N} n_{Si} \cdot \Delta_{Si} + n_{oi} \cdot \Delta_{oi}$$

where

n_{si} = number of stocks within the portfolio
Δ_{si} = delta of the stock (positive if long, negative if short)
n_{oi} and Δ_{oi} = number of options and the respective option delta; positive or negative as the case may be

Position Gammas indicate the sensitivity of portfolio deltas to changes in underlying stock values. Thus, knowing the position gamma can tell us the sensitivity of delta and therefore of the overall portfolio to changes in underlying asset values. Though individual options have positive gammas, position gammas which are computed as the weighted sum of both stocks and options within the portfolio can have negative gammas. A portfolio with a positive position gamma increases as underlying asset values increase. The opposite would be true for portfolios with negative position gammas.

As we end our discussion of option greeks, one final caveat needs to be reiterated. In all trading strategies based on option greeks, the objective is met only over finite or small changes. Though for illustrative purposes, large price changes in the underlying asset was used, the rule in calculus is that partial derivatives/differentiations only apply for small changes. Thus, all option greek based strategies must be dynamically managed with constant updates and revision of positions in order to be effective.

Appendix II

This appendix provides an overview of option models in addition to the binomial and BSOPM models in the chapter.

(1) A Multiperiod Binomial Model

We discussed the single period and two-period model of the BOPM which was given by the earlier Equations 1 and 2 in Section 9.2. We also extended Equation 2 for the case where there were three price changes in the underlying asset i.e. a three-period model. It is obvious that the model gets intractable for any further price changes. So, how does one mathematically solve for the case where there would realistically be several price changes in the underlying stock before maturity. A multiperiod model of the BOPM, which allows for several price changes, is shown below. This particular variant of the model automatically excludes price paths which would end with the option being out-of-the-money and considers only paths where the option would be in-the-money. The multi multiperiod model is as follows:

$$C_t = \frac{\sum_{j=m}^{n}\left[\frac{n!}{j!(n-j)!}\right]\left(\rho_u^j \rho_d^{n-j}\right)\left[U^j D^{A-j} S_t - K\right]}{r^n}$$

where

n = number of periods (number of times price changes)
j = number of up movements in stock price
m = minimum number of stock price increases needed for the option to be in-the-money
S_t = underlying stock price at time t
K = exercise price of option
r = risk-free discount rate/interest rate

(2) Pricing American-Style Options

As was argued in Chapter 7, though American-style options allow for early exercise, it never pays to exercise early an option on a nondividend paying stock. Selling rather than exercising such an option would mean realizing both the intrinsic and time values which constitute the option price, whereas exercising will only allow the realization of the IV alone. Thus, it was argued that though at first glance the early exercise feature of an American-style option looks very attractive, it is not really all that advantageous. The one situation when an American-style option has a clear advantage is in the presence of large dividends. Since dividend payments reduce the exdividend stock and call values, it would be advantageous to exercise the call just before the dividend is paid. In this particular case it may be worthwhile to forego the remaining time value since the fall in the exdividend value may be even larger.

The fact that an American-style option could be exercised at any point makes its valuation/pricing very difficult. Without a fix on maturity, a closed-form solution to pricing the option becomes difficult. Thus there is no generalized closed-form solution to pricing American-style options. Their pricing therefore is typically done in two ways: first, to approach the pricing from the viewpoint of a *compound option model* and second, to take an analytical approximation approach.

Compound Option Approach

A compound option is essentially an option on an option or an option which has yet another option within it. The compound option model is described briefly in the next section. The logic of using such a model for an American option is based on the view that aside from the original option, which if it is a call provides the right to buy the underlying asset, the holder also gets the option to exercise just before a dividend payment prior to maturity. Clearly such an option is not available to the holder of a European option. To put it simply, the compound option model in essence values the option within and adds that value to overall option value.

Analytical Approximation Approach

The second method of pricing American options uses approximations to arrive at the option value. Though available in several variants, a common analytical approximation technique is that proposed by Fischer Black (of the Black–Scholes Model).

Black's approximation procedure involves the calculation of *two* European options with features identical to that of the American option to be valued. The initial stock price (S_o), the interest rate (rf), exercise price (k), and volatility (σ) should be identical for the two European options and the American option to be valued. As for maturity, the two European options should have maturities as follows: one which has a maturity the same as that of the American option and the other with maturity just before the exdividend date which falls within the maturity of the first option. Thus the latter option has shorter maturity. The difference in the computed values of the two European options would reflect the trade off between foregoing time value by exercising early and taking advantage of early exercise to avoid diminution in value post dividend. If early exercise is advantageous, the shorter maturity option should have higher value. If however the dividend is tiny and the loss in value post dividend is smaller than time value lost, then the first, longer maturity option should be worth more. By this logic, Black's procedure prices the American option as being equivalent to the *higher* of the two European options valued.

(3) Other Stock/Index Option Models

Aside from the two models that we have seen, binomial and Black–Scholes, several other option pricing models are available. Although each of these models has its specific strengths, they also have weaknesses that render them less popular than the Black–Scholes model. In particular, the disadvantage is the added complexity of these models. Still, where there is a serious violation of the assumptions of the Black–Scholes model, these alternative models may be helpful. As an in-depth examination of these models is beyond the scope of this book, the following section provides a brief overview of four common models and cites a study comparing these alternative models with the Black–Scholes.

(a) The Compound Option Model

As mentioned in the last section, a compound option model can be used in valuing stock/index option, especially one with an American-style exercise. The compound option is appropriate where there may be other embedded options within an overall option. Thus, the model would be appropriate for valuing contingent claims or payoffs that depend on certain outcomes. The model as put forth by Geske (1979), assumes constant volatility as does the BSOPM. However, using the compound option model for stock option is more complicated than the BSOPM because the model requires additional information such as the face value and maturity of the firm's debt, etc.

(b) Merton's Continuous Dividend Model

Where a stock provides continuous dividends, the BSOPM may be less accurate since it assumes no dividend payments. In essence, Merton's model treats the dividends as a negative interest rate. This is based on the logic that dividend payments constitute a "leakage" in the value of a stock. The key difference between this model and BSOPM is in the treatment for dividend adjustment. While in the BSOPM we adjust by deducting the current stock price by the PV of expected dividends, in Merton's continuous dividend model, the adjustment is as follows:

$$e^{-\delta(T-t)} \cdot S_o$$

where δ is the continuous dividend rate and $(T-t)$ is the number of days left to option maturity.

In addition, δ is deducted from the risk-free interest rate when computing d_1. Thus, Merton's continuous dividend model is an extension of the BSOPM to adjust for the case of continuous dividends. The model is particularly suitable for valuing options on underlying assets such as foreign currencies. The continuous 'dividends' being treated as analogous to the foreign interest rate earned from the foreign currency.

(c) Merton's Jump-Diffusion Model

Robert Merton (1976) proposes an option pricing model for underlying stock with discontinuous returns, i.e., where the stock's price undergoes occasional large jumps. The Jump-Diffusion model as it came to be known assumes that stock returns are generated by a two-part stochastic process. The first part, a normal day to day Wiener/Brownian process and the second, a Poisson process generated-jump that though infrequent is large. This jump-generated return is assumed to be unsystematic.

The Jump-Diffusion model has been shown to be appropriate for valuation of long dated options with an equity underlying, e.g., the exchange traded LEAPs in the United States and Call Warrants in Malaysia. Since Call Warrants are essentially long dated call options on an underlying stock, the BSOPM may not be suited for their valuation. This is due to the fact the BSOPM assumes constant volatility of the underlying asset until option maturity. Clearly, such an assumption may not be appropriate where the maturity period is often more than a year. Furthermore, in volatile emerging markets such as Malaysia, a jump component may not be uncommon. The daily percentage returns for individual stocks can clearly be quite volatile. Though the Jump-Diffusion model gives rise to "fatter tail" distributions than that of the BSOPM, this may indeed be more appropriate for equities since stock returns do tend to portray fatter tails than that implied by a normal distribution.

(d) Stochastic Volatility Models

Since the constant volatility assumption of the BSOPM has been criticized as a key weakness, a number of models have appeared that assume underlying asset volatility to be stochastic. Of these, the most common is probably the model proposed by Hull and White (1987). They show that when volatility is stochastic, the BSOPM could misprice options with the mispricing being less acute for shorter maturities. Delta hedging too becomes much more difficult in the presence of stochastic volatilities.

Comparison of Models

Several academic studies have been carried out comparing the pricing "efficiency" of the various option pricing models. The studies have typically examined the theoretical prices derived from the models in relation to actual market/trading prices of the options. The most famous of such comparative studies is that of Mark Rubinstein. Rubinstein's study compared the BSOPM with the other option pricing models. Although some of the models outperformed the BSOPM in some respects, none did so consistently. Though Rubinstein also found certain biases with the BSOPM, he found none of the other models to be bias free. Though the BSOPM was found to have advantages in ease of use, etc. Rubinstein concludes that no one model is consistently superior over all other models in a generalized way.

CHAPTER · 10

Replication, Synthetics, and Arbitrage

Objectives

This chapter is designed to introduce *synthetics* and *arbitrage* and to explore in depth the put–call parity relationship. The chapter shows why these equilibrium relationships must hold and how arbitrage is possible when there is a disequilibrium. The possibility of arbitrage helps to ensure that equilibrium relationships hold. The chapter also shows how arbitrage can bring prices back into equilibrium. On completing the chapter you should have a good understanding of the role arbitrage plays in ensuring market efficiency. You should also appreciate how the flexibility of options enable the synthetization of assets making riskless arbitrage possible.

Introduction

We saw in Chapter 8 how versatile options can be. Given their flexibility, options could be combined in various ways to achieve different desired cash-flow objectives. For example, we saw how options could be used to hedge underlying exposure, how options could be used to take the advantage of extreme volatility, minimal volatility, etc. In this chapter, we examine yet another advantage arising from the flexible nature of options, i.e., the ability to replicate the cash flows of other assets/positions. The fact that options can be put together to provide different types of cash flows means that by using options an investor can replicate the payoffs/cash flows of other securities. This ability has two important implications: first, by being able to replicate the cash flows of another security, we are effectively able to "synthesize" the security. Thus, options can be used to synthesize other assets and achieve **cash-flow equivalence**. The second implication follows from the first, if we are able to synthesize another asset with options, then the cost of the synthetic position created using options must equal to the price of the asset, otherwise arbitrage would be possible. Thus, there must be **pricing equivalence**. While cash-flow equivalence occurs only at option maturity, pricing equivalence will hold at all times until option maturity.

Pricing equivalence implies that a pricing relationship must hold between an asset and options written on the asset. Should this relationship be violated then arbitrage would be possible. The presence of arbitrage in a way ensures that the pricing relationship will hold. In addition to the fact that synthesizing makes it possible to arbitrage, it makes it possible to overcome certain types of market regulation, for example, regulation preventing the short selling of stocks.

This chapter has two major parts. The first part examines the basics of synthesizing and the cash-flow equivalence. The second part discusses arbitrage and the put–call parity that describes pricing equivalence. We look at some of the strategies examined in Chapter 8 to prove the arbitrage relationship.

10.1 Replication and Synthetics

In this section, we look at how options can be used to replicate the cash flows of an asset and thereby effectively synthesize the asset. Recall from Chapter 6 that there are six basic strategies: (i) long stock, (ii) short stock, (iii) long call, (iv) short call, (v) long put, and (vi) short put. To see how **replication** is possible, we replicate or synthesize each of these basic six positions. Though the replication of more complex positions such as spreads, straddles, and other strategies covered in Chapter 8 is also possible, we shall keep our discussion here to the basic six positions. For the sake of clarity, we make two simplifying assumptions:

(a) We ignore interest rates and the timing difference between cash outlays now and option exercise.
(b) The underlying asset, exercise price, and maturity of both the calls and puts are the same.

Given these assumptions, we examine how to synthesize the assets that give rise to the six basic positions. We use the example of Maybank stock, and call and put options written on Maybank stock.

10.1.1 A Synthetic Long Stock Position

Using call and put options, a synthetic long stock position can be created by going long a call option and shorting a put option of the same exercise price. Suppose if the 30-day RM 12 call and put on Maybank stock are priced at RM 0.20 and RM 0.15, respectively, then the strategy and payoff are as shown in Figure 10.1.

Strategy: (to replicate long stock position)
- Long RM 12, Maybank call @ RM 0.20
- Short RM 12, Maybank put @ RM 0.15

Notice that the payoff to the combined option position at maturity is exactly that of a long stock position. The price at which the long stock position is established is RM 12.05. This is the exercise price plus the net premium. (Note that whether the call bought is exercised or put sold is assigned, we need to pay RM 12 at exercise.) Thus, the above option strategy replicated the cash flow/payoffs to a long position in Maybank stock at RM 12.05. If one buys Maybank stock today at RM 12.05 and holds it for 30 days, the payoff in 30 days would be

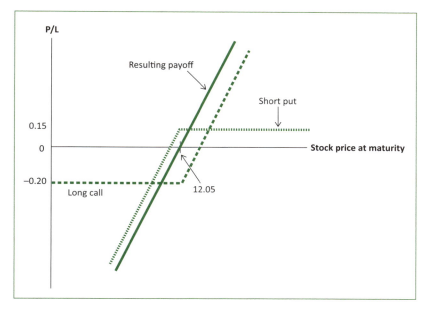

Figure 10.1 Synthetic Long Stock Position

exactly the same as that of the above option strategy. In essence, we had effectively gone long stock without touching the stock. To summarize, given our earlier assumptions:

Long Stock = Long Call + Short Put

10.1.2 A Synthetic Short Stock Position

A synthetic short stock position can be created by taking the opposite position in options as earlier. That is, by going short the call and long the put option. Suppose for the above Maybank stock options, we now do the following:

Strategy (to replicate short stock position)
- Short RM 12, Maybank call @ RM 0.20
- Long RM 12, Maybank put @ RM 0.15

Figure 10.2 shows the payoff to these positions.

The payoff to the combined option position at maturity is exactly that of a short position in Maybank stock at RM 12.05. Again, this effective price equals the exercise price plus net premium (RM 12 + 0.20 − 0.15). An investor who goes short Maybank stock at RM 12.05 will experience the same payoff as an investor who takes the above position in RM 12, 30-day Maybank call and put options. Thus, regulation preventing short selling of stock such as that existing in Malaysia currently would be meaningless when stock options are traded.

Short Stock = Long Put + Short Call

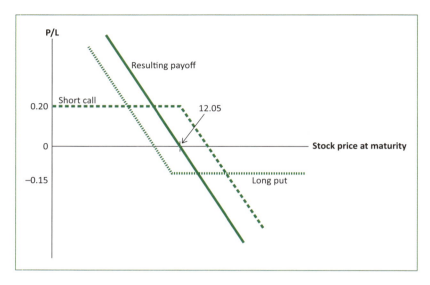

Figure 10.2   Synthetic Short Stock Position

10.1.3 A Synthetic Long Call Position

We saw in the earlier two examples how one could synthesize a position in the underlying asset by way of options. We now turn to synthesizing each of the basic four option positions: long call, short call, long put, and short put. The synthetic option position can be created by combining a position in the underlying stock/asset with an option position. Continuing with the example of Maybank stock and options, a synthetic long call position can be created by going long the stock and going long an at-the-money put option.

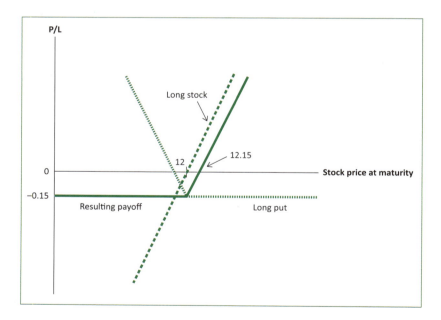

Figure 10.3   Synthetic Long Call Position

Strategy (to replicate a long call position)
- Long Maybank stock @ RM 12
- Long RM 12, Maybank put @ RM 0.15

The payoff to this combined position is shown in Figure 10.3.

The combined payoff has a limited downside, unlimited upside potential and breaks-even at RM 12.15 (RM 12 + RM 0.15). This is exactly the payoff one would have gotten by going long a 30-day RM 12 call option on Maybank stock at 15 sen premium. You should also recall that this **payoff profile** resembles that of the portfolio insurance strategy we saw in Chapter 8.

Long Call = Long Stock + Long Put

10.1.4 A Synthetic Short Call Position

A synthetic short call position can be established by taking the opposite of the above position. The short call is established by going short a stock and an at-the-money put.

Strategy (to replicate a short call position)
- Short Maybank stock @ RM 12
- Short RM 12 Maybank put @ RM 0.15

The payoff to this combined position is shown in Figure 10.4.

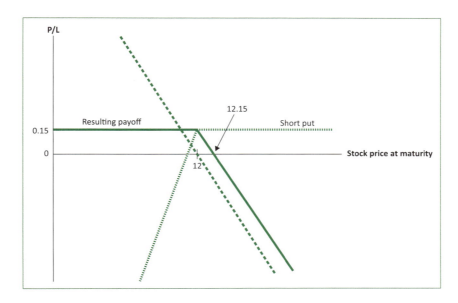

Figure 10.4   Synthetic Short Call Position

As the diagram shows, the short stock and short put position have a combined payoff equivalent to that of a short call. In effect, short an RM 12 call @ RM 0.15.

Short Call = Short Stock + Short Put

10.1.5 A Synthetic Long Put Position

A synthetic long put position is created by going long a call option and shorting the underlying stock. Recall that a long put position is intended to gain from falling underlying asset prices while simultaneously limiting the downside should prices rise instead.

Strategy (to replicate long put position)
- Short Maybank stock @ RM 12
- Long RM 12, Maybank call @ RM 0.20

Figure 10.5 shows the payoff to the resulting position.

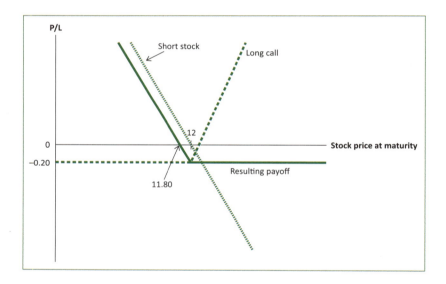

Figure 10.5   Synthetic Long Put Position

The resulting position has a payoff profile exactly that of a long put. In effect, by combining the RM 12 call and shorting the stock, we have created a long RM 12 put @ RM 0.20.

Long Put = Short Stock + Long Call

10.1.6 A Synthetic Short Put Position

A synthetic short put position is created by going long the underlying stock and going short the call option on the stock. The short put position is a neutral to bullish strategy that aims to profit from either stagnant underlying stock price or a marginal up movement.

Strategy (to replicate short put position)
- Long Maybank stock @ RM 12
- Short RM 12, Maybank call @ RM 0.20

The payoff to the resulting position is shown in Figure 10.6.

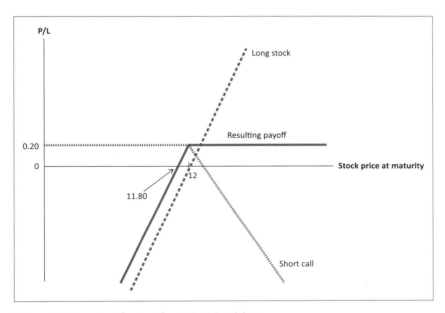

Figure 10.6   Synthetic Short Put Position

The resulting payoff has a payoff profile exactly that of an RM 12 put sold at 20 sen premium.

$$\textbf{\textit{Short Put = Long Stock + Short Call}}$$

The synthetic strategies outlined thus far are summarized in Table 10.1. The lower panel of Table 10.1 outlines the same relationship in algebraic form.

In algebraic versions of the relationships, a minus sign before the item means a short position in that item, otherwise a long position is assumed.

Figures 10.1 to 10.6 and Table 10.1 describe the synthetic strategies strictly from the viewpoint of **cash-flow equivalence**. In essence, the various synthetic strategies replicated the cash flows of the asset being synthesized. Equation (i) in Table 10.1 is often referred to as the **put–call parity**:

Note
Given the assumptions of the put–call parity, a long call and short put position have a cash-flow profile that is equivalent to that of a long position in the underlying stock.

$$S = C + -P$$

Table 10.1 Replicating Strategy and Resulting Synthetics

Replicating Strategy	Resulting Synthetic
(i) Buy call and sell put	Long stock
(ii) Sell call and buy put	Short stock
(iii) Buy put and buy stock	Long call
(iv) Sell put and short stock	Short call
(v) Buy call and short stock	Long put
(vi) Sell call and buy stock	Short put
(i) $S = C + -P$	
(ii) $-S = P + -C$	
(iii) $C = S + P$	
(iv) $-C = -S + -P$	
(v) $P = C + -S$	
(vi) $-P = -C + S$	

Note: The relationships assume the options to have the same underlying asset, maturity, and exercise price.

In essence, the equation states that a long stock position is equivalent to a long call and short put position.

Although the abovementioned six relationships are correct from a cash-flow equivalence point of view, keep in mind that we had ignored interest rates and the time difference in outlays. In the following section, we examine these relationships from a pricing equivalence viewpoint.

10.2 Put–Call Parity and Arbitrage

The put–call parity describes an equilibrium pricing relationship between calls and puts written on the same underlying asset, of the same maturity and exercise price. Here, we examine the equilibrium relationships from a pricing viewpoint. The connection between our earlier discussion of the relationships from a cash-flow equivalence viewpoint to the current pricing equivalence viewpoint can be described as follows: if a synthetic strategy produces a cash flow equivalent to that of the replicated asset, it follows that there must be a pricing equilibrium between the two. The put–call parity describes this pricing equilibrium, while equation (i) from Table 10.1 is a version of the put–call parity:

$$S = C + -P$$

Keep in mind this version ignores interest rates and the timing difference in cash outlays. For example, the above equation states that a long stock position is equivalent to the combination of a long call and short put position. Although this is indeed true from cash-flow equivalence as we saw in Figure 10.1, it ignores the fact that a long stock position will require an immediate cash outlay to purchase the stock. On the other hand, for the option positions, the cash outlay occurs only when one of the options is exercised at maturity. In our earlier example of Maybank stock and 30-day, at-the-money options, there will be a 30-day time difference between the long stock position and the equivalent option positions. Ignoring interest rates meant that this time difference did not matter. However, bringing interest rates into the picture, the present values (PV) of the two cash flows are not really equivalent. Thus, the earlier put–call parity can be rewritten as follows:

> **Note**
> The put–call parity describes a pricing equivalence/equilibrium that should hold between the underlying stock and options written on the stock.
> The risk-free interest rate plays a role in this equilibrium by adjusting for the time difference until option maturity.

$$S - PV \text{ of Exercise Price} = C + -P \quad (1)$$

or

$$S - K(1+r)^{-t} = C + -P \quad (2)$$

where

S = stock price (price of establishing long stock position)
r = annualized interest rate
K = exercise price of the options
t = days to maturity of option
C = call premium (cost of establishing long call position)
$-P$ = put premium (cost/amount received from establishing short put position)

There is an important implication of the earlier put–call parity. It implies that any deviation from the earlier relationship constitutes relative mispricing and would give rise to an arbitrage opportunity. The presence of arbitrage would therefore ensure that the put–call parity holds.

If $S - K(1+r)^{-t} \geq C + -P^{-t}$, then a riskless arbitrage profit can be made by taking advantage of the mispricing.

10.2.1 Put–Call Parity and Arbitrage: Illustration

To prove that a violation of the put–call parity will lead to pure arbitrage, we work through the following numerical example. Suppose Malaysian Oxygen Bhd. (MOX) has a current stock price of RM 11. RM 10 call and put options on the stock with 90 days to maturity are quoted at RM 1.77 for the call and RM 1 for the put. Assume the annualized risk-free interest rate is 10%. To see whether there is mispricing, we check the put–call parity using the earlier equation (2).

$$S - K(1+r)^{-t} \geq C + -P^{-t}$$

Using the inputs of the example, we get
RM 11 − RM 10(1.10)$^{-0.25}$ = RM 1.77 − RM 1
    RM 11 − RM 9.76 = RM 0.77
RM 1.24 > RM 0.77

Clearly, the put–call parity is violated. There is a mispricing differential of RM 0.47 (RM 1.24 − RM 0.77) or RM 470 of arbitrage profits to be made per lot/contract. But how should we arbitrage? Looking at the disparity, we note that the left side of the equation is greater than the right side (RM 1.24 versus RM 0.77). To take advantage, we sell/short the left side (lhs) of equation (2) and long the right side (rhs). In other words, we take the position as outlined in the rhs and take the **opposite** of the position outlined in the lhs. Going by this, our **arbitrage strategy** is therefore:

- Short stock
- Lend an amount equal to PV of exercise price
- Long call
- Short put

To prove that this strategy is riskless, we examine the cash flow today and under two stock price scenarios at option maturity. One scenario where MOX stock price goes higher to RM 15 and another where MOX stock price falls to RM 7 at option maturity.

Strategy	CF$_0$ (Today)	At Maturity MOX = RM 15 CF$_{90}$	At Maturity MOX = RM 7 CF$_{90}$
• Short MOX stock	RM 11	(RM 15)	(RM 7)
• Lend PV of exercise	(RM 9.76)	RM 10	RM 10
• Long call option	(RM 1.77)	RM 5[a]	0
• Short put option	RM 1	0	(RM 3)[b]
Net cash flow	RM 0.47	0	0

[a] Call is exercised for a profit of RM 5 (RM 15 − RM 10).
[b] Put sold is assigned, resulting in loss of RM 3 (RM 7 − RM 10). Amount in brackets signifies cash outflow.

Notice that a riskless profit of RM 0.47 per stock or RM 470 (RM 0.47 × 1,000 shares) per lot can be made. The strategy is riskless since the net cash flows at maturity is zero. That the above strategy is riskless, can also be shown by means of a diagram as in Figure 10.7.

The resulting payoff is a horizontal line at RM 0.47, meaning a profit of RM 0.47 regardless of what the underlying stock price is at maturity. It should be noted here that the figure really shows a **reverse conversion** strategy. Recall that we had seen the **conversion strategy** in Chapter 8. It was pointed out then that the conversion and reverse conversion are really arbitrage strategies. If there is no mispricing, then the resulting payoff to these strategies would be a horizontal line at zero, as we saw in Chapter 8.

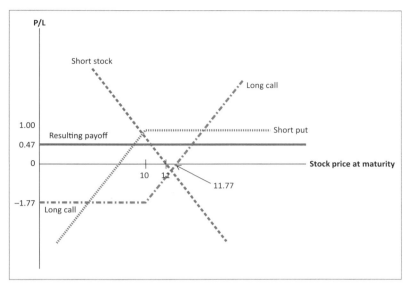

Figure 10.7   Arbitrage: Reverse Conversion

Yet another way to understand why the resulting payoff is a fixed amount, and how the strategy is riskless, is to view it in the context of replication. Note that there are a total of four steps in the arbitrage strategy. One of the four, lending the PV of exercise price has a fixed return of RM 0.24 (RM 10 − RM 9.76) and is independent of underlying stock price at maturity. It is not even shown in the earlier payoff simply to avoid clutter. If shown, it would be a horizontal line at 24 sen below the horizontal overall payoff line which is at 47 sen. When viewed from the replication viewpoint, the remaining three steps essentially offset one another leaving a net profit of 47 sen. Note that the two option positions, long call and short put together, replicate a long stock position. Thus, with the short stock position and the replicated long stock position there is effectively no net exposure in stocks — thus the strategy is riskless from a stock price risk viewpoint.

Note
The conversion and reverse conversion are strategies that can be used to arbitrage violations of the put–call parity.

The 47 sen profit can be explained as follows. In **replicating** the long stock position at an exercise of RM 10, we are buying the stock at RM 10. However, that stock had been shorted (sold) for RM 11 earlier, giving an RM 1.00 profit on exercise. Adjusting this for the difference in option premiums and interest earned on lending, we get:

- Proceeds from short stock   = RM 11
- Purchase price of stock on exercise   = (RM 10)
- Premium paid for call option   = (RM 1.77)
- Premium received for put option   = RM 1
- Interest earned on lending   = RM 0.24

                        Arbitrage profit = RM 0.47

10.2.2 Mispricing and Arbitrage: Another Illustration

In the previous example, mispricing occurred since the difference in option premiums (rhs of put–call parity equation) was lower than the difference between current stock price and PV of exercise price. The resulting arbitrage strategy used to take advantage of the mispricing was reverse conversion. We now use the same numerical example but at another form of mispricing. Suppose, now the put option has a premium of say 33 sen instead of RM 1 earlier. The put–call parity equation would now be:

$S - K(1 + r)^{-t} \quad = C + -P$
RM 11 − RM 9.76 = RM 1.77 − RM 0.33
RM 1.24 $\quad$ < RM 1.44

Since the option premium differential is greater than the stock minus PV of exercise price differential, we do the opposite of what we did earlier. Now, we go long the left side position and short the right side position. The arbitrage strategy is as follows:

- Long stock
- Borrow an amount equal to PV of exercise price
- Short call
- Long put

Note that these are exactly the opposite of our earlier arbitrage strategy. If earlier we used the reverse conversion, the appropriate arbitrage strategy here is the conversion strategy. To prove that this would be riskless yet provide a pure arbitrage profit, we work through the cash flows, again assuming MOX stock at maturity is either higher at RM 15 or lower at RM 7.

Strategy	CF_0 (today)	At Maturity	
		MOX = RM 15 CF_{90}	MOX = RM 7 CF_{90}
• Long stock	(RM 11)	RM 15	RM 7
• Borrow PV of exercise price	RM 9.76	(RM 10)	(RM 10)
• Short call option	RM 1.77	(RM 5)[a]	0
• Long put option	(RM 0.33)	0	RM 3[b]
Net cash flow	RM 0.20	0	0

[a]Call sold is assigned, resulting in a loss of RM 5.
[b]Put bought can be exercised to profit RM 3 (RM 10 − RM 7).

Note that the strategy enables us to profit 20 sen (per stock) today without any further net cash flows in the future. Since the cash flows at option maturity are netted off regardless of whether the stock price goes higher or lower, the profit we make today is riskless profit. The conversion strategy and its resulting payoff is shown in Figure 10.8.

In the conversion strategy, the short call and long put positions replicate a short stock position. Thus, when combined with a long stock position, the overall position is a horizontal line signifying no net exposure in stocks. The reason the horizontal line is at positive 20 sen and not at zero has to do with the inherent mispricing that enabled the 20 sen arbitrage profit.

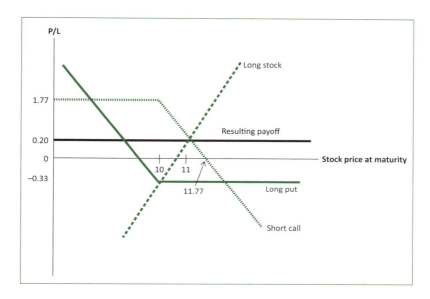

Figure 10.8 Arbitrage: Conversion Strategy

Box 10.1
Capital Flows and Regulatory Arbitrage

Recent events in Australia show the extent to which cross border capital flows can arbitrage regulatory hurdles. It appears that in an effort to rein in a burgeoning housing bubble, the Australian central bank, the Reserve Bank of Australia (RBA) had placed caps on bank lending to real estate developers. The policy, aimed largely at curbing purchases of Australian homes by foreigners through domestic borrowing, had initially been effective. In addition to foreign speculators, domestic housing developers too were hit hard. Such regulation would have essentially taken the wind out of a domestic housing bubble, had it not been for foreign hedge funds and private equity. Given free capital flows, these foreign entities that are really shadow banks stepped in to provide the needed funding, obviously at higher interest rates. At least for now, the foreign lenders appear to be making huge profits from the large interest spreads. Their currency exposure can be

(*Continued*)

Box 10.1
(Continued)

hedged using currency derivatives. For both the foreign lenders and the foreign speculators of Australian property, the ability to side step the regulation appears to be a win–win. The obvious loser is the Australian central bank, the RBA. Not only has its initiative to curb the housing bubble been rendered ineffective, its policy has given rise to profitable regulatory arbitrage. Interest rates on home financing, which were at about 6% prior to the RBA policy, were now being funded at 12%. A highly profitable 6% spread to the foreign capital providers with their currency exposure hedged. Thus, despite the fact that the underlying project risk was in no way any different post regulation, the foreign shadow banks were earning equity-like returns from low-risk home financing.

This episode amply illustrates the limits of regulation and policy-making in a globalized world with free capital flows. For central banks, in particular, domestic monetary policy becomes less effective if not impotent. And it arises from the classic "trilemma" in International finance, which argues that domestic monetary policy independence is not possible in the face of free capital flows and/or fixed exchange rates. Although Australia certainly does not have fixed exchange rates nor was the regulatory change above one of broad monetary policy but a targeted attempt at curbing excesses within a sector, it nevertheless resulted in regulation giving rise to arbitrage opportunity. Arbitrage opportunity arises whenever regulation tries to create artificial barriers. As implied by the "trilemma," an independent rate decision even for a specific sector is not possible with free capital flows. While domestic banks are subject to RBA requirements, foreign hedge funds are not. In the absence of capital controls, there is nothing to prevent them from stepping in to fill a vacuum created by regulation. The RBA may be the most obvious loser but there is more. Domestic banks that could not benefit from the enlarged spreads are losers too. So, too the Australian family looking to purchase a home of their own.

There are important lessons from the Australian episode for policymakers, particularly of emerging economies. The first and obvious lesson is the fact that in the globalized world that we now live in, regulation that seeks to distort or puts up barriers can be arbitraged away. Aside from eroding policy effectiveness, the outcomes may be diametrically opposite to what was intended. Second, policy options may not be as clear cut as they once were. The trade-offs are increasingly complex and their outcomes increasingly uncertain. The third key lesson is that with the advances in information technology, financial borders have become highly porous. Money and capital can be moved across borders in so many ways and with derivatives, the resulting currency exposure can be hedged. Regulation by way of licensing which by creating barriers

Box 10.1
(Continued)

increased the franchise values can now be arbitraged. Entire industries/sectors can be "uberized." Where the profit potential is large and the risks can be hedged using currency derivatives, speculative capital will seek out opportunities. The solution lies not in capital controls that can be hugely distortionary but in smart regulation that takes advantage of, rather than go against the grain of technological changes. Enlightened governments and clever policymakers should be able to see the writing on the wall.

Source: Adapted from the author's op-ed column.

10.2.3 Determining Arbitrage Strategy

We have seen how deviations from the put–call parity can be arbitraged. The deviations from parity imply relative mispricing. In deciding whether the conversion or reverse conversion strategy should be used in a particular situation, we could either use the method earlier of going long the "cheaper" side of the equation or by comparing each of the three traded assets (stock, call, and put) quoted price to the price implied by the put–call parity.

In the original scenario, MOX's stock price was RM 11, call premium = RM 1.77, put premium = RM 1, whereas PV of exercise price was RM 9.76. In determining the parity price of each of the assets, we can rearrange the put–call parity equation as follows:

$$S - K(1+r)^{-t} = C - P \qquad (2)$$

So

$$S = C - P + K(1+r)^{-t} \qquad 2.1$$
$$C = S + P - K(1+r)^{-t} \qquad 2.2$$
$$P = C - S + K(1+r)^{-t} \qquad 2.3$$
$$K(1+r)^{-t} = S + P - C \qquad 2.4$$

Using equations 2.1, 2.2, and 2.3 for the above prices, the parity values are S = RM 10.53, C = RM 2.24, and P = RM 0.53. Comparing these parity values to the quoted values implies that the stock is **overvalued** at the quoted RM 11 price (since it should be RM 10.53 for parity). The call is **undervalued**, whereas the put is **overvalued**. This automatically tells us what the arbitrage strategy should be. Since arbitrage always involves buying (long) the undervalued asset and selling (short) the overvalued asset, the arbitrage strategy here would be short stock, long call and short put. Which is exactly what we did, resulting in reverse conversion. As for the PV of exercise price $[K(1+r)^{-t}]$, whether we should lend or borrow as part of the arbitrage strategy is a residual issue and straight forward. Since it appears in equation 2 together with stock, our decision on whether we long or short the stock as part of arbitrage strategy determines whether we borrow or lend. If we short the stock, we will receive proceeds, which means we should lend. On the other hand, if we are to long (buy) the stock as part of the arbitrage strategy, then we borrow to part finance the stock purchase. The following table summarizes the mispricing.

Asset	Put–Call Parity	Parity Value	Quoted Price	Observation
Stock	$S = C - P + K(1+r)^{-t}$	RM 10.53	RM 11	Overvalued
Call	$C = S + P - K(1+r)^{-t}$	RM 2.24	RM 1.77	Undervalued
Put	$P = C - S + K(1+r)^{-t}$	RM 0.53	RM 1	Overvalued

In the second scenario, where the conversion strategy was used, we kept all prices the same as in the first scenario except to change one price, i.e., the put's quoted price was changed from RM 1 to RM 0.33. Using this set of prices, equations 2.1, 2.2, and 2.3 would show the following. The stock is undervalued (parity price = RM 11.20), call is overvalued (parity price = RM 1.57) and put is undervalued (parity price = RM 0.53). The following table shows the mispricing. This would imply the following steps for arbitrage: long stock, short call, and long put. Since we were long stock, we borrow the PV of exercise price. Recall that these were the exact steps in our arbitrage strategy. Thus the use of equations to determine the appropriate steps can be thought as an alternative and perhaps an easier way to determine the appropriate arbitrage strategy.

Asset	Put–Call Parity	Parity Value	Quoted Price	Observation
Stock	$S = C - P + K(1+r)^{-t}$	RM 11.20	RM 11	Undervalued
Call	$C = S + P - K(1+r)^{-t}$	RM 1.57	RM 1.77	Overvalued
Put	$P = C - S + K(1+r)^{-t}$	RM 0.53	RM 1	Undervalued

10.3 Put–Call Parity, Conversion, and Delta Neutral Trading

The put–call parity describes a pricing equilibrium between the underlying stock and the call and put option on the stock. When the pricing equilibrium does not hold, there is deviation from parity. Such a deviation, as we saw, leads to arbitrage opportunity. The strategy used to arbitrage such mispricing is the conversion or reverse conversion strategy as the case may be.

Although it is clear from Figures 10.7 and 10.8 that the reverse conversion and conversion strategies have payoffs that crossmatch and therefore net-off each other at option expiration, one may wonder whether the position is as riskless **prior** to option maturity. The answer is yes! The conversion and reverse conversion are known as **delta-neutral** strategies. A delta-neutral strategy is essentially a trading strategy that has an overall delta of zero for the whole position. Delta, as we saw in Chapter 9, determines the rate of change in option value for a given change in the underlying stock value. The delta of a long stock position in one underlying stock equals +1.0, that of a short stock position is −1.0. Recall from Chapter 9 that given the same underlying, maturity, and exercise price:

Call delta − Put delta = 1.0

It is easy to see how the conversion or reverse conversion is delta-neutral. In the conversion strategy, we go long the underlying stock while the option positions replicate a short stock position. Thus, the net delta = 0. Similarly, in a reverse conversion, we short the underlying stock while the option positions replicate a long stock position. The net position once again has a delta = 0 since the −1.0 delta of the short stock position is equally offset by +1.0 delta of the replicated long stock position.

As long as the underlying stock does not experience huge jumps, the delta-neutral position is considered riskless. Delta as we know is only applicable to small constant changes in price. Most option traders who perceive a mispriced option use such delta-neutral strategies to make arbitrage profits. This being safer than a one way bet of going long a perceived underpriced call, for example.

Note
The conversion and reverse conversion are delta-neutral trading strategies. Thus, ordinary changes in the underlying stock price will be equally offset by changes in the option positions, such that the overall value of strategy is unchanged.

Box 10.2
The Limits to Arbitrage

Although seamless arbitrage is possible in highly efficient markets, the reality is that there are limits to arbitrage. Long-Term Capital Management (LTCM), a US-based hedge fund, which was described in Box 8.1, was, in many ways, a victim of the limits of arbitrage. LTCM's arbitrage strategy was to short US treasuries (T-bills) and long Russian Government Bonds. The hedge fund was essentially betting that there will be a convergence in the spread between these two assets to traditional levels. That is, it was hoping that the Russian government bonds that were "undervalued" relative to US treasuries would rise in value such that the traditional spread between the two assets will prevail.

This bet however went sour when the Russian government, faced with a capital flight declared a moratorium on its debt — in essence, defaulting on its bonds. The spread that LTCM was hoping would converge widened instead. What made the situation untenable for LTCM was the huge amount of leverage that the hedge fund had used

(*Continued*)

> **Box 10.2**
> (Continued)
>
> to finance its various positions. As losses mounted on its Russian bonds position, it was faced with margin calls. To meet the margin calls, LTCM had to unwind its position, i.e., sell the Russian bonds it had gone long. To its horror, LTCM found that it could not find buyers for Russian bonds even at the sharply lower prices.
>
> Meanwhile, the US treasuries that it shorted had gone up in value, largely due to the flight to quality. This again triggered margin calls. Faced with this double jeopardy and a lack cash to stay afloat, the fund went under. When the dust settled and things went back to normal some months later, the convergence that had eluded LTCM did happen. LTCM simply did not have the liquidity to tide over the difficult period, vindicating Keynes famous saying that "markets can remain irrational for longer than one can remain liquid."
>
> Obviously, the "arbitrage" that LTCM had undertaken is not risk-free and not comparable to the arbitrage induced by violations in put–call parity. However, even in pure arbitrage situations, there are limits. Position limits and margin requirements may curtail the size of the arbitrage transaction. In addition, there are a number of risks that go with arbitrage opportunity. These are risks such as execution risks, regulatory risks, noise trader risk and other market idiosyncrasies. All of which limit the extent to which arbitrage positions can be established. Finally, there are transaction costs, bid-ask spreads and market impact costs that drive a wedge between theoretical and arbitrageable prices, thereby creating the no-arbitrage bounds described in Chapter 4.
>
> It is precisely due to these limitations to arbitrage that one sees mispricing even in efficient markets.

10.4 Put–Call Parity — Empirical Evidence

Although the put–call parity is a logical relationship that should always hold, deviations do occur. Empirical work has found that in most cases the deviations were the result of several institutional factors. In testing for put–call parity, one should therefore be careful to include factors such as bid-ask spreads and broker's commissions. In addition, deviations from parity may also be the result of regulations. For example, the short selling regulation in many countries prohibits the short selling of stocks. Often times, deviations from put–call parity may also be the result of nonsynchronous trading. Thus, using day-end close prices may show deviations, whereas intraday data may not. Finally, in establishing an arbitrage position to take the advantage of deviations from put–call parity, one should keep in mind the possibility of execution risk, especially in thin/illiquid derivative markets such as Malaysia.

SUMMARY

This chapter examined the use of options in replication, synthesizing, and arbitrage. These constitute yet another advantage of options arising from their inherent flexibility. By being able to replicate the cash flows of another asset, we are effectively able to synthesize the security. By replicating an asset, one is able to achieve cash-flow equivalence between the actual security and the synthetic option position. This cash-flow equivalence occurs at option maturity. The fact that there is cash-flow equivalence between assets implies that pricing equivalence or a pricing equilibrium must hold between the assets.

The first part of the chapter examined the basics of synthesizing and cash-flow equivalence. The six basic stock and option positions were replicated and the payoff equivalence were seen. The second part of the chapter examined the put–call parity and arbitrage. The put–call parity describes the pricing equivalence or pricing equilibrium between asset combinations. Violations to the put–call parity imply mispricing and pure arbitrage opportunity. The conversion and reverse conversion are the arbitrage strategies used where violations of the put–call parity occur. In a conversion strategy, we arbitrage by going long the "relatively underpriced" stock and use the options to synthesize a short stock position. The opposite is done in a reverse conversion. The profit earned from such mispricing is riskless since the cash flows offset one another. The appropriate arbitrage strategy can be determined by rearranging the put–call parity equation to value the stock and options and then comparing the computed values to actual quotes. The undervalued asset(s) are bought, whereas the overvalued one(s) shorted. The conversion and reverse conversion are delta-neutral strategies. A delta-neutral strategy is one that has an overall position delta that equals zero. As long as the underlying stock does not take big jumps, a delta-neutral strategy is riskless. Empirical evidence shows that deviations from put–call parity do exist, due mostly to institutional factors.

KEY TERMS

- Replication
- Payoff profile
- Put–call parity
- Synthetics
- Replicating strategy
- Arbitrage strategy
- Arbitrage
- Resulting synthetic
- Delta-neutral
- Cash-flow equivalence
- Conversion
- Call delta
- Pricing equivalence
- Reverse conversion
- Put delta

End-of-Chapter Questions

1. a. What is the put–call parity? What ensures that the parity will/should hold?
    b. Outline the circumstances under which one would use a conversion strategy as opposed to a reverse conversion.
    c. Differentiate between cash-flow equivalence and pricing equivalence.

2. You own five lots (each lot is 1,000 shares) of ABC Corp. stock currently selling at RM 5.25. The following options are available:
    - RM 4.50 call @ RM 0.85
    - RM 4.50 put @ RM 0.10

    Assume the RM 4.50 call has a delta of 0.80.

    State how you would hedge your stock portfolio. How many of the options would you use?

3. An investor who is currently long MAKRO Bhd. stocks, goes long an RM 8 put and shorts a RM 8 call on the stock. The stock is currently priced at RM 8. Assuming the call and put premiums are equal,
    a. Graph the strategy and show the overall position.
    b. What is the risk profile of the strategy?
    c. What is the objective of this strategy?

    What is the delta of the overall position (show proof)?

4. You are currently long an RM 6 call with a delta of 0.60. Suppose you then short an RM 6 put of the same maturity.
    (i) State and graph the overall position.
    (ii) What is the delta of the overall position?

5. A trader who is long THB 12 million of Thai stocks goes long call options on SET 50 Index and short the equivalent puts (both the calls and puts are at-the-money).
    (i) Can this be considered a hedge position?
    (ii) What must his expectation of the underlying market be?
    (iii) What is likely to happen if the market moves down?
    (iv) What is the delta of the option positions taken together?

6. Higher volatility of the underlying asset's price increases the value of an option. Yet, higher volatility means that underlying asset price could fall further. Using a long call position, clarify the paradox.

7. a. Suppose a European put option has a price higher than that dictated by the put–call parity.
        (i) Outline the appropriate arbitrage strategy.
        (ii) Graphically prove that the arbitrage is riskless.
    b. (i) Name the option/stock strategy used to proof the put–call parity.
       (ii) What would the extent of your profit in (a) depend on?

8. You subscribe to a data service that also provides historical standard deviations of stock prices. You note that the implied volatility of an at-the-money call option is much higher than the estimate of historical standard deviation.
    a. What does the disparity mean?

b. Describe how you would take advantage of the disparity above. (Be specific about the positions and the approximate number of options.)

9. Telekom Bhd. shares are currently at RM 15. Three-month call and put options with RM 15 exercise price are being quoted at RM 0.75 and RM 0.19, respectively. The rf rate is 12% per year.
   (i) Using put–call parity, prove that there is mispricing.
   (ii) Identify the security that is mispriced relative to the others.
   (iii) Outline the arbitrage strategy and show the arbitrage assuming you invested in one lot/contract.
   (iv) Graph the overall position.

10. You notice the following quotes for the SET 50 and the index options.
    - SET 50 = 840 points
    - 850 call = 8 points
    - 850 put = 3 points

    Assume you can long/short the spot index, the risk-free rate of 6% per year and 90-day maturity for the options.
    (i) Determine using the put–call parity, the nature of mispricing.
    (ii) Outline the arbitrage strategy and determine the arbitrage profit if you transacted in one contract equivalent.
    (iii) Graph your arbitrage strategy and the overall position.
    (iv) Show that your arbitrage strategy is indeed riskless.

11. You are a fund manager with MC Asset Management. It is now end-September and your current portfolio value is RM 7 million. You have done very well this year, having attained a 30% return thus far. However, you are worried about impending market volatility and wish to fully hedge your position over the next 3 months so as to ensure no erosion in your returns for the year. You have the following information:
    - rf = 6% per year
    - Portfolio beta = 1.0
    - Expected dividends = 0
    - FBM KLCI spot = 700 points
    - FBM KLCI 3-month futures = 710.27 (maturing December)

    FBM KLCI 90-day options
    - 680 December, put @ 2 points
    - 700 December, put @ 8 points
    - 720 December, put @ 22 points

    Assuming the FBM KLCI is at 630 points at end December (i.e., 90 days later).
    a. Show how you could have hedged using index futures and the value of the portfolio at end December (graph the strategy).
    b. Show how you could have hedged using options and the resulting portfolio value at end December. What is the cost of the strategy in Ringgit? Graph the strategy.

12. a. Refer to your response to Question 11. What are two advantages of using index futures instead of options? What are two disadvantages?
    b. Nikkei Stock Index futures contracts are traded contemporaneously in both the Singapore International Monetary Exchange (SIMEX) and Osaka Exchange, Inc. (OSE). Suppose you observe the following quotes, state whether arbitrage is possible and if so outline the strategy. What is the name of this strategy?

	SIMEX	OSE
December 99 Nikkei futures:	16,100.8	16,101.00
March 00 Nikkei futures:	16,240	16,248.8

13. On July 1, 1998, your company went long a *forward* contract with Citibank, KL, to purchase 30 million Japanese Yen on March 30, 1999. Then on September 1, 1998, your company shorted ¥en 30 million worth of *futures* contracts on SIMEX maturing on March 30, 1999. Assuming the exchange rate on both contracts are the same, graph each position and show the overall position.

14. A stock is selling at RM 6.10. An RM 6 call on the stock has a delta of 0.4. Suppose you want to synthesize the stock at RM 6 (long stock), outline the strategy.

15. You are in charge of risk management at an International Asset Management Company. Your company has exposure to Malaysian stocks. The following data has been provided.
    - Value of Malaysian portfolio = RM 15 million
    - Beta of Malaysian portfolio = 1.00
    - FBM KLCI current level = 1515 points
    - FBM KLCI 90-day, 1500 call @ 18 points; delta = 0.55
    - FBM KLCI 90-day, 1500 put @ 7 points; delta = 0.45

    a. Suppose, your company will hold the Malaysian position for at least the next 90 days, outline the strategy to fully hedge the position.
    b. If your company might unload all Malaysian stocks prior to the 90-day period, outline the hedge strategy.

16. Suppose, you notice a violation in an option price given the Black–Scholes option pricing model.
    a. Is arbitrage always possible? What might you want to re-examine before deciding to arbitrage?
    b. How would you arbitrage if a call option is overpriced?
    c. How would you arbitrage if the call is underpriced?
    d. How would you arbitrage if a put option were overpriced?

17. Maybank stock is currently selling at RM 10.80. The 3-month RM 10 call and put options on the stock are being quoted RM 1.50 and RM 0.90, respectively. Assume the *rf* rate is 10% per annum.
    (i) Prove that there is mispricing.
    (ii) Outline the arbitrage strategy and show the profit assuming the positions are for one contract or equivalent.
    (iii) Prove either mathematically or graphically, that your arbitrage position in (ii) has no net exposure.

18. a. RM 20 calls and puts on Nestle stock of 90-day maturity are available. Yesterday, you bought an RM 20 call on Nestle stock at RM 1.55. The stock price was RM 19.60. Today, the price has risen to RM 20. Assuming an *rf* rate of 8% and a standard deviation of 40%, determine the percentage return on your investment in the call option since yesterday.
    b. How does the % returns in (a) above compare with the % returns you would have gotten if you invested in the underlying stock? Briefly explain the difference.
    c. How would the call delta you computed in (a) compare with the call delta yesterday? Would it be higher or lower? Explain why.
    d. Your friend has 10 lots of Nestle stock (each lot = 1,000 shares) which he wants to hedge. Outline an appropriate hedge strategy using options. Determine the number of options that he should use.

19. Relative to its at-the-money options, a stock is overpriced according to the put–call parity.
    a. Outline the appropriate arbitrage strategy.
    b. Prove graphically that your arbitrage is riskless.
    c. Name the arbitrage strategy you have proposed.
    d. Show the overall payoff to your strategy.
    e. What are the underlying assumptions of the put-call parity condition?

20. As someone is always on the lookout for arbitrage opportunity, you notice the following price quotes:
    - MPI stock price = RM 18.50
    - 90-day MPI, RM 18 call = RM 1.02
    - 90-day MPI, RM 18 put = RM 0.60

    Assume that the risk-free rate is 8% annualized.
    a. Prove that arbitrage is possible.
    b. Outline your arbitrage strategy and show the profit made per contract (or equivalent).
    c. By means of a graph, prove that your strategy in (b) entails zero risk.

21. As the local fund manager for Tokyo Mutual, you have just watched the FBM KLCI break the 1,800 point level. Your screen shows the index level at 1,800.60 points. Your ebullience however is shattered by an instruction from Tokyo to fully hedge your entire portfolio. Your portfolio is currently worth RM 16 million.
    a. Assuming the 3-month FBM KLCI futures is being quoted at 816.61 points and your portfolio beta is 1.20, outline the appropriate hedge strategy using SIF contracts *(be specific, tenor, no. of contracts, etc.)*
    b. The 90-day, 1,800 point index call option has a delta of 0.5012. Outline the appropriate hedge strategy if options were used instead.
    c. Assuming the 90-day, 1,800 point index calls and puts are priced at 20 points and 11 points, respectively, determine the value of the hedged portfolio if in 90 days the index is at 1,818 points.
    d. Looking at the price quotes from the 90-day 1,800 point index calls and puts, what can you conclude about the overall market expectation for the next 90 days?

e. Separately, graph the hedge strategy in (a) using SIF contracts, and (b) in using options. Show the overall payoff.
f. Given you payoff diagrams in (e) above, which is the superior hedge strategy? Why?

22. You have just determined that a stock is overvalued relative to its at-the-money, call and put options.
   (i) Outline the appropriate arbitrage strategy.
   (ii) Graph your arbitrage strategy (carefully label all payoffs and axes.)
   (iii) Briefly explain why your strategy is riskless.
   (iv) State two factors that will determine the size of your arbitrage profit in this case.

23. Using a (+) to signify a positive impact, (−) for negative, and (0) for no impact, determine the impact of the following:

    An increase in interest rate on:
    - Long 3-month KLIBOR futures   _____
    - Long stock position   _____
    - Long call on stock   _____
    - Long put on stocks   _____
    - Long bond portfolio   _____

    An increase in dividends on:
    - Short stock position   _____
    - Long call on the stock   _____
    - Long put on the stock   _____
    - Long SIF position   _____

24. Outline the appropriate derivative strategy for each of the following (carefully state the contract that should be used, maturity and number of contracts where necessary):
   (i) Vesawit Bhd, a producer of palm oil-based cooking oil would have to replenish its inventory of CPO in 3 months. It normally purchases about 250 tones every 3 months.
   (ii) A speculator expects interest rates to rise over the next 3 months.
   (iii) A trader has just been quoted 95.3 points for the 3-month KLIBOR futures contract. Using implied forward rate (IFR), he has just determined that the correct quote should be 94.80.
   (iv) Currency futures and options are available on Korean Won. A Thai importer has just received a shipment of refrigerators from LG of South Korea. The invoice amount is 30 million Won, payable in 90 days.
   (v) A speculator is bullish about the Thai stock market and the SET 50 Index. However, he wants to establish a position that will limit his risk.
   (vi) A specialty chemical firm has just received 200 kg of pure silver. It will use the silver over the next 6 months. The company is worried that silver prices may come down. Its output price varies with the spot price of silver. Both options and futures contracts are available on silver at a contract size of 20 kg per contract.

CHAPTER · 11

Options in Corporate Finance and Real Options

Objectives

This chapter is designed to provide an options perspective to commonly used corporate financing methods such as debt. The motivational issues of capital structure and an examination of corporate finance instruments with option-like features are examined. The concept of real options and their increasing importance is analyzed. The chapter also provides a brief overview of exotic options and hybrid instruments such as irredeemable convertible unsecured loan stock (ICULS).

Introduction

In this chapter, we examine the issues and securities used in corporate finance from the perspective of options. Corporate financing modes such as debt and equity have payoff structures resembling those of options. The instruments used in raising debt securities such as bonds, warrants, etc., have option-like features. Thus, analyzing these instruments provides an interesting new perspective of their valuation and function. Such an analysis also throws new light on some of the behavioral and motivational issues of corporate finance.

The chapter is divided into three broad parts. The first part examines debt, equity, and issues related to capital structure from the options viewpoint. Securities with option-like features, instruments such as callable bonds, convertible bonds, **warrants**, etc., are also examined. The concept of **real options** and their use is examined in the second part. The third part of the chapter is devoted to an overview of exotic options. Instruments such as barrier options, Asian options, and other exotic options are described briefly.

11.1 Levered Equity: An Options Approach

Debt and equity financing are probably the two most common forms by which businesses finance themselves. Equity, as we know, represents ownership, whereas debt represents a financial obligation. For the purpose of our discussion that follows, it is important to keep in mind that **equity is perpetual and residual in claim**, whereas **debt is terminal and "fixed" in claim**. Equity has no maturity, thus it is perpetual. An equity holder has a claim on all assets owned by the company and is usually the last in line in the event of a liquidation of the firm, thus equity is residual in claim. Debt, however, has a predetermined maturity and has a claim fixed (equal) to the principal and accrued interest. Companies raise equity financing by issuing shares or common stock, whereas debt is raised typically through direct borrowing or through the issue of bonds.

A position in equity is essentially a position in a company stock. In previous chapters, we have seen the payoff to a long and short positions in stock. A sole proprietor who owns all the equity of an entirely equity financed company would face a payoff profile equivalent to that of a long stock position. However, what if the company adds debt to its capital structure? What is equity payoff when combined with debt? What is the potential payoff to the debt holders who lend to the company? We examine these two issues by working through the following simple example.

11.1.1 Payoff to Levered Equity

Assume a firm currently has RM 200,000 of equity. All of the firm's equity is owned by a single shareholder who is also the manager. The firm is now considering an investment in a new project. The investment needed for the project is RM 1,000,000. For simplicity, assume that the investment has a 1 year life, at the end of which the outcome is known and all financing partners get their respective returns. The equity holder seeks and receives RM 800,000 of debt financing at a 10% annual interest rate. The equity is now **levered equity**, what is its payoff?

Total value of firm = Value of equity + Value of debt
RM 1,000,000 = RM 200,000 + RM 800,000

The value of equity will depend on what the total firm value is at year end. Table 11.1 shows the payoff to the equity holder as total firm value changes.

Table 11.1 Firm Value and Payoff to Equity

Firm Value (RM)	Value of Equity (RM)
650,000	0
700,000	0
750,000	0
800,000	0
880,000	0
900,000	20,000
950,000	70,000
1,000,000	120,000
1,100,000	220,000
1,200,000	320,000

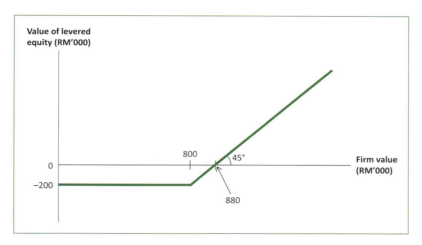

Figure 11.1 Payoff to Levered Equity

Notice that the equity holder losses all his equity for any firm value equal or below RM 880,000. This amount is essentially the "break- even point." It equals the principal of RM 800,000 plus the accrued 10% interest of RM 80,000 for the year. It is only when the firm value is above RM 880,000 that the equity holder gets anything for his original RM 200,000 investment in equity. His returns, however, get progressively higher as firm value gets higher beyond RM 880,000. Figure 11.1 plots the payoff shown in Table 11.1.

Since the value of levered equity is firm value less RM 880,000, **every RM 1** increase in firm value beyond that amount constitutes a RM 1 increase in the value of equity. This has to do with the fact that equity is residual in claim. On the other hand, the equity holder losses **all** his equity if firm value is less than RM 880,000. This is essentially the payoff to a long call position. Thus, **levered equity is really a call option on the firm**. It is essentially a European call option (since the outcome is only known at year end) with the following features.

Maturity = 1 year
Exercise price = RM 880,000
S_o (Asset value) = RM 1,000,000

If we knew the standard deviation of the project and the risk-free interest rate, the value of this option can be determined using the Black–Scholes option pricing model (BSOPM) as follows:

$$C = V_A \cdot N(d_1) - Ke^{-rt} N(d_2)$$

where

V_A = value of assets
K = repayable debt value

The implication of all of this is that, upon receipt of the loan, the equity holder will have RM 200,000 of equity and a call option on the firm. At loan "maturity," the equity holder can decide whether to "exercise" his call option by paying the loan and taking possession of the firm or not exercising by letting the debt holders take over the firm. The exercise price (loan repayment amount) has to be lower than the value of the firm for the equity holder to want to exercise by repaying.

Note
Levered equity represents a call option on the firm's assets. The payoff profit to equity holders of a leveraged firm has limited downside and unlimited upside.

11.1.2 Payoff to Debt

If the payoff to levered equity is that of a call option, what is the payoff to debt? The RM 800,000 debt will have a payoff as follows:

For any value below RM 880,000, notice that the payoff to debt equals firm value. This is because debt holders as senior claimants have priority to take all assets until their claim on the firm is satisfied. Thus, if firm value is RM 650,000, all of this amount goes to debt holders. Notice too that their claim on the company is fixed at RM 880,000. For firm values higher than RM 880,000, debt holders get no higher return. The break-even point is RM 800,000 since this is the original principal amount. Any firm value below this amount would mean that debt holders lose an amount equal to the difference between firm value and RM 800,000. Figure 11.2 plots the payoff shown in Table 11.2.

Clearly, debt holders have written (short) a put option on the firm. The reason their payoff is such is due to the fact that debt represents a "fixed" claim on the company. That is, a debt holder's claim on a company is limited on the upside to the total of the principal and

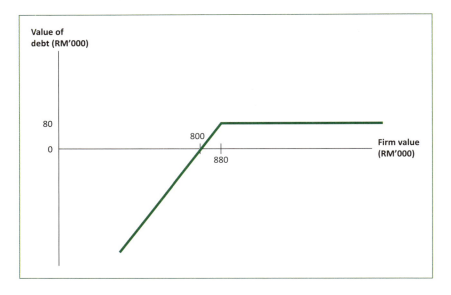

Figure 11.2   Payoff to Debt Holders

Table 11.2 Payoff to Debt Holders

Firm Value (RM)	Payoff to Debt (RM)	Gain/Loss (RM)
650,000	650,000	(150,000)
700,000	700,000	(100,000)
750,000	750,000	(50,000)
800,000	800,000	0
880,000	880,000	80,000
900,000	880,000	80,000
950,000	880,000	80,000
1,000,000	880,000	80,000
1,100,000	880,000	80,000
1,200,000	880,000	80,000

accumulated interest. Given that the outcome will be known at the end of the 1-year period, it is really a European put option with 1-year maturity. Once again, using the standard deviation of assets and the risk-free interest rate, the value of this option can be determined using BSOPM. Lenders to a firm essentially write a put option on the firm to the firm's equity holders.

Note
The payoff profile to lenders resembles that of a short put position. If the firm succeeds, debt holders receive their fixed returns and principal, otherwise they incur losses equivalent to the difference between loan principal and remaining firm value.

11.1.3 Payoff Profile and Incentive Effects

We have thus far established that (i) levered equity represents a call option on the firm, and (ii) debt financing constitutes a short put position. We now address the related issue of *incentive effects*.

Specifically, given what we know about options, if the levered equity holder is getting a call option, what kind of incentives will be provided to him by such an option? Recall that the risk profile of a call option is *limited downside risk and unlimited upside potential*. The maximum that the equity holder could lose is RM 200,000 (limited downside risk) but since equity is residual, he would get to keep everything above RM 880,000 (unlimited upside). Given this situation, the levered equity holder will have every incentive to undertake *high-risk, high-return* projects (i.e., even projects where the incremental return does not justify the incremental risk).

There are two equivalent ways to think about why this is so.

(a) A high-risk, high-return project will help to maximize the upside potential to the equity holder.
(b) In option terms, the value of the call option he holds will *increase* as the volatility (risk) of the firm's underlying assets increases.

This incentive to take on high-risk projects is often known as the agency problem of debt financing. The agency problem gets to be more acute, the higher the proportion of debt to equity. As an illustration, suppose the owner-manager in the earlier example is faced with a project that is as follows: the project requires an RM 1 million initial investment (which is the total firm value with the earlier debt financing of RM 800,000) and has two possible payoffs. The project pays RM 10 million if successful and 0 if it fails.

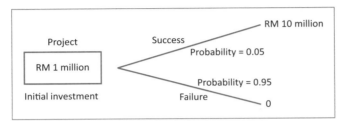

(For simplicity, assume project has 1 year life and all outcomes are known at the end of year.)

Under normal circumstances, such a project will never be given serious consideration. It has a certainty equivalent (CEV) to only RM 0.5 million (0.05 × RM 10 million + 0.95 × RM 0). This amount is obviously lower than the initial investment and thus an unworthy investment. However, from an options viewpoint, the equity holder may have the incentive to take the project even though the odds are clearly stacked against the project.

> **Note**
> The payoff profile to levered equity and the fact that equity holders keep everything beyond that due to debt holders can lead to moral hazard where leverage is high. Moral hazard is the incentive for equity holders to undertake high-risk, high-return projects.

This is because of two reasons:

(a) If the project fails, he stands to lose much less than the provider of debt (limited risk). (He loses RM 200,000 versus the RM 800,000 loss to debt holders.)
(b) Should the project succeed, he stands to gain RM 9.12 million. After paying the RM 880,000 due to debt holders, this translates into a percentage return of 4,460% on his investment of RM 200,000 (unlimited profit).

By undertaking such a high-risk, high-return project, the equity holder increases the volatility of the firm's assets and so he *increases the value of the call option he holds*. This incentive to take on higher risk is often known as the *moral hazard* problem. Such action on the part of equity holders essentially appropriates wealth from debt holders to equity holders. As a check on such motivational problems, transactions such as Leveraged Buyouts (LBOs), in which extensive debt financing is used, often use *securities* that are neither solely debt nor equity. Often times, securities known as "strips" which are part equity and part debt are used instead. Since post-LBO, all parties hold strips and not debt or equity, management has no incentive to take on excessive risk since such action does not enrich them at the expense of others.

11.2 A Rights Issue

A *rights issue* gives each shareholder the right to buy additional shares at a fixed exercise price. The number of shares offered being proportional to shares already owned. Given the time difference between the announcement of rights issue and final date of purchase, the issuing firm faces risk. The risk that not all of the rights will be taken up. One way in which an issuing firm can reduce this risk is by setting the exercise price at a deep discount, such that it would still be a discount on the expected ex-rights price. Viewed from the point of options, a shareholder who is offered rights really receives a call option on the company's stock.

Illustration

Suppose you own two lots of ABC Corp. stock and are offered a rights issue to purchase one lot at RM 5 (a 1 for 2 offer). The offer will expire in 30 days. (i) What is the payoff? (ii) How could the option be valued?

(a) Using a range of stock prices, the payoff profile would be that of a call option. If the stock price is less than the rights price, you would not exercise. But if the stock price is higher than rights price, you would exercise; profiting the difference.
(b) The value of the call option can be valued using the standard BSOPM with adjustments as follows:

C = value of one right to each new share
S = the ex-rights value of stock (adjust current stock price for increased number of stocks)
K = the exercise price or rights offer price
t = days between receipt of offer and final purchase date

11.3 The Value of Underwriting a Securities Issue

A common method by which a company issuing stocks protects itself from issuance failure is through the underwriting process. When a company arranges with a merchant bank to float its stocks and the bank underwrites the issue for a fee, the issuing company is in effect, long a put option with the premium for the put being the underwriting fee. Whether the fee is justified can easily be determined by finding the value of the put. Once again BSOPM (for put option) can be used. *(Note: With the exception of an initial public offer where stock price volatility is not apparent, the method can be used in all other situations, e.g., valuing the underwriting fee for a rights issue, a bond issue, etc.)* Suppose the underwriting is for a rights issue, then the value of underwriting is given by BSOPM as:

$$P = Ke^{-rt} \cdot N(-d_2) - SN(-d_1)$$

where P = value of put option per stock
K = underwritten price of rights
S = the ex-rights value of stock
t = days between initiation of agreement and floatation date

Multiplying the computed put value by the number of issued stock would give the "correct" value of the underwriting. An underwriting fee much higher than that derived earlier would imply that the merchant bank is "overcharging."

> **Note**
> A rights issue provides shareholders with a call option on additional new shares of the firm. An underwriting arrangement provides a long put position to the issuing firm on the securities to be issued.

11.4 Securities with Option-Like Features

Several commonly traded securities have embedded options or option-like features. Understanding option pricing helps in the valuation of such securities. In this subsection, we examine five such securities: ***transferable subscription rights*** (TSRSs)/warrants, ***call warrants***, ***callable bonds***, convertible bonds, and irredeemable convertible unsecured loan stock (ICULS).

(1) Transferable Subscription Rights

Warrants that were also referred to as TSRs were introduced in Malaysia in 1990. The first warrant was issued by Rashid Hussain Bhd. (RHB) in May 1990. Since then, several warrants/TSRs have been listed and traded on Bursa Malaysia. As of end December 2011, a total of 167 different warrants are listed and traded on Bursa Malaysia. A warrant/TSR can be thought of as a long-dated call option on the issuing company stock. Warrants/TSRs are instruments that are typically attached to loan stocks or bonds issued by a company. The idea being to make the bonds more attractive and marketable. The warrants/TSRs can be detached from the bonds and traded in a secondary market — Bursa Malaysia.

A warrant/TSR provides the holder the right but not the obligation to buy the issuing company's common stock at a predetermined price. The holder has the right to exercise the warrant at specified times until maturity. Though a substantial number of Malaysian warrants have maturities of 4–5 years, most appear to have been designed for a 10-year maturity. Interestingly, many warrants have experienced very active trading with occasions where their trading volumes have exceeded that of the underlying stock.

As mentioned earlier, warrants/TSRs are essentially long-dated call options. However, aside from maturity, there are a number of other differentiating features. Unlike equity options, which do not result in ownership ***dilution*** since there is no increase in the number of underlying stocks outstanding, the exercise of warrants/TSRs leads to dilution. When warrants/TSRs are exercised, the issuing company satisfies the exercise by issuing ***new***

> **Note**
> Warrants/TSRs are typically attached to loan stocks or bonds. They represent a long-dated call option on the issuing company stock.

stock to the warrant/TSR holders. Thus, unlike stock options, the exercise of warrants/TSRs leads to ownership dilution. This dilution effect obviously has an impact on the pricing of warrants. Therefore, in addition to adjusting for expected dividends, which is important given the long maturity of warrants, dilution has also to be adjusted for. Dubosky (1992) suggests the following adjustment for dilution in valuing warrants.

$$W = \frac{N}{\left(\dfrac{N}{\gamma} + M\right)} \cdot C$$

where

C = call value computed using BSOPM
N = number of stocks currently outstanding
M = number of warrants issued
γ = number of shares that can be purchased on exercise of each warrant

(2) Call Warrants

Call warrants were yet another security that had been introduced in Asian markets. Call warrants are essentially call options issued by a third party, usually a merchant bank, on a listed stock. For example, Malaysia's first call warrant was issued by Commerce International Merchant Bankers (CIMB) on Maybank stock. The call warrants had an 18-month maturity and could be exercised only at maturity at the stated exercise price of RM 19. Like call options, the holder has the right but not the obligation to buy the underlying asset at the predetermined exercise price. Thus there are a number of differences between call warrants and warrants/TSRs. The two main differences being (i) the issuer of call warrants is a merchant bank, whereas warrants/TSRs are issued by the companies themselves; (ii) unlike warrants/TSRs that cause dilution upon exercise of the warrants, the exercise of call warrants does not increase the outstanding number of shares. The investment bank that issued the call warrants will have to satisfy the exercise of the outstanding call warrants by first purchasing the underlying stock being traded on the stock exchange. A third difference is the fact that where warrants/TSRs come attached with other securities, call warrants are sold as stand-alone instruments.

(3) Callable Bonds

A callable bond is a bond that is callable or redeemable by the issuer at a predetermined price before maturity. The call provision in the bond provides a call option to the issuer. The exercise price is equal to the price at which the bond will be called. Thus, a callable bond arrangement is essentially the sale of a straight bond to the investor and the concurrent sale of a call option by the investor to the bond-issuing firm. As payment for this call option, the investor is "paid" with a higher coupon rate than that of a straight bond with the same features and risk class. Clearly, the embedded option is favorable to the issuer. Thus, the need to compensate investors with a higher coupon (yield). The issuer of a callable bond retains the option to refinance the bond by redeeming it if interest rates fall substantially in the future.

(4) Convertible Bonds

A convertible bond allows the **holder** to either receive the face value of the bond or convert the bond to a predetermined number of common stocks at maturity. The number of stocks that each bond can be converted to is predetermined and stated as the **conversion ratio**. Here, the option is given to the investor because he can choose to exercise the option at his preference on maturity. Clearly, the investor will only choose to convert if it is favorable for him to do so. With a convertible bond, the investor is assured a minimum payoff equal to the face value of the bond and potentially much more if the underlying stock rises. The investor is really getting a European call option since it is exercisable only at maturity. The investor "pays" for the call option by agreeing to receive a lower coupon rate than otherwise would have been. **Convertible bonds** therefore pay a lower coupon/yield relative to a straight bond with same features and risk level. (The valuation/pricing of convertible bonds is discussed in the appendix to this chapter.)

> **Note**
> A callable bond provides an option to the issuer to recall the bond for redemption before maturity. A convertible bond provides holders with the call option to exchange the bond for a given number of stocks according to the conversion ratio.

(5) Irredeemable Convertible Unsecured Loan Stock (ICULS)

An ICULS is a hybrid instrument that has the features of both debt and equity. In essence, it resembles a fixed income debt instrument until converted into equity at predetermined dates, at or prior to maturity. At first glance, one would be tempted to think of ICULS as being similar to convertible bonds. Indeed, its two variants, convertible unsecured loan stocks (CULS) and redeemable convertible loan stocks (RCLS), can be considered the Malaysian version of convertible bonds. What differentiates RCLS/CULS from ICULS is that the latter is "irredeemable," meaning cannot be redeemed for cash. The fact that ICULS **must be** converted to the underlying stock, substantially changes the risk profile of an ICULS from that of a convertible bond. As we will see in the appendix, this has important implications for cash flow and pricing. Similar to convertible bonds, ICULS carry fixed interest, coupons, payable either semiannually or annually. It is unsecured and normally subordinated to all other obligations of the company. ICULS have fixed maturity dates and holders of ICULS must convert their ICULS into the underlying ordinary shares either at predetermined exercise points before maturity or at maturity as specified by the issuer. Conversion is done automatically, regardless of whether the holder of ICULS surrenders them or not. This means that unlike convertible bonds where partial dilution is possible, ICULS ultimately result in full dilution.

The price at which the ICULS can be converted into the underlying shares is determined by the conversion price. The conversion price can be satisfied by tendering the ICULS or a combination of ICULS and cash. Thus, if the ICULS expire in-the-money, given the predetermined conversion price, the holder receives the stipulated number of shares without having to pay anymore. On the other hand, should the ICULS expire out-of-the-money, i.e., stock price is less than the conversion price, the holder will be required to pay the difference between the conversion price and the stock price in order to receive the underlying shares.

Thus, ICULS are never redeemable for cash. Although a holder may delay conversion when the ICULS are out-of-the-money, he ultimately has to convert. ICULS have a nominal value that is usually set at RM 1.00 and are tradeable in board lots of RM 1,000 nominal amounts.

Any new shares issued upon the conversion of ICULS will rank *pari passu* in all respects with the then existing shares. However, the new shares will not be entitled to dividend, rights, allotments, or other distributional entitlements which are before the conversion date of the ICULS. Neither would accrued interest since the last coupon date be payable. As ICULS are not redeemable for cash, the requirement for bond rating is exempted. This enables companies with weak financial standing to gain access to finding new capital. (On the other hand, CULS or RCLS which like convertible bonds can be redeemed for cash require ratings prior to issuance.)

In a sense, both ICULS and RCLS are convertible bonds since they both begin as debt securities. However, while RCLS like convertible bonds may be redeemed for cash, ICULS always end up being converted to the underlying stock. Thus, the issuer of ICULS not only has no further cash outflow at maturity but also could potentially have inflows if the ICULS expire out-of-the-money.

11.5 Real Options and Capital Budgeting

The term, **real options**, has become a popularly used term of late. Real options refers to options, often implicit that may be embedded within capital investments. Thus, real options are not a derivative instrument but constitute an actual option; *real*, because they are associated with investments in real/physical assets rather than financial assets. So, a real option using option terminology could be defined as **a right but not the obligation** to undertake a business initiative or to **exercise** favorable outcomes as they may occur in the future. This right often comes embedded within capital projects. Capital budgeting as we know refers to the process of identifying and evaluating investment projects. Traditional capital budgeting techniques such as net present value (NPV), internal rate of return (IRR), and payback period have a shortcoming. The shortcoming being that these techniques often only focus on apparent cash flows generated by the projects. What is often missed in discounted cash flow techniques is the embedded option implicit within the projects. For example, in comparing between two projects, the traditional methods would compare cash flows without considering flexibilities inherent in a project. Flexibilities within a project constitute **embedded options**. Since a real option provides a right but not the obligation, it provides flexibility in managerial decision-making. The value of the real option therefore is dependent on how valuable the flexibility is. In certain industries, this flexibility has a very high value; in others, so less so. Though such implicit options may have been evident, the difficulty of valuing such options has meant that they were often ignored. It is in bridging this gap that the real options framework comes handy. We quantify the value of this decision-making flexibility by applying the pricing logic of financial options.

Although financial options have their specifications clearly identified and stated in the option contract, real options embedded within investment projects must first be identified and specified in order to put a monetary value on them. Flexibilities arising from embedded options are often **contingent** in nature. That is, their availability depends on certain other outcomes. The real options approach therefore represents a strategic thinking process, one that attempts to proactively manage strategic investments. Capital budgeting and strategy that constitute a sequence of decisions are viewed as a series of options. In a world with increased turbulence and uncertainty, the need to be proactive and use uncertainty to provide competitive advantage has meant that many industries have resorted to "derivative thinkers." Such players have brought to bear financial engineering techniques to take advantage of real options. A related area has been the use of financial derivatives to provide customers with fixed price contracts for commodities with volatile market prices, thereby differentiating one's commodity-like product. The following section examines some of the likely embedded options in capital budgeting.

The typical real options embedded within investment projects are **growth options**, (ii) **exit options**, (iii) **guarantees**, (iv) **timing options**, etc. We examine the existence of such options within capital investment by means of a simple illustration.

> **Note**
> The real options approach uses the logic of financial option valuation to place a monetary value on options embedded/implicit in capital investment projects.

Illustration: Implicit Options in Capital Budgeting

Suppose you are a large Malaysian company involved in the manufacture of power generation equipment and electrical parts. You are now evaluating an investment to build and operate a plant that will produce and supply electrical parts for the National Electric Utility in Vietnam. In order to evaluate using NPV, you have determined the initial investment (RM 100 million), the types of parts to be produced, the expected annual demand, their inflation adjusted prices, etc. You are concerned however that you do not miss out implicit options that may be available. Suppose the following were available, identify the option.

(I) Government Guarantee

As part of its drive to attract foreign direct investment and given the necessity for your products, the Vietnamese government is offering a guarantee on your initial investment of RM 100 million.

What type of option is this? How should you adjust the NPV?

Answer: A government guarantee received is a long put option with exercise price of RM 100 million. The value of this put could be determined using BSOPM and the adjustment would be to ***add*** the put value to NPV. The period over which the guarantee is valid will be the maturity period. The project's standard deviation would be the volatility estimate to be used in the put valuation. While a guarantee received is equivalent to being long a put option with exercise price equal to guarantee amount, a guarantee extended or granted is equivalent to being short a put option.

(II) The Option to Abandon (Exit Option)

Your contract with the Vietnamese Utility allows you to pull out at the end of the third year by turning over all assets to the utility. The foreign utility will take over operations for a payment of RM 150 million.

What type of option is this? What adjustment is needed?

Answer: This is again a put option. The exercise price is RM 150 million with maturity equal to 3 years. The value of this long put option should be ***added*** to NPV.

(III) Possibility of Expansion (Growth Option)

You realize that if your company does well on this project, you could be awarded at least one other project to build and supply related electrical parts.

Alternatively, you may also be able to expand production for supply to neighboring countries such as Cambodia and Laos. You now have no sales to these markets. What kind of option is this? How should you adjust?

Answer: The option to expand is a call option. The exercise price will be the needed new investment and *S* will be the present value of cash flows that can be derived. The standard deviation will be the volatility of the new project cash flows. The value of this call option should be ***added*** to the NPV of the ***current project***.

(IV) Timing Option

Given Vietnam's economic and political risk, you feel uneasy about making too large a commitment. Rather than make a huge upfront investment to produce a multitude of products, you plan to go in small and then expand, if viable, in stages.

What kind of option is this?

Answer: This option to time investments by first waiting to see constitutes a series of call options. You will exercise the option to expand in stages if it becomes viable to do so. Should it not be viable, you will simply not exercise by not expanding.

(V) Flexibility Option

Suppose, in this investment you have two alternatives. The first alternative is to build one large plant in Vietnam to service both Vietnam and Cambodia. The second alternative is to build two smaller plants, one in each country. Which is the better alternative?

Answer: From a traditional discounted cash flow viewpoint, the first alternative may seem better. However, when viewed from an options viewpoint, in the light of the extensive economic and political risks in each country and where flexibility to move production capacity between countries is important, the second alternative might be more sensible. Having two small plants, one in each country not only limits your downside risk but provides for flexibility to shift production between plants should problems arise in any one country. The flexibility constitutes a call option.

Box 11.1
Can a Hedge Save an Economy?

Recent events in the oil market has sent the world's oil producers reeling. The collapse in oil prices was due largely to the freezing of economic activities following the global lockdown. Saudi Arabia's price war with Russia for market share only made matters worse. So much worse that at one point, the West Texas Intermediate (WTI) went to negative price, albeit for only a day. While the oil-dependent economies, the likes of Saudi Arabia, Russia, Nigeria, Algeria, the Gulf states, and even Malaysia, are all staring at massive potential budget deficits and economic pain, one key player, Mexico, appears to be largely unhurt, thanks to its use of oil derivative contracts to hedge itself. As with the other countries, revenue from oil accounts for a substantial part of the Mexican government budget. But unlike the others, Mexico had completely covered its expected 2020 output with a hedge program. The hedge involved the purchase by Mexico's finance ministry of put options on oil from a number of Wall Street banks. The fact that these were customized over-the-counter contracts meant that Mexico could get the size it wanted without moving markets and in total secrecy. It now appears that Mexico has been doing such hedging for many years. According to *World Oil*, a trade magazine, the hedge program has been a savior for Mexico several times. Apparently, Mexico made profits of US$ 5.1 billion in 2009 when oil price crashed due to the global financial crisis and again in 2015 when it made $6.4 billion and another $2.7 billion in 2016 from the hedge. The profit thus far this year is expected to be approximately $6.2 billion.

Box 11.1
(*Continued*)

The hedge in enabling Mexico to exercise the put, would allow it to sell its oil at the exercise price of $49 per barrel. Far higher than the current spot price for Mexican crude which now averages about $15.

By purchasing put options, Mexico was essentially buying insurance to protect itself from declines in the price of its key export — oil. What is interesting about put options is that unlike other derivatives like forwards and futures, which lock in the hedge price and protect only from unfavorable price movements, options enable the holder to benefit both ways. That is, a put option while protecting the holder against falling prices also allows for taking advantage of rising prices. This arises from the fact that options, unlike forwards and futures which are obligatory, need not be exercised. So when oil prices fall, the put option holder gets to exercise and sell oil at the predetermined exercise price but when oil prices rise, he does not exercise but simply sells the oil at the higher market price. Thus benefitting both ways. The put options essentially ensure that Mexico will receive *at least* $49 per barrel for its oil, but possibly more if spot prices are higher. This flexibility however comes at much higher cost. Options have higher transaction costs relative to forwards and futures. Mexico appears to have been paying about $1 billion per year on average for the put options. The cost for 2020 was estimated to be $1.37 billion, insurance that has paid off handsomely at a time of need.

The hedge program, aside from protecting its oil revenue has also provided Mexico with a huge strategic advantage in its dealings within OPEC. The current OPEC deal would have required Mexico to cut its production by 400,000 barrels per day, but with the hedge in place, Mexico could push back and insist on cutting a mere 100,000 barrels per day. Such leverage comes from the fact that Mexico knows that no matter how much oil prices fall, it is assured of its total hedged revenue. The current spot price of oil is quite irrelevant to its expected oil revenue given the hedge.

For all the other oil exporters, there is a huge lesson in this. It is one thing to be able to explore, extract, and export oil, but just as important is the ability to manage the price risk that comes with it. So while a confident Mexican finance ministry has publicly stated that its current year budget is unaffected by the oil price collapse, the other oil producers are scrambling for a solution. For them it is truly a double whammy. Revenue has fallen drastically at a time when spending needs have risen sharply. Yet, as the Mexican case shows, it wouldn't have been difficult for these countries to have reduced their risk if not eliminate it completely. Today, so many risk management tools are available both as exchange traded instruments and over-the-counter. In fact, the

(*Continued*)

> **Box 11.1**
> *(Continued)*
>
> flexibility that modern derivative instruments provide means that just about any exposure can be managed. One simply has to be clever enough to identify and enumerate the risk and structure the appropriate hedge. The instruments and skills are readily available, one however has to have the appreciation for their use. Mexico isn't exactly known for its financial savvy or prudence. Yet, its clever use of derivatives to insure its economy is certainly salutary.
>
> *Source:* Adapted from the author's op-ed column.

11.6 Exotic Options

Exotic options refer to nonstandard options traded in over-the-counter markets. Unlike normal options that have standard features, exotics are usually customized by financial engineers to meet the specific needs of corporate treasurers. Merchant banks are often willing to design and sell such options given the much higher profit margins. The need for such exotic options comes from either the need to hedge complicated cash flows, to get around regulations or simply to suit a finance managers perception of forecast events.

> **Note**
> Exotic options are non-standard options traded in over-the-counter markets. They are usually custom designed to meet specific needs.

As with normal options, exotics can have different underlying assets. However, going by past record, exotic options appear to be much more popular in foreign exchange markets with currencies being probably the most common underlying asset. Though numerous types of exotic options are in existence in developed markets, this section is intended to provide a brief overview of some of the more popular exotic options. We examine below four types of exotic options: **barrier options**, **forward start options**, binary options, and Asian options.

11.6.1 Barrier Options

A barrier option is an option whose payoff is triggered by the underlying asset reaching a certain predetermined price level. There are typically two kinds of barrier options: **knock-out options** and **knock-in options**. A knock-out option is usually designed to expire once the underlying asset reaches a certain price. A knock-in option, on the other hand, would begin once the underlying asset reaches the predetermined price. The option could be a call or a put. For example, an **up and out** call option would cease to exist once the underlying asset reaches a predetermined (barrier) price level. The barrier price level of the underlying is higher than it was when the call was initiated. An **up and in** call would begin to exist when the barrier price level is reached by the underlying asset. A **down and out** call and a **down and in** call would work the same way except that the barrier price level is set lower (down) from where the underlying asset price was at the time the option is initiated. Such barrier options may be attractive to certain investors either because of investor perception or exposure that may arise beyond certain price levels of the underlying asset. Often times, the attraction of barrier options may also be that they are cheaper than regular options.

11.6.2 Forward Start Options

Commonly used as part of incentive programs, e.g., employee stock option plans, forward start options are essentially options that will be activated at some future point in time. Thus, a forward start option may specify that the holder is entitled to buy one lot of issuing company stock at a price determined today but exercisable any time between 2 and 3 years from today. The exercise price is usually set to be at-the-money when the option is initiated. Often, forward start options may define more than one period over which the holder can exercise his right to buy the underlying. The idea being to make employee needs congruent to corporate objectives and rewarding loyalty.

11.6.3 Binary Options

Binary options typically have payoffs that **are all or nothing**. For example, **a cash or nothing call** option pays a fixed cash amount if the underlying assets price at maturity is above the exercise price but nothing if the asset price is below exercise. A **cash or nothing put** would payout a fixed cash amount if underlying asset price is below the exercise price and nothing otherwise. Thus the payoff profile to a long position is not unlimited profit potential as in a regular option but a limited one. Additionally, rather than a gradual increase in the payoff as the option gets more and more in-the-money, the holder of a binary receives a fixed limited payoff. Thus, the long position in a binary option has limited downside (premium paid) and a fixed limited upside potential. Analogously, the short position in a binary option also has limited profit and loss potential.

11.6.4 Asian Options

Asian options are an interesting and increasingly popular form of exotic option. An Asian option is one where the exercise price is not predetermined but arrived at by averaging the spot price of the underlying asset over a predetermined period until maturity. Though one is unsure about what price one would have to pay (call) or receive (put) at maturity, Asian options may actually be better suited to hedge underlying exposures where cash flows are spread evenly over a period of time. For example, a company that will be receiving payments in foreign currency on a weekly basis may be better hedged using Asian put options on the foreign currency. Similarly, a company with payables due in foreign currency with weekly or monthly payments, may be better off with Asian call options. Since the average price used in determining exercise price would be a closer reflection of the home currency cost of gradual cash flows, the Asian option would be a more effective hedge instrument than a regular option. Regular options would be suited for balloon payments or receivables.

11.6.5 Other Structured Products

There is an entire range of structured products that are built mainly on options but include other derivatives. One such product involves the combination of a forward and an option on the same underlying asset but with different maturities. Used typically for currencies, it might involve, for example, the combination of a 1-month forward and a 6-month option. One possible situation where such a product may be needed could be when an importer has two obligations due in the same currency but at different periods. Suppose, a Malaysian importer has to pay his German supplier in 1 month for goods he has already received and in 6 months for goods he has ordered and is to be shipped to him shortly. Assuming the payments are in Euro, the Malaysian importer may want to lock in his Malaysian Ringgit (MYR) cost of the 1-month payable but not the payable in 6 months. This could be because of his expectation that the Euro may fall beginning, say 3 months from now. In such a case, he stands to benefit from a depreciated Euro. If he wants to be hedged and still be able to take advantage of a lower Euro in 6 months, then a call option on the Euro of 6-month maturity may be better. Of course, the cost of using an option instead of a forward would be more expensive; however, the option allows the importer to protect against any appreciation of the Euro while at the same time take advantage of a potential decline of the Euro against the MYR.

11.6.6 Structured Warrants

Of late, structured warrants have become a relatively popular derivative product in Malaysia and other Asian countries. Often listed exchanges, structured warrants are essentially long-dated options written on stocks. In some cases, the underlying asset could also be a stock index such as the FBM KLCI or Hong Kong's stock index, the Hang Seng Index. The maturity can range from 6 months to 5 years. The typical maturity being 18 months. These structured warrants are issued by third parties such as a stock brokerage firm, an investment bank, an asset management firm of some other financial institution. For example, in Malaysia, Macquarie, an Australian asset management firm with a Malaysian subsidiary is probably the biggest issuer of structured warrants. CIMB, one of Malaysia's largest banks, and RHB, yet another bank, are active issuers. These three players account for most of the listed structured warrants in Malaysia. Being long-dated options on an equity underlying, the structured warrant can be either a call or a put. Functionally structured warrants operate exactly as options. A structured call warrant would provide the holder the right to buy the underlying asset at the predetermined exercise price at maturity. A structured put warrant would provide the right to sell. Since the issuer is a third party, there will be no dilution at maturity. The writer or issuer will have to deliver the underlying asset by purchasing them from the market. To protect itself, the issuer has to undertake dynamic hedging as explained in Chapter 10. Stocks that are chosen to be the underlying asset would usually be the larger capitalized and highly liquid stocks. Although structured warrants on company stocks are almost exclusively calls, the index warrants have both calls and puts. Being listed these warrants can be traded. In Malaysia, perhaps due to the requirement that the issuer must stand ready to be the market maker when needed, many of the warrants on the company stocks and especially the indexes are quite actively traded.

SUMMARY

This chapter examined issues and securities used in corporate finance from an options perspective. When equity is combined with debt, levered equity represents a call option on the firm. Since equity is residual and gets everything beyond the fixed claim of debt, levered equity has a payoff profile equivalent to that of a call option. Having taken on debt, equity holders receive a call option on the firm's assets. If firm value exceeds that of the amount due for debt repayment, it is profitable for equity holders to "exercise" by repaying the debt and taking full possession of the firm. Should firm value be lower than the debt amount due, equity holders could choose not to exercise by defaulting on the loan. Debt holders who have extended the debt financing face a payoff equivalent to that of a short put position. If the borrowing firm is not successful, debt holders stand to lose though they get first right to the firm's diminished assets; their loss being equal to difference between the loan principal and the amount realized from the firm's asset. The payoff profile to levered equity can provide the incentive for equity holders to take on increased risks. These motivational incentives to increase risk exposure are known as moral hazard and represent an agency problem of debt financing. The moral hazard problem becomes more acute as the degree of financial leverage increases.

When a firm issues rights to its shareholders, the existing shareholders effectively receive a call option. They receive the right but not the obligation to buy additional stock at the "rights" price. When a firm wanting to issue securities enters into an underwriting arrangement with a merchant bank for a fee, it is effectively buying a put option with the premium being the fee paid.

Many securities used in corporate finance have option-like features. Warrants/TSRs are instruments attached to securities such as loan stocks, bonds, etc. Warrants/TSRs are effectively long-dated call options on the issuing firm's new stock. Since new stock is issued to satisfy the exercise of outstanding warrants, there is dilution. This dilution has to be adjusted for in valuing warrants. Callable and convertible bonds also have embedded options; a callable bond provides a call option to the issuer, whereas a convertible bond provides a call option on the issuing firm's stock to bondholders. A callable bond pays a higher coupon/yield. The higher yield being compensation to bondholders for the call option that they have provided to the issuing firm. A convertible bond on the other hand provides a lower coupon/yield relative a similar straight bond. The difference in yield being the price paid by bondholders in exchange for the call option they receive.

Real options is the term used to describe options, often implicit that may be embedded within capital investments. Traditional discounted cash flow techniques of project evaluation often ignore these embedded options. The real options approach attempts to use the logic of financial option valuation to put a monetary value to these implicit options. The typical real options embedded within investment projects are growth options, exit options, guarantees, timing option, etc. A guarantee received is akin to a long put position, exercising the option to expand is like exercising a call option. Having the option to abandon is the possession of a long put position.

The final section of the chapter provides a brief overview of some exotic options. Exotic options are nonstandard options traded in over-the-counter markets. Exotics are customized options designed by merchant banks to meet the specific needs of corporate treasurers. Barrier options are options that will either begin or cease to exist once the underlying asset hits the predetermined "barrier" price. Forward start options are options that will be activated at some future point in time. Binary options are options that either pay a fixed cash amount or nothing. They have discontinuous payoff. An Asian option is one where the exercise price is not predetermined but arrived at by averaging the spot price of the underlying asset over a predetermined period until maturity.

KEY TERMS

- Levered equity
- Residual claim
- Incentive effect
- Moral hazard
- Rights issue
- Warrants
- Transferable subscription rights
- Dilution
- Securities underwriting
- Call warrants
- Callable bonds
- Conversion ratio

- Convertible bonds
- Real options
- Embedded options
- Growth options
- Exit option
- Guarantee
- Timing option
- Exotic options
- Barrier options
- Forward start options
- Binary options
- Asian options

End-of-Chapter Questions

1. Your company is considering an investment in Thailand. As part of its investment promotion, the Thai government is providing a guarantee on the initial investment. The guarantee is valid for 3 years. You have calculated the initial investment to be RM 100 million and the project NPV is RM 26 million.
   a. In option terms, identify the embedded option and graph the position.
   b. Briefly describe the adjustment needed to the NPV.

2. Chase Manhattan Bank has recently introduced a new type of savings account. The account pays either a 3% interest rate on outstanding balance or 50% of the *increase* in the S&P 500 stock index. The account pays the higher of the two. Identify the embedded option. Using % returns for the account on the vertical axis and the S&P 500 level on the horizontal axis, graph the payoff.

3. In a controversial stock-deal, United Engineers Malaysia (UEM) had purchased 32% of Renong stock at RM 3.20 from undisclosed sellers. At this shareholding level, the Takeover Code requires UEM to make a general offer for all outstanding Renong stocks at the same RM 3.20 price. Renong's current stock price is RM 1.80. UEM is seeking a waiver from having to make a general offer.
   a. From an options viewpoint, graphically show UEM's position and explain why they do not want to make a general offer.
   b. Graph the position from the viewpoint of a shareholder of Renong.

4. If levered equity is a call option on the firm, what incentive would a firm that is approaching financial distress have with regards to investment strategy?

5. How does a call warrant differ from a call option in terms of
   a. liquidity?
   b. exercise price intervals?
   c. maturity?
   d. payoff?
   e. impact on number of outstanding shares?

6. Three years ago, Company A, in a bid to raise financing had sold part of its shares to Company B which is an affiliate company. The shares came with put options exercisable at RM 3.50 per share. It is now close to maturity, but Company A does not have the money to pay for the shares. Company A's shares are now selling for RM 0.70. A director who sits on the board of both companies argues that the solution would be to lengthen the maturity of the put option. This he argues is a "win–win" situation to both companies, since Company A is given a reprieve while lengthening maturity increases option value and so Company B too benefits. Evaluate the argument.

7. A sole proprietor has RM 500,000 of equity in his firm. Suppose he borrows RM 4 million at 10% interest per year, show at the end of year 1,
   (i) the payoff to the proprietor.
   (ii) the payoff to the debt holder.

8. The *Wall Street Journal Asia* carried a banner article about a Malaysian company, Malaysian Resources Corporation Berhad's (MRCB) request to the Securities Commission for a waiver from the Takeover and Mergers Code. According to the article, MRCB had earlier made a commitment to make a general offer on stocks it did not own of New Straits Times (NST) and TV3. (Note: Both NST and TV3 are MRCB affiliates.) The offer had been for RM 15.20 per NST stock and RM 5.20 per TV3 stock. The article alludes that MRCB wants to be released from this commitment given the much lower current prices of NST and TV3. From an options viewpoint, analyze the situation.
   a. What is MRCB's position *vis-à-vis* minority shareholders of NST and TV3?
   b. Suppose you were a shareholder of NST or TV3, what is your position with respect to MRCB?

9. Learning that you have just completed a course in Risk Management, a friend comes to you for advice. He is faced with two investment choices.
   a. Place an RM 10,000 investment with an index fund for 1 year. (An index fund is a mutual fund that invests in a portfolio that tracks the index.)
   b. Place the RM 10,000 with an index linked bank deposit that a local bank is offering. Under this scheme, a depositor gets back his entire capital and zero interest if the FBM KLCI is lower than the day he placed his deposit. On the other hand, if the FBM KLCI rises, then the depositor gets his initial deposit **plus** 10% of the percentage rise in the FBM KLCI over the 1 year.
      (i) On a single diagram, show the payoff profile of each alternative.
      (ii) Describe the risk profile of each alternative.
      (iii) State two key factors that your friend ought to consider in deciding between the two alternatives.

10. a. A wealthy individual lends a firm RM 1 million for a 5-year period. An interest of 10% per annum is payable each year with the principal amount being repaid at the end of year 5 as a single bullet payment. At the end of the 5th year, both parties are allowed to negotiate whereby, instead of RM 1 million repayment of principal, the investor is given a 10% equity stake in the firm. Essentially, an equity for a debt swap. Show the payoff profile to the investor over the 5-year period during which the RM 1 million is a debt.
    b. Show the payoff profile when the investor gets the 10% equity stake in the firm.

11. Outline the appropriate hedge strategy using options for each of the following situations. (Assume calls and puts are available on the underlying asset.)
    a. A jeweler anticipates having to purchase gold for his inventory in 3 months.
    b. A Malaysian exporter anticipates receiving payment in ¥en in 3 months.
    c. A Malaysian bank has gone into a short position in a forward contact on British pounds with its customer. It wants to hedge its exposure.

12. For each of the following situations, outline the appropriate strategy using futures.
    a. A palm oil refiner intends to purchase 100 tons of CPO in 3 months.
    b. A banker whose cost of funds is fixed has agreed to lend RM 12 million in 3 months at KLIBOR +2%.
    c. A speculator believes the FBM KLCI is about to rise sharply over the next 3 months.
    d. A speculator believes interest rates are likely to fall over the next 3 months.
    e. A trader finds that the 3-month SIF contract which should have a price of 818 points is being quoted at 806 points.
    f. You think Malaysian Airline (MAS) stock will rise over the next 3 months. Assuming options are available on MAS stock, state three strategies (using only options), that will let you benefit from a rise while limiting downside risk.

13. Determine the total Ringgit profit or loss in each of the following cases. (One lot refers to 1,000 stocks. Ignore brokerage commissions.)
    a. Mr. Ali goes long one lot of MAS stock at RM 5. He then buys one at-the-money call option on MAS @ 22 sen. MAS stock price is RM 5.40 at option maturity.
    b. *Ceterus paribus*, if Mr. Ali had bought an at-the-money put option, what is his profit or loss?

c. Mr. A and Mr. B can agree on everything except market outlook. Mr. A goes long a 900 points index call @ 18 points and shorts a 900 points index put @ 12 points. Mr. B does the exact opposite. Determine the profit/loss to each for the following index value at option maturity.

Index Value	Mr. A	Mr. B
• 930 points	_____	_____
• 860 points	_____	_____
• 900 points	_____	_____

State who is bullish/bearish.

14. Mr. Lim is an investor who is always wavering in his decisions. On day 1, he went long 3 SIF contracts of June maturity. On day 2, he shorted 2 June SIF contracts. A few days later, he sold a June index call option and simultaneously bought a June index put option. Assuming all contracts were bought/sold at the same exercise/strike prices, what is Mr. Lim's net position now?

15. Regardless of country, previous experience consistently shows that when real estate bubbles burst, it always triggers a sharp increase in real estate loan defaults. Using the options perspective of this chapter, explain why this is to be expected.

Appendix

Pricing Convertible Bonds and ICULS[1]

This appendix examines the pricing of convertible bonds and ICULS.

Though ICULS are a convertible security, they differ from conventional convertible bonds in significant ways; especially from a cash flow viewpoint. A convertible bond, in its basic form is a combination of a straight bond and a call option on issuing company stock. Thus, the value of a convertible at exercise or maturity can be determined as follows:

Value of Convertible at Maturity/at Exercise

$$\sum_{t=1}^{n} \frac{C_t}{(1+r)^t} + \frac{FV_n}{(1+r)^n} + \left[[MPS - CP] \times \frac{FV}{CP} \right] \quad (1)$$

$$S \cdot t: MPS > CP; O$$

where

C_t = amount of coupon
FV_n = face value of bond
r = discount rate/required return

---

[1] The material is sourced from Luqman M. and Obiyathulla I. B. (2004). Pricing Hybrid Securities: The Case of Malaysian ICULS, *The International Journal of Finance*, Vol. 16, No. 3, pp. 3154–3172.

MPS is current market price of stock and CP is the conversion price.

Thus, the value of a convertible bond at maturity or at exercise (if exercise is before maturity) is equal to the value of the straight bond and conversion premium. In equation (1), the conversion premium is shown within brackets. This conversion value equals 0 if MPS, the current market price of stock is less than its conversion price. In other words, conversion premium is worthless if the convertible expires out-of-the-money.

The value of the convertible bond *prior* to exercise/maturity is given by:

$$\sum_{t=1}^{n} \frac{C_t}{(1+K)^t} + \frac{FV_n}{(1+K)^n} + [Call \text{ Value}] \qquad (2)$$

What differentiates equation (2) from equation (1) is that the call value in equation (2) includes the *"time value"* of the option whereas at maturity or at exercise time value is always zero. Since time value is always positive before maturity,[2] the call value in equation (2) will always be greater than the conversion value in equation (1).[3]

Figure 11.3 shows the value profile of a hypothetical convertible bond with the following features: 3 years to maturity, annual coupon of 10%, FV of RM 1,000, required return, *r* of 12% and a conversion ratio of 200 common shares or conversion price of RM 5 per share. (Note: The value of the straight bond using equations (1) or (2) will be RM 951.96.)

The payoff profile to the above convertible bond at maturity is given by Figure 11.4.

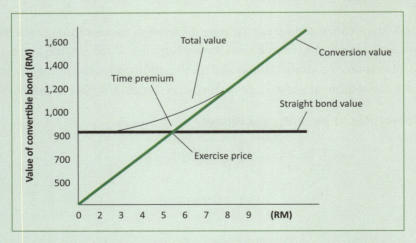

Figure 11.3   Conversion, Time, and Total Value for a Convertible Bond

---

[2] This is true even for deep out-of-the-money options.

[3] The logic here is the same as that of why it never makes sense in normal circumstances to exercise early an American-style option.

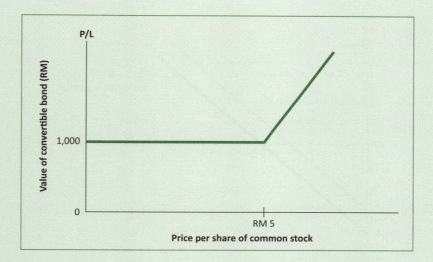

Figure 11.4   Payoff Profile to Convertible Bond at Maturity

Notice from Figure 11.4 that the payoff profile is a minimum RM 1,000 for common stock values below RM 5 and higher for subsequent common stock values. Note that this is precisely the payoff profile to a combined *long call* position on the stock at an exercise price of RM 5 and a long straight bond position with RM 1,000 face value.

Payoff Profile to ICULS

Recall from our description earlier that an ICULS provides fixed predetermined interest payments, much like the coupon above and has a conversion feature. Thus, at first glance it appears similar to a convertible bond. However, there is a key difference which consequently leads to a very different payoff profile for ICULS. This key difference is the fact that conversion is compulsory with ICULS. Unlike the convertible holder who can decide between either receiving the face value of the bond or converting to stocks, the holder of ICULS must convert to stocks even *if it is unfavorable* for him to do so. Thus, if as in the earlier example, an ICULS with a nominal value of RM 1,000 has a conversion ratio of 200 stocks implying a conversion price of RM 5, the holder has no choice but receive the 200 underlying stocks even if their current market price is less than RM 5. For example, if their current market price was RM 2, he effectively gets at maturity stocks worth RM 400 when converting the ICULS. Therefore, unlike convertible bonds where loss is not possible and a minimum value equivalent to the RM 1,000 face value is received, there is no such guarantee with ICULS. Losses are entirely possible.

Seen from the viewpoint of payoff profiles, the ICULS has a risk profile similar to that of a long stock position. In essence, when an investor buys an ICULS with a nominal value of RM 1,000, his exposure is essentially that of being invested in the stock for RM 1,000. Subsequent declines in stock prices hurt him while increases add to his potential profit. This potential gain/loss is independent of the fixed interest income. Thus, the difference between

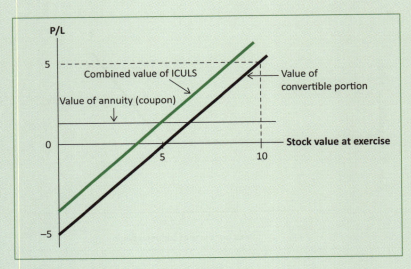

Figure 11.5　Payoff Profit to ICULS

a long stock and long ICULS position is the fixed interest received on ICULS. Where the ICULS has a zero coupon interest, the ICULS and long stock position would essentially be the same in risk profile terms.

In terms of component parts, ICULS like convertible bonds, have two parts: a fixed rate/annuity portion and a convertible portion. Algebraically:

$$ICULS = \sum \frac{C_t}{(1+r)^t} + CP \tag{3}$$

where

C_t = annual coupon amount
r = required return
CP = value of convertible portion

In terms of cash flow/payoff profile, these two components can be shown in Figure 11.5.

Notice that the value of the convertible portion is entirely dependent on the value of the underlying stock. Where the underlying stock has a value above RM 5, the ICULS is in-the-money and the convertible portion has positive value. On the other hand, when the underlying stock is less than RM 5, the ICULS is out-of-the-money and so the convertible portion has a negative value. The second component, the value of the fixed rate annuity portion, is constant regardless of underlying stock value. Combining the two payoffs gives us the overall payoff profile of ICULS. The bold line showing the combined value of the ICULS is to the left and parallel to the value of the convertible portion. The parallel distance between the two lines represents the value of the annuity portion.

There are two important implications from our analysis thus far. First, given the obligation to convert, the convertible portion of an ICULS has a payoff profile *identical* to that of a long position in the underlying stock at a price equal to the exercise price. The second implication comes from the first. Since an ICULS also has an annuity portion, a long ICULS position would always *dominate* a long stock position where the stock has been purchased at a price equal to the exercise price of the ICULS, i.e., RM 5 in our earlier example. To put it another way, if an ICULS had been issued at-the-money[4] and one investor had bought the ICULS while another the underlying stock, the holder of the ICULS would always be better off than the stockholder, regardless of subsequent stock price movement.

In arriving at a pricing model for ICULS, we have established one point, i.e., when the ICULS is at-the-money, its value must be higher than that of the underlying stock by the value of the annuity portion.

At-the-money:
ICULS – Stock Value = Value of annuity
or ICULS > Stock value; by the amount of annuity value

To arrive at a pricing model, let us first summarize three key points from our previous analysis.

(a) For ICULS at-the-money, we know that the premium of the ICULS must be worth at least the PV of the annuity. The PV of the annuity thus establishes the lower boundary.
(b) To the above value of the PV annuity, we must account for the fact that since there is time left to maturity, the ICULS could become in-the-money in the future (or otherwise) and therefore be more (less) profitable. This probability that more (less) profits are possible in the future has a value and is denoted "time value" in options literature.
(c) We know that with the exception of the annuity portion, ICULS have a payoff profile exactly as a long underlying stock position established at a price equal to the exercise price of the ICULS.

Taking all these into consideration, we turned to options literature on synthetics and replication for a pricing model. As a derivative, but one with compulsory conversion, the ICULS has a payoff profile similar to that of the long underlying position. Going by put–call parity which is:

$$S = C + -P \qquad (4)$$

or

$$S - \frac{K}{(1+r)^t} = C + -P \qquad (5)$$

---

[4] At-the-money means the exercise price of the ICULS equals the current value of the stock.

One could argue that the value of the convertible portion of an ICULS is equivalent to being long an at-the-money, call and short an at-the-money put on the underlying stock. Thus, the value of this convertible portion of the ICUL should equal the cost of the net premiums for the long call and short put. Since the ICULS has a fixed annuity portion, we add to this net premium the PV of annuity. Thus, the value of an ICULS given equation (5) is

$$ICULS - K(1+r)^{-t} = C + -P + \text{Value of annuity} \tag{6}$$

or rearranged as

$$ICULS = C + -P + K(1+r)^{-t} + \sum \frac{C_t}{(1+r)^t} \tag{7}$$

where

C = value of an at-the-money call on underlying
P = value of an at-the-money put on underlying stock
$K(1+r)^{-t}$ = PV of exercise price of call/put
C_t = RM amount of coupon received on ICULS

Since the exercise of ICULS results in the issuance new shares, there obviously is dilution. As conversion is compulsory, dilution is a certainty with ICULS. In accounting for this dilution, we multiply equation (7) by the ratio of the number of outstanding stocks pre- to post-dilution.

$$ICULS = \left[C + -P + K(1+r)^{-t} + \sum \frac{C_t}{(1+r)^t} \right] \cdot \left(\frac{\theta}{\pi} \right) \tag{8}$$

s•t: ICULS > 0

where

θ = number of existing shares pre dilution
π = number of shares post dilution
$\pi = (\theta + \text{Number of ICULS issued} \times \text{Conversion ratio})$

The logic of equations (7) and (8) is straight forward. The long call, short put, and PV of exercise price of options essentially replicate a long stock position. When the ICULS is in-the-money, the call premium is high while the put premium is low. This leads to a high value for the ICULS. When the ICULS is out-of-the-money, i.e. stock price is lower than ICULS exercise price, the call's value is lower whereas put value is high; thus the net premium would be negative making the combined value of ICULS *less than* its annuity value. As in the case of deep out-of-the-money options, the ICULS cannot have negative values; thus the "subject to" constraint.

CHAPTER · 12

Interest Rate Swaps, Credit, and Other Derivatives

Objectives

This chapter is designed to provide an overview of swaps, credit derivatives, forward rate agreements, nondeliverable forwards, and other derivatives. Following a description, the mechanics and application of these contracts are examined. The use of credit derivatives in managing credit risk is outlined with an emphasis on the structure of the contracts. On completing the chapter, readers should have a good understanding of the basic design and application of these derivatives in managing different risks.

Introduction

In this chapter, we examine additional financial derivatives such as swaps, forward rate agreements (FRAs), nondeliverable forwards (NDFs), contracts for differences (CFDs), and other derivatives. The chapter also describes at length credit derivatives. Credit derivatives, however, could also take the form of swaps, options, or instruments with embedded options. Swaps, FRAs, NDFs, and credit derivatives are not exchange-traded but are over-the-counter (OTC) instruments. Even so, these instruments have become increasingly popular in recent times. The customization that is possible with OTC instruments enhances their flexibility, with regards to size and tenor and probably contributes to their increased popularity. As will be evident in the chapter, these instruments have their own advantages and value added which would make them the instrument of choice in meeting specific needs.

12.1 Interest Rate Swaps

Interest rate swaps (IRS) belong to a category of derivatives known as ***swaps***. Swaps, as mentioned in Chapter 1, are customized bilateral transactions in which the parties agree to exchange cash flows at fixed periodic intervals, based on an underlying asset. Being customized, swaps are OTC instruments. Depending on the kind of underlying asset, there are different kinds of swaps. A currency swap, e.g., is one where parties exchange one currency for another; a commodity swap is one where parties exchange cash flows based either on a commodities index or the total return of a commodity in exchange for a return based on a market yield; and equity swaps constitute an exchange of cash flows based on different equity indices. An IRS, on the other hand, is a transaction in which the parties exchange cash flows based on two different interest rates.

Figure 12.1   A Fixed-for-Floating Interest Rate Swap

In its most common form, a ***fixed-for-floating swap***, one party pays an amount based on a fixed interest rate, whereas the other party pays, in exchange, an amount based on a floating interest rate. The size of the payment is determined by multiplying the interest rate with the ***notional principal***. The notional principal is the principal amount on which interest payments are calculated. The notional principal remains unchanged over the maturity of the swap. Typically, in an IRS, cash flows are swapped at fixed predetermined intervals over the tenor of the agreement. The fixed intervals, known as ***reset*** periods, may be six monthly, quarterly, etc., whereas the tenor or maturity of the swap may be 5 or 10 years. Figure 12.1 outlines the cash flows involved in a fixed-for-floating IRS of 5-year maturity and RM 100 million notional principal. If the ***reset frequency*** is 6 months, then a total of 10 cash flow swaps will occur over the 5 years. The fixed rate payer will pay an annualized 10% fixed rate, whereas the ***floating rate payer*** will pay 6-month Kuala Lumpur Interbank Offer Rate (KLIBOR) +1%.

The cash flow payment based on the interest rates will occur once every 6 months. Since the payments are to be made simultaneously, often the cash flows are netted such that only a single payment occurs. As to who pays whom would obviously depend on which rate is higher. If the floating rate, 6-month KLIBOR + 1% is higher than the fixed rate of 10%, the floating rate payer pays the difference. If the floating rate is lower than 10%, then the fixed payer pays 6-month KLIBOR is at 11.2%.

Note
In a fixed-for-floating swap, one party pays an amount based on a fixed interest rate, whereas the other pays based on a floating interest rate. The amount swapped is based on the notional principal.

Scenario 1: 6-month KLIBOR = 6%

The payment obligation for each party is as follows:

Fixed rate payer: [10% × RM 100,000,000]/2 = RM 5,000,000
Floating rate payer: [(6% + 1) × RM 100,000,000]/2 = RM 3,500,000
Since the fixed rate payer's obligation is higher by RM 1,500,000, he pays this amount. The netted cash flow will be:

```
                    RM 1,500,000 (net difference)
  Fixed rate payer  ─────────────────────────────▶  Floating rate payer
```

Scenario 2: 6-month KLIBOR = 11.2%

With changed floating interest rate, the payment obligation would now be:

Fixed rate payer: [10% × RM 100,000,000]/2 = RM 5,000,000

Floating rate payer: [(11.2% + 1%) × RM 100,000,000]/2 = RM 6,100,000

Here, since the floating rate payer's obligation is higher, he has to pay the fixed rate pay the net amount of RM 1,100,000. Now the cash flow will be:

There are two factors to note from the previous illustration. First, the notional principal is *never* exchanged. Second, only the net difference is paid. Thus, at any reset period, there will be a cash flow if the two rates are unequal. Since the fixed rate payer's obligation is known up front, it changes the floating interest rate that will determine the direction and quantum of payments.

Swap Terminology	
Fixed-rate payer	The counterparty in swap agreement who pays based on a fixed interest rate.
Floating rate payer	Counterparty who pays based on a floating interest rate.
Reset frequency	The time interval over which the floating rate is reviewed and reset.
Reference rate	The market interest rate on which the floating rate payer's payment will be based — typically an interbank rate like KLIBOR, London Interbank Offer rate (LIBOR), T-bill rate, etc.
Notional principal	The principal amount on which interest payment amounts are determined. Notional amount is never exchanged, only the interest amounts based on it.

12.1.1 Why Use IRS?

IRS grew out of parallel or back-to-back loans and **currency swaps** that multinational firms had used in the 1970s to access blocked funds or circumvent capital controls. Thus, the currency swap is the predecessor to IRS. Since its introduction in 1981, IRS have become extremely popular. Transacted volume, measured by total notional amount exceeds US$ 50 trillion according to the International Swaps and Derivatives Association (ISDA) in 2010. That IRS have become so popular in developed markets despite being an OTC instrument has to do with the initiatives of ISDA. ISDA had streamlined and standardized much of the paperwork for IRS, making the process much more simplified and thereby incurring lower costs. Though the fixed-for-floating or **plain vanilla swap** as it is often known is the most common, there are other variants. A **basis swap** is one where both rates are floating and parties try to lock in or profit from differences in swap spreads. A **forward-starting swap** enables parties to lock in current favorable yields for financing issues that will be carried out at a future date. An **amortizing swap** is one where the notional principal **reduces** over time, whereas a swap with an ***inverse floater*** is one where the floating rate is negatively correlated with a benchmark reference interest rate. Finally, there are also swaps with embedded options. Being customized products, any structural form or variant is possible as long as it is mutually agreed by the two parties. Though an intermediary is not necessary, it is very common. Intermediaries are usually merchant or commercial banks. Insurance firms too are common intermediaries. Intermediaries play one of these two roles: either as a ***broker*** or ***market maker***. As broker, an intermediary designs the swap and collects a fee. As market maker, the intermediary becomes the counterparty. Thus, they are not intermediaries in the strict sense. As market makers, these banks stand ready to undertake and enter into a swap transaction.

12.2 IRS — Applications

The huge popularity of IRS arises from the inherent flexibility that makes it possible to use IRS for multiple purposes. As is the case with all financial derivatives, IRS can be used for hedging, arbitrage, and speculation. However, in addition to these three common applications, an IRS can also be used to (i) lower the effective cost of borrowing, (ii) achieve higher potential yield on assets, and (iii) to manage asset–liability mismatches. In the discussion that follows, we examine the use of IRS in these applications.

> **Note**
> Aside from their use in hedging, arbitrage, and speculation, IRS can also be used to lower the cost of borrowing and manage asset–liability duration mismatches.

12.2.1 Arbitrage Using IRS

One of the first uses of IRS was as an instrument to take advantage of ***comparative advantage*** that companies may have across different credit markets. Despite integrated financial markets, credit assessment of companies, either due to informational asymmetries or coverage by analysts, may be different. Thus, differences may occur between the market for fixed versus floating loans or between short- versus long-term credit markets. These differences would translate into different funding costs for the same firm in the different credit markets. What is happening is, different markets are pricing credit differently based on their own assessment. It is this ***mispricing*** that can be ***arbitraged***.

Illustration: Arbitraging

Suppose two firms: Alfa and Beta are in the market for a $30 million, 5-year loan. Principal is to be paid in a single payment at the end of year 5 with semiannual interest payments in between. Alfa which has an AAA credit rating prefers a floating rate loan, whereas Beta which has an "A" rating wants a fixed rate loan. The rates available to each firm in the fixed and floating markets are as follows:

	Fixed rate market	Floating rate
Alfa	9%	LIBOR + 0.25%
Beta	10%	LIBOR + 0.75

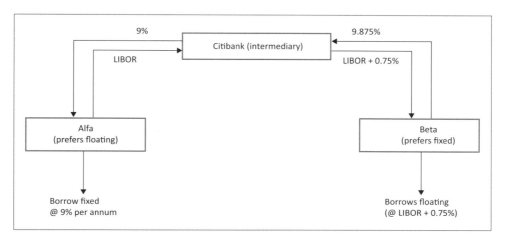

Figure 12.2   Arbitraging with IRS

Are these rates arbitrageable? Yes, notice the difference in spreads for the two firms in the different markets. In the fixed rate market, there is a 1% difference in yields, whereas in the floating rate market, the spread is half percent. Obviously, one of the two markets is not pricing the credit risk differential correctly. The 0.5% difference in spreads between the two markets can be thought of as **mispricing**. It is this mispricing of 0.5% that is arbitrageable with an IRS. With a commercial bank, let us say Citibank as intermediary, the IRS could be structured as shown in Figure 12.2.

Alfa which has higher credit rating has an absolute advantage in both markets *vis-à-vis* Beta (its cost is lower). However, it has a bigger comparative advantage in the fixed rate market where its cost advantage is 1% (10% − 9%). In structuring the swap, Alfa should be made to borrow in the market in which it has the bigger **comparative advantage**. However, Alfa wants a floating rate loan! This is where it swaps its fixed rate loan into a floating rate. Notice that with the IRS, two things happen: (i) each firm effectively ends up with the kind of loan it originally wanted, and (ii) they manage to get their preferred loan at a **lower cost** than if they had borrowed directly. The cost saving to each party is as follows:

	Alfa	Beta
Cost if borrowed directly	LIBOR + 1/4%	10.00 %
Cost of borrowing with IRS	LIBOR	9.875%
Cost saving from IRS	+ 0.25%	+ 0.125%

Gain to Citibank

Receive from Beta	9.875%
Pay to Alfa	(9.00%)
Receive from Alfa	LIBOR
Pay to Beta	(LIBOR + 0.75%)
Gain	+ 0.125%

Notice that the sum total of the gain to each party equals 0.50% (0.25% + 0.125% + 0.125%). This is no accident! The 0.50% total is essentially the percentage "mispricing" we saw earlier. (The difference in spreads across markets for the firms.) The three parties in the aforementioned IRS have divided the 0.50% mispricing among themselves. In this case, Alfa which had absolute advantage in both markets, gets the bigger portion. The proportion by which the mispricing differential is divided among the parties is obviously negotiated.

12.2.2 Hedging Interest Rate Risk with IRS

The second application of IRS is in hedging exposure to rate risk. There are three common ways by which IRS is used to manage rate risk: (i) to hedge against rising rates (borrowers); (ii) to hedge against falling rates (lenders); and (iii) to manage asset–liability **duration gaps**. We now discuss how IRS can be used in each of these three cases.

> **Note**
> In hedging, IRS can be used to hedge against rising rates, falling rates, and manage asset–liability duration gaps.

Illustration: Hedging Rising Interest Rates

Suppose a borrower, Syarikat ABC, has a 5-year, RM 10 million loan from Maybank. Maybank charges an interest based on 6-month KLIBOR + 2% payable semiannually. Syarikat ABC obviously has interest rate exposure. The firm's funding costs will increase as 6-month KLIBOR rises. How can the firm hedge? Using 3-month KLIBOR futures contracts as we saw in Chapter 5 will only help partially. The futures contract will only lock in rates over the next 3 months. Although a rollover strategy could be used, the rates locked in will be progressively higher as spot interest rates rise. A second problem with using interest rate futures is that most of the distant maturity contracts would be inactive. Given these circumstances, the logical way for Syarikat ABC to manage the rate risk would be through an IRS. Syarikat ABC should enter the swap as the ***fixed rate payer*** and ***floating rate receiver***. If the notional principal and reset frequency are structured to match the underlying position that it has with Maybank, then Syarikat ABC would have perfectly hedged its interest rate risk. The structure of the hedge is shown in Figure 12.3.

In the IRS, Syarikat ABC pays an annualized fixed rate of 8% every 6 months on RM 10 million notional [(0.08 × RM 10 million)/2].

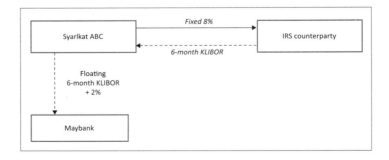

Figure 12.3 Hedging against Rising Rates with IRS

In exchange, it receives a cash flow equivalent to the prevailing spot 6-month KLIBOR rate on RM 10 million notional [(6-month KLIBOR × RM 10 million)/2].

Syarikat ABC protects itself from rising interest rates because its increased payments to Maybank will be **offset** by the increased payments it receives from the counterparty as interest rates rising. Since both the receivable from the counterparty and the payable to Maybank are referenced on 6-month KLIBOR, Syarikat ABC's inflows from the swap offset the outflow to Maybank. With the IRS, Syarikat ABC has effectively turned its floating rate payable into a fixed rate one. Effectively, it is a 10% annualized fixed rate loan (8% to swap counterparty and 2% spread over KLIBOR to Maybank).

Given the earlier example, it should be easy to see what needs to be done to hedge against falling interest rates. One should do the opposite of what Syarikat ABC did in the abovementioned IRS. That is, enter into an IRS as the ***floating rate payer***. The following example illustrates the logic.

Illustration: Hedging against Falling Interest Rates

KL Money Brokers (KLMB) manages a money-market fund for corporate clients. The size of the fund is RM 50 million, invested mostly in 3-month Malaysian Government Securities (MGS) and commercial papers. The returns approximate the 3-month KLIBOR. Based on its in-house research, KLMB expects short-term rates to fall over the next few years. The firm is worried that falling short-term rates will mean lower yields from its investments and reduced returns to its clients. To avoid the resulting withdrawals, KLMB wants to try and maintain current returns over the next 3 years. What can KLMB do to maintain steady returns in the face of falling short-term rates? Answer: Enter a 3-year IRS of RM 50 million notional principal as the floating rate payer. Figure 12.4 shows the structure of the proposed IRS.

In the swap, KLMB essentially passes through its earnings from 3-month paper to the counterparty as the 3-month KLIBOR. It receives in exchange a fixed rate of X%. As a result, KLMB can be assured of providing its clients with a return approximating X% even though short-term rates are falling. If the reset frequency is set to match the interval period(s) over which KLMB pays its clients, the company is well protected from falling rates.

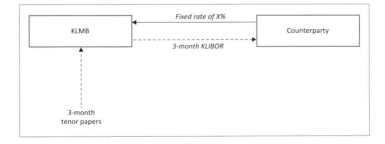

Figure 12.4 Hedging against Falling Interest Rates

12.2.3 Hedging Duration Gaps

Recall from our discussion in Chapter 5 that duration is a measure of interest rate sensitivity and that asset–liability mismatches in duration result in duration gaps. A financial institution with a positive gap (larger duration of assets relative to liabilities) will be susceptible to rising interest, whereas one with a negative gap to falling rates. Assume a bank has an asset–liability duration gap of positive 7.2 years, as in the Chapter 5 example. We saw in the example that a 5% rise in interest rates would reduce the bank's net worth by about 32.7%. It is obvious that the bank has significant exposure to rising interest rates. How can the bank protect itself?

To protect itself from rising rates, the bank would have to reduce the duration on the asset side of its balance sheet in order to reduce the positive gap and/or lengthen the duration on the liability side. One of the easiest ways to reduce the positive gap would be by entering an IRS as the fixed rate payer/floating rate receiver. Recall that interest is received by the bank on its assets, whereas it pays interest on its liabilities. Thus, from an earnings viewpoint, assets represent inflows, whereas liabilities outflows/payment. Therefore, entering into an IRS as floating rate receiver effectively reduces the overall duration of the asset side (and lengthens duration of liability side since the obligatory payments are fixed — fixed rate payer). Duration of the assets reduces because duration is simply the weighted average of the duration of individual items on the asset side of the balance sheet. Recall that the weighted average duration of assets in the Chapter 5 example was 9 years. Suppose the total assets of the bank in the example is RM 100 million; if the bank enters a 5-year, RM 100 million IRS with a 6-month reset period, then the duration of the receivable is simply 6 months.

> **Note**
> To reduce a positive duration gap, a bank should enter an IRS as the floating rate receiver. It can increase the positive gap or lengthen the duration of its assets by being the floating rate payer/fixed rate receiver in a long-dated IRS.

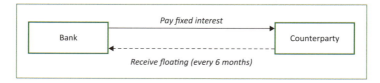

With this IRS, the new duration of the bank's assets will be 9 years for existing assets of RM 100 million, and 6 months for the newly created asset of RM 100 million (notional principal). The new weighted average duration of assets is now: 9.0 years × (0.5) + 0.5 years × (0.5) = 4.5 years + 0.25 years.

New duration of assets is therefore 4.75 years. Even if we hold the duration of liabilities to be unchanged at the original 1.8 years, the new duration gap is:

$$4.75 \text{ years} - 1.8 \text{ years} = 2.95 \text{ years}$$

The IRS therefore reduced the positive gap of the bank from 7.2 years previously to 2.95 years. Interest rate exposure as measured by the positive gap has been reduced to a third of what it was prior to the IRS.

12.2.4 Speculating with IRS

Though swaps are OTC instruments, using them for speculation is common. For example, IRS could be used to speculate on expected interest rate movements. However, unlike interest rate futures contracts, which being exchange-traded instruments could easily be reversed, swaps being customized, would require the consent of the counterparty in order to reverse. Still, IRS are used to speculate on rate movements over extended periods. Where plain vanilla, fixed-for-floating swaps are concerned, it is easy to see what the appropriate strategy should be to speculate on rate movements. Being a floating rate receiver would be the logical strategy if one expects interest rates to rise while the opposite will be true if rates are expected to fall.

Illustration: Speculating on Expected Increase in Interest Rates

Mr. Lee, a bond trader, has just completed his assessment of interest rate outlook. He is convinced that rates are likely to rise steadily over the next 2 years. To take advantage of this likely rise, Mr. Lee intends to enter into an IRS. What should his position be to benefit from rising rates?

Answer: He should enter the swap as the fixed rate payer and floating rate receiver.

Speculative Position: Rising Interest Rate Expectation

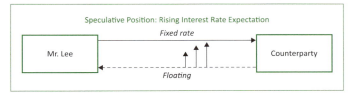

The logic in taking the earlier position is that while Mr. Lee will pay a fixed amount, the amount he receives will increase as interest rates rise. If his expectation of a steady increase comes true, Mr. Lee will be receiving steadily higher net cash flow at each future reset period. However, should his expectation not bear out and interest rates fall instead, Mr. Lee stands to lose in the IRS. The size of the potential profit or loss of the position will depend on the notional principal and the tenor of the swap.

Note
To take advantage of expected rising rates, a speculator enters an IRS as the floating rate receiver. If the expectation is falling interest rates, being the fixed rate receiver would be appropriate.

To speculate on expected falling interest rates, the speculator should establish the opposite of Mr. Lee's position earlier. To profit from an IRS from falling rates, one should enter as the floating rate payer and fixed rate receiver. If interest rates indeed fall, the speculator would have to pay progressively lower amounts but would receive the same fixed amount.

12.2.5 Duration Gaps and Interest Rate Expectation

Financial institutions often try to make a call on interest rate movements. For example, if a bank's assessment leads it to believe that interest rates are likely to fall, the bank might want to *increase* the positive duration gap between its assets–liabilities. A quick and easy way to achieve this would be by entering into a long dated IRS as the floating rate payer and fixed rate receiver. Notice that this is the exact opposite of the position the bank took in the hedging example earlier. While asset–liability mismatches are inevitable for banks, managing the gaps become easy with IRS. Based on its assessment, a bank may choose the type and size of gap it wants, for the period it wants by way of an IRS.

12.3 Pricing IRS

Pricing IRSs is a relatively complicated process requiring extrapolation and estimation. Thus, there is no formula providing a closed form solution. Instead, the process requires sourcing information from several sources, then estimating value using techniques such as bootstrapping and extrapolation. We outline below a description of the logic and the valuation process.

The underlying logic of valuing a swap is based on the premise that the transaction should, at its initiation, be a zero net present value (NPV) proposition. This logic is no different from the pricing of other financial instruments, e.g., bonds. Recall that the correct value of a bond is arrived at by discounting the bond's future cash flows by its appropriate discount rate or yield to maturity. The appropriate discount rate for the bond is determined based on the bond's credit rating. Once the correct price of the bond is arrived at, purchasing the bond would be a zero NPV investment. This is because deducting the price from the present value (PV) of cash flows would equal zero. Similarly, a fixed-for-floating swap is priced such that the PV of the fixed payments *equal* the PV of the *expected* cash flows of the floating rate.

It is obvious that a number of variables have to be estimated. First, to compute PVs, the appropriate discount rate has to be estimated. This is done by estimating the *swap spread*. The swap spread is essentially the premium above the treasury yield applicable for the swap. The swap spread therefore is directly dependent on the credit worthiness of the parties to the swap. Since the spread is a premium over treasury bills, a *swap curve* is often estimated based on the treasury yield curve. For long tenor swaps, the yield curve may have to be derived through extrapolation. The next task is to estimate the *potential* cash flows from the floating rate payer. Since this is dependent on the movements of the floating reference rate, a forecast has to be made of what the reference rate is likely to be in future periods. In highly liquid and deep markets, this is done by looking at the forward yield curve. The forward yield curve is typically derived from pricing of forward-based interest rate derivatives such as interest rate futures contracts. Often the trading in distant futures contract is not sufficiently active to get reliable prices. This is where the bootstrapping technique is used and estimates are then used as indicators of what future yields of the reference rate is likely to be. Once the **expected** future floating rate is estimated, the cash flow is determined by multiplying the estimated yield with the notional principal. This estimated cash flow is then discounted and set equal to the discounted cash flow arising from the fixed rate payment.

The earlier valuation method sets the value of an IRS to be net zero NPV at initiation. However, as market interest rates change, the value of the IRS would change. For example, if rates rise and the futures yield curve steepens, the fixed rate payer benefits as the floating rate payment will have to increase. Thus, the value of the IRS *increases* to the fixed rate payer (and decreases for the floating rate payer). For the fixed rate payer, the value of the IRS is now not zero but positive NPV. The Ringgit value of the positive NPV would simply be net NPV of the increase in payments he receives from the floating rate payer. If subsequent to initiating an IRS, interest rates fall instead, the opposite happens. That is, the IRS becomes more valuable to the floating rate payer since his outflows are now less.

Issues in IRS Markets

It is obvious that the huge popularity of IRS in the United States (US) and other developed markets has to do with the many benefits it offers. Some of the key advantages as mentioned earlier are flexibility that comes from the customization and the longer maturity that is feasible with IRS relative to other exchange-traded interest rate derivatives. In addition, there are two additional advantages: first, an IRS being a nonfunding transaction carries much lower credit risk. Since the notional principal never changes hands and cash flows at reset periods are exchanged simultaneously (or netted out), counterparty risk is minimized. Thus, parties could mutually choose to "walk away" from the deal. This does mean however that there is no counterparty risk — there can still be implied losses. Recall from our valuation discussion earlier that the value of the IRS changes to each party as interest rates change. One party stands to gain if rates subsequently rise while the other stands to lose and vice versa. As such, the party which stands to lose would have the incentive to default. If he does, then the counterparty loses the positive NPV that would have accrued to him. In addition to minimized credit risk, a second advantage of swaps is that it is off-balance-sheet. Thus, it will have no impact on a company's leverage or debt/equity ratios. Keep in mind that though an IRS is not a funding transaction, it can reduce the funding/borrowing cost (as we saw in the swap, e.g., of Alfa and Beta).

IRS are taking hold in Asia with merchant banks being active players. As an OTC transaction, however, it is difficult to estimate the overall size of the market or its growth rate. Given our discussion of the pricing process, it is clear that there are limitations to any kind of explosive growth seen in developed markets. Pricing requires the extrapolation of the yield curve and bootstrapping the forward yield curve. The lack of a deep market in bonds and a reference yield curve is a stumbling block. Much worse, however, is the fact that bootstrapping the forward yield curve is impossible given that there simply isn't a futures yield beyond a few months. So, pricing is probably based on quotes received from banks and other players.

12.4 Currency Swaps

A currency swap, as the name suggests, is essentially a transaction in which the parties agree to swap currencies at periodic intervals. One party agrees to pay a fixed amount of a currency in exchange for receiving fixed amounts of another currency. The rationale for such a transaction is to hedge currency risk and the interest rate risk that typically goes with it. The main difference between an IRS and a currency swap is that in an IRS, notional principal is never exchanged, whereas in a currency swap, the notional principal in two different currencies is exchanged. A first exchange of the two currencies occurs at the initiation of the swap contract. Typically, this first exchange is often based on prevailing spot exchange rates at the time. This initial exchange is then reversed at the end of the swap contract period. Since the amounts exchanged in both periods are exactly the same, exchange rate risk is eliminated. Companies often go into a currency swap in order to exchange a series of foreign currency denominated obligations into home currency ones. So, currency swaps may simply be the means to exchange debt obligations in one currency for another. In the process, both the currency risk and interest rate risks are being hedged. To better understand the mechanics of a currency swap, we work through the following example.

> **Note**
> A currency swap is a transaction in which two parties agree to exchange a fixed amount of one currency for another.

12.4.1 Illustration: A Currency Swap

Pacific Gloves Corporation (PGC), a Malaysian glove and rubber products manufacturer has a large and burgeoning market in Taiwan. Of late, it has had logistical problems with distribution. The company feels that it has to have its own warehouse and distribution center in Taiwan if current problems are to be overcome. Accordingly, it has identified an appropriate site outside Kaohsiung. The total cost for land, building and all shipping and handling equipment is expected to be TWD 200 million. This will be a one-off investment with subsequent capital expenditure expected to be minimal. Given its expected cash flows from Taiwan operations, PGC believes it can settle a TWD 200 million financing in 3 years. Accordingly, the company has negotiated with its Taiwanese banker, The National Bank of Taipei (NBOT), funding as follows:

Principle amount = TWD 200 million
Interest = Fixed 9% payable annually at year end
Loan tenor = 3 years; with lump sum principle payment at the end of 3rd year

Evergreen, the Taiwanese shipping and transportation giant, has operations at all of Malaysia's ports. It now wants to build its own handling facility at Malaysia's newest port, The Port of Tanjung Pelepas. The total investment needed will be RM 20 million. Evergreen's Malaysian banker, Public Bank Berhad (PBB) is willing to provide funding as follows:

Principal amount = RM 20 million
Interest = Fixed 6% payable annually at year end
Loan tenor = 3 years; with lump sum principle payment at the end of 3rd year

Since the two companies have opposite needs, i.e., PGC, a Malaysian company, needs funding for its project in Taiwan, whereas Evergreen, a Taiwanese company, needs funding in Malaysia; a currency swap can be a means by which both companies can get the funding they need while at the same time manage the exchange rate risk. Since we have assumed the terms of the respective loans to be the same, the currency swap would be a straightforward one as follows:

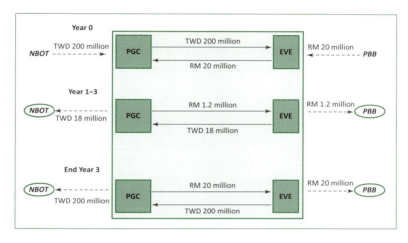

Figure 12.5   Mechanics of a Currency Swap — Cash Flows

If each firm takes the loan being offered by its bank without doing anything more, they face exchange rate risk on both the principal amount and the annual interest payments. If the currency they borrow in appreciates against their home currency, their effective cost increases. Additionally, since each firm's revenues are mostly in their respective home currency, having a large foreign currency denominated obligation causes a currency mismatch. For example, if Evergreen simply borrows from its Malaysian banker, PBB, to finance its new Taiwanese handling facility, without doing anything to hedge, then any appreciation of the Malaysian Ringgit against the TWD will hurt the company since its Ringgit liability in TWD terms will be higher. In addition, the appreciation of the Ringgit will also imply higher effective interest rate in TWD terms. So, not only does the liability increase but also the cost of funds.

To avoid these problems, both PGC and Evergreen could take the foreign currency loans they are being offered and then enter into a currency swap in order to overcome the exchange rate risk. To see how the swap can be structured, assume that the spot exchange rate between the TWD and the Ringgit is 10 TWD per Ringgit. To lock in the prevailing exchange rate and avoid any currency risk on both the principal and interest, the currency swap will work as shown in Figure 12.5. PGC takes the loan principal of TWD 200 million from NBOT and forwards it to Evergreen, which in turn gives PGC the RM 20 million it has received from

PBB. PGC now takes the RM 20 million received from Evergreen, converts it at the spot rate to TWD 200 million and uses these to finance its warehouse and distribution center in Kaohsiung. Evergreen does the same with the TWD it has received from PGC. These principal amounts are then reversed at the end of the 3rd year. In addition, at the end of each year, PGC gives RM 1.2 million being 6% interest on RM 20 million to Evergreen which in turn gives TWD 18 million as 9% interest on the TWD loan. Each company then simply passes on the payments received to their respective banks as fulfillment of their obligation.

The currency swap is shown as the shaded area in Figure 12.5. The payments to the respective banks are not part of the swap. They are shown here merely to show how the cash flows are all matched. Notice that each company gets back at end year 3 exactly the amount it gave at time 0 (initiation of swap).

Note
A currency swap enables a company to effectively switch a foreign currency denominated debt into an equivalent home currency loan.

In effect, the currency swap enables a company to switch a foreign currency denominated debt into an equivalent home currency loan. Thus, in the earlier example, the cash flows to PGC would be exactly equivalent to taking an RM 20 million, 3-year loan at 6% annual fixed interest.

Some readers may find it odd that in the earlier example, PGC is paying only (to Evergreen) 6% on the Ringgit loan but receiving 9% in exchange. Where is the compensation for the difference of 3%? The answer lies in interest-rate parity (IRP) and the international fisher effect, two parity conditions in international finance. Readers familiar with these parity conditions would realize that the Ringgit is likely to appreciate by 3%. (According to parity, the currency with the lower nominal interest rate should appreciate.) Since Evergreen is repaying the same amount of Ringgit 3 years later, it is indeed being compensated for the difference in interest rates.

The earlier was an example of how currency swaps could be used for hedging exchange rate risks. As was the case with IRSs, currency swaps can also be used to arbitrage across currencies or speculate on exchange rate movement. Speculators could use currency swaps to speculate on exchange rate movements. The simplest way would be to enter a swap as foreign currency receiver if that currency is expected to appreciate against home currency and vice versa if the expectation is opposite.

12.4.2 Arbitraging Credit Spreads with Currency Swaps

In addition to hedging exchange rate risks, currency swaps could also be used to arbitrage credit spreads. Companies doing cross-border transactions are often faced with different credit spreads on domestic versus foreign loans. This could simply be due to discrepancies between different credit/lending markets. For example, two companies from different countries but of the same risk category (credit worthiness) may be faced with interest rates on home and of foreign currency loans that have large spreads. Part of this differential could be due to the fact that a company would be better known in its home country but less well-known overseas. In such situations, a currency swap may be used to "arbitrage" this differential. The following is an illustration.

12.4.3 Illustration: Using a Currency Swap to Arbitrage

Malco, a Malaysian company, and HKCO, a Hong Kong-based company, have the same credit rating. However, they are offered the following interest rates for Ringgit and HK$ loans. For simplicity, assume the Ringgit, HK$ spot rate is HK$ 2.5 per Ringgit and the loan amounts are RM 10 million and HK$ 25 million, respectively.

	RM loan	HK$ loan
Malco	6%	9%
HKCO	9%	6%

Suppose Malco requires an HK$ 25 million loan to make an investment in Hong Kong, whereas HKCO needs an RM 10 million loan for its investment in Malaysia; then a currency swap would enable each party to get its desired loan currency but at home currency interest rates. This can be done as follows:

— Malco borrows in Malaysia RM 10 million at 6% interest.
— HKCO borrows in Hong Kong HK$ 25 million also at 6% interest.
— The companies now swap the currencies and undertake to reverse the cash flows at the end of 1 year (assuming they need the loan for only 1 year).

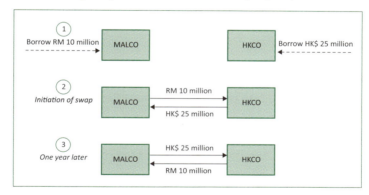

Notice that as a result of the swap both companies got the loan in the currency they wanted and at interest rates much lower than otherwise possible.

As in all cases of OTC derivatives, there is counterparty risk in this situation. Some readers may be tempted to ask whether the same result could have been reached if each company borrows in its home country at the lower interest and simply convert the currency for investment overseas. For example, suppose Malco borrows RM 10 million in Malaysia at 6%, converts it to HK$ 25 million and makes its investment in Hong Kong for 1 year, would the result not be the same? The answer is, it is not equivalent. While this method would eliminate counterparty risk, Malco will be carrying all the currency exposure. Suppose the HK$ depreciates over the next year, the Ringgit value of its Hong Kong investment would be lower — i.e., losses will be incurred in home currency terms. The currency swap in this example, not only allows the management of currency exposure but also achieving lower cost of funds. By means of the currency swap, Malco and HKCO have effectively arbitraged away the credit spreads they each faced with local versus foreign borrowing.

The pricing of a currency swap is done the same way as that of the IRS earlier. That is, value is determined by setting the transaction to have zero NPV at initiation. The process of extrapolating forward interest rates are also needed here. Except that here, interest rates of both currencies have to be extrapolated and estimated over the tenor of the swap.

12.5 Nondeliverable Forward Contracts

An nondeliverable forward (NDF) contract is a customized bilateral OTC contract typically with currencies as their underlying. Unlike a currency forward where the notional amounts of the two currencies are exchanged at maturity, with NDFs only the difference in rates is settled, not the full notional amount. Thus, the term nondeliverable. To understand the difference, we work through a simple illustration.

Suppose a Chinese manufacturer of toys has just exported a shipment to a US retail chain. The invoice amount of US$ 10 million is due in 90 days. To hedge his US$ exposure, the Chinese exporter could use either a currency forward or an NDF as follows.

Using 3-month US$/Chinese Renminbi Forward Contract
$t = 0$

Exporter goes into a 3-month currency forward with HSBC, shorting US$ 10 million at the bank's quoted 3-month forward rate of say 6.40 Chinese Renminbi (CNH) (yuan) per US$.

At Maturity $t = 90$

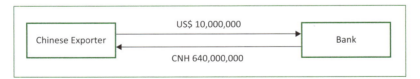

In the currency forward, the two currencies are exchanged at maturity. With the forward, the Chinese exporter "locks in" his CNH revenue of 64 million. If on the 90th day, the spot rate of CNH/US$ is say 6.60, the Chinese firm would have had an implied loss of CNH 2,000,000. This implied loss happens because the CNH had depreciated to 6.60 which is lower than the forward rate of 6.40. Had the Chinese exporter not hedged with the forward, the US$ 10 million he received could have been sold in the spot market for CNH 66,000,000, which is CNH 2 million higher.

However, if the CNH on day 90 turned out to be 6.20 per US$, then the Chinese firm would have had an implied gain from the forward of CNH 2 million. Here, the CNH had appreciated, or the US$ had depreciated. If he had not hedged with the forward, the export proceeds of US$ 10 million would only have fetched CNH 62,000,000. Thus, the implied gain from the forward of CNH 2 million.

Using a 3-Month US$/CNH NDF Contract
$t = 0$

Exporter goes into a 3-month NDF with HSBC, agreeing to sell a notional amount of US$ 10 million at CNH 6.40 (yuan) per US$. (HSBC as counterparty is obviously agreeing to buy US$ 10 million notional for the agreed rate of CNH 6.40.)

At Maturity $t = 90$

To understand how the NDF will be settled at maturity we look at two scenarios: (i) if CNH depreciates to 6.60 and (ii) if CNH appreciates to 6.20.

Scenario 1: CNH is at 6.60 on Day 90
In the NDF, only the difference — profit/loss will be exchanged to settle the contract. Here, since the US$ has appreciated the Chinese firm which is in the short position of having to deliver US$, is the losing party, whereas the bank is in the gaining position. Thus, the settlement of the NDF will be as follows:

NDF settlement amount = (Spot at maturity − Agreed rate) × Notional amount
$$= (6.60 - 6.40) \times 10{,}000{,}000$$
$$= \text{CNH } 2{,}000{,}000$$

Note that since the NDF does not require the Chinese firm to deliver the US$, to the bank, they can sell the US$ 10 million they received from their US customer at the spot rate of CNH 6.6 per US$. Their proceeds from the spot transaction will be CNH 66,000,000. Net of the loss incurred in the NDF, their proceeds is the same CNH 64,000,000 amount they would have locked in with a currency forward.

Scenario 2: CNH is at 6.20 on Day 90
Here, the CNH has appreciated or the US$ has depreciated relative to the agreed NDF rate of 6.40. Thus, the Chinese firm which is short US$ in the NDF is gainer while the bank which is long US$ is the losing party.

Thus, the settlement of the NDF will be as follows:
NDF settlement amount = (Spot at maturity − Agreed rate) × Notional amount
$$= (6.20 - 6.40) \times 10{,}000{,}000$$
$$= (\text{CNH } 2{,}000{,}000)$$

Here the bank being the losing party pays the CNH 2,000,000 to the Chinese firm.

Note that since the NDF does not require the Chinese firm to deliver the US$ to the bank, they can sell the US$ 10 million they received from their US customer at the spot rate of CNH 6.2 per US$. Their proceeds from the spot transaction will be CNH 62,000,000. However, with their net gain in the NDF of CNH 2 million, their total proceed is the same CNH 64,000,000 amount they would have locked in with a currency forward.

Thus, while the NDF is operationally different from the currency forward, notice that the same objective of hedging by locking in a revenue amount is achieved.

12.5.1 Why NDFs?

If the end result of the NDF is the same as that of a currency forward, one would be tempted to ask why we use NDFs when forwards can do the same. NDFs came about to meet the needs of investors with exposures in currencies that were subjected to some restriction. For example, currencies with capital controls, like the Yuan or with trading restrictions like the Indian Rupee, etc. Since hedging the exposure onshore was difficult, NDFs began to be offered in offshore financial centers like Singapore, Hong Kong, London, New York, etc. The fact NDFs do not require exchange of the notional amount but only profit/losses reduces counterparty risk. Additionally, the parties can agree to settle the profit/losses in the currency that is freely traded. Thus, in our previous example, the parties can agree to settle in US$ instead of CNH. These additional flexibilities make NDFs an attractive alternative.

12.5.2 NDF — Applications

Our earlier example illustrated how NDFs can be used to hedge currency exposures. The Chinese exporter was able to lock in his revenue in CNH. In addition to hedging, it is easy to see how NDFs can be used to speculate on expected currency movements. For example, a speculator who thinks the US$ will depreciate against the Indian Rupee over the next month, could go into the NDF as the party that will deliver (short) US$ and receive Indian Rupees.

Speculator Expects US$ to Depreciate Against Indian Rupee
— Enter NDF as US$ payer and receiver of Indian Rupee
  (effectively short US$ and long Indian Rupee)

Speculator Expects US$ to Appreciate Against Indian Rupee
— Enter NDF as US$ receiver and payer of Indian Rupee
  (effectively long US$ and short Indian Rupee)

Arbitraging with NDFs

Arbitraging with NDFs is possible but not easy. Since NDFs are OTC instruments, they do not have the liquidity nor flexibility of exchange-traded instruments. As such it would be difficult to use an NDF to arbitrage a mispriced asset.

12.6 Forward Rate Agreement

In addition to interest futures contracts and IRSs, another derivative instrument that could be used to hedge interest rate risk is the *forward rate agreement* (FRA). An FRA can be used to effectively lock in the interest rate on an underlying floating rate transaction. As the name suggests, an FRA is a *forward* contract in which two parties agree to *cash settle* the difference between a fixed rate and a floating reference rate based on a notional principal. So, the end result of an FRA is similar to that of a fixed-for-floating IRS. The party in the FRA who agrees to pay based on the fixed rate is known as the buyer, whereas the other party, the floating rate payer, is the seller. At the predetermined date, the difference between the two interest rates is cash settled. Being an OTC instrument, FRAs can be customized to meet specific needs. The seller/floating rate payer is typically a bank. Like other derivatives, FRAs are off-balance-sheet transactions. Being cash settled, counterparty risk is limited to the net payments due (i.e., the difference between the interest rates). As it should be evident, FRAs share many of the features of IRSs. But whereas an IRS involves a series of payments over several payment periods, the FRA is often a single payoff transaction. That is, the contract is fully settled on the single settlement date. As to who reimburse/pays whom and the net amount that is to be settled can be found as follows:

$$\text{Cash settlement amount} = \pi \left[\frac{(\text{Floating rate} - \text{Fixed}) \times \text{Tenor}/360}{1 + [(\text{Floating rate}) \times \text{Tenor}/360]} \right]$$

where

π = notional principal
Tenor = length of underlying borrowing/lending period

To see how an FRA can be used to lock in an interest cost, we work through the following example.

> **Note**
> An FRA is a forward contract in which two parties agree to cash-settle the difference between a fixed rate and a floating reference interest rate based on a notional principal.

Illustration: Hedging Borrowing Cost with an FRA

Suppose you are the CFO of XYZ Corporation. Your company has to make an RM 10 million payment to a supplier. The payment is due in 3 months. Since you do not have the funds available, you have arranged with your banker to get a 6-month loan of RM 10 million in 90 days. Your banker, Maybank, has agreed to provide the loan at 6-month KLIBOR + 1%. Having made the arrangement, you now worry that any increase in KLIBOR over the next 90 days would increase your cost of funds. The 6-month KLIBOR is now quoted at 8%.

In order to "lock in" your cost of funds, you might enter into an FRA with another bank (Citibank) on the following terms:

Notional principal: RM 10 million
Terms   : If 6-month KLIBOR exceeds 8%, bank pays Cash Flow (CF) equivalent of difference.
              If 6-month KLIBOR is less than 8%, your company pays CF equivalent of difference.
Maturity   : 180 days based on 6-month borrowing/lending.

Having entered the FRA as the buyer (fixed rate payer), you will be able to lock in a target 9% interest cost. (6-month KLIBOR rate + 1% spread of Maybank; 8% + 1%.) To see how your cost would be locked, we look at five possible interest rate scenarios for the 6-month KLIBOR rate on day 90. The rates range from 7% to 9%. The following table shows the range of interest rates and the reimbursement amount that each party would have to make. The amount is determined using the earlier formula.

6-Month KLIBOR on 90th Day	Cash Settled Reimbursement	
	Citibank to XYZ	XYZ to Citibank
7%	0	RM 48,309
7.5%	0	RM 24,096
8%	0	0
8.5%	RM 23,981	0
9%	RM 47,847	0

To see how you would have locked in, let us compute your "true cost" with the FRA if the 6-month KLIBOR rate rose to 9% annualized on day 90.

Effective Cost of Funds with FRA

Interest paid to Maybank on RM 10 million loan
$[(0.09 + 0.01) = 0.10]$
$$= \left[\frac{0.10 \times RM\ 10\ million}{2}\right]$$
$= RM\ 500,000$

Less
Reimbursement from Citibank = RM 47,847
Net interest payment = RM 452,153

Effective interest
$$= \frac{RM\ 452,153}{RM\ 10\ million}$$
$= 0.0452$ for 6 months

Annualized
$= 0.0452 \times 2$
$= 0.090$
$= 9\%$

Notice that the effective annualized interest rate of 9% is the rate you wanted to "lock in" initially (6-month KLIBOR was 8% + 1% = 9%).

It is easy to see how an FRA could also be used to speculate on rate movements. To take advantage of expected rising rates, one enters the FRA as floating rate receiver. If rates are expected to fall instead, one enters as a floating rate payer. As a final point, it is interesting to note that companies often use FRAs to offset unfavorable positions in IRSs. For example, if a company has entered a 5-year IRS as a floating rate payer and is now expecting to have to pay the counterparty in say the next 6 months, a higher payment because rates are expected to rise temporarily, it can partly reduce the damage by entering a one-off 6-month FRA as the floating rate receiver.

12.7 Credit Derivatives

Credit derivatives is the term used to refer collectively to derivative instruments used in managing credit risk. They are OTC products, custom designed to transfer and/or spread credit risk to other parties willing to accept them, either for a fee or for their own risk management purposes. From virtually nothing in the early 1990s, volume of traded business, which was approximately US$ 20 billion in 1995 has exploded to about $30 trillion in notional value in 2008.

Note
Credit derivatives are customized financial derivatives used in the management of credit risk.

While in the initial years *credit derivatives* mostly had sovereign debt as underlying asset, today corporate debt makes up the bulk of underlying assets. Given their explosive growth, credit derivatives are probably the most important financial product innovated over the last decade, at least until the subprime crisis of 2008.

Defined broadly, credit risk is essentially the probability that a borrower will default; i.e., a borrower is unable to meet financial obligations as they fall due. This inability could be due to firm-specific factors such as mismanagement, fraud, or systematic/economy-wide factors such as recessions. Therefore, credit risk can be attributed to firm-specific or macroeconomic factors or a combination of both. The sharp increase in nonperforming loans (NPLs) that we saw during the Asian currency crisis of 1997/98 was due to macroeconomic rather than firm-specific factors. Thus, business cycles have a huge influence on credit risk. During times of economic booms, credit risk falls. Firms are enjoying rapid revenue and cash flow growth and so have no problem meeting financial obligations. However, during recessions when revenues fall and cash flow is strained, meeting obligations could become difficult. Typically, a firm's credit risk is reflected in its credit rating. Thus, bond rating firms examine both firm-specific factors and the firm's susceptibility to macroeconomic events/cycles in arriving at a rating decision. A firm's credit rating is a qualitative measure of its credit worthiness or credit risk. Markets in pricing credit risk translate credit rating a qualitative measure into a quantitative one, the *credit risk premium*. The credit risk premium is essentially the premium or extra return required for investing in a firm's debt instrument, relative to the risk-free rate. Thus, if the current risk-free rate is 5% while the required return on a firm's bond is 8%, the credit risk premium is the difference of 3% (8% – 5%). Since credit risk is caused by both firm-specific and macro conditions, credit risk premiums change with changes in these factors. For example, aside from firm-specific negative events, credit risk premiums increase during recessions reflecting the higher probability of default.

We use different derivative instruments to manage different risks; credit derivatives are customized contracts designed to manage credit risk. Credit risk, however, can be of different shades. While the worst form is the risk of default or nonpayment, credit risk can also occur at intermediate levels, i.e., when a borrower is in financial distress. The loss that lenders to the distressed firm suffer, usually through diminution in the value of their claims is also credit risk. For example, when a firm is known to have financial problems, the credit worthiness of the firm suffers. If the company has bonds outstanding, their value falls as the market's required yield for the bond now increases. While a ratings downgrade on the bond may come later, the moment a bond is placed on **rating watch**, it can suffer if there is negative news about the company. There are three factors to note. First, credit risk occurs even if there is no technical bankruptcy. Second, market risk (i.e., change in market price of assets) and credit risk are interrelated. Markets react as a borrower's distress worsens and spreads on the company's debt instruments increase. Third, market risk, i.e., the change in the market price of a debt instrument could also be due to macro factors. For example, a rising interest rate regime increases the required return even though firm-specific factors are unchanged. Thus, market risk in this case is really interest rate risk. If the borrowing is from a bank, the lending bank suffers. The value of its loan ought to be marked down to reflect the borrower's distress. If the borrower goes into default, the value of the loan should equal realizable value (if any).

Until the recent advent of credit derivatives, banks managed credit risk by techniques such as **loan underwriting**, **loan syndication**, and **asset securitization**. In essence, these techniques allowed for the spreading of credit risk over a larger spectrum of investors/lenders. Credit risk concentration increases systemic risk, thus these techniques reduce systemic risk by spreading the risk. Despite their common use, techniques such as loan underwriting and syndication are limited by their complication and the narrow constituent of potential players. Loan syndication is typically limited to other commercial banks. In loans underwriting, credit risk is controlled for by controlling the terms of the loan. Securitization, on the other hand, is limited by the fact that it is only suited for loans with standardized features and similar risk profiles, for example, car loans, housing loans, etc. These limitations are overcome with credit derivatives. Standardized features aside, selling loans by securitization can be potentially damaging to bank–client relationships. Since selling off their loans implies that the bank wants to reduce their exposure to a client, it will not help with relationships.

Note
Currently, the three most common credit derivatives are credit default swaps, loan portfolio, and total return swaps.

Credit derivatives, as with most other derivatives these days, come in several forms. As OTC instruments, they can be custom designed to meet specific client purposes. Thus, merchant banks may design a credit derivative as a structured product to meet the needs of a specific commercial bank. While the customization implies that credit derivatives could take several forms, there are three common types. These are **credit swaps**, **credit options**, and **credit-linked notes**. We now turn to a brief discussion of each these.

12.8 Credit Swaps

Credit swaps as the name suggests are based on the logic of swaps. There are three common types of credit swaps: (i) *a credit default swap (CDS)*, (ii) *a loan portfolio swap*, and (iii) *a total return swap (TRS)*.

12.8.1 A Credit Default Swap

A *credit default swap* (CDS) is typically a bilateral arrangement between two parties wherein one party agrees to take on the credit risk in exchange for a periodic fee. The "buyer" in the arrangement pays the periodic fee to the seller who will reimburse the buyer if a prespecified "credit event" occurs. The "buyer" is typically a bank that wants to reduce specific credit risks. The seller in a CDS is often an insurance firm or merchant bank. The credit-event that could trigger a contingent payment by the seller to the buyer could be any one specified event, e.g., an insolvency or bankruptcy of a particular client of the bank, a downgrade of a client's credit rating, or even the rise in spreads between a predetermined risk class of bonds and treasury bills or MGS. Figure 12.6 shows the structure of a typical CDS between a commercial bank which is the buyer and an insurance firm which is the seller.

In essence, in a CDS, the bank is buying insurance to protect itself if a negative credit event occurs. The periodic payments the buyer makes to the seller is quite simply the "premium" for the insurance. The size of the premium would of course depend on the probability of the "negative event" occurring. The higher the probability, the higher the premium is likely to be. Occasionally, both the buyer and seller could be banks. In this case, the seller may be willing to take on the risk for two reasons. First, for the periodic fee it receives and second,

Figure 12.6   Credit Default Swap — Cash Flows

for the ability to diversify/alter its own credit risk profile. For example, if the "negative event" specified in the CDS is negatively correlated with its own credit risk profile or has low positive correlation, then selling the insurance in the CDS can be a sensible way to manage its own credit risk.

12.8.2 A Loan Portfolio Swap

A **loan portfolio swap** is a means by which banks can reduce the **concentration risk** of their loan portfolio by diversifying. As the name suggests, a loan portfolio swap is one in which two banks could exchange portions of their loan portfolio. Loan portfolio concentration can be either geographical or sectoral. That is, a regional bank may have all its loans given out within a certain region of the country — thus geographic concentration. Alternatively, a bank might have a huge portion of its loans extended to a particular industry or economic sector. For example, during the currency/banking crisis in the late 1990s, Malaysian banks had loan portfolios that were heavily concentrated on Broad Property Sector (BPS). With the onset of the crisis, the BPS sector being interest sensitive was severely affected. Local banks that had heavy concentration of construction/real estate loans suffered the most, whereas those with more diversified loan portfolios emerged unscathed.

Often times, concentration of loan portfolio may be inevitable. A bank may choose to specialize in lending to certain sectors. If it had invested in learning/analyzing the sector well, it would make sense to specialize in sectors it understands. Additionally, some banks by virtue of their strategy or mandate would inevitably have concentrations in some sectors. For example, it is inevitable that Agrobank would have heavy concentration of loans in the agricultural sector; Bank SME to the small business sector and the former Bank Industry to the manufacturing sector. While having loan portfolios heavily concentrated in some sectors of the economy is problematic from a risk-management viewpoint, risk reduction by means of diversification can be easily achieved by using a loan portfolio swap. The obvious advantage being that the bank does not have to force itself to lend to sectors it is not familiar with in order to diversify. Ironically, such diversification may actually be more risky since the bank is totally unfamiliar with the new industry/sector. To see how a loan portfolio swap would work, let us use the example of Agrobank and say Public Bank. Let us say Public Bank has a substantial portion of loans in the manufacturing/industrial sector but very little in agriculture/fisheries. Agrobank's loan portfolio on the other hand is heavily concentrated in agriculture/fisheries and very little in manufacturing. Obviously neither bank has the expertise nor the reach to access each other's sectors. Yet, each bank could change its risk profile by swapping a portion of their respective loan portfolios. Assuming the portion of their loans that each bank wants to swap is RM 200 million, a merchant bank that acts as intermediary could arrange the loan portfolio swap as shown in Figure 12.7.

In the loan portfolio swap, Public Bank forwards the payments it receives from its RM 200 million portion of loans to the merchant bank which passes the amount (less its fee) to Agrobank. Simultaneously, Agrobank forwards the payments it receives on its RM 200 million

Figure 12.7   A Loan Portfolio Swap

through the intermediary to Public Bank. Note that unlike securitization, the banks are not selling their loans but merely swapping the payments received from the loans. The net effect of the abovementioned swap is to provide each bank effective exposure in a new sector **without** lending directly in that sector. Given the very different credit risk profile, particularly the different macroeconomic risk, each bank is better off since they have effectively **diversified** their credit risk. From a risk management viewpoint, the absence of a high correlation between the industrial and agricultural sectors enhances the risk profile for both banks.

12.8.3 A Total Return Swap

A **total return swap** (TRS) is a little more complicated than the loan portfolio swap. In a loan portfolio swap, the parties only exchange the respective payments they receive on the portion of loan identified to be swapped; in a TRS both the interest payments received **and** the capital gains or losses are adjusted for in the swap cash flows. Suppose there are two insurance firms, Syarikat Insurans KL (SIKL) and Syarikat Insurans Sabah (SIS). SIKL has a large portion of its funds invested in corporate bonds and commercial papers. SIS, on the other hand, has not been able to purchase as much corporate bonds as it would like to. Thus, its bond portfolio is heavily invested in MGS. SIS feels that an RM 100 million re-allocation from MGS to corporate bonds would be appropriate.

> **Note**
> What differentiates a TRS from a loan portfolio swap is that in addition to the interest payments, capital gains/losses are adjusted for in the swap cash flows.

Rather than sell RM 100 million of MGS and buy corporate bonds, SIS can achieve the same goal at much lower transaction cost through a TRS with SIKL as the counterparty. In the TRS, SIKL will make periodic payments to SIS which will constitute the coupon interest it has received on its RM 100 million of corporate bonds **plus** the capital gains accrued as a result of increased market valuation of the bonds. In exchange for these periodic payments, SIS will pay a simultaneous payment made up of two things: an amount equal to the yield of the 5-year MGS **plus** the capital gain/loss, if any, incurred by SIKL on its RM 100 million of corporate bonds. Figure 12.8 shows the cash flows.

Figure 12.8   A Total Return Swap

What the TRS does in effect is enable each party to get a synthetic exposure in each other's bond portfolio. SIKL gets the stable return that exposure in MGS securities would while SIS gets the higher yield and market exposure (capital gains or losses) that corporate bonds provide.

Box 12.1
Of CDS, CDOs, and the Subprime Crisis

CDS have been at the epicenter of the 2007/2008 US subprime crisis. CDS were invented in the 1990s by Wall Street-based investment banks, largely to meet the demand for insurance against credit risk rising from Collateralized Debt Obligations (CDOs). CDOs were the result of the securitization of home mortgages or housing loans. Securitization is simply the pooling of housing loans bought from commercial banks and packaging them into tranches. For example, in Malaysia, CAGAMAS, the national home mortgage corporation, buys home loans carried on the balance sheets of commercial banks, packages them, and then issues CAGAMAS bonds or *sukuks*. Funds raised from these bonds/*sukuks* may be used to pay the banks. The monthly repayments on the loans are passed through by the banks to CAGAMAS, which in turn uses the funds received to service the bonds when coupon and redemptions are due. The US government pioneered this process with the establishment of two national agencies, Fannie Mae and Freddie Mac in the late 1960s, with the objective of expanding home ownership. Then, in the 1980s, the US government, realizing that banks were reluctant to extend home mortgages to the poor and lower income earners, made it compulsory for banks to extend a certain percentage of their loans to this category of borrowers. Since these were loans of lower quality, they were known as subprime. As motivation to the banks to fulfil their subprime quota, Fannie Mae and Freddie Mac offered to "insure" the credit risk of these loans by way of bilateral agreements with individual banks. As many securitized portfolios also included some subprime loans, a need for similar insurance arose. The investment banks met this requirement by innovating the CDS. Since the premium goes to the seller, CDS issuance was hugely profitable in the initial years when there were few, if any, defaults.

As CDS use expanded, an incentive problem arose. Since it was possible to buy insurance on the loans given out, banks had little incentive to be careful with who they give loans to. Furthermore, as subprime loans carried higher interest rates, they were more profitable than normal loans. With the higher default rates made painless by way of CDS, banks expanded their subprime loan portfolios very rapidly. The real risk takers in all of these were the writers or sellers of CDS. They were names like AIG, Lehman Brothers, Bear Sterns, and even Fannie and Freddie. With the bursting of the housing bubble, many home owners were effectively holding out-of-the-money options. There was little incentive to repay. Default rates spiked and the CDS issuers, institutions which were among the giants of the finance industry, were literally blown to pieces.

12.9 Credit Options

Credit options are essentially calls and puts with either an interest rate or debt instrument as the underlying asset. Just as options can be used to manage risk, **credit options** can be used to hedge credit risk. The underlying logic of using call options to seek protection from risk arising from upside movement and puts against falling prices/values applies. For example, if one would be hurt by rising interest rates, then going long call options on interest rates would

Note
Credit options are essentially calls and puts with either an interest rate or debt instrument as underlying asset.

be appropriate. On the other hand, if falling values would hurt, then going long put options would be sensible. The careful reader should realize that the CDS we saw earlier is really no different from going long a put option. The periodic fee the buyer pays the seller is the "premium" paid for buying the put. To see how credit options, calls, and put could be used, we look at the risk faced by two participants in credit markets: a company that has issued bonds and an investor who is holding a portfolio of bonds.

12.9.1 Illustration: Use of Credit Options Call Options on Credit Risk Premiums — for Bond Issuers

Call options on credit risk premiums are options that enable one to lock in a credit risk premium. For example, let us say Syarikat ABC which has an A3 credit rating has RM 50 million of 10-year bonds outstanding. Assume that these bonds pay a floating coupon rate based of the 10-year MGS + 3%. Currently, 10-year MGS is at 7%, thus Syarikat ABC pays 10%. The obvious risk for a bond issuer such as Syarikat ABC is rising risk premiums. Recall from our earlier discussion that risk premiums can rise either due to firm-specific or macroeconomic factors. Rising risk premiums would obviously increase Syarikat ABC's debt servicing costs. To protect itself and lock in its current cost of 10%, Syarikat ABC could long a call option on credit risk premium. In the US, such options are available on standard rating risk premiums. In Malaysia, Syarikat ABC would have to buy such an option OTC from perhaps a merchant bank or insurance firm.

The call option on credit risk premium will pay off if the premium rises but would expire out-of-the-money if risk premiums fall. In this case, Syarikat ABC could pay a premium of say RM 100,000 to buy the call option which would pay off the difference if the credit risk premium for A3 bonds goes above the 3% "strike price." If the maturity of the option is 1 year and the risk premium for A3 bonds rises to 3.8%, the call can be exercised to receive a payoff of RM 400,000 (0.008 × RM 50 million). The profit from exercise of the call option will offset the 0.8% increase in debt service cost to Syarikat ABC for that year. If the risk premium for A3 bonds is unchanged or reduces, the option expires worthless.

12.9.2 Put Options on Credit Risk Premiums — for Investors of Bond/Debt Instruments

If in the earlier example, an issuer of bonds could use call options to protect itself from rising credit risk premiums, a holder of such bonds could purchase put options to protect itself from falling bond values due to quality downgrades. Risk premiums and quality ratings are inversely related. A downgrade in ratings would increase the required return and thereby reduce bond value. As we saw earlier, this is a form of credit risk.

Illustration: Suppose, a bond fund manager has a portion of his investment in speculative grade BBB bonds. He had invested in them for the higher yield. However, he is now afraid that an increase in risk premium could wipe out the extra returns. Assume the current value of his investment in such bonds is RM 20 million. To protect himself, the fund manager could purchase customized put options from a merchant bank or insurance firm. Unlike the call option in the earlier example, where the strike price was the percentage risk premium, here the strike price should be bond value, i.e., the put options should be exercisable at RM 20 million. Suppose the fund manager pays a premium of RM 100,000 for the put options, he effectively limits his maximum downside risk to the RM 100,000 premium. He is fully protected because if risk premium on BBB bonds rise over the tenor of the put options, his capital loss on the bonds would be offset by the profit he makes on exercising the puts. Notice that in terms of cash flows, the long put option position here is identical to that of the CDS shown in Figure 12.6.

12.10 Credit-Linked Notes

Credit-linked notes can be thought of as debt instruments with embedded options exercisable by the issuer. A credit-linked note therefore would consist of a straight bond and an option. In a sense, this is similar to the callable bond we saw in Chapter 11. The difference here is that the issuer of a callable bond has an option to ***reduce*** the maturity of the bond by "calling" it for redemption earlier, whereas the issuer of the credit-linked note has the option to ***reduce*** the coupon interest of the bond. Just as the yield on a callable bond would be higher than that of a straight bond of the same risk class, the yield of a credit-linked note would be higher too. The higher yield is the "compensation" the issuer pays to the buyers of the note for the call option he has received. Investors in credit-linked notes would effectively have bought a straight bond while simultaneously selling a call option to the issuer.

Illustration: Hedging Credit Risk with Credit-Linked Notes

Easy Car Loan Bhd. (ECLB) is a company that finances car hire purchase; i.e., they lend to purchasers of new vehicles. ECLB wants to raise RM 20 million of new financing to expand its business. The company is obviously exposed to credit risk. Should economic conditions worsen, ECLB would be hard hit by increased default rates. To protect itself from such an eventuality, ECLB could issue credit-linked notes instead of straight bonds. The credit-linked note would pay the face value of RM 20 million at maturity just like a bond; however, the coupon interest is not fixed but may be adjusted lower at the option of ECLB. For example, the note may have two applicable coupon rates: 10% or 5% per year. If times are normal and the default rate on its car loans are below a certain threshold, ECLB would pay 10% coupon. However, if default rates in any particular year is above the threshold, the coupon paid will be reduced to 5%. What this arrangement does is reduce the impact of credit risk on ECLB. When times are bad and ECLB experiences higher default rates resulting in lower cash inflows, its debt servicing obligation is also reduced. The ability to reduce cost when needed is the key benefit of credit-linked notes to the issuer. However, the issuer pays for the benefit by paying a higher yield on the note.

The key players in credit derivatives are obviously those with credit risk exposure. As such, banks/financial institutions, corporates that have issued bonds, bond funds and bondholders, insurance companies, etc., would be key users. As with other derivatives, one could also use these instruments to speculate. For example, an insurance company might take the position of seller in a CDS for several reasons. First, for the periodic fee they would receive, second to take on exposure in credit markets and thereby influence their overall risk profile, or third, perhaps because their evaluation of the macroeconomic environment shows lower potential credit risk relative to their counterparty. As OTC contracts, arbitrage though possible, is less prevalent with credit derivatives.

Note
A credit-linked note is typically a debt instrument with embedded options. Like callable bonds which allow for early redemption, a credit-linked note allows the issuer to reduce the coupon interest rate.

Though the volume of trading in developed markets has increased exponentially, several practical difficulties with credit derivatives constrict their volume growth to anywhere near that of interest rate or equity derivatives. These practical difficulties have to do with issues like complexity of documentation, illiquidity, the lack of market makers and the difficulty in standardizing most credit exposures. Recently, ISDA has introduced new standardized formats for credit derivatives such as CDSs. However, while such standardization can help with disputes arising from interpretation of clauses, hurdles still remain. Perhaps the main difficulty with credit derivatives is determining the probability of default, downgrade, or negative credit event. Given that every customer and credit profile is different, information asymmetry makes it even more difficult for an outside counterparty to measure credit risk and probability of the triggering event occurring. For example, with credit-linked notes, unless the threshold default is very transparent and clearly measurable, it will be difficult to make a numerical assessment.

12.11 Contract for Difference

CFDs or a *contract for difference* is a fairly new OTC-traded derivative instrument. Developed by London-based investment banks in the 1990s as a substitute for an equity swap, it has now evolved into having underlying assets as diverse as commodities, indexes, bonds, etc. Some CFDs have a futures contract as underlying. A CFD is essentially a transaction between two parties in which one party agrees to pay the price difference if the price goes higher, whereas the other party agrees to pay the price difference if it goes lower. CFDs are usually offered by a stock brokerage or investment agencies. The offeror typically quotes bid–ask prices for a given underlying asset. An investor wanting to buy (long) a CFD on a given underlying asset, buys at the ask price and shorts at the quoted bid price. The counterparty is the brokerage that is offering the CFD. There is often no maturity in a CFD. So, one could buy a CFD today, hold it for a desired period and sell it back to the brokerage firm at whatever bid price is being quoted then. The absence of a maturity date is one of several key differences between a CFD and the other derivative instruments covered in this book. The financial institution that offers CFDs for trading, earns in several ways: (i) it earns the bid–ask spread, (ii) it collects margins from both the long and short positions which it holds without paying an interest, (iii) an entry and exit fee is charged as commission, and (iv) an overnight financing fee is charged for every position held overnight. This fee is based on a reference interest rate like LIBOR and would include the credit spread incurred by the broker. The overnight fee is determined as the difference between the total contract value and the margin posted. The overnight fee is debited to the margin account daily. In addition to debiting accounts for overnight fees, the margin accounts will also be adjusted as per marking to market requirements (see Chapter 3 for marking to market). Thus, depending on which way prices move, one could receive margin calls from the CFD offering firm. To understand how the CFD works, we work through the following example.

12.11.1 Illustration: Mechanics of a CFD

Assume a brokerage firm is offering a CFD on Maybank stock. The bid and ask prices are RM 12.50 and RM 12.70, respectively. Each CFD contract is for 1,000 stocks. An investor who is bullish about Maybank would go long the CFD by buying a contract at the ask price of RM 12.70 whereas someone bearish would short the CFD at the bid price of RM 12.50. Suppose you are bullish and so you go long a CFD contract. At entry, you pay the required margin. Unlike an exchange-traded contract where margins are predetermined, here the margin could depend on the brokerage firm's assessment of you. Let's say they require you to post 8% margin. Then the margin required is

$$\{[RM\ 12.70 \times 1,000] \times 0.08\} = RM\ 1,016$$

In addition, if the entry fee or commission is say 1.5%, then

$$\{[RM\ 12.70 \times 1,000] \times 0.015\} = RM\ 190.50$$

So, at entry, you need to pay a total of RM 1,206.50.

For every night that you keep the position open, a fee based on the annualized 3-month KLIBOR will be charged. If the 3-month KLIBOR is at 4% and the broker's spread is 1.5%, then the overnight fee would be

$$\{((RM\ 12.70 \times 1,000) - RM\ 1,016) \times 0.055))/365\} = RM\ 1.76.$$

The amount charged each night will vary according to changes in the ask price, which in turn depends on the closing price each day of Maybank stock.

If 3 weeks later when Maybank stock price had gone up and the bid-ask price is now RM 14.60 to 14.80, you decide to exit. Then, assuming the amount left in your margin account after overnight fee charge deductions is RM 970, the profit that will be credited to your margin account would be

$$(14.60 - 12.70 \times 1{,}000) = RM\ 1{,}900$$

Less exit fee/commission of 1.5% = (RM 14.60 × 1,000) × 0.015
$$= RM\ 219$$

Thus, RM 1,900 − RM 219 = RM 1,681 will be credited to your margin account and the position closed out.

In this example, it is obvious that if Maybank stock had gone down in value, it is not in the investor's interest to exit. He could choose to hold on until prices go higher, however, there is a cost to holding out. Notice that he will be charged overnight fees for each day he holds. These fees will erode his margin accounts. Also, as the underlying stock price falls, he could be receiving margin calls. Like other derivatives, there is in-built leverage. In fact, the leverage factor could be even higher as the initial margins maybe a smaller percentage then exchange traded derivatives.

The brokerage firm offering the CFD is technically an intermediary. If the number of short and long positions on a given CFD is equal, then there is no net exposure for the brokerage. However, in most cases, there would not be an equal number of longs and shorts, in such cases the brokerage will have to hedge its position. As the price of the underlying changes, so would its total exposure. Thus, the hedging has to be dynamic. Though many countries have allowed the trading of CFDs there are some that have not allowed them — this includes the US. The fact that CFDs allow for highly leveraged naked positions and can be a means to camouflage insider trading are concerns that regulators have.

Box 12.2
Debt and Derivatives Beget an Explosive Mixture

The blowup of Archegos, a US$ 50 billion edifice built on leverage that crumbled to nonexistence within a matter of days shocked US financial markets in April 2021. Established as a family office in 2013, it was neither a bank nor a hedge fund, and so escaped regulation. While banks and hedge funds are heavily regulated and have strict disclosure requirements as they use external/public investor's money, family offices

(Continued)

Box 12.2
(Continued)

are not. Archegos, it appears, took billion-dollar bets on a few stocks through derivatives like CFDs and equity TRSs. In exchange for a small fee, these instruments effectively enable one to "own" the underlying stock. Simply put, with equity TRSs, one receives cash flow equivalent to the sum of dividends and capital gains or losses of the underlying stock for a given period, in exchange for the premium. The inherent leverage that such instruments provide, meant that Archegos could build massive equity exposure, reportedly in excess of US$ 50 billion on a very small capital base. The counterparties to these transactions were investment banks like Credit Suisse, Morgan Stanley, and Nomura. It turns out that the use of such equity derivatives was beneficial in several ways to both parties in terms of regulation and compliance. For Archegos, it not only escaped the need to disclose its large positions but also saved costs on stamp duty exemptions, since the underlying stocks were not owned directly. For the counterparty, investment banks, it had the added advantage of not having to report and set aside capital as these derivative instruments were not covered under Basel III reporting requirements for capital adequacy. Archegos' extremely successful 7-year run ended abruptly because a single stock, Viacom CBS Inc., which announced a secondary stock offering, resulting in a 9% fall in its price. As Archegos had exposure to about 29% of Viacom's outstanding stock, it unravelled when margin calls on the equity TRSs could not be met.

An obvious question that arises is, how could someone take such large risks? The key to understanding such behavior lies in recognizing the perverse incentive that arises with situations of excessive debt/leverage. When a firm is highly leveraged, management is incentivized to take on risks as most of the money at stake is the externally sourced borrowed money. Failure would mean external debtholders stand to lose much more than equity holders, but success would mean huge profits to equity holders but the same interest rates to debtors. This skewed return payoff is what causes the perverse excessive risk-taking behavior.

Such incentives of leverage together with their ability to take advantage of regulatory loopholes meant that the build-up of risks could go unnoticed by regulators.

Financial markets become more fragile and prone to accidents because leverage magnifies fluctuation. Thus, a small setback in Viacom shares was enough to wipe out Archegos, a US$ 50 billion entity. This same build-up in vulnerability and magnification applies at the macrolevel too. And it is this macroeconomic vulnerability that worries regulators. Hong Kong's HKMA and SFC have recently announced new initiatives aimed

> **Box 12.2**
> (*Continued*)
>
> at precisely the Archegos type problem. Hong Kong, as Asia's premier financial center, is a natural choice for the setting up of family offices by Asia's wealthy elite. Aside from new regulation on family offices the initiative involves projects that will cross reference investment and market trading/clearing databases to identify large exposures by single entities.
>
> *Source:* Reproduced from an op-ed piece by the author titled "Recent Financial Blow Ups: Are They Canaries in the Coalmine?"

SUMMARY

This chapter provided an overview of swaps, NDFs, FRAs, and credit derivatives. All these derivatives are OTC instruments. Swaps involve the bilateral exchange of cash flows between counterparties at fixed periodic intervals. An IRS is a transaction in which parties exchange cash flows based on two different interest rates. In a fixed-for-floating swap, e.g., one party pays an amount based on a fixed interest rate, whereas the other party pays based on a floating interest rate. IRSs, like other derivatives, can be sued for hedging, arbitrage, and speculation. Examples of these applications were examined. IRS can also be used by financial institutions to manage asset–liability mismatches and duration gaps. Currency swaps are another type of swap examined in this chapter. In a currency swap, the parties exchange fixed amounts of one currency for another. The rationale being to hedge currency risk and the interest rate risk that goes with it. Unlike an IRS in which the notional principal is not exchanged, in a currency swap, the notional principal in the two different currencies is exchanged. The currency swap effectively enables a company to switch a foreign currency denominated debt into an equivalent home currency loan. An NDF is a customized bilateral transaction in which the notional amounts are not exchanged. At contract maturity, only the profit/loss resulting from the difference between the agreed rate and the spot rate at maturity is exchanged. FRAs can be used to effectively lock in the interest rate on an underlying floating rate transaction. An FRA is essentially a forward contract in which the parties agree to cash-settle the difference between a target fixed rate and a floating reference rate. Credit derivatives are instruments used in managing credit risk. Credit derivatives come in several forms. The three most common types are credit swaps, credit options, and credit-linked notes. Credit swaps can in turn be in the form of a CDS, loan portfolio swap or TRS. The CDS is essentially the purchase of a put option on credit risk. A loan portfolio swap can be an easy way by which banks can reduce the concentration risk of their loan portfolios. In a TRS, both the interest payments received and capital gains/losses, if any, are adjusted for in the swap cash flows. Credit options are essentially calls and puts with either an interest rate or debt instrument as the underlying asset. Credit-linked notes are debt instruments with embedded options exercisable by the issuer. It typically consists of a straight bond and an option.

KEY TERMS

- Interest rate swaps
- Currency swaps
- Notional principal
- Fixed for floating swap
- Comparative advantage
- Fixed/floating rate payer (receiver)
- Duration gaps
- Swap curve
- Swap spread
- Reset frequency/period
- Forward rate agreement
- Credit derivatives

- Credit risk premium
- Credit swaps
- Credit default swap
- Loan portfolio swap
- Total return swap
- Credit options
- Credit-linked notes
- Nondeliverable forwards

End-of-Chapter Questions

1. Both Syarikat KL Infra (KLI) and Ipoh Industries Bhd (IIB) are in the market for an RM 30 million, 5-year loan. Both companies have the same credit rating and have been offered the following rates for 5-year (balloon payment of principal) loan.

	KLI	IIB
Fixed	12.5%	12.5%
Floating	3-month KLIBOR + 2%	3-month KLIBOR + 2.75%
Preferred loan	Fixed	Floating

    You work for KL Merchant Bankers (KLMB), and think that the quoted rates are arbitrageable by means of an IRS. Design a fixed-for-floating swap. Show the percentage gain to each party assuming the "mispricing" is split equally among the three parties.

2. Bank Bumi Bhd (BBB) has total assets of RM 300 million and a positive duration gap of 8 years. The weighted duration of its assets is 8.8 years while that of its liabilities is 0.8 years. Assuming there is a credible counterparty willing to enter into an IRS with BBB for an RM 100 million notional and flexible tenor (maturity), design an IRS with 6-month reset by which BBB can reduce its positive duration gap. Assuming the duration of liabilities is unchanged, what is the new overall duration gap?

3. Mr. Tan, a very wealthy individual has just been told that interest rates are likely to rise over the next 2 years. He intends to enter an IRS in order to profit from rising rates.
    a. What should his position be in the swap? Fixed rate or floating rate payer?
    b. Assuming the notional principal is RM 10 million, and 6-month reset frequency, determine his profit or loss if rates increase 2% over the first 6 months. (Assume the current floating rate equals the proposed fixed rate at initiation.)
    c. What is his profit or loss if interest rates fall 1.5% over the first 6 months?

4. Melaka Food Industries Bhd. has requested an RM 20 million, 3-year loan from its bank, Maybank. Maybank however is willing to lend on a floating rate basis at 3-month KLIBOR + 1.5%. Assume the loan will have to be serviced quarterly. Encik Ali, the CFO of Melaka Foods, is worried having heard that interest rates are likely to rise over the foreseeable future. Advise Encik Ali on how he could use an IRS to hedge his company's interest rate exposure.

5. TNB has a 10-year, ¥en 50 million loan outstanding with a Japanese bank. The ¥en loan has a 2.5% annual interest rate. The loan was taken 5 years ago and so has 5 more years to go. Daibochi, a Japanese plastics maker with operations in Malaysia has just negotiated an RM 5 million, 5-year loan with Maybank at 7.5% annual interest. Both companies are worried about the foreign exchange exposure. Design a currency swap that will enable both companies to manage exchange rate risk. (Assume debt servicing will be on 6-monthly basis, the spot ¥en/Ringgit rate is ¥en 10/Ringgit.)

CHAPTER 12 Financial Derivatives: Markets and Applications

6. Design a 2-year currency swap between Cadbury (UK) and Trebor Malaysia Bhd. Both companies intend to finance a 2-year working capital requirement. Cadbury needs RM 12 million for its Malaysian subsidiary while Trebor needs £2 million for its UK subsidiary. The £ interest rate is 6% while the Ringgit rate is 8%.

7. Encik Aman, the CFO of Aman Swift Bhd., a local distributor of LG Electronics products, is a worried man. The company has just placed a large order with LG Korea for appliances worth RM 25 million. The payment will be due 60 days after their arrival. Encik Aman expects the products to arrive in 30 days. Accordingly, he had arranged with the company's banker, RHB Bank for working capital financing of 6-month duration. The loan of RM 25 million can be taken 90 days from now. The problem for Encik Aman is that RHB Bank would only agree to a floating rate loan priced at 3-month KLIBOR + 2.5%. His actual cost therefore will depend on prevailing interest rates 90 days from now. The 3-month KLIBOR is now 4.5%. Encik Aman wants to lock in the current rate of 7% (4.5% + 2.5%).

   You work for Bank of KL, a newly established bank known for its innovativeness. Encik Aman has approached you about locking in his cost of borrowing at 7%.
   a. Design a hedging strategy for Encik Aman using 3-month KLIBOR futures contracts. Show that a 2% increase in 3-month KLIBOR will have no effect on his cost.
   b. Structure an FRA to lock in the 7% cost.

   Show the cash flows (reimbursement) between Bank of KL and Aman Swift Bhd. if the 3-month KLIBOR is between 3.5% and 5.5% (use 1% increments).

8. Explain what is meant by a CDS. How different is it from buying credit put options?

9. How does a loan portfolio swap help banks diversify? What is the problem with loan portfolios that are concentrated either regionally or sectorally?

10. Compare and contrast the loan portfolio swap with a TRS. What are the similarities/differences?

11. You hold a medium-sized portfolio of money-market instruments: T-bills, NCDs, short-term Cagamas bonds and MGS. As these instruments are highly interest sensitive, you intend to hedge using derivative instruments.
    a. Assuming the following three interest derivatives are available, show how you would structure the hedge.
       (i) Interest rate futures
       (ii) Interest rate options
       (iii) IRSs
    b. In deciding on which derivative instrument to choose, state three factors/features that you should consider.

12. Your company, Syarikat IIUM, has been looking for an RM 60 million, 3-year loan. You have been quoted the following rates.
    - 3-year fixed rate @ 9.5% p.a.
    - Floating rate @ 3-month KLIBOR + 2.5%

    Your long-time friend, who is CFO of Zebra Holdings, tells you that his company has been quoted the followings rates for a similar loan.
    - 3-year fixed rate @ 8.70%
    - Floating rate @ 3-month KLIBOR + 2.25%

(i) Assuming both loans have principal balloon payments, what accounts for the lower quotes to Zebra Holdings?
(ii) Given the quotes, show that there is "mispricing."
(iii) Design an IRS between your company and Zebra Holdings that can "arbitrage" the mispricing equally (graph the swap).
(iv) Calculate the percentage gains to each company resulting from the swap.

13. A Japanese bank expects to lend 10 million Euros to a Spanish firm. If negotiations are successful, the loan will be made 1 month from today. The terms of the loan have already been established: the Spanish firm is to pay a fixed rate of 5%; the term of the loan will be 1 year; interest and principal, in euros, will be repaid to the bank 1 year after the loan is made. The Japanese bank is interested in maximizing the yen-denominated wealth of its Japanese stockholders.
   a. State the nature of the interest rate risk the Japanese bank faces.
   b. State how the Japanese bank can use FRAs to manage the interest rate risk it faces.
   c. State the nature of the foreign exchange rate risks the bank will face after the loan is actually made.
   d. Show how the bank can manage the exchange rate risk it will face by use of at least three different currency derivatives (clearly outline the strategy).

14. Consider a 3-year plain vanilla fixed-floating IRS. The notional principal is $20 million. The swap fixed rate is 6%. The floating rate is 6-month LIBOR. The payment dates are every 6 months, beginning 6 months hence. On the origination date, 6-month LIBOR is 5.5%. On subsequent dates, the 6-month LIBOR is:

Time	6-month LIBOR
5.5	5.25%
1	5.5%
5.5	6%
2	6.2%
5.5	5.44%

   a. Compute the cash flows that are exchanged between the two counterparties.
   b. If in hedging, you had entered the abovementioned IRS as the fixed rate payer, state the underlying exposure that you must have hedged.
   c. If you were the fixed rate payer, and the counterparty was speculating, briefly state what the counterparty's expectation must have been.
   d. As the hedger in (b) above, state two risks that you may still face.

15. Educorporation is seeking an RM 15 million loan to be drawn in 3 months. Its banker, Maybank, has agreed to provide the loan at KLIBOR + 2%. The 3-month KLIBOR is being quoted at 5% while the 3-month KLIBOR futures is 94.00.
   a. What target rate can Educorporation "lock in" using interest rates futures?
   b. Outline the hedge strategy using KLIBOR futures.
   c. Prove that the target rate has indeed been locked in, even if rates rise 2% over the next 3 months.
   d. Show how Educorporation could use an FRA to achieve the same goal of locking in a target interest rate? (Assume a counterparty and be specific about the terms.)

e. Show how Educorporation could have used an IRS to lock in the target rate (use a diagram, include/show the payments to Maybank).

16. Your company will be receiving £3 million in 90 days from its British customer. As CFO, you know that you have at least four possible means of hedging the exposure: (i) using currency forwards, (ii) using currency futures, (iii) currency options, and (iv) currency swap (assume the contract size is £1 million in all cases).
   a. State the position you would establish using each alternative (be specific).
   b. If you had to choose one alternative, which would you choose? State the factors you would consider in making the choice.

17. By means of an example, show how a call option on credit risk premiums can protect bond issuers, while a put option on credit risk premium can help bond investors.

18. What is a credit-linked note? Show its equivalence with straight bonds and options. How does a credit-linked note protect an issuer's credit exposure?

19. ATL Corp. and United Sabah Plantation (USP) are two large Bursa Malaysia listed companies. Both companies are in the process of sourcing an RM 50 million loan. Working for a local investment bank, your boss has asked you to design an IRS that your bank can "sell" to the two parties while acting as intermediary. You have been provided the following information.

	ATL Corp.	USP
Amount	RM 50 million	RM 50 million
Tenor	5 or 6 years	6 years
Preference	Floating	Fixed
Quoted floating	6-month KLIBOR + 1.5%	6-month KLIBOR
Quoted fixed rate	8.25%	7.5%

   a. Prove that there is an arbitrage opportunity.
   b. Structure an IRS with your bank as intermediary and assuming a 6-year tenor. (Show the figure and all cash flows carefully.)
   c. Assume the gains are shared equally among the three parties. Show the numerical breakdown of the gains to each party.

20. What is a CFD?
   a. How are CFDs different from options in terms of (i) transaction costs, (ii) margins, and (iii) risk profile.
   b. How would CFDs compare with futures contracts in terms of risk profile?

21. An Indian importer has a US$ 8 million payable in 30 days. Given restrictions in India on foreign currency contracts, he plans to undertake an NDF with DBS a Singapore Bank.
   a. Structure an appropriate NDF transaction for the Indian firm.
   b. If the agreed rate in the NDF is 65 Indian Rupees (INR) per US$, show the cash flow if the INR is at 72 per US$ in 30 days.
   c. Determine the resulting cash flow of the NDF, if the INR is at 60 per US$ on day 30.

CHAPTER · 13

Derivative Instruments and Islamic Finance

Objectives

This chapter provides an overview of Islamic financial contracts that have the features of modern-day derivatives. It also outlines some of the necessary features for an Islamic financial instrument and examines the opinion of Islamic jurists/scholars on the validity of modern derivative instruments. An in-depth description of several *Shariah*-compliant structured products is provided. The mechanics of their use in risk management is illustrated. On completing this chapter, you should have a good understanding of *Shariah*-compliant risk management tools.

Introduction

Malaysia is in many ways a pioneer in Islamic banking and finance. Growth in Islamic banking and, in particular, the amount of funds under the management of Islamic asset management and mutual funds has been impressive. A number of developments in the Malaysian financial sector over the last decade has provided an impetus to the growth of Islamic banking and finance. Among these have been the introduction of the Islamic Interbank Money Market, *Shariah*-compliant equity indices, and the development of *sukuks* and *sukuk* markets. These developments coupled with the fact that there has been a several fold increase in funds managed under Islamic mutual funds, and asset management companies has meant that Islamic finance invariably comes into contact with derivative instruments. Malaysia's Bursa Malaysia Derivatives Berhad has announced plans to launch an Islamic index futures contract. If introduced, it could be the world's first stock index futures contract based on an Islamic index. An Islamic equity index is essentially a stock index made up of stocks that have been designated as being *halal* or acceptable for investments by Muslim investors. Though Malaysia has made important strides in developing its Islamic banking and finance sector and is now on the verge of introducing Islamic equity derivatives, other Islamic countries have not been as "progressive." In fact, derivative instruments, especially the use of financial derivatives, have remained a controversial issue. That financial derivatives are necessary instruments for risk management, often appears to have been missed. The general stance (based on opinions of *fuqaha*) appears to be that where risk is concerned, **on-balance sheet** rather than **off-balance sheet** techniques (see Chapter 1) should be used. However, the inherent disadvantages associated with using on-balance sheet techniques, potential loss of competitiveness, customer inconvenience, etc., seem to have been ignored. The *Shariah* evaluation of derivatives is further clouded by the often contradictory stand of Islamic jurists and scholars with regard to derivative instruments. Still, a number of Islamic financial instruments/contracts exist that have derivative-like features. These being the *Ba'i Salam*, *Istisna*, *Joa'la*, and the *Istijrar* contracts.

This chapter is divided into three sections. The first section examines some of the necessary features for Islamic financial instruments. The second section provides a description of Islamic financial contracts that have the features of derivative instruments. The third section describes several **Shariah**-compliant risk management tools/derivatives that are available in Malaysia. This final section examines the views of Islamic scholars (***fuqaha***) on derivative instruments.

13.1 Necessary Features for Islamic Financial Instruments

Before going on to examine the existing instruments in Islamic finance that have derivative-like features, we examine here some of the necessary features for Islamic financial instruments. All Islamic financial instruments and transactions, in general, must meet a number of criteria to be considered *halal*. At a primary level, all financial instruments and transactions must be free of at least the following five items: (i) **riba** (usury), (ii) **rishwah** (corruption), (iii) **maysir** (gambling), (iv) **gharar** (unnecessary risk), and (v) **jahl** (ignorance). *Riba*, which literally translates to usury, is more commonly referred to as the charging of interest. *Riba* can be in different forms and is prohibited in all its forms. For example, *riba* can also occur when one gets a positive return without taking any risk. As for *gharar*, there appears to be no consensus on what *gharar* means. It has been taken to mean unnecessary risk, deception, or intentionally induced uncertainty. In the context of financial transactions, *gharar* could be thought of as looseness of the underlying contract such that one or both parties are uncertain about possible outcomes. Alternatively, that the contract could be read in a number of ways such that one party could easily deceive (deception) the other party. *Maysir* from a financial instrument viewpoint would be one where the outcome is purely dependent on chance alone — as in gambling. Finally, *jahl* refers to ignorance. From a financial transaction viewpoint, it would be unacceptable if one party to the transaction gains because of the other party's ignorance.

Though their exact definition may still be open to interpretation, there cannot be any doubt as to what is being intended by the *Shariah* in requiring that financial instruments and transactions be free of the above items. Clearly, what is being intended is fair play and justice to all parties to a transaction.

> **Note**
> In order to be compliant with the *Shariah*, financial instruments must avoid *riba* and *gharar*.

In addition to these requirements for financial instruments, the *Shariah* has some basic conditions with regards to the sale of an asset (in this case, a real asset as opposed to financial assets). Since a derivative instrument is a financial asset dependent on the value of its underlying asset (real asset in most cases), the *Shariah* conditions for the validity of a sale would also be relevant. Aside from the fact that the underlying asset must be *halal*, at least two conditions have to be met: (i) the underlying asset or commodity must currently exist in its physical sellable form, and (ii) the seller should have legal ownership of the asset in its final form. These conditions for the validity of a sale would obviously render impossible the trading of derivatives. However, the *Shariah* provides exceptions to these conditions to enable deferred sale where needed.

13.2 Islamic Finance Instruments with Features of Derivative Instruments

A number of instruments/contracts exist in Islamic finance that could be considered a basis for derivative contracts within an Islamic framework. In this section, we examine two such contracts: (a) the ***Ba'i Salam*** contract, and (b) the ***Istijrar*** contract. While the *Ba'i Salam* contract has provisions and precedence, the *Istijrar* is a recent innovation practiced in Pakistan. Two other contracts, the *Istisna* and *Joa'la,* which are related to the *Ba'i Salam* contract, are also briefly examined.

13.2.1 *Ba'i Salam*

Ba'i Salam is essentially a transaction where two parties agree to carry out a sale/purchase of an underlying asset at a predetermined future date but at a price determined and **fully paid** for today. The seller agrees to deliver the asset in the agreed quantity and quality to the buyer at the predetermined future date. This is similar to a conventional forward contract with the big difference being that in a *Salam* sale, the buyer pays the entire amount in **full at the time the contract is initiated**. The contract also stipulates that the payment must be in cash form. The idea behind such a "prepayment" requirement has to do with the fact that the objective in a *Ba'i Salam* contract is to help needy farmers and small businesses with working capital financing. Since there is full prepayment, a *Salam* sale is clearly beneficial to the seller. As such, the *Ba'i Salam* price is normally **lower** than the prevailing spot price. This price behavior is certainly different from that of conventional futures/forward contracts where the futures price is typically higher than the spot price by the amount of the carrying cost. The lower *Salam* price compared with spot is the "compensation" by the seller to the buyer for the privilege given to him.

The *Ba'i Salam* contract is subject to several conditions, of these the important ones are as follows:

(a) Full payment by buyer at the time of effecting the sale.
(b) The underlying asset must be standardizable, easily quantifiable, and of determinate quality.

(c) A *Salam* contract cannot be based on a uniquely identified underlying asset. This means that the underlying commodity cannot be based on a commodity from a particular farm/field, etc. (By definition such an underlying would not be standardizable.)
(d) Quantity, quality, maturity date, and place of delivery must be clearly enumerated in the *Salam* agreement.
(e) The underlying asset or commodity must be available and traded in the markets throughout the period of contract.

Given our earlier description of futures contracts, it should be clear that the current exchange-traded futures would conform to these conditions with the exception of the first, which requires full advance payment by the buyer. However, given the customized nature of *Ba'i Salam*, it would more closely resemble forwards rather than futures. Thus, some of the problems of forwards, namely "multiple-coincidence," potential for price squeeze and counterparty risk, can exist in the *Salam* sale. Counterparty risk, however, would be one-sided, in that, since the buyer has fully paid, it is only the buyer who faces the seller's default risk and not both ways as in forwards/futures. To overcome the potential for default on the part of the seller, the *Shariah* allows for the buyer to require security that may be in the form of a guarantee or mortgage.

> **Note**
> The *Ba'i Salam* is a transaction where two parties agree to carry out a sale/purchase of an underlying asset at a predetermined future date but at a price negotiated and fully paid today.

The contract could also form the basis for the provision of working capital financing by Islamic financial institutions (IFI). Since financial institutions would not want possession of the underlying commodity, parallel contracts may be used. Though not all jurists are in agreement about its permissibility, the literature cites two venues for parallel *Salam*.

The first is a parallel *Salam* with the original seller, whereas the other is an offsetting transaction by the financial institution with a third party. In the first alternative, the financial institution after entering into the original contract gets into a parallel *Salam* to sell the underlying commodity after a time lapse for the same maturity date to the original seller. The resale price would be higher and considered justifiable since there has been a time lapse. The difference between the two prices would constitute the bank's profit. The shorter the time left to maturity, the higher would be the price. However, the requirement is that both transactions should be independent of each other. The original transaction should not have been priced with the intention to do a subsequent parallel *Salam*. Under the second alternative, the bank that had gone into an original contract enters into a contract promising to sell the commodity to a third party on the maturity date of the contract. Since this second transaction is not a *Salam* contract, the bank does not receive advance payment.

13.2.2 *Istisna* and *Joa'la* Contracts

In addition to *Ba'i Salam*, there are two other contracts where a transaction is made on a "yet to" exist underlying asset. These are the *Istisna* and *Joa'la* contracts. The *Istisna* contract has, as its underlying, a product to be manufactured. Essentially, in an *Istisna*, a buyer contracts with a manufacturer to manufacture a needed product to his specifications. The price for the product is agreed upon and fixed. While the agreement may be canceled by either party before production begins, it cannot be canceled unilaterally once the manufacturer begins production. Unlike the *Salam* contract, the payment here is not made in advance. The time of delivery too is not fixed, but negotiated. Like the *Ba'i Salam*, a parallel contract is allowed for in *Istisna*. Thus, the *Istisna* contract may be used by Islamic banks for product financing.

Note
The *Istisna* and *Joa'la* contracts can be thought of as variants of the *Ba'i Salam*. They are for use in the case of a product yet to be manufactured and services to be performed, respectively. The parties agree on the price and terms for delivery in the future.

The *Joa'la* contract is essentially an *Istisna* but applicable for services as opposed to a manufactured product. Thus, for example, when a school wants to use the services of a tailor to make several hundred uniforms, the *Joa'la* contract would be an appropriate arrangement. The conditions described for the *Istisna* contract apply in the case of *Joa'la*.

13.2.3 The *Istijrar* Contract

The *Istijrar* contract is a recently introduced Islamic financing instrument. Introduced in Pakistan, the contract has embedded options that could be triggered if the underlying asset's price exceeds certain bounds. The contract is complex in that it constitutes a combination of options, average prices, and **Murabaha** or cost plus financing. The *Istijrar* involves two parties, a buyer who could be a company seeking financing to purchase the underlying asset and a financial institution.

A typical *Istijrar* transaction could be as follows: a company seeking short-term working capital to finance the purchase of a commodity like a needed raw material approaches a bank. The bank purchases the commodity at the current price (P_0) and resells it to the company for payment to be made at a mutually agreed-upon date in the future, e.g., in 3 months. The price at which settlement occurs on maturity is contingent on the underlying asset's price movement from t_0 to t_{90}, where t_0 is the day the contract was initiated and t_{90} is the 90th day that would be the maturity day.

Unlike a *Murabaha* contract where the settlement price would simply be a predetermined price, P^*, where $P^* = P_0(1+r)$, with r being the bank's required return/earning, the price at which the *Istijrar* is settled on maturity date could **either** be P^* or **an average price** ($\bar{P}$)

of the commodity between the period t_0 and t_{90}. As to which of the two prices will be used for settlement will depend on how prices have behaved and which party chooses to "*fix*" the settlement price. The embedded option is the right to choose to fix the price at which settlement will occur at any time before the contract mature. At the initiation of the contract, t_0, both parties agree on the following two items: (i) in the predetermined *Murabaha* price, P^*, and (ii) an upper and lower bound around the P_0 (bank's purchase price at t_0).

For better elucidation, the different prices are shown below in a continuum. Prices increase as one goes to the right.

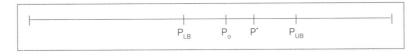

where P_0 = the price that bank pays to purchase underlying commodity
P^* = *Murabaha* price: $P^* = P_0(1+r)$
P_{LB} = the lower bound price
P_{UB} = the upper bound price

The settlement price (P_s) at t_{90} would be:
(i) $P_s = (\bar{P})$ if the underlying asset price remained within the bounds
or (ii) $Ps = P^*$ if the underlying asset exceeds the bounds and one of the parties chooses to exercise its option and use P^* as the price at which to settle at maturity

For either party to exercise its option and thereby fix the settlement price at P^*, the spot price during the term of the contract must have exceeded the bounds at any time. As to which party would exercise, of course, depend on the **direction** of the spot price movement. For example, if the spot price at any time breaks through the upper bound, the buyer would get worried. But whether he will exercise or not would depend on his expectations of the spot price over the remaining period of the contract. If he believes that the price is likely to keep increasing thereby causing the price at which settlement will occur to be greater than P^*, it will be in his interest to "exercise" by fixing the settlement price now at P^*. Essentially, he would notify the bank that he is exercising his option and that the settlement would be P^*. Should spot prices fall such that it breaks the **lower** bound, the seller, in this case the bank, would have the option to fix the settlement price at P^*.

Note
The *Istijrar* is a financing contract with embedded options. If the spot price of the underlying asset exceeds predetermined bounds, then the parties have the right to exercise the option to fix the settlement price at the predetermined *Murabaha* price.

The settlement price is determined as follows:

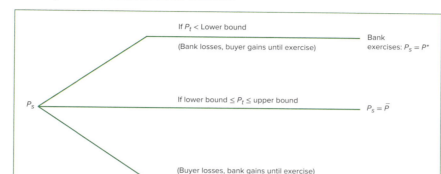

where P_s = settlement price at maturity
  $\bar{P}$ = average price; P_{t0} to P_{t90}
  P_t = spot price of underlying commodity on day t
  P^* = predetermined, cost plus or *Murabaha* price

Analyzing the *Istijrar* contract in its entirety from an option's viewpoint is complicated since it has two different exercise styles rolled into one. Such an instrument would be unusual in conventional finance. Still, for our purpose here, the embedded options in the *Istijrar* can simply be thought of as follows: The fact that the buyer gets to fix the buying price at P^* when the price goes higher implies that he has a **call option** at an exercise price of P^* while the bank has a **put option** at the same exercise price.

What the *Istijrar* contract attempts to do is to allow for the impact of price changes but to cap the benefits that accrue as a result. By definition, since price changes are allowed only within a band, the advantage to one party and the disadvantage to the other are capped. The maximum potential gain or loss is limited. Such a contract fulfills the need to avoid a fixed return on a riskless asset, which would be considered *riba* and also avoids *gharar*, in that both parties know up-front P^* and the range of other possible prices (by definition between the upper and lower bounds).

13.3 The *Ba'i Al-Urbun*

The *ba'i al-urbun* is one of the preexisting Islamic finance contracts that is often used by modern-day Islamic finance practitioners to justify the use of options. *Urbun,* which means a prepayment or advance in Arabic, is essentially a good faith deposit. In an *urbun* contract, the buyer of a product may place with the seller a small deposit in exchange for which the seller might grant a period of time, at the end of which the buyer forfeits his deposit. However, if the buyer goes ahead with the transaction within the stipulated time, then the buyer pays the agreed price *less* the *urbun* payment made earlier. That is, the difference between the selling price and the *urbun* amount paid earlier.

Thus, the *urbun* is essentially a portion of the agreed price. The typical period of time granted in an *urbun* is 3 days. One could argue that the *urbun* is like the granting of a call option for 3 days. However, there is a difference. In the case of options, regardless of whether it is exercised or not, the premium paid is never recovered (sunk cost). In the case of the *urbun*, the deposit placed is deducted from the agreed price in determining the price to be paid to take delivery from the seller, and thus the "premium" is recovered.

Ba'i al-urbun has two variants: a refundable *urbun* and a nonrefundable *urbun*. The nonrefundable *urbun* is one where the deposit placed is lost to the seller if the buyer decides not to go ahead with the transactions. This is also the variant which is more controversial, in that with the exception of the *Hanbali madzhab*, which permits it, the *Maliki*, *Shafii*, and *Hanafi madzhabs* find it objectionable. The refundable *urbun*, on the other hand, is acceptable to all four *madzhabs*. The refundable *urbun* is one where the deposit placed by the buyer is returned to the buyer if he chooses not to proceed.

Although the refundable *urbun* may have the acceptance of all four *madzhabs*, it obviously would not be workable as a basis for modern-day options. This has to do with the fact that being refundable there would be little compulsion on the buyer. The buyer is essentially getting a call option for free. As a result, there could be serious moral hazard on the part of the buyer.

13.4 The *Bai bil-Wafa* and *Bai bil-Istighlal* Contracts

The **Bai bil-wafa** is a financial contract that would resemble the conventional repurchase agreement (REPO). REPOs are commonly used with short-term/money market instruments. In a typical REPO, a money market trader sells commercial paper to another trader, promising to buy it back a few days later at a slightly higher price. In doing so, he gets temporary liquidity **without** selling the paper outright. He compensates the buyer with the higher price. The difference between the sale and the repurchase price is the interest cost for the borrowing. The *Bai bil-wafa* works in a similar way. One party sells an asset to another, promising to buy it back at a future period. The buyer can only resell the asset to the original party and not to a third party. Thus, the *Bai bil-wafa* is really a composite contract that has two elements — *Bai* (sale) and *rahnu* or *rihn* (pledge). The *rihn* element prevents the buyer from selling the asset to any other party. While the *Bai bil-wafa* resembles a REPO, there is a significant difference. Both the initial selling price and the repurchase prices are **equal**. This is unlike the REPO where the latter price is **always** higher. The REPO is a short-term financing transaction in which the party that first buys and then resells earns an interest return. In the *bil-wafa*, the only advantage to the party that buys and resells is *usufruct* or right of use of the asset.

A second difference between *Bai bil-wafa* and REPO is that, while a REPO is always of fixed maturity, the *bil-wafa* can be terminated by either party at any time. That is, the original seller can "redeem" his asset by repaying the sum he received earlier. Similarly, the buyer can at any time return the asset and require the seller to return his money. That the original seller can buy back the asset at any time by returning the money he had received resembles an embedded **American-style call option**. The exercise price being equivalent to the price he had received earlier from the buyer. Viewed from the viewpoint of the buyer, the fact that he can require repayment at any time by returning the asset implies that he has an embedded **American-style put option.** Since the prices are unchanged, the embedded options have been given/received at zero premium.

The **Bai bil-Istighlal** can be thought of as an extension of the *bil-wafa* contract that includes an *ijarah* (lease). In a *bil-Istighlal* contract, one party sells an asset to a buyer who immediately pays the sale price in full. Like the *bil-wafa*, the buyer agrees to resell the asset at the same price at a future date. However, in the *Bai bil-Istighlal* contract ownership changes, allowing the buyer to lease-back (*ijara*) the asset to the seller for fixed lease payments. The lease/*ijara* will be in effect until the original seller repurchases the asset. The *Bai bil-Istighlal* therefore would be a contract much more amenable for use in modern financial markets. The embedded options of the *bil-wafa* contract are still applicable; however, they can be subject to required stipulation as desired by both parties if not completely revoked.

Note
The *Bai bil-Istighla* combines the *bil-wafa* with an *ijarah*.

13.5 The Islamic Profit Rate Swap

Islamic banks in most countries including Malaysia operate within dual banking systems. They operate together with a larger conventional banking system, sharing a common customer base and ecosystem. As a result, when deposit rates change in the conventional banking system, the profit rates paid by Islamic banks have to also change, failing which there could be massive outflows. Thus, Islamic banks are inevitably exposed to interest rate risks as do conventional banks. Since interest rate changes, as discussed in the Appendix of Chapter 5, can play havoc with bank balance sheets, there is an obvious need for Islamic banks operating in dual banking systems to be able to manage such risks. It was precisely to manage such a need that Islamic profit rate swaps (IPRS) were innovated.

Approved by the National Shariah Advisory Council (NSAC) of Bank Negara Malaysia, the IPRS is now a key tool for IFI to manage their "interest rate" risk. Ironical as it may seem, Islamic banks in Malaysia operating within a dual banking system have substantial exposure to interest rate risk. While most of their assets (loans to customers) are fixed rate *Bai Bithamin Ajil* (BBA) or *Murabaha*-based, the cost of their deposits fluctuates. Studies have shown a very high correlation and a dependence of Islamic bank deposit rates on interest rates prevailing in the much larger conventional banking. As a result of this mismatch, one can expect large positive duration gaps in Islamic bank balance sheets. While conventional banks use floating or adjustable rate customer financing to reduce the duration of their assets, Islamic banks relying on deferred sale contracts like the BBA do not have that opportunity. In view of this huge potential risk, Bank Negara's Shariah Advisory Council (SAC) has approved the use of variable rate financing for Islamic banks. These, however, come with caps and conditions on how much of the risk can be passed on to customers. The IPRS should therefore be a timely instrument for the management of rate risk.

13.5.1 Mechanics of the IPRS

CIMB Bank's proposed swap involves two stages. In the first stage, the Islamic bank would sell an asset to a counterparty for a notional amount. The counterparty then resells the asset to the Islamic bank at notional principal **plus** a fixed markup profit rate. The net result of this stage is that the notional amounts cancel out, leaving the Islamic bank as the **fixed profit payer**. This fixed rate is payable according to the reset period, e.g., every quarter or 6 monthly. In the second stage of the transaction, the Islamic bank sells an asset to the counterparty for a notional amount **plus** a floating rate (based on an agreed-upon reference rate). In

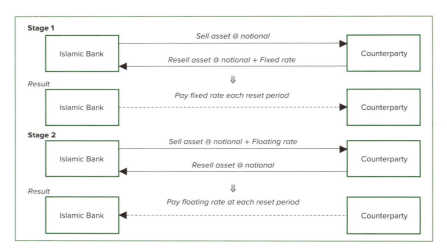

Result: Managing Rate Risk with IPRS

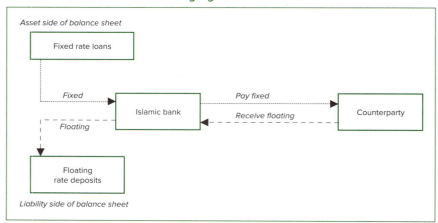

Figure 13.1 *Islamic Profit Rate Swap (IPRS)*

exchange, the counterparty resells the asset to the Islamic bank for the notional amount. The net result of this second stage is that the counterparty becomes the **floating profit rate payer**. Thus, on completion of both stages, the Islamic bank is the fixed profit rate payer and floating rate receiver while the counterparty is in the opposite position. For the Islamic bank, interest rate risk is being managed since the floating rate it receives from the swap would offset/move in line with its costs on the liability side of its balance sheet, i.e., customer deposits. On the other hand, the fixed rate payment it has to make in the swap would come from the fixed rate payments it receives from its customers. Figure 13.1 outlines the structure of the IPRS.

Readers of Chapter 12 would realize that the IPRS proposed above is essentially a plain vanilla, fixed-for-floating interest rate swap. Indeed, it is intended to achieve the same purpose, managing interest rate risk. The sale and resale of assets are to fulfill the *Shariah* requirement of the need for an underlying physical asset on which to base the cash flows.

> **Note**
> The IPRS can be used by IFI to manage rate risk and asset liability mismatches.

13.6 Islamic Structured Products

Islamic structured products are a fairly recent innovation. As the name suggests, they are purposefully designed by combining different derivatives and underlying assets to provide holders with an array of alternative payoff profiles, exposures, and risk profiles. They can be thought of as prepackaged investments customized to suit an investor's desired needs and risk profile. Often the profit payoff of the product is linked to the performance of an underlying reference such as a share, bond, basket of securities, commodities, etc.

Structured products are often the mainstay of the wealth management products offered by Islamic banks. Like real estate investment trusts (REITs) that offer investors bite-size pieces of the underlying real estate properties, structured products offer investors access to otherwise very large investments and the possibility of combining them with exposures in yet other assets. Thus, a structured product may offer an investor a unique risk-return profile that is otherwise not readily available.

A commonly marketed structured product is a capital or principal guaranteed product. Such capital guaranteed products are usually the result of combining a zero coupon bond with a call option on a stock. For example, a structured product with a principal of $50,000 and 1-year tenor may offer a principal guaranteed return, linked to the performance of Apple stock over the period, say 30% of the percentage rise in Apple shares over the year. At maturity, the investor's return is contingent on the performance of Apple stock.

If Apple stock had gone up 15% over the period, his returns would be $50,000 plus (0.15 × 0.30 = 5%).

If, however, Apple stock had fallen, he would simply get back his principal of $50,000, since it is a capital guaranteed product.

So, the advantage to the investor of this structured product is that he gets exposure to Apple stock without the equity risk.

In exchange for this advantage, his cost is that, in addition to any fees, he receives zero returns for his invested capital. The opportunity cost is the main cost. For the bank, there is risk when it sells the structured product. To protect itself, the bank would be investing in the needed zero coupon bond and either hold Apple stock or buy a call option on the stock or "synthesize" a call option on the stock. So, the bank often has to do dynamic hedging to ensure its exposure is well managed. Well-managed hedging with leveraged positioning can make structured profits highly profitable for banks.

13.6.1 Examples of Structured Products Offered by Islamic Banks

A number of structured products are offered by Islamic banks in Malaysia, the Middle East, and elsewhere. Most of these products are offered as part of their wealth management product portfolio. We examine below 4 such products offered by Islamic Banks in Malaysia.

1) **Islamic Callable Range Accrual** — Maybank Islamic

A principal protected deposit product, the return is determined by the performance of an underlying reference index. The investor only receives a return if the performance of the underlying reference index falls within a specified range. For example, the underlying reference index maybe the FBM KLCI with a specified range of say, 1,550–1,600 points. If the index never moves within the stipulated range, the investor receives nothing and only gets back his principal. If the index remains within the range for a brief period, he makes a small profit. If, however, the FBM KLCI index remains for a long period within the range, the investor makes huge profits.

Note that for the issuing bank, if the index remains within the range for an extended period, it can causes huge losses. The bank has to pay the investor his profits but even if it is holding the underlying stocks, it will not be making money from the stocks as they are simply within a range and not appreciating. In order for the bank to limit its losses, the product has an embedded call option, which enables the bank to recall the product for redemption.

Clearly, the objective of the investor in buying this product is to profit from the expected range trading of the FBM KLCI index. The contract is structured based on *tawarruq* and *wa'ad* as the underlying *Shariah* contracts.

Source: Maybank Islamic and FinCAD website.

2) **Range Accrual *Murabaha* Negotiable Certificate of Deposit-i (RA MNCD-i)** — RHB Islamic

This product is a commodity *Murabaha*-based deposit product. However, unlike the typical *Murabaha* where the profit markup fixed, here the profit is linked to the performance of an underlying reference index. The reference can be a currency pair or profit rate index, known as the *reference rate*. Like the *Istijrar* contract seen in Section 13.2.3 earlier, based on the expected volatility of the reference index, predetermined upper and lower limits are established. The profit return to the investor is based on the number of days the reference rate is within the range, i.e., between the upper and lower limits:

$$Lower\ Limit \leq Reference\ Rate \leq Upper\ Limit$$

The performance of the underlying reference is observed daily. The longer the reference remains within the range, the more profitable to the investor.

The investor receives the maximum profit rate if the reference rate is within the range **every day** during the specified time period. If the reference fails to fall within the range for all the days in the specified time period, the investor receives the minimum profit rate — which could be zero. If there are reference rate movements within and outside the range during the specified time period, the investor's return will be the participating profit rate, which is

$$Minimum\ Profit\ Rate \leq Participating\ Profit\ Rate \leq Maximum\ Profit\ Rate$$

Like the *Istijrar*, the objective here is to have an element of risk to perhaps justify the returns. For the investor, this is a product that will enable him to benefit from the range trading of the underlying index. Interestingly, the contract is transferable, and the last holder of the certificate will receive the final profit payment and the deposit on the maturity date.

Source: RHB Islamic.

3) **The Islamic Range Forward** — RHB Islamic

The Islamic Range Forward is a structured foreign exchange product. Currencies are exchanged not at a fixed but a rate based on the performance of the prevailing spot rate of the currency pair against a set of exchange rates or the "range."

The investor and bank agree up front on the range. The range is made of the upper strike rate or the upper limit, and lower strike rate or the lower limit. The underlying *Shariah* contracts are *wa'd* (unilateral promise undertaken by the investor) and *Bai' al-Sarf* on the settlement date, if investor chooses to exercise his options.

The investor's set of choices:

— If the spot rate at expiry ≤ the lower strike rate, the investor will exchange at the lower strike rate with the bank on settlement date.
— If the spot rate at expiry ≥ the upper strike rate, the investor will exchange at the upper strike rate.
— If the spot rate at expiry ≥ lower and ≤ upper strike rate, the investor has no obligation to exchange to another currency. He may choose instead to enter a foreign exchange contract with the bank at the prevailing spot rate.

— If the investor terminates the contract before the maturity date, he might incur unwinding costs for the termination, liquidation, or re-establishment of any hedging transaction related to the contract.

Illustration: Islamic Range Forward — Exchange Rate Scenarios and Payoffs

A Malaysian exporter with US$ receivables needs to hedge his exposure. He expects to receive US$ 1 million. He enters an Islamic range forward with a bank. To understand how settlement occurs, we examine 3 exchange rate scenarios on contract maturity date, as shown in the following table.

Exchange Rate Scenario	Spot Rate at Expiry	Lower Strike Rate	Upper Strike Rate	Principal Amount (US$)
1	4.18	4.20	4.24	1 million
2	4.25	4.20	4.24	1 million
3	4.23	4.20	4.24	1 million

- In the first scenario, the US$/RM spot rate is lower than the lower strike rate. The investor will sell US$ 1 million to the bank at the lower strike rate of RM 4.20 per US$ on the settlement date.
- In the second scenario, the US$/RM spot rate is higher that the upper strike rate. The investor will sell US$ 1 million to the bank at the upper strike rate of RM 4.24 per US$ on the settlement date.
- In the third scenario, the US$/RM spot rate is within the range. The investor has no obligation to sell his US$ 1 million to the bank. He can choose to sell at the spot rate of RM 4.23 to the bank if he chooses.

Clearly, what is happening with the Islamic range forward is that an investor can hedge his foreign currency within a range of rates. Unlike a currency forward or futures which will lock in a single exchange rate, here he has the potential to gain a little if rates move favorably, while also managing his exposure.

It is obvious that the size of the range is key to how much benefit the investor can get. But, it is likely the bank will want to charge a higher fee for a wider range. So, the key trade-off to the investor in deciding on this product is whether the marginally higher benefit he receives, relative to forwards and futures, justifies the incremental fee.

Source: RHB Islamic.

4) **Islamic Dual Currency Investment (IDCI)** — Maybank Islamic

This is a dual currency investment product that essentially combines foreign exchange options and *Murabaha* deposits. The product enables investors to gain from foreign exchange movements in addition to earning the profit rate for their murabaha deposit. To understand the mechanics of the product, we examine two scenarios, a first scenario where the currency option is in-the-money (ITM) at maturity and another where it is out-of-the money (OTM).

Scenario 1: Embedded Currency Option is ITM
If at maturity the embedded currency option is ITM (profitable), he can choose to exercise the option and receive the underlying foreign currency at the strike price for the amount of his outstanding *Murabaha* deposit. He can then choose to sell the foreign currency to the bank at the prevailing spot and be back in-home currency, making a profit in the process. The size of his profit will obviously depend on size of the exchange rate movement.

Scenario 2: Embedded Currency Option is OTM
If at maturity the embedded currency option is OTM and not profitable to exercise, then he simply gets the *Murabaha* profit from his deposit. Clearly, this is a structured product that enables the investor to participate in the potential upside rally of a foreign currency. For this advantage, he pays a fee to acquire the structured product. Obviously, the fee should equal the value of the embedded currency call option.

13.6.2 Risks Associated with Structured Products
As the majority of structured products are customized OTC instruments, they share many of the risks associated with nonexchange-traded instruments. The key risks would be

— counterparty/default risk
— liquidity risk
— pricing risk (possibility of hidden pricing — lack of transparency)
— valuation risk — inability to correctly value complex derivative instruments
— misselling — selling complex products to unwary customers (*jahl*)
— *Shariah* compliance risk

13.6.3 Islamic Structured Products — Challenges
Islamic structured products, even in a well-developed and highly supportive environment like Malaysia, are few and far in between when compared to conventional structured products. Going by Malaysian Securities Commission (SC) data, between 2013 and 2021 there were 149 lodged structured product programs with the SC. Of these 138 were conventional structured products programs amounting to RM 427 billion. By comparison, only 11 Islamic structured product programs amounting to RM 50.05 billion were lodged with the SC over the same period. Conventional structured products were therefore 12 times larger than Islamic products in terms of size, and 8 times larger in terms of value. As of January 2022, a total of 24 banks had lodged structured product programs with SC. Of these only 4 were Islamic banks. The lack of popularity of Islamic structured products among Muslim investors may be due to *Shariah* requirements. The need to avoid leverage, speculation, *riba*, and *gharar* preclude the use of many types of derivative-based structured products. Aside from *Shariah*-based limitations, lack of investor education, awareness, and small market size may be other reasons.

Box 13.1
Derivative Instruments, Risk Management, and *Shariah* Compliance

The acceptability of financial derivative instruments such as forwards, futures, options, and swaps for *Shariah*-compliant businesses remains unresolved. While the issue is still being debated and deliberated, risk management remains the soft underbelly of Islamic banking and finance. There has, however, been some progress. *Shariah* scholars have allowed the use of *wa'ad* (promise)-based contracts in the case of managing exchange rate risk. Today, *wa'ad*-based contracts that mimic currency forwards and currency options are available both in the Gulf and in Malaysia as *Shariah*-compliant ways of hedging exchange risk. The allowance for such an innovation came after years of debate and "pressure" on *Shariah* scholars in view of the obvious need for such instruments. The approval for the use of these instruments came with the requirement that the Islamic bank entering into these bilateral arrangements must ensure that customer is using the derivative solely for hedging. The bank verifies this by requiring the customer who will become the counterparty, to show documentary evidence of its underlying currency exposure. Even if this puts the onus on banks to ensure the derivatives are not misused for speculation, it is indeed a workable solution and has been well accepted. It is hard to imagine prohibition on the use of currency derivatives in a world with such volatile exchange rates.

Much of the reluctance that *Shariah* scholars have with derivatives arises from the fear that they can easily be used for speculation. While this fear is real and well placed, one needs to also consider the huge handicap placed on Muslim businesses from a blanket prohibition. Given the state of the world, businesses today face many complex risks. Often a risk is not visible until it hits. A classic case is that of contingent exposure, a common occurrence for companies involved in bidding for competitive international tenders. For example, when a company submits a bid to undertake a future foreign currency denominated transaction, and the outcome of the competitive bid will be known a month later, its foreign currency exposure is contingent upon its bid being selected. The bidding company does not know until a month later whether its bid has been accepted, yet, since the bid commits the firm to undertake a future transaction at a predetermined foreign currency amount, its currency exposure begins the very day it submits the bid. So, how does one hedge such exposure? The only way to hedge such contingent exposure is by way of currency options. In fact, derivatives evolved from forwards to futures and then to options precisely to enable the management of such complex risks.

Finally, the lack of a coordinated stand on the use of derivatives has resulted in the stunted growth of risk management within Islamic finance. Despite the huge strides that Islamic

(Continued)

Box 13.1
(Continued)

banking and finance have made in the last decades, *Shariah*-compliant risk management has not kept pace. Inadequate risk management capability will be a serious drag on Islamic banking and finance as it moves from infancy to growth. There is an obvious need for a well-considered and enlightened stand on the use of derivatives for hedging.

Source: Adapted from the author's op-ed column.

13.7 *Sukuk* with Embedded Options

Sukuk are a means by which businesses can raise nonequity, external financing in a *Shariah*-compliant way. *Sukuk*, which is plural for *sakk*, refers to investment certificates or "trust certificates" which are tradable. *Sukuks* have been used extensively by Muslim traders in the Middle Ages as papers denoting financial obligations arising from commercial activities. From a conventional finance viewpoint, *sukuks* are essentially a hybrid instrument, sharing features of both debt and equity. Despite their recent reincarnation, *sukuks* have become a very successful Islamic finance product. These days, there are many types of *sukuks*, including many exotic ones. Exotic *sukuks* are *sukuks* with complex structures. This has been the result of wanting to have altered risk profiles, different cash flows profiles, or cash flow profiles dependent on outcomes (contingent payoffs). The need for such cash flows is often the result of wanting to avoid fixed returns and faxed cash flows. Thus, we have seen of late *sukuks* that would have payoffs attached to commodity prices, *sukuks* that are exchangeable at maturity to equity of the *mudarib* or groups of stock of other companies, held by the *mudarib* (issuer — Khazanah Nasional, Malaysia). There has also been *sukuks* with embedded options. The options could be call options on the underlying asset made available to the *mudarib* or put options on the asset made available to the special purpose vehicle (SPV) (trustees). The following figure shows a *sukuk* structure with an embedded put option.

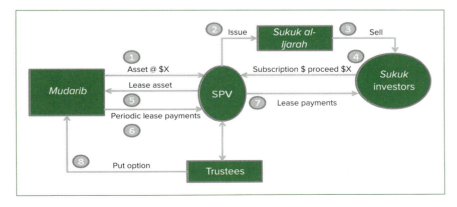

Figure 13.2   *Sukuk* with Embedded Put Option

Here, the embedded put option enables the trustees, who act on behalf of the *sukuk* holders, to exercise the put option by selling the underlying asset to the issuers at the exercise price. Notice that the *sukuk* holders will only want to exercise the put if it is in their favor to do so, i.e., if they cannot find a third party willing to pay more. Thus, with the embedded put option, there is no "guarantee" of what the cash flow at maturity is, ahead of time. Embedding options in *sukuk* allow issuers to overcome the issue of fixity in cash flows, which has been a source of unease among *Shariah* scholars. While the *Ijarah* (lease)-based *sukuk* had an embedded put option, there are also *sukuk* with embedded call options. One example would be the Khazanah exchangeable *sukuks* issued by Malaysia's Khazanah Nasional. These had stocks owned by Khazanah as the underlying asset of the *sukuk* and at maturity, *sukuk* holders could choose to exercise by redeeming the *sukuk* for a predetermined number of the underlying stocks.

A number of Middle Eastern entities, especially from the Gulf Cooperation Council (GCC) nations have issued sukuk with *"change of control put."* These are embedded options that will be triggered in the event of a change in ownership of the issuing entity. For example, many *sukuk*-issuing corporations are government-controlled entities, when these are privatized, ownership will change. *Sukuk* holders who do not want to continue with the new owners can exercise the put option and sell their *sukuk* to the issuing company at predetermined exercise prices. For example, DP World (a Dubai-based, government-linked entity that operates ports) issued a Wakala-based *sukuk* in 2016, which had an embedded put option giving *sukuk* holders the right to redeem the *sukuk* if a "change of control event" occurs. A change of control event was deemed to have occurred if the Government of Dubai ceases to own either directly or indirectly 50% of the issued share capital of DP World. The use of such an option can help reduce the funding costs as *sukuk* holders know they are protected from any potential change in ownership.

Following the global finance crisis of 2008/09, the Bank for International Settlements (BIS) came out with revised requirements for capital adequacy of banks. Known as the Basel III Framework, it was designed to address the deficiencies of Basel II, which were laid bare by the financial crisis. In essence, Basel III required banks to have much higher equity capital. Thus, banks in meeting the new requirements for Tier 1 capital could issue new common equity or quasi equity instruments that were subordinated, had no maturity, were loss absorbing, and had fully discretionary noncumulative dividends/repayment. A number of Islamic banks in the GCC region resorted to using "perpetual *sukuk*" to meet these additional capital adequacy requirements. **Abu Dhabi Islamic Bank (ADIB)** was the first to use a *Mudarabah*-based perpetual *sukuk* to raise funds under the Additional Tier 1 (AT1) category. These *Mudarabah sukuk*, however, came with embedded call options by which the issuing bank can call back portions of the issued *sukuk* at fixed intervals and at predetermined exercise prices. Following ADIB's successful use of the perpetual *sukuk* structure, a number of other Islamic banks in the Gulf and in other countries have used them to raise funds for their Tier 1 capital requirements.

13.8 *Shariah* Views on the Trading of Currency and *Shariah*-Compliant Tools for Managing Currency Risk

The *Shariah* viewpoint on the trading of currencies is based on the legal definition of the currency exchange (*sarf*) contract, which is *the exchange of one monetary form for another in the same or different genera, i.e., gold for gold coins, silver for silver, gold for silver, silver for gold, etc., whether it is in the form of jewelry or minted coins.* Such trading is permitted since the Prophet (PBUH) permitted such exchange. However, in addition to the five basic conditions that an instrument must avoid, *riba*, *gharar*, *masyir*, *rishwah*, and *jahl*, currency exchange contracts require the fulfillment of the following four additional conditions.

(a) Mutual receipt before the contracting parties' parting
(b) Equality of quantities if monies of the same genus are traded
(c) Inapplicability of additional conditions (*syart*)
(d) Nondeferment

The need for these conditions arise from the saying of the Prophet (PBUH): *"Gold for gold, in equal amounts, hand-to-hand; and silver for silver, in equal amounts, hand-to-hand,"* as well as his (PBUH) saying: *"Do not trade one of them absent (thus, deferred) for the other immediately delivered."*

These were authenticated by major narrators as *"Gold for gold, silver to silver, wheat for wheat, barley for barley, dates for dates, and salt for salt, in equal amounts, hand-to-hand; and if the genera differ (in an exchange), then trade as you wish provided it is hand-to-hand."*

Based on the abovementioned viewpoint, *fuqaha* had for long withheld permissibility of currency trading. Such a prohibition had obviously hindered Islamic businesses in their risk management needs. In view of the genuine need for hedging for companies in cross-border business, there had been much "pressure" on the *fuqaha* to review the prohibition. Perhaps, in response to these, there have been a number of developments that have made *Shariah*-compliant tools possible. The three key developments were the following:

(a) The convention of *Fiqh* scholars at its *Muktamar* in Kuwait (1409H) recommended that forward and future contracts be transacted based on Islamic nominate contracts such as *Salam Sarf* and *wa'ad*.
(b) The OIC's Islamic Fiqh Academy pronounced that the *wa'ad* is obligatory and can stand in a court of law if it is made as a unilateral promise in a commercial transaction and if violation of the promise can cause one to incur liabilities or losses. *(Note: By the Shariah, wa'ad which means promise may not be binding legally.)*
(c) BNM's Shariah council in its resolution of April 2005 pronounced that IFIs are allowed to enter forward currency transactions based on a unilateral binding promise (*wa'ad*).

In response to the previously stated developments, a number of IFI in the Gulf states and in Malaysia have developed several *wa'ad*-based products for managing currency risk. We examined the following two generic versions of *wa'ad*-based products.

(1) The Islamic FX Forward

The most popular *wa'ad*-based forex product is probably the Islamic FX forward. Known alternatively as the Islamic FX Outright, FX Forward *Wa'ad-I*, or by other names, it involves the use of a unilateral *wa'ad*. Under this arrangement, an IFI provides a unilateral promise (*wa'ad*) to a customer in return for a fee. Depending on the customer's needs, the *wa'ad* by the IFI could be either buy or sell a currency in exchange for another at a predetermined price and future date. Depending on the IFI's product structure, there may be another unilateral *wa'ad* by the customer to the IFI. The customers' *wa'ad* would obviously be in the opposite direction that is promising to deliver or take delivery of the currency from the IFI at a predetermined price/exchange rate.

By way of these *wa'ad* arrangements, a customer effectively "locks-in" the exchange rate at which he will buy or sell a currency to the IFI. In essence, this *wa'ad* arrangement replicates a conventional forward contract.

Illustration: Using Islamic Forward *Wa'ad* to Manage Currency Risk

A Malaysian importer has a KRW 60 million payable to Samsung Corporation of Korea for a shipment of electrical appliances. Payment is due in 60 days. The Malaysian company is afraid of any appreciation of the KRW against the Ringgit. To hedge this risk, the Malaysian company enters into an Islamic FX Forward *wa'ad* contract as follows with a Malaysia IFI.

Figure 13.3   Mechanics of the Islamic FX Forward

Assuming the IFI charges a fee of say RM 3,000 for the unilateral promise it makes to the Malaysian company, the importer would lock-in a MYR cost of:

KRW 60 million @ 0.05263	= RM 3,157,800
+ Fee charged	= RM 3,000
Hedged cost	= RM 3,160,800

Notice that the hedged cost of RM 3,160,800 to the Malaysian company is locked-in on day 0. Thus, over the following 60 days, the Malaysian company is unaffected by any changes in the RM/KRW exchange rate.

(2) The FX *Wa'ad* (FX Option)

This is another *Shariah*-compliant *wa'ad*-based foreign exchange risk management product offered by IFI. This structured product effectively replicates a conventional currency option. A customer intending to use this product will "buy" a promise from the IFI to either buy or sell one currency for another for a fee. In essence, the customer is buying the right to buy or sell a currency at a predetermined rate for a fee. At a future maturity date, the customer can "exercise" this right. If a customer buys the right to sell a foreign currency under this *wa'ad* arrangement, then from a conventional viewpoint, he is effectively purchasing a put option on the currency. A *wa'ad* arrangement to buy a currency would constitute a long-call position.

Illustration: Using an FX *Wa'ad* Option to Hedge Currency Risk

Suppose the Malaysian company in the earlier example wants to use a *wa'ad*-based option rather than the *wa'ad* forward, then the structure and cash flows would be as follows:

Step 1: t = day 0

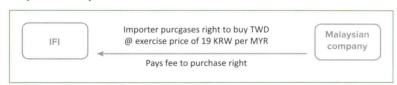

Step 2: t = day 60. If Malaysian company chooses to exercise

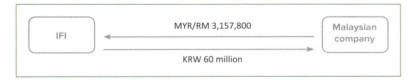

Figure 13.4   Mechanics of the Islamic FX Option

Here, the Malaysian company is effectively long a 60-day call option on KRW 60 million. The Malaysian company had paid a fee for the IFI's *wa'ad*. This fee is very much like the premium for a call option. Suppose the IFI charges a fee of RM 20,000 for the *wa'ad* option, then the Malaysian company is assured that its maximum cost on the shipment from Samsung is:

Payment on exercise	= RM 3,157,800
Fee (premium) paid to IFI	= RM 20,000
Maximum cost	= RM 3,177,800

Notice that with *wa'ad* option, one is not "locking-in" a cost as was the case with the *wa'ad*-based forward. With the option, one establishes instead a maximum cost or a "ceiling" on the payable. To see why this is so, suppose the KRW depreciates against the Ringgit over the next 60 days, it may be better for the Malaysian company to not exercise the *wa'ad* option with the IFI, but instead purchase the KRW at a lower spot rate. Depending on how much the Korean Won depreciated, the cost of the shipment would be lower.

For example, suppose the KRW depreciates against the Ringgit such that on day 60 the rate is:

Spot rate on day 60 = KRW 24 per RM
or = RM 0.04167 per KRW

It is obvious that not exercising the FX *wa'ad* option would be better for the company.

KRW 60 million/24 = RM 2,500,000

The cost of the KRW 60 million will be RM 2.5 million if purchased in the spot market. The company's total cost will be RM 2.502 million if the RM 20,000 fee paid to the IFI earlier is included.

Thus, with the *wa'ad* option, the Malaysian company is buying itself insurance against an appreciation of the KRW. While the forward protects against a KRW appreciation, it does not allow the company to take advantage of a potential depreciation. The FX *wa'ad* option contract does. As we saw in Chapter 6, it is this flexibility of options that makes it more attractive than forwards or futures. Since options allow one to hedge against unfavorable movements while also providing the opportunity to take advantage of favorable movements, their cost (premium) would obviously be higher. So, the fee paid to the IFI in the *wa'ad* forward would be much lower than that paid for the *wa'ad* option.

Given the latent demand for risk management products and the allowance in Malaysia for *wa'ad*-based products, there has been a substantial increase in their use. This popularity has to do with the fact that *wa'ad*-based products have straight forward structures with little need for complication and therefore can be cost effective. Over the last couple of years, a number of IFIs in Malaysia provide a range of *wa'ad*-based products.

13.9 Islamic View of Current-Day Derivative Instruments

Having discussed the necessary features for financial instruments to be *Shariah*-compliant and Islamic financial instruments with features of modern derivative instruments, we now turn to a brief discussion on the Islamic view of current-day derivatives. As any student of Islamic finance would agree, the jury is still out as far as a definitive opinion on derivatives is concerned. The validity and permissibility of these instruments appear to vary by scholar/jurists. Even where Islamic scholars have found them objectionable, their reasons for objection differs. There does not appear to be a consensus. Much of the work by Islamic scholars has been of a highly juridical nature. They examine derivatives within narrow confines of contractual arrangements and thereby miss the broader picture of why instruments such as futures and options are needed in modern business environments. Among Islamic countries, Malaysia appears to be the most accommodating and progressive in adapting modern financial instruments within its Islamic banking and financial system.

Though much of the existing work has been of a highly juridical nature, the approach taken by Islamic scholars appears to be different. In the case of options, for example, some have examined their validity under the Fiqh doctrine of **al-Khiyarat** or contractual stipulations while others have drawn parallels between options and **ba'i al-urbun**, **urbun** being a transaction in which a buyer places an initial good faith deposit with the seller. Should the buyer decide to go ahead with the transaction, the payment is adjusted for the initial deposit but is nonrefundable if the buyer decides not to proceed with the transaction. A third view has been to examine options in the light of *gharar* — or uncertainty. In at least one other situation (Abu Sulayman, 1992), options have been viewed as totally detached from the underlying asset.

When viewed solely as a promise to buy or sell an asset at a predetermined price within a stipulated period, *Shariah* scholars find nothing objectionable with options. However, it is in the trading of this promises and the charging of premiums that objections are raised. In the case of futures contracts, some *ulamas* have objected stating that deferred sale is not allowed while yet others cite precedents to deferred sale such as *ba'i salam* but have objection to futures on other grounds — mostly that it encourages speculation. The following is a sample list of opinions of *Shariah* scholars/councils.

Views of *Shariah* Scholars on Exchange-Traded Derivatives

Many *Shariah* scholars have provided their opinions on the validity or otherwise of exchange-traded derivatives. Since they are individual opinions, they are diverse and are often conflicting. As mentioned earlier, there is no consensus. While a definitive opinion, acceptable to all, may still be far off, there has been an obvious softening in the stance against derivative instruments, especially over-the-counter instruments such as forwards and swaps. The reluctance of *fuqaha* against exchange-traded derivatives appears to be rooted in the suspicion that they could be used easily for speculative purposes. The following is a list of some of the opinions.

13.9.1 Opinions on Futures Contracts
(1) Fatwa of Omam Al-Haramaini Al-Jauwaini
The trading of futures is *halal* if the practice is based on *Darurah* and the needs or *Hajaat* of the *ummah*.

(2) Shariah Advisory Council (SAC) of Securities Commission, Malaysia
- Futures trading of commodities is approved as long as underlying asset is *halal*.
- Crude Palm Oil futures contracts are approved for trading.
- For stock index futures (SIF) contract, the concept is approved.
  However, since the current FBM KLCI-based SIF has non-*halal* stocks, it is not approved.
Thus, it implies that an SIF contract of a *halal* index would be acceptable.

(3) Ustaz Ahmad Allam (Islamic Fiqh Academy — Jeddah, 1992)
- Stock index futures (SIF) trading is *haram*, since some of the underlying stocks are not *halal*.
- Until and unless the underlying asset or basket of securities in the SIF is all *halal*, SIF trading is not approved.

(4) Mufti Taqi Usmani (Fiqh Academy — Jeddah)
Futures transactions not permissible for two reasons:
- According to the *Shariah*, sale or purchase cannot be affected for a future date.
- In most futures transactions, delivery or possession is not intended.

13.9.2 Opinions on Option Contracts

(1) Ahmad Muhayyuddin Hassan (1986)
Objects to option trading for 2 reasons:
- Maturity beyond 3 days as in *al-khiyarat* is not acceptable.
- The buyer gets more benefits than the seller — injustice.

(2) Abu Sulayman (Fiqh Academy — Jeddah, 1992)
Acceptable when viewed in the light of *ba'i al-urbun* but considers options to have been detached and independent of the underlying asset — therefore, unacceptable.

(3) Mufti Taqi Usmani (Fiqh Academy — Jeddah)
- Promises as part of a contract is acceptable in *Shariah*; however, the trading and charging of a premium for the promise is *not acceptable*.
- Yet others have argued against options by invoking "*maisir*" or unearned gains; that is, the profits from options may be unearned.

(4) Mohamed Ali El Gari (1993) and Yusuf al-Qaradawi
- El Gari argues in favor of call options based on the framework of *ba'i al-urbun*.
- Yusuf Qaradawi argues that the ruling by Ibn Hanbal on *urbun* should be adapted to modern times. Implying that the use of options could be justified on the basis of *urbun*.

(5) Hashim Kamali (International Islamic University Malaysia, 1998)
Finds options acceptable.
- Invokes the *Hanbali* tradition, cites Hadiths of Barira (RA) and Habban Ibn Munqidh (RA).
- Also draws parallels with the *ba'i al-urbun* in arguing that premiums are acceptable.
- Cites that contemporary scholars such as Yusuf al-Qaradawi and Mustafa al-Zarqa have authenticated *ba'i al-urbun*.

(6) Shariah Advisory Council (SAC) Securities Commission, Malaysia
- No formal opinion on options. The fact that there are no equity options, only the index options available currently has meant that there is no urgency. Index options are disallowed based on the argument that some of the stocks in the FBM KLCI are non-*halal*.
- However, the SAC has approved as *halal* the trading of warrants/total shareholder returns (TSRs) as long as the underlying stock is designated as a *halal* stock.

Box 13.2
The Need for *Shariah*-Compliant Instruments for Equity Risk Management

The recent turmoil in global equity markets is a wake-up call to policymakers and Islamic equity market players. Equity and bond markets, having been fed on a steady diet of artificially low interest rates, have been at record highs. Now faced with the reality of rate normalization, both the bond and equity markets have reacted with extreme turbulence. The volatility index (VIX) which had been tepid the last few years has once again risen.

Equity markets are invariably volatile, which is why a whole range of risk management tools have been developed. Portfolio managers hedge equity risk in several ways, almost all of which use derivative instruments. With futures contracts, portfolio managers can hedge short-term fluctuations with stock index futures (SIF) contracts. Among others, SIF contracts can be used to alter portfolio betas and manage systematic risk and also replicate synthetic T-bill positions thereby neutralizing any volatility. With equity options, numerous hedge strategies are possible. Spread positions can be used to limit value change within a range, while straddles can be established to take advantage of extremes in market volatility. The most popular hedge strategy using options, however, is portfolio insurance. As the name suggests, the strategy can be used to preserve the value of an underlying portfolio regardless of market volatility. It involves combining the underlying portfolio with index put options. If the index puts were of 3-month maturity, the underlying portfolio's value is preserved for that period. The fund manager can be assured that a protective floor has been set for his portfolio should markets tank while simultaneously being able to participate in an upside rally, if markets rise. This is the advantage that options have over futures contracts. Options provide downside protection from unfavorable price movements while also enabling one to take advantage of favorable price movements.

(Continued)

Box 13.2
(Continued)

Broadly speaking, with derivatives, one can determine the magnitude and timing of the risk or exposure that one is willing to take. Thus, a hedger could choose to have more protection at some points and less at others. While risk management techniques and tools have seen tremendous development within the conventional finance space, little has happened within Islamic finance. This lack of risk management tools is particularly true for equity risk management. For the manager of a *Shariah*-compliant portfolio or mutual fund, there are little if any alternatives to protect his portfolio from market turbulence. As things now stand, the Islamic mutual fund manager is constrained to two traditional techniques, that of asset allocation and stock selection. Asset allocation seeks to time the market by allocating different proportions of investible funds among equities, bonds/*sukuk* and cash. The other traditional strategy of risk management, stock selection, involves identifying and allocating funds between growth stocks when bullish and defensive (low beta) stocks when bearish. Though seemingly obvious, the empirical evidence is that both stock selection and asset allocation are not only difficult and expensive but downright hazardous. There is an entire school of thought on stock price behavior, the random walk school, that debunks these traditional strategies.

While, there is no doubt that the *Shariah* requires one to take risk in order to justify the returns earned. The *Shariah* also prohibits the taking of unnecessary risks, and makes compulsory the preservation of wealth. Prudence is always an emphasis. Yet, prudence and preservation of wealth are not easy when one does have the needed tools of risk management. Today's financial markets can turn on a dime. Short-term risk events crop up often. Since the majority of *Shariah* scholars disallow the use of derivatives, for fear of their use in speculation, Islamic portfolio and mutual fund managers are unable to use the many risk management tools so heavily relied upon by conventional fund managers. In many ways, the *Shariah*-compliant fund managers may be competing with their hands tied. Yet, the ordinary investor takes little cognizance of this difference when evaluating Islamic fund managers against their conventional peers. This need not be the case.

The inability to hedge exposes investments to unnecessary risk. Aside from wealth preservation, there are larger and more serious consequences to the Islamic fund management industry. First, the susceptibility to wild fluctuations increases the required return to the equity investment. Second, individual investors, even those investing through mutual funds will shy away when the returns do not justify the risks. Third,

(Continued)

> **Box 13.2**
> *(Continued)*
>
> there could be an outflow of funds from the *Shariah*-compliant to the conventional sector or worse, overseas. Stock markets of the Muslim world, already tiny by international standards will not grow but may atrophy. These have huge consequences for developing countries. Volatile and underdeveloped equity markets have higher risk premiums which translates into higher costs of capital for businesses within. For nations and firms aspiring to compete internationally, this is unnecessary encumbrance.
>
> *Source*: Adapted from the author's op-ed column.

13.10 The Need for Harmonization

The fractious nature of the debate and opinions is obvious. It appears that any number of objections could be made for a given derivative instrument. The object of juridical analysis appears to be a microexamination of each and every feature of a derivative instrument to see if it passes an often subjective religious filter. The overall intended use of the instrument or the societal benefits that could accrue do not seem to have been given due consideration. Aside from individual interpretation, the differing opinions among *madzhabs*/imams complicate the situation further. Thus, an option contract may be found objectionable for exactly opposite reasons. For example, when seen from the viewpoint of subject of sale (*mahal al aqd*), the subject in options are rights/obligations, which some like Abu Sulayman (1992) find objectionable because rights/obligations are different (detached) from the underlying asset. When seen solely as conferring rights/obligations, options are **independent** of their underlying asset. While the sale/purchase of assets are entirely acceptable, the transaction of abstract things like rights and obligations are not recognized in the *Shariah*.

On the other hand, if options as derivatives are considered attached to the underlying asset, then objections have been made on the problem of paired contractual obligations (*'aqdayn fi aqd*). The existence of paired contractual obligations invalidates both the option contract and the sale contract of the underlying asset. Thus, an option may be found objectionable if it is deemed to be independent of its underlying asset and again objectionable if it is dependent and therefore paired. The irony that an instrument could be prohibited based on two diametrically opposite viewpoints appears to have been lost. Furthermore, unlike other prohibitions where the default position is one of impermissibility, the default position where financial transactions are concerned, according to most *fuqaha*, is permissibility, unless there is clear evidence of *riba*, *maysir*, or *gharar*.

The earlier example illustrates the difficulty in arriving at any form of consensus. While some *madzhabs* like the Hanbalis have been broader in their acceptance, the Shafi' and Hanafis have been less so. The Hanbalis, for example, are somewhat liberal when they come to option of stipulation (*khiyar-al-shart*). They hold that stipulations that remove a hardship, fulfill a legitimate need, provide a benefit or convenience, or facilitate the smooth flow of commercial transactions are generally valid as a matter of principle (Ibn Taymiyah, 1368 H: pp 16, 152).

SUMMARY

This chapter examined derivative instruments from the Islamic finance framework. The first section of the chapter outlined the necessary features for financial instruments to be *Shariah*-compliant. In order to be *halal*, all financial instruments must be free from five elements, namely *riba*, *rishwah*, *maysir*, *gharar*, and *jahl*. *Riba* that is commonly equated to interest must be avoided in all its forms. The *Shariah*'s objective in requiring the avoidance of these elements is to ensure social justice and fair play to all parties in a transaction. A number of instruments/contracts exist in Islamic finance that could be considered a basis for derivative contracts within an Islamic framework. The chapter examined in-depth, two such contracts, the *Ba'i Salam* contract and the *Istijrar*. The *Ba'i Salam* is a transaction where two parties agree to carry out a sale/purchase of an underlying asset at a predetermined future date but at a price negotiated and fully paid for today. While this is similar to conventional forward contracts, the key difference is in the timing of payment. In forward contracts, payment is on maturity, whereas in the *Salam* contract, full payment is at contract initiation. The logic of full up-front payment is based on the fact that the *Salam* contract is intended to help needy farmers and small businesses with working capital financing. Given the customized nature of the contract, *Salam* shares some of the problems associated with forward contracts. The *Istisna* and *Joa'la* are two other contracts where a transaction is made on a yet to exist underlying asset. The *Istisna* has as its underlying a product to be manufactured. The *Joa'la* is appropriate when contracting for services to be performed in the future.

The *Istijrar* is a financing contract with embedded options that could be triggered if the underlying asset's price exceeds certain bounds. The embedded option is the right to choose to fix the price at which settlement will occur at any time before contract maturity. For either party to exercise its option and thereby fix the settlement price at the *Murabaha* price (P^*), the spot price of the underlying asset must have exceeded the price bounds. By introducing an element of risk, the *Istijrar* tries to avoid a fixed return from a "riskless" arrangement that could be considered *riba*.

There appears to be neither a consensus nor a definite opinion on the acceptability of derivative instruments in Islamic finance. The validity and permissibility of these instruments appears to vary by scholar/jurists. Much of the evaluation has been of a highly juridical nature. Even where scholars have found derivatives to be objectionable, their reasons for objection differs. In Malaysia, the SAC of the Securities Commission has approved futures trading of Crude Palm Oil but not of stock index futures. The objection being that there are non-*halal* stocks in the underlying index — the FBM KLCI. Bursa Malaysia Derivatives Berhad (BMDB) is in the process of introducing an Islamic index futures contracts. The SAC has issued no formal opinion on options. However, it has approved as *halal* the trading of warrants/TSRs as long as the underlying stock is designated as *halal*.

KEY TERMS

- *Riba*
- *Istisna*
- *Ba'i al-Urbun*
- *Gharar*
- *Joa'la*
- *Maysir*
- *Shariah*
- *Halal* underlying asset
- *Rishwah*
- *Ba'i Salam*
- *Murabaha*
- *Jahl*
- *Istijrar*
- *Al-khiyarat*
- Price bounds
- *Bai bil-Wafa*
- *Bai bil-Istighlal*
- Islamic profit rate swap
- Floating profit rate payer
- Fixed profit payer

End-of-Chapter Questions

1. Compare and contrast the *Istijrar* contract with its closest conventional contract. What are the main similarities/differences?

2. Compare and contrast the *Ba'i Salam* contract with conventional derivatives. Which instrument does it resemble? What strong points and weaknesses can you attribute to the *Salam* contract?

3. Which conventional derivative contract does a *Ba'i Salam* contract closely resemble? What are the similarities and differences? What common problems are applicable to both *Ba'i Salam* and the conventional contract?

4. Contrast the *Ba'i Salam* contract with the modern-day futures contracts — specify the problems that remain with the former.

5. Differentiate between *Ba'i Salam*, *Istisna*, and *Joa'la* contracts. What are the similarities/differences?

6. Compare and contrast the pricing relationship between the conventional cost-of-carry model and *Ba'i Salam*. How and why does the pricing differ? Show the mathematical congruence between the two prices.

7. Evaluate conventional derivative instruments and their trading methods in light of the *Shariah* requirements. What are some of the concerns that Islamic scholars and jurists have with regards to derivatives?

8. a. What is the rationale of the need for full payment up-front by the long position in the *Ba'i Salam* contract?
   b. What would the cost-of-carry equation be for *Ba'i Salam* given full payment up-front?
   c. How much inbuilt leverage is there in the *Ba'i Salam*?
   d. The need to avoid *gharar* is a key requirement in Islamic finance. Define *gharar*. Briefly evaluate modern-day futures contracts from viewpoint of *gharar*.

9. Evaluate the *Ba'i Salam* contract in terms of its applicability for hedging, arbitrage, and speculation. Outline the possibilities and constraints of the contract for such applications.

10. a. Describe the *Ba'i Salam* contract. In what ways is it similar to modern-day futures; how is it different?
    b. Using the cost-of-carry model, justify why it is rational that the *Ba'i Salam* price is lower than the spot price.
11. What is the *Bai bil-Wafa* contract? How is it similar to conventional REPOs? What are the two key differences between the contracts?
12. In what way is the *Bai bil-Istighlal* an extension of the *Bai bil-Wafa*? Between the two contracts, which contract is more suited for practical use? Why?
13. An Islamic bank with a large positive duration gap (asset duration > liability side duration) intends to use a profit rate swap to reduce the mismatch. Show how this could be done.
14. Compare and contrast the profit rate swap with the fixed-for-floating interest rate swap described in Chapter 12. How different is the objective of use?
15. If an Islamic financial institution wishes to lengthen the duration of its assets and its overall positive gap, how can it use the profit rate swap to achieve this?
16. Compare and contrast the *Istijrar* contract from standard *Murabaha* contracts used in Malaysia. Why might proponents of the *Istijrar* consider it to be more in line with *Shariah* injunctions?
17. Mr. Brown who is chief strategist at Ponzi Asset Management Sdn. Berhad has just completed his analysis of forecast interest rate movements. He is convinced that interest rates are going to rise sharply over the near future. He wants to position his company to take advantage of this outlook.
    a. State three derivatives that Mr. Brown can use to position his company given his outlook.
    b. For each of the above, clearly describe the strategy that Mr. Brown should take.
18. a. Outline the relationship between the *Ba'i Salam* price and its underlying spot price. Prove/Argue that the relationship is logical even in a conventional sense.
    b. Would it be possible to use the *Ba'i Salam* as a means to speculate? Explain why or why not.
    c. Comment on the exercise style of an *Istijrar* contract. What style(s) is the exercise?
19. Philosophy and rationale dictate the design and workings of a derivative instrument. The rationale behind most conventional derivatives is risk management. Briefly explain the rationale/objective behind (i) the *Ba'i Salam* contract and (ii) the *Istijrar* contract. How is the instrument design influenced by the underlying rationale?
20. a. Briefly state:
       (i) At least four basic conditions for the *Ba'i Salam* contract.
       (ii) Difference between the *Joa'la* and *Istisna* contracts.
    b. If you were a seller (short), state one advantage and one disadvantage of the *Ba'i Salam* contract versus a conventional forward contract.
21. Assume a *Ba'i Salam* and a forward contract are both available on the same underlying asset.
    a. Describe the forward price relative to *Ba'i Salam*.
    b. Describe whether a trader who chooses a *salam* contract is better off than another who uses forward.

22. Evaluate the *Ba'i Salam* contract relative to a forward contract with regard to effectiveness in:
    (i) Hedging
    (ii) Speculating
23. Identify two Islamic structured products offered by banks.
    (i) Describe their structure and show what advantage there is to an investor.
    (ii) Why are Islamic structured products not as popular as conventional ones?
24. Can a speculator use the *Ba'i Salam* contract to speculate on:
    (i) Expected rising price of an agricultural commodity.
    (ii) How will the payoffs from the use of the *Salam* contract compare with that of a futures contract?
    (iii) Would the speculator be able to use the *Salam* contract to take advantage of an expected fall in the price of the agricultural product? Explain.
25. You work for a large fund management house. One of its newest and most successful funds is KLIMM, which is an Islamic money market fund. The fund has RM 300 million invested in Islamic money market instruments. Being rate sensitive instruments, your boss has asked you to find ways to manage the rate risk. The fund (KLIMM) pays investors a profit distribution every 6 months. Assuming your boss wants you to consider a 3-year horizon and the total fund size is expected to be at RM 300 million over that period:
    (i) Identify a *Shariah*-compliant way by which KLIMM can manage its profit exposure.
    (ii) Structure the hedge; show the exact cash flows, periodic intervals, and other details.
    (iii) Prove that KLIMM will be protected regardless of interest/profit rate movements. (Use a chart/figure if necessary)

Answers to Select End-of-Chapter Questions

Chapter 1

1. A derivative instrument is a financial asset that derives its value from its underlying asset. The underlying asset could be a commodity or another financial asset. Thus, unlike stocks and bonds that represent a direct claim, derivatives can be thought of as a claim on a claim.

3. Futures overcame the three problems of forwards: (i) multiple coincidence of needs, (ii) potential for price squeeze, and (iii) counterparty/default risk. While forwards/futures "locked-in" the underlying asset value, options have the advantage in that they provided both downside protection and upside profit potential.

5. Hedgers, arbitrageurs, and speculators. Hedgers, to manage risk; arbitrageurs, to take advantage of mispricing; speculators, to take positions based on their expectations.

7. (i) Reduced liquidity, reduced trading volume, and thus higher transaction cost.
   (ii) Lack of counterparties for hedgers to pass on their risk.

9. Commodity derivatives have underlying assets that are commodities/tangible assets and have physical settlement at maturity. Financial derivatives have financial assets as their underlying and have cash settlement at maturity.

11. (i) Market/price risk: Derivatives based on the appropriate underlying asset.
    (ii) Interest rate risk: Interest rate futures contracts, 3-month KLIBOR or 3-month BIBOR, and so on.
    (iii) Currency/exchange rate risk: Use currency forward contracts, currency options.

12. Off-balance sheet hedging methods are external to the business, typically using derivative instruments to hedge exposure arising from the business. On-balance sheet hedging attempts to restructure the way business is done in order to mitigate risk. Derivatives obviously belong to off-balance sheet methods.

14. The traded volume of interest rate derivatives has reduced substantially in recent years. This is mainly attributed to the fact that interest rates across the world had declined steadily. As interest rates get lower, the magnitude of interest rate risk reduces, thereby

reducing the need to hedge it. The fact that interest rate derivatives have seen much lower volumes is clear implication that they have traditionally been used for hedging.

Chapter 2

1. OTC instruments are customized over-the-counter instruments whereas exchange-traded instruments are standardized and traded on a centralized exchange.

3. The problems associated with the open outcry system is the main cause for this trend, in particular the errors in communication.

5. In an open outcry, trading is carried out on a trading floor with floor traders using hand signals and shouting out their orders. In a computerized system, buy–sell orders are keyed into distributed terminals. The computer matches the bids and executes transactions.

9. Derivative exchanges self-regulate by establishing internal mechanisms for control and compliance. Exchanges have their own internal committees that act as watchdog, arbitration, and disciplinary committees. To minimize potential conflicts of interest, these committees may include external parties.

11. There are several reasons: first, the imposition of capital controls and moratorium on capital outflow in 1998 led to a huge fall in volumes. Second, the subsequent opening up of China, India, Vietnam, and the like brought on players with huge economies of scale. Third, the unsettled issue of *Shariah* compliance has not helped in a Muslim country like Malaysia.

13. The increase in financial risks arising from factors such as changes in regulation, technological innovation, increased global competition, and enhanced cointegration of markets requires risk management. The ability to manage these newly arising risks through financial derivatives explains their popularity.

Chapter 3

1. Basis refers to the difference or spread between forward/futures and spot prices. By definition, basis should be zero at maturity unless there are mismatches. Mismatches could arise from (i) asset mismatch, (ii) maturity mismatch, and (iii) quantity mismatch.

2.
   - Total contract value $= (4 \times 25 \text{ tons}) \times \text{RM } 1{,}800$
     $= \text{RM } 180{,}000$
   - Initial margin $= \text{RM } 180{,}000 \times 0.10$
     $= \text{RM } 18{,}000$
   - Maintenance margin $= \text{RM } 18{,}000 \times 0.70$
     $= \text{RM } 12{,}600$

On Day 5:
Account balance = RM 19,000
Counterparty balance = RM 17,000

5. Like most other transactions, derivatives trading is a zero-sum game. Still, with well-developed derivative markets, society benefits in several ways. For example, producers are able to hedge easily and cheaply, thus making a nation more price competitive and arbitrageurs keep prices in line. Thus, free market systems are ensured equilibrium prices. Speculators are willing to take on risk and add to liquidity, thereby lower transaction costs for all players.

7. Total contract value = RM 200,000
Initial margin = RM 20,000
Maintenance margin = RM 14,000

	Your Account		Counterparty	
Day	Adjustment	Balance	Adjustment	Balance
0	20,000 (I.M.)	20,000	20,000 (I.M.)	20,000
1	+1,000	21,000	−1,000	19,000
2	−3,000	18,000	+3,000	22,000
3	−1,000	17,000	+1,000	23,000
4	+3,000	20,000	−3,000	20,000
5	+2,000	22,000	−2,000	18,000

9. (a) Since you are bullish, long rice futures contracts. With RM 10,000 available, you long 6 contracts, which would require an initial margin of RM 9,000 ⇒ [(RM 3 × 5,000) × 6] × 0.10. Thus, the initial investment is RM 9,000.
(b) Profit = [(RM 3.50 − RM 3) × 5,000 kg] × 6 contracts
= RM 15,000
% Profit = {(RM 15,000 − RM 9,000)/RM 9,000} × 100
= 66.7%
(c) Loss = RM 22,500
% Loss = 350% (loss on RM 22,500 on initial investment of RM 9,000)
(d) The huge fluctuation in profits, especially the percentage profits, has to do with the leverage inherent in derivatives. You are only paying the initial margin, not full cost.

11. Since you shorted at $0.92 and the Euro is at $0.93 on maturity day, you would have lost ($0.92 − $0.93) × 100,000 = $1,000.

13. Net position is zero.

17) (a) Based on the rates, the market's expectation is for the Ringgit to depreciate against the Pound.
(b) Since he has to pay (short), he has to go long Pounds in the forward.
(c) He should immediately lock in the 90-day forward today. Waiting longer could mean worse rates later.

Chapter 4

1) (a) (i) Lower transaction cost; (ii) Diversification benefits; (iii) Inbuilt leverage; and (iv) Exposure to overall markets.
   (b) (i) Systematic risk refers to nondiversifiable market risk. Unsystematic risk is company specific, random risk. (ii) Total risk, which is the combination of systematic and unsystematic risk. (iii) Only systematic risk.
   (c) (i) RM 1,020.56
       (ii) RM 1,031.24
   (d) Rising interest rates increases the carrying cost, and thus increases the price of SIF contracts.
   (e) Index multipliers are intended to make SIF contracts sufficiently large for institutional players.

3) (a) Calendar or time spread.
   (b) Bearish, but want some downside protection if the market moves against me.
   (c) Prices are going to fall. December contract will fall more than September contract.
   (d) Prices must fall. If the distant contract (December) falls more than the September contract, I make a net gain.

5) (a) Short 300 contracts (note: adjust for beta of 1.2).
   (b) Loss on portfolio = RM 2,400,000; Gain from short SIF position = RM 2,590,350; Dividends received = RM 50,000; thus net gain = RM 240,350. Hedged portfolio value will be higher by the net gain amount.

7) (a) This is a bear time spread. To make money, the distant contract must fall more than the nearby contract (i.e., June falls more than March contract).
   (b) Long KLSE CI futures contracts.
      Synthetic Stock = Long Futures + Long T-bills

9. Short 6 SIF contracts.
   $(1/1.60) = 0.625$
   $(1-0.625)$ THB 3.2 million = THB 1.2 million
   Thus, 1.2 million of the portfolio should be fully hedged. Since SET 50 multiplier is THB 200,
   (THB 1,200,000)/(1,000 pts × THB 200) = 6 SET 50 SIF contracts
   Note: (THB 2 million/THB 3.2 million)(1.60) = 1.0 beta overall portfolio beta

Answers to Select End-of-Chapter Questions

10) (a) Futures prices should be 754.18, so quoted futures price is underpriced.
    (b) Long futures, short spot.
    (c) Assuming the use of one SIF contract and equivalent spot position:
Profit from Long SIF	= RM 2,836
Loss on short spot	= (2,500)
Interest earned on lending	= RM 739
Replace borrowed dividends	= (RM 331.36)
Arbitrage profit	= RM 743.6
    (d) Arbitrage profit depends on the size of mispricing and not on the underlying index performance.

11) (a) Short 17.5 (18) SIF contracts. Thus RM 700,000 or 25% of portfolio will be neutralized.
    (b) (i) SIF is overvalued.
        (ii) Short SIF, long spot; borrow at rf to finance purchase of spot and receive and reinvest dividends. Arbitrage profit per contract would be RM 496 (762 − 752.08 × RM 50) (Actual − Theoretical × Index Multiplier).

13) (a) $\dfrac{\text{THB 150 million}}{\text{THB 160 million}} \times (0.90) + \dfrac{\text{THB 10 million}}{\text{THB 160 million}} \times (0) = 0.844$
    (b) $(0.6/0.844) = 0.711$
        $(1 - 0.711) \times$ THB 150 million = THB 43,350,000 of portfolio should be hedged.
        (THB 43,350,000)/(1,300 × THB 200) = 167 contracts.
        Short 167 SET 50 SIF contracts.
    (c) (THB 150,000,000)/(1,300 × THB 200) = 577 contracts
        Short 577 SET 50 SIF contracts, return will approximate the rf return since portfolio is fully hedged.

15) (a) The correct price should be 603 points. Thus, the SIF is overvalued by 5 points.
    (b) RM 250 per contract (5 points × RM 50 index multiplier).
    (c) The easiest way to convince would be to show that the arbitrage profit will be the same regardless of underlying market performance.

17) THB 15.91.

20) (a) Hedge by shorting Siam Cement SSF of 6-month maturity.
    (b) Long Berjaya Toto SSF, Short Genting SSF.
    (c) Short IOI Corp. Bhd. SSF.
    (d) Short Telekom Bhd SSF, worth half the value of his holding at RM 6.80.
    (e) Short CIMB Holdings SSF of 3-month maturity.

Chapter 5

1. (a) When interest rates ↑, required yields ↑, bond price ↓.
   (b) In its simplest form; interest rate risk refers to the change in asset values when interest rates change.
   (c) Most active tenor in interbank market, also in keeping with other internationally traded interest derivatives which are mostly of 3-month tenor.
   (d) (i) 6.25%, (ii) 8.72%, (iii) 5.40%, (iv) 7.70%.
   (e) 11.78%.

3. (a) Short 12 three-month KLIBOR futures contracts.
   (b) Profit from futures = RM 15,000
   Interest spread = RM 45,000
   Total earnings = RM 60,000, which is 2% annualized
   So, you lock-in the 2% spread.

5. (a) Short 20 three-month KLIBOR futures contracts.
   (b) Profit from futures = RM 50,000
   Interest spread = RM 50,000
   Total earnings = RM 100,000, which is 2% annualized spread (profit) that is locked-in

7. (Note: this question covers material in the Appendix of Chapter 5)
   (a) The 3-month bucket (RM 80 million has to be refinanced).
   (b) Short 80 three-month KLIBOR futures contracts.
   (c) Profit from futures = RM 200,000
   Refinancing cost = RM 1,400,000
   Net cost of funds = RM 1,200,000, which is effectively 1.5% for 3 months or 6% annualized

10. (a) By IFR, the correct yield = 9.10%, but the futures is yielding 7% (93.00), thus there is mispricing. Futures is overpriced.
    (b) Short the 3-month BIBOR futures; long 6-month BIBOR (spot).
    (c) Profit from futures = (0.02/4)
    $\qquad$ = 0.005 × THB 10 million
    $\qquad$ = THB 50,000
    Loss on Spot = (0.01/4)
    $\qquad$ = 0.0025 × THB 10 million
    $\qquad$ = (THB 25,000)
    Arbitrage Profit = THB 25,000

11. (a) Interest rate risk, you would be hurt by rising interest rates. To hedge (lock-in) your cost of funds, you should short 50 three-month KLIBOR futures contracts.

(b) When fully hedged, the cost will be 6% (i.e., 5.5% yield on futures + 0.5% spread of the banker). One can use any hypothetical interest rate change, to proof that the cost is locked-in.

13. (a) (i) Increase in cost of funds, (ii) deposit profile would change, (iii) income margin gets squeezed, and (iv) given the inherent maturity mismatch, net worth could also get squeezed.
    (b) Because the nature of banking is such that deposits have shorter maturity, whereas loans are necessarily of longer tenure.
    (c) Positively sloped; their cost of funds would be lower than interest they charge loans. $S_i < L_i$.

15. (a) Negatively.
    (b) Positively.
    (c) Assets would fall in value four times more than liabilities.
    (d) Negatively, net worth will be squeezed.

Chapter 6

1. Stock should end above RM 6.50; max profit = 0.10.

3. Call IV = 0.10; so TV must be 0.11.

5. Lower, since less time to maturity so lower TV.
   (a) Also lower since TV is less.
   (b) Put will be worth more since stock price will be lower ex-dividend thereby increasing the IV.

7. (b) (i) No change to IV, TV is higher.
       (ii) There should be a near parallel upward shift in the call value curve.

11. (a) 5.50 call and 6.50 put.
    (b) 6.00 call and 6.00 put.
    (c) Premiums would be higher for both the calls and the puts. IV is unchanged but TV is now higher.

13. (a) (i) 0.43 or 43 sen.
        (ii) 0.13 or 13 sen.
    (b) Call is in-the-money, but the put is out-of-the-money, so Put IV is zero.

15) (a) Highest RM 12 put, lowest RM 12 call.
    (b) RM 9 call and RM 12 call.
    (c) RM 12 put and RM 9 put.

17) For a given change in underlying asset price, the call and put values will change in opposite directions. The magnitude of change will depend on their respective deltas.

Chapter 7

1) (a) RM 6,110; (b) RM 10.89; (c) unlimited since long call; (d) $0.89 \times 1,000 =$ RM 890.

3) In futures, both long and short positions have to post margins. In options, only the short position is margined since the long can only lose a maximum equal to premium paid.

5) Yes; depreciating ¥en can cause losses. Futures; since cheapest and most liquid relatively.

7) Put IV = 0; Call IV = 0.30; Put IV = 0.10; Call TV = 0.20. Call is in-the-money, whereas the put is out-of-the-money.

9) Exchanges would list at least one ITM, one ATM, and one OTM option for trading at any time. Additionally, options of various exercise prices will be demanded by participants in order to establish different strategies.

11) (a) Any factor that could cause the underlying stock's value to fall would lead to early exercise. For example, the payment of a large unexpected dividend or the possibility of an unexpected negative event.
    (b) The European put would increase in value if it is currently out-of-the-money, and vice versa when time to expiration is lengthened. A European put which is currently in-the-money would decrease in value.

13) Selling the option is better as the price will include IV and TV. Exercising will only get you IV.

15) (a) Futures are obligatory if held to maturity but options are not. No margins for long position of options.
    (b) Both could be used to hedge widely diversified or stock portfolios that resemble the index.
    (c) First, the long option does not require capital; second, options are better if the probability of prices going against you is high.

17) (a) If the underlying index rises substantially instead of falling.
    (b) Futures, being obligatory, are cheaper.

Chapter 8

1) (a) Long 950 ninety-day straddle.
   (b) See graph of straddle in text.
   (c) The long straddle would benefit either way.

3) (a) 58 sen.
   (b) 18 sen.
   (c) 58 sen + 18 sen = 76 sen.

5) (a) The 6.00 put cancels out; leaving a RM 5.50 – 6.00 short straddle position.
   (b) RM 0.35.
   (c) RM 5.15 and RM 6.35.
   (d) The stock price must have fallen since the value of RM 6 put has increased on day 2.

7) (a) Bear put spread.
   (b) RM 7.70.
   (c) Neutral to bearish.
   (d) RM 0.70.
   (e) Neither option is exercised.

9) (a) Long 680 index put options @ 7 points.
   (b) THB 1,400 per contract (7 pts × THB 200).
   (c) THB 1,400 (premium paid).

11) The appropriate strategy is a covered call write (short a call on the stock owned).

13) Hedge the short stock position by going long, call options on Promet. At-the-money calls would be appropriate.

15) (i) A long straddle, long 7.00 call and 7.00 put; breakeven, RM 6.56 and RM 7.44.
    (ii) A long strangle, long 7.50 call and 7.00 put; breakeven, RM 6.73 and RM 7.77.

17) Strategy: portfolio insurance; combine current long stock position with long 15 RM 4.25 puts @ 0.15.

19) Strategy: covered call write. Combine current long stock position with short RM 3.80 call @ 0.30.

21) (a) Net long 20 million Pounds (the original receivable remains unhedged).
    (b) Bear time spread, bearish about CPO price. The 6-month falls more than 3-month contract.

23) (1) Long straddle, (2) Long strangle, (3) Short butterfly.

25) Box spread; limited profit, limited loss.

Chapter 9

1) 667 calls (400/0.60); 1,000 puts (400/0.40), since call delta = 0.60, put delta must equal 0.40 (Call delta − Put delta = 1.0).

3) $d_1 = 1.02, d_2 = 0.81$
   $N(d_1) = 0.8461, N(d_2) = 0.79$
   Call Value = RM 7.80.

5) (i) Long RM 5 put options on the stock.
   Put delta must = 0.20 since call delta = 0.80; thus, 5 puts needed to hedge each lot. For 4 lots of stocks; 20 puts needed.

6) $d_1 = 0.7177, d_2 = 0.5677$
   $N(d_1) = 0.7642, N(d_2) = 0.7157$ (Present value of dividends = RM 2.97)
   Call value = RM 1.83

7) $P = Ke^{-rt} \cdot N(-d_2) - S \cdot N(-d_1)$
   Since steps 1 and 2 are the same as in call option pricing, we simply use the computed numbers in Question 6 and go directly to step 3, which is to plug in and solve for value. However, we invoke here a rule of normal distributions, that is, that being symmetrical, if $N(d_1) = x$ then the area under the curve for $N(-d_1)$ must be 1 − x.

   Thus, since $N(d_1)$ and $N(d_2)$ in the earlier question was determined to be 0.7642 and 0.7157.

   $N(-d_1) = (1 − 0.7642) = 0.2358$
   $N(-d_2) = (1 − 0.7157) = 0.2843$

   Solving for put value using this variable gives a put value of RM 0.36 or 36 sen. The reason for this much lower put value relative to the call is that whereas the call is in the money by RM 4, the put is out of the money by that amount. (Note that although the call is in the money by RM 4, its value is only RM 1.83 because of the adjustment for dividend of RM 3 per share.)

9) A higher interest rate is favorable to call holder since the present value of exercise price to be paid is lower. Since a put holder receives the present value of exercise price, lower present value means he receives less. Thus, unfavorable to puts.

11) (a) (i) RM 1.56, (ii) also RM 1.56.
    (b) Constant volatility assumption. Stock price volatility need not be constant over option maturity.

13) (a) Value of call = RM 9.47.
    (b) Put value is RM 0.11.
    (c) (i) Call ITM whereas put is OTM, (ii) the probability of up movement is higher, this favors the call.

15)
	Call	Put
(i)	+	−
(ii)	+	+
(iii)	−	+
(iv)	−	+
(v)	+	+

16) A call benefits from rising value of underlying asset and since delta is the correlation between the two, call delta is always positive. Put delta is negative since puts benefit when underlying asset value falls.

18) Value of call = 59 points. In RM = 59 pts × RM 50 = RM 2,950.

Chapter 10

1) (a) The put–call parity describes an equilibrium relationship between an underlying asset and options on the asset. The options must be of same maturity and exercise price. Since deviations from put–call parity can be arbitraged risklessly, arbitrage will ensure that the parity holds.
   (b) Generally, given the put–call parity equation, if the rhs of the equation is higher than; a reverse conversion (if rhs > lhs). However, if rhs < lhs then the conversion strategy is used.
   (c) Cash flow equivalence describes the similarity of payoffs at maturity. Pricing equivalence describes the pricing equilibrium that must hold until maturity. Should pricing equivalence not hold, riskless arbitrage is possible.

3) (a) Conversion strategy; overall position is the horizontal axis (since both call and put premiums are equal).
   (b) Zero profit, zero loss.
   (c) Hedge strategy, intended to stay covered until option maturity. Upon maturity of options, back to long stock position. Delta of overall position is zero.

5) (a) Resulting position is double long stock.
   (b) Extremely bullish.
   (c) He will lose substantially, double the losses of the original long stock position.
   (d) Delta of option position = 1.0.

7) (a) Short put, long call, short stock ⇒ reverse conversion.
    (b) (i) Conversion or reverse conversion.
    (ii) Profit will depend on the extent of mispricing.

9) (a) Going by put–call parity; stock is undervalued (it should be RM 15.14), call is overvalued (it should be 0.61), put is undervalued (it should be 0.33).
    (b) Long stock, long put, and short call (conversion strategy). Arbitrage profit will be RM 0.14 or RM 140 per lot/contract.
    (c) Conversion strategy with overall resulting position a horizontal line at RM 0.14.

12) (a) Advantage: Lower transaction cost; higher liquidity.
    Disadvantage: Locks-in value, cannot take advantage of favorable upside movement; margins have to be paid for index futures but not for long position in options.
    (b) Both the Nikkei futures contracts are overpriced on OSE relative to SIMEX. The December 99 contract has very small mispricing, arbitrage may not be possible given transaction costs. The March 00 could be arbitraged; short the contract on OSE and Long it on SIMEX. Since underling is same-riskless arbitrage.

13) Long forward has payoff equivalent to long underlying, short futures has payoff equivalent to short underlying. Thus, the net position = zero (no profit, no loss).

15) (a) Long 300 ninety-day 500 put @ 7 points.
    (b) Now, there is maturity mismatch; adjust for option delta. Put delta = 0.45; thus 1/0.45 = 2.22 puts to hedge each stock. So, 300 contracts × 2.22 = 667 put option contracts.

16) (a) Not necessarily; re-examine the "implied volatility" or your estimate of volatility in arriving at your option value.
    (b) Short the call, then — Long $N(d_1)$ of stock
                              — Short $Ke^{-rt} \cdot N(d_2)$ of bonds
    (c) Long the call, then — Short $N(d_1)$ of stock
                              — Long $Ke^{-rt} \cdot N(d_2)$ of bonds
    (d) Short the put, then — Short $N(-d_1)$ of stock
                              — Long $Ke^{-rt} \cdot N(-d_2)$ of bonds
    The position in options combined with the synthesized opposite positions will ensure riskless arbitrage profit.

17) (a) 1.04 > 0.60; thus parity is violated; (b) Short stock, long call, and short put. Profit = RM 0.44 or RM 440 per contract; (c) Reverse conversion.

19) (a) Short stock, long call, and short put. (b)–(d) Graph of reverse conversion, overall payoff will be horizontal line above 0. (e) Same underlying asset, same maturity, and exercise price of the options.

21) (a) Short 480 three-month KLSE CI futures contracts.
    (b) Long 800 three-month 800 point index puts.
    (c) RM 19,432,000.
    (d) Bullish.
    (e) Diagram.
    (f) Using options; unlimited upside, limited downside.

24) (a) Long 10 three-month CPO futures; (b) Short 3-month KLIBOR futures; (c) Short 3-month KLIBOR futures, long 6-month KLIBOR; (d) Long 3-month futures on Won for 30 million; (e) Long index call or bull call spread; (f) Short 10 six-month silver futures.

Chapter 11

1) (a) Long put option; a zero premium long put with RM 100 million. Exercise price, maturity = 3 years.
   (b) Value the put option and add the value to the computed net present value.

3) (a) UEM is short puts. It has received no premium for the puts it sold to Renong shareholders.
   At any price below RM 3.20, they will be swamped with Renong stock, but if Renong's stock price happens to be above the RM 3.20 ex. price, none will be offered. UEM has zero upside, but unlimited downside potential.
   (b) Renong shareholders are long put options for which they have paid no premium. They have zero downside potential but unlimited upside potential.

5) (a) In developed markets, call warrants are generally less liquid than listed call options.
   (b) Warrants, single exercise price but call options of different exercise price intervals would be available.
   (c) Much longer maturity for warrants.
   (d) Payoff profile at maturity is essentially the same.
   (e) Being third-party issues, call warrants like call options have no impact on number of stocks outstanding.

7) (a) Long call option with exercise price of RM 4.4 million and breakeven of RM 4.9 million. Max loss possible is the equity of RM 0.5 million.
   (b) Short put position, with exercise price of RM 4.4 million, breakeven of RM 4 million, max upside is RM 0.4 million (interest) but max loss is RM 4 million (principal).

9) (a) Graph — essentially long equity.
   (b) (i) Unlimited profit, unlimited downside for alternative (A); (ii) unlimited upside and zero downside for alternative (B); (iii) Transaction costs and expectation of market performance.

11) (a) Long 3-month call options on gold.
    (b) Short 3-month put options on ¥en.
    (c) Long call options on Pounds or long call and short put options on Pounds.

13) (a) RM 580.
    (b) RM 180 (assuming put premium is 22 sen).
    (c) Assuming index multiplier of RM 100:
        930 pts; A RM 2,400   B (RM 2,400)
        860 pts; A (RM 4,600)   B RM 4,600
        900 pts; A (RM 600)   B RM 600
        A is bullish, B is bearish.

Chapter 12

1) KLI should borrow floating and IIB borrow fixed. They then swap. KLI is the floating rate receiver and IIB the fixed rate receiver. Since the difference in rates is 0.75%, each party will gain 0.25% if the gains are to be split equally among the three parties.

3) (a) Mr. Tan should go in as the fixed rate payer/floating rate receiver.
   (b) RM 10 million × 0.02 = RM 200,000 profit.
   (c) RM 10 million × 0.015 = RM 150,000 loss.

6) Trebor Malaysia borrows RM 12 million from its bank in Malaysia and forwards the amount to Cadbury which gives £ 2 million in return (Cadbury, like Trebor may or may not have borrowed the amount from its bank). Additionally, in each year interest differential of 2% should be fulfilled by Cadbury paying Trebor 2% of RM 12 million.

8) A credit default swap is one in which the "buyer" pays a periodic fee to the seller who will reimburse the buyer if a prespecified "credit-event" occurs. A credit put option requires a single payment of premium and has a fixed maturity and exercise price.

10) In a loan portfolio swap, the parties only exchange the respective payments they receive on the portion of loan identified to be swapped. In a total return swap, both the interest payments received and the capital gains or losses are adjusted in the swap cash flows.

13) (a) Since the Japanese bank is to receive fixed interest, but its costs will be floating (since the deposit rate, it pays in Euros would be dependent on short-term Euro rates), the bank would be hurt if the interest rates on Euro increase.
    (b) It can go into an FRA in which it receives "compensation" if Euro interest rates (1-year tenor) goes above 5% but will have to pay if rates go below 5%.
    (c) After the loan is made, the Japanese bank has a Euro receivable, which is an asset. Any depreciation of the Euro against the Japanese ¥en, will mean a diminution in the value of an asset and so a loss in ¥en terms (currency transaction exposure).

(d) Using currency forwards — short Euro, long ¥en (match amount ant time).
   Using currency swap — agree to swap Euro for ¥en in 1 year.
   Using currency options — long 1-year put options of Euro (or roll over if 1-year put options are not available).

15) (a) 8% (6% yield on futures + 2%).
    (b) Short 15 three-month KLIBOR futures contracts.
    (c) See proofs in Chapter 5.
    (d) Educorporation receives compensation if interest rate goes above 6% and pays compensation of the difference if rate is below 6% (6% target rate in FRA and RM 15 million notional principle).

16) (a) (i) Using forwards: short £ 3 million.
        (ii) Using futures: short 3 ninety-day Euros futures contracts.
        (iii) Options: long 3 ninety-day put options on Euros.
        (iv) Swap: enter as the party that receives Ringgit and pays Euros.

18) Credit-linked notes are debt instruments with embedded options exercisable by the issuer. Essentially, buyers are long a straight bond and short a call option to the issuer.

20) (a) Unlike options which are exchange-traded, CFDs are an OTC transaction. Unlike options, they have bid–ask spreads, margins that are dependent on the offeror's assessment of your credit worthiness, has entry and exit fees and overnight charges based on period that the contract is held. Margins are applicable for both long and short, as opposed to options where it only applies to short position. Also, unlike options, there is no fixed maturity. As the margins can be eroded and margin calls possible, there is unlimited downside, unlike options.
    (b) The risk profile of CFDs can be similar to futures, unlimited both ways.

Chapter 13

1) *Istijrar* has embedded options but is Asian in style of exercise for a given price range (average of spot prices). If exercised at *Murabaha* price, then it has a predetermined exercise price. In some ways, it has limited upside and downside like a spread. However, it is also American in style since it can be "exercised" to fix price any time before maturity.

3) *Ba'i Salam* mostly closely resembles forward contracts. Customized, negotiated price. It has the three shortcomings common to forwards, though default is possible only by the seller, since there is full payment at contract initiation.

5) They are similar in operation/design but intended for different purposes. *Istisna* is for products yet to be manufactured whereas *Joala* is for services to be performed in the future.

8) (a) Intended to help famers with working capital (short-term) financing.
   (b) *Ba'i Salam* price $= S_o[1-(rf+c)]t$; since upfront payment; thus *Salam* price would lower than spot by this relationship.
   (c) None, since there is full upfront payment.
   (d) *Gharar* can be defined as intentionally induced uncertainty, or a contract that is deliberately designed to be loose and therefore subject to various interpretation with intention to deceive. Since modern-day futures contracts have elaborate and clearly defined contract specifications, gharar is minimal.

9) Hedging to lock-in the price of a needed underlying asset in the future is possible but not hedging a current long position in the underlying, since one cannot "short" the *Ba'i Salam*. Similarly, one could "speculate" to take advantage of perceived future increase in the price of the underlying but not take advantage of expected falling prices. Both speculation and arbitrage are restricted since the capital outlay involved with full prepayment is substantial. Furthermore, as a customized contract, there would be little liquidity and opportunity to offset/reverse out of a position.

11) A financial contract that resembles conventional REPO, but the initial selling and repurchase prices are equal, whereas in a Repo, the repurchase price is always higher.

13) As in Figure 13.1 of text.

15) Opposite of swap shown in Figure 13.1.

17) (i) 3-month KLIBOR futures, interest rate swaps (IRS), and FRA.
    (ii) Short 3-month KLIBOR futures, enter IRS as the floating rate receiver. In FRA, enter as party that will receive compensation if rate goes higher than agreed target rate.

19) *Ba'i Salam* — underlying philosophy is social justice, objective is to provide working capital (to farmers).
    Istijrar — underlying philosophy is to introduce an element of risk in order to "justify" the profit rate earned; objective: to provide working capital/short-term financing.

21) (i) Forward price should be higher than *Ba'i Salam* price (since forward always has positive net carry whereas a *Salam* would imply negative net carry).
    (ii) No, since with *Salam* you pay upfront (and earn the net carry) whereas with forwards you pay later and incur the net carry.

24) (i) Yes, he can use a *Salam* contract to lock-in his purchase price and then sell at the expected higher price upon receiving delivery to make a profit.
    (ii) Since the *Salam* contract requires full payment and so has zero leverage, it will be less profitable than using a futures contract where he only needs to post a margin.
    (iii) No, he cannot try to take advantage of expected falling prices since he cannot short the underlying in a *Salam* contract.

Table: Cumulative Normal Distribution

d	N(d)	d	N(d)	d	N(d)	d	N(d)	d	N(d)	d	N(d)
−3.00	0.0013	−1.58	0.0571	−0.76	0.2236	0.06	0.5239	0.86	0.8051	1.66	0.9515
−2.95	0.0016	−1.56	0.0594	−0.74	0.2297	0.08	0.5319	0.88	0.8106	1.68	0.9535
−2.90	0.0019	−1.54	0.0618	−0.72	0.2358	0.10	0.5398	0.90	0.8159	1.70	0.9554
−2.85	0.0022	−1.52	0.0643	−0.70	0.2420	0.12	0.5478	0.92	0.8212	1.72	0.9573
−2.80	0.0026	−1.50	0.0668	−0.68	0.2483	0.14	0.5557	0.94	0.8264	1.74	0.9591
−2.75	0.0030	−1.48	0.0694	−0.66	0.2546	0.16	0.5636	0.96	0.8315	1.76	0.9608
−2.70	0.0035	−1.46	0.0721	−0.64	0.2611	0.18	0.5714	0.98	0.8365	1.78	0.9625
−2.65	0.0040	−1.44	0.0749	−0.62	0.2676	0.20	0.5793	1.00	0.8414	1.80	0.9641
−2.60	0.0047	−1.42	0.0778	−0.60	0.2743	0.22	0.5871	1.02	0.8461	1.82	0.9656
−2.55	0.0054	−1.40	0.0808	−0.58	0.2810	0.24	0.5948	1.04	0.8508	1.84	0.9671
−2.50	0.0062	−1.38	0.0838	−0.56	0.2877	0.26	0.6026	1.06	0.8554	1.86	0.9686
−2.45	0.0071	−1.36	0.0869	−0.54	0.2946	0.28	0.6103	1.08	0.8599	1.88	0.9699
−2.40	0.0082	−1.34	0.0901	−0.52	0.3015	0.30	0.6179	1.10	0.8643	1.90	0.9713
−2.35	0.0094	−1.32	0.0934	−0.50	0.3085	0.32	0.6255	1.12	0.8686	1.92	0.9726
−2.30	0.0107	−1.30	0.0968	−0.48	0.3156	0.34	0.6331	1.14	0.8729	1.94	0.9738
−2.25	0.0122	−1.28	0.1003	−0.46	0.3228	0.36	0.6406	1.16	0.8770	1.96	0.9750
−2.20	0.0139	−1.26	0.1038	−0.44	0.3300	0.38	0.6480	1.18	0.8810	1.98	0.9761
−2.15	0.0158	−1.24	0.1075	−0.42	0.3373	0.40	0.6554	1.20	0.8849	2.00	0.9772
−2.10	0.0179	−1.22	0.1112	−0.40	0.3446	0.42	0.6628	1.22	0.8888	2.05	0.9798
−2.05	0.0202	−1.20	0.1151	−0.38	0.3520	0.44	0.6700	1.24	0.8925	2.10	0.9821
−2.00	0.0228	−1.18	0.1190	−0.36	0.3594	0.46	0.6773	1.26	0.8962	2.15	0.9842
−1.98	0.0239	−1.16	0.1230	−0.34	0.3669	0.48	0.6844	1.28	0.8997	2.20	0.9861
−1.96	0.0250	−1.14	0.1271	−0.32	0.3745	0.50	0.6915	1.30	0.9032	2.25	0.9878
−1.94	0.0262	−1.12	0.1314	−0.30	0.3821	0.52	0.6985	1.32	0.9066	2.30	0.9893
−1.92	0.0274	−1.10	0.1357	−0.28	0.3897	0.54	0.7054	1.34	0.9099	2.35	0.9906
−1.90	0.0287	−1.08	0.1401	−0.26	0.3974	0.56	0.7123	1.36	0.9131	2.40	0.9918
−1.88	0.0301	−1.06	0.1446	−0.24	0.4052	0.58	0.7191	1.38	0.9162	2.45	0.9929
−1.86	0.0314	−1.04	0.1492	−0.22	0.4129	0.60	0.7258	1.40	0.9192	2.50	0.9938
−1.84	0.0329	−1.02	0.1539	−0.20	0.4207	0.62	0.7324	1.42	0.9222	2.55	0.9946
−1.82	0.0344	−1.00	0.1587	−0.18	0.4286	0.64	0.7389	1.44	0.9251	2.60	0.9953
−1.80	0.0359	−0.98	0.1635	−0.16	0.4365	0.66	0.7454	1.46	0.9279	2.65	0.9960
−1.78	0.0375	−0.96	0.1685	−0.14	0.4443	0.68	0.7518	1.48	0.9306	2.70	0.9965
−1.76	0.0392	−0.94	0.1736	−0.12	0.4523	0.70	0.7580	1.50	0.9332	2.75	0.9970
−1.74	0.0409	−0.92	0.1788	−0.10	0.4602	0.72	0.7642	1.52	0.9357	2.80	0.9974
−1.72	0.0427	−0.90	0.1841	−0.08	0.4681	0.74	0.7704	1.54	0.9382	2.85	0.9978
−1.70	0.0446	−0.88	0.1894	−0.06	0.4761	0.76	0.7764	1.56	0.9406	2.90	0.9981
−1.68	0.0465	−0.86	0.1949	−0.04	0.4841	0.78	0.7823	1.58	0.9429	2.95	0.9984
−1.66	0.0485	−0.84	0.2005	−0.02	0.4920	0.80	0.7882	1.60	0.9452	3.00	0.9986
−1.64	0.0505	−0.82	0.2061	0.00	0.5000	0.82	0.7939	1.62	0.9474	3.05	0.9989
−1.62	0.0526	−0.80	0.2119	0.02	0.5080	0.84	0.7996	1.64	0.9495		
−1.60	0.0548	−0.78	0.2177	0.04	0.5160						

This table shows the probability [N(d)] of observing a value less than or equal to d. For example, as illustrated, if d is −0.24, then N(d) is 0.4052.

References and Further Reading

- Ayoub, S. (2014), *Derivatives in Islamic Finance: Examining the Market Risk Management Framework*, Edinburgh University Press.
- Bank Negara Malaysia, www.bnm.gov.my.
- Bursa Malaysia, www.bursamalaysia.com.
- Chance, D. M. (1998), *An Introduction to Derivatives*, 4th edition, Dryden Press, Orlando, FL.
- Cox, J. C. & Rubinstein, M. (1985), *Options Markets*, Prentice Hall, Englewood Cliffs, NJ.
- Daigler, R. T. (1994), *Financial Futures & Options Markets: Concepts and Strategies*, Harper Collins, New York, NY.
- Dubofsky, D. A. (1992), *Options and Financial Futures: Valuation and Uses*, McGraw-Hill International Editions, Singapore.
- Edil, M. & Obiyathulla, I. B. (2010), Pricing Efficiency of Stock Rights Issues in Malaysia. *Applied Financial Economics*, Vol. 20, No. 22, pp. 1751–1760.
- Fabozzi, F. J. & Kipnis, G. M. (1989), *The Handbook of Stock Index Futures and Options*, Dow Jones-Irwin, Homewood, IL.
- Futures Industry Association, https://fia.org/www.futuresindustry.org.
- Geske, R. & Shastri, K. (1985), Valuation by Approximation: A Comparison of Alternative Option Valuation Techniques. *The Journal of Financial and Quantitative Analysis*, Vol. 20, No. 1, pp. 45–71.
- Geske, R. & Roll, R. (1984), On Valuing American Call Options with the Black-Scholes European Formula. *The Journal of Finance*, Vol. 39, No. 2, pp. 443–455.
- Gibson, R. (1991), *Option Valuation: Analyzing and Pricing Standardized Option Contracts*, McGraw-Hill, Singapore.
- Hong Kong Exchanges and Clearing — HKEX — www.hkex.com.
- Hull, J. C. (2000), *Options, Futures & Other Derivatives*, 4th edition, Prentice Hall, Upper Saddle River, NJ.
- Obiyathulla, I. B, Abdul, J. O., & Othman, K. (1999), Issues in Stock Index Futures Introduction and Trading. Evidence from the Malaysian Index Futures Market. *Capital Markets Review*, Vol. 7, Nos. 1–2, pp. 1–46.
- Jarrow, R. & Turnbull, S. (2000), *Derivative Securities*, South-Western College Publishing, Thomson Learning, Cincinnati, OH.
- Kamali, M. H., (2002), *Islamic Commercial Law: An Analysis of Futures and Options*, Ilmiah Publishers, Kuala Lumpur, Malaysia.
- Kolb, R. W. (1992), *The Financial Derivatives Reader*, Kolb Publishing, Miami, FL.
- Kolb, R. W. (1993), *Financial Derivatives*, New York Institute of Finance, Paramus, NJ.
- Kolb, R. W. (1994), *Options: An Introduction*, 2nd edition, Kolb Publishing, Miami, FL.

- Lukman, H. & Obiyathulla, I. B. (2004), Pricing Hybrid Securities: The Case of Malaysian ICULS. *The Journal of International Finance*, Vol. 16, No. 3, pp. 3154–3172.
- Mallaby, S. (2011), *More Money than God: Hedge Funds and the Making of a New Elite*, Bloomsbury, London.
- Marina, M. & Obiyathulla, I. B (2009), Pricing Efficiency of the 3-month KLIBOR Futures Contracts: An Empirical Analysis. *Applied Financial Economics*, Vol. 19, No. 6, pp. 445–462.
- Martha, A. & Nalin, K. (1999), *Real Options: Managing Strategic Investment in an Uncertain World*, Harvard Business School Press, Boston, MA.
- Merton, R. (1990), *Continuous Time Finance*, Basil Blackwell Inc, Cambridge, MA.
- Obiyathulla, I. B. (2010), *Risk Management Issues in Islamic Banking and Finance*, UPM/INCEIF-ISRA, 2nd Annual Symposium, Kuala Lumpur, March 8–10, 2010.
- Obiyathulla I. B. & Mirakhor, A. (2019), *Islamic Capital Markets: A Comparative Approach*, 2nd edition, World Scientific Publishing, Singapore
- Obiyathulla, B. & Villa, A. (1994), Futures Markets, Regulation and Volatility: The Nikkei Stock Index Futures Markets. *Pacific Basin Finance Journal*, Vol. 2, Nos. 2–3, pp. 201–225.
- Obiyathulla, B. & Villa, A. (1994), *Lead/Lag Relationships in a Multi Market Context: The Nikkei Stock Index Futures*, Routledge Press, UK.
- Obiyathulla, B. & Villa, A. (1996), Futures Innovation, Market Structure and Systematic Patterns in the Nikkei Stock Index Futures Markets, 1986–1992. *The International Journal of Finance*.
- Obiyathulla, B. & Villa, A. (1996), Multi-Market Trading and Patterns in Volume and Mispricing: The Nikkei Stock Index Futures. *Journal of International Financial Markets, Institutions and Money*, Vol. 6, No. 1, pp. 1–38.
- Obiyathulla, B. & Villa, A. (1997), Derivative Instruments and Islamic Finance: Some Thoughts for a Reconsideration. *International Journal of Islamic Financial Services*, Vol. 1, No. 1, pp. 9–25.
- Obiyathulla, B. (1997), Adapting Mudarabah Financing to Contemporary Realities: A Proposed Financing Structure. *The Journal of Accounting, Commerce & Finance*, Vol. 1, No. 1, pp. 26–54.
- Park, K. K. H & Schoenfeld, S.A. (1992), *The Pacific Rim Futures and Options Markets*, Probus Publishing, Chicago, IL.
- Ritchken, P. (1996), *Derivative Markets: Theory, Strategy and Applications*, Harper Collins, New York, NY.
- Saleem, M. Y. (2013), *Islamic Commercial Law*, John Wiley & Sons, Singapore.
- Securities Commission Malaysia, www.sc.gov.my.
- SGX — Singapore Exchange, www.sgx.com.
- Sharifah, R., Azhar M., Eskandar, R., & Obiyathulla, I. B. (2009), Granting Employee Stock Options (ESOs), Market Reaction and Financial Performance. *Asian Academy of Management Journal of Accounting & Finance*, Vol. 5, No. 1, pp.117–138.
- Siegel, D. R. & Siegel, D. F. (1990), *Futures Markets*, Dryden Press, Orlando, FL.
- Sutcliffe, C. (1997), *Stock Index Futures: Theories and International Evidence*, 2nd edition, International Thomson Business Press, London.
- TFX — Thailand Futures Exchange, www.tfex.co.th.
- Taufiq, H., Shamsher, M., Mohamad, A., & Annuar, M. N. (2007), Stock Index Futures Prices and the Asian Financial Crisis. *International Review of Finance*, Vol. 7, No. 3–4, pp. 119–141.
- Thomson Reuters, www.thomsonreuters.com.
- WFE Derivatives Report 2020, World Federation of Exchanges www.world-exchanges.org.

Formulas

Derivatives: Introduction and Overview

$$F_{t,T} = S_O(1 + r_f + c - y)^{t,T}$$

$$F_{t,T} = S_O(1 + r_f - d)^{t,T}$$

$$\text{Nmber of contracts} = \frac{\text{RM value of portfolio} \times \text{Beta}}{\text{RM value of index}}$$

Long Syn. T-bill = Short futures + Long stocks
Long Syn. stock = Long futures + Long T-bills
Long futures   = Long T-bills = Short stock

No arbitrage bounds:

Upper bound: $F_t^+ = S_t(1 + C^+)(1 + r - d)^{t,T}$
Lower bound: $F_t^- = S_t(1 + C^-)(1 + r - d)^{t,T}$
Mispricing: $M_t = (F_t - F_t^*) / F_t^*$

Interest Rate Futures

$$\text{Bond value} = \sum_{t=1}^{n} \frac{C_t}{(1+y)^t} + \frac{FV_n}{(1+y)^n}$$

$$\text{Duration} = \sum t \cdot \left[\left(\frac{C_t}{(1+y)^t} \right) \Big/ P_n \right]$$

$$\%\Delta \text{ price} = -D \cdot \left[\frac{\Delta i}{(1+i)} \right]$$

$$\text{Gap} = \text{RSA} - \text{RSL}$$

$$\Delta \text{Value of assets} = -D_A \cdot \left[\frac{\Delta i}{(1+i)} \right]$$

$$\Delta \text{Value of liability} = -D_L \cdot \left[\frac{\Delta i}{(1+i)}\right]$$

$$\%\Delta NW = -D_{GAP} \cdot \left[\frac{\Delta i}{(1+i)}\right]$$

$$IFR = [1 + IFR \times (Tenor/360)]$$

$$= \frac{[1 + Long\ rate\ (Long\ tenor/360)]}{[1 + Short\ rate\ (Short\ tenor/360)]}$$

$$MGS\ settlement\ price = \{c/y[1-(1+y/2)^{-2N}] + (1+y/2)^{-2N}\} \times 100$$

Introduction to Options & Option Contracts

Premium $= IV + TV$

$$\text{Unassigned returns} = \left[\frac{Premium\ received}{Purchase\ price\ of\ stock - Premium\ received}\right] \times \left[\frac{360}{Call\ mat.}\right]$$

$$\text{Returns with assignment} = \left[\frac{Premium\ received + Capital\ gain}{Purchase\ price\ of\ stock - Premium\ received}\right]$$

Option Pricing

Single period BOPM: $C_t = \dfrac{\rho_u \cdot C_u + \rho_d \cdot C_d}{(1+r)^t}$

Two-period BOPM: $C_t = \dfrac{\rho_{uu} \cdot C_{uu} + \rho_{ud} \cdot C_{ud} + \rho_{du} \cdot C_{du} + \rho_{dd} \cdot C_{dd}}{\left(1+\dfrac{r}{2}\right)^2}$

Multi period BOPM: $C_t = \dfrac{\sum_{j=m}^{n}\left[\dfrac{n!}{j!(n-j)!}\right](\rho_u^j \rho_d^{n-j})[U^j D^{A-j} S_t - K]}{r^n}$

BSOPM:

$$Call = S \cdot N(d_1) - Ke^{-rt} \cdot N(d_2)$$

$$d_1 = \frac{\ln(S/K) + [r + (\sigma^2/2)]T}{\sigma \sqrt{T}}$$

$$d_2 = d_1 - \sigma \sqrt{T}$$

$$Put = Ke^{-rt} \cdot N(-d_2) - S \cdot N(-d_1)$$

Call IV $= S - \dfrac{Exercise\ price}{(1+r)^t}$

Put IV $= \dfrac{Exercise\ price}{(1+r)^t} - S$

Option Greeks

Variable	Formula for Calls		Formula for Puts	
Exercise price, K	$\dfrac{\partial C}{\partial K}$	$-e^{-rt}N(d_2)$	$\dfrac{\partial P}{\partial K}$	$\dfrac{\partial C}{\partial K}+e^{-rt}$
Volatility (vega)	$\dfrac{\partial C}{\partial \sigma}$	$S\sqrt{T}\cdot N'(d_1)$	$\dfrac{\partial P}{\partial \sigma}$	$S\sqrt{T}\cdot N'(d_1)$
Interest rate (rho)	$\dfrac{\partial C}{\partial r}$	$TKe^{-rt}\cdot N(d_2)$	$\dfrac{\partial P}{\partial r}$	$\dfrac{\partial C}{\partial r}-TKe^{-rt}$
Time (theta)	$\dfrac{\partial C}{\partial T}$	$Ke^{-rt}\left[\dfrac{\sigma N'(d_2)}{2\sqrt{T}}+rN(d_2)\right]$	$\dfrac{\partial P}{\partial T}$	$\dfrac{\partial C}{\partial T}-rKe^{-rt}$
Stock price (delta)	$\dfrac{\partial C}{\partial S}$	$N'(d_1)$	$\dfrac{\partial P}{\partial S}$	$\dfrac{\partial C}{\partial S}-1=N(d_1)-1$
Gamma	$\dfrac{\partial^2 C}{\partial S^2}$	$\dfrac{N'(d_1)}{S\sigma\sqrt{T}}$	$\dfrac{\partial^2 P}{\partial S^2}$	$\dfrac{N'(d_1)}{S\sigma\sqrt{T}}$

Pricing Stock Index Call Options

$$C = Se^{-qt} N(d1) - Ke^{-rt} \cdot N(d2)$$

$$d_1 = \frac{\ln(S/K)+[(r-q)(\sigma^2/2)]T}{\sigma\sqrt{T}}$$

$$d_2 = d_1 - \sigma\sqrt{T}$$

Pricing Stock Index Put Options

$$P = Ke^{-rt} N(-d2) - Se^{-qt} N(-d1)$$

where

S = current value of the stock index
K = exercise price
q = expected dividend yield
σ = estimate of index volatility
r = risk-free rate
T = time to maturity of option

Pricing Call Options on Stock Index Futures

$$C = \Omega \times N(d_1) - Ke^{-rt} \times N(d_2)$$

$$d_1 = \frac{\ln(\Omega/K)+[r+(\sigma^2/2)]T}{\sigma\sqrt{T}}$$

$$d_2 = d_1 - \sigma\sqrt{T}$$

The Garman–Kohlhagen Currency Call Option Model

$$C = S_o e^{-r_f T} \times N(d_1) - K e^{-r_d T} \times N(d_2)$$

$$d_1 = \frac{\ln(S_o/K) + [(r_d - r_f)(\sigma^2/2)]T}{\sigma \sqrt{T}}$$

$$d_2 = d_1 - \sigma \sqrt{T}$$

where

S_o = current (spot) underlying exchange rate
K = exercise exchange rate
$N(.)$ = cumulative standard normal distribution function
T = time to maturity of option
σ = volatility of the exchange rate
r_d = domestic risk-free interest rate
r_f = foreign risk-free interest rate

$\ln(S_o/K)$ = natural logarithm of S/K

Value of Currency Put Option

$$P = K e^{-r_d T} \times N(-d_2) - S_o e^{-r_f T} \times N(-d_1)$$

Replication, Synthetics and Arbitrage

$$
\begin{aligned}
S &= C + -P \\
-S &= P + -C \\
C &= S + P \\
-C &= -S + P \\
P &= C + -S \\
-P &= -C + S \\
S - K(1+r)^{-t} &= C + -P \\
S &= C - P + K(1+r)^{-t} \\
C &= S + P - K(1+r)^{-t} \\
P &= C - S + K(1+r)^{-t} \\
K(1+r)^{-t} &= S + P - C
\end{aligned}
$$

Options in Corporate Finance and Real Options

$$W = \frac{N}{(N/Y + M)} \cdot C$$

Value of convertible at maturity $= \sum_{t=1}^{n} \frac{C_t}{(1+r)^t} + \frac{FV_n}{(1+r)^n} + \left[[MPS - CP] \times \frac{FV}{CP} \right]$

$S \bullet t : MPS > CP; O$

Value of convertible prior to maturity $= \sum_{t=1}^{n} \frac{C_t}{(1+K)^t} + \frac{FV_n}{(1+K)^n} + [Call\ value]$

$$ICULS = \sum \frac{C_t}{(1+r)^t} + CP$$

$$ICULS = \left[C + -P + K(1+r)^{-t} + \sum \frac{C_t}{(1+r)^t} \right] \cdot \left(\frac{\theta}{\pi} \right)$$

$$s \cdot t : ICUL > 0$$

Interest Rate Swaps, FRAS, and Credit Derivatives

$$FRA\ cash\ settlement\ amount = \pi \cdot \left[\frac{(Floating\ rate - Fixed) \times Tenor/360}{1 + [(Floating\ rate) \times Tenor/360]} \right]$$

IRS payment obligation – 6-month reset

Fixed rate payer: [Fixed rate × Notional amount]/2

Floating rate payer: [(1 + Floating rate) × Notional amount]/2

Index

agricultural commodity, 63
al-Khiyarat, 493
American option, 202
American style, 202, 203
American-style option, 334
amortizing swap, 435
annualized, 181
annualized volatility, 351
anticipatory hedge, 55
anticipatory loss, 12
arbitrage, 9
arbitrage pricing logic, 335
arbitrage strategy, 182
arbitrageur, 8, 55
Asian option, 405, 420
asset allocation, 114
asset–liability mismatch, 440
asset match, 46
asset price distribution, 334
asset securitization, 454
assignment, 203
at-the-money, 219
auction method, 19
automatic leverage, 84
average annual dividend, 93

back-to-back loan, 435
backwardation, 63
ba'i al-urbun, 477, 493
Bai bil-Istighlal, 479
Bai bil-wafa, 478
Bai Bithamin Ajil (BBA), 479
Ba'i Salam, 472
Bangkok Interbank Offer Rate (BIBOR), 141
Bangkok Stock Exchange, 35
banker's acceptance (BA), 146
Bank for International Settlements (BIS), 488
Bank of Japan (BOJ), 164

Barings PLC, 121
barrier option, 405, 420
base hedge, 98
Basel III Framework, 488
basis, 61
basis risk, 61
basis swap, 435
bear call spread, 288
bearish, 205
bearish expectation, 102
bear put spread, 288
bear spread, 288
bear time spread, 103
Behavioral Finance, 68
benchmark, 436
bid–ask spread, 181, 462
bid (buy), 21
bilateral transaction, 7
binary option, 420, 421
binomial option pricing model (BOPM), 324, 325
Black–Scholes option pricing model (BSOPM), 324, 325
bond portfolio, 161
bond's rating, 143
bond yield, 143
bootstrapping, 443
box spread, 313
break-even point, 207, 283
Bretton Woods, 171
brokerage cost, 181
Brownian motion, 357
bull call spread, 288
bullish, 204
bullish expectation, 101
bullish to neutral, 208
bull put spread, 288
bull spread, 288

bull time spread, 103
Bursa Malaysia Derivatives, 26
business cycle, 453
butterfly spread, 308
buy-stop, 66

calendar spread, 103
callable bond, 412, 413
call delta, 397
call option, 201
call ratio spread, 312
call warrant, 412, 413
capital budgeting, 416
capital guaranteed product, 481
capitalization weighted index, 86
Capital Market and Services Act, 2007, 27
carrying cost, 47, 58
cash and carry arbitrage, 97, 108
cash-flow equivalence, 381, 387
cash or nothing call option, 421
cash or nothing put, 421
cash-settled, 81
cash settlement, 11, 232
change of control event, 488
change of control put, 488
Chartism, 64
Chicago Board of Trade (CBOT), 140
Chicago Board Options Exchange (CBOE), 201
Chicago Mercantile Exchange (CME), 26, 33, 82, 139
Chinese Renminbi (CNH), 172
circuit-breaker, 89, 106
class of option, 240
clearing, 23
clearinghouse, 23, 50
clearing-member, 21
closed-form solution, 329, 341
combination strategy, 280
commodity derivative, 26
commodity spread, 288
commodity swap, 433
comparative advantage, 436
compound option, 377

computerized method, 19
concentration risk, 456
condor strategy, 310
constituent stock, 353
contango, 63
contingent, 416, 481
contingent claim, 215
contingent liability, 215
continuous time model, 324
contract for difference (CFD), 433, 461
contract month, 90, 107, 242
contract size, 258
contract specifications, 7, 48, 88
contract value, 52
convenience yield, 58
convergence property, 59
conversion ratio, 414
conversion strategy, 286, 390
convertible bond, 412, 414
corporate finance
    behavioral, 405
    motivational issues, 405
cost-of-carry model (COC), 59, 92
cost of funds, 140
cost of margin, 181
cost of storage, 58
counterparty, 49
counterparty risk, 5, 23, 46, 178, 443, 474
coupon, 414
covered call strategy, 303
covered call write, 215, 303
credit default swap, 455
credit derivative, 433, 453
credit event, 455
credit-linked note, 455, 460
credit option, 455, 459
credit rating, 442, 453
credit risk, 12, 453
credit risk premium, 453
credit swap, 455
Cross-hedging, 61
Crude Palm Oil futures, 26
cumulative probability, 328
currency crisis, 453

currency derivative, 171
currency option, 7, 231, 257
currency risk, 12, 444
currency swap, 433, 435, 444
customized agreement, 45

daily marking-to-market, 6
daily price limit, 89
daily volatility, 351
day order, 68
day trader, 56
debt
    fixed in claim, 405
    terminal, 405
debt ratio, 443
decision tree, 327
default risk, 8, 12, 46
deferred contract, 61
delta, 342, 368
delta-neutral strategy, 373, 396
derivatives, 1
derive, 2
desired objective, 306
dilution, 412
discount rate, 442
discrete time model, 324
dispersion, 351
diversification, 84, 457
dividend index, 34
dividend yield, 92
divisibility, 49
down and in call, 421
down and out call, 421
dual exchange rate, 174
dual risk-free interest rate, 357
duration, 144
duration gap, 438
dynamic hedging, 349

economic cycle, 166
efficient market, 338
Efficient Market Hypothesis (EMH), 68
embedded call option, 488
embedded currency option, 485

embedded option, 415
embedded put option, 488
equally weighted index, 86
equity, 405
    perpetual, 405
    residual in claim, 405
equity derivative, 26
equity index option, 231
equity indices, 7
equity option, 201, 231
equity ratio, 443
equity swap, 433
ETF option, 246
European style, 202
exchange rate risk, 12
exchange-traded derivative, 7
exchange-traded forward contract, 46
execution-related order, 66
execution risk, 118
exercise, 201
exercise price, 202
exercise price interval, 242
exercise style, 202, 242
exit fee, 462
exit option, 416, 417
exotic option, 405
expiration day, 120
exposure, 176

Fatwa, 493
Federation of Exchanges (WFE), 35
fill order, 67
final settlement price, 107
final settlement value, 90
financial engineering, 6
financials, 10
firm-specific condition, 454
Fisherian Equation, 166
fixed-for-floating swap, 434
fixed-income securities, 161
fixed profit payer, 480
fixed rate payer, 434
flexibility option, 418
floating exchange rate, 140

floating interest rate, 141
floating profit rate payer, 481
floating rate payer, 434
floor trader, 20
foreign exchange, 34
forward discount, 174
forward premium, 174
forward rate agreement (FRA), 433, 451
forwards, 2
forward-starting swap, 435
forward start options, 420, 421
framing, 69
frictionless trading, 338
front-loading, 21
FTSE Bursa Malaysia KLCI (FBM KLCI), 26
FTSE China A50 index futures contract, 35
fuqaha, 472, 497
futures, 2
futures broker, 20
futures contract, 46
futures option, 241
future volatility, 350
FX Forward *Wa'ad-I*, 490
FX option, 491
FX *wa'ad*, 491, 492

gamma, 368
Garman–Kohlhagen currency option model, 357
Garman–Kohlhagen model, 262
geometrically weighted index, 86
gharar, 472
GLOBEX, 26
gold parity, 171
Good till Canceled order, 67
gross domestic product (GDP), 260
growth option, 416, 417
guarantee, 50, 416

halal, 471
Hanafi, 478
Hanbali, 478
hand signal, 20
Hang Seng Index (HSI) Futures, 29

hedge, 9, 46
hedge position, 280
hedger, 8, 54
hedge ratio, 346
hedging strategy, 176
heuristics, 69
historical volatility, 350
HKEX futures contract, 31
HKEX option, 244
HKEX option contract, 32
HKFE Clearing Corporation (HKCC), 30
Hong Kong Exchanges and Clearing (HKEX), 29, 30
Hong Kong Interbank Offered Rate (HIBOR) futures, 29
Hong Kong Interbank Offer Rate (HIBOR), 141
Hong Kong Monetary Authority (HKMA), 175
HSCEI futures, 32
HSI futures, 32
HSI options, 33

Ibn Taymiyah, 498
ijara, 479
ijarah, 479
implied forward rate (IFR), 149
implied gain, 53
implied loss, 47, 53
implied volatility, 346, 350
inbuilt leverage, 62, 179
incentive effect, 409
index arbitrage, 94
index multiplier, 88, 233
inflation rate, 140
inflation risk, 11
information asymmetry, 215
initial margin, 50
interbank market, 146
interest rate derivative, 26
Interest rate futures (IRF), 139
interest rate parity (IRP), 171
interest rate risk, 11, 152, 444
interest rate swap (IRS), 7, 433
intermarket spread, 103, 120, 288
internal rate of return (IRR), 415

International Monetary Market (IMM), 139
International Swaps and Derivatives Association, 7
International Swaps and Derivatives Association (ISDA), 435
in-the-money, 218
intrinsic value, 219
inverse floater, 436
inversely correlated, 235
inverse relationship, 143
irredeemable convertible unsecured loan stock, 414
irredeemable convertible unsecured loan stock (ICULS), 412
Islamic Dual Currency Investment (IDCI), 484
Islamic FX forward, 490
Islamic FX outright, 490
Islamic mutual funds, 471
Islamic profit rate swap, 479
Islamic range forward, 483
Islamic structured product, 481
Istijrar, 472
Istijrar contract, 475
Istisna, 472, 475

jahl, 472
Joa'la, 472, 475

Khazanah exchangeable *sukuk*, 488
Khazanah Nasional, 488
khiyar-al-shart, 498
kill order, 67
knock-in option, 420
knock-out option, 420
Kuala Lumpur Interbank Offer Rate (KLIBOR), 141

lead–lag relationship, 120
leverage, 62
leveraged naked position, 463
levered equity, 406
    call option on the firm, 407
levered stock position, 336
limit order, 66

liquidity, 10, 50
liquidity risk, 12
loan portfolio swap, 456
loan syndication, 454
loan underwriting, 454
local, 20
locking-in, 46
logarithmic price relative, 351
lognormal distribution, 358
log normally distributed, 338
London Interbank Offer Rate (LIBOR), 141, 462
long butterfly spread, 308
long call position, 206
long condor, 310
long position, 45
long put position, 207
long stock position, 204
long straddle, 295
long strangle, 298, 300
losing position, 180

3-month BIBOR futures contract, 146
3-month KLIBOR futures, 26
macro condition, 454
madzhabs, 478
maintenance margin, 50
Maliki, 478
manual trading, 20
margin call, 52, 463
margin forfeited, 53
margining, 50
margining process, 6
market anomaly, 69
market-clearing, 50
market friction, 120
Market if Touched (MIT) order, 67
market impact cost, 21
market maker, 436
Market on Close (MOC) Order, 67
Market on Open (MOO) Order, 67
market order, 66
market risk, 11
marking-to-market process, 50
maturity match, 46

maysir, 472
Merton's continuous dividend model, 378
Merton's Jump-Diffusion model, 378
Mini FTSE Bursa Malaysia Mid 70 Index Futures (FM70), 122
Mini-HSI futures, 32
Mini-HSI options, 33
minimum price fluctuation, 89
mispriced, 56
mispricing, 94, 337
moral hazard, 410
Mudarabah sukuk, 488
mudarib, 487
multiperiod binomial model, 376
Multiperiod BOPM, 329
multiple-coincidence, 4, 474
multiple coincidence of need, 46
Murabaha, 475, 479
mutual offset system, 33

naked position, 179, 280
National Shariah Advisory Council (NSAC), 479
nearby contract, 61
negative delta, 374
negative gap, 440
negative position gamma, 375
negative time delay, 227
negative vega position, 374
net present value (NPV), 415
neutral to bearish, 213, 314
neutral to bullish, 213, 314
Nikkei 225 futures contract, 33
Nikkei 225 Index option, 231
no-arbitrage bound, 117
nominal interest rate, 140
nondeliverable forward contract, 448
nondeliverable forward (NDF), 433
nonrefundable urbun, 478
notional principal, 258, 434
novation principle, 5, 23

off-balance sheet, 13, 471
off-balance-sheet transaction, 451

offeror, 462
offer (sell), 21
offsetting position, 102
on-balance sheet, 13, 471
One-Cancels-the-Other (OCO) order, 67
open interest, 63
open-outcry, 19
opportunity cost, 58
option delta, 346
option greeks, 341, 375
option moneyness, 218, 240
option premium, 203
options, 2, 201
option series, 240
option theta, 344
option to abandon, 417
order imbalance, 118
order routing, 20
OTC instrument, 433
OTC market, 19
out-of-the-money, 219
over hedged, 178
over-the-counter, 6

paired-trading, 131
parallel *Salam*, 474
partial derivative, 341
payoff, 203, 325
payoff diagram, 213
pegged, 359
perfectly correlated, 61
perpetual *sukuk*, 488
physicals, 10
physical settlement, 10, 232
plain vanilla swap, 435
political risk, 12
portfolio beta, 114, 375
portfolio insurance, 248, 281
position limit, 90, 242
position trader, 56
positive delta, 374
positive gamma, 375
positive gap, 440
positively correlated, 235

Index | 535

positive position, 375
positive time decay, 224
positive vega, 374
potential for price squeeze, 474
premium tick size, 241
price path, 328
price-related order, 66
price risk, 11, 44, 46
price squeeze, 46
pricing efficiency, 180
pricing equivalence, 381
principal guaranteed product, 481
profit on exercise, 234
program trading, 56
put–call parity, 387
put–call parity condition, 253
put–call ratio, 214
put delta, 397
put option, 202

quantity match, 46
quasi arbitrage, 97
quasi-index arbitrage, 97

rahnu, 478
Range Accrual Murabaha Negotiable Certificate of Deposit-i (RA MNCD-i), 482
ratings downgrade, 454
rating watch, 454
ratio spread, 312
real estate investment trust (REIT), 481
real interest rate, 167
real option, 405, 415
rebalancing, 373
redemption, 460
reference rate, 435
refinancing risk, 141
refundable urbun, 478
reinvestment risk, 141
replicate, 381
replicated, 97
replication, 100
reportable position, 90
repurchase agreement (REPO), 146, 478

reset frequency, 434, 435
reset period, 434
return with assignment, 304
reverse cash and carry arbitrage, 96, 109
reverse conversion, 390
rho, 343
riba, 472
rights issue, 411
rihn, 478
rishwah, 472
risk-based margining, 62, 242
risk-free arbitrage, 255
risk-free rate, 113, 336
riskless asset, 113
riskless hedge, 336
riskless hedged portfolio, 337
risk management, 12, 23
risk profile, 204, 283
risk-return trade off, 13

sakk, 487
Salam Sarf, 489
scalper, 56
screen-based method, 19
Securities Commission Act, 1993, 27
securitization, 454
self-regulatory organization (SRO), 27
sell-stop, 66
semi-strong-form EMH, 68
sensitivity, 144
SET 50 Index option, 246
SET composite index, 36
settlement, 49
settlement value, 233
SGX Mini JGB futures, 160
Shafii, 478
Shanghai–Hong Kong Stock Connect, 31
Shariah compliance risk, 485
Shariah-compliant, 471
Shanghai Interbank Offered Rate (SHIBOR), 358
short butterfly strategy, 309
short call position, 208
short condor, 311
short hedge, 97, 99

short position, 45
short put, 208
short stock position, 205
short straddle, 297
short strangle, 301, 302
Singapore Exchange (SGX), 34
Singapore International Monetary Exchange (SIMEX), 33
Single Period BOPM, 326
single stock futures (SSF), 26, 32, 81, 123
speculate, 9
speculative grade, 460
speculator, 8, 56
spot exchange rate, 357
spot-futures parity, 59
spot-futures party condition, 91
spot price, 47
spread, 280
spread strategy, 288
spread trading, 103
standard deviation, 11, 351
standardization, 48
standardized forward contract, 46
statutory reserve ratio, 166
stochastic volatility model, 379
stock bought on margin, 305
Stock Exchange of Hong Kong Options Clearing House (SEOCH), 30
Stock Exchange of Thailand (SET), 35
stock index futures contracts (SIF), 81
stock index option, 353
stock market volatility, 119
stock option, 231
stop order, 66
straddle, 295
straddle strategy, 295
straight bond, 413
strangle, 295
strangle strategy, 298
strike price, 202
strong-form EMH, 68
structured product, 422, 455
structured warrant, 422
sukuk, 471, 487

swap contract, 3
swap curve, 442
swap spread, 442
synthesize, 381
synthetic, 253
synthetic cash position, 100
synthetic futures position, 101
synthetic long call position, 384
synthetic long put position, 386
synthetic long stock position, 382
synthetic position, 100, 381
synthetic short call position, 385
synthetic short put position, 386
synthetic short stock position, 383
synthetic stock position, 101
synthetic T-bill position, 101
systematic risk, 84

target sell price, 131
T-bill, 146
T-bill rate, 358
Technical Analysis, 64
TFEX futures contract, 37
TFEX option contract, 38
Thailand Futures Exchange (TFEX), 36
Theoretical Intermarket Margining, 242
tick-rule, 118
tick size, 89
time decay, 224
time-related order, 66
time spread, 103
time stamped, 21
time value, 219
timing option, 416, 417
total return swap, 457
trading floor, 20
trading hour, 90
trading pit, 20
trading restriction, 450
trading volume, 10, 63
transferable subscription right, 412
transparency, 178
treasury bill, 139
treasury yield, 442

triple-witching day, 119
true value, 329

unassigned return, 304
uncovered position, 280
underlying assets, 1
underwriting fee, 411
unfair price, 5
unhedged, 178
unilateral promise, 489
unsystematic risk, 84
urbun contract, 477
US$/CNH currency option, 257
US$/CNH futures contract, 174
U-shaped pattern, 120
US T-bill rate, 170

valuation risk, 485
value weighted index, 86

vega, 342
volatility, 324
volume migration, 120

wa'ad, 489
Wakala, 488
warrant, 405
wasting asset, 224
weak-form EMH, 68

10-year Mini JGB futures, 160
10-year Mini Japanese Government Bond (JGB) futures, 144
yield curve, 143

zero coupon bond, 481
zero sum game, 53, 212